中国教育统计年鉴

EDUCATIONAL STATISTICS YEARBOOK OF CHINA

2003

中华人民共和国
教育部发展规划司

DEPARTMENT OF DEVELOPMENT & PLANNING
MINISTRY OF EDUCATION
THE PEOPLE'S REPUBLIC OF CHINA

图书在版编目（CIP）数据

中国教育统计年鉴. 2003/教育部发展规划司编.
—北京：人民教育出版社，2004
ISBN 7-107-18107-6

Ⅰ. 中...
Ⅱ. 教...
Ⅲ. 教育统计—统计资料—中国—2003—年鉴
Ⅳ. G526. 6-54

中国版本图书馆 CIP 数据核字（2004）第 112166 号

人民教育出版社出版发行
（北京沙滩后街 55 号　邮编：100009）
网址：http://www.pep.com.cn
山东新华印刷厂德州厂印装　全国新华书店经销
2004 年 11 月第 1 版　2004 年 11 月第 1 次印刷
开本：787 毫米×1 092 毫米　1/16　印张：43. 75
字数：918 千字　印数：0 001 ~ 2 000 册
定价：90. 00 元

《中国教育统计年鉴》
编辑委员会名单

说　明

《中国教育统计年鉴》(2003)是一本全面反映中华人民共和国教育事业发展情况的资料性年鉴，是由教育部发展规划司根据全国各省、自治区、直辖市教育委员会、教育厅填报的学校基层报表数字整理汇编而成的。教育部教育管理信息中心承担了数据的计算机处理汇总工作。

本年鉴包括以下部分：综合部分、高等教育、中等教育、初等教育、幼儿教育、特殊教育、全国各级各类学校的分布情况、办学条件、科学研究等。

本年鉴是各有关部门研究教育改革和发展的必备资料工具书，是教育界各机关、学校指导部门制定教育计划、指导教育改革必不可少的依据。

本年鉴所列资料，暂缺台湾省、香港特别行政区和澳门特别行政区的数字；凡未注明年份的均为2003年的数字。

Notes from the Compiler

The Educational Statistics Yearbook of China for 2003 is an informational yearbook comprehensively reflecting the development of the educational undertaking of the People's Republic of China, and it was compiled by the Department of Development and Planning of Ministry of Education, based on the synthetic statistical returns relating to schools of various types and levels completed by the Educational Commissions (or the Bureaus of Education) of the provincial governments and the goverments of various autonomous regions and municipalities directly under the State Council All data were processed and calculated usin Computers by the Educational Management Information Center of Ministry of Education.

The yearbook is composed of the following parts: summary tables, higher education, secondary education, primary education, pre-primary education, special education, geographical distribution of schools by type and level, Physical Facilities, Scientific Research Activities.

The yearbook is a requisite reference for all departments concerned with the study of educational reform and development, and provides indispensable factual information to the educational community (circles), the state organs, and all supervisory bodies of education (schools) engaged in curricular development and the guidance of educational reform.

The yearbook lacks the data of Taiwan Province. Hong Kong and Macao. Data in tables are for 2003, unless otherwise notified.

目　录

第一部分　教育事业发展

一、综合部分

全国各级各类学校校数、教职工、专任教师情况 …… 2
全国各级各类学历教育学生情况 …… 3
全国各级各类非学历教育学生情况 …… 4
全国各级民办教育基本情况 …… 4
各级普通学校女学生和女教职工数 …… 5
各级普通学校少数民族学生和少数民族教职工数 …… 6
分年度各级各类学校校数 …… 7
分年度各级各类学历教育学生数 …… 8
分年度各级各类学历教育招生数 …… 9
分年度各级各类学校教职工数 …… 10
分年度各级各类学校专任教师数 …… 11
高中阶段教育学生数的构成 …… 12
教育规模 …… 12
小学学龄儿童入学率 …… 13
各级教育毛入学率 …… 13
各级普通学校毕业生升学率 …… 14
每十万人口各级学校平均在校生数 …… 14
各级普通学校生师比 …… 15
普通高等学校校均规模 …… 15
全国各级自学考试基本情况 …… 16

二、高等教育

高等教育学校(机构)数 …… 18
普通高等学校校数 …… 19
普通高等学校规模 …… 19
高等学校设置专业数 …… 20
普通高等学校(机构)学生数 …… 21
分部门、分计划研究生数(总计) …… 22
分部门、分计划研究生数(普通高校) …… 22
分部门、分计划研究生数(科研机构) …… 24
分学科研究生数(总计) …… 24
分学科研究生数(普通高校) …… 26
分学科研究生数(科研机构) …… 26
在职人员攻读博士、硕士学位分学科学生数 …… 28
普通高等学校工科分大类学生数 …… 29
普通、成人本、专科分举办者学生数 …… 30

普通本、专科分性质类别学生数 …… 30
成人本、专科分性质类别学生数 …… 32
普通本、专科分学科学生数 …… 32
成人本、专科分学科学生数 …… 34
网络本、专科分学科学生数 …… 36
高等教育学生变动情况 …… 36
高等教育非学历教育学生情况 …… 38
高等教育其他学生情况 …… 39
外国留学生情况 …… 40
高等教育学校(机构)教职工情况(总计) …… 42
高等教育学校(机构)教职工情况(普通高校) …… 42
高等教育学校(机构)教职工情况(成人高校) …… 44
研究生指导教师情况(总计) …… 46
研究生指导教师情况(普通高校) …… 46
分学科专任教师数(总计) …… 48
分学科专任教师数(普通高校) …… 49
分学科专任教师数(成人高校) …… 50
分学科专任教师数(民办的其他高等教育机构) …… 51
专任教师、聘请校外教师学历情况(总计) …… 52
专任教师、聘请校外教师学历情况(普通高校) …… 52
专任教师、聘请校外教师学历情况(成人高校) …… 53
专任教师、聘请校外教师学历情况(民办的其他高等教育机构) …… 53
专任教师年龄情况(总计) …… 54
专任教师年龄情况(普通高校) …… 54
专任教师年龄情况(成人高校) …… 55
专任教师年龄情况(民办的其他高等教育机构) …… 55
专任教师、聘请校外教师岗位分类情况 …… 56
专任教师变动情况 …… 58
资产情况 …… 58
校舍情况(总计) …… 60
校舍情况(普通高校) …… 61
校舍情况(成人高校) …… 62
校舍情况(民办的其他高等教育机构) …… 63

三、中等教育

(一)高中阶段教育

普通高中校数、班数 …… 65
普通高中班额情况 …… 65
普通高中学生数 …… 66
普通中学教职工数 …… 67
普通高中分课程专任教师学历情况 …… 68
普通高中专任教师专业技术职称、年龄结构情况 …… 68
普通高中专任教师变动情况 …… 70
普通高中学生、教职工政治面貌及其他 …… 70
普通高中办学条件(一) …… 72

普通高中办学条件(二) …… 72
普通高中办学条件(三) …… 74
成人高中基本情况 …… 74
中等职业学校(机构)数 …… 75
中等职业学校分办学类型及举办者的中职学生及教职工情况 …… 76
中等职业学校(机构)各类学生数 …… 78
中等职业学校(机构)各类女学生数 …… 78
中等职业学校(机构)学生分科类情况(总计) …… 80
中等职业学校(机构)学生分科类情况(其中:全日制学生) …… 81
中等职业学校(机构)学生分科类情况(普通中专) …… 82
中等职业学校(机构)学生分科类情况(成人中专) …… 83
中等职业学校(机构)学生分科类情况(职业高中) …… 84
中等职业学校(机构)分年龄学生数 …… 85
中等职业学校(机构)分年龄女学生数 …… 85
中等职业学校(机构)学生变动情况 …… 86
中等职业学校(机构)女学生变动情况 …… 86
中等职业学校(机构)其他学生情况 …… 88
中等职业学校(机构)培训学生情况 …… 88
中等职业学校(机构)外国留学生情况 …… 89
中等职业学校(机构)教职工数(总计) …… 90
中等职业学校(机构)教职工数(普通中专) …… 90
中等职业学校(机构)教职工数(成人中专) …… 92
中等职业学校(机构)教职工数(职业高中) …… 92
中等职业学校(机构)教职工数(其他机构) …… 94
中等职业学校(机构)分科专任教师数(总计) …… 96
中等职业学校(机构)分科专任教师数(普通中专) …… 97
中等职业学校(机构)分科专任教师数(成人中专) …… 98
中等职业学校(机构)分科专任教师数(职业高中) …… 99
中等职业学校(机构)分科专任教师数(其他机构) …… 100
中等职业学校(机构)专任教师、聘请校外教师学历情况(合计) …… 101
中等职业学校(机构)专任教师、聘请校外教师学历情况(普通中专学校) …… 102
中等职业学校(机构)专任教师、聘请校外教师学历情况(成人中专学校) …… 103
中等职业学校(机构)专任教师、聘请校外教师学历情况(职业高中) …… 104
中等职业学校(机构)专任教师、聘请校外教师学历情况(其他机构) …… 105
中等职业学校(机构)专任教师分年龄情况 …… 106
中等职业学校(机构)专任教师、聘请校外教师岗位分类情况 …… 108
中等职业学校(机构)专任教师变动情况 …… 110
中等职业学校(机构)资产情况 …… 112
中等职业学校(机构)教职工中其他情况 …… 114
中等职业学校(机构)校舍情况(总计) …… 115
中等职业学校(机构)校舍情况(普通中专学校) …… 116
中等职业学校(机构)校舍情况(成人中专学校) …… 117
中等职业学校(机构)校舍情况(职业高中学校) …… 118
中等职业学校(机构)校舍情况(其他机构) …… 119
职业技术培训机构基本情况 …… 120

职业技术培训机构资产情况……………………………………………………………………………………………… 122

(二)初中阶段教育

普通初中校数、班数 ………………………………………………………………………………………………… 124
职业初中校数、班数 ………………………………………………………………………………………………… 125
普通初中班额情况……………………………………………………………………………………………………… 126
职业初中班额情况……………………………………………………………………………………………………… 127
普通初中学生数…… 128
职业初中学生数…… 130
初中阶段分年龄在校学生情况………………………………………………………………………………………… 132
职业初中教职工数……………………………………………………………………………………………………… 134
普通初中分课程专任教师学历情况…………………………………………………………………………………… 136
职业初中分课程专任教师学历情况…………………………………………………………………………………… 136
普通初中专任教师专业技术职称、年龄结构情况 ………………………………………………………………… 138
职业初中专任教师专业技术职称、年龄结构情况 ………………………………………………………………… 138
职业初中专任教师变动情况…………………………………………………………………………………………… 140
普通初中专任教师变动情况…………………………………………………………………………………………… 140
普通初中学生、教职工政治面貌及其他 …………………………………………………………………………… 142
职业初中学生、教职工政治面貌及其他 …………………………………………………………………………… 143
普通初中办学条件(一)………………………………………………………………………………………………… 144
普通初中办学条件(二)………………………………………………………………………………………………… 144
普通初中办学条件(三)………………………………………………………………………………………………… 144
职业初中办学条件(一)………………………………………………………………………………………………… 146
职业初中办学条件(二)………………………………………………………………………………………………… 146
职业初中办学条件(三)………………………………………………………………………………………………… 148
成人初中基本情况……………………………………………………………………………………………………… 148

(三)初等教育

小学校数、教学点数、班数 ………………………………………………………………………………………… 150
小学班额情况……… 151
小学学生数…… 152
小学学龄人口入学及在校生情况……………………………………………………………………………………… 154
小学教职工数……… 158
小学专任教师学历情况………………………………………………………………………………………………… 160
小学专任教师专业技术职称、年龄结构情况………………………………………………………………………… 160
小学专任教师变动情况………………………………………………………………………………………………… 162
小学学生、教职工政治面貌及其他 ………………………………………………………………………………… 162
小学办学条件(一)……………………………………………………………………………………………………… 164
小学办学条件(二)……………………………………………………………………………………………………… 164
小学办学条件(三)……………………………………………………………………………………………………… 166
成人小学基本情况……………………………………………………………………………………………………… 166

四、工读学校

工读学校基本情况……………………………………………………………………………………………………… 168

五、特殊教育

特殊教育基本情况……170
特殊教育在校学生中职业技术班学生及少数民族学生情况……172
特殊教育教职工数……172
特殊教育学校专任教师学历、职称情况……174
特殊教育专任教师变动情况……174
特殊教育办学条件……174

六、幼儿教育

幼儿园园数、班数……177
幼儿教育分年龄学生数……178
幼儿教育分年龄学生数(续)……179
幼儿园教职工数……180
幼儿园园长、专任教师学历、职称情况……182
幼儿园教职工和专任教师政治面貌及其他……182
幼儿园校舍及其他情况……184

七、各级各类学校分布情况

高等教育学校(机构)数……187
高等学校(机构)研究生总计……188
普通高校研究生数……190
科研机构研究生数……192
高等教育本、专科学生数……194
高等教育普通本、专科学生数……196
高等教育成人本、专科学生数……198
高等教育网络本、专学生数……200
综合大学本科、专科生学生数……202
高等理工院校本科、专科生学生数……204
高等农业院校本科、专科生学生数……206
高等林业院校生科、专科生学生数……208
高等医药院校本科、专科生学生数……210
高等师范院校本科、专科生学生数……212
高等语文院校本科、专科生学生数……214
高等财经院校本科、专科生学生数……216
高等政法院校本科、专科生学生数……218
高等体育院校本科、专科生学生数……220
高等艺术院校本科、专科生学生数……222
高等民族院校本科、专科生学生数……224
职业技术学院本科、专科生学生数……226
广播电视大学本、专科学生数……228
职工高等学校本、专科学生数……230
农民高等学校本、专科学生数……232
独立函授学院本、专科学生数……234
教育学院本、专科学生数……236

管理干部学院本、专科学生数 …………………………………………………………………… 238
其他机构本、专科学生数 ………………………………………………………………………… 240
普通高等学校举办函授、业余、脱产分本专科学生数…………………………………………… 242
在职人员攻读博士、硕士学位学生情况 ………………………………………………………… 244
高等教育非学历教育学生情况(总计)……………………………………………………………… 246
高等教育非学历教育学生情况(普通高校)………………………………………………………… 248
高等教育非学历教育学生情况(成人高校)………………………………………………………… 250
高等教育非学历教育学生情况(民办非学历高等教育机构)……………………………………… 252
高等教育非学历教育学生情况(科研机构)………………………………………………………… 254
外国留学生情况……………………………………………………………………………………… 256
高等教育学校(机构)教职工情况(总计)…………………………………………………………… 258
高等教育学校(机构)女教职工情况(总计)………………………………………………………… 260
高等教育学校(机构)教职工情况(普通高校)……………………………………………………… 262
高等教育学校(机构)女教职工情况(普通高校)…………………………………………………… 264
高等教育学校(机构)教职工情况(成人高校)……………………………………………………… 266
高等教育学校(机构)女教职工情况(成人高校)…………………………………………………… 268
高等教育学校(机构)教职工情况(民办的其他高等教育机构)…………………………………… 270
高等教育学校(机构)女教职工情况(民办的其他高等教育机构)………………………………… 272
专任教师学历、职称情况(总计) ………………………………………………………………… 274
专任教师学历、职称情况(普通高校) …………………………………………………………… 275
专任教师学历、职称情况(成人高校) …………………………………………………………… 276
专任教师学历、职称情况(民办的其他高等教育机构) ………………………………………… 277
聘请校外教师学历情况(总计)……………………………………………………………………… 278
聘请校外教师学历情况(普通高校)………………………………………………………………… 279
聘请校外教师学历情况(成人高校)………………………………………………………………… 280
聘请校外教师学历情况(民办的其他高等教育机构)……………………………………………… 281
资产情况(学校产权)(总计)………………………………………………………………………… 282
资产情况(学校产权)(普通高校)…………………………………………………………………… 284
资产情况(学校产权)(成人高校)…………………………………………………………………… 286
资产情况(学校产权)(民办的其他高等教育机构)………………………………………………… 288
资产情况(非学校产权)(总计)……………………………………………………………………… 290
资产情况(非学校产权)(普通高校)………………………………………………………………… 292
资产情况(非学校产权)(成人高校)………………………………………………………………… 294
资产情况(非学校产权)(民办的其他高等教育机构)……………………………………………… 296
校舍情况(总计)……………………………………………………………………………………… 298
校舍情况(普通高校)………………………………………………………………………………… 299
校舍情况(成人高校)………………………………………………………………………………… 300
校舍情况(民办的其他高等教育机构)……………………………………………………………… 301
普通高中校数、班数(总计) ……………………………………………………………………… 302
普通高中校数、班数(城市) ……………………………………………………………………… 303
普通高中校数、班数(县镇) ……………………………………………………………………… 304
普通高中校数、班数(农村) ……………………………………………………………………… 305
普通高中学生数(总计)……………………………………………………………………………… 306
普通高中学生数(城市)……………………………………………………………………………… 307
普通高中学生数(县镇)……………………………………………………………………………… 308

普通高中学生数(农村)……309
普通高中女学生数……310
普通中学教职工数(总计)……311
普通中学职工数(城市)……312
普通中学教职工数(县镇)……313
普通中学教职工数(农村)……314
普通中学女教职工数……315
普通中学教职工总数中社会力量办教职工数……316
普通高中专任教师学历、职称情况(总计)……318
普通高中专任教师学历、职称情况(城市)……320
普通高中专任教师学历、职称情况(县镇)……322
普通高中专任教师学历、职称情况(农村)……324
普通高中办学条件(一)(总计)……326
普通高中办学条件(一)(城市)……328
普通高中办学条件(一)(县镇)……330
普通高中办学条件(一)(农村)……332
普通高中办学条件(二)(总计)……334
普通高中办学条件(二)(城市)……336
普通高中办学条件(二)(县镇)……338
普通高中办学条件(二)(农村)……340
中等职业学校(机构)数……342
中等职业学校(机构)学生数……344
中等职业学校(机构)女学生数……346
普通中等专业学校学生数……348
普通中等专业学校女学生数……350
成人中等专业学校学生数……352
成人中等专业学校女学生数……354
职业高中学校学生数……356
职业高中学校女学生数……358
中等职业学校(机构)分年龄学生数……360
中等职业学校(机构)分年龄女学生数……362
中等职业学校(机构)培训学生结业情况……364
中等职业学校(机构)培训学生注册情况……366
中等职业学校(机构)学生变动情况……368
中等职业学校(机构)学生变动情况(女)……370
中等职业学校(机构)外国留学生情况……372
中等职业学校(机构)教职工数……374
中等职业学校(机构)女教职工数……376
普通中等专业学校教职工数……378
普通中等专业学校女教职工数……380
成人中等专业学校教职工数……382
成人中等专业学校女教职工数……384
职业高中学校教职工数……386
职业高中学校女教职工数……388
其他机构教职工数……390

其他机构女教职工数…………………………………………………………………………………… 392
中等职业学校(机构)专任教师职称、学历情况 ……………………………………………………… 394
普通中等专业学校专任教师职称、学历情况 ………………………………………………………… 396
成人中等专业学校专任教师职称、学历情况 ………………………………………………………… 398
职业高中学校专任教师职称、学历情况 ……………………………………………………………… 400
其他机构专任教师职称、学历情况 …………………………………………………………………… 402
中等职业学校(机构)情况(学校产权)……………………………………………………………… 404
中等职业学校(机构)资产情况(非学校产权中独立使用)………………………………………… 406
普通中专学校资产情况(学校产权)………………………………………………………………… 408
普通中专学校资产情况(非学校产权中独立使用)………………………………………………… 410
成人中专学校资产情况(学校产权)………………………………………………………………… 412
成人中专学校资产情况(非学校产权中独立使用)………………………………………………… 414
职业高中学校资产情况(学校产权)………………………………………………………………… 416
职业高中学校资产情况(非学校产权中独立使用)………………………………………………… 418
其他机构资产情况(学校产权)……………………………………………………………………… 420
其他机构资产情况(非学校产权中独立使用)……………………………………………………… 422
中等职业学校(机构)校舍情况(总计)……………………………………………………………… 424
普通中专学校校舍情况………………………………………………………………………………… 425
成人中专学校校舍情况………………………………………………………………………………… 426
职业高中学校校舍情况………………………………………………………………………………… 427
其他机构………………………………………………………………………………………………… 428
校舍情况………………………………………………………………………………………………… 429
职业技术培训机构基本情况(总计)………………………………………………………………… 430
职业技术培训学校基本情况…………………………………………………………………………… 432
农村成人文化技术培训学校基本情况………………………………………………………………… 434
其他培训机构基本情况………………………………………………………………………………… 436
职业技术培训机构资产情况…………………………………………………………………………… 438
职工技术培训学校资产情况…………………………………………………………………………… 440
农村成人文化技术培训学校资产情况………………………………………………………………… 442
其他培训机构资产情况………………………………………………………………………………… 444
普通初中校数、班数(总计) ………………………………………………………………………… 446
普通初中校数、班数(城市) ………………………………………………………………………… 447
普通初中校数、班数(县镇) ………………………………………………………………………… 448
普通初中校数、班数(农村) ………………………………………………………………………… 449
职业初中校数、班数(总计) ………………………………………………………………………… 450
职业初中校数、班数(城市) ………………………………………………………………………… 451
职业初中校数、班数(县镇) ………………………………………………………………………… 452
职业初中校数、班数(农村) ………………………………………………………………………… 453
普通初中学生数(总计)……………………………………………………………………………… 454
普通初中学生数(城市)……………………………………………………………………………… 455
普通初中学生数(县镇)……………………………………………………………………………… 456
普通初中学生数(农村)……………………………………………………………………………… 457
普通初中女学生数……………………………………………………………………………………… 458
职业初中学生数(总计)……………………………………………………………………………… 459
职业初中学生数(城市)……………………………………………………………………………… 460

职业初中学生数(县镇)……………………………………………………………………… 461
职业初中学生数(农村)……………………………………………………………………… 462
职业初中女学生数……………………………………………………………………………… 463
职业初中教职工数(总计)…………………………………………………………………… 464
职业初中教职工数(城市)…………………………………………………………………… 465
职业初中教职工数(县镇)…………………………………………………………………… 466
职业初中教职工数(农村)…………………………………………………………………… 467
职业初中教职工总数中社会力量办教职工数……………………………………………… 468
职业初中女教职工数………………………………………………………………………… 469
普通初中专任教师学历、职称情况(总计) ………………………………………………… 470
普通初中专任教师学历、职称情况(城市) ………………………………………………… 472
普通初中专任教师学历、职称情况(县镇) ………………………………………………… 474
普通初中专任教师学历、职称情况(农村) ………………………………………………… 476
职业初中专任教师学历、职称情况(总计) ………………………………………………… 478
职业初中专任教师学历、职称情况(城市) ………………………………………………… 480
职业初中专任教师学历、职称情况(县镇) ………………………………………………… 482
职业初中专任教师学历、职称情况(农村) ………………………………………………… 484
普通初中办学条件(一)(总计)…………………………………………………………… 486
普通初中办学条件(一)(城市)…………………………………………………………… 488
普通初中办学条件(一)(县镇)…………………………………………………………… 490
普通初中办学条件(一)(农村)…………………………………………………………… 492
职业初中办学条件(一)(总计)…………………………………………………………… 494
职业初中办学条件(一)(城市)…………………………………………………………… 496
职业初中办学条件(一)(县镇)…………………………………………………………… 498
职业初中办学条件(一)(农村)…………………………………………………………… 500
普通初中办学条件(二)(总计)…………………………………………………………… 502
普通初中办学条件(二)(城市)…………………………………………………………… 504
普通初中办学条件(二)(县镇)…………………………………………………………… 506
普通初中办学条件(二)(农村)…………………………………………………………… 508
职业初中办学条件(二)(总计)…………………………………………………………… 510
职业初中办学条件(二)(城市)…………………………………………………………… 512
职业初中办学条件(二)(县镇)…………………………………………………………… 514
职业初中办学条件(二)(农村)…………………………………………………………… 516
小学校数、教学点数及班数(总计) ………………………………………………………… 518
小学校数、教学点数及班数(城市) ………………………………………………………… 520
小学校数、教学点数及班数(县镇) ………………………………………………………… 522
小学校数、教学点数及班数(农村) ………………………………………………………… 524
小学学生数(总计)…………………………………………………………………………… 526
小学学生数(城市)…………………………………………………………………………… 528
小学学生数(县镇)…………………………………………………………………………… 530
小学学生数(农村)…………………………………………………………………………… 532
六年制小学学生数……………………………………………………………………………… 534
小学女学生数…………………………………………………………………………………… 536
小学教职工数(总计)………………………………………………………………………… 538
小学教职工数(城市)………………………………………………………………………… 540

小学教职工数(县镇)……………………………………………………………………………… 542
小学教职工数(农村)……………………………………………………………………………… 544
小学教职工总数中社会力量办教职工数…………………………………………………………… 546
小学女教职工数……………………………………………………………………………………… 548
小学专任教师学历、职称情况(总计)……………………………………………………………… 550
小学专任教师学历、职称情况(城市)……………………………………………………………… 552
小学专任教师学历、职称情况(县镇)……………………………………………………………… 554
小学专任教师学历、职称情况(农村)……………………………………………………………… 556
小学办学条件(一)(总计)………………………………………………………………………… 558
小学办学条件(一)(城市)………………………………………………………………………… 560
小学办学条件(一)(县镇)………………………………………………………………………… 562
小学办学条件(一)(农村)………………………………………………………………………… 564
小学办学条件(二)(总计)………………………………………………………………………… 566
小学办学条件(二)(城市)………………………………………………………………………… 568
小学办学条件(二)(县镇)………………………………………………………………………… 570
小学办学条件(二)(农村)………………………………………………………………………… 572
工读学校基本情况…………………………………………………………………………………… 574
特殊教育基本情况(总计)…………………………………………………………………………… 576
特殊教育基本情况(城市)…………………………………………………………………………… 578
特殊教育基本情况(县镇)…………………………………………………………………………… 580
特殊教育基本情况(农村)…………………………………………………………………………… 582
特殊教育女学生数…………………………………………………………………………………… 584
特殊教育教职工数…………………………………………………………………………………… 586
特殊教育女教职工数………………………………………………………………………………… 587
特殊教育学校专任教师学历、职称情况 …………………………………………………………… 588
特殊教育办学条件…………………………………………………………………………………… 590
幼儿教育基本情况(总计)…………………………………………………………………………… 592
幼儿教育基本情况(城市)…………………………………………………………………………… 594
幼儿教育基本情况(县镇)…………………………………………………………………………… 596
幼儿教育基本情况(农村)…………………………………………………………………………… 598
幼儿教育中女儿童数………………………………………………………………………………… 600
幼儿教育教职工数(总计)…………………………………………………………………………… 601
幼儿教育教职工数(城市)…………………………………………………………………………… 602
幼儿教育教职工数(县镇)…………………………………………………………………………… 603
幼儿教育教职工数(农村)…………………………………………………………………………… 604
幼儿教育女教职工数………………………………………………………………………………… 605
幼儿园园长、专任教师学历、职称情况(总计)……………………………………………………… 606
幼儿园园长、专任教师学历、职称情况(城市)……………………………………………………… 608
幼儿园园长、专任教师学历、职称情况(县镇)……………………………………………………… 610
幼儿园园长、专任教师学历、职称情况(农村)……………………………………………………… 612
幼儿园校舍及其他情况(总计)……………………………………………………………………… 614
幼儿园校舍及其他情况(城市)……………………………………………………………………… 616
幼儿园校舍及其他情况(县镇)……………………………………………………………………… 618
幼儿园校舍及其他情况(农村)……………………………………………………………………… 620

第二部分 办学条件

一、教育经费

各地区教育经费来源和支出情况(2002 年) …… 624
各类学校教育经费来源和支出情况(2002 年) …… 626

二、教育基本建设投资

教育基本建设投资完成情况 …… 630
地方所属各级学校基本建设投资省完成情况 …… 632

三、仪器设备

普通高等学校教育、科研仪器设备分省情况 …… 636

第三部分 科学研究活动及其他

一、自然科学与技术

普通高等学校科技人力情况 …… 638
普通高等学校人力中科学家和工程师技术职务(职称)情况 …… 640
普通高等学校科技经费情况 …… 642
普通高等学校研究与发展课题、成果情况 …… 644

二、社会科学

普通高等学校人文、社会科学人力情况 …… 648
普通高等学校人文、社会科学研究与发展经费情况 …… 650
普通高等学校人文、社会科学研究与发展课题、成果情况 …… 652
普通高等学校招生报名情况(2002 年) …… 654
普通高等学校招生报名情况(2003 年) …… 660

附表:

国民生产总值 …… 666
各地区国内生产总值 …… 667
国家财政收支总额及增长速度 …… 668
中央财政和地方财政收支总额 …… 669
人口数及构成 …… 670
各地区分性别的 15 岁及 15 岁以上文盲半文盲人口 …… 671
各地区按性别和受教育程度分的人口 …… 672

CONTENTS

PARt Ⅰ

THE DEVELOPMENT OF THE EDUCTIONAL UNDERTAKING

SUMMARY TABLES

The Number of Schools of all Types and Levels Staffs and Full time Teachers (2)
Number of Graduates, Entrants, Data Enrolment, of Schools of All Types and Level Providing Formal Programs (3)
Data on Students Enrdment in Non-formal Programmes of All Types and Levels (4)
Number of Female Students, Teachers, Staff & Workers of schools of All Levels & Types (5)
Number of Minority Students Enrolled, Teachers, Staff & Workers of Schools of All Levels & Types. (6)
Number of Schools of All Levels & Types (7)
Number of Enrolment of Schools of All Types and Level Providing Formal Programs (8)
Number of New Entrants of Schools of All Types and Level Providing Formal Programs (9)
Number of Staff and Workers of Schools of All Levels & Types (10)
Number of Fulltime Teachers of Schools of All Levels & Types (11)
Composition of Students in Senior Sec. Schools (12)
Size of Education (12)
Net Enrolment Ratio of School-age Children in Primary Schools (13)
Gross Enrolment Rate of Schools of All Levels (13)
Promotion Rate of Graduates of Regular School of All Levels & Types (14)
Number of Students of Per 100, 000 Inhabitants of All Levels (14)
Pupil-Teacher Ratio of Regular Schools of All levels (15)
Average Size of Regular Inst of Highter Education (15)
Basic Statistics of Applicants for State-administered Examination Self-learners by Level (16)

HIGHER EDUCATION

Number of Higher Education Institutions (18)
Number of Regular Higher Educational Institutions (19)
Breakdown of Regular Higher Educational Institutions by Size of Enrolments (19)
Number of Specialities and Number of Educational Programmes Estabished by Field of Study in Regular Higher Educational Institutions (20)
Data on Students in Regular Higher Education Institutions (21)
Total Number of Postgraduate Students by Sector and Program (Total) (22)
Number of Postgraduate Students by Sector and Program (Regular HEIs) (22)
Number of Postgraduate Students by Sector and Program (Research Institutes) (24)
Total Number of Postgraduate Students by Academic Field (24)
Number of Postgraduate Students by Academic Field (Regular HEIs) (26)
Number of Postgraduate Students by Academic Field (Research Institutes) (26)
Number of Postgraduate Students Studying for Advanced Degrees Without Leaving Their Jobs (28)
Breakdown of Engineering Students by Subfield of Study in Regular Higher Educational Institutions (29)

Number of Undergraduate Students by Type of Courses in Regular Higher Educational Institutions (30)
Number of Undergraduate Students by Type of Courses in Regular Higher Educational Institutions (30)
Number of Students by type of Schools in all Adult Higher Educational Institutions (32)
Number of Students in Regular HEIs by Field of Study (32)
Number of Students by Field of Study in Adult Higher Educational Institutions (34)
Number of Students in Adult HEIs by Field of Study (36)
Changes in Higher Educations Enrolment (36)
Data on Students Enrolled in Non-formal Programmes of HEIS (38)
Data on Other Students Enrolled of HEIS (39)
Information on Foreign Students (40)
Aggregate Data on Staff and Workers in HEIs (Total) (42)
Aggregate Data on Staff and Workers in Regular HEIs (42)
Data on Staff and Workers in Adult HEIs (44)
Aggregate Data on Supervisors of Postgraduate Programs (46)
Data on Supervisors of Postgraduate Programs (Regular HEIs) (46)
Total Number of Full-time Teachers by Field of Study (48)
Number of Full-time Teachers by Field of Study in Regular Higher Educational Institutions (49)
Number of Full-time Teachers by Field of Study in Adult Higher Educational Institutions (50)
Number of Full-time Teachers by Field of Study in Non-state/private HEIs (51)
Aggregate Data on Academic Qualifications of Full-time and Part-time Teachers in HEIs (52)
Data on Academic Qualifications of Full-time and Part-time Teachers in Adult HEIs (52)
Data on Academic Qualifications of Full-time and Part-time Teachers in Higher Educational Institutions for Adults (53)
Data on Academic Qualifications of Full-time and Part-time Teachers in Non-state/private HEIs (53)
Breakdown of Full-time Teachers by Age (Regional Aggregates) (54)
Breakdown of Full-time Teachers by Age (Regular HEIs) (54)
Breakdown of Full-time Teachers by Age in Adult HEIs (55)
Breakdown of Full-time Teachers by Age (Non-state/private HEIs) (55)
Data on Academic Qualification of Full－time and Invited from other Institutions Invited Teachers Classified by Teaching Content (56)
Changes of Full-time Teachers in Higher Educational Institutions (58)
Condition of Fixed Assets and Teaching Resources (58)
Conditions of School Buidings (Total) (60)
Conditions of School Buidings (Regular HEIs) (61)
Conditions of School Buidings in Adult Higher Educational Institutions (62)
Conditions of School Buidings in Non-state/private HEIs (63)

Secondary Education

Senior Seconday

Number of Senior Secondary Schools and Classes (65)
Size of Senior Secondary Schools Classes (65)
Number of Students in Senior Secondary Schools (66)
Number of Teachers, Staff & Workers in General Secondary Schools (67)
Number of Full-time Senior Secondary School Teachers by Subject Taught & Educational Attainment (68)
Full-time Teachers in Senior Secondary Schools Broken Down by Rank and Age (68)
Changes of Full-time Teachers in General Secondary Schools (70)
Supplementary Information on Students and Full-time Teachers of Senior Secondary Schools (70)
Condition of School Buildings in Senior Secondary Schools (1) (72)

Condition of School Buildings in Senior Secondary Schools (2) (72)
Condition of School Buildings in Senior Secondary Schools (3) (74)
Basic Statistics of Adult Schools by Province (74)
Number of Secondary Vocational Schools (75)
Data on Students and Staff and Workers of Secondary Vocational Schools by Types and Providers of Schools (77)
Number of Students in Secondary Vocational Schools (Institutions) (78)
Number of Female Students in Secondary Vocational Schools (Institutions) (78)
Data on Secondary Vocational Schools by Field of Study (Total) (80)
Data on Secondary Vocational Schools by Field of Study (of which: fulltime students) (81)
Data on Secondary Vocational Schools by Field of Study (Specialized Secondary Schools) (82)
Data on Secondary Vocational Schools by Field of Study (Adult Specialized Secondary Schools) (83)
Data on Secondary Vocational Schools by Field of Study (High Vocational Schools) (84)
Number of Students by age in Secondary Vocational Schools (Institutions) Vocational Schools (Institutions) (85)
Number of Female Students by age in Secondary Vocational Schools (Institutions) (85)
Changes in Enrolment of Secondary Vocational Schools (Institutions) (86)
Changes in Female Enrolment of Secondary Vocational Schools (Institutions) (86)
Other Students in Secondary Vocational Schools (Institution) (88)
Training Students inSecondary Vocational Schools (Institutions) (88)
Information on Foreign Students in Secondary Vocational Schools (Institutions) (89)
Number of Teachers, Staff & Workers in Secondary Vocational Schools (Institutions) (Total) (90)
Number of Teachers, Staff & Workers in Secondary Vocational Schools (Institutions) (SSSs) (90)
Number of Teachers, Staff & Workers in Secondary Vocational Schools (Institutions) (Adult SSSs) (92)
Number of Teachers, Staff & Workers in Secondary Vocational Schools (Institutions) (High Vocational Schools) (92)
Number of Teachers, Staff & Workers in Secondary Vocational Schools (Institutions) (Other Institutions) (94)
Number of Full-time Teachers by Field of Study in Secondary Vocational Schools (Institutions) (Total) (96)
Number of Full-time Teachers by Field of Study in Secondary Vocational Schools (SSSs) (97)
Number of Full-time Teachers by Field of Study in Secondary Vocational Schools (Adult SSSs) (98)
Number of Full-time Teachers by Field of Study Schools) in Secondary Vocational Schools (High Vocational Schools) (99)
Number of Full-time Teachers by Field of Study in Secondary Vocational Schools (Other Institutions) (100)
Data on Academic Qualifications of Full-time and Part-time Teachers in Secondary Vocational Schools (Institutions) (101)
Data on Academic Qualifications of Full-time and Part-time Teachers in Secondary Vocational Schools (SSSs) (102)
Data on Academic Qualifications of Full-time and Part-time Teachers in Secondary Vocational Schools (Adult SSSs) (103)
Data on Academic Qualifications of Full-time and Part-time Teachers in Secondary Vocational Schools (High Vocational Schools) (104)
Data on Academic Qualifications of Full-time and Part-time Teachers in Secondary Vocational Schools (Other Institutions) (105)
Breakdown of Full-time Teachers by Age in Secondary Vocational Schools (Institutions) (106)
Data on the Numbers by Teaching Course of Full-time and Part-time Teachers in Secondary Vocational Schools (108)
Changes of Full-time Teachers in Secondary Vocational Schools (Institutions) (110)
Condition of Fixed Assets and Teaching Resources in Secondary Vocational Schools (Institutions) (112)
Other Teachers, Staff & Workers in Secondary Vocational Schools (Institutions) (114)
Conditions of School Buidings in Secondary Vocational Schools (Total) (115)
Conditions of School Buidings in Secondary Vocational Schools (SSSs) (116)
Conditions of School Buidings in Secondary Vocational Schools (Adult SSSs) (117)
Conditions of School Buidings in Secondary Vocational Schools (High Vocational Schools) (118)
Conditions of School Buidings in Secondary Vocational Schools (Other Institutions) (119)
Basic Statistics of Vocational-Technical Training Institutions (120)

Condition of Fixed Assets and Teaching Resources in Vocational-Technical Training Institutions (122)

Junior Secondary Education

Number of Junior Schools and Classes (124)
Number of Schools, Classes Admitted in Vocational Schools (125)
Size of Junior Secondary Schools Classes (126)
Size of Vocational Junior Secondary Schools Classes (127)
Number of Students in Junior Secondary Schools (128)
Number of Students in Junior Secondary Schools (130)
Number of School－age Population. Enrolment of Junior Schools (132)
Number of School－age Population. Enrolment of Junior Schools (133)
Number of Teachers, Staff & Workers in Vocational Schools (134)
Number of Full-time Junior Secondary School Teachers by Subject Taught & Educational Attainment (136)
Number of Full-time Vocational Schools Teachers by Subjeot Taught Educational Attainment (136)
Full-time Teachers in Junior Secondary Schools Broken Down by Rank and Age (138)
Full-time Teachers in Vocational Secondary Schools Broken Down by Rank and Age (138)
Changes of Full-time Teachers in Junior Secondary Schools (140)
Changes of Full-time Teachers in Vocational Junior Secondary Schools (140)
Supplementary Information on Students and Full-time Teachers of Junior Secondary Schools (142)
Supplementary Information on Students and Full-time Teachers of Vocational Junior Secondary Schools (143)
Condition of School Buildings in Junior Secondary Schools (1) (144)
Condition of School Buildings in Junior Secondary Schools (2) (144)
Condition of School Buildings in Junior Secondary Schools (3) (144)
Condition of School Buildings in Vocational Junior Secondary Schools (1) (146)
Condition of School Buildings in Vocational Junior Secondary Schools (2) (146)
Condition of School Buildings in Vocational Junior Secondary Schools (3) (148)
Basic Statistics of Adult Schools by Province (148)

PRIMARY EDUCATION (PRIMARY SCHOOLS)

Number of Schools, Extemal Teachingsites & Classes in Primary Schools (150)
Size of Primary Classes (151)
Number of Students in Primary Schools (152)
Number on School－age Population of Primary Schools (154)
Number of Teachers, Staff & Workers in Primary Schools (158)
Breakdown of Full-time Primary School Teachers by Educational Attainment (160)
Full-time Teachers in Primary Schools Broken Down by Rank and Age (160)
Changes of Full-time Teachers in Primary Schools (162)
Supplementary Information on Students and Staff & Workers of Primary Schools (162)
Condition of School Buildings in Primary Schools (1) (164)
Condition of School Buildings in Primary Schools (2) (164)
Condition of School Buildings in Primary Schools (3) (166)
Basic Statistics of Adult Primary Schools by Province (166)

COMUNTIY HOUSE

Basic Statistics of Correctional Work-study Schools (168)

SPECIAL DUCATION

Basic Statistics of Special Education (170)
Condition of Minorities and Vocational & Skill Students in special Edu. Schools (172)
Number of Teachers, Staff and Workers in Special Education Schools (172)
Full-time Teachers in Special Education Schools Broken Down by Rank and Age (174)
Changes of Full-time Teachers in Special Education Schools (174)
Condition of School Buildings in Special Education Schools (174)

PRE - PRIMARY EDUCATION

Number of Kindergartens, Classes in Pre-Primary Education (177)
Number of Pre-school Education by Ages (178)
Number of Teachers, Staff & Workers in Kindergarten (180)
Breakdown of Kindergarten Heads and Teachers by Educational Attainment and Rank (182)
Supplementary Information on Staff & Workers and full-time teachers of Kindergarten (182)
Statistics of Kindergarten Buildings and Others (184)

CEOGRAPHICAL DISTRIBUTION OF SCHOOLS BY TYRE AND LEVEL

Number of Higher Education Institutions (187)
Data on Postgraduates in Higher Education Institutions (Total) (188)
Data on Postgraduates in Higher Education Institutions (190)
Data on Postgraduates in Higher Education Institutions (192)
Data on Students Enrolled in Normal and Short - cycle Courses in Higher Education (194)
Data on Students Enrolled in Regular Normal and Short - cycle Courses in Higher Education (196)
Data on Students Enrolled in Normal and Short - cycle Courses Provided by Adult HEIs in Higher Education (198)
Data on Students Enrolled in Normal and Short - cycle Courses Provided by Web - based Programs in Higher Education (200)
Data on Students of Comprehensive Universities (202)
Data on Students of of Institutions of Science & Technology (204)
Data on Students of of Institutions of Agriculture (206)
Data on Students of Institutions of Forestry (208)
Data on Students of Institutions of Medicine & Pharmacy (210)
Data on Students of Institutions of Teachers Colleges (212)
Data on Students of Institutions of Languages & Literatures (214)
Data on Students of Institutions of Finance & Economics (216)
Data on Students of Institutions of Political Science & Law (218)
Data on Students of Institutions of Physical Culture (220)
Data on Students of Institutions of Art (222)
Data on Students of Institutions of Art (224)
Data on Students of Short-cycle Vocational Colleges (226)
Number of Students in Radio/TV Universities by Type of Courses (228)
Number of Students in Workers' Colleges by Type of Courses (230)
Number of Students in Peasants Colleges (232)
Number of Students in Independent Correspondence Colleges (234)

Number of Students in Educational Colleges by Type of Courses (236)
Number of Students in Institutes for Administration by Type of Courses (238)
Number of Students by Type of Courses in Correspondence Divisions、Sparetime Schools & Short-cycle Courses for Adults run by Regular Institutions of Higher Education (242)
Number of Postgraduate Students Studying Without Leaving Their Jobs (244)
Data on Students Enrolled in Non-formal Programmes of HEIS (Total) (246)
Data on Students Enrolled in Non-formal Programmes of HEIS (Regular HEIs) (248)
Data on Students Enrolled in Non-formal Programmes of HEIS (HEIs for Adults) (250)
Data on Students Enrolled in Non-formal Programmes of HEIS (Non-state/Private HEIs) (252)
Data on Students Enrolled in Non-formal Programmes of HEIS (Research Institutes) (254)
Information on Foreign Students (256)
Aggregate Data on Staff and Workers in HEIs (258)
Aggregate Data on Female Staff and Workers in HEIs (260)
Aggregate Data on Staff and Workers in HEIs (Regular HEIs) (262)
Aggregate Data on Female Staff and Workers in HEIs (Regular HEIs) (264)
Aggregate Data on Staff and Workers in HEIs (HEIs for Adults) (266)
Aggregate Data on Female Staff and Workers in HEIs (HEIs for Adults) (268)
Aggregate Data on Female Staff and Workers in HEIs (Non-state/private HEIs) (270)
Aggregate Data on Female Staff and Workers in HEIs (Non-state/private HEIs) (272)
Data on Academic Qualifications、Rank of Full-time Teacher (Total) (274)
Data on Academic Qualifications、Rank of Full-time Teacher (HEIs) (275)
Data on Academic Qualifications、Rank of Full-time Teacher (HEIs for Adults) (276)
Data on Academic Qualifications、Rank of Full-time Teacher (Non-state/private HEIs) (277)
Aggregate Data on Academic Qualifications of Part-time Teachers in HEIs (278)
Aggregate Data on Academic Qualifications of Part-time Teachers in HEIs (279)
Aggregate Data on Academic Qualifications of Part-time Teachers in HEIs for Adults (280)
Aggregate Data on Academic Qualifications of Part-time Teachers in Non-state/private HEIs (281)
Condition of Fixed Assets and Teaching Resources (Owned by HEIs) (Total) (282)
Condition of Fixed Assets and Teaching Resources (Owned by HEIs) (HEIs) (284)
Condition of Fixed Assets and Teaching Resources (Owned by HEIs) (HEIs for Adults) (286)
Condition of Fixed Assets and Teaching Resources (Owned by HEIs) (Non-state/private HEIs) (288)
Condition of Fixed Assets and Teaching Resources (Not Owend by HEIs) (Total) (290)
Condition of Fixed Assets and Teaching Resources (Not Owned by HEIs) (HEIs) (292)
Condition of Fixed Assets and Teaching Resources (Not Owned by HEIs) (HEIs for Adults) (294)
Condition of Fixed Assets and Teaching Resources (Not Owned by HEIs) (Non-state/private HEIs) (296)
Conditions of School Buidings (Regional Aggregates) (298)
Conditions of School Buidings (HEIs) (299)
Conditions of School Buidings (HEIs for Adults) (300)
Conditions of School Buidings (Non-state/Private HEIs) (301)
Number of Senior Secondary Schools and Classes (Regional Aggregates) (302)
Number of Senior Secondary Schools and Classes (Urban) (303)
Number of Senior Secondary Schools and Classes (County Seats & Towns) (304)
Number of Senior Secondary Schools and Classes (Rural) (305)
Number of Students in Senior Secondary Schools (Regional Aggregates) (306)
Number of Students in Senior Secondary Schools (Urban) (307)
Number of Students in Senior Secondary Schools (County Seats & Towns) (308)
Number of Students in Senior Secondary Schools (Rural) (309)
Number of Female Students in Senior Secondary Schools (310)

Number of Teachers, Staff & Workers in General Secondary School (Regional Aggregates) (311)
Number of Teachers, Staff & Workers in General Secondary Schools (Urban) (312)
Number of Teachers, Staff & Workers in General Secondary Schools (County Seats & Towns) (313)
Number of Teachers, Staff & Workers in Grneral Secondary Schools (Rural) (314)
Number of Fenale Teachers, Staff & Workers in General Secondary Schools (315)
Number of General Secondary Schools Teachers, Staff & Workers Maintained by the Communities (316)
Breakdown of Senior Secondary Schools Heads and Teachers by Educational Attainment (Regional Aggregates) (318)
Breakdown of Senior Secondary Schools Heads and Teachers by Educational Attainment (Urban) (320)
Breakdown of Senior Secondary Schools Heads and Teachers by Educational Attainment (County Seats & Towns) (322)
Breakdown of Senior Secondary Schools Heads and Teachers by Educational Attainment (Rural) (324)
Condition of School Buildings in Senior Secondary Schools (1) (Regional Aggregates) (326)
Condition of School Buildings in Senior Secondary Schools (1) (Urban) (328)
Condition of School Buildings in Senior Secondary Schools (1) (County Seats & Towns) (330)
Condition of School Buildings in Senior Secondary Schools (1) (Rural) (332)
Condition of School Buildings in Senior Secondary Schools (2) (Regional Aggregates) (334)
Condition of School Buildings in Senior Secondary Schools (2) (Urban) (336)
Condition of School Buildings in Senior Secondary Schools (2) (Cornty Seats & Towns) (338)
Condition of School Buildings in Senior Secondary Schools (2) (Rural) (340)
Number of Secondary Vocational Schools (342)
Number of Students in Secondary Vocational Schools (Institutions) (344)
Number of Female Students in Secondary Vocational Schools (Institutions) (346)
Number of Students in Reg Specialized Sec. Schools (348)
Number of Female students in Reg. Specialized Sec. Schools (350)
Number of Students in Specialezed Sec. Schools for Adults (352)
Number of Female Students in Specialized Sec. Schools for Adults (354)
Number of Students in Vocational High Schools (356)
Number of Female Students in Vocational High Schools (358)
Number of Students by age in Secondary Vocational Schools (Institutions) (360)
Number of Female Students by age in Secondary Vocational Schools (Institutions) (362)
Data on Training Students of in Graduation Secondary Vocational Schools (Institutions) (364)
Data on Training Students of Enrolment in Secondary Vocational Schools (Institutions) (366)
Changes of Enrolment in Secondary Vocational Schools (Institutions) (368)
Changes of Female Enrolment in Secondary Vocational Schools (Institutions) (370)
Information on Foreign Students in Secondary Vocational Schools (Institutions) (372)
Number of Teachers, Staff & Workers in Secondary Vocational Schools (Institutions) (374)
Number of Femal Teachers, Staff & Workers in Secondary Vocational Schools (Institutions) (376)
Number of Teachers, Staff & Workers in Reg. Specialized Sec. Schools (378)
Number of Female Teachers, Staff & Workers in Reg. Specialized Sec. Schools (380)
Number of Teachers, Staff & Workers Specialized Sec. Schools for Adults (382)
Number of Female Teachers, Staff & Workers in Specialized Sec. Schools for Adults (384)
Number of Teachers, Staff & Workers in Vocational High Schools (386)
Number of Female Teachers, Staff & Workers in Vocational High Schools (388)
Number of Teachers, Staff & Workers in Other Institutions (390)
Number of Female Teachers, Staff & Workers in Other Institutions (392)
Data on Rank、Academic Qualifications of Full-time Teachers in Secondary Vocational Schools (Institutions) (394)
Data on Rank、Academic Qualifications of Full-time Teachers in Reb. Specialized Sec. Schools (396)
Data on Rank、Academic Qualifications of Full-time Teachers in Specialized Sec. Schools for Adults (398)
Data on Rank、Academic Qualifications of Full-time Teachers in Vocational High Schools (400)

Data on Rank、Academic Qualifications of Full-time Teachers in Other Institutions (402)
Condition of Fixed Assets and Teaching Resources in Secondary Vocational Schools (Institutions) (Owned by HEIs) (404)
Condition of Fixed Assets and Teaching Resources in Secondary Vocational Schools (Institutions) (Not Owned by HEIs) (406)
Condition of Fixed Assets and Teaching Resources in SSSs (Owned by HEIs) (408)
Condition of Fixed Assets and Teaching Resources in SSSs (Not Owned by HEIs) (410)
Condition of Fixed Assets and Teaching Resources in Adult SSSs (Owned by HEIs) (412)
Condition of Fixed Assets and Teaching Resources in Adult SSSs (Not Owned by HEIs) (414)
Condition of Fixed Assets and Teaching Resources in High Vocational Schools (Owned by HEIs) (416)
Condition of Fixed Assets and Teaching Resources in High Vocational Schools (Not Owned by HEIs) (418)
Condition of Fixed Assets and Teaching Resources in Other Institutions (Owned by HEIs) (420)
Condition of Fixed Assets and Teaching Resources in Other Institutions (Not Owned by HEIs) (422)
Conditions of School Buidings in Secondary Vocational Schools (Regional Aggregates) (424)
Conditions of School Buidings in Specialized Sec. Schools (425)
Conditions of School Buidings in Specialized Sec. Schools for Adults (426)
Conditions of School Buidings in Vocational High Schools (427)
Conditions of School Buidings in Other Institutions (428)
Basic Statistics of Vocaktional Technical Training Institutions (Total) (430)
Basic Statistics of Vocaktional Technical Training Schools (432)
Basic Statistics of Technical Training Schools for Peasants (434)
Basic Statistics of Others (436)
Condition of Fixed Assets and Teaching Resources in Vocational Technical Training Institutions (438)
Condition of Fixed Assets and Teaching Resources in Technical Training Schools (440)
Cndition of Fixed Assets and Teaching Resources in Technical Training Schools for Peasants (442)
Condition of Fixed Assets and Teaching Resources in Others (444)
Number of Junior Schools and Classes (Regional Aggregates) (445)
Number of Junior Schools and Classes (Urban) (447)
Number of Junior Schools and Classes (County Seats & Towns) (448)
Number of Junior Schools and Classes (Rural) (449)
Number of Schools, Classes Admitted in Vocational Schools (Regional Aggregates) (450)
Number of Schools, Classes Admitted in Vocational Schools (Urban) (451)
Number of Schools, Classes Admitted in Vocational Schools (County Seats & Towns) (452)
Number of Schools, Classes Admitted in Vocational Schools (Rural) (453)
Number of Students in Junior Secondary Schools (Regional Aggregates) (454)
Number of Students in Junior Secondary Schools (Urban) (455)
Number of Students in Junior Secondary Schools (County Seats & Towns) (456)
Number of Students in Junior Secondary Schools (Rural) (457)
Number of Female Students in Junior Secondary Schools (458)
Number of Students in Junior Secondary Schools (Regional Aggregates) (459)
Number of Students in Junior Secondary Schools (Urban) (460)
Number of Students in Junior Secondary Schools (County Seats & Towns) (461)
Number of Students in Junior Secondary Schools (Rural) (462)
Number of Female Students in Junior Secondary Schools (463)
Number of Teachers, Staff & Workers in Vocational Schools (Regional Aggregates) (464)
Number of Teachers, Staff & Workers in Vocational Schools (Urban) (465)

Number of Teachers, Staff & Workers in Vocational Schools (County Seats & Towns) (466)
Number of Teachers, Staff & Workers in Vocational Schools (Rural) (467)
Number of Female Teachers, Staff & Workers in Vocational Schools (468)
Number of General Secondary Schools Teachers, Staff & Workers Maintained by the Communities (469)
Breakdown of Junior Secondary Schools Heads and Teachers by Educational Attainment (Regional Aggregates) (470)
Breakdown of Junior Secondary Schools Heads and Teachers by Educational Attainment (Urban) (472)
Breakdown of Junior Secondary Schools Heads and Teachers by Educational Attainment (County Seats & Towns) (474)
Breakdown of Junior Secondary Schools Heads and Teachers by Educational Attainment (Rural) (476)
Breakdown of Vocational Junior Secondary Schools Heads and Teachers by Educational Attainment (Regional Aggregates) (478)
Breakdown of Vocational Junior Secondary Schools Heads and Teachers by Educational Attainment (Urban) (480)
Breakdown of Vocational Junior Secondary Schools Heads and Teachers by Educational Attainment (County Seats & Towns) (482)
Breakdown of Vocational Junior Secondary Schools Heads and Teachers by Educational Attainment (Rural) (484)
Condition of School Buildings in Junior Secondary Schools (1) (Regional Aggregates) (486)
Condition of School Buildings in Junior Secondary Schools (1) (Urban) (488)
Condition of School Buildings in Junior Secondary Schools (1) (County Seats & Towns) (490)
Cndition of School Buildings in Junior Secondary Schools (1) (Rural) (492)
Condition of School Buildings in Vocational Junior Secondary Schools (1) (Regional Aggrgates) (494)
Condition of School Buildings in Vocational Junior Secondary Schools (1) (Urban) (496)
Condition of School Buildings in Vocational Junior Secondary Schools (1) (County Seats & Towns) (498)
Condition of School Buildings in Vocational Junior Secondary Schools (1) (Rural) (500)
Condition of School Buildings in Junior Secondary Schools (2) (Regional Aggregates) (502)
Condition of School Buildings in Junior Secondary Schools (2) (Urban) (504)
Condition of School Buildings in Junior Secondary Schools (2) (County Seats & Towns) (506)
Condition of School Buildings in Junior Secondary Schools (2) (Rural) (508)
Condition of School Buildings in Vocational Junior Secondary Schools (2) (Regional Aggregates) (510)
Condition of School Buildings in Vocational Junior Secondary Schools (2) (Urban) (512)
Condition of School Buildings in Vocational Junior Secondary Schools (2) (County Seats & Towns) (514)
Condition of School Buildings in Vocational Junior Secondary Schools (2) (Rural) (516)
Number of Schools, External Teachingsites & Classes in Primary Schools (Regional Aggregates) (518)
Number of Schools, External Teachingsites & Classes in Primary Schools (Urban) (520)
Number of Schools, External Teachingsites & Classes in Primary Schools (County seats & Towns) (522)
Number of Schools, External Teachingsites & Classes in Primary Schools (Rural) (524)
Number of Students in Primary Schools (Regional Aggregates) (526)
Number of Students in Primary Schools (Urban) (528)
Number of Students in Primary Schools (County Seats & Towns) (530)
Number of Students in Primary Schools (Rural) (532)
Number of Students in 6-year Primary Schools (534)
Number of Female Students in Primary Schools (536)
Number of Teachers, Saff & Workers in Primary Schools (Regional Aggregates) (538)
Number of Teachers, Saff & Workers in Primary Schools (Urban) (540)
Number of Teachers, Staff &Workers in Primary Schools (County Seats & Towns) (542)
Number of Teachers, Staff &Workers in Primary Schools (Rural) (544)
Number of Primary Schools Teachers, Staff & Workers Maintained by the Comrounities (546)
Number of Female Teachers, Staff &Workers in Primary Schools (548)
Breakdown of Primary Schools Heads and Teachers by Educational Attainment (Regional Aggregates) (550)
Breakdown of Primary Schools Heads and Teachers by Educational Attainment (Urban) (552)

Breakdown of Primary Schools Heads and Teachers by Educational Attainment (County Seats & Towns) (554)
Breakdown of Primary Schools Heads and Teachers by Educational Attainment (Rural) (556)
Condition of School Buildings in Primary Schools (1) (Regiônal Aggregates) (558)
Condition of School Buildings in Primary Schools (1) (Urban) (560)
Condition of School Buildings in Primary Schools (1) (County Seats & Towns) (562)
Condition of School Buildings in Primary Schools (1) (Rural) (564)
Condition of School Buildings in Primary Schools (2) (Regional Aggregates) (566)
Condition of School Buildings in Primary Schools (2) (Urban) (568)
Condition of School Buildings in Primary Schools (2) (County Seats & Towns) (570)
Condition of School Buildings in Primary Schools (2) (Rural) (572)
Basic Statistics of Correctional Work-study Schools (574)
Basic Statistics of Special Education (Regional Aggregates) (576)
Basic Statistics of Special Education (Urban) (578)
Basic Statistics of Special Education (County Seats & Towns) (580)
Basic Statistics of Special Education (Rural) (582)
Number Of Female Studentsin Special Education (584)
Number of Teachers, Staff and Workers in Special Education Schools (Regional Aggregates) (586)
Number of Female Teachers, Staff and Workers in Special Education Schools (587)
Full-time Teachers in Special Education Schools Broken Down by Rank and Age (588)
Condition of School Buildings in Special Education Schools (590)
Basic Statistics of Kindergartens (Regional Aggregates) (592)
Basic Statistics of Kindergartens (Urban) (594)
Basic Statistics of Kindergartens (County Seats & Towns) (596)
Basic Statistics of Kindergartens (Rural) (598)
Number of Female Children in Kindergartens (600)
Number of Teachers, Staff & Workers in Kindergarten (Regional Aggregates) (601)
Number of Teachers, Staff & Workers in Kindergarten (Urban) (602)
Number of Teachers, Staff & Workers in Kindergarten (County Seats & Towns) (603)
Number of Teachers, Staff & Workers in Kindergarten (Rural) (604)
Number of Female Teachers, Staff & Workers in Kindergarten (605)
Breakdown of Kindergarten Heads and Teachers by Educational Attainment and Rank (Regional Aggregates) (606)
Breakdown of Kindergarten Heads and Teachersby Educational Attainment and Rank (Urban) (608)
Breakdown of Kindergarten Heads and Teachers by Educational Attainment and Rank (County Seats & Towns) (610)
Breakdown of Kindergarten Heads and Teachers by Educational Attainment and Rank (Rural) (612)
Statistics of Kindergarten Buildings and Others (Regional Aggregates) (614)
Statistics of Kindergarten Buildings and Others (Urban) (616)
Statistics of Kindergarten Buildings and Others (County Seats & Towns) (618)
Statistics of Kindergarten Buildings and Others (Rural) (620)

Part Ⅱ

Physical Facilities

Public Expenditure on Education

Statistics of Kindergarten Buildings and Others (Raral) (623)
Sources of Educational Fund and Expenditure for Education (624)
Sources of Educational Fund and Expenditure for Education by Region (2002) (626)

Capital Construction Investment in the Educational Sector

Sources of Educational Fund and Expenditure Education in Various Schools (2002) (630)
Data on the Completion of Capital Construction Investment in the Educational Sector (632)

Instrument and Equipment

Data on the Completion of Capital Construction Investment in the Educational Sector (636)

Part Ⅲ

Scientific Research Activites & Other

Natural Science and Technology

Scientific and Technical Manpowerin Regular HEIs (638)
Statistics of Scientists and Engineer Among S & T Manpower in Regular HEIs by Level of Post (640)
S & T Expenditure in Regular HEIs (642)
Statistics of R & D Projects and Achievements in Regular HEIs (644)

Social Science

Professional Manpower in Regular HEIs in the Fields of the Humanities and Social Acience (648)
Humanities and Social Sciences R & D Expenditure in Regular HEIs (650)
Basic Statistics of Humunities and Social Sciences R & D and Achievements in Regular HEIs (652)
Applicants of Student for Regular Higher Educational Institutions (2002) (654)
Applicants of Student for Regular Higher Educational Institutions (2003) (660)

Appendixes

Gross Domestic Product (666)
Gross Domestic Product by Region (2002) (667)
Total Government Revernue and Expenditures and Their Increase Rate (668)
Total Revenue and Expenditures of Central and Local Governments (669)
Population and Its Composition (670)
Illterate and Semi-Literate Population Aged 15 and Over by Gender and Region (671)
Population by Gender, Educational Level and Region (672)

第一部分
Part I

教育事业发展
The Development of the Educational Undertaking

一、综合部分
Summary Tables

全国各级各类学校校数、教职工、专任教师情况

The Number of Schools of all Types and Levels Staffs and Fulltime Teachers

	学校数(所) No. of Schools	教职工数(人) Staff & Workers	专任教师(人) Full-time Teachers
一、高等教育 Higher Education			
(一)研究生培养机构(不计校数) Institutions Providing Postgraduate Programs	720		
1. 普通高校 Regular HEIs	407		
2. 科研机构 Research Institutes	313		
(二)普通高等学校 Regular HEIs	1552	1452623	724658
1. 本科院校 University	644	1060628	502458
2. 专科院校 Non-university Tertiry	908	350636	196872
其中:职业技术学院 Of Which: Tertiary Vocational-technical Colleges	711	268239	149473
3. 其他机构(点)(不计校数) Other Institutions	284	41359	25328
(三)成人高等学校 Adult HEIs	558	158397	85141
(四)民办的其他高等教育机构 Non-state/private HEIs	1104	52537	24543
1. 学历文凭考试机构 Institutions Adm. Exams for Formal	384	29733	13733
2. 非学历文凭考试机构 Institutions Adm. Exams for Non-formal	720	22804	10810
二、中等教育 Secondary Education			
(一)高中阶段教育 Senior Secondary	31778	6588332	1789541
1. 高中 Senior Secondary Schools	17096	5505370	1076629
普通高中 Regular Schools	15779	5496535	1070575
成人高中 Adult Schools	1317	8835	6054
2. 中等职业教育 Secondary Vocational Schools	14682	1082962	712912
普通中专 Regular Specialized Sec. Schools	3065	347013	198550
成人中专 Adult SSSs	2823	126113	75341
职业高中 Vocational High Schools	5824	363312	257945
技工学校 Skilled Workers Schools	2970	202190	152960
其他机构(教学点)(不计校数) Other Institutions	2275	44334	28116
(二)初中阶段教育 Junior Secondary Education			
1. 普通初中 Regular Junior Secondary Schools	63711		3466735
2. 职业初中 Vocational JSSs	1019	36300	30788
3. 成人初中 Adult JSSs	1920	8203	4801
三、初等教育 Primary Education			
(一)普通小学 Regular Primary Schools	425846	6256185	5702750
(二)成人小学 Adult Primary Schools	82713	124059	47609
其中:扫盲班 Of Which: Literacy Classes	55901	86317	28674
四、工读学校 Correctional Work-Study Schools	82	2636	1580
五、特殊教育 Special Education Schools	1551	40853	30349
六、学前教育 Pre-school Education Institutions	116390	973159	612856

注:普通高中的教职工数中包含普通初中的教职工数。

Note: Data on Staff and workers in regular junior secondary schools are included in the data of regular senior secondary schools.

全国各级各类学历教育学生情况

The Number of Graduates, Entrants, Enrolment of Schools of All Types and Level Providing Formal Programs

	毕业生数(人) Graduats	招生数(人) Entrants	在校生数(人) Enrolments
一、高等教育 Higher Education			
(一)研究生 Postgraduates	111091	268925	651260
(二)普通本专科 Undergraduates in Regular HEIs	1877492	3821701	11085642
(三)成人本专科 Undergraduates in Adult HEIs	1593358		5591573
(四)其他各类高等学历教育 Students Enrolled in Other Formal Programs			
1. 在职人员攻读博士、硕士学位 Employed People Enrolled in Doctoral and Master's Degree Programs		59747	149695
2. 网络本专科生 Web-based Undergraduates	144408	841496	1860749
3. 学历文凭考试 Students Preparing for Exams Awarding Formal Qualifications	99671	157967	393759
二、中等教育 Secondary Education			
(一)高中阶段教育 Senior Secondary	8210081	12678793	32433993
1. 高中 Senior Secondary Schools			
普通高中 Regular Schools	4581235	7521264	19648261
成人高中 Adult Schools	164842		218468
2. 中等职业教育 Secondary Vocational Schools	3464004	5157529	12567264
普通中专 Regular Specialized Sec. Schools	1484471	1838777	5023708
成人中专 Adult SSSs	400315	429818	1054511
职业高中 Vocational High Schools	1126652	1972571	4557622
技工学校 Skilled Workers Schools	452566	916363	1931423
(二)初中阶段教育 Junior Secondary Education			
1. 普通初中 Regular Junior Secondary Schools	19955825	21953113	66184186
2. 职业初中 Vocational JSSs	228816	248172	724087
3. 成人初中 Adult JSSs	613854		528155
三、初等教育 Primary Education			
(一)普通小学 Regular Primary Schools	22678857	18293875	116897395
(二)成人小学 Adult Primary Schools	3933231		3814850
其中:扫盲班 Of Which: Literacy Classes	2031417		1952204
四、工读学校 Correctional Work-Study Schools	3390	3373	7452
五、特殊教育 Special Education Schools	44533	48840	364740
六、学前教育 Pre-school Education Institutions	10719922	13167889	20039061

注:成人本专科在校生数为2002年数据,2003年成人本专科无招生数,下同。

Note: Data on enrolment figures of adult HEIs are 2002 data, There is no enrolment in 2003. same as the followings.

全国各级各类非学历教育学生情况

Data on Students Enrdment in Non-formal Programmes of All Types and Levels

	毕(结)业生数(人) Corupleters	招生数(人) Entrants	在校生数(人) Enrolment
一、高等教育 Higher Education	3532533	2943758	2395186
(一)研究生课程进修班 Postgraduate Courses	104355	102623	172169
(二)自考助学班 Classes run by Non-state/private HEIs for Students Preparing for State-administered Examinations for Self-directed Leacners	220554	286065	764010
(三)普通预科生 College preparatory Classes	12169	22186	22151
(四)证书教育 Programs Awarding Certificates on Completion of Courses	291922	252334	219050
(五)岗位培训 Job-related Training	1773468	1202767	620513
(六)进修及培训 In-service Training	1130065	1077783	597293
二、中等教育 Secondary Education	72420768		56772232
(一)中等职业教育 Secondary Vocational Schools	5646046		2972650
(二)职业技术培训机构 Other Vocational-technical Training Institutions	66774722		53799582

全国各级民办教育基本情况

Data on Non-state/private Schools

	学校数(所) Schools	毕业生数(人) Graduates	招生数(人) Entrants	在校生数(人) Enrollment	教职工数(人) Staff & Worker	专任教师(人) Fulltime Teacher
一、民办高等教育 Non-state/private HEIs						
(一)普通高校 Regular HEIs	173	52061	375658	810030	86743	50143
(二)成人高校 Adult HEIs	2	687	566	2046	253	128
(三)民办的其他高等教育机构 Other Categories of Non-state/private HEIs	1104	836121	880289	1004048	52537	24543
二、民办中等教育机构 Non-state/private Secondary Schools						
(一)高中阶段教育 Senior Secondary						
其中:民办普通高中 Of Which: Non-state/private General Secondary Schools	2679	253327	634945	1413680	291604	201421
民办中等职业教育 Non-state/private Secondary Vocational Schools	1382	185967	388943	793804	62779	36585
(二)初中阶段教育 Junior Secondary						
其中:民办普通初中 Of Which: Non-state/private General Secondary Schools	3651	534789	938817	2565747		
民办职业初中 Non-state/private Secondary Vocational Schools	53	5339	8709	22786	1253	879
三、民办普通小学 Non-state/private Primary Schools	5676	374728	474421	2749341	162825	117239
四、民办幼儿园 Non-state/private Kindergartens	55536	1784947	2664739	4802297	383942	228791

注:民办普通高中的教职工数包含民办普通初中的教职工数据。

Note: Data on staff and workers in Non-state/private Junior secondary schools are included in the data of non-state/private senior secondary schools.

各级各类学校女学生和女教职工数

Number of Female Students, Teachers, Staff & Workers of Schools of All Levels & Types

单位:万人

Unit:in 10 thousand

	女学生 Female Students		女教职工 Female Teachers, Staff & Workers		女专任教师 Female Full-time Teachers	
	人数 Number	占学生总数的比重(%) Percentage	人数 Number	占教职工总数的比重(%) Percentage	人数 Number	占专任教师总数的比重(%) Percentage
普通高等学校 Regular HEIs	474.12	44.52	61.68	42.46	30.23	41.71
成人高等学校 HEIs for Adults	65.47	51.89	7.06	44.55	3.91	45.91
民办的其他高等教育机构 Non-state/private HEIs	45.81	45.62	2.20	41.90	1.03	42.04
普通高中 Regular Senior Sec. Schools	885.72	45.08	230.90	42.01	43.06	40.22
成人高中 Senior Sec. Schools for Adults	10.55	48.27				
中等职业学校 Sec. Voc. Schools	551.83	51.88	38.55	43.77	25.84	46.15
普通初中 Regular Junior Sec. Schools	3138.14	47.42			157.00	45.29
职业初中 Junior Sec. Vocational Schools	33.73	46.58	1.22	33.51	1.10	35.71
成人初中 Junior Sec. Schools for Adults	33.17	47.59				
小学 Primary Schools	5503.76	47.08	323.73	51.75	305.42	53.56
成人小学 Primary Schools for Adults	195.97	51.37				
工读学校 Correctional Work Study Schools	0.09	11.59	0.08	30.12	0.05	29.11
特殊教育学校 Special Education	12.74	34.93	2.73	66.90	2.20	72.51
幼儿园 Kindergartens	906.76	45.25	91.01	93.52	60.22	98.27

注:普通高中女教职工数包括普通初中女教职工数。

普通高校不包括成人本专科的数据。成人高校学生数为2002年数据。

Note:Data on female teachers,staff and workers of junior secondary schools are included in the data of senior secondary schools.

Data of regular do not include the data of adult HEIs senior. Data of adult HEIs students are the statistics of 2002.

各级各类学校少数民族学生和少数民族教职工数

Number of Minority Students Enrolled, Teachers, Staff & Workers of Schools of All Levels & Types.

单位:万人

Unit:in 10 thousand

	少数民族学生 Minority Students		少数民族教职工 Minority Teachers, Staff & Workers		少数民族专任教师 Minority Full-time Teachers	
	人数 Number	占学生总数的比重(%) Percentage	人数 Number	占教职工总数的比重(%) Percentage	人数 Number	占专任教师总数的比重(%) Percentage
普通高等学校 Regular HEIs	69.76	6.55	6.77	4.66	3.63	5.01
成人高等学校 HEIs for Adults	12.00	9.51	0.83	5.25	0.46	5.42
民办的其他高等教育机构 Non-state/private HEIs			0.06	1.17	0.03	1.11
普通高中 Regular Senior Sec. Schools	128.13	6.52	39.97	7.27	6.61	6.18
中等职业学校 Secondary Voc. Schools	56.49	5.31	4.39	4.99	2.79	4.98
普通初中 Regular Junior Sec. Schools	526.33	7.95			26.73	7.71
职业初中 Junior Sec. Vcational Schools	8.74	12.07	0.35	9.72	0.30	9.72
小学 Primary Schools	1120.70	9.59	62.70	10.02	57.09	10.01
特殊教育 Special Education	2.56	7.01	0.21	5.06	0.15	5.09
幼儿园 Kindergartens	117.75	5.88	3.93	4.04	2.62	4.28

注:普通高中少数民族教职工数包括普通初中少数民族教职工数。

普通高校不包括成人本专科的数据。成人高校学生数为 2002 年数据。

Note:The number of minority teachers,staff and workers employed by junior secondary schools is included in that employ by senior secondary schools.

Data of regular do not include the data of adult HEIs senior. Data of adult HEIs students are the statistics of 2002.

各级各类学校校数

Number of Schools of All Levels & Types

单位:所

Unit : Number of Schools

	1949	1965	1978	1980	1985	2000	2002	2003
一、高等教育 Higher Education								
(一)研究生培养机构(不计校数) Institutions Providing Postgraduate Programs						738	728	720
1. 普通高校 Regular HEIs						415	408	407
2. 科研机构 Research Institutes						323	320	313
(二)普通高等学校 Regular HEIs	205	434	598	675	1016	1041	1396	1552
1. 本科院校 University						599	629	644
2. 专科院校 Non-university Tertiry						442	767	908
其中:职业技术学院 Of Which: Tertiary Vocational-technical Colleges						548		711
3. 分校、大专班(点)(不计校数) Branch Schools & SCHE Classes								284
(三)成人高等学校 Adult HEIs	1	964	10395	2775	1216	772	607	558
(四)民办的其他高等教育机构 Non-state/private HEIs								1104
1. 学历文凭考试机构 Institutions Adm. Exams for Formal								384
2. 非学历文凭考试机构 Institutions Adm. Exams for Non-formal								720
二、中等教育 Secondary Education								
(一)高中阶段教育 Senior Secondary								31883
1. 高中 Senior Secondary Schools								17096
普通高中 Regular Schools	1597	4112	49215	31300	17318	14564	15406	15779
成人高中 Adult Schools						1939	1463	1317
2. 中等职业教育 Secondary Vocational Schools								14787
普通中专 Regular Specialized Sec. Schools	1171	1265	2760	3069	3557	3646	2953	3065
成人中专 Adult SSSs						4634	3473	2823
职业高中 Vocational High Schools						7655	6418	5824
技工学校 Skilled Workers Schools	3	281	2013	3305	3548	3792	3075	3075
其他机构(教学点)(不计校数) Other Institutions								2275
(二)初中阶段教育 Junior Secondary Education								
1. 普通初中 Regular Junior Secondary Schools	2448	13990	113130	87077	75903	62704	64661	63711
2. 职业初中 Vocational JSSs						1194	984	1019
3. 成人初中 Adult JSSs						2001	1802	1920
三、初等教育 Primary Education								
(一)普通小学 Regular Primary Schools	346769	1681939	949323	917316	832309	553622	456903	425846
(二)成人小学 Adult Primary Schools					100337	156839	106398	82713
其中:扫盲班 Of Which: Literacy Classes					176076	104863	70346	55901
四、工读学校 Correctional Work-Study Schools	–	–	–	–	98	74	76	82
五、特殊教育 Special Education Schools	–	266	292	292	375	1539	1540	1551
六、学前教育 Pre-school Education Institutions	–	19226	163952	170419	172262	175836	111752	116390

各级各类学历教育学生数

Number of Enrolment of Schools of All Types and Level Providing Formal Programs

单位:万人

Unit:in 10 Thousand

	1949	1965	1978	1980	1985	2000	2002	2003
一、高等教育 Higher Education								
(一)研究生(人) Postgraduates(Person)	629	4546	10934	21604	87331	301239	500980	651260
(二)普通本专科 Undergraduates in Regular HEIs	11.65	67.44	85.63	114.37	170.31	556.09	903.36	1108.56
(三)成人本专科 Undergraduates in Adult HEIs	0.01	41.30	140.8	155.4	172.50	353.64	559.16	559.16
(四)其他各类高等学历教育 Students Enrolled in Other Formal Programs								
1. 在职人员攻读博士、硕士学位 Employed People Enrolled in Doctoral and Master's Degree Programs								14.97
2. 网络本专科生 Web-based Undergraduates								121.14
3. 学历文凭考试 Students Preparing for Exams Awarding Formal Qualifications								39.38
二、中等教育 Secondary Education								
(一)高中阶段教育 Senior Secondary								3243.40
1. 高中 Senior Secondary Schools								
普通高中 Regular Schools	20.72	130.82	1553.08	969.79	741.13	1201.26	1683.81	1964.83
成人高中 Adult Schools				75.12	138.98	32.40	33.52	21.85
2. 中等职业教育 Secondary Vocational Schools								1256.73
普通中专 Regular Specialized Sec. Schools	22.88	54.74	88.92	124.34	157.11	489.52	456.35	502.37
成人中专 Adult SSSs	0.01	351.8	123.9	449.4		169.26	153.28	105.45
职业高中 Vocational High Schools	–	77.50	...	31.92	184.34	414.56	428.13	455.76
技工学校 Skilled Workers Schools	0.27	10.10	38.20	70.04	74.17	140.1	152.99	193.14
(二)初中阶段教育 Junior Secondary Education								
1. 普通初中 Regular Junior Secondary Schools	83.18	802.97	4995.17	4538.29	3964.83	6167.65	6604.06	6618.42
2. 职业初中 Vocational JSSs	–	365.84	...	13.45	45.23	88.64	83.37	72.41
3. 成人初中 Adult JSSs				302.57	273.30	18.77	25.01	52.82
三、初等教育 Primary Education								
(一)普通小学 Regular Primary Schools	2439.10	11620.90	14624.00	14627.00	13370.20	13013.25	12156.71	11689.74
(二)成人小学 Adult Primary Schools	1326.8	823.7	6467.2	1646.1	303.23	480.88	467.83	381.49
其中:扫盲班 Of Which: Literacy Classes	1326.8		1806.7	1220.9	518.98	249.32	177.39	195.22
四、工读学校 Correctional Work-Study Schools	–	–	–	...	0.65	0.77	0.79	0.75
五、特殊教育 Special Education Schools	...	2.29	3.09	3.31	4.17	37.76	37.45	36.47
六、学前教育 Pre-school Education Institutions	...	171.30	787.70	1150.80	1479.70	2244.18	2036.02	2003.91

注:2003 年成人本专科学生为 2002 年数据。

Note:Data on 2003 undergraduates in Adult HEIs are the statistics of 2002.

各级各类学历教育招生数

Number of New Entrants of Schools of All Types and Level Providing Formal Programs

单位:万人

Unit:in 10 Thousand

	1949	1965	1978	1980	1985	2000	2002	2003
一、高等教育 Higher Education								
(一)研究生(人) Postgraduates(person)	242	1456	10708	3616	46871	128484	202611	268925
(二)普通本专科 Undergraduates in Regular HEIs	3.06	16.42	40.15	28.12	61.92	220.61	320.50	382.17
(三)成人本专科 Undergraduates in Adult HEIs					78.78	156.15	222.32	
(四)其他各类高等学历教育 Students Enrolled in Other Formal Programs								
1. 在职人员攻读博士、硕士学位 Employed People Enrolled in Doctoral and Master's Degree Programs								5.97
2. 网络本专科生 Web-based Undergraduates								22.39
3. 学历文凭考试 Students Preparing for Exams Awarding Formal Qualifications								15.80
二、中等教育 Secondary Education								
(一)高中阶段教育 Senior Secondary								1267.88
1. 高中 Senior Secondary Schools								
普通高中 Regular Schools	7.11	45.89	692.91	383.40	257.51	472.69	676.70	752.13
成人高中 Adult Schools				50.05	107.61	30.47	30.49	
2. 中等职业教育 Secondary Vocational Schools								515.75
普通中专 Regular Specialized Sec. Schools	9.74	20.85	44.70	46.76	66.83	132.59	155.31	183.88
成人中专 Adult SSSs				152.22		53.39	57.55	42.98
职业高中 Vocational High Schools	–	55.67	...	24.06	98.49	150.39	187.36	197.26
技工学校 Skilled Workers Schools	...	...	25.70	33.13	35.54	50.38	73.33	91.64
(二)初中阶段教育 Junior Secondary Education								
1. 普通初中 Regular Junior Secondary Schools	34.12	299.89	2005.98	1550.91	1349.40	2263.3	2252.30	2195.31
2. 职业初中 Vocational JSSs	–	250.81	...	6.66	17.61	32.27	29.52	24.82
3. 成人初中 Adult JSSs				194.81	237.02	14.67	17.77	
三、初等教育 Primary Education								
(一)普通小学 Regular Primary Schools	680.00	3296.02	3315.36	2942.34	2298.17	1946.47	1952.80	1829.39
(二)成人小学 Adult Primary Schools				248.29	194.95	452.52	432.96	
其中:扫盲班 Of Which: Literacy Classes				720.48	326.14	210.61	146.81	
四、工读学校 Correctional Work-Study Schools	–	–	–	...	0.32	0.44	0.52	0.34
五、特殊教育 Special Education Schools	...	...	0.59	0.59	0.92	5.29	5.29	4.88
六、学前教育 Pre-school Education Institutions	...					1531.11	1373.61	1316.79

各级各类学校教职工数

Number of Staff and Workers of Schools of All Levels & Types

单位:万人

Unit : in 10 thousand

	1949	1965	1978	1980	1985	2000	2002	2003
一、高等教育 Higher Education								
(一)研究生培养机构(不计校数) Institutions Providing Postgraduate Programs								
1. 普通高校 Regular HEIs								
2. 科研机构 Research Institutes								
(二)普通高等学校 Regular HEIs	4.60	33.30	51.80	63.20	87.06	111.28	130.36	145.26
1. 本科院校 University						92.69	100.11	106.06
2. 专科院校 Non-university Tertiry						17.50	28.71	35.06
其中:职业技术学院 of Which: Tertiary Vocational-technical Colleges								26.82
3. 分校、大专班(点)(不计校数) Branch Schools & SCHE Classes						1.08	1.54	4.14
(三)成人高等学校 Adult HEIs				6.45	14.34	18.70	16.81	15.84
(四)民办的其他高等教育机构 Non-state/private HEIs								5.25
1. 学历文凭考试机构 Institutions Adm. Exams for Formal								2.97
2. 非学历文凭考试机构 Institutions Adm. Exams for Non-formal								2.28
二、中等教育 Secondary Education								
(一)高中阶段教育 Senior Secondary								658.83
1. 高中 Senior Secondary Schools								550.54
普通高中 Regular Schools	10.40	67.70	391.70	389.70	355.69	491.1	533.48	549.65
成人高中 Adult Schools					5.65	2.17	1.62	0.88
2. 中等职业教育 Secondary Vocational Schools								108.30
普通中专 Regular Specialized Sec. Schools	2.40	12.20	23.70	29.80	40.32	48.81	38.15	34.70
成人中专 Adult SSSs				3.19		20.84	14.52	12.61
职业高中 Vocational High Schools	–	30.60	...	4.10	21.59	44.69	43.03	36.33
技工学校 Skilled Workers Schools	...	...	6.66	13.61	21.53	23.96	20.34	20.22
其他机构(教学点)(不计校数) Other Institutions								4.43
(二)初中阶段教育 Junior Secondary Education								
1. 普通初中 Regular Junior Secondary Schools								
2. 职业初中 Vocational JSSs								3.63
3. 成人初中 Adult JSSs					7.29	0.79	0.80	0.82
三、初等教育 Primary Education								
(一)普通小学 Regular Primary Schools	84.90	407.50	562.00	605.40	602.10	645.49	634.02	625.62
(二)成人小学 Adult Primary Schools				2.02		16.24	11.68	12.41
其中:扫盲班 Of Which: Literacy Classes				7.40		11.01	8.07	8.63
四、工读学校 Correctional Work-Study Schools	–	–	–	...	0.32	0.27	0.25	0.26
五、特殊教育 Special Education Schools	...	0.37	0.69	0.80	1.15	4.37	4.04	4.09
六、学前教育 Pre-school Education Institutions	...	16.20	46.90	61.00	79.80	114.43	90.33	97.32

各级各类学校专任教师数

Number of Fulltime Teachers of Schools of All Levels & Types

单位:万人

Unit : in 10 thousand

	1949	1965	1978	1980	1985	2000	2002	2003
一、高等教育 Higher Education								
(一)研究生培养机构(不计校数) Institutions Providing Postgraduate Programs								
1. 普通高校 Regular HEIs								
2. 科研机构 Research Institutes								
(二)普通高等学校 Regular HEIs	1.61	13.81	20.63	24.69	34.43	46.28	61.84	72.47
1. 本科院校 University						37.08	45.49	50.25
2. 专科院校 Non-university Tertiry						8.66	15.59	19.69
其中:职业技术学院 Of Which: Tertiary Vocational-technical Colleges								14.95
3. 分校、大专班(点)(不计校数) Branch Schools & SCHE Classes						0.53	0.77	2.53
(三)成人高等学校 Adult HEIs				3.32	6.93	9.34	8.89	8.51
(四)民办的其他高等教育机构 Non-state/private HEIs								2.45
1. 学历文凭考试机构 Institutions Adm. Exams for Formal								1.37
2. 非学历文凭考试机构 Institutions Adm. Exams for Non-formal								1.08
二、中等教育 Secondary Education								
(一)高中阶段教育 Senior Secondary								178.95
1. 高中 Senior Secondary Schools								107.66
普通高中 Regular Schools	1.40	7.79	74.13	57.07	49.17	75.69	94.6	107.06
成人高中 Adult Schools					3.23	1.35	1.01	0.61
2. 中等职业教育 Secondary Vocational Schools								71.29
普通中专 Regular Specialized Sec. Schools	1.56	5.51	9.96	12.87	17.40	25.64	20.78	19.86
成人中专 Adult SSSs				1.78		11.83	8.41	7.53
职业高中 Vocational High Schools	–	5.29	...	1.65	11.58	28.18	27.27	25.79
技工学校 Skilled Workers Schools	...	...	2.80	6.14	8.89	14	12.6	15.30
其他机构(教学点)(不计校数) Other Institutions								2.81
(二)初中阶段教育 Junior Secondary Education								
1. 普通初中 Regular Junior Secondary Schools	5.26	37.92	244.07	244.90	215.99	324.86	343.03	346.67
2. 职业初中 Vocational JSSs	–	14.42	...	0.67	2.49	3.83	3.74	3.08
3. 成人初中 Adult JSSs					5.00	0.43	0.49	0.48
三、初等教育 Primary Education								
(一)普通小学 Regular Primary Schools	83.60	385.71	522.55	549.94	537.68	586.03	577.89	570.28
(二)成人小学 Adult Primary Schools				1.65	2.87	4.76	3.64	4.76
其中:扫盲班 Of Which: Literacy Classes				4.83	4.26	2.93	2.28	2.87
四、工读学校 Correctional Work-Study Schools	–	–	–	...	0.13	0.15	0.15	0.16
五、特殊教育 Special Education Schools	...	0.26	0.42	0.48	0.73	3.2	2.98	3.03
六、学前教育 Pre-school Education Institutions	...	6.18	27.75	41.07	54.99	85.65	57.12	61.29

高中阶段教育学生数的构成

Composition of Students in Senior Sec. Schools

	合计 Total	普通高中 Senior General Secondary Schools	成人高中 Adult Secondary Schools	中等职业教育 Secondary Vocational Schools				
				小计 Subtotal	中等专业学校 Specialized Sec. Schools	成人中专 Adult SSSs	职业高中 Vocational High Schools	技工学校 Skilled Worker Schools
学生数(万人) No. of Students (in 10 thousand)								
1965	622.9	130.8		492.1	52.7	351.8	77.5	10.1
1980	1720.5	969.8	75.1	675.6	124.3	449.4	31.9	70.0
1985	1295.7	741.1	139.0	415.6	157.1		184.3	74.2
1990	1528.6	717.3	47.8	763.5	224.4	158.8	247.1	133.2
2000	2463.2	1201.3	32.4	1229.5	489.5	169.3	414.6	156.1
2001	2606.3	1405.0	31.0	1170.3	457.9	189.2	383.1	140.1
2002	2889.8	1683.8	33.5	1172.5	456.4	153.3	428.1	134.7
2003	3243.4	1964.8	21.5	1256.7	502.4	105.5	455.7	193.1
比重(%)Percentage								
1965	100	21.0		79.0	8.5	56.5	12.4	1.6
1980	100	56.4	4.4	39.3	7.2	26.1	1.9	4.1
1985	100	57.2	10.7	32.1	12.1		14.2	5.7
1990	100	46.9	3.1	49.9	14.7	10.4	16.2	8.7
2000	100	48.8	1.3	49.9	19.9	6.9	16.8	6.3
2001	100	53.9	1.2	44.9	17.6	7.3	14.7	5.4
2002	100	58.3	1.2	40.6	15.8	5.3	14.8	4.7
2003	100	60.6	0.7	38.7	15.5	3.3	14.1	5.9

教育规模

Size of Education

单位:万人

Unit : in 10 thousand person

年份 Year	学校数(万所) Schools (in 10 Thousand)	学生数 Enrolment	教职工数 Teachers Scaff & Workers	教育人口 Educational Population	教育人口比重(%) Propotion of Education Population
1985	144	21753	1261	23014	22.0
1990	136	23654	1432	25086	22.2
1996	155	30401	1549	31950	26.2
1997	157	31076	1577	32653	26.7
1998	155	31809	1580	33389	27.0
1999	159	32672	1596	34268	27.5
2000	149	32093	1592	33685	26.8
2001	135	32135	1574	33709	26.6
2002	117	31873	1579	33452	26.2
2003	96	31989	1610	33599	26.2

小学学龄儿童入学率

Net Enrolment Ratio of School-age Children in Primary Schools

单位:万人

Unit:in 10 Thousand person

年　份 Year	学龄儿童入学率 Net Enrolment Ratio of School-age Children in various regions.		
	全国学龄儿童数 Total No. of School-age Children	已入学学龄儿童数 No. of School-age Children Enrolled	入学率(%) Net Enrolment Ratio
1965	11603.2	9829.1	84.7
1980	12219.6	11478.2	93.0
1985	10362.3	9942.8	95.9
1990	9740.7	9529.7	97.8
1999	12991.4	12872.8	99.1
2000	12445.3	12333.9	99.1
2001	11766.4	11561.2	99.1
2002	11310.4	11150.0	98.6
2003	10908.3	10761.6	98.7

* 1991 年以前的入学率是按 7 - 11 周岁统一计算的。从 1991 年起入学率是按各地不同入学年龄和学制分别计算的。

Enrolment Ratio of school-age children before 1991 was calculated on the basis of primary school pupils aged 7 - 11 enroled. From 1991 onwards its calculation has taken account of the age of entry and the lenth of schooling prevailing.

各级教育毛入学率

Gross Enrolment Rate of Schools of All Levels

单位:%

Unit: %

年　份 Year	小学 Primary 按各地相应学龄计算 According to provincial entrant age primary Schools years	初中 Junior 12 - 14 周岁 the age of 12 - 14	高中阶段 Senior 15 - 17 周岁 the age of 15 - 17		高等教育 IHEs 18 - 22 周岁 the age of 18 - 22
			职前	全口径	
1990	111.0	66.7	21.9		3.4
1991	109.5	69.7	23.9		3.5
1992	109.4	71.8	22.6	26.0	3.9
1993	107.3	73.1	24.1	28.4	5.0
1994	108.7	73.8	26.2	30.7	6.0
1995	106.6	78.4	28.8	33.6	7.2
1996	105.7	82.4	31.4	38.0	8.3
1997	104.9	87.1	33.8	40.6	9.1
1998	104.3	87.3	34.4	40.7	9.8
1999	104.3	88.6	35.8	41.0	10.5
2000	104.6	88.6	38.2	42.8	12.5
2001	104.5	88.7	38.6	42.8	13.3
2002	107.5	90.0	38.4	42.8	15.0
2003	107.2	92.7	42.1	43.8	17.0

各级普通学校毕业生升学率

Promotion Rate of Graduates of Regular School of All Levels & Types

年 份 Year	小学升初中(%) Promotion Rate of Primary School Graduates	初中升高级中学(%) Promotion Rate of Junior Sec. School Graduates	高中升高等教育(%) Promotion Rate of Senior Sec. School Graduates
1990	74.6	40.6	27.3
1991	77.7	42.6	28.7
1992	79.7	43.6	34.9
1993	81.8	44.1	43.3
1994	86.6	47.8	46.7
1995	90.8	50.3	49.9
1996	92.6	49.8	51.0
1997	93.7	51.5	48.6
1998	94.3	50.7	46.1
1999	94.4	50.0	63.8
2000	94.9	51.2	73.2
2001	95.5	52.9	78.8
2002	97.0	58.3	83.5
2003	97.9	59.6	83.4

注:高中升学率为普通高校招生数(含电大普通班)与普通高中毕业生数之比。

Note: Promotion rate of senior secondary school graduates is the ratio of total number of new entrants admitted to HEIs (including those admitled into the regular fulltime courses run by RTVUs) to the total number of graduates of regular senior secondary schools of the current year.

每十万人口各级学校平均在校生数

Number of Students of Per 100,000 Inhabitants of All Levels

单位:人
Unit: Person

年 份 Year	高等学校 Higher Education	高中阶段 Senior	初中阶段 Junior	小 学 Primary	幼儿园 Kindergarten
1990	326	1337	3426	10707	1725
1991	304	1355	3465	10502	1907
1992	313	1365	3518	10413	2072
1993	376	1448	3599	10656	2190
1994	433	1293	3681	10819	2219
1995	457	1610	3945	11010	2262
1996	470	1780	4180	11273	2208
1997	482	1905	4289	11435	2058
1998	519	1978	4408	11287	1944
1999	594	2032	4656	10855	1864
2000	723	2000	4969	10335	1782
2001	931	2021	5161	9937	1602
2002	1146	2283	5240	9525	1595
2003	1298	2523	5209	9100	1560

各级普通学校生师比

Pupil-Teacher Ratio of Regular Schools of All levels

单位：%
Unit：%

年份 Year	小学 Primary	初中 Junior	普通高中 Senior	职业高中 Vacational Secondary Schools	普通中专 Regular Secondary Schools	普通高校 Regular Inst. of Higher Educations		
						全国 Total	本科院校 University	专科院校 Non-university Tertiry
1992	20.07	15.85	12.24	13.82	14.60	6.83	6.63	7.30
1993	22.37	15.65	14.96	13.86	14.55	8.00	7.82	8.61
1994	22.85	16.07	12.16	14.66	15.07	9.25	9.00	10.10
1995	23.30	16.73	12.95	15.35	15.95	9.83	9.71	10.16
1996	23.73	17.18	13.45	15.38	16.43	10.36	10.32	10.20
1997	24.16	17.33	14.05	15.88	16.71	10.87	10.80	10.85
1998	23.98	17.56	14.60	16.13	17.82	11.62	11.63	11.09
1999	23.12	18.17	15.16	15.91	17.88	13.37	13.67	12.23
2000	22.21	19.03	15.87	14.71	19.09	16.30	16.04	17.65
2001	21.64	19.24	16.73	14.26	19.91	18.22	18.47	17.15
2002	21.04	19.25	17.80	16.50	21.96	19.00	20.60	14.20
2003	20.50	19.13	18.35	17.67	25.30	17.00	21.07	14.75

普通高等学校校均规模

Average Size of Regular Inst. of Highter Education

单位：人
Unit：Person

	1992	1993	1994	1995	1996	1997	1998	1999	2000	2001	2002	2003
全国 Total	2074	2381	2591	2758	2927	3112	3335	3815	5289	5870	6471	7143
本科院校 University	2676	3094	3418	3632	3857	4062	4418	5275	6916	8730	10454	11662
专科院校 Non-university Tertiry	1051	1235	1338	1405	1466	1594	1701	1975	2282	2337	2523	2893

全国各级自学考试基本情况

Basic Statistics of Applicants for State-administered Examination for Self-learners by Level

		83-2000 年 合计 Total	2001 上半年 First half year	2001 下半年 Second half year	2002 上半年 First half year	2002 下半年 Second half year	2003 上半年 First half year	2003 下半年 Second half year
毕业生人数	Gradutes							
本科	Nonmal course	336434	73130	88506	232591	121670	184789	153719
专科	Short-Cycle course	2739875	213555	265847	661563	278341	172815	193211
中专	Specialized Secondary	403467	870	774	949	84	10	8
单科合格科次数	Passed Main-courses							
本科	Nonmal course	14040591	2545065	2357131	2744221	2609694	3119915	2658986
专科	Short-Cycle course	82006621	3573156	3248698	3394816	2497491	2016762	1967873
中专	Specialized Secondary	4939318	23877	1197	247	153	41	26
报考人数	Applicants							
计	Total							
本科	Nonmal course	14770330	2347089	2441547	2693547	2877525	3011183	2690625
专科	Short-Cycle course	118627085	4367392	4148303	3753833	3525605	3103200	2754066
中专	Specialized Secondary	5499782	10313	1444	351	230	1815	842
首次报考人数	First Time							
本科	Nonmal course	5020891	731805	606143	828202	704459	630324	491321
专科	Short-Cycle course	31712703	980880	893524	896314	715840	466105	461862
中专	Specialized Secondary	1436507	744	96	41	35		1
报考科次	Main-courses to be Examined							
本科	Nonmal course	44401517	6048851	5765261	6294005	6759658	7348088	6622991
专科	Short-Cycle course	239564642	10250842	9378904	8894268	8296085	7415830	6571647
中专	Specialized Secondary	9909387	33890	2558	523	325	5667	2120
实考人数	Actural Examined							
本科	Nonmal course	10939344	1938347	1906783	2127149	2230816	2384484	2080732
专科	Short-Cycle course	81827187	3528505	3249569	2954655	2647007	2022183	1850164
中专	Specialized Secondary	3486356	8713	1205	284	181	52	39
实考科次	Actural Main-courses Examined							
本科	Nonmal course	25086964	4585818	4281323	4745404	5083830	5496026	4793017
专科	Short-Cycle course	176118877	7913893	7001861	6680018	6074949	4509259	4127024
中专	Specialized Secondary	7977887	29937	2191	411	247	72	49
在档考生人数	Exmainees on File							
累计数	Sum。							
本科	Nonmal course	16241391	4037236	4643379	5471581	6176040	6806364	7297685
专科	Short-Cycle course	160319158	13353898	14247422	15143736	15859576	16325681	16787543
中专	Specialized Secondary	10943852	137889	137985	138026	138061	138061	138062
其中:新生数	of Which: Curent session							
本科	Nonmal course	2299796	731805	606143	828202	704459	630324	491321
专科	Short-Cycle course	14062838	980880	893524	896314	715840	466105	461862
中专	Specialized Secondary	958261	744	96	41	35		1

二、高等教育
Higher Education

高等教育学校(机构)数

Number of Higher Education Institutions

单位:所

Unit: Institutions

	计 Total	中央部委 HEIs under Central Ministries & Agencies			地方部门 HEIs under Local Auth.			民办 Nongove－state/private
		计 Total	教育部 HEIs under MOE	其他部委 HEIs under Other Central Agencies	计 Total	教育部门 HEIs under MOE	非教育部门 Run by Non－ed. Dept.	
1.研究生培养机构 Luetitatims Prov. Graduate Programs	720	371	73	298	349	295	54	
普通高校 Regular HEIs	407	94	73	21	313	292	21	
科研机构 Research Institutes	313	277		277	36	3	33	
2.普通高校 Regular HEIs	1552	111	73	38	1268	767	501	173
本科院校 University	644	104	73	31	531	470	61	9
高职(专科)院校 Non-university Tertiry Voc. Colleges	908	7		7	737	297	440	164
其中:高职院校 Of which: Tertiary Vocational-technical Colleges	711	2		2	554	195	359	155
3.成人高等学校 HEIs for Adults	558	19	1	18	537	250	287	2
4.民办的其他高等教育机构 Non－state/private HEIs	1104							1104
其中:学历文凭考试机构 Of which: Institutions authorized to offer State－recognized credits for part of their Programs	384							384

普通高等学校校数

Number of Regular Higher Educational Institutions

单位:所

Unit: Institutions

	合计 Total	大学、专门学院 University	专科学校 Non-university Tertiry	职业技术学院 Tertiary Vocational-technical Colleges
总计 Total	**1552**	**644**	**197**	**711**
综合大学 Comprehensive University	121	112	9	0
理工院校 Natural Sciences & Technology	223	180	43	0
农业院校 Agriculture	37	33	4	0
林业院校 Forestry	6	6	0	0
医药院校 Medicine & Pharmacy	97	76	21	0
师范院校 Teacher Training	188	113	75	0
语文院校 Language & Literature	16	13	3	0
财经院校 Finance & Economics	64	42	22	0
政法院校 Political Science & Law	33	14	19	0
体育院校 Physical Culture	15	14	1	0
艺术院校 Art	29	29	0	0
民族院校 Ethnic National lities	12	12	0	0
职业技术学院 Tertiary Vocational-technical Colleges	711	0	0	711
合计中民办学院 Of which: Non-state/private Colleges	173	9	9	155

普通高等学校规模

Breakdown of Regular Higher Educational Institutions by Size of Enrolments

单位:所

Unit: Institutions

	学校数 Institutions	300人及以下 300 and under	301-500人 301 to 500	501-1000人 501 to 1000	1001-1500人 1001 to 1500	1501-2000人 1501 to 2000	2001-3000人 2001 to 3000	3001-4000人 3001 to 4000	4001-5000人 4001 to 5000	5001人及以上 5001 and over
总计 Total	**1552**	**99**	**51**	**92**	**86**	**81**	**153**	**171**	**92**	**727**
综合大学 Comprehensive University	121	1	0	0	0	1	1	5	2	111
理工院校 Natural Sciences & Technology	223	2	0	2	3	1	2	11	6	196
农业院校 Agriculture	37	1	0	0	0	0	0	1	0	35
林业院校 Forestry	6	0	0	0	0	0	0	0	0	6
医药院校 Medicine & Pharmacy	97	3	0	2	2	2	5	12	13	58
师范院校 Teacher Training	188	2	0	2	4	2	11	21	13	133
语文院校 Language & Literature	16	0	0	1	0	0	2	4	1	8
财经院校 Finance & Economics	64	2	0	0	1	0	3	5	5	48
政法院校 Political Science & Law	33	1	1	0	3	3	7	5	7	6
体育院校 Physical Culture	15	0	0	0	0	2	1	5	3	4
艺术院校 Art	29	0	0	2	6	6	5	5	3	2
民族院校 Ethnic National Lities	12	0	0	0	0	0	0	1	0	11
职业技术院校 Tertiary Vocational-technical Colleges	711	87	50	83	67	64	116	96	39	109

普通高等学校设置专业数

Number of Specialities and Number of Educational Programmes Estabished by Field of Study in Regular Higher Educational Institutions

单位:个

Unit

	合计 Total	哲学 Philosophy	经济 Economics	法学 Law	教育 Education	文学 Literature	历史 History	理学 Science	工学 Engineering	农学 Agriculture	医学 Medicine	管理学 Administrators	其他 other
研究生													
种数 No. of Sp.	475	10	21	32	22	35	8	61	159	35	67	23	2
点数 No. of Ed. Prog.	12045	282	598	684	386	925	274	1935	4060	567	1566	762	6
普通高等教育													
种数 No. of Sp.	527	5	16	26	55	86	8	65	150	36	42	38	0
点数 No. of Ed. Prog.	41190	59	2086	1791	2899	6484	309	4665	12268	1251	1857	7521	0
成人高等教育													
种数 No. of Sp.	438	5	14	24	51	54	5	49	132	32	36	36	0
点数 No. of Ed. Prog.	20582	8	1426	1155	1782	3192	166	1555	5148	434	1102	4614	0

注:成人高等教育为2002年数据。

Note: Data of adult HEIs are th statistics of 2002.

高等学校(机构)学生数

Data on Students in Higher Education Institutions

单位:人

Unit: in Persons

	毕(结)业生数 Graduates	授予学位数 Degrees Awarded	招生数 Entrants			在校学生数 Enrolment	预计毕业生数 Anticipated Graduates for Next Year
			计 Total	其中 Of which: 应届生 Autumn Session	其中 Of which: 春季招生 Spring Session		
研究生 Postgraduates	**111091**	**108109**	**268925**	**133688**		**651260**	**178748**
博　士 Doctor's Degrees	18806	17362	48740	17762		136687	45636
硕　士 Master's Degrees	92285	90747	220185	115926		514573	133112
普通本、专科 Undergraduates in Regular HEIs	**1877492**	**814759**	**3821701**	**3246536**	**24312**	**11085642**	**2477931**
本　科 Normal Courses	929598	814759	1825262	1511627	8788	6292089	1235436
专　科 Short-cycle Courses	947894		1996439	1734909	15524	4793553	1242495
成人本、专科 Undergraduates in Adult HEIs	**1593358**	**64067**				**5591573**	**1968374**
本　科 Normal Courses	386142	64067				1542743	544500
专　科 Short-cycle Courses	1207216					4048830	1423874
网络本科、专科生 Web-based Undergraduates	**144408**	**3600**	**841496**	**149148**	**363646**	**1860749**	
本　科 Normal Courses	66309	3600	426563	87329	186601	976545	
专　科 Short-cycle Courses	78099		414933	61819	177045	884204	
研究生课程进修班 Postgraduates Courses	104355		102623			172169	
在职人员攻读博士硕士学位 Advanced degree Programs for persons in Employment		17663	59747			149695	
学历文凭考试 Students Enrolled in State Recognized Credit Programs Provided by Non-state/private HEIs	99671		157967			393759	
电大注册视听生 Registeyed Viewers/auditors of Programs Provided by RTVUs	64123		30920			178773	
自考助学班 Classes run by Non-state/private HEIs for Students Preparing for State-administered Examinations for Self-directed Learners	220554		286065			764010	
普通预科生 College-preparatory Classes	12169		22186			22151	
证书教育 Programs Awarding Certificates on Completion of Courses	291922		252334			219050	
岗位培训 Job-related Training	1773468		1202767			620513	
进修及培训 In-service Training	1130065		1077783			597293	
留学生 Foreign Students	34349	2901	40165		13913	53461	

分部门、分计划

Total Number of Postgraduate

	学校(机构)数(所) No. of Inst.	毕业生数 Graduates				招生数 Entrants		
		计 Total	博士 Doctor's Degrees	硕士 Master's Degrees	研究生班 Postgraduate Coruses	计 Total	博士 Doctor's Degrees	硕士 Master's Degrees
总 计 Total	**720**	**111091**	**18806**	**92241**	**44**	**268925**	**48740**	**220007**
国家任务 State-planned Programs		68377	13358	55019		150684	31701	118983
委托培养 Contractual Programs		16486	3653	12833		28242	10805	1743
自筹经费 Self-financed Programs		26228	1795	24389	44	89999	6234	83587
一、中央部委所属 Under Central Ministries & Agencies	**371**	**77144**	**16145**	**60999**		**180122**	**41174**	**138948**
1.教育部 Under MOE	73	62723	11977	50746		143980	30782	113198
2.其他部委 Under Other Central Agencies	298	14421	4168	10253		36142	10392	25750
二、地方所属 Under Local Auth.	**349**	**33947**	**2661**	**31242**	**44**	**88803**	**7566**	**81059**
1.教育部门 Edu. Dept.	295	32390	2530	29816	44	84788	7217	77393
2.其他部门 Run by Non-ed. Dept.	54	1557	131	1426		4015	349	3666

分部门、分计划

Number of Postgraduate Students

	学校(机构)数(所) No. of Inst.	毕业生数 Graduates				招生数 Entrants		
		计 Total	博士 Doctor's Degrees	硕士 Master's Degrees	研究生班 Postgraduate Coruses	计 Total	博士 Doctor's Degrees	硕士 Master's Degrees
总 计 Total	**407**	**105387**	**16401**	**88942**	**44**	**255335**	**43315**	**211842**
国家任务 State-planned Programs		62830	11058	51772		137451	26430	111021
委托培养 Contractual Programs		16360	3556	12804		28036	10661	17375
自筹经费 Self-financed Programs		26197	1787	24366	44	89848	6224	83446
一、中央部委所属 Under Central Ministries & Agencies	**94**	**71766**	**13763**	**58003**		**167216**	**35806**	**131410**
1.教育部 Under MOE	73	62723	11977	50746		143980	30782	113198
2.其他部委 Under Other Central Agencies	21	9043	1786	7257		23236	5024	18212
二、地方所属 Under Local Auth.	**313**	**33621**	**2638**	**30939**	**44**	**88119**	**7509**	**80432**
1.教育部门 Edu. Dept.	292	32365	2530	29791	44	84742	7209	77355
2.其他部门 Run by Non-ed. Dept.	21	1256	108	1148		3377	300	3077

研究生数(总计)

Students by Sector and Program (Total)

单位:人

Unit:in Persons

研究生班 Postgraduate Coruses	在校学生数 Enrolment				预计毕业生数 Graduates for Next Year			
	计 Total	博士 Doctor's Degrees	硕士 Master's Degrees	研究生班 Postgraduate Coruses	计 Total	博士 Doctor's Degrees	硕士 Master's Degrees	研究生班 Postgraduate Coruses
178	**651260**	**136687**	**514115**	**458**	**178748**	**45636**	**132946**	**166**
	377461	88808	288610	43	104730	29310	75420	
	79922	30710	49212		27496	10335	17161	
178	193877	17169	176293	415	46522	5991	40365	166
	450694	**117438**	**333256**		**128507**	**39477**	**89030**	
	360196	88362	271834		103141	29464	73677	
	90498	29076	61422		25366	10013	15353	
178	**200566**	**19249**	**180859**	**458**	**50241**	**6159**	**43916**	**166**
178	191562	18417	172687	458	48010	5908	41936	166
	9004	832	8172		2231	251	1980	

研究生数(普通高校)

by Sector and Program (Regular HEIs)

单位:人

Unit:in Persons

研究生班 Postgraduate Coruses	在校学生数 Enrolment				预计毕业生数 Graduates for Next Year			
	计 Total	博士 Doctor's Degrees	硕士 Master's Degrees	研究生班 Postgraduate Coruses	计 Total	博士 Doctor's Degrees	硕士 Master's Degrees	研究生班 Postgraduate Coruses
178	**617544**	**122381**	**494705**	**458**	**169722**	**41077**	**128479**	**166**
	344747	74997	269707	43	96028	24940	71088	
	79289	30260	49029		27283	10168	17115	
178	193508	17124	175969	415	46411	5969	40276	166
	418576	**103282**	**315294**		**119909**	**34975**	**84934**	
	360196	88362	271834		103141	29464	73677	
	58380	14920	43460		16768	5511	11257	
178	**198968**	**19099**	**179411**	**458**	**49813**	**6102**	**43545**	**166**
178	191440	18392	172590	458	47966	5895	41905	166
	7528	707	6821		1847	207	1640	

分部门、分计划

Number of Postgraduate Students

	学校(机构)数(所) No. of Inst.	毕业生数 Graduates				招生数 Entrants		
		计 Total	博 士 Doctor's Degrees	硕 士 Master's Degrees	研究生班 Postgraduate Coruses	计 Total	博 士 Doctor's Degrees	硕 士 Master's Degrees
总 计 Total	**313**	**5704**	**2405**	**3299**		**13590**	**5425**	**8165**
国家任务 State-planned Programs		5547	2300	3247		13233	5271	7962
委托培养 Contractual Programs		126	97	29		206	144	62
自筹经费 Self-financed Programs		31	8	23		151	10	141
一、中央部委所属 Under Central Ministries & Agencies	**277**	**5378**	**2382**	**2996**		**12906**	**5368**	**7538**
1.教育部 Under MOE								
2.其他部委 Under Other Central Agencies	277	5378	2382	2996		12906	5368	7538
二、地方所属 Under Local Auth.	**36**	**326**	**23**	**303**		**684**	**57**	**627**
1.教育部门 Edu. Dept.	3	25		25		46	8	38
2.其他部门 Run by Non-ed. Dept	33	301	23	278		638	49	589

分学科研

Total Number of Postgraduate

	毕业生数 Graduates				招生数 Entrants		
	计 Total	博 士 Doctor's Degrees	硕 士 Master's Degrees	研究生班 Postgraduate Coruses	计 Total	博 士 Doctor's Degrees	硕 士 Master's Degrees
总计 Total	**111091**	**18806**	**92241**	**44**	**268925**	**48740**	**220007**
其中:女 Of Which: Female	41291	5321	35960	10	112295	15299	96914
哲学 Philosophy	1562	348	1214		3103	592	2511
经济学 Economics	6578	1204	5374		14423	2575	11836
法学 Law	7484	770	6714		18489	2034	16438
教育学 Education	2764	307	2457		7671	791	6880
文学 Literature	7426	837	6589		18926	2022	16870
历史学 History	1926	454	1472		3634	823	2811
理学 Science	13220	3705	9515		33969	8872	25097
工学 Engineering	41337	6573	34764		103212	18941	84230
农学 Agriculture	3849	756	3093		9693	1961	7732
医学 Medicine	12207	2825	9382		26501	5764	20737
军事学 Military Science	32	6	26		124	38	86
管理学 Administrators	12706	1021	11641	44	29180	4327	24779

研究生数(科研机构)

by Sector and Program (Research Institutes)

单位:人

Unit:in Persons

研究生班 Postgraduate Coruses	在校学生数 Enrolment 计 Total	博士 Doctor's Degrees	硕士 Master's Degrees	研究生班 Postgraduate Coruses	预计毕业生数 Graduates for Next Year 计 Total	博士 Doctor's Degrees	硕士 Master's Degrees	研究生班 Postgraduate Coruses
	33716	**14306**	**19410**		**9026**	**4559**	**4467**	
	32714	13811	18903		8702	4370	4332	
	633	450	183		213	167	46	
	369	45	324		111	22	89	
	32118	**14156**	**17962**		**8598**	**4502**	**4096**	
	32118	14156	17962		8598	4502	4096	
	1598	**150**	**1448**		**428**	**57**	**371**	
	122	25	97		44	13	31	
	1476	125	1351		384	44	340	

究生数(总计)

Students by Academic Field (Total)

单位:人

Unit:in Persons

研究生班 Postgraduate Coruses	在校学生数 Enrolment 计 Total	博士 Doctor's Degrees	硕士 Master's Degrees	研究生班 Postgraduate Coruses	预计毕业生数 Graduates for Next Year 计 Total	博士 Doctor's Degrees	硕士 Master's Degrees	研究生班 Postgraduate Coruses
178	**651260**	**136687**	**514115**	**458**	**178748**	**45636**	**132946**	**166**
82	256763	39666	216919	178	64717	11706	52965	46
	7747	1896	5851		2265	730	1535	
12	34675	7312	27351	12	9670	2554	7116	
17	43718	5376	38325	17	12258	1663	10595	
	17425	1960	15465		4491	584	3907	
34	43459	5184	38198	77	11266	1563	9703	
	9259	2351	6908		2821	827	1994	
	82125	23481	58644		21710	7377	14333	
41	255754	57793	197920	41	70932	20724	50208	
	22105	4906	17199		5902	1525	4377	
	63939	14690	49249		17009	4301	12708	
	315	93	222		73	25	48	
74	70739	11645	58783	311	20351	3763	16422	166

分学科研

Number of Postgraduate Students

	毕业生数 Graduates				招生数 Entrants		
	计 Total	博士 Doctor's Degrees	硕士 Master's Degrees	研究生班 Postgraduate Coruses	计 Total	博士 Doctor's Degrees	硕士 Master's Degrees
总计 Total	**105387**	**16401**	**88942**	**44**	**255335**	**43315**	**211842**
其中:女 Of Which: Female	39720	4743	34967	10	107941	13703	94156
哲学 Philosophy	1494	318	1176		2976	554	2422
经济学 Economics	6273	1073	5200		13928	2368	11548
法学 Law	7283	701	6582		18124	1917	16190
教育学 Education	2741	295	2446		7620	767	6853
文学 Literature	7341	808	6533		18762	1972	16756
历史学 History	1881	439	1442		3569	799	2770
理学 Science	11064	2458	8606		28220	6069	22151
工学 Engineering	39090	5881	33209		97964	17213	80710
农学 Agriculture	3737	699	3038		9331	1807	7524
医学 Medicine	11876	2742	9134		25842	5590	20252
军事学 Military Science	32	6	26		122	38	84
管理学 Administrators	12575	981	11550	44	28877	4221	24582

分学科研

Number of Postgraduate Students

	毕业生数 Graduates				招生数 Entrants		
	计 Total	博士 Doctor's Degrees	硕士 Master's Degrees	研究生班 Postgraduate Coruses	计 Total	博士 Doctor's Degrees	硕士 Master's Degrees
总计 Total	**5704**	**2405**	**3299**		**13590**	**5425**	**8165**
其中:女 Of Which: Female	1571	578	993		4354	1596	2758
哲学 Philosophy	68	30	38		127	38	89
经济学 Economics	305	131	174		495	207	288
法学 Law	201	69	132		365	117	248
教育学 Education	23	12	11		51	24	27
文学 Literature	85	29	56		164	50	114
历史学 History	45	15	30		65	24	41
理学 Science	2156	1247	909		5749	2803	2946
工学 Engineering	2247	692	1555		5248	1728	3520
农学 Agriculture	112	57	55		362	154	208
医学 Medicine	331	83	248		659	174	485
军事学 Military Science					2		2
管理学 Administrators	131	40	91		303	106	197

究生数(普通高校)
by Academic Field (Regular HEIs)

单位:人
Unit:in Persons

研究生班 Postgraduate Coruses	在校学生数 Enrolment 计 Total	博士 Doctor's Degrees	硕士 Master's Degrees	研究生班 Postgraduate Coruses	预计毕业生数 Graduates for Next Year 计 Total	博士 Doctor's Degrees	硕士 Master's Degrees	研究生班 Postgraduate Coruses
178	**617544**	**122381**	**494705**	**458**	**169722**	**41077**	**128479**	**166**
82	246459	35711	210570	178	62236	10592	51598	46
	7450	1794	5656		2183	700	1483	
12	33386	6735	26639	12	9295	2365	6930	
17	42737	5056	37664	17	11960	1561	10399	
	17291	1893	15398		4458	565	3893	
34	43077	5053	37947	77	11162	1523	9639	
	9091	2293	6798		2766	805	1961	
	67817	16099	51718		17979	5017	12962	
41	242624	53142	189441	41	67374	19223	48151	
	21303	4536	16767		5696	1418	4278	
	62346	14270	48076		16574	4172	12402	
	310	93	217		73	25	48	
74	70112	11417	58384	311	20202	3703	16333	166

究生数(科研机构)
by Academic Field (Research Institutes)

单位:人
Unit:in Persons

研究生班 Postgraduate Coruses	在校学生数 Enrolment 计 Total	博士 Doctor's Degrees	硕士 Master's Degrees	研究生班 Postgraduate Coruses	预计毕业生数 Graduates for Next Year 计 Total	博士 Doctor's Degrees	硕士 Master's Degrees	研究生班 Postgraduate Coruses
	33716	**14306**	**19410**		**9026**	**4559**	**4467**	
	10304	3955	6349		2481	1114	1367	
	297	102	195		82	30	52	
	1289	577	712		375	189	186	
	981	320	661		298	102	196	
	134	67	67		33	19	14	
	382	131	251		104	40	64	
	168	58	110		55	22	33	
	14308	7382	6926		3731	2360	1371	
	13130	4651	8479		3558	1501	2057	
	802	370	432		206	107	99	
	1593	420	1173		435	129	306	
	5		5					
	627	228	399		149	60	89	

在职人员攻读博士、硕士学位分学科学生数

Number of Postgraduate Students Studying for Advanced Degrees Without Leaving Their Jobs

单位：人

Unit: in Person

	授予学位数 Degrees Awarded			招生数 Entrants			在校学生数 Enrolment		
	计 Total	博士 Doctor's Degrees	硕士 Master's Degrees	计 Total	博士 Doctor's Degrees	硕士 Master's Degrees	计 Total	博士 Doctor's Degrees	硕士 Master's Degrees
总计 Total	**17663**	**640**	**17023**	**59747**	**1687**	**58060**	**149695**	**4729**	**144966**
其中：女 Of Which: Female	5058	137	4921	17457	504	16953	40088	1246	38842
哲学 Philosophy	82	7	75	181	2	179	495	6	489
经济学 Economics	383	24	359	802	10	792	1790	44	1746
法学 Law	1285	11	1274	4311	41	4270	10876	96	10780
教育学 Education	1357	4	1353	4799	10	4789	12007	26	11981
文学 Literature	580	12	568	1540	53	1487	3239	101	3138
历史学 History	99	5	94	132	5	127	339	11	328
理学 Science	766	162	604	1017	152	865	3089	497	2592
工学 Engineering	6218	144	6074	25359	715	24644	69213	2276	66937
农学 Agriculture	279	4	275	3153	61	3092	8942	172	8770
医学 Medicine	2322	234	2088	4822	518	4304	10950	1250	9700
军事学 Military Science									
管理学 Administrators	4292	33	4259	13631	120	13511	28755	250	28505

普通高等学校工科分大类学生数

Breakdown of Engineering Students by Subfield of Study in Regular Higher Educational Institutions

单位：人

Unit: in person

	毕业生数 Graduates	招生数 Entrants	在校学生数 Enrolment
总计 Total	**644106**	**1242426**	**3693401**
工学 Engineering	68	522	1028
地矿类 Applied Gelolgy	6696	11690	34979
材料类 Materials Science	19773	34066	106957
机械类 Mechanical Engineering	97987	195293	539092
仪器仪表类 Instrument & Meter	8919	15509	50134
能源动力类 Thermal & Nuclear Energy	11520	18296	57410
电气信息类 Electronics & Information	321363	623361	1885221
土建类 Civil Engineering & Architcture	74298	136562	402514
水利类 Hydraulics	6876	13603	40136
测绘类 Sruvey & Measure	3287	5928	17519
环境与安全类 Environment and Safety	13096	29755	90834
化工与制药类 Chernical Engineering & Pharmaceutics	19293	32946	102662
交通运输类 Transportation	14347	35946	96093
海洋工程类 Marine Engineering	1568	3146	8789
轻工纺织食品类 Light Industry, Textile and Food	24526	42641	128470
航空航天类 Aeronautics & Astronautics	2704	5046	14868
武器类 Weaponry	538	2028	6599
工程力学类 Engineering Mechanics	1307	3212	10090
生物工程类 Biotechnology	5870	19862	53431
农业工程类 Agriculture Engineering	4974	5795	22949
林业工程类 Forestry Engineering	1894	2304	8487
公安技术类 Public Security technology	3202	4915	15139

普通、成人本、专科

Number of Undergraduate Students by Type of

	毕业生数 Graduates			招生数 Entrants	
	合计 Total	本科 Normal Courses	专科 Short-cycle Courses	合计 Total	本科 Normal Courses
普通本、专科总计 Total	**1877492**	**929598**	**947894**	**3821701**	**1825262**
中央教委所属院校 Inst. Under SEDC	300810	255634	45176	411100	362920
其中：教育部所属院校 of which: Inst. Under MOE of Education	239504	210773	28731	313324	290097
地方所属学校 Inst. Under Local Auth.	1524621	667148	857473	3034313	1320632
民办 Non-State/private	52061	6816	45245	376288	141710
成人本、专科总计 Total	**1169983**	**339377**	**830606**		
中央教委所属院校 Inst. Under SEDC	245088	106049	139039		
其中：教育部所属院校 of which: Inst. Under MOE of Education	203148	92849	110299		
地方所属学校 Inst. Under Local Auth.	919215	233248	685967		
民办 Non-State/private	5680	80	5600		

普通本、专科分

Number of Undergraduate Students by Type of

	毕业生数 Graduates			招生数 Entrants	
	合计 Total	本科 Normal Courses	专科 Short-cycle Courses	合计 Total	本科 Normal Courses
总计 Total	**1877492**	**929598**	**947894**	**3821701**	**1825262**
其中：女 Of Which: Female	831472	386191	445281	1736809	798579
一、普通高等学校 Reg. Inst. of High Education	**1773441**	**928035**	**845406**	**3646382**	**1822091**
本科院校 University	1345328	919169	426159	2235218	1672923
高职(专科)院校 Non-university Tertiry	402652	490	402162	1181496	1863
其他 Other	25461	8376	17085	229668	147305
综合大学 Comprehensive Universities	374264	252079	122185	584710	423617
理工院校 Natural Sciences & Tech.	487436	316350	171086	904629	637074
农业院校 Agriculture	78507	52270	26237	151900	111547
林业院校 Forestry	9961	8182	1779	22016	20360
医药院校 Medicine & Pharmacy	72758	40980	31778	185264	103279
师范院校 Teacher Training	325273	149376	175897	551724	298331
语文院校 Language & Literature	17055	10608	6447	31542	21688
财经院校 Finance & Economics	109438	58717	50721	205374	115401
政法院校 Political Science & Law	29751	10874	18877	44291	19377
体育院校 Physical Culture	10224	8348	1876	20942	17975
艺术院校 Art	10893	8017	2876	27776	23286
民族院校 Ethnic Minorities	15003	12067	2936	32366	29243
职业技术学院 Tertiary Vocational-technical Colleges	232878	167	232711	883848	913
二、成人高等学校 Higher Educational Institutions for Adults	**104051**	**1563**	**102488**	**175319**	**3171**

分举办者学生数

Courses in Regular Higher Educational Institutions

单位:人

Unit: in Person

	在校学生数 Enrolment			毕业班学生数 Graduates for Next Year		
专　科 Short-cycle	合　计 Total	本　科 Normal Courses	专　科 Short-cycle Courses	合　计 Total	本　科 Normal Courses	专　科 Short-cycle Courses
1996439	**11085642**	**6292089**	**4793553**	**2477931**	**1235436**	**1242495**
48180	1502345	1365215	137130	356109	309424	46685
23227	1181647	1111323	70324	279267	254659	24608
1713681	8771582	4607134	4164448	1998562	906773	1091789
234578	811715	319740	491975	123260	19239	104021
	5591573	**1542743**	**4048830**	**1495357**	**487346**	**1008011**
	898834	413781	485053	294683	139022	155661
	705418	341001	364417	240637	117215	123422
	4668888	1128188	3540700	1192813	348141	844672
	23851	774	23077	7861	183	7678

性质类别学生数

Courses in Regular Higher Educational Institutions

单位:人

Unit: in Person

	在校学生数 Enrolment			毕业班学生数 Graduates for Next Year		
专　科 Short-cycle	合　计 Total	本　科 Normal Courses	专　科 Short-cycle Courses	合　计 Total	本　科 Normal Courses	专　科 Short-cycle Courses
1996439	**11085642**	**6292089**	**4793553**	**2477931**	**1235436**	**1242495**
938230	4970504	2686315	2284189	1063143	493587	569556
1824291	**10648820**	**6280547**	**4368273**	**2352011**	**1232940**	**1119071**
562295	7510090	5941391	1568699	1699285	1211170	488115
1179633	2627093	2973	2624120	587170	333	586837
82363	511637	336183	175454	65556	21437	44119
161093	1977522	1527134	450388	456582	321481	135101
267555	2887038	2169464	717574	642459	429984	212475
40353	469857	367006	102851	98636	68535	30101
1656	72608	67633	4975	13851	12249	1602
81985	585510	399237	186273	106233	62695	43538
253393	1673209	1009584	663625	397569	196047	201522
9854	88411	63472	24939	20470	12822	7648
89973	623257	393252	230005	140253	77199	63054
24914	127015	59791	67224	32518	12819	19699
2967	61576	55853	5723	13015	10604	2411
4490	82177	72292	9885	15690	11579	4111
3123	102781	93923	8858	19249	16690	2559
882935	1897859	1906	1895953	395486	236	395250
172148	**436822**	**11542**	**425280**	**125920**	**2496**	**123424**

成人本、专科分

Number of Students by type of Schools in

	毕业生数 Graduates			招生数 Entrants	
	合计 Total	本科 Normal Courses	专科 Short-cycle Courses	合计 Total	本科 Normal Courses
总计 Total	**1593358**	**386142**	**1207216**		
其中:女 Of Which:Female	786098				
一、成人高等学校 Adult Higher Educational Institutions	**423375**	**46765**	**376610**		
其中:全脱产 of Which:Full-time	227183	13713	213470		
职工高等学校 Workers' Colleges	101192	1754	99438		
农民高等学校 Peasants' Colleges	316	0	316		
管理干部学院 Institutes for Administration	50878	4340	46538		
教育学院 Educational Colleges	109602	39224	70378		
独立函授学院 Independent Correspondence Colleges	4672	556	4116		
广播电视大学 Radio/TV Universities	152691	539	152152		
其他机构	4024	352	3672		
二、普通高等学校办 Run by Regular HEIs	**1169983**	**339377**	**830606**		
函授 Divisions of Correspondence	636345	207331	429014		
业余 Sparetime Schools	199493	62583	136910		
脱产 Shrot-cycle Courses for Adults	334145	69463	264682		

普通本、专科分

Number of Students in Regular

	毕业生数 Graduates			招生数 Entrants	
	合计 Total	本科 Normal Courses	专科 Short-cycle Courses	合计 Total	本科 Normal Courses
总计 Total	**1877492**	**929598**	**947894**	**3821701**	**1825262**
其中:女 of Which: Female	831472	386191	445281	1736809	798579
哲学 Philosophy	1196	1127	69	1520	1446
经济学 Economics	88181	48878	39303	221410	114545
法学 Law	110416	52756	57660	185999	91920
教育学 Education	117072	30977	86095	218575	69682
文学 Literature	286889	126087	160802	612021	297002
其中:外语 of which:Foreign Language	115421	48947	66474	263490	106602
历史学 History	13905	8791	5114	16330	11496
理学 Science	173031	103409	69622	329656	220157
工学 Engineering	644106	351537	292569	1242426	595398
农学 Agriculture	50057	29758	20299	81619	41637
医学 Medicine	111356	55927	55429	257681	119270
管理学 Administrators	281283	120351	160932	654464	262709
总计中:师范生 of Total:Students Enrolled in Teacher Training Institutions	346965	158569	188396	486997	237745

性质类别学生数

all Adult Higher Educational Institutions

单位:人

Unit: in Person

	在校学生数 Enrolment			毕业班学生数 Anticipated Graduatstes for Next Year		
专　科 Short-cycle	合　计 Total	本　科 Normal Courses	专　科 Short-cycle Courses	合　计 Total	本　科 Normal Courses	专　科 Short-cycle Courses
	5591573	**1542743**	**4048830**	**1968374**	**544500**	**1423874**
	2818909			919217	0	0
	1261789	**142005**	**1119784**	**473017**	**57154**	**415863**
	593105	28804	564301	252376	14811	237565
	367280	6121	361159	131180	2390	128790
	1008	0	1008	552	0	552
	155538	12852	142686	54823	5841	48982
	326380	119489	206891	116558	46816	69742
	10032	0	10032	5326	831	4495
	385130	2432	382698	159500	1044	158456
	16421	1111	15310	5078	232	4846
	4329784	**1400738**	**2929046**	**1495357**	**487346**	**1008011**
	2472060	864379	1607681	827145	301090	526055
	860982	263854	597128	265832	86212	179620
	996742	272505	724237	402380	100044	302336

学科学生数

HEIs by Field of Study

单位:人

Unit: in Person

	在校学生数 Enrolment			毕业班学生数 Graduates for Next Year		
专　科 Short-cycle	合　计 Total	本　科 Normal Courses	专　科 Short-cycle Courses	合　计 Total	本　科 Normal Courses	专　科 Short-cycle Courses
1996439	**11085642**	**6292089**	**4793553**	**2477931**	**1235436**	**1242495**
938230	4970504	2686315	2284189	1063143	493587	569556
74	5974	5558	416	1322	1285	37
106865	604135	360683	243452	118536	63699	54837
94079	560916	313131	247785	137903	64237	73666
148893	592123	223837	368286	153895	41414	112481
315019	1719230	950274	768956	377788	171632	206156
156888	726691	348813	377878	160474	65476	94998
4834	56673	42543	14130	15092	10380	4712
109499	1004506	723579	280927	216286	138985	77301
647028	3693401	2156584	1536817	846609	462798	383811
39982	249671	151756	97915	62081	35197	26884
138411	814741	496136	318605	158293	82548	75745
391755	1784272	868008	916264	390126	163261	226865
249252	1585900	902639	683261	415426	197808	217618

成人本、专科

Number of Students by Field of Study in

	毕业生数 Graduates			招生数 Entrants	
	合 计 Total	本 科 Normal Courses	专 科 Short-cycle Courses	合 计 Total	本 科 Normal Courses
总计 Total	**1593358**	**386142**	**1207216**		
其中:女 of which: Female	786098	0	0		
成人高等学校 Adult Higher Educations	**423375**	**46765**	**376610**		
哲学 Philosophy	0	0	0		
经济学 Economics	38144	1134	37010		
法学 Law	39583	5294	34289		
教育学 Education	40501	3608	36893		
文学 Literature	93807	16944	76863		
其中:外语 of which:Foreign Language	15738	5498	10240		
历史学 History	1776	1122	654		
理学 Science	15383	8786	6597		
工学 Engineering	51374	1650	49724		
农学 Agriculture	898	0	898		
医学 Medicine	31936	1072	30864		
管理学 Administrators	109973	7155	102818		
总计中:师范 of the Total: Teacher Training	103027	37627	65400		
普通高等学校办 Run by Regular HEIs	**1169983**	**339377**	**830606**		
哲学 Philosophy					
经济学 Economics	76738	19728	57010		
法学 Law	80768	32218	48550		
教育学 Education	95201	17945	77256		
文学 Literature	240140	68093	172047		
其中:外语 of which:Foreign Language	47931	23949	23982		
历史学 History	7004	4402	2602		
理学 Science	52897	32465	20432		
工学 Engineering	219264	64296	154968		
农学 Agriculture	15608	1954	13654		
医学 Medicine	110907	32472	78435		
管理学 Administrators	271456	65804	205652		
总计中:师范 of the Total: Teacher Training	308389	107015	201374		

分学科学生数

Adult Higher Educational Institutions

单位:人

Unit: in Person

	在校学生数 Enrolment			毕业班学生数 Graduates for Next Year		
专科 Short-cycle	合计 Total	本科 Normal Courses	专科 Short-cycle Courses	合计 Total	本科 Normal Courses	专科 Short-cycle Courses
	5591573	**1542743**	**4048830**	**1968374**	**544500**	**1423874**
	2818909	0	0	919217	0	0
	1261789	**142005**	**1119784**	**473017**	**57154**	**415863**
	0	0	0	9	0	9
	95295	3748	91547	39766	1412	38354
	95771	12543	83228	39301	5687	33614
	117996	16258	101738	41631	7441	34190
	258207	55135	203072	98342	22590	75752
	54465	18857	35608	22346	8004	14342
	4655	3206	1449	1911	1229	682
	49700	28090	21610	18510	11774	6736
	190049	4989	185060	60766	1942	58824
	2348	0	2348	1042	0	1042
	133612	4333	129279	42765	1445	41320
	314156	13703	300453	128974	3634	125340
	280943	111515	169428	107056	45198	61858
	4329784	**1400738**	**2929046**	**1495357**	**487346**	**1008011**
	4537	718	3819	26	26	0
	252108	74410	177698	93237	26909	66328
	266270	130970	135300	96995	44750	52245
	318839	68528	250311	108278	20586	87692
	813650	301242	512408	309397	116595	192802
	190207	105430	84777	73792	40708	33084
	20349	13927	6422	7043	5095	1948
	193828	129240	64588	70294	47700	22594
	874059	283518	590541	284384	90348	194036
	67774	12716	55058	23337	3371	19966
	565146	134435	430711	167185	49899	117286
	953224	251034	702190	335181	82067	253114
	1062890	448080	614810	366557	152009	214548

网络本、专科

Number of Students in

	毕业生数 Graduates		
	合计 Total	本科 Normal Courses	专科 Short-cycle Courses
总计 Total	**144408**	**66309**	**78099**
其中：女 Of Which: Female	69481		
哲学 Philosophy			
经济学 Economics	38331	22226	16105
法学 Law	22693	16648	6045
教育学 Education	24363	110	24253
文学 Literature	7535	5168	2367
其中：外语 Of which: Foreign Language	4665	3968	697
历史学 History			
理学 Science	257	207	50
工学 Engineering	10411	5491	4920
农学 Agriculture	4804	51	4753
医学 Medicine	357	73	284
管理学 Administrators	35657	16335	19322
总计中：师范生 Of Total: Students Enrolled in Teacher Training Institutions	950		950

高等教育学生

Changes in Higher

	上学年初报表在校学生数 Total enrolment at beginning of previous academic year	增加学生数 Factors of Increase					
		计 Total	招生 No. of Students Admitted	复学 Students Resuming Studies	转入 Transfers from Other Inst.	其他 Others	计 Total
博士生 Doctor's Degrees	108598	49509	48740	144	120	505	21420
硕士生 Master's Degrees	391917	222914	220007	383	425	2099	100716
研究生班学生 Postgraduate Courses	362	180	178	0	0	2	84
普通本科、专科生 Students Enrolled in Normal and Short-cycle Courses	9051171	4256614	3821701	12463	199829	222621	2222143
成人本科、专科生 Students Enrolled in Normal and Short-cycle Courses Provided by Adult HEIs	4546372	2422485	2223211	15406	37433	146435	1377284
网络本科、专科生 Students Earolled in Normal and Short-cycle Courses Provided by Web-based Programs	1198175	908247	841496	13708	6869	46174	245673

分学科学生数

Adult HEIs by Field of Study

单位:人

Unit: in Person

招生数 Entrants			在校学生数 Enrolment		
合计 Total	本科 Normal Courses	专科 Short – cycle Courses	合计 Total	本科 Normal Courses	专科 Short – cycle Courses
841496	**426563**	**414933**	**1860749**	**976545**	**884204**
393310			881258		
54318	28624	25694	183911	89834	94077
173514	92227	81287	352874	213980	138894
49403	12438	36965	143158	16723	126435
103663	76822	26841	230484	176126	54358
34429	21018	13411	88843	62137	26706
122	122		122	122	
10618	9950	668	22383	21122	1261
79590	44531	35059	213456	119994	93462
10314	765	9549	25652	1669	23983
21860	6324	15536	62730	18302	44428
338094	154760	183334	625979	318673	307306
26338	23489	2849	56855	51510	5345

数变动情况

Educations Enrolment

单位:人

Unit: in Person

减少学生数 Factors of Decrease									本学年初报表在校学生数 Total enrolment at beginning of current academic year
毕业 Graduates	结业 Completers of Courses without formal awards	休学 Suspended	退学 Quitting	开除 Expelled	死亡 Dead	转出 Transfers to Other Inst.	其他 Others		
18806	35	140	512	10	13	48	1856		136687
92241	85	384	871	17	41	1637	5440		514115
44	40	0	0	0	0	0	0		458
1877492	19559	18133	31530	2712	775	115407	156535		11085642
1174979	33480	11477	36233	1012	190	22018	97895		5591573
144408	7950	10233	25516	88	33	13422	44023		1860749

高等教育非学历教育学生情况

Data on Students Enrolled in Non-formal Programmes of HEIS

单位：人
Unit: in Person

	毕(结)业生数 Corupleters	招生数 New Entrants	在校生数 Total Enrolment
研究生课程进修班 Postgraduate Courses	104355	102623	172169
其中:女 Of which: Female	44845	38219	73471
自考助学班			
Classes run by Non-state/private HEIs for Students Preparing for State-administered Examinations for Self-directed Leacners	220554	286065	764010
其中:女 Of which: Female	104161	130252	323555
普通预科生 College-preparatory Classes	12169	22186	22151
其中:女 Of which: Female	5335	9222	8894
证书教育 Programs Awarding Certiticates on Completion of Courses			
单科班 Programs Awarding Certificateson Completion of Courses	172949	139629	79298
其中:女 Of which: Female	60896	62850	25679
专业证书班	118973	112705	139752
其中:女 Of which: Female	50313	42200	49271
岗位培训 Job－related Training			
资格性培训 Job-related Training	1100242	758414	349214
其中:女 Of which: Female	453469	312857	160555
适应性培训	673226	444353	271299
其中:女 Of which: Female	278487	196076	116697
进修及培训 In－service Training			
一周至三个月以下 In-service Training: a week to 3 months under	737394	657541	290190
其中:女 Of which: Female	298841	308720	141781
三个月至半年以下 3 months to half year under	180506	184968	91966
其中:女 Of which: Female	101000	104185	49934
半年至一年以下 half year to one year under	152545	149117	101694
其中:女 Of which: Female	66802	66485	43207
一年以上 One year and over	59620	86157	113443
其中:女 Of which: Female	19930	29349	42278

高等教育其他学生情况

Data on Other Students Enrolled of HEIS

单位：人
Unit：in Person

	共产党员 Member of C.P.A	共青团员 Member of C.Y.L	民主党派	华侨 Overseas Chinese	港澳台 From HK, Macao and Taiwan	少数民族 Minorities
总 计 Total	**1291892**	**13050386**	**16724**	**3509**	**14811**	**1154117**
博士生 Doctor's Degrees	49094	28000	1263	5	1172	6509
硕士生 Master's Degrees	149725	262053	1255	16	2329	21983
研究生班学生 Postgraduate Courses	172	68	1	0	0	11
普通本科、专科生 Undergraduates in Regular HEIs	374755	9609712	1671	1638	8796	669465
成人本科、专科生 Undergraduates in Adult HEIs	414554	2381990	8220	1311	2425	333559
网络本科、专科生 Web－based Undergraduates	238334	510976	3151	418	60	71603

	毕(结)业生数 Graduates	授予学位数 Degrees Awarded	招生数 Entrants 计 Total	其中:春季招生 Of Which: Spring term
总计 Total	**34349**	**2901**	**40165**	**13913**
其中:女 Of Which:Female	17640	1122	19170	6697
分层次 By level of training				
博士 Doctor's Degrees	300	259	468	54
硕士 Master's Degrees	699	636	1166	91
本科 Normal Courses	2855	2006	7569	719
专科 Short-cycle Courese	125	0	244	83
培训 In-service Training	30370	0	29671	12367
分大洲 By continent				
亚洲 Asia	27735	2402	32849	11819
非洲 Africa	574	288	585	55
欧洲 Europe	3580	146	3254	816
北美洲 North America	2043	38	1963	489
南美洲 South America	90	10	153	32
澳洲 Australia	327	17	314	103
分经费来源 By Sources of Support				
国际组织资助 Aided by IGOs	123	0	5	0
中国政府资助 Aided by Chinese government	2453	666	2442	92
本国政府资助 Aided by home government	148	14	127	11
学校间交换 Aided by inter-institutional exchanges	1783	15	1741	572
自费 Self-supporting	29842	2206	34803	12639

生情况

Foreign Students

单位:人

Unit: in Person

在校学生数 Enrolment					
计 Total	第一年 1st year	第二年 2nd year	第三年 3rd year	第四年 4th year	第五年 5th year
53461	**35069**	**10379**	**4530**	**2592**	**891**
24021	16228	4608	1847	1054	284
0	**0**	**0**	**0**	**0**	**0**
1425	469	369	329	144	114
3108	1207	1054	700	117	30
17030	6558	4707	2937	2161	667
469	**240**	**195**	**33**	**1**	**0**
31429	26595	4054	531	169	80
0	**0**	**0**	**0**	**0**	**0**
44970	29337	8859	3805	2229	740
1492	594	381	289	162	66
3871	2897	545	232	129	68
2492	1827	465	135	51	14
240	147	56	22	14	1
396	267	73	47	7	2
0	0	0	0	0	0
132	48	47	26	8	3
4835	2452	1096	707	429	151
332	135	168	25	2	2
2038	1675	269	48	46	0
46124	30759	8799	3724	2107	735

高等教育学校(机构)
Aggregate Data on Staff

	计 Total	校本部 Teacher, staff & Workers 计 Total	专任教师 计 Total	专任教师 正高级 Senior	专任教师 副高级 Sub-senior
总　计 Total	**1663557**	**1475680**	**834342**	**75636**	**245795**
其中:女 Of Which: Female	749310	671332	374292	14011	95274
普通高校 Regular HEIs	1452623	1271567	724658	70063	216161
成人高校 Adult HEIs	158397	153504	85141	2050	22758
民办的其他高等教育机构 Non-state/private HEIs	52537	50609	24543	3523	6876

高等教育学校(机构)
Aggregate Data on Staff

	计 Total	校本部 Teacher, staff & Workers 计 Total	专任教师 计 Total	专任教师 正高级 Senior	专任教师 副高级 Sub-senior
总　计 Total	**1452623**	**1271567**	**724658**	**70063**	**216161**
其中:女 Of Which: Female	616825	542967	302257	12332	78922
分类型:本科院校 By Type of HEIs: HEIs Offening Degree Level Programs	1060628	899193	502458	61950	156302
高职(专科)院校 Short-cycle HEIs and Teitiary Vocational Colleges	350636	332349	196872	5962	51885
其他机构 Other	41359	40025	25328	2151	7974
分举办者:1.中央部委所属 By Providers: Central Ministries & Agencies	337882	257415	132186	25911	45147
教育部 MOE	269192	206644	107541	21831	36582
其他部委 Other Coutral Agencies	68690	50771	24645	4080	8565
2.地方所属 Local Authorities	1027998	930446	542329	38665	157158
教育部门 Ed. Dept.	794207	710705	413130	35105	121100
其他部门 Non-Ed. Dept.	233791	219741	129199	3560	36058
3.民办 Non-state/private	86743	83706	50143	5487	13856

教职工情况(总计)
and Workers in HEIs (Total)

单位:人
Unit: in Person

教职工数 Teacher, staff & Workers / 教职工 in College or Uni. Proper / Full-time Teachers / 中级 Middle	初级 Junior	无职称 No Rank	行政人员 Adm. Personnel	教辅人员 Supporting Staff	工勤人员 Workers	科研机构人员 Personnel in Affiliated Research Org.	校办企业职工 Employees in School-run Factories & Farms	其他附设机构人员 Personnel in Others Subsidiary Units
285286	**168943**	**58682**	**271139**	**184163**	**186036**	**42971**	**60385**	**84521**
140003	92214	32790	123363	102092	71585	15506	20011	42461
240555	146092	51787	225725	160180	161004	42240	57166	81650
36795	18917	4621	32151	18308	17904	525	2101	2267
7936	3934	2274	13263	5675	7128	206	1118	604

教职工情况(普通高校)
and Workers in Regular HEIs

单位:人
Unit: in Person

教职工数 Teacher, staff & Workers / 教职工 in College or Uni. Proper / Full-time Teachers / 中级 Middle	初级 Junior	无职称 No Rank	行政人员 Adm. Personnel	教辅人员 Supporting Staff	工勤人员 Workers	科研机构人员 Personnel in Affiliated Research Org.	校办企业职工 Employees in School-run Factories & Farms	其他附设机构人员 Personnel in Others Subsidiary Units
240555	**146092**	**51787**	**225725**	**160180**	**161004**	**42240**	**57166**	**81650**
108809	74568	27626	96853	84582	59275	15165	18411	40282
159012	92610	32584	160381	122202	114152	40224	46928	74283
73330	48401	17294	58342	34368	42767	1893	9729	6665
8213	5081	1909	7002	3610	4085	123	509	702
40019	16382	4727	46866	41571	36792	29226	19941	31300
32781	12410	3937	37079	32549	29475	18999	17500	26049
7238	3972	790	9787	9022	7317	10227	2441	5251
186417	118174	41915	162966	110510	114641	12520	35731	49301
136929	88377	31619	124282	86840	86453	10899	29227	43376
49488	29797	10296	38684	23670	28188	1621	6504	5925
14119	11536	5145	15893	8099	9571	494	1494	1049

高等教育学校(机构)
Data on Staff and

	合计 Total	校本部 Teacher, staff & Workers			
		计 Sub－Total	专任教师		
			小计 Sub－Total	正高级 Senior	副高级 Sub-senior
总　计 Total	**158397**	**153504**	**85141**	**2050**	**22758**
其中:女 Of which: Female	70573	68421	39089	510	9074
分类型:By type:职工高等学校 Workers' Colleges	45816	43656	24749	608	6970
农民高等学校 Peasants' College	259	259	165	0	22
管理干部学院 Institutes for Administration	22374	21525	10927	570	3469
教育学院 Educational College	22364	21735	12999	384	4100
独立函授学院 Independent Correspon－dence Colleges	517	517	389	15	63
广播电视大学 Radio/Tv Universities	64411	63232	34524	449	7769
其他机构 Other Institutions	2656	2580	1388	24	365
分举办者:By Provider:1. 中央部委所属 Under Central Ministries & Agencies	4789	4703	1881	165	522
教育部 MOE	422	415	123	11	63
其他部委 Other Central Agencies	4367	4288	1758	154	459
2. 地方所属 Local Auth.	153355	148548	83132	1871	22180
教育部门 Ed. Dept.	101833	99570	55710	1059	14099
其他部门 Non-ed. Dept.	51522	48978	27422	812	8081
3. 民办 Non-state/private	253	253	128	14	56

教职工情况(成人高校)
Workers in Adult HEIs

单位:人
Unit: in Person

教职工数 Teachers, staff & Workers								
教职工 in College or Uni. Proper						科研机构人员 Personnel in Affiliated Research Org.	校办企业职工 Employees in School-run Enterprise	其他附设机构人员 Personnel in Others Subsidiary Units
Full-time Teachers			行政人员 Adm. Personnel	教辅人员 Supporting Staff	工勤人员 Workers			
中级 Middle	初级 Junior	无职称 No Rank						
36795	**18917**	**4621**	**32151**	**18308**	**17904**	**525**	**2101**	**2267**
17603	9518	2384	13642	9442	6248	174	794	1184
11636	4513	1022	8722	4591	5594	77	885	1198
72	66	5	44	19	31	0	0	0
4024	2155	709	4949	2513	3136	162	514	173
5056	2665	794	3863	2335	2538	120	159	350
203	94	14	104	0	24	0	0	0
15148	9158	2000	13898	8550	6260	164	504	511
656	266	77	571	300	321	2	39	35
812	301	81	1393	707	722	13	42	31
40	9	0	132	105	55	7	0	0
772	292	81	1261	602	667	6	42	31
35944	18602	4535	30694	17571	17151	512	2059	2236
23943	13402	3207	20814	12472	10574	348	768	1147
12001	5200	1328	9880	5099	6577	164	1291	1089
39	14	5	64	30	31	0	0	0

研究生指导
Aggregate Data on Supervisors

	计 Total	30岁及以下 30 and under	31—35岁 31 to 35	36—40岁 36 to 40	41—45岁 41 to 45
总　计 Total	**128652**	**500**	**7340**	**33232**	**25242**
其中:女 Of Which: Female	25651	98	1711	7424	5172
分职称:By Rank:					
正高级 Senior	66603	51	1143	10091	11978
副高级 Sub-senior	62049	449	6197	23141	13264
分指导关系:By Level of Programs Supervised:					
博士导师 Supervisors of doctoral Programs	10620		102	1034	1279
其中:女 Of Which: Female	1104		5	78	116
硕士导师 Supervisors of Master's Degree Programs	99727	497	6934	29184	20658
其中:女 Of Which: Female	22721	98	1677	7115	4775
博士、硕士导师 Supervisors of Doc. & Mas. Degree Programs	18305	3	304	3014	3305
其中:女 Of Which: Female	1826		29	231	281

研究生指导教
Data on Supervisors of Postgraduate

	计 Total	30岁及以下 30 and under	31—35岁 31 to 35	36—40岁 36 to 40
总　　计 Total	**115401**	**441**	**6283**	**29702**
其中:女 Of Which: Female	24003	92	1568	6999
分职称: By Rank:				
正高级 Senior	57497	38	841	8156
副高级 Sub-senior	57904	403	5442	21546
分指导关系:By Level of Programs Supervised:				
博士导师 Supervisors of doctoral Programs	8229		60	747
其中:女 Of Which: Female	888		3	59
硕士导师 Supervisors of Master's Degree Programs	91197	439	6029	26510
其中:女 Of Which: Female	21503	92	1543	6747
博士、硕士导师 Supervisors of Doc. & Mas. Degree Programs	15975	2	194	2445
其中:女 Of Which: Female	1612		22	193

教师情况(总计)
of Postgraduate Programs

单位:人
Unit:in Person

46—50岁 46 to 50	51—55岁 51 to 55	56—60岁 56 to 60	61—65岁 61 to 65	66岁及以上 66 and over
22239	**13119**	**14051**	**8075**	**4854**
4760	2619	2396	1042	429
12833	8144	10337	7380	4646
9406	4975	3714	695	208
1384	1011	1672	1978	2160
154	134	213	206	198
17714	10258	9615	3778	1089
4264	2267	1825	590	110
3141	1850	2764	2319	1605
342	218	358	246	121

师情况(普通高校)
Programs (Regular HEIs)

单位:人
Unit: in Person

41—45岁 41 to 45	46—50岁 46 to 50	51—55岁 51 to 55	56—60岁 56 to 60	61—65岁 61 to 65	66岁及以上 66 and over
22821	**20527**	**12037**	**12722**	**6689**	**4179**
4859	4506	2429	2232	930	388
10249	11616	7350	9186	6083	3978
12572	8911	4687	3536	606	201
998	1139	825	1335	1428	1697
95	123	109	171	164	164
18894	16535	9538	8953	3282	1017
4516	4069	2137	1740	552	107
2929	2853	1674	2434	1979	1465
248	314	183	321	214	117

分学科专任教师数(总计)

Total Number of Full-time Teachers by Field of Study

单位:人
Unit: in Person

	计 Total	正高级 Senior	副高级 Sub-Senior	中级 Middle	初级 Junior	无职称 No Rank
总计 Total	**834342**	**75636**	**245795**	**285286**	**168943**	**58682**
其中:女 Of Which: Female	351618	13745	90481	130086	86102	31204
哲学 Philosophy	28389	2667	9724	10656	4035	1307
经济学 Economics	54722	4479	15354	20833	10571	3485
法学 Law	34644	2733	9394	12867	7295	2355
教育学 Education	74222	3218	20611	27692	16847	5854
其中:体育 Of which: Sport	39540	1451	10998	15094	9157	2840
文学 Literature	176618	10429	43327	61183	44971	16708
其中:外语 Of which: Foreign Language	81695	3343	18171	28804	22345	9032
其中:艺术 Of which: Art	43313	2485	9053	14125	13427	4223
历史学 History	11809	1470	3920	4263	1662	494
理学 Science	113307	12702	39053	36018	19060	6474
工学 Engineering	222009	22940	67164	73335	43441	15129
其中:计算机 Of which: Computer	58869	3033	13607	19808	16275	6146
农学 Agriculture	22253	2914	7527	7245	3442	1125
其中:林学	3812	460	1301	1195	657	199
医学 Medicine	54904	8379	17993	16366	9478	2688
管理学 Administrators	41465	3705	11728	14828	8141	3063

分学科专任教师数(普通高校)

Number of Full-time Teachers by Field of Study in Regular Higher Educational Institutions

单位:人
Unit: in Person

	计 Total	正高级 Senior	副高级 Sub-Senior	中级 Middle	初级 Junior	无职称 No Rank
总计 Total	**724658**	**70063**	**216161**	**240555**	**146092**	**51787**
其中:女 Of Which: Female	302257	12332	78922	108809	74568	27626
哲学 Philosophy	23157	2267	7966	8462	3318	1144
经济学 Economics	42705	3803	12110	15662	8253	2877
法学 Law	27331	2248	7546	9965	5678	1894
教育学 Education	65307	2941	18400	23865	14813	5288
其中:体育 Of which: Sport	35874	1388	10289	13463	8173	2561
文学 Literature	152301	9250	37332	51575	39453	14691
其中:外语 Of which: Foreign Language	71415	2940	15902	24645	19876	8052
其中:艺术 Of which: Art	38830	2168	8135	12540	12168	3819
历史学 History	9735	1393	3282	3326	1306	428
理学 Science	100976	12277	34957	30879	16912	5951
工学 Engineering	197531	22116	61189	63272	37704	13250
其中:计算机 Of which: Computer	47535	2657	11224	15454	13170	5030
农学 Agriculture	21453	2857	7255	6964	3283	1094
其中:林学	3551	424	1149	1151	631	196
医学 Medicine	49666	7714	16166	14645	8654	2487
管理学 Administrators	34496	3197	9958	11940	6718	2683

分学科专任教师数(成人高校)

Number of Full-time Teachers by Field of Study in Adult Higher Educational Institutions

单位:人
Unit: in Person

	计 Total	正高级 Senior	副高级 Sub-Senior	中级 Middle	初级 Junior	无职称 No Rank
总计 Total	**85141**	**2050**	**22758**	**36795**	**18917**	**4621**
其中:女 Of Which: Female	39089	510	9074	17603	9518	2384
哲学 Philosophy	4166	175	1382	1884	605	120
经济学 Economics	9351	262	2434	4254	1944	457
法学 Law	6035	242	1475	2506	1428	384
教育学 Education	7604	158	1893	3371	1777	405
其中:体育 Of which:Sport	3063	33	625	1407	823	175
文学 Literature	18400	424	4509	7718	4486	1263
其中:外语 Of which:Foreign Language	6963	83	1477	3040	1815	548
其中:艺术 Of which:Art	3237	76	590	1271	1059	241
历史学 History	1870	53	570	876	317	54
理学 Science	10771	226	3638	4641	1873	393
工学 Engineering	18866	174	4599	8153	4788	1152
其中:计算机 Of which:Computer	8229	76	1596	3321	2549	687
农学 Agriculture	569	14	126	256	148	25
其中:林学	100	1	31	42	24	2
医学 Medicine	2615	161	903	944	494	113
管理学 Administrators	4894	161	1229	2192	1057	255

分学科专任教师数(民办的其他高等教育机构)

Number of Full-time Teachers by Field of Study in Non-state/private HEIs

单位:人
Unit: in Person

	计 Total	正高级 Senior	副高级 Sub-Senior	中级 Middle	初级 Junior	无职称 No Rank
总计 Total	**24543**	**3523**	**6876**	**7936**	**3934**	**2274**
其中:女 Of Which: Female	10272	903	2485	3674	2016	1194
哲学 Philosophy	1066	225	376	310	112	43
经济学 Economics	2666	414	810	917	374	151
法学 Law	1278	243	373	396	189	77
教育学 Education	1311	119	318	456	257	161
其中:体育 Of which: Sport	603	30	84	224	161	104
文学 Literature	5917	755	1486	1890	1032	754
其中:外语 Of which: Foreign Language	3317	320	792	1119	654	432
其中:艺术 Of which: Art	1246	241	328	314	200	163
历史学 History	204	24	68	61	39	12
理学 Science	1560	199	458	498	275	130
工学 Engineering	5612	650	1376	1910	949	727
其中:计算机 Of which: Computer	3105	300	787	1033	556	429
农学 Agriculture	231	43	146	25	11	6
其中:林学	161	35	121	2	2	1
医学 Medicine	2623	504	924	777	330	88
管理学 Administrators	2075	347	541	696	366	125

专任教师、聘请校外教师学历情况(总计)

Aggregate Data on Academic Qualifications of Full-time and Part-time Teachers in HEIs

单位:人

Unit:in Person

	计 Total	博士 Doctor's Degrees	硕士 Master's Degrees	本科 Normal Courses	专科及以下 Short-cycle Courses and Under
1.专任教师 Full-time Teachers	834342	54790	192123	544083	43346
其中:女 Of Which: Female	351618	10810	77951	244619	18238
正高级 Senior	75636	20062	19633	34372	1569
副高级 Sub-senior	245795	22396	59964	154199	9236
中级 Middle	285286	10534	73601	184017	17134
初级 Junior	168943	534	29424	127759	11226
无职称 No Rank	58682	1264	9501	43736	4181
2.聘请校外教师 Part-time Teachers	229257	12811	50121	149369	16956
其中:女 Of Which: Female	82584	2440	17312	56606	6226
正高级 Senior	38071	7239	10616	19452	764
副高级 Sub-senior	82738	3849	19112	55589	4188
中级 Middle	82128	1341	14889	56464	9434
初级 Junior	17951	138	3004	13143	1666
无职称 No Rank	8369	244	2500	4721	904
聘请校外教师中:外教 Foreign Teachers Among Part-time Teachers ones	4969	765	1495	2659	50

专任教师、聘请校外教师学历情况(普通高校)

Data on Academic Qualifications of Full-time and Part-time Teachers in Adult HEIs

单位:人

Unit:in Person

	计 Total	博士 Doctor's Degrees	硕士 Master's Degrees	本科 Normal Courses	专科及以下 Short-cycle Courses and Under
1.专任教师 Full-time Teachers	724658	53612	182517	458522	30007
其中:女 Of Which: Female	302257	10484	74059	205518	12196
正高级 Senior	70063	19598	18359	30732	1374
副高级 Sub-senior	216161	21905	56262	130230	7764
中级 Middle	240555	10339	70142	148507	11567
初级 Junior	146092	520	28585	110185	6802
无职称 No Rank	51787	1250	9169	38868	2500
2.聘请校外教师 Part-time Teachers	134250	9815	33123	85505	5807
其中:女 Of Which: Female	48452	1811	11368	32639	2634
正高级 Senior	26603	5801	7302	13027	473
副高级 Sub-senior	48518	2846	11976	31800	1896
中级 Middle	40693	876	9656	28237	1924
初级 Junior	12268	107	2270	8921	970
无职称 No Rank	6168	185	1919	3520	544
聘请校外教师中:外教 Foreign Teachers Among Part-time Teachers ones	4576	726	1365	2443	42

专任教师、聘请校外教师学历情况(成人高校)

Data on Academic Qualifications of Full-time and Part-time Teachers in Higher Educational Institutions for Adults

单位:人
Unit:in Person

	计 Total	博士 Doctor's Degrees	硕士 Master's Degrees	本科 Normal Courses	专科及以下 Short-cycle Courses and Under
1.专任教师 Full-time Teachers	85141	514	6453	68761	9413
其中:女 Of Which:Female	39089	150	2746	32000	4193
正高级 Senior	2050	143	449	1364	94
副高级 Sub-senior	22758	238	2409	18970	1141
中级 Middle	36795	114	2618	29812	4251
初级 Junior	18917	12	702	14977	3226
无职称 No Rank	4621	7	275	3638	701
2.聘请校外教师 Part-time Teachers	44437	852	7516	34132	1937
其中:女 Of Which:Female	15568	145	2510	12206	707
正高级 Senior	2858	315	842	1636	65
副高级 Sub-senior	15699	325	3205	11824	345
中级 Middle	20755	164	2682	16870	1039
初级 Junior	3854	20	427	3052	355
无职称 No Rank	1271	28	360	750	133
聘请校外教师中外教 Foreign Teachers Among Part-time Teachers ones	131	11	44	71	5

专任教师、聘请校外教师学历情况(民办的其他高等教育机构)

Data on Academic Qualifications of Full-time and Part-time Teachers in Non-state/private HEIs

单位:人
Unit:in Person

	计 Total	博士 Doctor's Degrees	硕士 Master's Degrees	本科 Normal Courses	专科及以下 Short-cycle Courses and Under
1.专任教师 Full-time Teachers	24543	664	3153	16800	3926
其中:女 Of Which: Female	10272	176	1146	7101	1849
正高级 Senior	3523	321	825	2276	101
副高级 Sub-senior	6876	253	1293	4999	331
中级 Middle	7936	81	841	5698	1316
初级 Junior	3934	2	137	2597	1198
无职称 No Rank	2274	7	57	1230	980
2.聘请校外教师 Part-time Teachers	50570	2144	9482	29732	9212
其中:女 Of Which: Female	18564	484	3434	11761	2885
正高级 Senior	8610	1123	2472	4789	226
副高级 Sub-senior	18521	678	3931	11965	1947
中级 Middle	20680	301	2551	11357	6471
初级 Junior	1829	11	307	1170	341
无职称 No Rank	930	31	221	451	227
聘请校外教师中:外教 Foreign Teachers Among Part-time Teachers ones	262	28	86	145	3

专任教师年龄情况(总计)

Breakdown of Full-time Teachers by Age (Regional Aggregates)

单位:人

Unit: in Person

	计 Total	30岁及以下 30 and under	31—35岁 31 to 35	36—40岁 36 to 40	41—45岁 41 to 45	46—50岁 46 to 50	51—55岁 51 to 55	56—60岁 56 to 60	61—65岁 61 to 65	66岁及以上 66 and over
总　计 Total	**834342**	**232318**	**154458**	**173619**	**96723**	**75502**	**44095**	**40247**	**13112**	**4268**
其中:女 Of Which: Female	351618	123371	72304	70840	34844	26415	13188	8128	2062	466
正高级 Senior	75636	96	842	9613	12926	15844	10185	13935	8771	3424
副高级 Sub-senior	245795	1114	16926	81390	53254	41938	24787	21874	3721	791
中级 Middle	285286	44891	108683	75022	27615	16033	8354	4115	527	46
初级 Junior	168943	132676	24914	6580	2546	1385	596	215	27	4
无职称 No Rank	58682	53541	3093	1014	382	302	173	108	66	3

专任教师年龄情况(普通高校)

Breakdown of Full-time Teachers by Age (Regular HEIs)

单位:人

Unit: in Person

	计 Total	30岁及以下 30 and under	31—35岁 31 to 35	36—40岁 36 to 40	41—45岁 41 to 45	46—50岁 46 to 50	51—55岁 51 to 55	56—60岁 56 to 60	61—65岁 61 to 65	66岁及以上 66 and over
总　计 Total	**724658**	**206107**	**134745**	**151790**	**82615**	**64593**	**36170**	**34081**	**10879**	**3678**
其中:女 Of Which: Female	302257	109162	62290	60406	28778	21949	10666	6951	1658	397
正高级 Senior	70063	50	734	9306	12324	15023	9158	12682	7704	3082
副高级 Sub-senior	216161	886	15664	74505	46852	36180	20485	18273	2745	571
中级 Middle	240555	40144	95519	62136	21293	12125	6039	2923	354	22
初级 Junior	146092	117378	20250	5030	1867	1042	368	136	20	1
无职称 No Rank	51787	47649	2578	813	279	223	120	67	56	2

专任教师年龄情况(成人高校)

Breakdown of Full-time Teachers by Age in Adult HEIs

单位:人
Unit: in Person

	计 Total	30岁及以下 30 and under	31—35岁 31 to 35	36—40岁 36 to 40	41—45岁 41 to 45	46—50岁 46 to 50	51—55岁 51 to 55	56—60岁 56 to 60	61—65岁 61 to 65	66岁及以上 66 and over
总　计 Total	**85141**	**20293**	**16089**	**18356**	**11237**	**8615**	**5805**	**4228**	**468**	**50**
其中:女 Of Which: Female	39089	11019	8257	8887	4900	3528	1796	639	62	1
正高级 Senior	2050		6	112	303	464	414	528	193	30
副高级 Sub-senior	22758	55	820	5883	5220	4597	3278	2658	228	19
中级 Middle	36795	3426	11058	11030	5138	3247	1897	952	46	1
初级 Junior	18917	12676	3957	1249	522	268	180	64	1	
无职称 No Rank	4621	4136	248	82	54	39	36	26		

专任教师年龄情况(民办的其他高等教育机构)

Breakdown of Full-time Teachers by Age (Non-state/private HEIs)

单位:人
Unit: in Person

	计 Total	30岁及以下 30 and under	31—35岁 31 to 35	36—40岁 36 to 40	41—45岁 41 to 45	46—50岁 46 to 50	51—55岁 51 to 55	56—60岁 56 to 60	61—65岁 61 to 65	66岁及以上 66 and over
总　计 Total	**24543**	**5918**	**3624**	**3473**	**2871**	**2294**	**2120**	**1938**	**1765**	**540**
其中:女 Of Which: Female	10272	3190	1757	1547	1166	938	726	538	342	68
正高级 Senior	3523	46	102	195	299	357	613	725	874	312
副高级 Sub-senior	6876	173	442	1002	1182	1161	1024	943	748	201
中级 Middle	7936	1321	2106	1856	1184	661	418	240	127	23
初级 Junior	3934	2622	707	301	157	75	48	15	6	3
无职称 No Rank	2274	1756	267	119	49	40	17	15	10	1

专任教师、聘请校外教

Data on Academic Qualification of Full－time and Invited from other Institutions

	专任教师中按授课内容分 Full－time teachers classified by teaching content			
	计 Total	公共课 Common Required Course	专业课 Specialied Course	
		基础课	计 Total	其中：双师型 Double－teacher Type
总　　计 Total	**801595**	**241850**	**559745**	**53899**
其中：女 Of Which：Female	339186	114690	224496	18696
正高级 Senior	73516	14318	59198	3740
副高级 Sub-senior	238134	67844	170290	19653
中级 Middle	272766	85553	187213	24025
初级 Junior	160775	53993	106782	5745
无职称 No Rank	56404	20142	36262	736
普通高校 Regular HEIs	693832	204719	489113	44017
其中：女 Of Which：Female	290666	97112	193554	15155
正高级 Senior	67992	12613	55379	3091
副高级 Sub-senior	208970	57885	151085	16199
中级 Middle	228874	70289	158585	19535
初级 Junior	138365	46332	92033	4651
无职称 No Rank	49631	17600	32031	541
成人高校 Adult HEIs	83719	28375	55344	7310
其中：女 Of Which：Female	38466	13703	24763	2744
正高级 Senior	2040	531	1509	237
副高级 Sub-senior	22368	7399	14969	2642
中级 Middle	36189	12409	23780	3523
初级 Junior	18580	6330	12250	811
无职称 No Rank	4542	1706	2836	97
民办的其他高等教育机构 Non-state/private HEIs	24044	8756	15288	2572
其中：女 Of Which：Female	10054	3875	6179	797
正高级 Senior	3484	1174	2310	412
副高级 Sub-senior	6796	2560	4236	812
中级 Middle	7703	2855	4848	967
初级 Junior	3830	1331	2499	283
无职称 No Rank	2231	836	1395	98

师岗位分类情况

Invited Teachers Classified by Teaching Content

单位：人

Unit: in Person

聘请校外教师按授课内容分 Invited Teachers Classified by Teaching Coneent				专任教师中不任课人数 Full－time Teacher by nonteaching				
计 Total	公共课 基础课 Common Requ－ired Course	专业课 Specialied Course		计 Total	进修 In-service	科研 Research	病休 Sick Leave	其他 Others
		计 Total	其中：双师型 Double－teach－er Type					
229275	**62692**	**166583**	**19749**	**32747**	**20783**	**3290**	**860**	**7814**
82589	25681	56908	5814	12432	8071	797	316	3248
38080	7673	30407	3597	2120	874	758	80	408
82743	22273	60470	8886	7661	4496	1230	191	1744
82132	22795	59337	6452	12520	8429	868	342	2881
17951	6493	11458	671	8168	5981	310	213	1664
8369	3458	4911	143	2278	1003	124	34	1117
134250	39093	95157	12573	30826	20167	3072	740	6847
48452	16454	31998	3623	11591	7765	711	265	2850
26603	4795	21808	2399	2071	866	743	77	385
48518	13671	34847	5691	7191	4423	1116	158	1494
40693	13402	27291	3958	11681	8117	806	285	2473
12268	4410	7858	456	7727	5786	285	188	1468
6168	2815	3353	69	2156	975	122	32	1027
44437	11955	32482	3740	1422	371	195	107	749
15568	4576	10992	1012	623	177	80	42	324
2858	643	2215	326	10	3	5	0	2
15699	4041	11658	1654	390	56	107	28	199
20755	5372	15383	1629	606	168	58	54	326
3854	1502	2352	127	337	132	24	24	157
1271	397	874	4	79	12	1	1	65
50588	11644	38944	3436	499	245	23	13	218
18569	4651	13918	1179	218	129	6	9	74
8619	2235	6384	872	39	5	10	3	21
18526	4561	13965	1541	80	17	7	5	51
20684	4021	16663	865	233	144	4	3	82
1829	581	1248	88	104	63	1	1	39
930	246	684	70	43	16	1	1	25

高等学校专任
Changes of Full-time Teachers in

	上学年初报表专任教师数 Total number of full-time teachers at beginning of previous academic year	增加专任 Factors of			
		合计 Total	录用毕业生 New recruits from current year graduates		
			计 Total	其中:Of which:	
				研究生 completing doc. & mas. deg. Prog.	本 科 completing 1st degree courses
总计 Total	**729400**	**152565**	**64341**	**23485**	**39440**
其中:女 Of Which: Female	300258	69311	33032	10776	20684
普通高校 Regular HEIs	626911	134855	58422	22751	34742
其中:女 Of Which: Female	255020	61048	29892	10419	18261
成人高校 Adult HEIs	82392	9782	3664	519	2884
其中:女 Of Which: Female	36953	4945	2001	285	1524
民办的其他高等教育机构 Non-state/private HEIs	20097	7928	2255	215	1814
其中:女 Of Which: Female	8285	3318	1139	72	899

资 产
Condition of Fixed Assets

	学校占地面积(平方米) Area of School sites (m^2)			图书音像 Audio-visual	
				一般图书(万册) Books & Magazines in Libraries(10 Thouand Volume)	
	计 Total	其中:绿化用地面积 Of Which: Green Arens	其中:运动场地面积 Of Which: Sports Areas	计 Total	当年新增 New Floor Space Added in Current Year
总计 Total					
学校产权 Owned by HEIs	1132873054	256248743	79379123	97919.11	9725.46
非学校产权中独立使用 Not Owned by HEIs	59939206	11770732	5658170	46915.44	21381.44
普通高校 Regular HEIs					
学校产权 Owned by HEIs	1035638801	235175170	69633469	83649.02	6936.20
非学校产权中独立使用 Not Owned by HEIs	44685738	8155877	3459639	2192.34	324.62
成人高校 Adult HEIs					
学校产权 Owned by HEIs	72093070	15699337	6922975	10135.88	1560.32
非学校产权中独立使用 Not Owned by HEIs	3429334	815288	487302	246.90	18.75
民办的其他高等教育机构 Non-state/private HEIs					
学校产权 Owned by HEIs	25141183	5374236	2822679	4134.21	1228.94
非学校产权中独立使用 Not Owned by HEIs	11824134	2799567	1711229	44476.20	21038.07

教师变动情况

Higher Educational Institutions

单位：人

Unit: in Person

教师数 Increase				减少专任教师数 Factors of Decrease				本学年初报表专任教师数 Total number of full-time teachers at beginning of current academic year
外单位教师调入 Teachers recruited from other units		校内、外非教师调入 Non-teaching personnel changed into teachers		合 计 Total	自然减员 Retired from their posts during previcus academic year	调离教师岗位 Transferred from teaching to non－teaching posts	其 他 Others	
计 Total	其中：高校调入 Of Which: from reg. HEIs	计 Total	其中：本校调整 Of Which: with change of status in their own institutions					
63630	**31224**	**24594**	**15245**	**47623**	**13062**	**9709**	**24852**	**834342**
26743	12113	9536	5830	17951	4399	3817	9735	351618
54904	28387	21529	13562	37108	10925	8301	17882	724658
23051	10937	8105	5023	13811	3599	3265	6947	302257
4006	1352	2112	1359	7033	1474	906	4653	85141
1943	598	1001	664	2809	544	360	1905	39089
4720	1485	953	324	3482	663	502	2317	24543
1749	578	430	143	1331	256	192	883	10272

情　　况

and Teaching Resources

资料情况 ed. Resources		拥有教学用计算机（台） No. of computers used for Instruction	语音实验室座位数（个） No. of Seats in Audio Labs	多媒体教室座位数（个） No. of Seats in Multimedia Class rooms	网上教学课程数（种） No. of Web-Based Courses	固定资产值（万元） Fixed Assets (in 10000 yuan)		
电子图书（片） Electronic Books & Magazines in Libraries(Disk)						合 计 Total	其中：教学、科研仪器设备资产 of which: Teaching Equipment & Instruments	
计 Total	当年新增 New Floor Space Added in Current Year						计 Total	当年新增 New Floor Space Added in Current Year
45546551	20502002	2563538	879077	4908240	52241	39741265.74	8912671.18	1625536.84
734431	179148	94654	45753	150620	2345	1434370.81	344914.30	56948.03
42790841	19142440	2158221	737531	4393919	17171	35783341.45	8112916.24	1480608.44
634914	164415	72377	36684	127979	267	1282006.61	306390.39	45545.01
1716508	814644	297903	94835	407923	29592	2901143.60	604961.71	92181.34
32046	452	9504	3700	9302	993	67099.10	17580.10	2210.41
1039202	544918	107414	46711	106398	5478	1056780.69	194793.23	52747.06
67471	14281	12773	5369	13339	1085	85265.10	20943.81	9192.61

校舍情况(总计)

Conditions of School Buidings (Total)

单位:平方米

Unit:m²

	学校产权建筑面积 Floor Area of School Building Owned by HEIs				正在施工面积 Floor Area Under Construction	独立使用非学校产权建筑面积 Floor Area of School Building Not Owned by HEIs
	计 Subtotal	其中:危房 Of Which: Dilapidated Buildings	其中:当年新增 Of Which: Newly Added in Current Year	其中:被外单位借用 Of Which: Floor Space Hired by OtherSchools or Units		
总计 Total	**426007768**	**1965975**	**54392904**	**1260003**	**47624638**	**41815149**
一、教学及辅助用房 Buildings for Instraction and Ancillary Uses	**165976371**	**576695**	**24857600**	**394611**	**24560626**	**15605667**
教室 Classroom	76489574	207220	12027256	202669	10657445	9241192
图书馆 Library	19199349	27145	3090222	29075	4318367	1054998
实验室、实习场所 Lab. And Practice Facilities	57009011	307670	8055809	139789	7325925	4239494
体育馆 Gymnasium	8881574	10999	1260183	15904	1870672	649159
会堂 Hall	4396863	23661	424130	7174	388217	420824
二、行政办公用房 Administritive	**20622328**	**136744**	**2121748**	**79845**	**2060277**	**1669549**
三、生活用房 Residential Buildings	**151487742**	**645563**	**23105580**	**455864**	**15742352**	**23072647**
学生宿舍(公寓) Students' Dormitories	99300564	257650	17621784	232485	11922348	18982195
学生食堂 Students' Dining Halls	17275064	44147	2836392	44426	1919079	1970103
教工单身宿舍 Apartments for Single	6104673	116295	662045	35810	318856	513961
教工食堂 Dining Halls for Teachers, Staff and Workers	1750859	5458	87701	4377	60758	113208
生活福利及其他用房 Residential, Welfare and Anxiliary Buildings	27056582	222013	1897658	138766	1521311	1493180
四、教工住宅 Residential Quarters for Teachers & Workers	**87921327**	**606973**	**4307976**	**329683**	**5261383**	**1467286**

校舍情况(普通高校)

Conditions of School Buidings (Regular HEIs)

单位:平方米

Unit: m^2

	学校产权建筑面积 Floor Area of School Building Owned by HEIs				正在施工面积 Floor Area Under Construction	独立使用非学校产权建筑面积 Floor Area of School Building Not Owned by HEIs
	计 Subtotal	其中:危房 Of Which: Dilapidated Buildings	其中:当年新增 Of Which: Newly Added in Current Year	其中:被外单位借用 Of Which: Floor Space Hired by OtherSchools or Units		
总计 Total	**382017582**	**1857033**	**50655732**	**1114358**	**44019739**	**34542433**
一、教学及辅助用房 Buildings for Instraction and Ancillary Uses	**146806522**	**545416**	**23195058**	**341183**	**22551777**	**12397224**
教室 Classroom	65897832	182393	11050707	163790	9477522	7051320
图书馆 Library	17501576	26210	2930398	23297	4037407	861744
实验室、实习场所 Lab. And Practice Facilities	52815803	303905	7700626	135318	7003128	3699204
体育馆 Gymnasium	7000997	9559	1145407	12404	1683691	493060
会堂 Hall	3590314	23349	367920	6374	350029	291896
二、行政办公用房 Administritive	**17066478**	**130143**	**1886891**	**68426**	**1862220**	**1100134**
三、生活用房 Residential Buildings	**136404988**	**581049**	**21433259**	**383142**	**14449409**	**19609478**
学生宿舍(公寓) Students' Dormitories	89979879	223094	16418493	192460	11028334	16357133
学生食堂 Students' Dining Halls	15244409	33886	2628064	31266	1734468	1623078
教工单身宿舍 Apartments for Single	5369704	108289	578048	29242	255453	359285
教工食堂 Dining Halls for Teachers, Staff and Workers	1347884	5216	73520	3927	47312	63397
生活福利及其他用房 Residential, Welfare and Anxiliary Buildings	24463112	210564	1735134	126247	1383842	1206585
四、教工住宅 Residential Quarters for Teachers & Workers	**81739594**	**600425**	**4140524**	**321607**	**5156333**	**1435597**

校舍情况(成人高校)

Conditions of School Buidings in Adult Higher Educational Institutions

单位:平方米

Unit: m^2

	学校产权建筑面积 Floor Area of School Building Owned by HEIs				正在施工面积 Floor Area Under Construction	独立使用非学校产权建筑面积 Floor Area of School Building Not Owned by HEIs
	计 Subtotal	其中:危房 Of Which: Dilapidated Buildings	其中:当年新增 Of Which: Newly Added in Current Year	其中:被外单位借用 Of Which: Floor Space Hired by OtherSchools or Units		
总　计 Total	**34738545**	**72542**	**2372703**	**127177**	**2036111**	**2207072**
一、教学及辅助用房 Buildings for Instraction and Ancillary Uses	**14731070**	**14279**	**1042951**	**38564**	**1171654**	**1036649**
教室 Classroom	8328411	7827	605633	24015	737402	656394
图书馆 Library	1378292	935	92138	5778	121895	62413
实验室、实习场所 Lab. And Practice Facilities	3529005	3765	264684	4471	186278	261954
体育馆 Gymnasium	889750	1440	52608	3500	105826	28490
会堂 Hall	605612	312	27888	800	20253	27398
二、行政办公用房 Administritive	**2935098**	**6601**	**165328**	**11204**	**123609**	**136458**
三、生活用房 Residential Buildings	**11376300**	**45114**	**1029409**	**69333**	**701165**	**1030565**
学生宿舍(公寓) Students' Dormitories	6879261	24056	751959	39725	476424	874224
学生食堂 Students' Dining Halls	1529902	1361	143054	13160	97180	67304
教工单身宿舍 Apartments for Single	489617	8006	47515	6508	29061	23811
教工食堂 Dining Halls for Teachers, Staff and Workers	342562	242	5970	450	3956	9643
生活福利及其他用房 Residential, Welfare and Anxiliary Buildings	2134958	11449	80911	9490	94544	55583
四、教工住宅 Residential Quarters for Teachers & Workers	**5696077**	**6548**	**135015**	**8076**	**39683**	**3400**

校舍情况(民办的其他高等教育机构)

Conditions of School Buidings in Non-state/private HEIs

单位:平方米

Unit:m²

	学校产权建筑面积 Floor Area of School Building Owned by HEIs				正在施工面积 Floor Area Under Construction	独立使用非学校产权建筑面积 Floor Area of School Building Not Owned by HEIs
	计 Subtotal	其中:危房 Of Which: Dilapidated Buildings	其中:当年新增 Of Which: Newly Added in Current Year	其中:被外单位借用 Of Which: Floor Space Hired by OtherSchools or Units		
总　　计 Total	**9251641**	**36400**	**1364469**	**18468**	**1568788**	**5065644**
一、教学及辅助用房 Buildings for Instraction and Ancillary Uses	**4438779**	**17000**	**619591**	**14864**	**837195**	**2171794**
教室 Classroom	2263331	17000	370916	14864	442521	1533478
图书馆 Library	319481	0	67686	0	159065	130841
实验室、实习场所 Lab. And Practice Facilities	664203	0	90499	0	136519	278336
体育馆 Gymnasium	990827	0	62168	0	81155	127609
会堂 Hall	200937	0	28322	0	17935	101530
二、行政办公用房 Administritive	**620752**	**0**	**69529**	**215**	**74448**	**432957**
三、生活用房 Residential Buildings	**3706454**	**19400**	**642912**	**3389**	**591778**	**2432604**
学生宿舍(公寓) Students' Dormitories	2441424	10500	451332	300	417590	1750838
学生食堂 Students' Dining Halls	500753	8900	65274	0	87431	279721
教工单身宿舍 Apartments for Single	245352	0	36482	60	34342	130865
教工食堂 Dining Halls for Teachers, Staff and Workers	60413	0	8211	0	9490	40168
生活福利及其他用房 Residential, Welfare and Anxiliary Buildings	458512	0	81613	3029	42925	231012
四、教工住宅 Residential Quarters for Teachers & Workers	**485656**	**0**	**32437**	**0**	**65367**	**28289**

三、中等教育
Secondary Education

(一)高中阶段教育
Senior Secondary

普通高中校数、班数

Number of Senior Secondary Schools and Classes

	学校数(所) Schools			班数(个) Classes
	合 计 Total	高级中学 Senior Sec. Schools	完全中学 Complete Sec. Schools	
总 计 Total	**15779**	**5868**	**9911**	**344059**
教育部门和集体办 Run by Ed. Dept. & Communities	11755	4701	7054	296559
社会力量办 Non-state/private	2679	927	1752	29749
其他部门办 Run by Non-ed. Dept.	1345	240	1105	17751
城市 Urban	6300	2142	4158	135188
教育部门和集体办 Run by Ed. Dept. & Communities	3896	1429	2467	105223
社会力量办 Non-state/private	1545	564	981	17223
其他部门办 Run by Non-ed. Dept.	859	149	710	12742
县镇 Counties & Towns	7191	3013	4178	173161
教育部门和集体办 Run by Ed. Dept. & Communities	5994	2655	3339	159524
社会力量办 Non-state/private	931	305	626	10738
其他部门办 Run by Non-ed. Dept.	266	53	213	2899
农村 Rural	2288	713	1575	35710
教育部门和集体办 Run by Ed. Dept. & Communities	1865	617	1248	31812
社会力量办 Non-state/private	203	58	145	1788
其他部门办 Run by Non-ed. Dept.	220	38	182	2110
总计中:其他学校附设初中班 Junior Sec. Classes Attached to Others Schools	–	–	–	5707
独立设置少数民族学校 Inde. Sec. Schools for Minorities	2340	–	–	7131

普通高中班额情况

Size of Senior Secondary Schools Classes

单位:个

	计 Subtotal	一年级 Grade 1	二年级 Grade 2	三年级 Grade 3
总 计 Total	**344059**	**129584**	**114038**	**100437**
城市:urban 25 人及以下	2047	485	721	841
26 - 35 人	5324	1670	1695	1959
36 - 45 人	17454	6072	5538	5844
46 - 55 人	49248	19090	16021	14137
56 - 65 人	38853	15454	13159	10240
66 人及以上	22262	7894	7893	6475
县镇:Counties & Towns 25 人及以下	1107	200	331	576
26 - 35 人	2624	674	803	1147
36 - 45 人	10535	3247	3294	3994
46 - 55 人	43803	16767	13870	13166
56 - 65 人	56653	22385	18658	15610
66 人及以上	58439	22248	20180	16011
农村:Rural 25 人及以下	548	106	157	285
26 - 35 人	1202	311	408	483
36 - 45 人	3045	845	997	1203
46 - 55 人	9202	3429	2946	2827
56 - 65 人	11452	4385	3846	3221
66 人及以上	10261	4322	3521	2418

普通高中学生数

Number of Students in Snior Secondary Schools

单位:人

Unit:in Person

	毕业生数 Graduates	招生数 Students Admitted	在校学生数 Enrolment				
			合　计 Total	其中女 Of Which: Female	一年级 Grade 1	二年级 Grade 2	三年级 Grade 3
总　计 Total	**4581235**	**7521264**	**19648261**	**8857158**	**7528644**	**6574860**	**5544757**
其中女 Of Which: Female	1978861	3448819	8857158	–	3450778	2955553	2450827
教育部门和集体办 Run by Ed. Dept. & Communities	4110364	6544134	17336280	7801777	6550157	5830778	4955345
社会力量办 Non-state/private	253327	634945	1413680	614116	636072	441281	336327
其他部门办 Run by Non－ed. Dept.	217544	342185	898301	441265	342415	302801	253085
城市 Urban	1691793	2698002	7090958	3362427	2700048	2379140	2011770
教育部门和集体办 Run by Ed. Dept. & Communities	1394482	2135024	5711492	2716591	2136328	1929562	1645602
社会力量办 Non-state/private	142134	314971	730083	325349	315591	230516	183976
其他部门办 Run by Non-ed. Dept.	155177	248007	649383	320487	248129	219062	182192
县镇 Counties & Towns	2411586	4009038	10453499	4583972	4013730	3488144	2951625
教育部门和集体办 Run by Ed. Dept. & Communities	2277459	3673068	9707158	4258854	3677165	3253719	2776274
社会力量办 Non-state/private	96708	280278	598162	253427	280767	184083	133312
其他部门办 Run by Non-ed. Dept.	37419	55692	148179	71691	55798	50342	42039
农村 Rural	477856	814224	2103804	910759	814866	707576	581362
教育部门和集体办 Run by Ed. Dept. & Communities	438479	736042	1917630	826332	736664	647497	533469
社会力量办 Non-state/private	14429	39696	85435	35340	39714	26682	19039
其他部门办 Run by Non-ed. Dept.	24948	38486	100739	49087	38488	33397	28854
总计中:其他学校附设初中班 Classes Attached to Others Schools	49308	126218	287031	135777	126312	95221	65498
重读生 Repeaters			152482	58448	7380	6706	138396
重读中女 Of Which: Female			58448	–	1959	2237	54252
少数民族学生 Minority Students	282002	502318	1281311	528887	503667	421763	355881
独立设置少数民族学校 Inde. Sec. Schools for Minorities	81531	142601	360144	183654	142731	117976	99437

普通中学教职工数

Number of Teachers, Staff & Workers in General Secondary Schools

单位:人

Unit:in Person

	教职工数 Teachers, Staff & Workers						代课教师 Substitute Teachers	兼任教师 Part-time Teachers
	合　计 Total	专任教师 Full-time Teachers	行政人员 Adm. Personnel	教辅人员 Supporting Staff	工勤人员 Workers	校办工厂、农(林)场职工 Employees in School-run Factories & Farms		
总　　计 Total	**5496535**	**4537310**	**360888**	**227448**	**356318**	**14571**	**119041**	**36532**
其中女 Of Which: Female	2308993	2000679	77040	103285	122764	5225	56420	12359
少数民族 Minority	399670	333481	25605	13041	27133	410	9278	1570
教育部门和集体办 Run by Ed. Dept. & Communities	4944927	4137757	310480	199665	284394	12631	98640	18885
社会力量办 Non-state/private	291604	201421	25175	15633	48601	774	14933	15560
其他部门办 Run by Non-ed. Dept.	260004	198132	25233	12150	23323	1166	5468	2087
城市 Urban	1416121	1096706	129601	79817	102675	7322	31246	19116
教育部门和集体办 Run by Ed. Dept. & Communities	1104249	870381	98016	63012	66579	6261	20595	7555
社会力量办 Non-state/private	147284	99075	14684	8812	24419	294	6886	10012
其他部门办 Run by Non-ed. Dept.	164588	127250	16901	7993	11677	767	3765	1549
县镇 Counties & Towns	2134433	1748178	126652	99930	154396	5277	35960	10401
教育部门和集体办 Run by Ed. Dept. & Communities	1982185	1638169	114787	92624	131772	4833	30237	5882
社会力量办 Non-state/private	107955	76560	7872	5251	17975	297	5066	4199
其他部门办 Run by Non-ed. Dept.	44293	33449	3993	2055	4649	147	657	320
农村 Rural	1945981	1692426	104635	47701	99247	1972	51835	7015
教育部门和集体办 Run by Ed. Dept. & Communities	1858495	1629207	97677	44031	86043	1537	47808	5448
社会力量办 Non-state/private	36363	25786	2619	1568	6207	183	2981	1349
其他部门办 Run by Non-ed. Dept.	51123	37433	4339	2102	6997	252	1046	218

普通高中分课程专

Number of Full-time Senior Secondary School Teachers

	总计 Total	其中女 Of Which: Female	政治 Politics	语文 Language & Literature	数学 Mathematics	物理 Physics	化学 Chemistry	生物 Biology
合计 Total	**1070575**	**430638**	**70732**	**172905**	**168533**	**106681**	**101313**	**47486**
研究生毕业 Graduate	9244	3643	737	1817	1629	916	1007	462
本科毕业 Under-graduate	801276	333515	55910	137615	131669	82222	79546	36703
专科毕业 Associate Bachelor	254026	92081	13809	32985	34811	23209	20475	10169
高中阶段毕业 High School Graduate	5837	1369	265	471	418	328	279	150
高中阶段毕业以下 Below High School Graduate	192	30	11	17	6	6	6	2
合计中：女 Of Total: Female	430638		29279	78106	54127	27910	38888	20225
少数民族 Minorities	66142	26400	4889	10997	10258	6527	6123	2848
城市 Urban	407063	191997	25920	64446	63334	40428	38538	17718
县镇 County & Towns	549200	201309	36742	89471	87047	55088	52162	24482
农村 Rural	114312	37332	8070	18988	18152	11165	10613	5286

普通高中专任教师专业技术

Full-time Teachers in Senior Secondary

	合计 Total	其中女 Of the Total: Female	25岁及以下 25 Years and Under	26－30	31－35
总计 Total	**1070575**	**430638**	**179571**	**235904**	**240488**
中学高级 Senior	191670	53449	158	489	8522
中学一级 1st Grade	377317	141887	1530	31600	143590
中学二级 2nd Grade	350104	158105	59323	176543	84997
中学三级 3rd Grade	33982	14856	18560	12638	1842
未评职称 Rank Undecided	117502	62341	100000	14634	1537
总计中：女 Of Which: Female	430638		97121	111489	100687
少数民族 Minorities	66142	26400	7847	15270	16829
城市 Urban	407063	191997	65043	81060	85788
县镇 County & Towns	549200	201309	92186	124216	128963
农村 Rural	114312	37332	22342	30628	25737

任教师学历情况
by Subject Taught & Educational Attainment

单位:人
Unit: in Person

地　理 Geography	历　史 History	外　语 Foreign Languages	信息技术 Infor. Technique	体　育 Physical Culture	音　乐 Music	美　术 Fine Arts	劳动技术 Skills Teaching	其　他 Others	当年不任课 No Teaching Load in Currentyear
46729	**59848**	**158795**	**27655**	**56079**	**13418**	**14412**	**3501**	**7212**	**15276**
318	543	1168	138	210	47	74	13	69	96
34251	46980	111532	17258	37181	6806	8167	1739	4143	9554
11970	12162	45609	10041	17557	6248	5965	1550	2609	4857
188	153	477	214	1097	309	199	188	370	731
2	10	9	4	34	8	7	11	21	38
17938	25160	97693	9783	9281	8110	5019	767	3147	5205
2953	3951	7885	1494	3526	847	721	171	1756	1196
17499	22281	60993	11046	22267	5804	6184	1399	3161	6045
24053	30848	81420	13547	28140	6492	6868	1731	3416	7693
5177	6719	16382	3062	5672	1122	1360	371	635	1538

职称、年龄结构情况
Schools Broken Down by Rank and Age

单位:人
Unit:in Person

36－40	41－45	46－50	51－55	56－60	61岁及以上 61 Years and Over
208001	**80984**	**51731**	**36991**	**31267**	**5638**
54487	39127	31870	26344	25513	5160
130920	37050	17677	9426	5152	372
21472	4372	1940	1010	402	45
469	197	94	96	63	23
653	238	150	115	137	38
71533	23703	14412	8524	2615	554
14734	5477	2954	1647	1164	220
81263	34349	23297	16978	15737	3548
108416	39831	24236	16742	12882	1728
18322	6804	4198	3271	2648	362

普通高中专任

Changes of Full-time Teachers in

	上学年初报表专任教师数 Total Number of Full-time Teachers at Beginning of Previous Academic	增加教师 Factors of Increase				
		合计 Total	录用毕业生 New recruits from Current Year Graduates	调入 Teachers Recruited from Other Units	校内调整 of which with change of status in their own institutions	其他 Others
合计 Total	**946356**	**211617**	**77171**	**79399**	**38882**	**16165**
其中女 Of Which: Female	366107	95604	42192	31300	16176	5936
城市 Urban	360014	80597	28150	27831	15343	9273
其中女 Of Which: Female	166281	39767	16706	12046	7353	3662
县镇 Counties & Towns	481380	107797	39996	43072	19122	5607
其中女 Of Which: Female	167522	46518	20967	16249	7382	1920
农村 Rural	104973	23212	9025	8485	4417	1285
其中女 Of Which: Female	32312	9311	4519	2997	1441	354

普通高中学生、教职工

Supplementary Information on Students and Full-time

	在校学生中 Of Total Students		
	共产党员 Member of C.P.C.	共青团员 Member of C.Y.L.	华侨 Overseas Chinese
合计 Total	**45802**	**13015047**	**5337**
其中女 Of Which: Female	19282	6072031	2574
城市 Urban	11123	4754112	2097
其中女 Of Which: Female	5411	2352059	1034
县镇 Counties & Towns	29027	6918922	3150
其中女 Of Which: Female	11383	3122809	1495
农村 Rural	5652	1342013	90
其中女 Of Which: Female	2488	597163	45

教师变动情况
General Secondary Schools

单位:人
Unit: in Person

减少教师 Factors of Decrease					本学年初报表专任教师数 Total Number of Full-time Teachers at Beginning of Current Academic Year
计 Total	自然减员 Retired from their posts during previous academic	调出 Transterred from teaching to non－teaching posts	校内调整 of which with Change of status in their own institutions	其他 Others	
87398	**9410**	**42464**	**19670**	**15854**	**1070575**
31073	2930	15916	6480	5747	430638
33548	4964	14454	7250	6880	407063
14051	1909	6367	2826	2949	191997
39977	3679	20705	9389	6204	549200
12731	846	7150	2849	1886	201309
13873	767	7305	3031	2770	114312
4291	175	2399	805	912	37332

政治面貌及其他
Teachers of Senior Secondary Schools

单位:人
Unit: in Person

专任教师中 Of Total Full-time Teachers			
共产党员 Member of C.P.C.	共青团员 Member of C.Y.L.	民主党派 Member of Non－communist Parties	华侨 Overseas Chinese
277285	208603	19544	231
80428	104598	7157	80
116313	76928	13585	157
44535	43747	5522	59
135593	104986	5356	64
31148	49340	1504	19
25379	26689	603	10
4745	11511	131	2

普通高中

Condition of School Buildings in

	学校占地面积 Areas Occupied	校舍建筑面积 Floor Space	教学及辅 Teaching & Assistant			
			合计 Total	其中		
				普通教室 classroom	实验室 Laboratory	图书室 Library
合　计 Total	**766396702**	**273613355**	**107640441**	**66428898**	**17644795**	**7604951**
城市 Urban	275515752	116544856	48369871	27649671	8287027	3871151
县镇 County Seats & Towns	381506400	127158950	48138785	31083557	7790242	3180888
农村 Rural	109374550	29909549	11131785	7695670	1567526	552912

普通高中

Condition of School Buildings in

	体育运动场(馆)面积(平方米) Sports Areas (m^2)	计算机(台) PC (set)	图书藏量(册) Books & Magazines in Libraries (Volume)	电子图书藏量(片) Electronic Books & Magazines in Libraries (disk)
合　计 Total	**182625764**	**1813251**	**444803404**	**8808254**
城市 Urban	70726957	925855	201338080	4943639
县镇 County Seats & Towns	86451604	725155	195164121	3425279
农村 Rural	25447203	162241	48301203	439336

办学条件(一)
Senior Secondary Schools (1)

单位:平方米

Unit: m^2

助用房 Buildings Of Which 微机室 PC-room	语音室 Linguistic	行政办公用房 Administritive 计 Total	其中教师办公室 Of Which: for Teachers	生活用房 Residential and Welfare	其他用房 Rooms for Other Purposes	校舍面积中 Of the Floor Space 危房面积 Floor Space of Dilapidated Buildings	当年新增 New Floor Space Added in Current Year
3885833	**2112256**	**27508583**	**16109548**	**107418962**	**31045369**	**5371839**	**19464077**
1889175	999978	12552060	7067798	39475644	16147281	1046979	8236462
1646772	939947	12149070	7281923	54803021	12068074	3165245	9540073
349886	172331	2807453	1759827	13140297	2830014	1159615	1687542

办学条件(二)
Senior Secondary Schools (2)

固定资产总值(万元) Total Volue of Fixed Asset (in 10 thousand yuan) 合计 Total	其中:仪器设备总值(万元) Of Which: Total Volue of Equip & Instru. (in 10 thousand yuan) 小计 Sub Total	专业实验设备 For Prefession	专业实习设备 For Practice
21524438.56	**2401690.83**	**1526799.76**	**302713.52**
10625443.73	1354080.41	858037.96	145423.43
9078184.97	853343.68	546772.90	127123.60
1820809.86	194266.74	121988.90	30166.49

普通高中办学条件(三)

Condition of School Buildings in Senior Secondary Schools (3)

单位:所

Unit: School

	体育运动场(馆)面积达标校数 Schools No: Sprots Areas Reached Standard	体育器械配备达标校数 Schools No: Sports Equip. Reached Standard	音乐器械配备达标校数 Schools No: Musical Instru. Reached Standard	美术器械配备达标校数 Schools No: Fine Arts Instru. Reached Standard	理科实验仪器达标校数 Schools No: Equip. of Natural Sci. Reached Standard	建立校园网校数 Schools No: Campus Networks Set
合　计 Total	**11594**	**11687**	**10394**	**10356**	**12423**	**7062**
城市 Urban	4621	4969	4656	4601	5227	3565
县镇 County Seats & Towns	5327	5207	4520	4515	5565	2890
农村 Rural	1646	1511	1218	1240	1631	607

成人高中

Basic Statistics of Adult

	学校数(所) Schools	教学班(点)(个) External Teaching Sites	毕(结)业生数 Graduates	
			计 Total	其中:女 Of which: Female
合　计 Total	**1317**	**5324**	**164842**	**79767**
职工高中 Senior Sec. Schools for Staff & workers	330	1606	60590	32491
农民高中 Senior Sec. Shools for Peasants	987	3718	104252	47276

中等职业学校机构数

Number of Secondary Vocational Schools

单位:人
Unit:in Person

	计 Total	中央部门 HEIs under Central Ministries & Agencies	地方部门 HEIs under Local Auth.			民办 Non-state/private
			计 Total	教育部门 Run by Ed. Dept.	非教育部门 Run by Non-ed. Dept.	
中等职业学校 Secondary Vocational Schools	11712	98	10232	7075	3157	1382
其中:普通中等专业学校 Of which: Reg. Specialized Sec. Schools	3065	65	2811	1283	1528	189
成人中等专业学校 Specialized Sec. Schools for Adults	2823	27	2673	1806	867	123
职业高中学校 Vocational High Schools	5824	6	4748	3986	762	1070
其他机构(教学点)(不计校数) Other Institutions	2275	15	2062	1417	645	198

注:中等职业学校数据不含技工学校数据,下同。

Note:Data on Skilled Workers Schools are not included. same as the followings.

基本情况

Schools by Province

单位:人(人次)
Unit:in Person

注册学生数 enrolment		教职工数 Teachers,Staff & Workers		聘请校外教师 Part-time Teachers
计 Total	其中:女 Of which:Female	计 Total	其中:专任教师 Of which:Full-time Teacher	
218468	**105455**	**8835**	**6054**	**7650**
94456	49785	3864	2524	2023
124012	55670	4971	3530	5627

	计 Total			中职全日制学生 Fulltime Students of SVSs		
	毕业生数 Graduates	招生数 Entrants	在校学生数 Enrolment	毕业生数 Graduates	招生数 Entrants	在校学生数 Enrolment
总计 Total	**3011438**	**4241166**	**10635841**	**2848330**	**4090725**	**10278823**
其中：女 Of Which: Female	1587363	2138863	5518321	1504232	2065493	5344223
分办学类型 By Types:						
普通中专学校 Reg. Specialized Sec. Schools	1050931	1389517	3722201	1039143	1374808	3684236
成人中专学校 Specialized Sec. Schools for Adults	336076	396068	930470	197665	276342	649464
职业高中学校 Vocational High Schools	1047631	1851188	4269988	1044826	1847852	4262874
其他机构 Other Institutions	576800	604393	1713182	566696	591723	1682249
分举办者 By Providers:						
1.中央部门 Under Central Ministries & Agencies	35878	39707	120461	30313	33408	99220
2.地方部门 Under Local Authorities	2789593	3812516	9721576	2634836	3671623	9393326
教育部门 Under Ed. Dept	1765264	2570382	6412302	1679202	2489404	6239253
非教育部门 Run by Non-ed. Dept	1024329	1242134	3309274	955634	1182219	3154073
3.民办 Non-state/private	185967	388943	793804	183181	385694	786277

注：SVSs＝中等职业学校，下同。

Note: SVSs = Secondary Vocational Schools. Same as the followings.

举办者的中职学生及教职工情况

Secondary Vocational Schools by Types and Providers of Schools

单位：人

Unit：in Person

中职非全日制学生 Parttime Students of SVSs			教职工数 Teachers，Staff & Workers							聘请校外教师 Part-time Teachers
				其中：专任教师 of which：Full-time Teachers						
毕业生数 Graduates	招生数 Entrants	在校学生数 Enrolment	计 Total	计 Total	正高级 Senior	副高级 Sub-senior	中级 Middle	初级 Junior	无职称 No Rank	
163108	**150441**	**357018**	**880772**	**559952**	**4732**	**90536**	**227281**	**190089**	**47314**	**78888**
83131	73370	174098	385493	258413	1558	35890	104760	92290	23915	30297
11788	14709	37965	347013	198550	1395	43269	84165	56797	12924	27986
138411	119726	281006	126113	75341	1021	13497	36217	20653	3953	26477
2805	3336	7114	363312	257945	2013	28496	95931	104123	27382	20134
10104	12670	30933	44334	28116	303	5274	10968	8516	3055	4291
5565	6299	21241	13804	6237	48	1419	3130	1436	204	1737
154757	140893	328250	804189	517130	2197	83506	212255	181393	37779	65326
86062	80978	173049	528585	364725	1289	50687	144754	139609	28386	28245
68695	59915	155201	275604	152405	908	32819	67501	41784	9393	37081
2786	3249	7527	62779	36585	2487	5611	11896	7260	9331	11825

中等职业学校

Number of Students in Secondary

	毕业生数 Graduates		招生数 Entrants		
	计 Total	其中:获得职业资格证书 Of which: Reciptents of Vocational qualifications	计 Total	其中:初中毕业 of which: Junior Sec. School Graduates 计 Total	其中:初中毕业 of which: Junior Sec. School Graduates 应届毕业生 Autumn Session
合　计 Total	**3011438**	**1393781**	**4241166**	**3927843**	**3706506**
其中:中职全日制学生 Of which: fulltime students	2848330	1339581	4090725	3888370	3692215
中职非全日制学生 parttime students	163108	54200	150441	39473	14291
1.普通中专学生 Students of Regular SSSs	1484471	603232	1838777	1764773	1669399
2.成人中专学生 Students of Adult SSSs	400315	158417	429818	284395	240683
3.职业高中学生 Students of High Vocational Schools	1126652	632132	1972571	1878675	1796424
二、培训学生 Traning students	5646046				
三、外国留学生 Foreign Students	2652				

注:SSSs＝中等专业学校,下同。

Note: SSSs＝Specialized Secondary Schools, the same below.

中等职业学校

Number of Female Students in Secondary

	毕业生数 Graduates		招生数 Entrants		
	计 Total	其中:获得职业资格证书 Of which: Reciptents of Vocational qualifications	计 Total	其中:初中毕业 of which: Junior Sec. School Graduates 计 Total	其中:初中毕业 of which: Junior Sec. School Graduates 应届毕业生 Autumn Session
一、中职学生计 Students of SVSs	1587363	701644	2138863	1990870	1882504
其中:中职全日制学生 Of which: fulltime students	1504232	672617	2065493	1973601	1876721
中职非全日制学生 parttime students	83131	29027	73370	17269	5783
1.普通中专学生 Students of Regular SSSs	835780	318628	996449	961620	911965
2.成人中专学生 Students of Adult SSSs	205117	77600	209126	139283	118915
3.职业高中学生 Students of High Vocational Schools	546466	305416	933288	889967	851624
二、培训学生 Traning students	2511467				
三、外国留学生 Foreign Students	1111				

(机构)各类学生数

Vocational Schools (Institutions)

单位:人

Unit: in Person

在校学生数 Enrolment					
计 Total	一年级 Grade 1	二年级 Grade 2	三年级 Grade 3	四年级及以上 Over Grade 4	预计毕业生数 Graduates for Next Year
10635841	**4254287**	**3530848**	**2567389**	**283317**	**3029702**
10278823	4100866	3407932	2488986	281039	2870815
357018	153421	122916	78403	2278	158887
5023708	1844565	1626312	1285290	267541	1419617
1054511	433258	374697	241277	5279	389185
4557622	1976464	1529839	1040822	10497	1220900
2972650					
835					

(机构)各类女学生数

Vocational Schools (Institutions)

单位:人

Unit: in Person

在校学生数 Enrolment					
计 Total	一年级 Grade 1	二年级 Grade 2	三年级 Grade 3	四年级及以上 Over Grade 4	预计毕业生数 Graduates for Next Year
5518321	2149509	1837743	1361612	169457	1556694
5344223	2073326	1778317	1324279	168301	1480873
174098	76183	59426	37333	1156	75821
2811533	1000768	914664	735629	160472	788219
523450	212614	184958	123067	2811	187855
2183338	936127	738121	502916	6174	580620
1299506					
443					

中等职业学校(机构)学生分科类情况(总计)

Data on Secondary Vocational Schools by Field of Study (Total)

单位:人

Unit:in Person

	毕业生数 Graduates		招生数 Entrants			在校学生数 Enrolment	预计毕业生数 Graduates for Next Year
	计 Total	其中:获得职业资格证书 Of which: Reciptents of Vocational qualifications	计 Total	其中:初中毕业 of which:Junior Sec. School Graduates			
				计 Total	应届毕业生 Autumn Session		
总 计 Total	**3011438**	**1393781**	**4241166**	**3927843**	**3706506**	**10635841**	**3029702**
其中:女 Of Which: Female	1587363	701644	2138863	1990870	1882504	5518321	1556694
农林类 Aqri. & Forestry	191007	79269	200497	175030	154571	534167	176971
资源与环境类 Resources & Environment	23946	10580	19239	17534	15554	55222	16935
能源类 Energy	22735	9573	28655	23203	21164	66158	18236
土木水利工程类 Civil & Hydraulic Engineering	93018	44304	97006	87502	81734	247975	70782
加工制造类 Manufacturing	333388	186141	622448	599886	567562	1331800	320051
交通运输类 Commu. & Transpor.	70062	40224	118567	104327	100276	270090	67635
信息技术类 Infor. Technologies	694028	368082	1117834	1064930	1018614	2715631	758649
医药卫生类 Medicine & Health	302174	68945	359361	331919	303698	1081853	338018
商贸与旅游类 Trade & Tourism	248547	133534	393712	381125	367975	1022987	279226
财经类 Finance & Economics	295717	145750	300854	263649	247386	786959	248650
文化艺术与体育类 Culture, Arts & Physical Edu.	199719	80905	250391	232832	218021	684737	196212
社会公共事物类 Public Affairs	149821	70639	162733	140093	127870	418763	138483
师范类 Teacher Training	262085	104969	256913	224492	212740	750362	241389
其他 Other	125191	50866	312956	281321	269341	669137	158465

中等职业学校(机构)学生分科类情况(其中:全日制学生)

Data on Secondary Vocational Schools by Field of Study (of which: full-time students)

单位:人
Unit: in Person

	毕业生数 Graduates		招生数 Entrants			在校学生数 Enrolment	预计毕业生数 Graduates for Next Year
	计 Total	其中:获得职业资格证书 Of which: Recipients of Vocational qualifications	计 Total	其中:初中毕业 of which: Junior Sec. School Graduates			
				计 Total	应届毕业生 Autumn Session		
总 计 Total	**2848330**	**1339581**	**4090725**	**3888370**	**3692215**	**10278823**	**2870815**
其中:女 Of Which: Female	1504232	672617	2065493	1973601	1876721	5344223	1480873
农林类 Aqri. & Forestry	171075	74746	184141	167330	153620	488190	152151
资源与环境类 Resources & Environment	23914	10580	19239	17534	15554	55061	16843
能源类 Energy	18024	9410	24486	22418	21114	56032	14675
土木水利工程类 Civil & Hydraulic Engineering	91325	43664	93706	87187	81574	241400	68210
加工制造类 Manufacturing	329573	184287	619714	598380	566713	1323629	316070
交通运输类 Commu. & Transpor.	66941	39647	115018	103896	100236	259000	64022
信息技术类 Infor. Technologies	679509	359667	1102867	1058540	1015313	2690207	743759
医药卫生类 Medicine & Health	291019	67376	345356	326818	303121	1048278	327760
商贸与旅游类 Trade & Tourism	246257	133204	392115	380160	367444	1017044	276492
财经类 Finance & Economics	251268	132291	266764	254789	243822	697999	211034
文化艺术与体育类 Culture, Arts & Physical Edu.	199076	80643	249838	232576	217921	683447	195804
社会公共事物类 Public Affairs	144842	69811	153373	136855	125491	395504	127584
师范类 Teacher Training	221776	89178	231320	221929	211624	684248	208578
其他 Other	113731	45077	292788	279958	268668	638784	147833

中等职业学校(机构)学生分科类情况(普通中专)

Data on Secondary Vocational Schools by Field of Study (Specialized Secondary Schools)

单位:人

Unit: in Person

	毕业生数 Graduates		招生数 Entrants			在校学生数 Enrolment	预计毕业生数 Graduates for Next Year
	计 Total	其中:获得职业资格证书 Of which: Recíptents of Vocational qualifications	计 Total	其中:初中毕业 of which: Junior Sec. School Graduates			
				计 Total	应届毕业生 Autumn Session		
总　计 Total	**1484471**	**603232**	**1838777**	**1764773**	**1669399**	**5023708**	**1419617**
其中:女 Of Which: Female	835780	318628	996449	961620	911965	2811533	788219
农林类 Aqri. & Forestry	76096	35333	53309	49591	45215	172880	56994
资源与环境类 Resources & Environment	21025	8983	13589	12717	11666	41153	12931
能源类 Energy	13156	6615	16351	14783	14382	39122	9211
土木水利工程类 Civil & Hydraulic Engineering	72141	33150	63616	58584	54824	173248	50161
加工制造类 Manufacturing	168418	83013	273526	267831	254464	610391	140472
交通运输类 Commu. & Transpor.	28634	14787	49866	43487	41860	116310	26166
信息技术类 Infor. Technologies	284149	127039	384084	373384	357394	1045066	295448
医药卫生类 Medicine & Health	199333	39480	278469	267971	250150	825873	250454
商贸与旅游类 Trade & Tourism	112448	49557	188410	183879	176948	499297	131439
财经类 Finance & Economics	138937	69190	125612	122031	115819	339546	100204
文化艺术与体育类 Culture, Arts & Physical Edu.	105002	33473	110030	100619	93423	341285	99449
社会公共事物类 Public Affairs	73842	30459	60809	54941	49348	176357	59382
师范类 Teacher Training	165732	63275	160824	156988	149766	508028	154214
其他 Other	25558	8878	60282	57967	54140	135152	33092

中等职业学校(机构)学生分科类情况(成人中专)

Data on Secondary Vocational Schools by Field of Study (Adult Specialized Secondary Schools)

单位:人
Unit:in Person

	毕业生数 Graduates		招生数 Entrants			在校学生数 Enrolment	预计毕业生数 Graduates for Next Year
	计 Total	其中:获得职业资格证书 Of which: Recipients of Vocational qualifications	计 Total	其中:初中毕业 of which: Junior Sec. School Graduates			
				计 Total	应届毕业生 Autumn Session		
总 计 Total	**400315**	**158417**	**429818**	**284395**	**240683**	**1054511**	**389185**
其中:女 Of Which: Female	205117	77600	209126	139283	118915	523450	187855
农林类 Aqri. & Forestry	27141	7704	23791	14047	6104	66327	33430
资源与环境类 Resources & Environment	518	366	1415	802	675	3038	789
能源类 Energy	7443	1605	5210	1789	900	15217	6669
土木水利工程类 Civil & Hydraulic Engineering	6102	2767	8901	5357	4349	18894	5979
加工制造类 Manufacturing	29922	17836	54443	48382	44394	116579	32023
交通运输类 Commu. & Transpor.	10823	6085	11521	7265	6460	29688	9054
信息技术类 Infor. Technologies	72468	35890	100896	87803	81142	230648	77972
医药卫生类 Medicine & Health	47822	9952	33981	22546	15062	113946	39296
商贸与旅游类 Trade & Tourism	17671	7412	22711	20374	19154	60088	19444
财经类 Finance & Economics	68436	23033	56934	28185	21769	144265	59407
文化艺术与体育类 Culture, Arts & Physical Edu.	7191	1991	7761	6560	5897	19975	7143
社会公共事物类 Public Affairs	25413	12365	32801	18979	15512	77723	30051
师范类 Teacher Training	62447	23897	42253	16230	14334	114277	52614
其他 Other	16918	7514	27200	6076	4931	43846	15314

中等职业学校(机构)学生分科类情况(职业高中)

Data on Secondary Vocational Schools by Field of Study (High Vocational Schools)

单位:人
Unit: in Person

	毕业生数 Graduates		招生数 Entrants			在校学生数 Enrolment	预计毕业生数 Graduates for Next Year
	计 Total	其中:获得职业资格证书 Of which: Recipients of Vocational qualifications	计 Total	其中:初中毕业 of which: Junior Sec. School Graduates			
				计 Total	应届毕业生 Autumn Session		
总　计 Total	**1126652**	**632132**	**1972571**	**1878675**	**1796424**	**4557622**	**1220900**
其中:女 Of Which: Female	546466	305416	933288	889967	851624	2183338	580620
农林类 Aqri. & Forestry	87770	36232	123397	111392	103252	294960	86547
资源与环境类 Resources & Environment	2403	1231	4235	4015	3213	11031	3215
能源类 Energy	2136	1353	7094	6631	5882	11819	2356
土木水利工程类 Civil & Hydraulic Engineering	14775	8387	24489	23561	22561	55833	14642
加工制造类 Manufacturing	135048	85292	294479	283673	268704	604830	147556
交通运输类 Commu. & Transpor.	30605	19352	57180	53575	51956	124092	32415
信息技术类 Infor. Technologies	337411	205153	632854	603743	580078	1439917	385229
医药卫生类 Medicine & Health	55019	19513	46911	41402	38486	142034	48268
商贸与旅游类 Trade & Tourism	118428	76565	182591	176872	171873	463602	128343
财经类 Finance & Economics	88344	53527	118308	113433	109798	303148	89039
文化艺术与体育类 Culture, Arts & Physical Edu.	87526	45441	132600	125653	118701	323477	89620
社会公共事物类 Public Affairs	50566	27815	69123	66173	63010	164683	49050
师范类 Teacher Training	33906	17797	53836	51274	48640	128057	34561
其他 Other	82715	34474	225474	217278	210270	490139	110059

中等职业学校(机构)分年龄学生数

Number of Students by age in Secondary Vocational Schools (Institutions)

单位:人

Unit:in Person

	计 Total	14岁及以下 14 years and under	15岁 15 years	16岁 16 years	17岁 17 years	18岁 18 years	19岁 19 years	20岁 20 years	21岁 21 years	22岁及以上 22 years and over
合　计 Total	**10635841**	**173193**	**1299001**	**2914114**	**2891838**	**1877682**	**753323**	**252692**	**106285**	**367713**
其中:中职全日制学生 Of which: fulltime students	10278823	173174	1288251	2907809	2883800	1861965	736899	230900	87823	108202
中职非全日制学生 parttime students	357018	19	10750	6305	8038	15717	16424	21792	18462	259511
1.普通中专学生 Students of Regular SSSs	5023708	93334	609111	1330497	1368053	945732	436592	149372	48746	42271
2.成人中专学生 Students of Adult SSSs	1054511	7862	88906	188223	183258	134744	64756	47510	40272	298980
3.职业高中学生 Students of High Vocational Schools	4557622	71997	600984	1395394	1340527	797206	251975	55810	17267	26462

中等职业学校(机构)分年龄女学生数

Number of Female Students by age in Secondary Vocational Schools (Institutions)

单位:人

Unit:in Person

	计 Total	14岁及以下 14 years and under	15岁 15 years	16岁 16 years	17岁 17 years	18岁 18 years	19岁 19 years	20岁 20 years	21岁 21 years	22岁及以上 22 years and over
合　计 Total	5518321	96594	683379	1526153	1519343	973953	385225	120449	44532	168693
其中:中职全日制学生 Of which: fulltime students	5344223	96585	678820	1523112	1515336	966513	377405	109254	34274	42924
中职非全日制学生 parttime students	174098	9	4559	3041	4007	7440	7820	11195	10258	125769
1.普通中专学生 Students of Regular SSSs	2811533	57207	350775	751665	774834	527380	236746	75041	21625	16260
2.成人中专学生 Students of Adult SSSs	523450	4367	43073	98730	98204	67558	32792	21383	15633	141710
3.职业高中学生 Students of High Vocational Schools	2183338	35020	289531	675758	646305	379015	115687	24025	7274	10723

中等职业学校(机构)
Changes in Enrolment of Secondary

	上学年初报表在校学生数 Total enrolment at beginning of previous academic year	增加学生数 Factors of Increase				
		计 Total	招生 No. of Students Admitted	复学 Students Resuming Studies	转入 Transfers from Other Inst.	其他 Others
合计 Total	**9894205**	**4696097**	**4241166**	**7846**	**180704**	**266381**
其中:中职全日制学生 Of which: fulltime students	9515564	4506134	4090725	7225	169427	238757
中职非全日制学生 parttime students	378641	189963	150441	621	11277	27624
1.普通中专学生 Students of Regular SSSs	4909314	2017088	1838777	3340	71251	103720
2.成人中专学生 Students of Adult SSSs	1033218	530782	429818	1831	22772	76361
3.职业高中学生 Students of High Vocational Schools	3951673	2148227	1972571	2675	86681	86300

中等职业学校(机构)
Changes in Female Enrolment of

	上学年初报表在校学生数 Total enrolment at beginning of previous academic year	增加学生数 Factors of Increase				
		计 Total	招生 No. of Students Admitted	复学 Students Resuming Studies	转入 Transfers from Other Inst.	其他 Others
合计 Total	**5152382**	**2364058**	**2138863**	**3448**	**92786**	**128961**
其中:中职全日制学生 Of which: fulltime students	4973592	2272341	2065493	3033	87349	116466
中职非全日制学生 parttime students	178790	91717	73370	415	5437	12495
1.普通中专学生 Students of Regular SSSs	2745886	1093599	996449	1412	41818	53920
2.成人中专学生 Students of Adult SSSs	511012	257879	209126	1009	11503	36241
3.职业高中学生 Students of High Vocational Schools	1895484	1012580	933288	1027	39465	38800

学生变动情况
Vocational Schools (Institutions)

单位:人
Unit: in Person

减少学生数 Factors of Decrease									本学年初报表在校学生数
计 Total	毕业 Graduates	结业 Completers of Courses without formal awards	休学 Suspended	退学 Quitting	开除 Expelled	死亡 Dead	转出 Transfers to Other Inst.	其他 Others	Total enrolment at beginning of current academic year
3954461	**3011438**	**81977**	**19096**	**193855**	**7873**	**549**	**324871**	**314802**	**10635841**
3742875	2848330	68903	18082	189585	7867	549	307053	302506	10278823
211586	163108	13074	1014	4270	6	0	17818	12296	357018
1902694	1484471	11995	8583	76065	4786	285	171341	145168	5023708
509489	400315	18669	2044	21209	468	23	26903	39858	1054511
1542278	1126652	51313	8469	96581	2619	241	126627	129776	4557622

女学生变动情况
Secondary Vocational Schools (Institutions)

单位:人
Unit: in Person

减少学生数 Factors of Decrease									本学年初报表在校学生数
计 Total	毕业 Graduates	结业 Completers of Courses without formal awards	休学 Suspended	退学 Quitting	开除 Expelled	死亡 Dead	转出 Transfers to Other Inst.	其他 Others	Total enrolment at beginning of current academic year
1998119	**1587363**	**35757**	**8013**	**80744**	**1719**	**190**	**150705**	**133628**	**5518321**
1901710	1504232	29175	7591	78764	1718	190	148586	131454	5344223
96409	83131	6582	422	1980	1	0	2119	2174	174098
1027952	835780	3253	3499	31982	1000	98	89306	63034	2811533
245441	205117	9971	835	9583	94	6	5282	14553	523450
724726	546466	22533	3679	39179	625	86	56117	56041	2183338

中等职业学校(机构)其他学生情况

Other Students in Secondary Vocational Schools (Institution)

单位:人
Unit: in person

	共产党员 Member of C.P.A	共青团员 Member of C.Y.L	华侨 Overseas Chinese	港澳台 From HK, Macao and Taiwan	少数民族 Minorities	残疾人 Disabled
合　计 Total	**65276**	**6216216**	**2773**	**366**	**564916**	**7747**
其中:女 Of Which: Female	23621	3212753	1332	151	272886	2629
中职全日制学生 full-time students	30549	6131240	2772	366	540360	7712
中职非全日制学生 part-time students	34727	84976	1	0	24556	35
1.普通中专学生 Students of Regular SSSs	17765	3219350	1136	134	342683	3978
2.成人中专学生 Students of Adult SSSs	41458	472604	347	19	55700	788
3.职业高中学生 Students of High Vocational Schools	6053	2524262	1290	213	166533	2981

中等职业学校(机构)培训学生情况

Training Students inSecondary Vocational Schools (Institutions)

单位:人次
Unit: in person

	结业生数 Graduates		注册学生数 Enrolment	
	计 Total	其中:女 Of Which: Female	计 Total	其中:女 Of Which: Female
总　计 Total	**5646046**	**2511467**	**2972650**	**1299506**
其中:少数民族 Of Which: Minority	314491	133738	194311	83109
一周至一个月以下 from one week to a month under	3321071	1439994	1381863	587465
一个月至半年以下 from one month to half year under	1643031	775410	895596	403000
半年以上 over half a year	681944	296063	695191	309041
总计中 Of Which: 资格证书培训	1663205	719277	837250	375852
岗位证书培训 Job-related Training	1425562	626483	657081	274570
总计中 Of Which: 外语 Foreign language	187751	113385	128897	82119
会计 Accountant	562465	368119	154806	105733
计算机 Computer	1011251	500376	546811	277515
农业技术 Agriculture Technology	979239	260279	488802	131130

中等职业学校(机构)外国留学生情况

Information on Foreign Students in Secondary Vocational Schools (Institutions)

单位:人

Unit:in persons

	结业生数 Graduates		注册学生数 Enrolment	
	计 Total	其中:女 Of Which: Female	计 Total	其中:女 Of Which: Female
总　计 Total	**2652**	**1111**	**835**	**443**
分时间:By Time:				
一周至一个月以下 from one week to a month nuder	178	33	0	0
一个月至半年以下 from one month to half yeaw under	2209	957	53	20
半年以上 over half a year	265	121	782	423
分地区 By continent:				
亚洲 Asia	2449	1030	700	400
非洲 Africa	40	0	58	7
欧洲 Europe	129	70	73	32
北美洲 North America	25	8	0	0
南美洲 South America	2	1	1	1
澳洲 Australia	7	2	3	3

中等职业学校

Number of Teachers, Staff & Workers in

	教职工数 Teachers,		
		校本部 Teacher, staff & Workers in	
	计 Total	计 Total	专任教师 Full-time Teachers
总 计 Total	**880772**	**854035**	**559952**
其中:女 Of Which: Female	385493	373266	258413
正高级 Senior	6664	6529	4732
副高级 Sub-senior	120786	119673	90536
中 级 Middle	302635	297554	227281
初 级 Junior	259916	253842	190089
无职称 No Rank	190771	176437	47314
总计中聘任制: Of Which: Part-time Teachers	172756	168160	114761
其中:女 Of Which: Female	74752	72811	52225
正高级 Senior	1863	1820	1385
副高级 Sub-senior	22373	22177	17010
中 级 Middle	57021	56356	44135
初 级 Junior	51194	50308	38759
无职称 No Rank	40305	37499	13472

中等职业学校(机构)

Number of Teachers, Staff & Workers in

	教职工数 Teachers,		
		校本部 Teacher, staff & Workers in	
	计 Total	计 Total	专任教师 Full-time Teachers
总 计 Total	**347013**	**330934**	**198550**
其中:女 Of Which: Female	155050	146931	92629
正高级 Senior	1939	1866	1395
副高级 Sub-senior	54601	53840	43269
中 级 Middle	115678	112038	84165
初 级 Junior	88064	83997	56797
无职称 No Rank	86731	79193	12924
总计中聘任制: Of Which: Part-time Teachers	60729	58090	36206
其中:女 Of Which: Female	26715	25468	16538
正高级 Senior	461	426	338
副高级 Sub-senior	9102	9019	7291
中 级 Middle	19954	19517	15002
初 级 Junior	15506	15020	10428
无职称 No Rank	15706	14108	3147

(机构)教职工数(总计)

Secondary Vocational Schools (Institutions)(Total)

单位:人

Unit:in person

Staff & Workers 教职工 College or Uni. Proper 行政人员 Adm. Personnel	教辅人员 Supporting Staff	工勤人员 Workers	校办企业职工 Employees in School-run Factories & Farms	其他附设机构人员 Personnel in Others Subsidiary Units	聘请校外教师 Part-time Teachers
120985	**66811**	**106287**	**13468**	**13269**	**78888**
42283	35027	37543	5161	7066	30297
1418	152	227	53	82	4214
22393	3457	3287	298	815	22678
40775	20924	8574	1483	3598	33659
25493	24515	13745	2092	3982	9974
30906	17763	80454	9542	4792	8363
21713	12553	19133	3053	1543	0
7461	6328	6797	1259	682	0
371	29	35	31	12	0
4171	544	452	111	85	0
7235	3563	1423	319	346	0
4376	4702	2471	444	442	0
5560	3715	14752	2148	658	0

教职工数(普通中专)

Secondary Vocational Schools (Institutions)(SSSs)

单位:人

Unit:in person

Staff & Workers 教职工 College or Uni. Proper 行政人员 Adm. Personnel	教辅人员 Supporting Staff	工勤人员 Workers	校办企业职工 Employees in School-run Factories & Farms	其他附设机构人员 Personnel in Others Subsidiary Units	聘请校外教师 Part-time Teachers
55932	**28314**	**48138**	**6429**	**9650**	**27986**
21972	15752	16578	2552	5567	11281
341	47	83	32	41	1293
8152	1225	1194	137	624	9043
16290	8983	2600	711	2929	11131
12909	10292	3999	863	3204	3749
18240	7767	40262	4686	2852	2770
9240	5071	7573	1904	735	0
3554	2657	2719	816	431	0
72	11	5	30	5	0
1419	171	138	44	39	0
2650	1547	318	216	221	0
2081	1880	631	223	263	0
3018	1462	6481	1391	207	0

中等职业学校(机构)

Number of Teachers, Staff & Workers in

	教职工数 Teachers,		
		校本部 Teacher, staff & Workers in	
	计 Total	计 Total	专任教师 Full-time Teachers
总计 Total	**126113**	**123465**	**75341**
其中:女 Of Which: Female	52681	51662	32970
正高级 Senior	1408	1390	1021
副高级 Sub-senior	18609	18534	13497
中级 Middle	49163	48826	36217
初级 Junior	32398	32029	20653
无职称 No Rank	24535	22686	3953
总计中聘任制: Of Which: Part-time Teachers	24510	23934	15455
其中:女 Of Which: Female	9759	9590	6526
正高级 Senior	302	297	217
副高级 Sub-senior	3659	3646	2666
中级 Middle	9096	9015	6881
初级 Junior	6310	6191	4220
无职称 No Rank	5143	4785	1471

中等职业学校(机构)

Number of Teachers, Staff & Workers in

	教职工数 Teachers,		
		校本部 Teacher, staff & Workers in	
	计 Total	计 Total	专任教师 Full-time Teachers
总计 Total	**363312**	**356506**	**257945**
其中:女 Of Which: Female	158334	155814	119817
正高级 Senior	2954	2911	2013
副高级 Sub-senior	40681	40455	28496
中级 Middle	122976	122079	95931
初级 Junior	127857	126441	104123
无职称 No Rank	68844	64620	27382
总计中聘任制: Of Which: Part-time Teachers	77909	76686	56678
其中:女 Of Which: Female	34079	33599	26193
正高级 Senior	934	932	688
副高级 Sub-senior	7994	7919	5775
中级 Middle	24772	24650	19857
初级 Junior	26939	26697	22329
无职称 No Rank	17270	16488	8029

教职工数(成人中专)

Secondary Vocational Schools (Institutions)(Adult SSSs)

单位:人
Unit:in person

Staff & Workers 教职工 College or Uni. Proper			校办企业职工 Employees in School-run Factories & Farms	其他附设机构人员 Personnel in Others Subsidiary Units	聘请校外教师 Part-time Teachers
行政人员 Adm. Personnel	教辅人员 Supporting Staff	工勤人员 Workers			
20064	**12806**	**15254**	**1781**	**867**	**26477**
6389	6621	5682	729	290	9111
298	49	22	5	13	1250
3827	793	417	42	33	7520
6878	4227	1504	151	186	13606
4207	4665	2504	160	209	2968
4854	3072	10807	1423	426	1133
3444	2270	2765	277	299	0
1009	1118	937	114	55	0
67	8	5	0	5	0
736	171	73	11	2	0
1164	676	294	20	61	0
703	818	450	27	92	0
774	597	1943	219	139	0

教职工数(职业高中)

Secondary Vocational Schools (Institutions)(High Vocational Schools)

单位:人
Unit:in person

Staff & Workers 教职工 College or Uni. Proper			校办企业职工 Employees in School-run Factories & Farms	其他附设机构人员 Personnel in Others Subsidiary Units	聘请校外教师 Part-time Teachers
行政人员 Adm. Personnel	教辅人员 Supporting Staff	工勤人员 Workers			
38621	**22442**	**37498**	**4768**	**2038**	**20134**
11706	10912	13379	1707	813	8205
728	52	118	16	27	1448
9261	1237	1461	112	114	4810
15346	6648	4154	556	341	7178
7032	8491	6795	988	428	2764
6254	6014	24970	3096	1128	3934
7685	4521	7802	839	384	0
2411	2208	2787	321	159	0
213	6	25	1	1	0
1735	170	239	56	19	0
2924	1105	764	80	42	0
1332	1778	1258	191	51	0
1481	1462	5516	511	271	0

中等职业学校(机构)

Number of Teachers, Staff & Workers in

	教职工数 Teachers,		
	计 Total	校本部 Teacher, staff & Workers in	
		计 Total	专任教师 Full-time Teachers
总　计 Total	**44334**	**43130**	**28116**
其中:女 Of Which: Female	19428	18859	12997
正高级 Senior	363	362	303
副高级 Sub-senior	6895	6844	5274
中　级 Middle	14818	14611	10968
初　级 Junior	11597	11375	8516
无职称 No Rank	10661	9938	3055
总中聘任制: Of Which: Part-time Teachers	9608	9450	6422
其中:女 Of Which: Female	4199	4154	2968
正高级 Senior	166	165	142
副高级 Sub-senior	1618	1593	1278
中　级 Middle	3199	3174	2395
初　级 Junior	2439	2400	1782
无职称 No Rank	2186	2118	825

教职工数(其他机构)

Secondary Vocational Schools (Institutions)(Other Institutions)

单位:人

Unit:in person

Staff & Workers 教 职 工 College or Uni. Proper					
行政人员 Adm. Personnel	教辅人员 Supporting Staff	工勤人员 Workers	校办企业职工 Employees in School-run Factories & Farms	其他附设机构人员 Personnel in Others Subsidiary Units	聘请校外教师 Part-time Teachers
6368	**3249**	**5397**	**490**	**714**	**4291**
2216	1742	1904	173	396	1700
51	4	4	0	1	223
1153	202	215	7	44	1305
2261	1066	316	65	142	1744
1345	1067	447	81	141	493
1558	910	4415	337	386	526
1344	691	993	33	125	0
487	345	354	8	37	0
19	4	0	0	1	0
281	32	2	0	25	0
497	235	47	3	22	0
260	226	132	3	36	0
287	194	812	27	41	0

中等职业学校(机构)分科专任教师数(总计)

Number of Full-time Teachers by Field of Study in Secondary Vocational Schools (Institutions) (Total)

单位:人

Unit: in Person

	计 Total	其中:女 Of Which: Female	正高级 Senior	副高级 Sub-Senior	中级 Middle	初级 Junior	无职称 No Rank
总计 Total	**559952**	**258413**	**4732**	**90536**	**227281**	**190089**	**47314**
其中:女 Of Which: Female	258413	–	1558	35890	104760	92290	23915
文化基础课 Common Required Subject	268316	130547	2007	45690	110805	87695	22119
专业课 Specialized Subject:	274974	122612	2617	43645	110052	95518	23142
农林类 Aqri. & Forestry	17648	6340	50	3039	7884	5956	719
资源与环境类 Resources & Environment	1806	668	7	453	805	476	65
能源类 Energy	2208	842	16	610	993	490	99
土木水利工程类 Civil & Hydraulic Engineering	7559	3021	31	1510	3353	2390	275
加工制造类 Manufacturing	24332	8547	159	4492	10117	7883	1681
交通运输类 Commu. & Transpor.	6384	1922	43	977	2786	2088	490
信息技术类 Infor. Technologies	51589	21443	493	5407	18263	21146	6280
医药卫生类 Medicine & Health	26325	14129	627	7069	10858	6577	1194
商贸与旅游类 Trade & Tourism	16203	9568	161	2124	6292	5898	1728
财经类 Finance & Economics	29219	15415	143	4395	13114	9681	1886
文化艺术与体育类 Culture, Arts & Physical Edu.	36795	16395	553	4882	13464	14120	3776
社会公共事物类 Public Affairs	7268	3088	46	1053	2917	2497	755
师范类 Teacher Training	28633	13328	135	5067	12193	9124	2114
其他 Other	19005	7906	153	2567	7013	7192	2080
实习指导课 Practice Course	16662	5254	108	1201	6424	6876	2053

中等职业学校(机构)分科专任教师数(普通中专)

Number of Full-time Teachers by Field of Study in Secondary Vocational Schools (SSSs)

单位:人
Unit:in Person

	计 Total	其中:女 Of Which: Female	正高级 Senior	副高级 Sub-Senior	中级 Middle	初级 Junior	无职称 No Rank
总计 Total	**198550**	**92629**	**1395**	**43269**	**84165**	**56797**	**12924**
其中:女 Of Which: Female	92629	–	495	18008	40150	27351	6625
文化基础课 Common Required Subject	79056	39334	477	18055	34133	21262	5129
专业课 Specialized Subject	112002	50822	899	24628	46889	32447	7139
农林类 Aqri. & Forestry	6625	2546	19	1772	2946	1685	203
资源与环境类 Resources & Environment	1062	390	2	321	492	220	27
能源类 Energy	1320	517	3	429	608	231	49
土木水利工程类 Civil & Hydraulic Engineering	4157	1725	8	966	1886	1159	138
加工制造类 Manufacturing	9347	3705	40	2494	4196	2216	401
交通运输类 Commu. & Transpor.	2308	763	11	490	1115	579	113
信息技术类 Infor. Technologies	14995	6232	101	2445	5866	5236	1347
医药卫生类 Medicine & Health	17516	9563	270	5475	7138	3894	739
商贸与旅游类 Trade & Tourism	5374	3054	37	951	2224	1709	453
财经类 Finance & Economics	12351	6589	62	2545	5881	3357	506
文化艺术与体育类 Culture, Arts & Physical Edu.	17715	7394	264	2935	6878	6056	1582
社会公共事物类 Public Affairs	3365	1410	23	654	1452	965	271
师范类 Teacher Training	11508	5149	28	2319	4521	3658	982
其他 Other	4359	1785	31	832	1686	1482	328
实习指导课 Practice Course	7492	2473	19	586	3143	3088	656

中等职业学校(机构)分科专任教师数(成人中专)

Number of Full-time Teachers by Field of Study in Secondary Vocational Schools (Adult SSSs)

单位:人

Unit: in Person

	计 Total	其中:女 Of Which: Female	正高级 Senior	副高级 Sub-Senior	中级 Middle	初级 Junior	无职称 No Rank
总计 Total	**75341**	**32970**	**1021**	**13497**	**36217**	**20653**	**3953**
其中:女 Of Which: Female	32970	–	341	4843	16502	9566	1718
文化基础课 Common Required Subject	36395	16564	371	7225	17874	9412	1513
专业课 Specialized Subject	36753	15812	627	6098	17390	10478	2160
农林类 Aqri. & Forestry	3227	1251	14	587	1608	898	120
资源与环境类 Resources & Environment	231	98	5	49	108	56	13
能源类 Energy	317	128	5	72	145	64	31
土木水利工程类 Civil & Hydraulic Engineering	722	317	13	150	351	188	20
加工制造类 Manufacturing	2303	753	42	487	1080	554	140
交通运输类 Commu. & Transpor.	704	211	10	131	338	193	32
信息技术类 Infor. Technologies	4662	1878	132	552	1907	1545	526
医药卫生类 Medicine & Health	3355	1797	212	806	1452	820	65
商贸与旅游类 Trade & Tourism	1095	580	25	150	536	291	93
财经类 Finance & Economics	5128	2425	38	675	2663	1356	396
文化艺术与体育类 Culture, Arts & Physical Edu.	1592	670	16	179	657	583	157
社会公共事物类 Public Affairs	762	310	4	101	378	199	80
师范类 Teacher Training	9838	4276	77	1702	4890	2861	308
其他 Other	2817	1118	34	457	1277	870	179
实习指导课 Practice Course	2193	594	23	174	953	763	280

中等职业学校(机构)分科专任教师数(职业高中)

Number of Full-time Teachers by Field of Study Schools) in Secondary Vocational Schools (High Vocational Schools)

单位:人

Unit:in Person

	合计 Total	其中:女 Of Which: Female	正高级 Senior	副高级 Sub-Senior	中 级 Middle	初 级 Junior	无职称 No Rank
总 计 Total	**257945**	**119817**	**2013**	**28496**	**95931**	**104123**	**27382**
其中:女 Of Which: Female	119817	–	648	10922	43077	51221	13949
文化基础课 Common Required Subject	139079	67890	1049	17836	53317	52902	13975
专业课 Specialized Subject	112402	49880	900	10260	40474	48361	12407
农林类 Aqri. & Forestry	7397	2403	15	594	3145	3263	380
资源与环境类 Resources & Environment	343	111	0	53	151	127	12
能源类 Energy	511	176	6	86	224	179	16
土木水利工程类 Civil & Hydraulic Engineering	2072	719	8	195	872	888	109
加工制造类 Manufacturing	11656	3699	73	1225	4439	4861	1058
交通运输类 Commu. & Transpor.	3099	877	17	314	1207	1227	334
信息技术类 Infor. Technologies	29734	12475	224	2127	9736	13575	4072
医药卫生类 Medicine & Health	4653	2323	78	552	1985	1707	331
商贸与旅游类 Trade & Tourism	9211	5648	89	957	3308	3740	1117
财经类 Finance & Economics	10422	5761	33	958	4059	4550	822
文化艺术与体育类 Culture, Arts & Physical Edu.	15079	7266	231	1337	5017	6670	1824
社会公共事物类 Public Affairs	2880	1269	16	246	989	1252	377
师范类 Teacher Training	4576	2585	26	526	1693	1841	490
其他 Other	10769	4568	84	1090	3649	4481	1465
实习指导课 Practice Course	6464	2047	64	400	2140	2860	1000

中等职业学校(机构)分科专任教师数(其他机构)

Number of Full-time Teachers by Field of Study in Secondary Vocational Schools (Other Institutions)

单位:人

Unit: in Person

	合计 Total	其中:女 Of Which: Female	正高级 Senior	副高级 Sub-Senior	中级 Middle	初级 Junior	无职称 No Rank
总计 Total	**28116**	**12997**	**303**	**5274**	**10968**	**8516**	**3055**
其中:女 Of Which: Female	12997	–	74	2117	5031	4152	1623
文化基础课 Common Required Subject	13786	6759	110	2574	5481	4119	1502
专业课 Specialized Subject	13817	6098	191	2659	5299	4232	1436
农林类 Aqri. & Forestry	399	140	2	86	185	110	16
资源与环境类 Resources & Environment	170	69	0	30	54	73	13
能源类 Energy	60	21	2	23	16	16	3
土木水利工程类 Civil & Hydraulic Engineering	608	260	2	199	244	155	8
加工制造类 Manufacturing	1026	390	4	286	402	252	82
交通运输类 Commu. & Transpor.	273	71	5	42	126	89	11
信息技术类 Infor. Technologies	2198	858	36	283	754	790	335
医药卫生类 Medicine & Health	801	446	67	236	283	156	59
商贸与旅游类 Trade & Tourism	523	286	10	66	224	158	65
财经类 Finance & Economics	1318	640	10	217	511	418	162
文化艺术与体育类 Culture, Arts & Physical Edu.	2409	1065	42	431	912	811	213
社会公共事物类 Public Affairs	261	99	3	52	98	81	27
师范类 Teacher Training	2711	1318	4	520	1089	764	334
其他 Other	1060	435	4	188	401	359	108
实习指导课 Practice Course	513	140	2	41	188	165	117

中等职业学校(机构)专任教师、聘请校外教师学历情况(合计)

Data on Academic Qualifications of Full-time and Part-time Teachers in Secondary Vocational Schools (Institutions)

单位:人
Unit:in Person

	计 Total	博士 Doctor's Degrees	硕士 Master's Degrees	本科 Normal Courses	专科 Short-cycle Courses	高中阶段及以下 Below High School Graduate
1.专任教师 Full-time Teacher	559952	179	5870	366529	169043	18331
其中:女 Of Which: Female	258413	48	2400	174980	74433	6552
正高级 Senior	4732	89	393	3499	691	60
副高级 Sub-senior	90536	62	2183	73866	13380	1045
中　级 Middle	227281	24	2555	158493	60157	6052
初　级 Junior	190089	1	559	107588	74620	7321
无职称 No Rank	47314	3	180	23083	20195	3853
其中:实习指导课教师 Of Which:Practice Course Teacher	16662	1	53	6514	7820	2274
2.聘请校外教师 Part-time Teacher	78888	301	3328	53538	19322	2399
其中:女 Of Which: Female	30297	63	1109	20384	7951	790
正高级 Senior	4214	145	574	3037	368	90
副高级 Sub-senior	22678	112	1438	18202	2549	377
中　级 Middle	33659	34	884	24070	8098	573
初　级 Junior	9974	1	223	5192	4199	359
无职称 No Rank	8363	9	209	3037	4108	1000
其中:实习指导课教师 Of Which:Practice Course Teacher	4727	4	111	3001	1193	418
聘请校外教师中:外教 Foreign Teachers Among Part-time Teachers ones	402	4	60	254	66	18

中等职业学校(机构)专任教师、聘请校外教师学历情况(普通中专学校)

Data on Academic Qualifications of Full-time and Part-time Teachers in Secondary Vocational Schools (SSSs)

单位:人

Unit: in Person

	计 Total	博士 Doctor's Degrees	硕士 Master's Degrees	本科 Normal Courses	专科 Short-cycle Courses	高中阶段及以下 Below High School Graduate
1. 专任教师 Full-time Teacher	198550	56	3272	148082	40932	6208
其中:女 Of Which: Female	92629	12	1373	71025	17904	2315
正高级 Senior	1395	17	83	1044	216	35
副高级 Sub-senior	43269	26	1254	36967	4450	572
中　级 Middle	84165	11	1490	64250	15926	2488
初　级 Junior	56797	1	330	37908	16388	2170
无职称 No Rank	12924	1	115	7913	3952	943
其中:实习指导课教师 Of Which: Practice Course Teacher	7492	0	29	3109	3335	1019
2. 聘请校外教师 Part-time Teacher	27986	116	1383	20719	4927	841
其中:女 Of Which: Female	11281	12	523	8298	2126	322
正高级 Senior	1293	54	165	948	68	58
副高级 Sub-senior	9043	44	442	7608	744	205
中　级 Middle	11131	12	468	8332	2043	276
初　级 Junior	3749	1	158	2338	1126	126
无职称 No Rank	2770	5	150	1493	946	176
其中:实习指导课教师 Of Which: Practice Course Teacher	1452	2	55	926	320	149
聘请校外教师中:外教 Foreign Teachers Among Part-time Teachers ones	229	1	33	171	20	4

中等职业学校(机构)专任教师、聘请校外教师学历情况(成人中专学校)

Data on Academic Qualifications of Full-time and Part-time Teachers in Secondary Vocational Schools (Adult SSSs)

单位:人
Unit:in Person

	计 Total	博士 Doctor's Degrees	硕士 Master's Degrees	本科 Normal Courses	专科 Short-cycle Courses	高中阶段及以下 Below High School Graduate
1.专任教师 Full-time Teacher	75341	58	972	46199	24862	3250
其中:女 Of Which: Female	32970	14	379	20351	10975	1251
正高级 Senior	1021	40	187	720	72	2
副高级 Sub-senior	13497	8	382	10880	2083	144
中级 Middle	36217	10	350	23469	11242	1146
初级 Junior	20653	0	35	9672	9519	1427
无职称 No Rank	3953	0	18	1458	1946	531
其中:实习指导课教师 Of Which:Practice Course Teacher	2193	0	9	773	1060	351
2.聘请校外教师 Part-time Teacher	26477	112	1096	18514	6306	449
其中:女 Of Which: Female	9111	27	262	6339	2377	106
正高级 Senior	1250	53	219	874	101	3
副高级 Sub-senior	7520	45	637	5809	928	101
中级 Middle	13606	14	213	9932	3357	90
初级 Junior	2968	0	8	1565	1339	56
无职称 No Rank	1133	0	19	334	581	199
其中:实习指导课教师 Of Which:Practice Course Teacher	1681	0	23	1288	299	71
聘请校外教师中:外教 Foreign Teachers Among Part-time Teachers ones	17	0	6	9	2	0

中等职业学校(机构)专任教师、聘请校外教师学历情况(职业高中)

Data on Academic Qualifications of Full-time and Part-time Teachers in Secondary Vocational Schools (High Vocational Schools)

单位:人
Unit:in Person

	计 Total	博士 Doctor's Degrees	硕士 Master's Degrees	本科 Normal Courses	专科 Short-cycle Courses	高中阶段及以下 Below High School Graduate
1.专任教师 Full-time Teacher	257945	44	1053	152092	96644	8112
其中:女 Of Which: Female	119817	18	406	73887	42783	2723
正高级 Senior	2013	21	95	1538	347	12
副高级 Sub-senior	28496	21	359	21616	6265	235
中级 Middle	95931	0	424	62685	30683	2139
初级 Junior	104123	0	133	54403	46069	3518
无职称 No Rank	27382	2	42	11850	13280	2208
其中:实习指导课教师 Of Which:Practice Course Teacher	6464	1	12	2396	3223	832
2.聘请校外教师 Part-time Teacher	20134	57	545	11320	7214	998
其中:女 Of Which: Female	8205	22	208	4532	3125	318
正高级 Senior	1448	28	173	1047	176	24
副高级 Sub-senior	4810	21	222	3749	775	43
中级 Middle	7178	4	104	4560	2339	171
初级 Junior	2764	0	27	1032	1541	164
无职称 No Rank	3934	4	19	932	2383	596
其中:实习指导课教师 Of Which:Practice Course Teacher	1468	2	27	709	538	192
聘请校外教师中:外教 Foreign Teachers Among Part-time Teachers ones	135	1	12	64	44	14

中等职业学校(机构)专任教师、聘请校外教师学历情况(其他机构)

Data on Academic Qualifications of Full-time and Part-time Teachers in Secondary Vocational Schools (Other Institutions)

单位:人

Unit: in Person

	计 Total	博士 Doctor's Degrees	硕士 Master's Degrees	本科 Normal Courses	专科 Short-cycle Courses	高中阶段及以下 Below High School Graduate
1. 专任教师 Full-time Teacher	28116	21	573	20156	6605	761
其中:女 Of Which: Female	12997	4	242	9717	2771	263
正高级 Senior	303	11	28	197	56	11
副高级 Sub-senior	5274	7	188	4403	582	94
中　级 Middle	10968	3	291	8089	2306	279
初　级 Junior	8516	0	61	5605	2644	206
无职称 No Rank	3055	0	5	1862	1017	171
其中:实习指导课教师 Of Which: Practice Course Teacher	513	0	3	236	202	72
2. 聘请校外教师 Part-time Teacher	4291	16	304	2985	875	111
其中:女 Of Which: Female	1700	2	116	1215	323	44
正高级 Senior	223	10	17	168	23	5
副高级 Sub-senior	1305	2	137	1036	102	28
中　级 Middle	1744	4	99	1246	359	36
初　级 Junior	493	0	30	257	193	13
无职称 No Rank	526	0	21	278	198	29
其中:实习指导课教师 Of Which: Practice Course Teacher	126	0	6	78	36	6
聘请校外教师中:外教 Foreign Teachers Among Part-time Teachers ones	21	2	9	10	0	0

中等职业学校(机构)

Breakdown of Full-time Teachers by Age in Secondary

	计 Total	30岁及以下 30 and under	31—35岁 31 to 35	36—40岁 36 to 40
总　计 Total	**559952**	**164840**	**127344**	**112356**
其中:女 Of Which: Female	258413	90241	63215	50524
正高级 Senior	4732	91	140	414
副高级 Sub-senior	90536	298	3360	21626
中　级 Middle	227281	16397	68482	70445
初　级 Junior	190089	107400	51950	18513
无职称 No Rank	47314	40654	3412	1358
普通中专学校 SSSs	198550	51467	44073	44417
其中:女 Of Which: Female	92629	28152	22027	20623
正高级 Senior	1395	29	55	147
副高级 Sub-senior	43269	68	1512	12096
中　级 Middle	84165	6208	26942	26922
初　级 Junior	56797	33874	14747	4895
无职称 No Rank	12924	11288	817	357
成人中专学校 Adult SSSs	75341	14056	15482	16799
其中:女 Of Which: Female	32970	7294	7906	7823
正高级 Senior	1021	3	25	84
副高级 Sub-senior	13497	73	504	2457
中　级 Middle	36217	1886	8468	11029
初　级 Junior	20653	9202	6007	3007
无职称 No Rank	3953	2892	478	222
职业高中学校 High Vocational Schools	257945	90241	61813	45707
其中:女 Of Which: Female	119817	49823	30276	19647
正高级 Senior	2013	48	56	165
副高级 Sub-senior	28496	123	1157	5706
中　级 Middle	95931	7229	29628	29230
初　级 Junior	104123	59107	29017	9890
无职称 No Rank	27382	23734	1955	716
其他机构 Other Institutions	28116	9076	5976	5433
其中:女 Of Which: Female	12997	4972	3006	2431
正高级 Senior	303	11	4	18
副高级 Sub-senior	5274	34	187	1367
中　级 Middle	10968	1074	3444	3264
初　级 Junior	8516	5217	2179	721
无职称 No Rank	3055	2740	162	63

专任教师分年龄情况

Vocational Schools (Institutions)

单位:人

Unit:in Person

41—45 岁 41 to 45	46—50 岁 46 to 50	51—55 岁 51 to 55	56—60 岁 56 to 60	61 岁及 以上 66 and over
58687	**45200**	**30333**	**18847**	**2345**
23979	17862	10175	1908	509
732	796	944	977	638
19003	19333	14924	10829	1163
32063	21068	12251	6106	469
6204	3458	1847	692	25
685	545	367	243	50
22629	17709	10838	6757	660
9736	7404	3793	742	152
247	242	231	257	187
9443	9159	6154	4464	373
11019	7282	3901	1800	91
1732	893	471	182	3
188	133	81	54	6
11226	8201	5715	3453	409
4662	3242	1676	299	68
168	196	253	185	107
2924	2930	2485	1903	221
6739	4305	2525	1190	75
1250	678	373	131	5
145	92	79	44	1
22096	17071	12231	7685	1101
8446	6399	4206	765	255
292	317	403	477	255
5563	6143	5436	3865	503
12911	8537	5260	2851	285
3007	1790	941	354	17
323	284	191	138	41
2736	2219	1549	952	175
1135	817	500	102	34
25	41	57	58	89
1073	1101	849	597	66
1394	944	565	265	18
215	97	62	25	
29	36	16	7	2

中等职业学校(机构)专任教师、

Data on the Numbers by Teaching Conrse of Full-time and

	专任教师中按授课内容分 Full-time Teacher by Teaching Content			
	计 Total	文化基础课 Common Required Subject	专业课、实习指导课 Specialized Practice Subject 计 Total	其中:双师型 Double-teacher Type
总　计 Total	**553047**	**265431**	**287616**	**55609**
其中:女 Of Which: Female	255608	129412	126196	21515
正高级 Senior	4683	2000	2683	692
副高级 Sub-senior	89407	45120	44287	11235
中　级 Middle	224554	109690	114864	26263
初　级 Junior	187519	86667	100852	15305
无职称 No Rank	46884	21954	24930	2114
普通中专学校 SSSs	196521	78307	118214	24558
其中:女 Of Which: Female	91781	39011	52770	9892
正高级 Senior	1390	475	915	262
副高级 Sub-senior	42861	17888	24973	6742
中　级 Middle	83311	33835	49476	12245
初　级 Junior	56151	21019	35132	4937
无职称 No Rank	12808	5090	7718	372
成人中专学校 Adult SSSs	74020	36164	37856	6752
其中:女 Of Which: Female	32418	16505	15913	2479
正高级 Senior	999	371	628	197
副高级 Sub-senior	13336	7190	6146	1422
中　级 Middle	35602	17754	17848	3352
初　级 Junior	20204	9353	10851	1464
无职称 No Rank	3879	1496	2383	317
职业高中学校 High Vocational Schools	254629	137285	117344	22414
其中:女 Of Which: Female	118508	67184	51324	8424
正高级 Senior	1995	1044	951	202
副高级 Sub-senior	27972	17483	10489	2580
中　级 Middle	94781	52664	42117	9787
初　级 Junior	102720	52211	50509	8479
无职称 No Rank	27161	13883	13278	1366
其他机构 Other Institutions	27877	13675	14202	1885
其中:女 Of Which: Female	12901	6712	6189	720
正高级 Senior	299	110	189	31
副高级 Sub-senior	5238	2559	2679	491
中　级 Middle	10860	5437	5423	879
初　级 Junior	8444	4084	4360	425
无职称 No Rank	3036	1485	1551	59

聘请校外教师岗位分类情况

Part-time Teachers in Secondary Vocational Schools

单位:人

Unit:in Person

聘请校外教师按授课内容分 Part-time Teacher by Teaching content				专任教师中不任课人数 Full - time Teacher by nonteaching			
计 Total	文化基础课 Common Required Subject	专业课、实习指导课 Special Subject、Practice Course		计 Total	进修 In-service	病休 Sick Leave	其他 Others
		计 Total	其中:双师型 Double - teacher Type				
78888	**28702**	**50186**	**9757**	**6905**	**1180**	**836**	**4889**
30297	12719	17578	2933	2805	588	361	1856
4214	1170	3044	719	49	5	5	39
22678	8183	14495	3595	1129	75	161	893
33659	11948	21711	4126	2727	418	352	1957
9974	4053	5921	856	2570	554	275	1741
8363	3348	5015	461	430	128	43	259
27986	11813	16173	3070	2029	605	204	1220
11281	5345	5936	863	848	308	94	446
1293	242	1051	256	5	0	0	5
9043	3888	5155	1204	408	48	27	333
11131	4733	6398	1251	854	268	108	478
3749	1750	1999	252	646	237	66	343
2770	1200	1570	107	116	52	3	61
26477	6939	19538	3960	1321	115	69	1137
9111	2814	6297	1265	552	55	31	466
1250	286	964	233	22	2	1	19
7520	1786	5734	1563	161	10	16	135
13606	3677	9929	1730	615	35	30	550
2968	939	2029	341	449	48	20	381
1133	251	882	93	74	20	2	52
20134	8334	11800	2151	3316	385	549	2382
8205	3856	4349	606	1309	176	229	904
1448	582	866	217	18	0	3	15
4810	2061	2749	614	524	9	114	401
7178	2887	4291	853	1150	86	209	855
2764	1144	1620	220	1403	238	185	980
3934	1660	2274	247	221	52	38	131
4291	1616	2675	576	239	75	14	150
1700	704	996	199	96	49	7	40
223	60	163	13	4	3	1	0
1305	448	857	214	36	8	4	24
1744	651	1093	292	108	29	5	74
493	220	273	43	72	31	4	37
526	237	289	14	19	4	0	15

中等职业学校(机构)

Changes of Full-time Teachers in Secondary

	上学年初报表专任教师数 Total number of full-time teachers at beginning of previous academic year	合 计 Total	录用毕业生 New recruits from current year graduates			增加专任 Factors of 外单位 Teachers recruited
			计 Total	研究生 completing doc, & mas. deg. Prog.	本科生 completing 1st degree courses	计 Total
总计 Total	**551209**	**87840**	**26938**	**462**	**20692**	**27930**
其中:女 Of Which: Female	250310	40537	15057	286	11434	12345
普通中专学校 SSSs	193342	23768	8755	175	7711	5591
其中:女 Of Which: Female	89052	11191	4945	109	4300	2490
成人中专学校 Adult SSSs	73463	11424	1979	99	1544	3596
其中:女 Of Which: Female	31171	4996	1019	75	773	1593
职业高中学校 High Vocational Schools	243265	46009	14250	165	9763	17060
其中:女 Of Which: Female	111730	21460	8024	93	5439	7592
其他机构 Other Institutions	41139	6639	1954	23	1674	1683
其中:女 Of Which: Female	18357	2890	1069	9	922	670

专任教师变动情况

Vocational Schools (Institutions)

单位:人

Unit: in Person

教师数 Increase 教师调入 from other units 其中:中职学校调入 Of Which: from other SVSs	非教师调入 Non-teaching personnel changed into teachers 计 Total	非教师调入 其中:本校调整 Of Which: with change of status in their own institutions	其他 Others	减少专任教师数 Factors of Decrease 合计 Total	自然减员 Retired from their posts during previcus academic year	调离教师岗位人员 Transferred from teaching to non-teaching posts	其他 Others	本学年初报表专任教师数 Total number of full-time teachers at beginning of current academic year
8614	**15162**	**11872**	**17810**	**79097**	**8265**	**13454**	**57378**	**559952**
3729	5844	4498	7291	32434	3343	5716	23375	258413
2409	4850	3919	4572	18560	2633	3294	12633	198550
1083	1820	1446	1936	7614	1054	1312	5248	92629
1175	1955	1240	3894	9546	1459	1558	6529	75341
537	704	471	1680	3197	467	585	2145	32970
4639	7133	5689	7566	31329	3714	7594	20021	257945
1969	2860	2201	2984	13373	1628	3389	8356	119817
391	1224	1024	1778	19662	459	1008	18195	28116
140	460	380	691	8250	194	430	7626	12997

	学校占地面积(平方米) Area of School sites (m^2)			图书音像 Audio-visual 一般图书(万册) Books & Magazines in Libraries(10 Thouand Volume)	
	计 Total	其中:绿化用地面积 Of Which: Green Arens	其中:运动场地面积 Of Which: Sports Areas	计 Total	当年新增 New Floor Space Added in Current Year
总计 Total					
学校产权 Owned by HEIs	488927373	91670027	73222352	301304013	19543197
非学校产权中独立使用 Not Owned by HEIs	24916634	4308027	4242666	26524797	497723
普通中专学校 SSSs					
学校产权 Owned by HEIs	205915959	38731111	30454339	155830843	8006780
非学校产权中独立使用 Not Owned by HEIs	7703655	1258837	1041561	2110099	170484
成人中专学校 Adult SSSs					
学校产权 Owned by HEIs	47834298	8002007	5906533	35685726	2107232
非学校产权中独立使用 Not Owned by HEIs	3581377	522558	681196	21271006	91975
职业高中学校 High Vocational Schools					
学校产权 Owned by HEIs	211526994	39762169	33939944	94656674	8562305
非学校产权中独立使用 Not Owned by HEIs	11855692	1845331	2294176	2689687	227414
其他机构 Other Institutions					
学校产权 Owned by HEIs	23650122	5174740	2921536	15130770	866880
非学校产权中独立使用 Not Owned by HEIs	1775910	681301	225733	454005	7850

(机构)资产情况

Secondary Vocational Schools (Institutions)

资料情况 ed. Resources		拥有教学用计算机(台) No. of Computers used for Instruction	语音实验室座位数(个) No. of Seats in Audio-Labs	多媒体教室座位数(个) No. of Seats in Multimedia Class rooms	网上教学课程数(种) No. of Web-Based Courses	固定资产值(万元) Fixed Assets (in 10000 yuan)		
电子图书(片) Electronic Books & Magazines in Libraries(Disk)						合计 Total	其中:教学、科研仪器设备资产 of which: Teaching Equipment & Instruments	
计 Total	当年新增 New Floor Space Added in Current Year						计 Total	当年新增 New Floor SpaceAdded in Current Year
12952879	4520551	1380820	404771	1201176	44230	13319121.04	3120588.01	329421.14
170944	48701	41031	13067	26385	1465	9131438.33	8361517.57	362147.65
7313340	2625953	547360	168718	561043	22588	6190272.73	1453967.19	167299.05
54389	27440	11829	3413	10358	412	8899252.89	8319442.67	355349.31
1520828	405653	182647	56781	182915	6192	1910961.66	527189.04	33009.59
9256	3142	7419	2251	6289	232	91891.32	6463.70	815.06
3871545	1390885	583307	154996	401019	12366	4211802.92	758625.10	109414.96
106861	18038	19936	6772	8755	758	117237.95	30941.40	5646.18
247166	98060	67506	24276	56199	3084	1006083.73	380806.68	19697.54
438	81	1847	631	983	63	23056.17	4669.80	337.10

中等职业学校(机构)教职工中其他情况

Other Teachers, Staff & Workers in Secondary Vocational Schools (Institutions)

单位:人

Unit: in person

	共产党员 Member of C.P.A	共青团员 Member of C.Y.L	民主党派 Non-communict parties	华侨 Overseas Chinese	港澳台 From HK, Macao and Taiwan	少数民族 Minorities
总计 Total						
教职工 Teachers, Staff & Workers	280515	108387	12423	352	126	43914
其中:女 Of Which: Female	91574	57134	5198	139	59	19049
专任教师 Full-time Teachers	166244	85422	9296	192	54	27874
其中:女 Of Which: Female	58353	45879	4105	89	23	12379
普通中专学校 SSSs						
教职工 Teachers, Staff & Workers	122427	35524	6574	190	89	22478
其中:女 Of Which: Female	42752	18660	2778	69	38	9759
专任教师 Full-time Teachers	65361	25373	5043	103	37	13614
其中:女 Of Which: Female	24777	13619	2250	46	15	6003
成人中专学校 Adult SSSs						
教职工 Teachers, Staff & Workers	45888	10224	1333	42	14	6497
其中:女 Of Which: Female	14245	4977	517	18	8	2635
专任教师 Full-time Teachers	28794	6831	961	25	3	4051
其中:女 Of Which: Female	9505	3531	373	9	1	1622
职业高中学校 High Vocational Schools						
教职工 Teachers, Staff & Workers	97626	56740	3811	107	18	13457
其中:女 Of Which: Female	29776	30365	1621	47	10	5959
专任教师 Full-time Teachers	63814	48642	2739	54	11	9278
其中:女 Of Which: Female	21105	26219	1257	29	6	4286
其他机构 Other Institutions						
教职工 Teachers, Staff & Workers	14574	5899	705	13	5	1482
其中:女 Of Which: Female	4801	3132	282	5	3	696
专任教师 Full-time Teachers	8275	4576	553	10	3	931
其中:女 Of Which: Female	2966	2510	225	5	1	468

中等职业学校(机构)校舍情况(总计)

Conditions of School Buildings in Secondary Vocational Schools (Total)

单位:平方米

Unit: m^2

	学校产权建筑面积 Floor Area of School Building Owned by HEIs				正在施工面积 Floor Area Under Construction	独立使用非学校产权建筑面积 Floor Area of School Building Not Owned by HEIs
	合计 Subtotal	其中:危房 Of Which: Dilapidated Buildings	其中:当年新增 Of Which: Newly Added in Current Year	其中:被外单位借用 Of Which: Floor Space Hired by Other Schools or Units		
总计 Total	**161490486**	**1579309**	**8487882**	**610543**	**5545278**	**7841276**
一、教学及辅助用房 Buildings for Instraction and Ancillary Uses	65843674	444150	3776866	277951	2744190	3586907
教室 Classroom	35762619	314767	2106249	142729	1507604	2311021
图书馆 Library	5150531	11572	282190	5573	283954	184172
实验室、实习场所 Lab. And Practice Facilities	18457474	94209	918179	120040	648867	698585
体育馆 Gymnasium	3782499	925	348614	4545	216619	246878
会堂 Hall	2690551	22677	121634	5064	87146	146251
二、行政办公用房 Administritive	12342126	113828	466249	40340	348029	699359
三、生活用房 Residential Buildings	59952763	858476	3562414	270374	1893986	3547569
学生宿舍(公寓) Students' Dormitories	34298650	349426	2602929	118571	1314450	2322634
学生食堂 Students' Dining Halls	7955379	82960	458620	20152	331009	397899
教工单身宿舍 Apartments for Single	3463348	128197	111910	9250	97078	244901
教工食堂 Dining Halls for Teachers, Staff and Workers	1577294	11781	41531	3519	77648	84413
生活福利及其他用房 Residential, Welfare and Anxiliary Buildings	12658092	286112	347424	118882	73801	497722
四、教工住宅 Residential Quarters for Teachers & Workers	23351923	162855	682353	21878	559073	7441

中等职业学校(机构)校舍情况(普通中专学校)

Conditions of School Buidings in Secondary Vocational Schools (SSSs)

单位:平方米
Unit:m²

	学校产权建筑面积 Floor Area of School Building Owned by HEIs				正在施工面积 Floor Area Under Construction	独立使用非学校产权建筑面积 Floor Area of School Building Not Owned by HEIs
	合计 Subtotal	其中:危房 Of Which: Dilapidated Buildings	其中:当年新增 Of Which: Newly Added in Current Year	其中:被外单位借用 Of Which: Floor Space Hired by Other Schools or Units		
总 计 Total	**77693422**	**435867**	**3446001**	**294927**	**2916091**	**2408806**
一、教学及辅助用房 Buildings for Instraction and Ancillary Uses	30679038	113038	1638695	150178	1527984	1070377
教室 Classroom	14579149	57029	833046	43364	804932	553803
图书馆 Library	2809273	3414	142710	308	185672	55904
实验室、实习场所 Lab. And Practice Facilities	9276852	39403	371206	101961	366637	274045
体育馆 Gymnasium	2568621	0	248668	4545	115366	148959
会堂 Hall	1445143	13192	43065	0	55377	37666
二、行政办公用房 Administritive	4842493	27747	184074	12986	151277	209464
三、生活用房 Residential Buildings	28950944	238820	1346793	122040	957062	1126815
学生宿舍(公寓) Students' Dormitories	17240587	103731	1027595	44025	651553	779349
学生食堂 Students' Dining Halls	3802516	20279	131922	5940	158320	101093
教工单身宿舍 Apartments for Single	1321756	28307	31687	4459	49910	57961
教工食堂 Dining Halls for Teachers, Staff and Workers	1012838	4730	13701	1361	65525	14760
生活福利及其他用房 Residential, Welfare and Anxiliary Buildings	5573247	81773	141888	66255	31754	173652
四、教工住宅 Residential Quarters for Teachers & Workers	13220947	56262	276439	9723	279768	2150

中等职业学校(机构)校舍情况(成人中专学校)

Conditions of School Buidings in Secondary Vocational Schools (Adult SSSs)

单位:平方米

Unit: m^2

	学校产权建筑面积 Floor Area of School Building Owned by HEIs				正在施工面积 Floor Area Under Construction	独立使用非学校产权建筑面积 Floor Area of School Building Not Owned by HEIs
	合计 Subtotal	其中:危房 Of Which: Dilapidated Buildings	其中:当年新增 Of Which: Newly Added in Current Year	其中:被外单位借用 Of Which: Floor Space Hired by Other Schools or Units		
总计 Total	**19071998**	**131941**	**745278**	**89751**	**478689**	**1660792**
一、教学及辅助用房 Buildings for Instraction and Ancillary Uses	7687127	33796	324391	40861	196664	827133
教室 Classroom	4901755	28614	197325	37394	119620	637786
图书馆 Library	512466	941	19224	565	19162	37591
实验室、实习场所 Lab. And Practice Facilities	1696114	1826	86980	1346	23072	102896
体育馆 Gymnasium	271961	75	4561	0	28030	26835
会堂 Hall	304831	2340	16301	1556	6780	22025
二、行政办公用房 Administritive	1916805	12147	38068	12612	40568	189109
三、生活用房 Residential Buildings	6713153	62687	307596	34944	172146	644355
学生宿舍(公寓) Students' Dormitories	3773917	25977	234941	17832	120184	378887
学生食堂 Students' Dining Halls	808938	12954	35493	4878	24653	66108
教工单身宿舍 Apartments for Single	410974	6730	7434	874	13699	51370
教工食堂 Dining Halls for Teachers, Staff and Workers	132306	964	3888	1075	2812	41047
生活福利及其他用房 Residential, Welfare and Anxiliary Buildings	1587018	16062	25840	10285	10798	106943
四、教工住宅 Residential Quarters for Teachers & Workers	2754913	23311	75223	1334	69311	195

中等职业学校(机构)校舍情况(职业高中学校)

Conditions of School Buidings in Secondary Vocational Schools (High Vocational Schools)

单位:平方米

Unit: m^2

	学校产权建筑面积 Floor Area of School Building Owned by HEIs				正在施工面积 Floor Area Under Construction	独立使用非学校产权建筑面积 Floor Area of School Building Not Owned by HEIs
	合计 Subtotal	其中:危房 Of Which: Dilapidated Buildings	其中:当年新增 Of Which: Newly Added in Current Year	其中:被外单位借用 Of Which: Floor Space Hired by Other Schools or Units		
总　计 Total	**56005517**	**975124**	**3694603**	**173613**	**1849582**	**3325895**
一、教学及辅助用房 Buildings for Instraction and Ancillary Uses	23933106	289632	1506045	69396	853061	1503595
教室 Classroom	14360580	224071	914885	52364	475634	1017531
图书馆 Library	1487246	6137	82485	184	62095	77414
实验室、实习场所 Lab. And Practice Facilities	6565494	51429	380434	15283	232036	267207
体育馆 Gymnasium	730544	850	70568	0	61132	62268
会堂 Hall	789242	7145	57673	1565	22164	79175
二、行政办公用房 Administritive	4968538	73662	215549	8842	147789	266260
三、生活用房 Residential Buildings	21135916	544371	1675169	90023	672817	1550944
学生宿舍(公寓) Students' Dormitories	11378974	212653	1161087	42772	479003	1010255
学生食堂 Students' Dining Halls	2864938	49523	261477	7427	135767	199075
教工单身宿舍 Apartments for Single	1606165	90089	67609	3917	32083	123591
教工食堂 Dining Halls for Teachers, Staff and Workers	347765	6087	21375	620	2111	23101
生活福利及其他用房 Residential, Welfare and Anxiliary Buildings	4938074	186019	163621	35287	23853	194922
四、教工住宅 Residential Quarters for Teachers & Workers	5967957	67459	297840	5352	175915	5096

中等职业学校(机构)校舍情况(其他机构)

Conditions of School Buidings in Secondary Vocational Schools (Other Institutions)

单位:平方米

Unit:m²

	学校产权建筑面积 Floor Area of School Building Owned by HEIs				正在施工面积 Floor Area Under Construction	独立使用非学校产权建筑面积 Floor Area of School Building Not Owned by HEIs
	合计 Subtotal	其中:危房 Of Which: Dilapidated Buildings	其中:当年新增 Of Which: Newly Added in Current Year	其中:被外单位借用 Of Which: Floor Space Hired by Other Schools or Units		
总　计 Total	**8719549**	**36377**	**602000**	**52252**	**300916**	**445783**
一、教学及辅助用房 Buildings for Instraction and Ancillary Uses	3544403	7684	307735	17516	166481	185802
教室 Classroom	1921135	5053	160993	9607	107418	101901
图书馆 Library	341546	1080	37771	4516	17025	13263
实验室、实习场所 Lab. And Practice Facilities	919014	1551	79559	1450	27122	54437
体育馆 Gymnasium	211373	0	24817	0	12091	8816
会堂 Hall	151335	0	4595	1943	2825	7385
二、行政办公用房 Administritive	614290	272	28558	5900	8395	34526
三、生活用房 Residential Buildings	3152750	12598	232856	23367	91961	225455
学生宿舍(公寓) Students' Dormitories	1905172	7065	179306	13942	63710	154143
学生食堂 Students' Dining Halls	478987	204	29728	1907	12269	31623
教工单身宿舍 Apartments for Single	124453	3071	5180	0	1386	11979
教工食堂 Dining Halls for Teachers, Staff and Workers	84385	0	2567	463	7200	5505
生活福利及其他用房 Residential, Welfare and Anxiliary Buildings	559753	2258	16075	7055	7396	22205
四、教工住宅 Residential Quarters for Teachers & Workers	1408106	15823	32851	5469	34079	0

职业技术培训

Basic Statistics of Vocational-Technical

	学校数（所）Schools	教学班(点)(个) External Teaching Sites (classes)	结业生数 计 Total
总　计 Total	230667	668538	66774722
职工技术培训学校(机构) Vocational-Technical Training Schools	4944	42828	3164059
教育部门和集体办 Run by Ed. Dept. & Collectives	2503	23488	1665916
其他部门办 Run by Non-Ed. Dept.	1738	16340	1311299
民办 Non-state/private	703	3000	186844
农村成人文化技术培训学校(机构) Technical Training Schools for Peasants	214529	535023	57654793
教育部门和集体办 Run by Ed. Dept. & Collectives	206314	501198	54886337
其中:县办 Of which:County-run	2004	10315	1669641
乡办 Of which:Township-run	29748	167260	23357039
村办 Of which:Village-run	174562	323623	29859657
其他部门办 Run by Non-Ed. Dept.	6667	29294	2355498
民办 Non-state/private	1548	4531	412958
其他培训机构(含社会培训机构) Others	11194	90687	5955870
教育部门和集体办 Run by Ed. Dept. & Collectives	1251	11362	611495
其他部门办 Run by Non-Ed. Dept.	1563	26171	1540649
民办 Non-state/private	8380	53154	3803726
总计中:少数民族 Total of: Minority	3042	10586	3794047
培训时间 Length of training:			
一周至一个月以下 from one week to a month under	0	0	46883933
一个月至半年以下 from one month to halfyeew under	0	0	14815966
半年以上 over half a year	0	0	5074823
培训形式 Mode of training:			
资格证书培训 For Certificates of Vocational qualifications	0	0	4112871
岗位证书培训 For Certificates of Job-related qualifications	0	0	7022506
培训科目:Subjects of training:			
外语 Foreign language	0	0	1348065
会计 Accounting	0	0	741774
计算机 Computer	0	0	1709900
农业技术 Agricultural techniques	0	0	32651491

机构基本情况

Training Institutions

单位：人次
Unit: in Person

Graduates	注册学生数 Enrolment		教职工数 Teachers, Staff & Workers		聘请校外教师 Part-time Teachers
其中：女 Of which: Female	计 total	其中：女 Of which: Female	计 Total	其中：专任教师 Of which: Full-time Teacher	
29521906	**53799582**	**24107405**	**457157**	**205952**	**458585**
1323552	2812372	1256456	44899	28507	24916
737876	1432931	694333	18880	12331	11677
498444	1150968	456984	18657	10527	11625
87232	228473	105139	7362	5649	1614
25301441	45494316	20122905	277559	109941	366158
24110386	42902016	19009996	259960	102561	352015
713451	1165580	437693	11168	6146	7424
10096573	17802038	7787857	81509	42680	116248
13300362	23934398	10784446	167283	53735	228343
1028857	2298785	983466	12841	3675	12846
162198	293515	129443	4758	3705	1297
2896913	5492894	2728044	134699	67504	67511
314433	752008	375576	10412	4731	4144
680239	1324727	597919	15770	7111	9692
1902241	3416159	1754549	108517	55662	53675
1643198	2950593	1261851	14397	3219	15878
20247580	36908906	16175328	0	0	0
6783108	12511721	5838184	0	0	0
2491218	4378955	2093893	0	0	0
1785077	3611598	1617986	0	0	0
2997546	5399253	2395278	0	0	0
638651	1045590	559670	0	0	0
431987	652280	405264	0	0	0
846191	1526000	773435	0	0	0
14141518	26172424	11590038	0	0	0

职业技术培训机构资产情况

Condition of Fixed Assets and Teaching Resources in Vocational-Technical Training Institutions

	总　计 Total	职工技术培训学校(机构) Vocational-Technical Training Institutions	农村成人文化技术培训学校(机构) Technical Training Schools for Peasants	其他培训机构(含社会培训机构) Others
占地面积(平方米) Area of School sites (m^2)	117339904	14791082	80471559	22077263
教学行政用房建筑面积(平方米)Administritive (m^2)	33593632	4900248	19456915	9236469
图书藏量(册)Books (Volume)	95731304	10217319	38638244	46875741
教学用计算机(台)No. of computers used for Instruction	364646	65002	112582	187062
语音实验室座位数(个) No. of Seats in Audio-Labs	104127	17232	37108	49787
多媒体教室座位数(个) No. of Seats in Multimedia Classrooms	262660	46295	103579	112786
固定资产总值(万元) Fixed Assets (in 10000 yuan)	239032807	1758263	5418116	231856428
其中:教学、实习仪器设备资产值 of which: Teaching Equipment & Instruments	108552038	114272	1335154	107102612

(二)初中阶段教育
Junior Secondary Education

普通初中校数、班数

Number of Junior Schools and Classes

	学校数(所) Schools			班数(个) Classes				
	合 计 Total	初级中学 Junior Sec. Schools	九年一贯制学校 9-Year Sec. Schools	合 计 Total	一年级 Grade 1	二年级 Grade 2	三年级 Grade 3	四年级 Grade 4
总 计 Total	**63711**	**55327**	**8384**	**1165041**	**390110**	**384723**	**369305**	**20903**
教育部门和集体办 Run by Ed. Dept. & Communities	56911	51344	5567	1067607	356935	353107	340157	17408
社会力量办 Non-state/private	3651	2344	1307	52372	19549	17395	14937	491
其他部门办 Run by Non-ed. Dept.	3149	1639	1510	45062	13626	14221	14211	3004
城市 Urban	8989	6850	2139	222960	71750	72730	72085	6395
教育部门和集体办 Run by Ed. Dept. & Communities	6033	5329	704	171614	54983	56072	56311	4248
社会力量办 Non-state/private	1293	700	593	23498	8286	7904	6920	388
其他部门办 Run by Non-ed. Dept.	1663	821	842	27848	8481	8754	8854	1759
县镇 Counties & Towns	17471	15889	1582	397249	133835	130718	126541	6155
教育部门和集体办 Run by Ed. Dept. & Communities	15682	14728	954	370858	124282	122024	118978	5574
社会力量办 Non-state/private	1252	855	397	19431	7537	6485	5350	59
其他部门办 Run by Non-ed. Dept.	537	306	231	6960	2016	2209	2213	522
农村 Rural	37251	32588	4663	544832	184525	181275	170679	8353
教育部门和集体办 Run by Ed. Dept. & Communities	35196	31287	3909	525135	177670	175011	164868	7586
社会力量办 Non-state/private	1106	789	317	9443	3726	3006	2667	44
其他部门办 Run by Non-ed. Dept.	949	512	437	10254	3129	3258	3144	723
总计中:四年制初中 Of the Total:4-YearJunior Sec. School	–	–	–	75325	14565	18882	21549	20329
其他学校附设初中班 Junior Sec. Classes Attached to Others Schools	–	–	–	24176	8519	8187	7392	78
独立设置少数民族学校 Inde. Sec. Schools for Minorities	–	–	–	29080	10573	9417	8777	313

职业初中校数、班数

Number of Schools, Classes Admitted in Vocational Schools

	学校数(所) Schools	班数(个) Classes 计 Total	一年级 Grade 1	二年级 Grade 2	三年级 Grade 3	四年级 Grade 4
总计 Total	**1019**	**12415**	**4187**	**4076**	**3788**	**364**
教育部门和集体办 Run by Ed. Dept. & Communities	956	11942	4014	3914	3654	360
社会力量办 Non-state/private	53	424	155	148	117	4
其他部门办 Run by Non-ed. Dept.	10	49	18	14	17	0
城市 Urban	48	455	147	155	140	13
教育部门和集体办 Run by Ed. Dept. & Communities	28	357	113	123	109	12
社会力量办 Non-state/private	14	61	21	21	18	1
其他部门办 Run by Non-ed. Dept.	6	37	13	11	13	0
县镇 Counties & Towns	231	3207	1099	1064	976	68
教育部门和集体办 Run by Ed. Dept. & Communities	216	3048	1037	1008	935	68
社会力量办 Non-state/private	11	147	57	53	37	0
其他部门办 Run by Non-ed. Dept.	4	12	5	3	4	0
农村 Rural	740	8753	2941	2857	2672	283
教育部门和集体办 Run by Ed. Dept. & Communities	712	8537	2864	2783	2610	280
社会力量办 Non-state/private	28	216	77	74	62	3
其他部门办 Run by Non-ed. Dept.	0	0	0	0	0	0
总计中:四年制 Of the Total:4-Year	–	969	131	260	254	324
普通中学附设班 Classes Attached to General Sec. Schools	–	1240	359	370	464	47
其他单位(学校)办班 Classes Run by Other Unit (or Schools)	–	1352	450	473	394	35
独立设置少数民族学校 Inde. Sec. Schools for Minorities	30	252	81	82	74	15

普通初中班额情况

Size of Junior Secondary Schools Classes

单位:个

Unit:Class

	合 计 Total	一年级 Grade 1	二年级 Grade 2	三年级 Grade 3	四年级 Grade 4
合 计 Total	**1165041**	**390110**	**384723**	**369305**	**20903**
城市:Urban:					
25 人及以下 under 25 years	4659	1700	1359	1434	166
26 - 35 人 between 26 - 35	15481	5435	4589	4969	488
36 - 45 人 between 36 - 45	43703	14742	13540	14050	1371
46 - 55 人 between 36 - 55	73429	23730	23817	23719	2163
56 - 65 人 between 56 - 65	51636	16053	17266	16860	1457
66 人及以上 over 66 years	34052	10090	12159	11053	750
县镇:Counties & Toun:					
25 人及以下 Under 25 years	2621	829	751	955	86
26 - 35 人 between 26 - 35	9589	3215	2753	3273	348
36 - 45 人 between 36 - 45	41843	13233	12951	14472	1187
46 - 55 人 between 46 - 55	118272	39249	38036	39029	1958
56 - 65 人 between 56 - 65	117925	39623	39279	37168	1855
66 人及以上 over 66 years	106999	37686	36948	31644	721
农村:Rural:					
25 人及以下 under 25 years	5580	1768	1677	1951	184
26 - 35 人 between 26 - 35	17081	5126	5130	6211	614
36 - 45 人 between 36 - 45	65304	20352	20677	22533	1742
46 - 55 人 between 46 - 55	163934	53170	53841	53952	2971
56 - 65 人 between 56 - 65	153159	52414	51653	47198	1894
66 人及以上 over 66 years	139774	51695	48297	38834	948

职业初中班额情况

Size of Vocational Junior Secondary Schools Classes

单位:个
Unit:Class

	合 计 Total	一年级 Grade 1	二年级 Grade 1	三年级 Grade 1	四年级 Grade 1
合 计 Total	**12415**	**4187**	**4076**	**3788**	**364**
城市:Urban:					
25 人及以下 under 25 years	60	18	20	21	1
26－35 人 between 26－35	58	19	19	15	5
36－45 人 between 36－45	51	17	16	12	6
46－55 人 between 46－55	128	34	48	45	1
56－65 人 between 56－65	88	28	32	28	0
66 人及以上 over 66 years	70	31	20	19	0
县镇:Counties & Toun:					
25 人及以下 under 25 years	93	31	18	34	10
26－35 人 between 26－35	243	63	74	93	13
36－45 人 between 36－45	478	136	187	135	20
46－55 人 between 46－55	801	296	233	254	18
56－65 人 between 56－65	856	300	311	243	2
66 人及以上 over 66 years	736	273	241	217	5
农村:Rural:					
25 人及以下 under 25 years	216	47	63	70	36
26－35 人 under 25 years	551	159	153	190	49
36－45 人 between 36－45	1167	325	351	424	67
46－55 人 between 46－55	1892	610	602	629	51
56－65 人 between 56－65	1905	667	624	578	36
66 人及以上 over 66 years	3022	1133	1064	781	44

普通初中
Number of Students in

	毕业生数 Graduates	招生数 Students Admitted	合 计 Total	其中女 Of Which: Female
总　计 Total	**19955825**	**21953113**	**66184186**	**31381370**
其中女 Of Which: Female	9504902	10382894	31381370	–
教育部门和集体办 Run by Ed. Dept. & Communities	18827262	20402324	61569214	29325284
社会力量办 Non-state/private	534789	938817	2565747	1071803
其他部门办 Run by Non-ed. Dept.	593774	611972	2049225	984283
城市 Urban	3488014	3591798	11439364	5458427
教育部门和集体办 Run by Ed. Dept. & Communities	2883111	2842963	9107631	4390148
社会力量办 Non-state/private	228790	369992	1058314	453206
其他部门办 Run by Non-ed. Dept.	376113	378843	1273419	615073
县镇 Counties & Towns	7093950	7725374	23140839	10924001
教育部门和集体办 Run by Ed. Dept. & Communities	6790481	7240580	21796067	10354831
社会力量办 Non-state/private	209763	389728	1023275	416874
其他部门办 Run by Non-ed. Dept.	93706	95066	321497	152296
农村 Rural	9373861	10635941	31603983	14998942
教育部门和集体办 Run by Ed. Dept. & Communities	9153452	10318781	30665516	14580305
社会力量办 Non-state/private	96284	179097	484158	201723
其他部门办 Run by Non-ed. Dept.	124125	138063	454309	216914
总计中:四年制 Of the Total:4-Year	0	0	4031193	1807680
九年一贯制学校 9-Year Sec. Schools	839273	1076775	3089485	1432585
其他学校附设初中班 Junior Sec. Classes Attached to Others Schools	393961	469599	1312125	608291
重读生 Repeaters			108119	38333
重读中女 Of Which: Female			38333	–
少数民族学生 Minority Students	1475203	1878679	5263295	2224510
独立设置少数民族学校 Inde. Sec. Schools for Minorities	387775	477672	1355751	661300

学生数

Junior Secondary Schools

单位：人

Unit:in Person

在校学生数 Enrolment				毕业班学生数 Graduates for Next Year
一年级 Grade 1	二年级 Grade 2	三年级 Grade 3	四年级 Grade 4	
22010411	**22135558**	**20906121**	**1132096**	**20854262**
10401189	10466292	9961821	552068	9852206
20454982	20609907	19527848	976477	19494240
942417	862973	737911	22446	728734
613012	662678	640362	133173	631288
3599294	3798285	3709604	332181	3690684
2849706	3027413	2996926	233586	2988614
370403	358560	311214	18137	304296
379185	412312	401464	80458	397774
7744497	7713589	7343162	339591	7322121
7257155	7265100	6958905	314907	6940893
392190	344874	283579	2632	282302
95152	103615	100678	22052	98926
10666620	10623684	9853355	460324	9841457
10348121	10317394	9572017	427984	9564733
179824	159539	143118	1677	142136
138675	146751	138220	30663	134588
713801	1002338	1185086	1129968	1125237
1079783	1029186	921565	58951	916095
470523	448218	389673	3711	388898
57298	20713	29524	584	
18295	7691	12140	207	
1888000	1741819	1576644	56832	1567180
478590	449535	413525	14101	413439

职业初中

Number of Students in

	毕业生数 Graduates	招生数 Students Admitted	在校学生数 合计 Total	其中女 Of Which: Female
总　计 Total	**228816**	**248172**	**724087**	**337287**
其中女 Of Which: Female	105244	115157	337287	–
教育部门和集体办 Run by Ed. Dept. & Communities	222654	238828	699459	328817
社会力量办 Non-state/private	5339	8709	22786	7637
其他部门办 Run by Non-ed. Dept.	823	635	1842	833
城市 Urban	6893	7270	21825	9336
教育部门和集体办 Run by Ed. Dept. & Communities	5598	6047	18071	8119
社会力量办 Non-state/private	530	695	2200	501
其他部门办 Run by Non-ed. Dept.	765	528	1554	716
县镇 Counties & Towns	65120	61334	179138	83642
教育部门和集体办 Run by Ed. Dept. & Communities	62542	58010	170827	81377
社会力量办 Non-state/private	2520	3217	8023	2148
其他部门办 Run by Non-ed. Dept.	58	107	288	117
农村 Rural	156803	179568	523124	244309
教育部门和集体办 Run by Ed. Dept. & Communities	154514	174771	510561	239321
社会力量办 Non-state/private	2289	4797	12563	4988
其他部门办 Run by Non-ed. Dept.	0	0	0	0
总计中:四年制 Of the Total:4-Year	0	0	57117	25941
普通中学附设班 Classes Attached to General Sec. Schools	32681	17131	59400	27624
其他单位(学校)办班 Classes Run by Other Unit(or Schools)	34477	25949	76940	34199
重读生 Repeaters			1411	551
重读中女 Of Which: Female			551	–
少数民族学生 Minority Students	29108	28441	87404	37723
独立设置少数民族学校 Inde. Sec. Schools for Minorities	2987	3656	10579	4841

学生数
Junior Secondary Schools

单位:人
Unit:in Person

在校学生数 Enrolment				毕业班学生数 Graduates for Next Year
一年级 Grade 1	二年级 Grade 2	三年级 Grade 3	四年级 Grade 4	
249085	**240953**	**216738**	**17311**	**218345**
115489	112632	100997	8169	99693
239738	232429	210178	17114	211887
8712	7960	5917	197	5815
635	564	643	0	643
7323	7495	6538	469	6963
6097	6234	5326	414	5761
698	794	653	55	643
528	467	559	0	559
61984	59095	54987	3072	55801
58660	56201	52894	3072	53708
3217	2797	2009	0	2009
107	97	84	0	84
179778	174363	155213	13770	155581
174981	169994	151958	13628	152418
4797	4369	3255	142	3163
0	0	0	0	0
9298	15587	15854	16378	16364
17166	17429	21556	3249	24257
26127	27013	22120	1680	21963
913	93	405		
332	38	181		
28903	28080	29120	1301	28408
3656	3539	3028	356	3021

初中阶段学学龄人口及在校学生情况

Number of School－age Population and Enrolment of Junior Schools

单位:人

Unit:in Person

	在校学龄人口数 School－age Population		在校学生数 Enrolment					
	计 Total	其中:女 Of Which: Female	计 Total	其中:女 Of Which: Female	一年级 Grade 1	二年级 Grade 2	三年级 Grade 3	四年级 Grade 4
合　计 Total	**57918516**	**27620598**	**66908273**	**31718657**	**22259496**	**22376511**	**21122859**	**1149407**
10岁及以下 under 10 years	0	0	33730	16004	32916	793	21	0
11岁	147445	72477	960395	461493	906400	51810	2178	7
12岁	7825206	3754408	9478968	4555529	8236962	1162137	78965	904
13岁	20790864	9945800	20795044	9947825	10565464	8949994	1266327	13259
14岁	20808190	9906626	20831087	9917218	2047486	9889805	8644253	249543
15岁	8339425	3937939	12124401	5684502	391547	1947627	9075188	710039
16岁	7386	3348	2284711	984192	63953	321434	1750024	149300
17岁	0	0	348937	133976	11189	44279	269180	24289
18岁及以上 Over 18 years	0	0	51000	17918	3579	8632	36723	2066
城市 Urban	9612782	4611668	11461189	5467763	3606617	3805780	3716142	332650
10岁及以下 under 10 years	0	0	6300	3247	6143	150	7	0
11岁	77111	38386	223000	111440	212612	9620	761	7
12岁	1455735	706628	1746741	851474	1474891	255138	15987	725
13岁	3506603	1687915	3507020	1688226	1582922	1634574	283412	6112
14岁	3551311	1695831	3560869	1700163	288287	1574588	1598455	99539
15岁	1021773	482785	2022497	947573	37456	293847	1510708	180486
16岁	249	123	353093	150090	3874	34073	274935	40211
17岁	0	0	38611	14509	380	3445	29443	5343
18岁及以上 Over 18 years	0	0	3058	1041	52	345	2434	227

注:初中阶段包括普通初中和职业初中,下同。

Note :Data on General and Vocational Schools are included,the same below.

初中阶段学龄人口及在校学生情况(续)

Number of School－age Population and Enrolment of Junior Schools

单位:人

Unit:in Person

	在校学龄人口数		在校学生数 Enrolment					
	计 Total	其中:女 Of Which: Female	计 Total	其中:女 Of Which: Female	一年级 Grade 1	二年级 Grade 2	三年级 Grade 3	四年级 Grade 4
县镇 Counties & Towns	20303495	9636032	23319977	11007643	7806481	7772684	7398149	342663
10 岁及以下	0	0	12841	6060	12598	236	7	0
11 岁	37507	18321	349028	167191	328590	19721	717	0
12 岁	2562939	1218771	3208683	1531582	2761794	416566	30242	81
13 岁	7310393	3480879	7313140	3482141	3853637	2997771	458040	3692
14 岁	7247405	3437266	7254684	3440699	695712	3557067	2926491	75414
15 岁	3143507	1479938	4291598	2005428	128828	658994	3291815	211961
16 岁	1744	857	762029	326682	21150	105095	591380	44404
17 岁	0	0	111620	41989	3067	14394	87437	6722
18 岁及以上	0	0	16354	5871	1105	2840	12020	389
农村 Rural	28002239	13372898	32127107	15243251	10846398	10798047	10008568	474094
10 岁及以下	0	0	14636	6715	14222	407	7	0
11 岁	32686	15770	388359	182837	365232	22427	700	0
12 岁	3806694	1828992	4523447	2172333	4000135	490469	32745	98
13 岁	9973705	4777018	9974932	4777600	5128966	4317657	524854	3455
14 岁	10009623	4773534	10015544	4776361	1063487	4758148	4119319	74590
15 岁	4174138	1975216	5810306	2731587	225263	994786	4272665	317592
16 岁	5393	2368	1169589	507334	38929	182266	883709	64685
17 岁	0	0	198706	77478	7742	26440	152300	12224
18 岁及以上	0	0	31588	11006	2422	5447	22269	1450

职业初中

Number of Teachers, Staff & Workers

	教职工数 Teachers, Staff & Workers			
	合计 Total	专任教师 Full-time Teachers	行政人员 Adm. Personnel	教辅人员 Supporting Staff
总计 Total	**36300**	**30788**	**1945**	**1112**
其中女 Of Which: Female	12164	10995	169	410
少数民族 Minority	3529	2993	184	83
教育部门和集体办 Run by Ed. Dept. & Communities	34838	29781	1760	1061
社会力量办 Non-state/private	1253	879	149	44
其他部门办 Run by Non-ed. Dept.	209	128	36	7
城市 Urban	1631	1177	186	77
教育部门和集体办 Run by Ed. Dept. & Communities	1111	887	81	57
社会力量办 Non-state/private	345	187	69	13
其他部门办 Run by Non-ed. Dept.	175	103	36	7
县镇 Counties & Towns	10155	8432	620	342
教育部门和集体办 Run by Ed. Dept. & Communities	9608	8034	570	317
社会力量办 Non-state/private	513	373	50	25
其他部门办 Run by Non-ed. Dept.	34	25	0	0
农村 Rural	24514	21179	1139	693
教育部门和集体办 Run by Ed. Dept. & Communities	24119	20860	1109	687
社会力量办 Non-state/private	395	319	30	6
其他部门办 Run by Non-ed. Dept.	0	0	0	0

教职工数

in Vocational Schools

单位:人

Unit: in Person

工勤人员 Workers	校办工厂、农(林)场职工 Employees in School-run Factories & Farms	代课教师 Substitute Teachers	兼任教师 Part-time Teachers
2310	145	1311	777
571	19	556	227
259	10	145	227
2098	138	1131	702
178	3	180	61
34	4	0	14
182	9	60	39
81	5	43	19
76	0	17	16
25	4	0	4
666	95	303	254
592	95	303	231
65	0	0	13
9	0	0	10
1462	41	948	484
1425	38	785	452
37	3	163	32
0	0	0	0

普通初中分课程专

Number of Full-time Junior Secondary School Teachers

	总 计 Total	其中女 Of Which: Female	政 治 Politics	语 文 Language & Literature	数 学 Mathematics	物 理 Physics	化 学 Chemistry	生 物 Biology
合 计 Total	**3466735**	**1570041**	**241917**	**691644**	**650045**	**251173**	**155477**	**130509**
研究生毕业 Graduate	4991	2679	450	1127	836	339	231	240
本科毕业 Under-graduate	821025	428568	66208	196312	148259	59833	41501	30579
专科毕业 Associate Bachelor	2364815	1043026	157930	455600	457426	178047	107106	85833
高中阶段毕业 High School Graduate	269273	94383	16867	38006	42999	12785	6549	13564
高中阶段毕业以下 Below High School Graduate	6631	1385	462	599	525	169	90	293
合计中:女 Of Total:Female	1570041		98843	349461	266627	71304	56665	60297
少数民族 Minorities	267339	112546	20892	53948	47604	19222	12408	10326
城市 Urban	689643	421190	44315	124331	121399	49582	31348	26653
县镇 County & Towns	1198978	546871	84829	234043	222144	86422	53363	46170
农村 Rural	1578114	601980	112773	333270	306502	115169	70766	57686

职业初中分课程专任

Number of Full-time Vocational

	总 计 Total	其中女 Of Which: Female	文化课 Cultural Subject	专 业 课				
				农林类 Aqri. & Forestry	资源与环境类 Resources & Environment	能源类 Energy	土木水利工程类 Civil & Water Engineering	加 工 制造类 Manufactruing
合 计 Total	**30788**	**10995**	**27562**	**862**	**81**	**28**	**51**	**61**
研究生毕业 Graduate	34	13	31	1	0	0	0	0
本科毕业 Under-graduate	5277	2101	4809	131	3	3	10	5
专科毕业 Associate Bachelor	20838	7547	18780	557	65	19	38	42
高中阶段毕业 High School Graduate	4542	1316	3874	169	13	5	3	14
高中阶段毕业以下 Below High School Graduate	97	18	68	4	0	1	0	0
合计中:女 Of Total:Female	10995	0	9975	251	40	11	19	14
少数民族 Minorities	2993	1136	2577	83	5	2	4	9

任教师学历情况

by Subject Taught & Educational Attainment

单位:人

Unit: in Person

地 理 Geography	历史 History	外 语 Foreign Languages	信息技术 Infor. Technique	体 育 Physical Culture	音 乐 Music	美 术 Fine Arts	劳动技术 Skills Teaching	其 他 Others	当年不任课 No Teaching Load in Currentyear
125119	158835	531950	70136	165003	78384	74025	41594	31479	69445
162	299	699	109	169	54	68	24	63	121
25402	39344	116007	15418	36492	11329	11923	4202	6122	12094
84723	104271	383938	48652	106271	53672	51390	27538	19270	43148
14458	14543	30855	5873	21370	13060	10367	9305	5491	13181
374	378	451	84	701	269	277	525	533	901
51619	68563	361285	26063	27078	52009	30694	11838	13008	24687
9834	11876	32681	4358	13822	6628	5519	2900	8804	6517
24223	32503	112947	17128	37870	18037	16954	7501	6537	18315
44325	56031	185349	25011	58048	28013	26460	14512	11038	23220
56571	70301	233654	27997	69085	32334	30611	19581	13904	27910

教师学历情况

Schools Teachers by Subject Taught Educational Attainment

单位:人

Unit:in Person

Subjects									
交通运输类 Commu. & Trancpor.	信息技术类 Infor. Technique	医药卫生类 Medicine & Health	商贸与旅游类 Trade & Travel	财经类 Finance & Economics	文化艺术与体育类 Cultural. Arts & Physical Edu.	社会公共事业类 Public Affairs	其 他 Others	实习指导 Practical Guiding	当年不任课 No Teaching Load in Current Year
35	270	102	25	78	995	68	204	41	325
0	0	0	0	0	0	0	1	0	1
3	42	13	4	17	152	6	14	2	63
25	178	77	19	51	612	42	115	31	187
5	50	12	2	10	228	17	60	7	73
2	0	0	0	0	3	3	14	1	1
13	96	48	6	36	300	25	65	8	88
6	22	10	2	10	122	23	50	5	63

普通初中专任教师专业技术

Full-time Teachers in Junior Secondary

	合 计 Total	其中女 Of the Total: Female	25岁及以下 25 Years and Under	26－30	31－35
总 计 Total	**3466735**	**1570041**	**613759**	**867547**	**735490**
中学高级 Senior	169283	74662	165	394	5156
中学一级 1st Grade	1119241	444465	3184	51910	289001
中学二级 2nd Grade	1477150	686342	146038	637185	407419
中学三级 3rd Grade	358052	176695	202953	119171	21834
未评职称 Rank Undecided	343009	187877	261419	58887	12080
总计中:女 Of Which: Female	1570041	–	348606	436625	346213
少数民族 Minorities	267339	112546	44085	77414	62049
城市 Urban	689643	421190	95666	147054	154870
县镇 County & Towns	1198978	546871	193519	303191	271751
农村 Rural	1578114	601980	324575	417302	308868

职业初中专任教师专业技术

Full-time Teachers in Vocational Secondary

	合 计 Total	其中女 Of the Total: Female	25岁及以下 25 Years and Under	26－30	31－35
总 计 Total	**30788**	**10995**	**5577**	**8185**	**6381**
中学高级 Senior	540	101	0	3	32
中学一级 1st Grade	8214	2059	27	338	1784
中学二级 2nd Grade	14250	5316	1073	5424	4093
中学三级 3rd Grade	4345	1863	2198	1583	327
未评职称 Rank Undecided	3439	1656	2279	837	145
总计中:女 Of Which: Female	10995	–	2748	3603	2361
少数民族 Minorities	2993	1136	562	887	639

职称、年龄结构情况

Schools Broken Down by Rank and Age

单位:人

Unit:in Person

36－40	41－45	46－50	51－55	56－60	61岁及以上 61 Years and Over
517829	**258604**	**230407**	**158212**	**81966**	**2921**
28697	30113	41770	39804	21580	1604
314301	166110	147473	95898	50294	1070
162145	57274	37712	20333	8918	126
7317	3087	1975	1180	511	24
5369	2020	1477	997	663	97
219852	91304	77057	45806	4167	411
40398	17517	13865	8277	3608	126
115388	56372	56905	44194	17905	1289
191578	90258	73617	48445	25648	971
210863	111974	99885	65573	38413	661

职称、年龄结构情况

Schools Broken Down by Rank and Age

单位:人

Unit:in Person

36－40	41－45	46－50	51－55	56－60	61岁及以上 61 Years and Over
4581	**2338**	**1883**	**1135**	**653**	**55**
87	110	127	104	63	14
2348	1347	1179	721	439	31
1932	784	527	282	130	5
129	57	30	11	8	2
85	40	20	17	13	3
1329	511	302	122	19	0
438	227	142	67	24	7

普通初中专任

Changes of Full-time Teachers in

	上学年初报表专任教师数 Total Number of Full-time Teachers at Beginning of Previous Academic Year	增加教师 Factors of Increase				
		计 Total	录用毕业生 New from Current Year Graduates	调入 Teachers Recruited from Other Units	校内调整 of which with change of status in their own institutions	其他 Others
合计 Total	**3429985**	**427379**	**108195**	**213766**	**65107**	**40311**
其中女 Of Which: Female	1529496	202242	60048	100146	24355	17693
城市 Urban	677508	91170	23331	40816	13825	13198
其中女 Of Which: Female	411783	52827	15105	23876	6451	7395
县镇 Counties & Towns	1191227	144509	34203	79303	21707	9296
其中女 Of Which: Female	534119	68065	18688	37381	8350	3646
农村 Rural	1561239	191711	50661	93658	29575	17817
其中女 Of Which: Female	583586	81358	26255	38897	9554	6652

职业初中专任

Changes of Full-time Teachers in

	上学年初报表专任教师数 Total Number of Full-time Teachers at Beginning of Previous Academic Year	增加教师 Factors of Increase				
		计 Total	录用毕业生 New Recruits from Current Year Graduates	调入 Teachers Recruited from Other Units	校内调整 of which with change of status in their own institutions	其他 Others
合计 Total	**35107**	**4543**	**882**	**2118**	**1079**	**464**
其中女 Of Which: Female	12302	1929	465	895	435	134
城市 Urban	1688	382	23	91	137	131
其中女 Of Which: Female	897	192	11	47	70	64
县镇 Counties & Towns	10599	1381	218	703	397	63
其中女 Of Which: Female	4471	660	117	360	168	15
农村 Rural	22820	2780	641	1324	545	270
其中女 Of Which: Female	6934	1077	337	488	197	55

教师变动情况
Junior Secondary Schools

单位：人
Unit: in Person

减少教师 Factors of Decrease					本学年初报表专任教师数 Total Number of Full-time Teachers at Beginning of Current Academic Year
计 Total	自然减员 Retired from their posts during previcus academic year	调出 Transterred from teaching to non－teaching posts	校内调整 of which with change of status in their own institutions	其　他 Others	
390629	**37992**	**216803**	**85337**	**50497**	**3466735**
161697	14535	94053	32043	21066	1570041
79035	12690	31381	21564	13400	689643
43420	7737	17603	10667	7413	421190
136758	10800	72896	33841	19221	1198978
55313	3622	32198	12135	7358	546871
174836	14502	112526	29932	17876	1578114
62964	3176	44252	9241	6295	601980

教师变动情况
Vocational Junior Secondary Schools

单位：人
Unit: in Person

减少教师 Factors of Decrease					本学年初报表专任教师数 Total Number of Full-time Teachers at Beginning of Current Academic Year
计 Total	自然减员 Retired from their posts during previcus academic year	调出 Transterred from teaching to non－teaching posts	校内调整 of which with change of status in their own institutions	其　他 Others	
8862	**216**	**3772**	**2283**	**2591**	**30788**
3236	68	1427	730	1011	10995
893	24	160	213	496	1177
460	18	88	92	262	629
3548	32	1200	908	1408	8432
1397	6	462	345	584	3734
4421	160	2412	1162	687	21179
1379	44	877	293	165	6632

普通初中学生、专任教师政治面貌及其他

Supplementary Information on Students and Full-time Teachers of Junior Secondary Schools

单位：人

Unit: in Person

	在校学生中 Of Total Students			专任教师中 Of Total Full-time Teachers			
	共产党员 Member of C.P.C.	共青团员 Member of C.Y.L.	华侨 Overseas Chinese	共产党员 Member of C.P.C.	共青团员 Member of C.Y.L.	民主党派 Non-com-munict Parties	华侨 Overseas Chinese
合　计 Total	**37901**	**14095454**	**9953**	**717690**	**755159**	**19392**	**427**
其中女 Of Which: Female	18565	7147248	4967	202630	395462	9820	195
城市 Urban	4104	1921401	2785	157542	136373	12308	235
其中女 Of Which: Female	2215	1047745	1413	78553	88416	6988	130
县镇 Counties & Towns	14719	5198101	4089	248912	252222	4390	83
其中女 Of Which: Female	7119	2628590	2117	66025	131019	1838	28
农村 Rural	19078	6975952	3079	311236	366564	2694	109
其中女 Of Which: Female	9231	3470913	1437	58052	176027	994	37

职业初中学生、专任教师政治面貌及其他

Supplementary Information on Students and Full-time Teachers of Vocational Junior Secondary Schools

单位：人

Unit: in Person

	在校学生中 Of Total Students			专任教师中 Of Total Full-time Teachers			
	共产党员 Member of C.P.C.	共青团员 Member of C.Y.L.	华侨 Overseas Chinese	共产党员 Member of C.P.C.	共青团员 Member of C.Y.L.	民主党派 Member of Dem. Parties	华侨 Overseas Chinese
合　计 Total	**419**	**160771**	**162**	**6967**	**5984**	**22**	**0**
其中女 Of Which: Female	210	78426	86	1126	2763	7	0
城市 Urban	0	3321	0	224	190	11	0
其中女 Of Which: Female	0	1581	0	99	104	4	0
县镇 Counties & Towns	32	43491	0	1815	1627	7	0
其中女 Of Which: Female	4	21580	0	414	847	3	0
农村 Rural	387	113959	162	4928	4167	4	0
其中女 Of Which: Female	206	55265	86	613	1812	0	0

普通初中

Condition of School Buildings in

	学校占地面积 Areas Occupied	校舍建筑面积 Floor Space	教学及辅助用房 Teaching & Assistant Buildings				
			计 Total	其中 Of Which			
				普通教室 classroom	实验室 Laboratory	图书室 Library	微机室 PC-room
合　计 Total	**1422218450**	**334730429**	**152832033**	**109677136**	**19558728**	**6556132**	**4688197**
城市 Urban	173209444	61055332	30301984	19102894	4261819	1494536	1123326
县镇 County Seats & Towns	460096404	115015174	51011788	36820224	6526906	2088227	1556518
农村 Rural	788912602	158659923	71518261	53754018	8770003	2973369	2008353

普通初中

Condition of School Buildings in

	体育运动场(馆)面积(平方米) Sports Areas (m^2)	计算机(台) PC (set)	图书藏量(册) Books & Magazines in Libraries (Volume)
合计 Total	**400443980**	**2118469**	**820437062**
城市 Urban	56927114	582643	139857939
县镇 County Seats & Towns	127028526	696135	273429015
农村 Rural	216488340	839691	407150108

普通初中办学

Condition of School Buildings

	体育运动场(馆)面积达标校数 Schools No:Sprots Areas Reached Standard	体育器械配备达标校数 Schools No:Sports Equip. Reached Standard
合计 Total	**41847**	**40297**
城市 Urban	5789	6223
县镇 County Seats & Towns	12324	12156
农村 Rural	23734	21918

办学条件(一)
Junior Secondary Schools (1)

单位:平方米

Unit:m²

语言室 Linguistic	行政办公用房 Administritive 计 Total	其中教师办公室 Of Which: for Teachers	生活用房 Residential and Welfare	其他用房 Rooms for Other Purposes	校舍面积中 Of the Floor Space 危房面积 Floor Space of Dilapidated Buildings	当年新增 New Floor Space Added in Current Year
2017740	**37430396**	**25807112**	**110412789**	**34055211**	**15625863**	**12084968**
575535	8180481	5000829	13349742	9223125	1031100	2427064
721203	11917062	8076637	41241628	10844696	4545619	4719890
721002	17332853	12729646	55821419	13987390	10049144	4938014

办学条件(二)
Junior Secondary Schools (2)

电子图书藏量(片) Electronic Books & Magazines in Libraries (disk)	固定资产总值(万元) Total Volue of Fixed Asset (in 10 thousand yuan) 计 Total	其中:仪器设备总值(万元) Of Which: Total Volue of Equip & Instru. (in 10 thousand yuan) 计 Sub Total	专业实验设备 For Prefession	专业实习设备 For Practice
7028617	**20429204.56**	**2096011.52**	**1307276.66**	**279949.93**
2768020	5118095.10	669862.65	428491.94	68684.81
2165951	6965522.57	579778.86	375687.88	85305.11
2094646	8345586.89	846370.01	503096.84	125960.01

条件(三)
in Junior Secondary Schools(3)

单位:所

Unit: School

音乐器械配备达标校数 Schools No:Musical Instru. ReachedStandard	美术器械配备达标校数 Schools No:Fine Arts Instru. Reached Standard	理科实验仪器达标校数 Schools No:Equip. of Natural Sci. Reached Standard	建立校园网校数 Schools No:Campus Networks Set
34369	**33401**	**44708**	**10132**
5917	5751	6673	3221
10573	10385	13252	3377
17879	17265	24783	3534

职业初中

Condition of School Buildings in

	学校占地面积 Areas Occupied	校舍建筑面积 Floor Space	教学及辅助用房 Teaching & Assistant Buildings				
			计 Total	其中 Of Which			
				普通教室 classroom	实验室 Laboratory	图书室 Library	微机室 PC-room
合计 Total	**24518236**	**3307053**	**1452978**	**1077849**	**186087**	**81753**	**43819**
城市 Urban	649486	180969	77653	46931	14249	6147	4981
县镇 County Seats & Towns	6613063	1036605	440684	302121	67993	28019	13724
农村 Rural	17255687	2089479	934641	728797	103845	47587	25114

职业初中

Condition of School Buildings in

	体育运动场(馆)面积(平方米) Sports Areas (m^2)	计算机(台) PC (set)	图书藏量(册) Books & Magazines in Libraries (Volume)	电子图书藏量(片) Electronic Books & Magazines in Libraries (disk)
合计 Total	**5891546**	**16210**	**7577227**	**22683**
城市 Urban	197340	1509	246688	5325
县镇 County Seats & Towns	1786092	6417	1926652	4104
农村 Rural	3908114	8284	5403887	13254

办学条件(一)

Vocational Junior Secondary Schools (1)

单位:平方米

Unit: m^2

语言室 Linguistic	行政办公用房 Administritive 计 Total	其中教师办公室 Of Which: for Teachers	生活用房 Residential and Welfare	其他用房 Rooms for Other Purposes	校舍面积中 Of the Floor Space 危房面积 Floor Space of Dilapidated Buildings	当年新增 New Floor Space Added in Current Year	实习工厂(农场)面积
14143	**372811**	**276711**	**1181724**	**299540**	**308520**	**97722**	**40405**
1833	22764	11798	63203	17349	5527	295	8145
5067	109205	83496	376492	110224	69152	39990	8084
7243	240842	181417	742029	171967	233841	57437	24176

办学条件(二)

Vocational Junior Secondary Schools (2)

固定资产总值(万元) Total Value of Fixed Asset (in 10 thousand yuan) 计 Total	其中:仪器设备总值(万元) Of Which: Total Volue of Equip & Instru. (in 10 thousand yuan) 计 Sub Total	专业实验设备 For Prefession	专业实习设备 For Practice
144403.80	**14803.21**	**9479.10**	**2921.45**
11250.58	2358.03	1634.42	585.41
42795.04	5349.45	3292.65	1168.26
90358.18	7095.73	4552.03	1167.78

职业初中办学条件(三)

Condition of School Buildings in Vocational Junior Secondary Schools (3)

单位:所

Unit: School

	体育运动场(馆)面积达标校数 Schools No: Sprots Areas Reached Standard	体育器械配备达标校数 Schools No: Sports Equip. Reached Standard	音乐器械配备达标校数 Schools No: Musical Instru. Reached Standard	美术器械配备达标校数 Schools No: Fine Arts Instru. Reached Standard	理科实验仪器达标校数 Schools No: Equip. of Natural Sci. Reached Standard	建立校园网校数 Schools No: Campus Networks Set
合计 Total	**571**	**478**	**389**	**371**	**507**	**72**
城市 Urban	25	24	15	14	18	8
县镇 County Seats & Towns	139	118	105	95	125	26
农村 Rural	407	336	269	262	364	38

成人初中基本情况

Basic Statistics of Adult Schools by Province

单位:人(人次)

Unit:in Person

	学校数(所) Schools	教学班(点)(个) External Teaching Sites	毕(结)业生数 Graduates		注册学生数 enrolment		教职工数 Teachers,Staff & Workers		聘请校外教师 Part-time Teachers
			计 Total	其中:女 Of which: Female	计 Total	其中:女 Of which: Female	计 Total	其中:专任教师 Of which: Full-time Teacher	
合 计 Total	**1920**	**7365**	**613854**	**268918**	**528155**	**244555**	**8203**	**4801**	**8008**
职工初中 Junior Sec. Schools for Staff & workers	147	678	15675	7244	19498	9059	1090	786	511
农民初中 Junior Sec. Shools for Peasants	1773	6687	598179	261674	508657	235496	7113	4015	7497

（三）初等教育（小学）

Pbimary Education

（Primary Schools）

小学校数、教学点数及班数
Number of Schools, Extemal Teachingsites & Classes in Primary Schools

	学校数(所) Schools	教学点数(个) Extemal Teachingsites	班数(个) Classes
总　计 Total	**425846**	**105679**	**3364094**
教育部门和集体办 Run by Ed. Dept. & Communities	414486	103165	3195744
社会力量办 Non-state/private	5676	2014	76240
其他部门办 Run by Non-ed. Dept.	5684	500	92110
城市 Urban	25473	806	404623
教育部门和集体办 Run by Ed. Dept. & Communities	21328	749	321973
社会力量办 Non-state/private	1680	19	32809
其他部门办 Run by Non-ed. Dept.	2465	38	49841
县镇 Counties & Towns	40007	3199	501310
教育部门和集体办 Run by Ed. Dept. & Communities	38075	3127	470919
社会力量办 Non-state/private	1053	37	17210
其他部门办 Run by Non-ed. Dept.	879	35	13181
农村 Rural	360366	101674	2458161
教育部门和集体办 Run by Ed. Dept. & Communities	355083	99289	2402852
社会力量办 Non-state/private	2943	1958	26221
其他部门办 Run by Non-ed. Dept.	2340	427	29088
总计中:六年制 Of the Total:6-Year			3145148
一贯制学校小学部 Primary Schools for 6-Year			95469
其他学校附设 Other Primary Schools Attached			11556
独立设置的少数民族学校 Inde. Sec. Schools for Minorities	14302		88339

小学班额情况
Size of Primary Classes

单位：个
Unit:Calss

	合计 Total	一年级 Grade 1	二年级 Grade 2	三年级 Grade 3	四年级 Grade 4	五年级 Grade 5	六年级 Grade 6	复式班 Multiple-grade Classes
合　计 Total	**3364094**	**577809**	**573563**	**557847**	**547464**	**545526**	**440128**	**121757**
城市:Urban:								
25 人及以下 under 25 years	36930	8422	7530	6485	5531	4986	3775	201
26－35 人 between 26－35	64418	12259	12237	11142	10397	9934	8432	17
36－45 人 between 36－45	102163	17955	17786	17001	17217	17241	14955	8
46－55 人 between 46－55	106066	17519	17886	18271	18282	18483	15625	0
56－65 人 between 46－55	61192	9097	9703	10658	11416	11247	9071	0
66 人及以上 over 66 years	33854	4450	5119	6328	6453	6431	5067	6
县镇:Counties & Toun:								
25 人及以下 under 25 years	63593	15434	13015	11063	9247	7585	4680	2569
26－35 人 between 26－35	83848	15465	14867	14001	14055	14161	10829	470
36－45 人 between 36－45	120619	19499	19520	14001	14055	14161	10829	470
46－55 人 between 46－55	116010	16820	18474	14001	14055	14161	10829	470
56－65 人 between 55－65	69564	9785	11151	14001	14055	14161	10829	470
66 人及以上 over 66 years	47676	6799	7330	14001	14055	14161	10829	470
农村:Rural:								
25 人及以下 under 25 years	957724	210914	189820	158847	130584	101238	67157	99164
26－35 人 between 26－35	596365	96932	100099	101615	102415	101327	80318	13659
36－45 人 between 36－45	466146	63661	69318	75231	83070	92856	78097	3913
46－55 人 between 46－55	273649	33133	38053	42616	48713	58182	51916	1036
56－65 人 between 56－65	114194	13415	15053	17828	20106	24387	23099	306
66 人及以上 over 66 years	50083	6250	6602	7783	8645	10754	9853	196

	毕业生数 Graduates	招生数 Entrants		合计 Total	其中女 Of Which: Female
		计 Total	其中受过学前教育 of which: never receiv - ed the pre - school education		
总　计 Total	**22678857**	**18293875**	**14960487**	**116897395**	**55037589**
其中女 Of Which: Female	10759948	8573945	6933168	55037589	–
教育部门和集体办 Run by Ed. Dept. & Communities	21670739	17238585	14062443	110614777	52209882
社会力量办 Non-state/private	374728	474421	376419	2749341	1154346
其他部门办 Run by Non-ed. Dept.	633390	580869	521625	3533277	1673361
城市 Urban	3179926	2966115	2716715	18076855	8473273
教育部门和集体办 Run by Ed. Dept. & Communities	2636849	2387330	2206957	14742480	6954121
社会力量办 Non-state/private	165060	230647	189720	1230434	520793
其他部门办 Run by Non-ed. Dept.	378017	348138	320038	2103941	998359
县镇 Counties & Towns	4265248	3403283	3051795	21929021	10241977
教育部门和集体办 Run by Ed. Dept. & Communities	4092694	3231482	2900874	20846937	9774231
社会力量办 Non-state/private	85473	90976	75274	591292	232525
其他部门办 Run by Non-ed. Dept.	87081	80825	75647	490792	235221
农村 Rural	15233683	11924477	9191977	76891519	36322339
教育部门和集体办 Run by Ed. Dept. & Communities	14941196	11619790	8954629	75025411	35481554
社会力量办 Non-state/private	124195	152798	111333	927615	401028
其他部门办 Run by Non-ed. Dept.	168292	151889	126015	938493	439757
总计中:六年制 Of the Total: 6-Year	21149172	16989890	13944899	109765576	51645581
一贯制学校小学部 Primary Schools for 6-Year	765377	586189	494420	3859206	1770831
其他学校附设 Other Attached Primary Schools	195495	50392	41957	437654	193651
少数民族 Minorities	1963076	1893373	968512	11206997	5045733
重读生 Repeaters	0	0	0	366734	148689
重读中女 Of Which: Female	0	0	0	148689	–
小学教学点 Teaching Places of Primary Schools	577550	1181678	761922	4990074	2350619
复式班 Morning & Afternoon Shift Classes	0	359295	183835	1688643	773468

学 生 数
in Primary Schools

单位:人
Unit:in Person

在校学生数 Enrolment						毕业班学生数 Graduates for Next Year
一年级 Grade 1	二年级 Grade 2	三年级 Grade 3	四年级 Grade 4	五年级 Grade 5	六年级 Grade 6	
18560820	**19518737**	**19829825**	**20246141**	**21119095**	**17622777**	**21444969**
8684618	9171903	9334472	9558844	9961214	8326538	10086211
17502130	18452863	18730847	19146608	20019079	16763250	20367557
475439	465408	476518	470473	474531	386972	465306
583251	600466	622460	629060	625485	472555	612106
2968231	3048710	3136941	3164935	3143958	2614080	3075170
2388819	2475153	2550443	2584375	2573592	2170098	2519070
230794	215543	212617	203494	196310	171676	191756
348618	358014	373881	377066	374056	272306	364344
3432963	3608019	3706961	3786084	4023642	3371352	4081721
3260901	3432985	3523030	3595781	3823193	3211047	3879899
91076	91982	98606	103128	113838	92662	117088
80986	83052	85325	87175	86611	67643	84734
12159626	12862008	12985923	13295122	13951495	11637345	14288078
11852427	12544743	12657390	12966452	13622294	11382105	13968588
153569	157883	165295	163851	164383	122634	156462
153630	159382	163238	164819	164818	132606	163028
17221736	18141917	18447064	18828040	19529801	17597018	19898700
591263	601321	629946	658379	716081	662216	766333
50417	49927	53509	57910	69623	156268	167960
1959204	1924138	1873784	1847462	1874838	1727571	1834832
266945	33730	28677	20459	14584	2339	0
110673	12855	10883	7953	5540	785	0
1212707	1216505	967787	712411	504157	376507	404893
456344	513920	354642	239377	89029	35331	48213

小学学龄人口入学数

Number on School - age Population

	在校学龄人口数 School - age Population		招生数 Entrants		
	计 Total	其中女 Of Which: Female	计 Total	其中受过学前教育 of Which never received the pre - school education	计 Total
合 计 Total	**107615792**	**50760456**	**18293875**	**14960487**	**116897395**
5 岁及以下 under 5 years	0	0	469324	367740	484436
6 岁	6273499	2945502	8339123	7260078	8828798
7 岁	17019067	7986228	8802591	6961282	17022225
8 岁	18193650	8571143	546985	323904	18193890
9 岁	18665824	8825060	91255	36803	18665824
10 岁	19680851	9309803	26608	7220	19680851
11 岁	19388006	9164569	10093	2019	19517191
12 岁	8394361	3957921	5275	912	11966136
13 岁	477	206	1796	384	1958085
14 岁	57	24	598	116	451364
15 岁及以上 over 15 years	0	0	227	29	128595
城市 Urban	16674482	7832702	2966115	2716715	18076855
5 岁及以下 under 5 years	0	0	66737	59589	67178
6 岁	1463791	689459	1851582	1717231	1926588
7 岁	2793887	1308288	981121	885340	2793900
8 岁	2923482	1373779	58160	48190	2923482
9 岁	2971962	1400593	6474	4886	2971962
10 岁	3019644	1420343	1508	1153	3019644
11 岁	2744664	1287961	319	209	2806601
12 岁	756860	352190	137	77	1352969
13 岁	192	89	54	26	184150
14 岁	0	0	20	13	26313
15 岁及以上 over 15 years	0	0	3	1	4068

学及在校生情况

of Primary Schools.

单位:人

Unit: in Person

其中女 Of Which: Female	在校学生数 Enrolment 一年级 Grade 1	二年级 Grade 2	三年级 Grade 3	四年级 Grade 4	五年级 Grade 5	六年级 Grade 6
55037589	**18560820**	**19518737**	**19829825**	**20246141**	**21119095**	**17622777**
232551	476146	8105	168	10	6	1
4157780	8370846	448032	9674	229	15	2
7987735	8910892	7676041	424691	10186	396	19
8571262	638370	10180429	6982065	381336	11286	404
8825060	109935	935026	10780032	6451277	376649	12905
9309803	32431	188640	1244682	11426673	6435507	352918
9225543	12522	51110	274557	1473389	12022900	5682713
5619521	6530	20013	77401	367862	1696700	9797630
862097	2146	7902	25394	99280	438684	1384679
192615	702	2477	8110	26514	106009	307552
53622	300	962	3051	9385	30943	83954
8473273	2968231	3048710	3136941	3164935	3143958	2614080
34478	66636	523	18	1	0	0
912510	1850501	75074	999	12	2	0
1308294	983042	1735251	74251	1192	160	4
1373779	59381	1135525	1659170	68083	1273	50
1400593	6570	89621	1252665	1558120	63840	1146
1420343	1555	10256	128726	1352566	1472166	54375
1316518	322	1636	16847	157022	1400273	1230501
619541	142	607	3252	22927	173395	1152646
75936	55	174	775	4088	28051	151007
9885	23	30	177	732	4089	21262
1396	4	13	61	192	709	3089

	在校学龄人口数 School－age Population		招生数 Entrants		
	计 Total	其中女 Of Which: Female	计 Total	其中受过学前教育 of Which never received the pre－school education	计 Total
县镇 Counties & Towns	20165948	9426296	3403283	3051795	21929021
5岁及以下 under 5 years	0	0	105240	91828	107936
6岁	1270683	591813	1733404	1587800	1855883
7岁	3217853	1498579	1470947	1305298	3218071
8岁	3405433	1591611	78159	59144	3405449
9岁	3472580	1628443	10648	6164	3472580
10岁	3665915	1719110	2702	955	3665915
11岁	3609354	1689390	1144	299	3625631
12岁	1524105	707344	846	244	2202388
13岁	20	4	126	48	305711
14岁	5	2	44	10	56673
15岁及以上 over 15 years	0	0	23	5	12784
农村 Rural	70775362	33501458	11924477	9191977	76891519
5岁及以下 under 5 years	0	0	297013	216236	308950
6岁	3539025	1664230	4754352	3955054	5046575
7岁	11007327	5179361	6350637	4770717	11010378
8岁	11864735	5605753	410669	216576	11864959
9岁	12221282	5796024	74134	25754	12221282
10岁	12995292	6170350	22398	5112	12995292
11岁	13033988	6187218	8630	1511	13084959
12岁	6113396	2898387	4293	591	8410789
13岁	265	113	1616	310	1468214
14岁	52	22	534	93	368378
15岁及以上 over 15 years	0	0	201	23	111743

学及在校生情况(续)

单位:人
Unit:in Person

在校学生数 Enrolment						
其中女 Of Which: Female	一年级 Grade 1	二年级 Grade 2	三年级 Grade 3	四年级 Grade 4	五年级 Grade 5	六年级 Grade 6
10241977	3432963	3608019	3706961	3786084	4023642	3371352
53202	106388	1522	25	1	0	0
873022	1738397	115407	2024	52	3	0
1498685	1483704	1619107	113192	2036	32	0
1591617	86767	1705954	1510157	100076	2436	59
1628443	12103	134011	1844854	1379521	99444	2647
1719110	3145	23378	188787	2006405	1359406	84794
1697220	1332	5537	36175	234182	2198810	1149595
1020129	912	2279	8473	49720	288326	1852678
132010	143	575	2248	10911	59603	232231
23447	49	155	752	2414	12406	40897
5092	23	94	274	766	3176	8451
36322339	12159626	12862008	12985923	13295122	13951495	11637345
144660	302758	6052	125	8	6	1
2372386	4782290	257461	6647	165	10	2
5180829	6444175	4321918	237121	6945	204	15
5605866	492215	7338813	3813008	213075	7553	295
5796024	91262	711394	7682374	3514009	213151	9092
6170350	27731	155006	927169	8067444	3604354	213588
6211805	10868	43937	221535	1082185	8423636	3302798
3979851	5476	17127	65676	295215	1234989	6792306
654151	1948	7153	22371	84281	351020	1001441
159283	630	2292	7181	23368	89514	245393
47134	273	855	2716	8427	27058	72414

小学教

Number of Teachers, Staff &

	教职 Teachers,			
	合 计 Total	专任教师 Full-time Teachers	行政人员 Adm. Personnel	教辅人员 Teaching Auxiliarg
总　计 Total	**6256185**	**5702750**	**325470**	**77662**
其中女 Of Which: Female	3237320	3054234	80533	36688
少数民族 Minorities	626962	570947	32741	4866
教育部门和集体办 Run by Ed. Dept. & Communities	5850398	5379242	298270	64861
社会力量办 Non-state/private	162825	117239	10771	7555
其他部门办 Run by Non-ed. Dept.	242962	206269	16429	5246
城市 Urban	1080931	936396	77314	23312
教育部门和集体办 Run by Ed. Dept. & Communities	858410	757957	61579	15925
社会力量办 Non-state/private	85475	60223	6125	4392
其他部门办 Run by Non-ed. Dept.	137046	118216	9610	2995
县镇 Counties & Towns	1260445	1120663	72317	24283
教育部门和集体办 Run by Ed. Dept. & Communities	1182043	1060717	67014	21391
社会力量办 Non-state/private	41021	28869	2597	2111
其他部门办 Run by Non-ed. Dept.	37381	31077	2706	781
农村 Rural	3914809	3645691	175839	30067
教育部门和集体办 Run by Ed. Dept. & Communities	3809945	3560568	169677	27545
社会力量办 Non-state/private	36329	28147	2049	1052
其他部门办 Run by Non-ed. Dept.	68535	56976	4113	1470

职工数
Workers in Primary Schools

单位:人
Unit:in Person

工数 Staff & Workers		代课教师 Substitute Teachers	兼任教师 Part-time Teachers
工勤人员 Workers	校办工厂、农场职工 Employees in School-run Factories & Farms		
145709	**4594**	**423857**	**20496**
64176	1689	249851	9710
18135	273	67085	1522
104298	3727	404637	16951
26989	271	13380	2524
14422	596	5840	1021
42123	1786	32004	4130
21642	1307	25224	2292
14614	121	3454	1175
5867	358	3326	663
41812	1370	27208	3318
31693	1228	24142	2488
7372	72	2415	654
2747	70	651	176
61774	1438	364645	13048
50963	1192	355271	12171
5003	78	7511	695
5808	168	1863	182

小学专任教师
Breakdown of Full-time Primary School

	总　计 Total	其中女 Of Which: Female	思想品德 Moral Edu.	语　文 Language & Literature	数　学 Mathematics	外　语 Foreign Languages	自　然 Natural Science
合　　计 Total	**5702750**	**3054234**	**122362**	**2554628**	**1852343**	**167263**	**150983**
研究生毕业 Graduate	1018	553	83	344	209	77	35
本科毕业 Under-graduate	175263	116876	5077	73800	42265	13457	4516
专科毕业 Associate Bachelor	2134696	1365336	41041	973900	651096	100375	49002
高中阶段毕业 High School Graduate	3269207	1542031	72407	1455114	1119431	52785	93612
高中阶段毕业以下 Below High School Graduate	122566	29438	3754	51470	39342	569	3818
合计中:女 Of Total:Female	3054234	–	51855	1511304	891397	129599	58810
少数民族 Minorities	570947	258475	14538	256974	178148	11291	15758

小学专任教师专业
Full-time Teachers in Primary Schools

	合　计 Total	其中女 Of Which Female	25岁及以下 25 Years and Under	26－30 26 to 30	31－35 31 to 35
合　　计 Total	**5702750**	**3054234**	**978627**	**906758**	**784258**
中学高级 Senior Secondary	15813	7059	40	116	724
小学高级 Senior Primary	2037609	999080	2907	52824	243191
小学一级 1st Grade Primary	2534656	1343820	246387	658736	465046
小学二级 2st Grade Primary	703780	438655	450347	135392	45629
小学三级 3st Grade Primary	39083	21137	19391	7026	3511
未评职称 Rank Undecided	371809	244483	259555	52664	26157
总计中:女 Of the Total:Female	3054234	–	679096	598808	505044
少数民族 Minorities	570947	258475	103204	106032	87541

学历情况
Teachers by Educational Attainment

单位:人
Unit: in Person

社 会 Social Science	信息技术 Information Technique	体 育 Physical Culture	音 乐 Music	美 术 Arts	劳 动 Skills Teaching	其 他 Others	当年不任课 No Teaching Load in Current Year
86224	**63015**	**178138**	**129412**	**108333**	**40415**	**108946**	**140688**
30	41	34	35	28	7	36	59
2409	5053	8936	6334	5794	947	3518	3157
27141	37162	72499	58687	47902	11802	34488	29601
54367	20562	93425	62743	52726	26030	66644	99361
2277	197	3244	1613	1883	1629	4260	8510
34880	26986	38163	96578	58903	19561	70173	66025
9054	4067	17503	12393	9304	3913	22567	15437

技术职称、年龄结构情况
Broken Down by Rank and Age

单位:人
Unit:in Person

36－40 36 to 40	41－45 41 to 45	46－50 46 to 50	51－55 51 to 55	56－60 56 to 60	61岁及以上 61 Years And Over
721448	**674801**	**825681**	**584136**	**223672**	**3369**
2198	2601	3941	3877	2043	273
309040	360689	519982	397306	149830	1840
365405	285196	280486	167846	64625	929
26748	16475	13850	10335	4874	130
2801	2023	1923	1638	734	36
15256	7817	5499	3134	1566	161
415043	325013	330747	191988	8025	470
79486	63857	70863	43968	15585	411

小学专任教

Changes of Full-time

	上学年初报表专任教师数 Total Number of Full-time Teachers at Beginning of Previous Academic Year	增加教师 Factors of Increase				
		合计 Total	录用毕业生 New Recruits from Current Year Graduates	调入 Teachers Recruited from Other Units	校内调整 of which with change of status in their own institutions	其他 Others
合计 Total	**5778269**	**745598**	**98467**	**428298**	**162763**	**56070**
其中女 Of Which: Female	3057247	372080	62475	212473	65145	31987
城市 Urban	928027	109519	19497	58090	14177	17755
其中女 Of Which: Female	712901	77161	14415	42011	8080	12655
县镇 Counties & Towns	1127851	133730	15570	77332	31047	9781
其中女 Of Which: Female	746718	78206	10749	47381	14933	5143
农村 Rural	3722391	502349	63400	292876	117539	28534
其中女 Of Which: Female	1597628	216713	37311	123081	42132	14189

小学学生、教职工

Supplementary Information on Students and

	在校学生中 Of Total Students		教职 Of Total Staff	
	共青团员 Member of C.Y.L.	华侨 Overseas Chinese	共产党员 Member of C.P.C.	共青团员 Member of C.Y.L.
合计 Total	**55472**	**9973**	**1292686**	**1020467**
其中女 Of Which: Female	27227	4295	445247	693466
城市 Urban	8173	2794	236331	249790
其中女 Of Which: Female	4293	1157	149738	197327
县镇 Counties & Towns	10493	1562	281892	215670
其中女 Of Which: Female	5533	726	123827	159748
农村 Rural	36806	5617	774463	555007
其中女 Of Which: Female	17401	2412	171682	336391

师变动情况

Teachers in Primary Schools

单位：人

Unit: in Person

减少教师 Factors of Decrease					本学年初报表专任教师数 Total Number of Full-time Teachers at Beginning of Current Academic Year
计 Total	自然减员 Retired from their posts during previous academic	调出 Transterred from teaching to won - teaching posts	校内调整 of which with change of status in their own institutions	其他 Others	
821117	**116938**	**450198**	**174201**	**79780**	**5702750**
375093	50115	213419	70745	40814	3054234
101150	21436	47201	15123	17390	936396
69725	15491	32916	9223	12095	720337
140918	21619	71942	29293	18064	1120663
77849	12194	40990	14212	10453	747075
579049	73883	331055	129785	44326	3645691
227519	22430	139513	47310	18266	1586822

政治面貌及其他

Staff & Workers of Primary Schools

单位：人

Unit: in Person

工中 & Workers		专任教师中 Of Total Full-time Teachers			
民主党派 Member of Dem. Parties	华侨 Overseas Chinese	共产党员 Member of C.P.C.	共青团员 Member of C.Y.L.	民主党派 Member of Dem. Parties	华侨 Overseas Chinese
17645	**1678**	**1052473**	**981403**	**15157**	**892**
10363	890	380408	668027	9109	515
6642	424	176885	238342	5503	235
4700	310	118255	188421	4006	161
3924	316	222751	208300	3335	159
2626	183	107008	154250	2351	105
7079	938	652837	534761	6319	498
3037	397	155145	325356	2752	249

小学办学

Condition of School Buildings

	学校占地面积 Areas Occupied	校舍建筑面积 Floor Space	教学及辅 Teaching & Assistant				
			计 Total	其中			
				普通教室 classroom	实验室 Laboratory	图书室 Library	微机室 PC-room
合 计 Total	**2741459179**	**577161373**	**356746150**	**300882851**	**15589831**	**13593797**	**5713346**
城市 Urban	243729669	92705295	54331893	40390255	2624309	2007985	1690093
县镇 County Seats & Towns	379368313	104007051	61075687	50376566	2632859	2105422	1455068
农村 Rural	2118361197	380449027	241338570	210116030	10332663	9480390	2568185

小 学 办

Condition of School Buildings

	体育运动场(馆)面积(平方米) Sports Areas (m^2)	计算机(台) PC (set)	图书藏量(册) Books & Magazines in Libraries (Volume)
合 计 Total	**900379183**	**2678411**	**1410676033**
城市 Urban	85461015	950323	281729681
县镇 County Seats & Towns	127249845	693268	290465291
农村 Rural	687668323	1034820	838481061

条件(一)
in Primary Schools (1)

单位:平方米

Unit: m^2

助用房 Buildings	行政办公用房 Administritive		生活用房 Residential and Welfare	其他用房 Rooms for Other Purposes	校舍面积中 Of the Floor Space	
Of Which 语音室 Linguistic	计 Total	其中教师办公室 Of Which: for Teachers			危房面积 Floor Space of Dilapidated Buildings	当年新增 New Floor Space Added in Current Year
1838991	**63228981**	**49322861**	**99565233**	**57621009**	**38568116**	**14999875**
688520	10740954	6941537	14047540	13584908	1726612	2945354
529920	11033858	7991345	20863186	11034320	4362712	3220021
620551	41454169	34389979	64654507	33001781	32478792	8834500

学条件(二)
in Primary Schools (2)

电子图书藏量(片) Electronic Books & Magazines in Libraries (disk)	固定资产总值(万元) Total Value of Fixed Asset (in 10 thousand yuan)			
	计 Total	其中:仪器设备总值(万元) Of Which: Total Volue of Equip & Instru. (in 10 thousand yuan)		
		计 Sub Total	专业实验设备 For Prefession	专业实习设备 For Practice
12346850	**31983379.16**	**3097495.11**	**1849806.00**	**376217.42**
5882816	8083194.47	1199200.68	751565.09	138417.83
2287107	6660174.04	581776.85	360941.38	68922.57
4176927	17240010.65	1316517.58	737299.53	168877.02

小学办学条件(三)

Condition of School Buildings in Primary Schools (3)

单位:所

Unit: School

	体育运动场(馆)面积达标校数 Schools No: Sprots Areas Reached Standard	体育器械配备达标校数 Schools No: Sports Equip. Reached Standard	音乐器械配备达标校数 Schools No: Musical Instru. Reached Standard	美术器械配备达标校数 Schools No: Fine Arts Instru. Reached Standard	教学自然实验仪器达标校数 Schools No: Equip. of Natural Sci. Reached Standard	建立校园网校数 Schools No: Campus Networks Set
合　计 Total	**213785**	**188942**	**164651**	**156231**	**212072**	**17483**
城市 Urban	15160	17188	16581	15657	17679	6196
县镇 County Seats & Towns	23971	24209	22360	21172	26900	4145
农村 Rural	174654	147545	125710	119402	167493	7142

成人小学基本情况

Basic Statistics of Adult Primary Schools by Province

单位:人(人次)

Unit:in Person

	学校数(所) Schools	教学班(点)(个) External Teaching Sites	毕(结)业生数 Graduates		注册学生数 enrolment		教职工数 Teachers, Staff & Workers		聘请校外教师 Part-time Teachers
			计 Total	其中:女 Of which: Female	计 Total	其中:女 Of which: Female	计 Total	其中:专任教师 Of which: Full-time Teacher	
合计 Total	**82713**	**152165**	**3933231**	**2010078**	**3814850**	**1959749**	**124059**	**47609**	**138407**
其中:少数民族 Of which: Minority	2339	7735	409278	210145	416638	204134	12622	2308	12928
职工小学 General Primary Schools for Staff & workers	908	1861	78417	36591	64869	29375	3553	835	2560
农民小学 General Primary Schools for Peasants	81805	150304	3854814	1973487	3749981	1930374	120506	46774	135847
其中:of which:									
小学班 Primary Classes	25904	42759	1823397	915330	1797777	881931	34189	18100	36053
扫盲班 Literacy Classes	55901	107545	2031417	1058157	1952204	1048443	86317	28674	99794

四、工读学校
Community House

工读学校基本情况

Basic Statistics of Correctional Work-study Schools

单位：人

Unit: in Person

	学校数（所）Schools	班 数（个）Classes	离校人数 School Leavers	入校人数 No. of Persons Entered	在校生数 Enrolment	教职工数 Teachers, Staff & Workers	
						计 Total	其中专任教师 Of Which: Full-time Teachers
合 计 Total	**82**	**450**	**3390**	**3373**	**7452**	**2636**	**1580**
其中女 Of Which: Female			370	305	864	794	460

五、特殊教育
Special Eoucation

特殊教育

Basic Statistics of

	学校数 (所) Schools	班数 (个) Classes	毕业生数 Graduates	招生数 Entrants	合计 Total	一年级 Grade 1	二年级 Grade 2
总　计 Total	**1551**	**12881**	**44533**	**48840**	**364740**	**44774**	**47836**
其中女 Of Which Female			16043	17677	127415	15438	16385
盲人学校 Schools for the Blind	37	784			38299	3377	4023
聋人学校 Schools for the Deaf-mute	669	8063			109771	15018	14704
弱智学校 Schools for Retarded	375	4034			216670	26379	29109
特殊教育学校 Schools For Special Edu.	470	12146	10599	17759	123169	18973	16884
盲人学校 Schools for the Blind		772			7030	1136	1026
聋人学校 Schools for the Deaf-mute		7979			82633	11668	10849
弱智学校 Schools for Retarded		3395			33506	6169	5009
小学附设特教班 Classes Attached to Primary Schools		727	599	794	5094	887	821
盲人学校 Schools for the Blind		12			79	17	12
聋人学校 Schools for the Deaf-mute		82			568	154	120
弱智学校 Schools for Retarded		633			4447	716	689
小学随班就读 Followers in Primary Schools			20758	17788	190324	24914	30131
盲人学校 Schools for the Blind					18023	2224	2985
聋人学校 Schools for the Deaf-mute					21353	3196	3735
弱智学校 Schools for Retarded					150948	19494	23411
普通(职业)初中附设特教 Special Classes Attached to Junior High (Vacational) Schools		8	56	1	66		
盲人学校 Schools for the Blind					0		
聋人学校 Schools for the Deaf-mute		2			12		
弱智学校 Schools for Retarded		6			54		
普通(职业)初中随班就读 Followers in Junior High(Vacational) Schools			12521	12498	46087		
盲人学校 Schools for the Blind					13167		
聋人学校 Schools for the Deaf-mute					5205		
弱智学校 Schools for Retarded					27715		
总计中：Of the Total：							
城市 Urban	705	7031	14892	15173	109776	12632	12265
县镇 County Seats & Towns	774	5293	11868	14444	97157	12572	12695
农村 Rural	72	557	17773	19223	157807	19570	22876

基本情况
Special Education

单位：人

Unit: in Person

在校学生数 Enrolment							
三年级 Grade 3	四年级 Grade 4	五年级 Grade 5	六年级 Grade 6	七年级 Grade 7	八年级 Grade 8	九年级 Grade 9	十年级 Grade 10
50710	**50075**	**49647**	**43318**	**25005**	**25364**	**23814**	**4197**
17420	17040	16841	14663	9451	9463	9048	1666
4173	4018	4037	3162	4423	4976	5283	827
14938	13745	12867	11472	9391	8183	7001	2452
31599	32312	32743	28684	11191	12205	11530	918
16008	14313	12968	11838	10526	9472	8113	4074
736	685	633	472	521	493	509	819
10834	9839	9160	8473	7613	6416	5342	2439
4438	3789	3175	2893	2392	2563	2262	816
857	859	908	720	39	0	3	0
10	12	13	15	0	0	0	0
76	101	49	68	0	0	0	0
771	746	846	637	39	0	3	0
33845	34903	35771	30760		0	0	0
3427	3321	3391	2675		0	0	0
4028	3805	3658	2931		0	0	0
26390	27777	28722	25154		0	0	0
					36	30	0
					0	0	0
					3	9	0
					33	21	0
				14440	15856	15668	123
				3902	4483	4774	8
				1778	1764	1650	13
				8760	9609	9244	102
12691	12282	12398	12106	9910	10939	10668	3885
13071	12738	12344	11146	8297	7655	6484	155
24948	25055	24905	20066	6798	6770	6662	157

特殊教育在校学生中职业技术

Condition of Minorities and Vocational &

	合 计 Total	其中:女 Of Which Female	一年级 Grade 1	二年级 Grade 2	三年级 Grade 3
职业技术班 Voca. & Skill Class	5457	1461	49	101	114
少数民族 Minorities	25554	88	3542	3807	3803

特殊教育学

Number of Teachers, Staff and Workers

	教 职 Teachers, Staff		
	合 计 Total	专任教师 Full-time Teachers	行政人员 Adm. Personnel
合 计 Total	**40853**	**30349**	**3963**
其中:女 Of Which: Female	27331	22005	1824
少数民族 Minorities	2066	1544	199

班学生及少数民族学生情况

Skill Students in special Edu. Schools

单位:人

Unit:in Person

四年级 Grade 4	五年级 Grade 5	六年级 Grade 6	七年级 Grade 7	八年级 Grade 8	九年级 Grade 9	十年级 Grade 10
109	252	397	785	1033	1247	1370
3442	3185	2492	2095	1765	1341	82

校教职工数

in Special Education Schools

单位:人

Unit:in Person

工　数 & Workers		代课教师 Substitute Teachers	兼任教师 Part-time Teachers
教辅人员 Teaching Auxiliarg	工勤人员 Workers		
2140	**4401**	**831**	**378**
1357	2145	508	195
90	233	20	11

特殊教育学校专任

Full-time Teachers in Special Education

	合 计 Total	按学历分 Broken down by Educational Attainment				
		研究生毕业 Graduate	本科毕业 Under-graduate	专科毕业 Associate Bachelor	高中阶段毕业 High School Graduate	高中阶段毕业以下 Below High School Graduate
合　计 Total	**30349**	**48**	**3757**	**15023**	**11140**	**381**
其中:女 Of Which:Female	22005	31	2535	10924	8267	248
受过特教专业培训	15475	15	1992	8084	5283	101

特殊教育专任

Changes of Full-time Teachers in

	上学年初报表专任教师数 Total Number of Full-time Teachers at Beginning of Previous Academic Year	增 加 教 师 Factors of Increase				
		合 计 Total	录用毕业生 New Recruits from Current Year Graduates	调 入 Teachers Recruited from Other Units	校内调整 Of which with change of statrs in their own institutions	其 他 Others
合　计 Total	**29812**	**2569**	**684**	**1049**	**615**	**221**
其中女 Of Which: Female	21597	1705	489	723	349	144

特殊教育学

Condition of School Buildings

	学校占地面积 Areas Occupied	校舍建筑面积 Floor Space	教学及辅助用房 Teaching & Assistant Buildings					
			计 Total	其中 Of Which				
				普通教室 classroom	实验室 Laboratory	图书室 Library	微机室 PC-room	专用教室
合计 Total	**10222485**	**3801428**	**1593941**	**1019758**	**67460**	**58770**	**40639**	**231301**

教师学历、职称情况

Schools Broken Down by Rank and Age

单位:人

Unit:in Person

按职称分 Brokendown by Rank					
中学高级 Senior Secondary	小学高级 Senior Primary	小学一级 1st Grade Primary	小学二级 2st Grade Primary	小学三级 3st Grade Primary	未评职称 Rank Undecided
729	**12321**	**11950**	**3223**	**250**	**1876**
383	9051	8657	2380	167	1367
341	5326	6872	1943	93	900

教师变动情况

Special Education Schools

单位:人

Unit: in Person

减少教师 Factors of Decrease					本学年初报表专任教师数 Total Number of Full-time Teachers at Beginning of Current Academic Year
计 Total	自然减员 Retired from their posts during previcus academic	调出 Transterred from teaching to non-teaching posts	校内调整 Of which with change of status in their own institutions	其他 Others	
2032	**511**	**616**	**610**	**295**	**30349**
1297	355	414	339	189	22005

校办学条件

in Special Education Schools

单位:平方米

Unit:m^2

行政办公用房 Administritive		生活用房 Residential and Welfare	其他用房 Rooms for Other Purposes	校舍面积中 Of the Floor Space		图书(册) Books & Magazines in Libraries (Volume)	教学用录像录音带(盘)
计 Total	其中教师办公室 Of Which: for Teachers			危房面积 Floor Space of Dilapidated Buildings	当年新增 New Floor Space Added in Current Year		
450994	266632	1212656	543837	119247	106642	2785328	87729

六、幼儿教育
Pre－Primary Education

幼儿园园数、班数

Number of Kindergartens, Classes in Pre-Primary Education

	园数(所) Kindergartens		班数(个) Classes	
	计 Total	其中少数民族幼儿园 Of Which: Minorities	计 Total	其中学前班 Of Which: Pre-School
总　计 Total	**116390**	**568**	**728511**	**325182**
教育部门和集体办 Run by Ed. Dept. & Communities	51774	396	479541	284977
社会力量办 Non-state/private	55536	147	188618	29474
其他部门办 Run by Non-ed. Dept.	9080	25	60352	10731
城市 Urban	31652	104	180872	33461
教育部门和集体办 Run by Ed. Dept. & Communities	8482	64	65196	18956
社会力量办 Non-state/private	16816	28	71352	9058
其他部门办 Run by Non-ed. Dept.	6354	12	44324	5447
县镇 Counties & Towns	34177	231	174666	47655
教育部门和集体办 Run by Ed. Dept. & Communities	12518	143	96982	36787
社会力量办 Non-state/private	20140	78	68642	8886
其他部门办 Run by Non-ed. Dept.	1519	10	9042	1982
农村 Rural	50561	233	372973	244066
教育部门和集体办 Run by Ed. Dept. & Communities	30774	189	317363	229234
社会力量办 Non-state/private	18580	41	48624	11530
其他部门办 Run by Non-ed. Dept.	1207	3	6986	3302
合计中:独立设置幼儿园、小学附设幼儿园、独立设置学前班 Of Total: Inde. Kinder., Kinder. Attached to Primary School and Inde. Pre-school Classes			429673	65446
小学附设幼儿班、学前班 Kinder. And Pre-school Classes Attached to Primary School			298838	259736

幼儿教育分年龄学生数

Number of Pre-school Education by Ages

单位:人

Unit: in Person

	入园(班)人数 Enrollment		在园(班)人数 Retained		离园(班)人数 Leavers	
	计 Total	其中学前班 Of Which: Pre-School	计 Total	其中学前班 Of Which: Pre-School	计 Total	其中学前班 Of Which: Pre-School
总　计 Total	**13167889**	**7684152**	**20039061**	**9002399**	**10719922**	**7216334**
其中:女 Of Which:Female	5912419	3459476	9067576	4055739	4847968	3274190
少数民族 Minorities	953923	746849	1177471	800624	655674	562374
教育部门和集体办 Run by Ed. Dept. & Communities	9673241	6866196	13423070	7827997	8225129	6280328
3岁以下 Under 3 years	282789	25340	353818	29361	13242	3865
3-5岁 3-5 years	4000702	1948143	6160775	2275171	632831	405771
5岁以上 Over 5 years	5389750	4892713	6908477	5523465	7579056	5870692
社会力量办 Non-state/private	2664739	582617	4802297	831847	1784947	644391
3岁以下 Under 3 years	360878	8449	502095	9688	29297	1061
3-5岁 3-5 years	1539650	141460	2871893	202741	257969	42441
5岁以上 Over 5 years	764211	432708	1428309	619418	1497681	600889
其他部门办 Run by Non-ed. Dept.	829909	235339	1813694	342555	709846	291615
3岁以下 Under 3 years	141548	1191	187676	2026	9014	312
3-5岁 3-5 years	426216	44411	1027715	59504	77249	12711
5岁以上 Over 5 years	262145	189737	598303	281025	623583	278592
城市 Urban	2594719	834321	5256140	1129987	2094055	886769
其中:女 Of Which:Female	1159129	369913	2388108	501498	931609	392107
少数民族 Minorities	91731	46802	154911	53966	62882	37429
教育部门和集体办 Run by Ed. Dept. & Communities	1176536	557667	2157242	690604	1023862	543490
3岁以下 Under 3 years	102862	2068	131540	2795	4694	591
3-5岁 3-5 years	551150	124387	1137951	149068	89143	33840
5岁以上 Over 5 years	522524	431212	887751	538741	930025	509059
社会力量办 Non-government/private	855348	154805	1750076	246612	577646	183499
3岁以下 Under 3 years	155851	2118	226211	2613	14115	463
3-5岁 3-5 years	474464	30528	1016271	44052	80506	9115
5岁以上 Over 5 years	225033	122159	507594	199947	483025	173921
其他部门办 Run by Non-ed. Dept.	562835	121849	1348822	192771	492547	159780
3岁以下 Under 3 years	112220	518	148889	896	7449	263
3-5岁 3-5 years	303239	24404	789735	33728	57294	6389
5岁以上 Over 5 years	147376	96927	410198	158147	427804	153128

幼儿教育分年龄学生数(续)

单位:人

Unit: in Person

	人园(班)人数 Enrollment		在园(班)人数 Retained		离园(班)人数 Leavers	
	计 Total	其中学前班 Of Which: Pre-School	计 Total	其中学前班 Of Which: Pre-School	计 Total	其中学前班 Of Which: Pre-School
县镇 Counties & Towns	3246035	1395859	5378954	1705034	2566085	1388874
其中:女 Of Which:Female	1447863	623490	2423025	763099	1144843	620295
少数民族 Minorities	234859	134629	339056	149816	159383	112664
教育部门和集体办 Run by Ed. Dept. & Communities	2080950	1168299	3311298	1388449	1813671	1145035
3岁以下 Under 3 years	107795	5464	130170	6499	4387	837
3-5岁 3-5 years	976511	315515	1715481	382399	168723	82873
5岁以上 Over 5 years	996644	847320	1465647	999551	1640561	1061325
社会力量办 Non-state/private	1025432	187334	1792654	258246	637502	191148
3岁以下 Under 3 years	139716	5300	187023	5654	11069	333
3-5岁 3-5 years	616270	41932	1121547	56519	99914	11332
5岁以上 Over 5 years	269446	140102	484084	196073	526519	179483
其他部门办 Run by Non-ed. Dept.	139653	40226	275002	58339	114912	52691
3岁以下 Undre 3 years	20397	353	26636	366	1103	41
3-5岁 3-5 years	73447	7950	153802	10242	12120	2428
5岁以上 Over 5 years	45809	31923	94564	47731	101689	50222
农村 Rural	7327135	5453972	9403967	6167378	6059782	4940691
其中:女 Of Which:Female	3305594	2466080	4256626	2791115	2771494	2261788
少数民族 Minorities	627454	565539	683625	596963	433535	412366
教育部门和集体办 Run by Ed. Dept. & Communities	6415755	5140230	7954530	5748944	5387596	4591803
3岁以下 Under 3 years	72132	17808	92108	20067	4161	2437
3-5岁 3-5 years	2473041	1508241	3305346	1743704	374965	289410
5岁以上 Over 5 years	3870582	3614181	4557076	3985173	5008470	4299956
社会力量办 Non-state/private	783959	240478	1259567	326989	569817	269744
3岁以下 Under 3 years	67311	3031	90861	3421	4113	275
3-5岁 3-5 years	448916	69000	734075	102170	77549	22114
5岁以上 Over 5 years	267732	168447	434631	221398	488155	247355
其他部门办 Run by Non-ed. Dept.	127421	73264	189870	91445	102369	79144
3岁以下 Under 3 years	8931	320	12151	764	462	8
3-5岁 3-5 years	49530	12057	84178	15534	7868	3927
5岁以上 Over 5 years	68960	60887	93541	75147	94039	75209

幼儿园教

Number of Teachers, Staff

	教职 Teachers, Staff	
	合计 Total	园长 Kindergarten heads
总计 Total	**973159**	**96219**
教育部门和集体办 Run by Ed. Dept. & Communities	398437	34252
社会力量办 Non-state/private	383942	48844
其他部门办 Run by Non-ed. Dept.	190780	13123
城市 Urban	487151	40978
教育部门和集体办 Run by Ed. Dept. & Communities	152180	10921
社会力量办 Non-state/private	179689	19861
其他部门办 Run by Non-ed. Dept.	155282	10196
县镇 Counties & Towns	305443	30564
教育部门和集体办 Run by Ed. Dept. & Communities	149558	10787
社会力量办 Non-state/private	131923	17847
其他部门办 Run by Non-ed. Dept.	23962	1930
农村 Rural	180565	24677
教育部门和集体办 Run by Ed. Dept. & Communities	96699	12544
社会力量办 Non-state/private	72330	11136
其他部门办 Run by Non-ed. Dept.	11536	997
其中:女 Of Which: Female	910125	89649
幼教专业毕业 Graduates of Pre-school Education Programmes	517029	54785
少数民族 Minorities	39334	3735

职工数

& Workers in Kindergarten

单位:人

Unit:in Person

工　数 & Workers			代课教师 Substitute Teachers	兼任教师 Part-time Teachers
专任教师 Full-time Teachers	保健员 Health Nurses	其　他 Other		
612856	**63620**	**200464**	**67750**	**11680**
282054	17560	64571	41823	4151
228791	33615	72692	17617	5735
102011	12445	63201	8310	1794
278633	33687	133853	18556	5313
95909	7962	37388	7551	1472
101064	15977	42787	4779	2405
81660	9748	53678	6226	1436
206556	20863	47460	19494	3707
111803	6854	20114	12043	1233
81040	12273	20763	6143	2208
13713	1736	6583	1308	266
127667	9070	19151	29700	2660
74342	2744	7069	22229	1446
46687	5365	9142	6695	1122
6638	961	2940	776	92
602235	59763	158478	62403	9344
436638	9031	16575	30723	3764
26221	2406	6972	2237	291

幼儿园园长、专任教师

Breakdown of Kindergarten Heads and Teachers

	合 计 Total	按学历分 by Educational Attainment				
		研究生毕业 Graduate	本科毕业 Under-graduate	专科毕业 Associate Bachelor	高中阶段毕业 High School Graduate	高中阶段以下毕业 Below High School Graduate
合 计 Total	**709075**	**857**	**25446**	**264567**	**379839**	**38366**
园长 Kinder-garten Heads	96219	461	7633	39906	43978	4241
专任教师 Teachers	612856	396	17813	224661	335861	34125
城市 Urban	319611	704	17388	146078	144960	10481
园长 Kinder-garten Heads	40978	375	5126	19965	14240	1272
专任教师 Teachers	278633	329	12262	126113	130720	9209
县镇 Counties & Towns	237120	105	6312	83436	135109	12158
园长 Kinder-garten Heads	30564	64	1854	12242	15046	1358
专任教师 Teachers	206556	41	4458	71194	120063	10800
农村 Rural	152344	48	1746	35053	99770	15727
园长 Kinder-garten Heads	24677	22	653	7699	14692	1611
专任教师 Teachers	127667	26	1093	27354	85078	14116

幼儿园教职工和专任

Supplementary Information on Staff &

	教职工中 Of Total Staff & Workers		
	共产党员 Member of C.P.C.	共青团员 Member of C.Y.L.	民主党派 Non-communist
合 计 Total	**100177**	**300845**	**2934**
其中女 Of Which: Female	89737	292186	2654
城市 Urban	53831	147612	1389
其中女 Of Which: Female	48627	143110	1231
县镇 Counties & Towns	33253	99315	1252
其中女 Of Which: Female	29889	96740	1163
农村 Rural	13093	53918	293
其中女 Of Which: Female	11221	52336	260

学历、职称情况

by Educational Attainment and Rank

单位:人
Unit:in Person

按职称分 by Rank					
中学高级 Senior Secondary	小学高级 Senior Primary	小学一级 1st Grade Primary	小学二级 2st Grade Primary	小学三级 3st Grade Primary	未评职称 Rank Undecided
3803	**107427**	**159506**	**69058**	**11672**	**357609**
2181	26549	15235	4285	1012	46957
1622	80878	144271	64773	10660	310652
2440	59355	79507	34780	6418	137111
1514	14117	6847	1791	480	16229
926	45238	72660	32989	5938	120882
1087	37372	56860	22560	3247	115994
510	8318	4399	1262	242	15833
577	29054	52461	21298	3005	100161
276	10700	23139	11718	2007	104504
157	4114	3989	1232	290	14895
119	6586	19150	10486	1717	89609

教师政治面貌及其他

Workers and full - time teachers of Kindergarten

单位:人
Unit: in Person

	专任教师中 = Of Total Full-time Teachers			
华侨 Overseas Chinese	共产党员 Member of C.P.C.	共青团员 Member of C.Y.L.	民主党派 Member of Dem. Parties	华侨 Overseas Chinese
390	**52936**	**256986**	**1733**	**173**
358	50698	251637	1647	170
214	25611	125954	709	84
198	24781	122988	684	82
110	19810	85414	847	50
96	18911	83860	799	49
66	7515	45618	177	39
64	7006	44789	164	39

幼儿园校舍

Statistics of Kindergarten

	学校占地面积 Areas Occupied	校舍建筑面积 Floor Space	教学及辅助用房 Teaching & Assistant Buildings				
			计 Total	其中 Of Which			
				活动室 Recreational	睡眠室 Bed Room	保健室 Health Care	图书室 Pictare Books
合计 Total	**147001228**	**72243577**	**47398161**	**27740756**	**12070832**	**1449363**	**1536522**
城市 Urban	55249740	34211605	21731865	12155616	6491720	583493	637798
县镇 County Seats & Towns	44336636	22217540	14880413	8715377	3694165	488403	468838
农村 Rural	47414852	15814432	10785883	6869763	1884947	377467	429886

及其他情况
Buildings and Others

单位:平方米
Unit:m^2

行政办公用房 Administritive		生活用房 Residential and Welfare	其他用房 Forother Purposes	校舍面积中 Of Hoor Space:		幼儿园中户外活动场 Areas for Out Door Activities	图书(册) Picture Books	教学用录像录音带(盒) Tapes for Teaching
计 Total	其中教师办公室 Of Which: Office			危房面积 Floor Space of Dilapidated Buildings	当年新增 New Floor Space Added in Current Year			
6126689	**3691762**	**8209309**	**10509418**	**347495**	**1571719**	**62989085**	**51989114**	**6508602**
2719644	1330608	4034552	5725544	94164	731991	23179126	24372954	3456468
1855399	1178310	2636583	2845145	175224	545120	19357983	15697954	1806869
1551646	1182844	1538174	1938729	78107	294608	20451976	11918206	1245265

七、各级各类学校分布情况

Ceographical Distribution of Schools by Type and Level

高等教育学校(机构)数

Number of Higher Education Institutions

单位:所

Unit: Institutions

地区 Region	普通高校 Regular HEIs				成人高等学校 HEIs for Adults		民办的其他高等教育机构 Non-state/private HEIs	
	计 Total	其中:中央部委 Of which: HEIs under Central Ministries & Agencies	本科院校 HEIs Providing Degree-level	高职(专科)院校 Short-cycle HEIs and Teitiary Voc. Colleges	计 Total	其中:中央部委 Of which: HEIs under Central Ministries & Agencies	计 Total	其中:学历文凭考试机构 Of which: Institutions authorized to offer State-recognized credits for part of their Programs
总计 Total	**1552**	**111**	**644**	**908**	**558**	**19**	**1104**	**384**
北京 Beijing	73	33	56	17	33	9	72	32
天津 Tianjin	37	3	18	19	22	0	46	
河北 Hebei	83	5	26	57	14	0	67	21
山西 Shanxi	45		14	31	16	0	45	4
内蒙古 Inner Mongolia	27		10	17	7	0	39	5
辽宁 Li aoning	70	5	38	32	40	2	27	27
吉林 Jilin	40	2	22	18	21	1	24	7
黑龙江 Heilongjiang	54	3	22	32	37	2	41	6
上海 Shanghai	56	9	26	30	27	1	196	19
江苏 Jiangsu	94	10	42	52	29	1	12	12
浙江 Zhejiang	64	2	23	41	16	0	37	36
安徽 Anhui	73	2	24	49	11	0	8	
福建 Fujian	39	2	14	25	16	0	11	11
江西 Jiangxi	54		17	37	15	0	34	24
山东 Shandong	85	2	33	52	28	0	106	35
河南 Henan	71	1	24	47	24	0	81	20
湖北 Hubei	75	8	31	44	23	0	15	
湖南 Hunan	73	3	22	51	22	0	60	23
广东 Guangdong	77	4	31	46	35	1	63	51
广西 Guangxi	45		14	31	8	0	4	1
海南 Hainan	11		4	7	1	0	1	1
重庆 Chongqing	34	2	16	18	12	0	15	3
四川 Sichuan	62	6	27	35	32	1	32	18
贵州 Guizhou	34		10	24	7	0	3	
云南 Yunnan	34		16	18	7	0	2	2
西藏 Tibet	4		3	1	0	0		
陕西 Shaanxi	57	6	30	27	25	1	37	26
甘肃 Gansu	31	2	13	18	12	0	25	
青海 Qinghai	12		4	8	2	0	1	
宁夏 Ningxia	12	1	3	9	1	0		
新疆 Xinjiang	26		11	15	15	0		

高等学校(机

Data on Postgraduates in

地区 Region	毕(结)业生数 Graduates 计 Total	其中:女 Of which: Female	博士 Doctor's Degrees	硕士 Master's Degrees	授予学位数 Degrees Awarded	招生数 计 Total	其中:女 Of which: Female
总计 Total	**111091**	**41291**	**18806**	**92241**	**108109**	**268925**	**112295**
北京 Beijing	21917	8091	5179	16738	21243	45970	19062
天津 Tianjin	3252	1320	585	2667	3651	8506	3732
河北 Hebei	2012	987	139	1873	2003	5022	2636
山西 Shanxi	1158	556	87	1071	1146	2979	1507
内蒙古 Inner Mongolia	624	331	26	598	613	1734	921
辽宁 Liaoning	5256	2312	747	4509	5345	13882	6787
吉林 Jilin	4403	2102	1136	3267	3618	10071	5088
黑龙江 Heilongjiang	3862	1662	543	3319	3807	9906	4238
上海 Shanghai	10079	3598	2027	8052	9677	22524	9386
江苏 Jiangsu	9035	2973	1652	7383	8433	22023	8808
浙江 Zhejiang	3514	1105	642	2872	3507	6863	2597
安徽 Anhui	2149	562	434	1715	1762	5883	1679
福建 Fujian	1871	728	200	1671	2075	5860	2486
江西 Jiangxi	973	292	25	948	950	2562	984
山东 Shandong	3694	1655	478	3216	3672	9764	4230
河南 Henan	1488	706	66	1422	1482	3818	1748
湖北 Hubei	9079	2963	1377	7702	8922	22191	8973
湖南 Hunan	3099	1029	384	2715	3104	8597	2366
广东 Guangdong	4701	1754	777	3924	4718	11619	4938
广西 Guangxi	886	363	11	875	863	2643	1227
海南 Hainan	64	28	12	52	62	204	99
重庆 Chongqing	2715	772	326	2389	2692	6392	2618
四川 Sichuan	5128	1764	782	4346	4990	13648	5517
贵州 Guizhou	444	160	20	424	440	1458	587
云南 Yunnan	1169	409	117	1052	1076	3307	1498
西藏 Tibet	14			14	14	17	1
陕西 Shaanxi	6500	2312	792	5664	6340	15722	5931
甘肃 Gansu	1349	446	218	1131	1281	3634	1500
青海 Qinghai	45	19	6	39	43	172	70
宁夏 Ningxia	90	44		90	95	290	165
新疆 Xinjiang	521	248	18	503	485	1664	916

构)研究生数(总计)

Higher Education Institutions (Total)

单位:人
Unit:in Person

Entrants		在校学生数 Enrolment				预计毕业生数 Anticipated Graduates for Next Year			
博士 Doctor's Degrees	硕士 Master's Degrees	计 Total	其中:女 Of which: Female	博士 Doctor's Degrees	硕士 Master's Degrees	计 Total	其中:女 Of which: Female	博士 Doctor's Degrees	硕士 Master's Degrees
48740	**220007**	**651260**	**256763**	**136687**	**514115**	**178748**	**64717**	**45636**	**132946**
11451	34415	116522	45885	33230	83145	33904	13047	10486	23418
1680	6826	20657	8552	4304	16353	5481	2141	1250	4231
448	4574	11171	5669	1144	10027	2792	1356	388	2404
274	2705	6669	3492	727	5942	1673	862	266	1407
77	1657	3848	2084	255	3593	942	511	103	839
2249	11633	33627	15154	7030	26597	8926	3875	2278	6648
1972	8099	23684	11519	4672	19012	6044	2902	1259	4785
1836	8070	23630	9520	5249	18381	6577	2438	2047	4530
5103	17421	59090	22715	15002	44088	17990	6204	5574	12416
4309	17714	53633	19596	12042	41591	14651	4709	3973	10678
1536	5327	19269	6573	5144	14125	5227	1592	1006	4221
958	4925	13535	3743	2312	11223	3461	833	658	2803
688	5172	13266	5347	1674	11592	3191	1179	459	2732
102	2460	5711	1999	237	5474	1350	429	62	1288
1399	8365	21910	9636	3293	18617	5485	2448	963	4522
157	3661	8465	3775	380	8085	2020	915	101	1919
4230	17961	52297	18884	10839	41458	14457	4700	3674	10783
1410	7187	19421	7094	3456	15965	5063	1144	1115	3948
2124	9495	27896	11325	5541	22355	7939	3032	1950	5989
63	2580	5774	2571	159	5615	1389	581	52	1337
19	185	442	208	46	396	96	49	13	83
816	5576	14763	5410	2306	12457	3979	1072	1054	2925
2221	11427	32171	11842	6401	25770	8258	2739	2266	5992
55	1403	2966	1185	114	2852	632	249	25	607
282	3025	7406	3139	667	6739	1808	719	185	1623
	17	59	8		59	22	4		22
2591	13057	40213	13946	8646	31256	12107	3600	3797	8144
583	3051	8555	3416	1594	6961	2231	847	573	1658
16	156	387	147	37	350	86	26	8	78
	290	594	327		594	122	63		122
91	1573	3629	2002	186	3443	845	451	51	794

普通高校

Data on Postgraduates in

地区 Region	毕(结)业生数 Graduates 计 Total	其中:女 Of which: Female	博士 Doctor's Degrees	硕士 Master's Degrees	授予学位数 Degrees Awarded	招生数 计 Total	其中:女 Of which: Female
总计 Total	**105373**	**39720**	**16401**	**88928**	**102662**	**255318**	**107940**
北京 Beijing	18855	7238	3796	15059	18296	39379	16946
天津 Tianjin	3252	1320	585	2667	3651	8506	3732
河北 Hebei	1998	983	139	1859	1989	4991	2621
山西 Shanxi	1113	536	67	1046	1101	2842	1457
内蒙古 Inner Mongolia	622	331	26	596	611	1729	920
辽宁 Liaoning	5027	2240	632	4395	5119	13242	6576
吉林 Jilin	4227	2060	1034	3193	3441	9590	4916
黑龙江 Heilongjiang	3797	1636	537	3260	3740	9806	4200
上海 Shanghai	9501	3447	1724	7777	9157	20767	8805
江苏 Jiangsu	8918	2948	1610	7308	8328	21705	8729
浙江 Zhejiang	3493	1096	642	2851	3487	6806	2579
安徽 Anhui	1989	539	370	1619	1604	5542	1603
福建 Fujian	1853	724	192	1661	2053	5762	2449
江西 Jiangxi	973	292	25	948	950	2562	984
山东 Shandong	3585	1611	445	3140	3573	9519	4134
河南 Henan	1460	701	66	1394	1454	3770	1735
湖北 Hubei	8874	2915	1313	7561	8734	21642	8800
湖南 Hunan	3081	1027	384	2697	3083	8543	2350
广东 Guangdong	4561	1718	733	3828	4582	11158	4783
广西 Guangxi	886	363	11	875	863	2643	1227
海南 Hainan	64	28	12	52	62	204	99
重庆 Chongqing	2713	772	326	2387	2691	6390	2618
四川 Sichuan	4964	1724	737	4227	4826	13214	5382
贵州 Guizhou	419	154		419	415	1374	562
云南 Yunnan	1079	372	68	1011	994	3090	1416
西藏 Tibet							
陕西 Shaanxi	6304	2260	768	5492	6149	15279	5815
甘肃 Gansu	1171	402	141	1030	1141	3296	1396
青海 Qinghai	19	8		19	19	108	49
宁夏 Ningxia	90	44		90	95	290	165
新疆 Xinjiang	485	231	18	467	454	1569	892

研究生数

Higher Education Institutions

单位:人

Unit:in Person

Entrants		在校学生数 Enrolment				预计毕业生数 Anticipated Graduates for Next Year			
博士 Doctor's Degrees	硕士 Master's Degrees	计 Total	其中:女 Of which: Female	博士 Doctor's Degrees	硕士 Master's Degrees	计 Total	其中:女 Of which: Female	博士 Doctor's Degrees	硕士 Master's Degrees
43315	**211825**	**617485**	**246451**	**122381**	**494646**	**169700**	**62232**	**41077**	**128457**
8488	30787	99893	40798	25408	74338	29280	11768	8015	21265
1680	6826	20657	8552	4304	16353	5481	2141	1250	4231
448	4543	11097	5642	1144	9953	2773	1349	388	2385
224	2618	6334	3377	590	5744	1582	840	218	1364
77	1652	3838	2081	255	3583	940	510	103	837
1975	11267	31796	14577	6102	25694	8351	3708	1875	6476
1755	7835	22472	11099	4030	18442	5737	2807	1038	4699
1824	7982	23375	9423	5205	18170	6500	2411	2024	4476
4396	16371	55092	21497	13308	41784	17099	5967	5098	12001
4220	17485	52875	19409	11796	41079	14421	4658	3886	10535
1534	5272	19151	6540	5141	14010	5200	1588	1006	4194
829	4713	12614	3535	1934	10680	3206	775	545	2661
648	5114	13053	5271	1591	11462	3156	1171	441	2715
102	2460	5711	1999	237	5474	1350	429	62	1288
1325	8194	21310	9418	3096	18214	5316	2396	893	4423
156	3614	8345	3747	378	7967	1990	910	101	1889
4067	17575	50994	18503	10413	40581	14132	4624	3546	10586
1410	7133	19304	7060	3456	15848	5036	1137	1115	3921
1928	9230	26855	10979	5139	21716	7692	2953	1856	5836
63	2580	5774	2571	159	5615	1389	581	52	1337
19	185	442	208	46	396	96	49	13	83
816	5574	14758	5410	2306	12452	3978	1072	1054	2924
2091	11123	31123	11525	6117	25006	8002	2664	2201	5801
16	1358	2796	1132	23	2773	603	239		603
207	2883	6866	2932	477	6389	1666	672	128	1538
2507	12698	39068	13652	8386	30371	11795	3527	3709	7920
430	2866	7660	3159	1164	6496	1943	765	409	1534
	108	224	102	1	223	44	19		44
	290	594	327		594	122	63		122
80	1489	3414	1926	175	3239	820	439	51	769

地 区 Region	毕(结)业生数 Graduates 计 Total	其中:女 Of which: Female	博 士 Doctor's Degrees	硕 士 Master's Degrees	授予学位数 Degrees Awarded	招生数 计 Total	其中:女 Of which: Female
总 计 Total	**5704**	**1571**	**2405**	**3299**	**5433**	**13590**	**4354**
北 京 Beijing	3062	853	1383	1679	2947	6591	2116
天 津 Tianjin							
河 北 Hebei	14	4		14	14	31	15
山 西 Shanxi	45	20	20	25	45	137	50
内蒙古 Inner Mongolia	2			2	2	5	1
辽 宁 Liaoning	229	72	115	114	226	640	211
吉 林 Jilin	176	42	102	74	177	481	172
黑龙江 Heilongjiang	65	26	6	59	67	100	38
上 海 Shanghai	578	151	303	275	520	1757	581
江 苏 Jiangsu	117	25	42	75	105	318	79
浙 江 Zhejiang	21	9		21	20	57	18
安 徽 Anhui	160	23	64	96	158	341	76
福 建 Fujian	18	4	8	10	22	98	37
江 西 Jiangxi							
山 东 Shandong	109	44	33	76	99	245	96
河 南 Henan	28	5		28	28	48	13
湖 北 Hubei	205	48	64	141	188	549	173
湖 南 Hunan	18	2		18	21	54	16
广 东 Guangdong	140	36	44	96	136	461	155
广 西 Guangxi							
海 南 Hainan							
重 庆 Chongqing	2			2	1	2	
四 川 Sichuan	164	40	45	119	164	434	135
贵 州 Guizhou	25	6	20	5	25	84	25
云 南 Yunnan	90	37	49	41	82	217	82
西 藏 Tibet							
陕 西 Shaanxi	196	52	24	172	191	443	116
甘 肃 Gansu	178	44	77	101	140	338	104
青 海 Qinghai	26	11	6	20	24	64	21
宁 夏 Ningxia							
新 疆 Xinjiang	36	17		36	31	95	24

研究生数
Higher Education Institutions

单位：人
Unit: in Person

Entrants		在校学生数 Enrolment				预计毕业生数 Anticipated Graduates for Next Year			
博士 Doctor's Degrees	硕士 Master's Degrees	计 Total	其中:女 Of which: Female	博士 Doctor's Degrees	硕士 Master's Degrees	计 Total	其中:女 Of which: Female	博士 Doctor's Degrees	硕士 Master's Degrees
5425	**8165**	**33716**	**10304**	**14306**	**19410**	**9026**	**2481**	**4559**	**4467**
2963	3628	16629	5087	7822	8807	4624	1279	2471	2153
	31	74	27		74	19	7		19
50	87	335	115	137	198	91	22	48	43
	5	10	3		10	2	1		2
274	366	1831	577	928	903	575	167	403	172
217	264	1212	420	642	570	307	95	221	86
12	88	255	97	44	211	77	27	23	54
707	1050	3998	1218	1694	2304	891	237	476	415
89	229	758	187	246	512	230	51	87	143
2	55	118	33	3	115	27	4		27
129	212	921	208	378	543	255	58	113	142
40	58	213	76	83	130	35	8	18	17
74	171	600	218	197	403	169	52	70	99
1	47	120	28	2	118	30	5		30
163	386	1303	381	426	877	325	76	128	197
	54	117	34		117	27	7		27
196	265	1041	346	402	639	247	79	94	153
	2	5			5	1			1
130	304	1048	317	284	764	256	75	65	191
39	45	170	53	91	79	29	10	25	4
75	142	540	207	190	350	142	47	57	85
84	359	1145	294	260	885	312	73	88	224
153	185	895	257	430	465	288	82	164	124
16	48	163	45	36	127	42	7	8	34
11	84	215	76	11	204	25	12		25

Data on Students Enrolled in Normal and Short－cycle

地区 Region	毕(结)业生数 Graduates				授予学位数 Degrees Awarded	招生数	
	计 Total	其中:女 Of which: Female	本科 Normal Courses	专科 Short-cycle Courses		计 Total	其中:女 Of which: Female
总 计 Total	**3470850**	**1617570**	**1315740**	**2155110**	**877894**	**3821701**	**1736809**
北 京 Beijing	180821	84154	92554	88267	64208	141790	67666
天 津 Tianjin	67932	35864	29717	38215	19851	86115	41902
河 北 Hebei	194066	96816	54871	139195	41979	203826	101437
山 西 Shanxi	83655	41974	28770	54885	19937	91283	43705
内蒙古 Inner Mongolia	50698	26488	19840	30858	10320	59450	30892
辽 宁 Liaoning	162881	81294	76486	86395	54792	163802	80216
吉 林 Jilin	99731	47908	51592	48139	35173	107125	46754
黑龙江 Heilongjiang	124534	60546	55920	68614	39650	121984	59022
上 海 Shanghai	113589	56174	54553	59036	37864	120269	57077
江 苏 Jiangsu	225970	99955	103136	122834	71901	256595	110204
浙 江 Zhejiang	151723	79263	57687	94036	27674	168167	87226
安 徽 Anhui	118805	45857	37250	81555	25920	142361	58626
福 建 Fujian	71082	30534	22806	48276	14767	106715	47474
江 西 Jiangxi	84666	33955	34823	49843	22825	141571	55299
山 东 Shandong	196771	92211	72716	124055	51216	273894	128228
河 南 Henan	171826	80351	45432	126394	33272	190214	89142
湖 北 Hubei	214308	89874	100401	113907	68167	250198	106064
湖 南 Hunan	183212	79891	57518	125694	40169	193830	89648
广 东 Guangdong	172965	78553	50576	122389	38032	225837	95754
广 西 Guangxi	82250	38886	19491	62759	12851	82537	37693
海 南 Hainan	12366	6276	3637	8729	1485	17006	6993
重 庆 Chongqing	79807	38107	29311	50496	17881	85474	38348
四 川 Sichuan	215312	98272	67169	148143	37488	180308	78364
贵 州 Guizhou	64548	28184	19126	45422	9142	53318	22647
云 南 Yunnan	55293	25674	20789	34504	12045	62176	29454
西 藏 Tibet	2758	1271	626	2132	392	4279	1085
陕 西 Shaanxi	143326	63378	65994	77332	46898	168127	70173
甘 肃 Gansu	55858	24200	17357	38501	10696	60069	23486
青 海 Qinghai	10863	5496	2391	8472	1642	9075	4610
宁 夏 Ningxia	14913	8036	4800	10113	2709	11237	5602
新 疆 Xinjiang	64321	38128	18401	45920	6948	43069	22018

本、专科学生数(总计)

Courses in Higher Education Institutions

单位:人

Unit:in Person

Entrants		在校学生数 Enrolment				预计毕业生数 Anticipated Graduates for Next Year			
本科 Normal Courses	专科 Short-cycle Courses	计 Total	其中:女 Of which: Female	本科 Normal Courses	专科 Short-cycle Courses	计 Total	其中:女 Of which: Female	本科 Normal Courses	专科 Short-cycle Courses
1825262	**1996439**	**16677215**	**7789413**	**7834832**	**8842383**	**4446305**	**1982360**	**1779936**	**2666369**
98396	43394	814124	405365	486862	327262	229576	108464	120100	109476
44427	41688	349483	175464	175058	174425	92580	45337	40818	51762
67233	136593	871104	437783	312580	558524	246636	118196	71251	175385
40200	51083	429285	210777	174563	254722	110633	52128	38876	71757
28114	31336	250745	130059	117277	133468	68264	32824	24812	43452
99543	64259	715493	349477	423547	291946	190544	90018	99722	90822
69955	37170	473618	225657	295614	178004	125792	51313	68978	56814
69705	52279	564686	273788	319526	245160	152177	71625	72389	79788
61674	58595	549369	270054	286765	262604	145888	69868	67934	77954
140139	116456	1186895	539954	610166	576729	324782	139870	140536	184246
75554	92613	760129	394394	353339	406790	208034	108727	79698	128336
60886	81475	581882	232642	244326	337556	145836	56581	53675	92161
48859	57856	343336	156041	159596	183740	86597	38781	33572	53025
57019	84552	501758	198270	226925	274833	112383	40240	46796	65587
115932	157962	1078022	503322	477205	600817	280874	133486	114396	166478
75925	114289	811256	373678	303304	507952	227585	91950	64141	163444
113002	137196	1041177	437036	543253	497924	249422	101891	129770	119652
84066	109764	839000	384984	338076	500924	230868	97530	73851	157017
90370	135467	876771	415057	335027	541744	216261	93856	68858	147403
30931	51606	400586	194112	129673	270913	110955	44979	28290	82665
6966	10040	66371	29083	26958	39413	17398	7642	5516	11882
45859	39615	362597	162067	187063	175534	92963	38872	39689	53274
84737	95571	870503	395499	394017	476486	243591	109343	87935	155656
27349	25969	258959	110336	113583	145376	73699	29551	23442	50257
32533	29643	298988	142285	137127	161861	76502	34894	27997	48505
2289	1990	15520	7942	6496	9024	3885	2102	960	2925
85187	82940	704675	307414	355278	349397	193676	82534	90963	102713
31771	28298	269292	114563	123088	146204	74406	28079	26547	47859
4638	4437	44205	22840	19566	24639	12724	5789	4653	8071
6888	4349	71928	36457	29889	42039	22454	11296	7231	15223
25115	17954	275458	153013	129085	146373	79320	44594	26540	52780

Data on Students Enrolled in Regular Normal and Short

地区 Region	毕(结)业生数 Graduates				授予学位数 Degrees Awarded	招生数	
	计 Total	其中:女 Of which: Female	本科 Normal Courses	专科 Short-cycle Courses		计 Total	其中:女 Of which: Female
总计 Total	**1877492**	**831472**	**929598**	**947894**	**814759**	**3821701**	**1736809**
北京 Beijing	82828	37671	59473	23355	52785	141790	67666
天津 Tianjin	40221	20400	22756	17465	19045	86115	41902
河北 Hebei	113442	57879	41629	71813	37655	203826	101437
山西 Shanxi	40779	18370	21682	19097	18512	91283	43705
内蒙古 Inner Mongolia	24919	12966	11183	13736	10198	59450	30892
辽宁 Liaoning	98908	48171	56704	42204	53096	163802	80216
吉林 Jilin	52605	23535	34961	17644	31339	107125	46754
黑龙江 Heilongjiang	69050	32153	38389	30661	36366	121984	59022
上海 Shanghai	71158	35319	39952	31206	34903	120269	57077
江苏 Jiangsu	137048	56991	79041	58007	62953	256595	110204
浙江 Zhejiang	78685	38079	28751	49934	24714	168167	87226
安徽 Anhui	65685	23298	28318	37367	24928	142361	58626
福建 Fujian	47792	19473	16870	30922	14515	106715	47474
江西 Jiangxi	47167	17150	24689	22478	20697	141571	55299
山东 Shandong	117253	52454	54329	62924	49974	273894	128228
河南 Henan	108975	48712	35346	73629	30960	190214	89142
湖北 Hubei	119118	47889	66120	52998	61023	250198	106064
湖南 Hunan	90035	37988	42160	47875	38301	193830	89648
广东 Guangdong	105533	43604	39268	66265	36406	225837	95754
广西 Guangxi	40178	16996	14462	25716	11584	82537	37693
海南 Hainan	5846	2519	2669	3177	1485	17006	6993
重庆 Chongqing	42653	19082	22184	20469	17706	85474	38348
四川 Sichuan	74307	31831	43525	30782	36911	180308	78364
贵州 Guizhou	25362	11284	11082	14280	8976	53318	22647
云南 Yunnan	31337	14381	15590	15747	11508	62176	29454
西藏 Tibet	1745	847	491	1254	348	4279	1085
陕西 Shaanxi	79785	31394	51018	28767	46472	168127	70173
甘肃 Gansu	29582	11660	12067	17515	10293	60069	23486
青海 Qinghai	4771	2563	1890	2881	1449	9075	4610
宁夏 Ningxia	5461	2727	3368	2093	2709	11237	5602
新疆 Xinjiang	25264	14086	9631	15633	6948	43069	22018

普通本、专科学生数

-cycle Courses in Higher Education

单位:人

Unit: in Person

Entrants		在校学生数 Enrolment				预计毕业生数 Anticipated Graduates for Next Year			
本 科 Normal Courses	专 科 Short-cycle Courses	计 Total	其中:女 Of which: Female	本 科 Normal Courses	专 科 Short-cycle Courses	计 Total	其中:女 Of which: Female	本 科 Normal Courses	专 科 Short-cycle Courses
1825262	**1996439**	**11085642**	**4970504**	**6292089**	**4793553**	**2477931**	**1063143**	**1235436**	**1242495**
98396	43394	454480	215473	354268	100212	103757	48094	74805	28952
44427	41688	245213	117858	145159	100054	53277	25576	29992	23285
67233	136593	575542	283764	255688	319854	148067	72061	51748	96319
40200	51083	272967	123291	147579	125388	56229	24628	29584	26645
28114	31336	157602	81251	83931	73671	33089	16348	13949	19140
99543	64259	514191	245928	344672	169519	119445	55082	72045	47400
69955	37170	319504	146609	234830	84674	69488	29814	46623	22865
69705	52279	392246	183171	260067	132179	89278	40316	52075	37203
61674	58595	378517	188602	223893	154624	93154	46064	49445	43709
140139	116456	859674	379092	505929	353745	212185	89384	102819	109366
75554	92613	484135	236963	252310	231825	106435	52209	41903	64532
60886	81475	410041	158953	209916	200125	90705	33180	40077	50628
48859	57856	257417	114336	131737	125680	57198	23974	24120	33078
57019	84552	358622	133696	185742	172880	64919	22530	33088	31831
115932	157962	761417	341397	383954	377463	171784	77046	71028	100756
75925	114289	557240	245426	259558	297682	136660	53173	49619	87041
113002	137196	721513	300581	423446	298067	145201	56413	88683	56518
84066	109764	537220	238490	279150	258070	114931	46552	53964	60967
90370	135467	587779	257779	277707	310072	128054	49094	51138	76916
30931	51606	227257	99210	103209	124048	51224	20799	18734	32490
6966	10040	43498	18252	21941	21557	7776	3207	3481	4295
45859	39615	240503	107268	149660	90843	52750	21289	28395	24355
84737	95571	512663	218924	325062	187601	99651	42492	63949	35702
27349	25969	149444	59936	90655	58789	31404	11872	15190	16214
32533	29643	175255	81440	105671	69584	36313	15309	18484	17829
2289	1990	10409	5175	6138	4271	2133	989	906	1227
85187	82940	499017	209143	295810	203207	116990	48157	69427	47563
31771	28298	173391	69172	100392	72999	39528	13184	17563	21965
4638	4437	26124	13197	16828	9296	5856	2856	3198	2658
6888	4349	35134	17065	24421	10713	7842	3379	4899	2943
25115	17954	147627	79062	92766	54861	32608	18072	14505	18103

Data on Students Enrolled in Normal and Short-cycle Courses

地 区 Region	毕(结)业生数 Graduates				授予学位数 Degrees Awarded	招生数	
	计 Total	其中:女 Of which: Female	本 科 Normal Courses	专 科 Short-cycle Courses		计 Total	其中:女 Of which: Female
总 计 Total	**1593358**	**786098**	**386142**	**1207216**	**63135**		
北 京 Beijing	97993	46483	33081	64912	11423		
天 津 Tianjin	27711	15464	6961	20750	806		
河 北 Hebei	80624	38937	13242	67382	4324		
山 西 Shanxi	42876	23604	7088	35788	1425		
内蒙古 Inner Mongolia	25779	13522	8657	17122	122		
辽 宁 Liaoning	63973	33123	19782	44191	1696		
吉 林 Jilin	47126	24373	16631	30495	3834		
黑龙江 Heilongjiang	55484	28393	17531	37953	3284		
上 海 Shanghai	42431	20855	14601	27830	2961		
江 苏 Jiangsu	88922	42964	24095	64827	8948		
浙 江 Zhejiang	73038	41184	28936	44102	2960		
安 徽 Anhui	53120	22559	8932	44188	992		
福 建 Fujian	23290	11061	5936	17354	252		
江 西 Jiangxi	37499	16805	10134	27365	2128		
山 东 Shandong	79518	39757	18387	61131	1242		
河 南 Henan	62851	31639	10086	52765	2312		
湖 北 Hubei	95190	41985	34281	60909	7144		
湖 南 Hunan	93177	41903	15358	77819	1868		
广 东 Guangdong	67432	34949	11308	56124	1626		
广 西 Guangxi	42072	21890	5029	37043	1267		
海 南 Hainan	6520	3757	968	5552			
重 庆 Chongqing	37154	19025	7127	30027	175		
四 川 Sichuan	141005	66441	23644	117361	577		
贵 州 Guizhou	39186	16900	8044	31142	166		
云 南 Yunnan	23956	11293	5199	18757	537		
西 藏 Tibet	1013	424	135	878	44		
陕 西 Shaanxi	63541	31984	14976	48565	426		
甘 肃 Gansu	26276	12540	5290	20986	403		
青 海 Qinghai	6092	2933	501	5591	193		
宁 夏 Ningxia	9452	5309	1432	8020			
新 疆 Xinjiang	39057	24042	8770	30287			

成人本、专科学生数

Provided by Adult HEIs in Higher Education

单位:人

Unit:in Person

Entrants		在校学生数 Enrolment				预计毕业生数 Anticipated Graduates for Next Year			
本 科 Normal Courses	专 科 Short-cycle Courses	计 Total	其中:女 Of which: Female	本 科 Normal Courses	专 科 Short-cycle Courses	计 Total	其中:女 Of which: Female	本 科 Normal Courses	专 科 Short-cycle Courses
		5591573	2818909	1542743	4048830	1968374	919217	544500	1423874
		359644	189892	132594	227050	125819	60370	45295	80524
		104270	57606	29899	74371	39303	19761	10826	28477
		295562	154019	56892	238670	98569	46135	19503	79066
		156318	87486	26984	129334	54404	27500	9292	45112
		93143	48808	33346	59797	35175	16476	10863	24312
		201302	103549	78875	122427	71099	34936	27677	43422
		154114	79048	60784	93330	56304	21499	22355	33949
		172440	90617	59459	112981	62899	31309	20314	42585
		170852	81452	62872	107980	52734	23804	18489	34245
		327221	160862	104237	222984	112597	50486	37717	74880
		275994	157431	101029	174965	101599	56518	37795	63804
		171841	73689	34410	137431	55131	23401	13598	41533
		85919	41705	27859	58060	29399	14807	9452	19947
		143136	64574	41183	101953	47464	17710	13708	33756
		316605	161925	93251	223354	109090	56440	43368	65722
		254016	128252	43746	210270	90925	38777	14522	76403
		319664	136455	119807	199857	104221	45478	41087	63134
		301780	146494	58926	242854	115937	50978	19887	96050
		288992	157278	57320	231672	88207	44762	17720	70487
		173329	94902	26464	146865	59731	24180	9556	50175
		22873	10831	5017	17856	9622	4435	2035	7587
		122094	54799	37403	84691	40213	17583	11294	28919
		357840	176575	68955	288885	143940	66851	23986	119954
		109515	50400	22928	86587	42295	17679	8252	34043
		123733	60845	31456	92277	40189	19585	9513	30676
		5111	2767	358	4753	1752	1113	54	1698
		205658	98271	59468	146190	76686	34377	21536	55150
		95901	45391	22696	73205	34878	14895	8984	25894
		18081	9643	2738	15343	6868	2933	1455	5413
		36794	19392	5468	31326	14612	7917	2332	12280
		127831	73951	36319	91512	46712	26522	12035	34677

高等教育网络本、

Data on Students Enrolled in Normal and Short-cycle Courses Provided

地　区 Region	毕(结)业生数 Graduates 计 Total	其中:女 Of which: Female	本　科 Normal Courses	专　科 Short-cycle Courses	授予学位数 Degrees Awarded	招生 计 Total
总　计 Total	**144408**	**69481**	**66309**	**78099**	**3600**	**841496**
北　京 Beijing	118847	58304	60202	58645	2365	605187
天　津 Tianjin	196	104	182	14	47	4987
河　北 Hebei						
山　西 Shaanxi						
内蒙古 Inner Mongolia						
辽　宁 Liaoning	185	70	185		162	9568
吉　林 Jilin						3142
黑龙江 Heilongjiang	6122	2752	1860	4262	303	28663
上　海 Shanghai	1404	684	1356	48	189	14198
江　苏 Jiangsu						8431
浙　江 Zhejiang	12767	5809	1423	11344	210	42912
安　徽 Anhui						
福　建 Fujian						8226
江　西 Jiangxi						
山　东 Shandong	97	37	97			5182
河　南 Henan						1524
湖　北 Hubei	2875	858	121	2754	53	27412
湖　南 Hunan	950	490		950		8049
广　东 Guangdong	778	308	696	82	265	11908
广　西 Guangxi						
海　南 Hainan						
重　庆 Chongqing						18122
四　川 Sichuan	50	13	50		6	19906
贵　州 Guizhou						
云　南 Yunnan						
西　藏 Tibet						513
陕　西 Shaanxi	137	52	137			16956
甘　肃 Gansu						4322
青　海 Qinghai						2288
宁　夏 Ningxia						
新　疆 Xinjiang						

专学生数

by Web-based Programs in Higher Education Institutions

单位:人

Unit:in Person

数 Entrants			在校学生数 Enrolment			
其中:女 Of which: Female	本科 Normal Courses	专科 Short-cycle Courses	计 Total	其中:女 Of which: Female	本科 Normal Courses	专科 Short-cycle Courses
393310	**426563**	**414933**	**1860749**	**881258**	**976545**	**884204**
288003	278464	326723	1338630	640870	645146	693484
2362	4708	279	8683	4124	7927	756
3932	8428	1140	21061	9658	19728	1333
1245	2936	206	6351	2464	5835	516
14637	10769	17894	71838	35091	26119	45719
7991	12568	1630	29472	14873	27543	1929
3564	7856	575	10632	4134	9854	778
22839	7794	35118	107030	60429	23325	83705
3698	7282	944	29942	13327	26783	3159
2461	5182		18824	8661	18598	226
597	1447	77	3020	1183	2943	77
6902	13316	14096	50794	18502	29639	21155
3794	8049		24156	9655	20516	3640
4905	9969	1939	23924	9586	21703	2221
8202	16126	1996	36366	16386	30448	5918
8311	14983	4923	42052	16519	33854	8198
286	94	419	880	484	241	639
7167	12270	4686	19836	8451	15051	4785
1322	4322		11814	4278	11292	522
1092		2288	5444	2583		5444

综合大学本科、专科生

Data on Students of Comprehensive

地区 Region	毕(结)业生数 Graduates			招生数 Entrants		
	计 Total	本科 Normal Courses	专科 Short-cycle Courses	计 Total	本科 Normal Courses	专科 Short-cycle Courses
总计 Total	**374264**	**252079**	**122185**	**584710**	**423617**	**161093**
北京 Beijing	22292	15399	6893	30316	21120	9196
天津 Tianjin	2834	2270	564	3390	3390	
河北 Hebei	5369	3267	2102	9419	5450	3969
山西 Shanxi	4285	2951	1334	6602	3848	2754
内蒙古 Inner Mongolia	2693	1618	1075	3839	2908	931
辽宁 Liaoning	13770	10514	3256	19655	15252	4403
吉林 Jilin	18341	15895	2446	26990	22451	4539
黑龙江 Heilongjiang	15224	8259	6965	22795	15994	6801
上海 Shanghai	10085	7959	2126	11754	9739	2015
江苏 Jiangsu	30821	24836	5985	37201	33554	3647
浙江 Zhejiang	12643	9548	3095	14272	10276	3996
安徽 Anhui	3347	2610	737	5367	4178	1189
福建 Fujian	6159	5042	1117	13031	12105	926
江西 Jiangxi	15448	6020	9428	40891	16500	24391
山东 Shandong	36817	24114	12703	66974	47915	19059
河南 Henan	16265	11701	4564	20479	18564	1915
湖北 Hubei	28494	20943	7551	38997	30192	8805
湖南 Hunan	20818	18578	2240	27839	25303	2536
广东 Guangdong	34125	13198	20927	61096	38488	22608
广西 Guangxi	4339	3929	410	5317	5317	
海南 Hainan	1305	821	484	3534	2260	1274
重庆 Chongqing	10103	5857	4246	14432	10776	3656
四川 Sichuan	17025	9137	7888	32038	17773	14265
贵州 Guizhou	4003	3337	666	6019	5176	843
云南 Yunnan	4869	3109	1760	11622	8787	2835
西藏 Tibet	584	162	422	971	795	176
陕西 Shaanxi	16576	11303	5273	26959	16220	10739
甘肃 Gansu	4179	2342	1837	5763	4370	1393
青海 Qinghai	1609	751	858	2258	1344	914
宁夏 Ningxia	3556	2326	1230	4531	4350	181
新疆 Xinjiang	6286	4283	2003	10359	9222	1137

学生数
Universities

单位：人
Unit：in Person

在校学生数 Enrolment			预计毕业生数 Anticipated Graduates for Next Year		
计 Total	本科 Normal Courses	专科 Short-cycle Courses	计 Total	本科 Normal Courses	专科 Short-cycle Courses
1977522	**1527134**	**450388**	**456582**	**321481**	**135101**
103610	77953	25657	25392	17394	7998
12432	11859	573	3180	2688	492
29386	21293	8093	7435	4422	3013
24815	16724	8091	5750	3422	2328
12880	10172	2708	3106	2030	1076
67372	54417	12955	16117	12214	3903
97337	85563	11774	24264	20454	3810
91509	67170	24339	23006	13967	9039
46218	40319	5899	12086	10156	1930
140236	127583	12653	33793	28322	5471
55289	43618	11671	14685	10884	3801
19551	14849	4702	4700	3218	1482
34670	32026	2644	7046	6065	981
109283	49811	59472	21246	8335	12911
227971	165335	62636	52421	31000	21421
75336	67590	7746	17657	14332	3325
149212	124707	24505	35081	29736	5345
107519	100043	7476	25626	23059	2567
172807	116037	56770	34732	19126	15606
20494	19448	1046	5208	4712	496
10218	7018	3200	1704	1124	580
49144	37887	11257	11372	7338	4034
92922	61196	31726	19023	11703	7320
20400	18526	1874	4561	4034	527
34183	26473	7710	6380	3948	2432
3164	2460	704	565	401	164
87617	59029	28588	22130	14566	7564
18822	14047	4775	4411	2600	1811
6875	5261	1614	1834	1335	499
16941	15252	1689	3916	3260	656
39309	33468	5841	8155	5636	2519

高等理工院校本科、

Data on Students of of Institutions

地区 Region	毕(结)业生数 Graduates			招生数	
	计 Total	本科 Normal Courses	专科 Short-cycle Courses	计 Total	本科 Normal Courses
总计 Total	**487436**	**316350**	**171086**	**904629**	**637074**
北京 Beijing	25333	20470	4863	45995	37150
天津 Tianjin	15417	10782	4635	22942	20001
河北 Hebei	34980	17777	17203	58143	31630
山西 Shanxi	9540	7875	1665	19254	15022
内蒙古 Inner Mongolia	7502	3053	4449	16736	10126
辽宁 Liaoning	38679	27933	10746	63909	49734
吉林 Jilin	11352	7581	3771	26860	20368
黑龙江 Heilongjiang	20320	16082	4238	29850	24448
上海 Shanghai	29255	19152	10103	38545	28697
江苏 Jiangsu	40814	29327	11487	66901	58617
浙江 Zhejiang	14966	7267	7699	37207	27661
安徽 Anhui	18047	11861	6186	30479	23408
福建 Fujian	13557	5316	8241	30359	19977
江西 Jiangxi	11105	7944	3161	29219	19059
山东 Shandong	16426	9069	7357	29312	21724
河南 Henan	27748	10616	17132	49699	25353
湖北 Hubei	33877	27093	6784	72084	50496
湖南 Hunan	24347	11212	13135	50296	33372
广东 Guangdong	9058	6070	2988	18981	10755
广西 Guangxi	7243	4267	2976	14241	9276
海南 Hainan					
重庆 Chongqing	8269	3881	4388	17605	8416
四川 Sichuan	24403	16496	7907	53987	31189
贵州 Guizhou	2245	1919	326	4551	4400
云南 Yunnan	5364	3726	1638	7535	5436
西藏 Tibet					
陕西 Shaanxi	31328	25740	5588	57151	42024
甘肃 Gansu	5253	3636	1617	11692	8735
青海 Qinghai					
宁夏 Ningxia					
新疆 Xinjiang	1008	205	803	1096	

专科生学生数

of Science & Technology

单位:人

Unit:in Person

Entrants	在校学生数 Enrolment			预计毕业生数 Anticipated Graduates for Next Year		
专科 Short-cycle Courses	计 Total	本科 Normal Courses	专科 Short-cycle Courses	计 Total	本科 Normal Courses	专科 Short-cycle Courses
267555	**2887038**	**2169464**	**717574**	**642459**	**429984**	**212475**
8845	155403	134626	20777	34683	27907	6776
2941	76550	66236	10314	18948	14539	4409
26513	187752	112431	75321	47529	22020	25509
4232	62197	51453	10744	12770	10245	2525
6610	46489	27427	19062	9841	4125	5716
14175	210324	171636	38688	48831	37111	11720
6492	79304	62286	17018	15794	10337	5457
5402	106447	90863	15584	24070	18965	5105
9848	134324	103735	30589	33884	23362	10522
8284	239541	207846	31695	54656	42551	12105
9546	116923	88713	28210	21999	13310	8689
7071	100699	79663	21036	22182	15536	6646
10382	74052	48111	25941	18075	8670	9405
10160	81066	60022	21044	15297	11058	4239
7588	100510	69756	30754	25047	12403	12644
24346	151102	81832	69270	37713	15225	22488
21588	234942	187568	47374	44916	37305	7611
16924	146345	100379	45966	30286	16642	13644
8226	55500	37144	18356	12562	8132	4430
4965	45083	29055	16028	9701	5056	4645
9189	50867	28564	22303	11011	5122	5889
22798	168338	120779	47559	33775	23948	9827
151	15268	14663	605	2901	2633	268
2099	24663	19113	5550	5420	3858	1562
15127	183076	147293	35783	41930	34422	7508
2957	36888	28270	8618	7705	5502	2203
1096	3385		3385	933		933

高等农业院校本科、

Data on Students of of Institutions

地区 Region	毕(结)业生数 Graduates			招生数	
	计 Total	本科 Normal Courses	专科 Short-cycle Courses	计 Total	本科 Normal Courses
总计 Total	**78507**	**52270**	**26237**	**151900**	**111547**
北京 Beijing	3597	2578	1019	6163	5007
天津 Tianjin	693	367	326	2769	1865
河北 Hebei	3574	2208	1366	9934	3982
山西 Shanxi	1994	1686	308	5326	3608
内蒙古 Inner Mongolia	2875	2096	779	5291	4094
辽宁 Liaoning	4219	2503	1716	7725	5103
吉林 Jilin	2829	1926	903	5957	3911
黑龙江 Heilongjiang	6034	3660	2374	7835	6450
上海 Shanghai	1365	1036	329	3362	3178
江苏 Jiangsu	2670	2202	468	3760	3244
浙江 Zhejiang	1481	594	887	2655	1853
安徽 Anhui	2066	1490	576	6304	3898
福建 Fujian	3484	2103	1381	4329	3892
江西 Jiangxi	2416	1933	483	4107	3442
山东 Shandong	5581	3509	2072	12126	9218
河南 Henan	5662	2182	3480	8472	3218
湖北 Hubei	2163	2045	118	3900	3700
湖南 Hunan	2307	2118	189	4785	4249
广东 Guangdong	7197	4619	2578	15360	12958
广西 Guangxi					
海南 Hainan	1205	916	289	3102	1867
重庆 Chongqing	3482	2238	1244	5377	3950
四川 Sichuan	1957	1756	201	5697	4481
贵州 Guizhou					
云南 Yunnan	1617	1237	380	2546	2019
西藏 Tibet	254	65	189	376	252
陕西 Shaanxi	3223	2761	462	5279	4353
甘肃 Gansu	1730	982	748	2740	2408
青海 Qinghai					
宁夏 Ningxia					
新疆 Xinjiang	2832	1460	1372	6623	5347

专科生学生数
of Agriculture

单位:人
Unit: in Person

Entrants	在校学生数 Enrolment			预计毕业生数 Anticipated Graduates for Next Year		
专科 Short-cycle Courses	计 Total	本科 Normal Courses	专科 Short-cycle Courses	计 Total	本科 Normal Courses	专科 Short-cycle Courses
40353	**469857**	**367006**	**102851**	**98636**	**68535**	**30101**
1156	21720	18950	2770	4695	3789	906
904	6568	4334	2234	1115	542	573
5952	25167	13983	11184	4232	2556	1676
1718	15682	11647	4035	3042	2179	863
1197	16559	13027	3532	3502	2362	1140
2622	23430	16991	6439	5049	3557	1492
2046	17852	13167	4685	4068	2815	1253
1385	26640	22562	4078	6049	4292	1757
184	12159	10829	1330	2339	1472	867
516	12900	11864	1036	2984	2464	520
802	7525	5375	2150	1350	759	591
2406	19590	13451	6139	4014	2698	1316
437	15776	13705	2071	4011	2916	1095
665	13260	11860	1400	2608	2252	356
2908	36986	28648	8338	8323	5434	2889
5254	26028	12187	13841	6936	2633	4303
200	13183	12208	975	2606	2174	432
536	15493	14723	770	2629	2515	114
2402	40576	33342	7234	7672	5131	2541
1235	9270	6462	2808	1753	1196	557
1427	16069	13096	2973	3457	2631	826
1216	18730	15769	2961	3354	2931	423
527	8221	6711	1510	1715	1377	338
124	1265	865	400	289	196	93
926	18670	16056	2614	4612	3906	706
332	8712	7622	1090	1946	1300	646
1276	21826	17572	4254	4286	2458	1828

高等林业院校本科、

Data on Students of

地 区 Region	毕(结)业生数 Graduates			招生数	
	计 Total	本 科 Normal Courses	专 科 Short-cycle Courses	计 Total	本 科 Normal Courses
总 计 Total	**9961**	**8182**	**1779**	**22016**	**20360**
北 京 Beijing	1780	1445	335	3672	3154
天 津 Tianjin					
河 北 Hebei					
山 西 Shanxi					
内蒙古 Inner Mongolia					
辽 宁 Liaoning					
吉 林 Jilin					
黑龙江 Heilongjiang	2186	2045	141	4410	3948
上 海 Shanghai					
江 苏 Jiangsu	2027	1476	551	4121	3943
浙 江 Zhejiang	1434	885	549	3459	3330
安 徽 Anhui					
福 建 Fujian					
江 西 Jiangxi					
山 东 Shandong					
河 南 Henan					
湖 北 Hubei					
湖 南 Hunan	1595	1435	160	4160	4160
广 东 Guangdong					
广 西 Guangxi					
海 南 Hainan					
重 庆 Chongqing					
四 川 Sichuan					
贵 州 Guizhou					
云 南 Yunnan	939	896	43	2194	1825
西 藏 Tibet					
陕 西 Shaanxi					
甘 肃 Gansu					
青 海 Qinghai					
宁 夏 Ningxia					
新 疆 Xinjiang					

专科生学生数

Institutions of Forestry

单位:人
Unit:in Person

Entrants	在校学生数 Enrolment			预计毕业生数 Anticipated Graduates for Next Year		
专科 Short-cycle Courses	计 Total	本科 Normal Courses	专科 Short-cycle Courses	计 Total	本科 Normal Courses	专科 Short-cycle Courses
1656	**72608**	**67633**	**4975**	**13851**	**12249**	**1602**
518	12662	11716	946	2585	2232	353
462	15910	14763	1147	3407	3079	328
178	14203	13254	949	2710	2383	327
129	10092	9174	918	1696	1186	510
	12912	12912		2298	2298	
369	6829	5814	1015	1155	1071	84

高等医药院校本科、

Data on Students of Institutions

地 区 Region	毕(结)业生数 Graduates			招生数	
	计 Total	本 科 Normal Courses	专 科 Short-cycle Courses	计 Total	本 科 Normal Courses
总 计 Total	**72758**	**40980**	**31778**	**185264**	**103279**
北 京 Beijing	1678	930	748	3543	2080
天 津 Tianjin	2094	1075	1019	4229	2397
河 北 Hebei	7958	3012	4946	15561	6337
山 西 Shanxi	2889	1507	1382	9697	4120
内蒙古 Inner Mongolia	563	506	57	1307	912
辽 宁 Liaoning	3507	2990	517	12527	7454
吉 林 Jilin	1592	380	1212	3944	1203
黑龙江 Heilongjiang	3395	2111	1284	7388	4708
上 海 Shanghai	1822	1119	703	2263	1493
江 苏 Jiangsu	3566	3191	375	9819	8787
浙 江 Zhejiang	1744	841	903	6180	4149
安 徽 Anhui	4354	2810	1544	10631	5585
福 建 Fujian	2457	917	1540	3809	2489
江 西 Jiangxi	2034	1553	481	6753	4163
山 东 Shandong	6266	3295	2971	17551	9081
河 南 Henan	1526	867	659	3669	2668
湖 北 Hubei	1471	980	491	5622	1944
湖 南 Hunan	2002	628	1374	6425	1783
广 东 Guangdong	4582	2812	1770	11263	6714
广 西 Guangxi	3543	1928	1615	7038	4140
海 南 Hainan	344	104	240	1041	661
重 庆 Chongqing	1428	655	773	3759	1381
四 川 Sichuan	2993	2238	755	8736	5906
贵 州 Guizhou	2419	1471	948	7450	4878
云 南 Yunnan	1330	1037	293	3270	2361
西 藏 Tibet	24		24	231	192
陕 西 Shaanxi	1630	357	1273	3966	841
甘 肃 Gansu	1771	666	1105	3812	2498
青 海 Qinghai	336	271	65	680	570
宁 夏 Ningxia	358	227	131	1161	728
新 疆 Xinjiang	1082	502	580	1939	1056

专科生学生数
of Medicine & Pharmacy

单位:人
Unit:in Person

Entrants	在校学生数 Enrolment			预计毕业生数 Anticipated Graduates for Next Year		
专科 Short-cycle Courses	计 Total	本科 Normal Courses	专科 Short-cycle Courses	计 Total	本科 Normal Courses	专科 Short-cycle Courses
81985	**585510**	**399237**	**186273**	**106233**	**62695**	**43538**
1463	11538	7907	3631	1908	1115	793
1832	12673	8195	4478	2494	1436	1058
9224	50336	28378	21958	10813	5102	5711
5577	30786	19375	11411	5693	3512	2181
395	4306	3812	494	641	582	59
5073	38004	28402	9602	6147	4589	1558
2741	9997	4003	5994	2284	605	1679
2680	25633	19080	6553	4643	2950	1693
770	7860	5693	2167	1672	1037	635
1032	32308	29274	3034	5455	4429	1026
2031	19473	14184	5289	2747	1510	1237
5046	35017	24492	10525	6570	4091	2479
1320	12516	8549	3967	2952	1473	1479
2590	20955	16327	4628	3429	2644	785
8470	51129	28644	22485	10583	4357	6226
1001	14964	12511	2453	2644	1951	693
3678	17416	9513	7903	2399	1688	711
4642	17015	6609	10406	3566	1131	2435
4549	30049	21368	8681	4985	3434	1551
2898	23762	17402	6360	4480	2915	1565
380	3142	2174	968	459	219	240
2378	9490	5027	4463	1754	694	1060
2830	29904	25129	4775	3993	3257	736
2572	24506	19188	5318	4133	2854	1279
909	11817	9343	2474	2253	1388	865
39	594	401	193	79	27	52
3125	11927	4130	7797	2712	900	1812
1314	12714	9351	3363	2056	1155	901
110	2892	2782	110	390	390	
433	4087	2966	1121	694	432	262
883	8700	5028	3672	1605	828	777

高等师范院校本科、

Data on Students of Institutions

地　区 Region	毕(结)业生数 Graduates 计 Total	本　科 Normal Courses	专　科 Short-cycle Courses	招生数 计 Total	本　科 Normal Courses
总　计 Total	**325273**	**149376**	**175897**	**551724**	**298331**
北　京 Beijing	4221	3675	546	4974	4974
天　津 Tianjin	4721	3196	1525	7513	5690
河　北 Hebei	29911	8865	21046	34632	10979
山　西 Shanxi	11310	4764	6546	18470	9202
内蒙古 Inner Mongolia	6934	3015	3919	15850	8601
辽　宁 Liaoning	11044	6451	4593	15351	9142
吉　林 Jilin	10077	7480	2597	21972	15227
黑龙江 Heilongjiang	8470	4031	4439	16213	8559
上　海 Shanghai	7416	5284	2132	8795	7654
江　苏 Jiangsu	17953	13259	4694	25648	20126
浙　江 Zhejiang	12392	6064	6328	25093	17108
安　徽 Anhui	22437	7636	14801	37013	19716
福　建 Fujian	11617	3492	8125	21747	9919
江　西 Jiangxi	7560	4917	2643	13674	9625
山　东 Shandong	18547	10258	8289	39539	17661
河　南 Henan	27176	6382	20794	43345	20787
湖　北 Hubei	10034	6020	4014	13601	7612
湖　南 Hunan	13829	6994	6835	23239	12144
广　东 Guangdong	10254	6792	3462	21708	11763
广　西 Guangxi	12509	2849	9660	19687	8203
海　南 Hainan	1664	828	836	4086	2178
重　庆 Chongqing	6980	3926	3054	13721	9444
四　川 Sichuan	14450	9278	5172	32889	15050
贵　州 Guizhou	9959	2032	7927	14601	7322
云　南 Yunnan	8633	2582	6051	14613	6422
西　藏 Tibet	354		354	676	
陕　西 Shaanxi	7930	4572	3358	16181	9637
甘　肃 Gansu	8938	1926	7012	14158	5424
青　海 Qinghai	837	454	383	1867	1582
宁　夏 Ningxia	630		630	1210	
新　疆 Xinjiang	6486	2354	4132	9658	6580

专科生学生数
of Teachers Colleges

单位：人
Unit: in Person

Entrants	在校学生数 Enrolment			预计毕业生数 Anticipated Graduates for Next Year		
专科 Short-cycle Courses	计 Total	本科 Normal Courses	专科 Short-cycle Courses	计 Total	本科 Normal Courses	专科 Short-cycle Courses
253393	**1673209**	**1009584**	**663625**	**397569**	**196047**	**201522**
	18574	18252	322	4207	4207	
1823	23648	19344	4304	5657	4221	1436
23653	105585	44245	61340	30806	9119	21687
9268	63231	35422	27809	15701	7884	7817
7249	44191	24969	19222	9456	3875	5581
6209	48366	31899	16467	12725	7151	5574
6745	62640	49525	13115	12221	9122	3099
7654	45955	27692	18263	9795	5057	4738
1141	34235	30143	4092	9104	7222	1882
5522	97583	75911	21672	24498	15945	8553
7985	78335	56505	21830	16556	8582	7974
17297	112255	64456	47799	27737	12249	15488
11828	57216	28784	28432	12435	4970	7465
4049	41973	32430	9543	8546	6352	2194
21878	109671	59982	49689	26038	11978	14060
22558	130640	64554	66086	32172	10553	21619
5989	45645	29698	15947	10493	6972	3521
11095	63242	34597	28645	14948	6990	7958
9945	58468	36520	21948	11704	7407	4297
11484	57903	25126	32777	14423	3995	10428
1908	11080	6287	4793	2126	942	1184
4277	36432	27051	9381	7333	4807	2526
17839	101886	65718	36168	23127	15054	8073
7279	42873	21465	21408	10409	2740	7669
8191	41077	20515	20562	8742	3236	5506
676	1286		1286	610		610
6544	50491	31015	19476	13189	7349	5840
8734	42783	17299	25484	12303	3415	8888
285	5565	4654	911	1137	725	412
1210	3145		3145	840		840
3078	37235	25526	11709	8531	3928	4603

高等语文院校本科、

Data on Students of Institutions

地 区 Region	毕(结)业生数 Graduates			招生数	
	计 Total	本 科 Normal Courses	专 科 Short-cycle Courses	计 Total	本 科 Normal Courses
总 计 Total	**17055**	**10608**	**6447**	**31542**	**21688**
北 京 Beijing	6544	3800	2744	9765	6585
天 津 Tianjin	1140	732	408	2102	2075
河 北 Hebei					
山 西 Shanxi					
内蒙古 Inner Mongolia	979		979	1487	
辽 宁 Liaoning	1159	1159		1988	1988
吉 林 Jilin	422		422	1883	1016
黑龙江 Heilongjiang					
上 海 Shanghai	1472	983	489	1711	1408
江 苏 Jiangsu					
浙 江 Zhejiang	845		845	2074	234
安 徽 Anhui					
福 建 Fujian					
江 西 Jiangxi					
山 东 Shandong					
河 南 Henan					
湖 北 Hubei					
湖 南 Hunan					
广 东 Guangdong	2164	2164		3368	3368
广 西 Guangxi					
海 南 Hainan					
重 庆 Chongqing	933	701	232	4184	2684
四 川 Sichuan					
贵 州 Guizhou					
云 南 Yunnan					
西 藏 Tibet					
陕 西 Shaanxi	1397	1069	328	2980	2330
甘 肃 Gansu					
青 海 Qinghai					
宁 夏 Ningxia					
新 疆 Xinjiang					

专科生学生数
of Languages & Literatures

单位：人
Unit: in Person

Entrants	在校学生数 Enrolment			预计毕业生数 Anticipated Graduates for Next Year		
专科 Short-cycle Courses	计 Total	本科 Normal Courses	专科 Short-cycle Courses	计 Total	本科 Normal Courses	专科 Short-cycle Courses
9854	**88411**	**63472**	**24939**	**20470**	**12822**	**7648**
3180	28733	21370	7363	7542	4692	2850
27	6175	5502	673	1363	945	418
1487	3151		3151	822		822
	7168	7168		1449	1449	
867	3694	1620	2074	576		576
303	6069	4861	1208	1452	1042	410
1840	4764	250	4514	1123		1123
	10166	10166		2432	2432	
1500	10275	6390	3885	1763	966	797
650	8216	6145	2071	1948	1296	652

高等财经院校本科、

Data on Students of Institutions

地区 Region	毕(结)业生数 Graduates 计 Total	 本科 Normal Courses	 专科 Short-cycle Courses	 计 Total	招生数 本科 Normal Courses
总计 Total	**109438**	**58717**	**50721**	**205374**	**115401**
北京 Beijing	5210	4407	803	8210	6689
天津 Tianjin	5486	3395	2091	8757	6150
河北 Hebei	7833	5603	2230	12697	6428
山西 Shanxi	3679	2899	780	9658	4400
内蒙古 Inner Mongolia	936	895	41	2670	1473
辽宁 Liaoning	7158	1718	5440	9045	3552
吉林 Jilin	3490	924	2566	6924	2226
黑龙江 Heilongjiang	4241	1632	2609	7264	4498
上海 Shanghai	7676	1864	5812	12538	5850
江苏 Jiangsu	3490	2735	755	6960	6596
浙江 Zhejiang	5932	3299	2633	10588	8899
安徽 Anhui	3387	1911	1476	6663	4101
福建 Fujian	686		686	1630	
江西 Jiangxi	2514	2322	192	5813	4230
山东 Shandong	3338	2911	427	8386	6910
河南 Henan	7655	3598	4057	11558	5335
湖北 Hubei	9291	4498	4793	17477	8398
湖南 Hunan	3725	1195	2530	7023	3055
广东 Guangdong	4462	1890	2572	11005	3237
广西 Guangxi	3346		3346	8237	411
海南 Hainan					
重庆 Chongqing	3892	2511	1381	6382	5139
四川 Sichuan	2415	2067	348	4113	3018
贵州 Guizhou	2688	1184	1504	5683	2889
云南 Yunnan	1509	1426	83	2552	2376
西藏 Tibet					
陕西 Shaanxi	2810	1963	847	5805	3385
甘肃 Gansu	1395	1171	224	5030	3781
青海 Qinghai					
宁夏 Ningxia					
新疆 Xinjiang	1194	699	495	2706	2375

专科生学生数

of Finance & Economics

单位:人

Unit:in Person

Entrants	在校学生数 Enrolment			预计毕业生数 Anticipated Graduates for Next Year		
专科 Short-cycle Courses	计 Total	本科 Normal Courses	专科 Short-cycle Courses	计 Total	本科 Normal Courses	专科 Short-cycle Courses
89973	**623257**	**393252**	**230005**	**140253**	**77199**	**63054**
1521	28765	24599	4166	7104	5664	1440
2607	28754	21634	7120	6565	4388	2177
6269	41744	27598	14146	11286	6874	4412
5258	24702	12958	11744	4256	2342	1914
1197	7549	4524	3025	1688	975	713
5493	27243	12283	14960	6930	2150	4780
4698	20004	8332	11672	4693	2009	2684
2766	24248	14663	9585	6013	3164	2849
6688	36459	16416	20043	9067	2342	6725
364	25749	23865	1884	5514	4312	1202
1689	35217	29185	6032	7507	5224	2283
2562	19456	13005	6451	4163	2285	1878
1630	3341		3341	666		666
1583	18174	15292	2882	2730	2447	283
1476	26061	22305	3756	5341	4146	1195
6223	37676	20884	16792	9986	4925	5061
9079	46507	27080	19427	8451	4952	3499
3968	17996	9887	8109	3168	1329	1839
7768	29580	12249	17331	6709	2766	3943
7826	20231	728	19503	4946	30	4916
1243	21420	17921	3499	5267	3949	1318
1095	13707	11421	2286	3018	2613	405
2794	15774	8207	7567	3583	1383	2200
176	7961	7435	526	1620	1518	102
2420	18296	10332	7964	5197	2596	2601
1249	15911	11116	4795	3056	1526	1530
331	10732	9333	1399	1729	1290	439

高等政法院校本科、

Data on Students of Institutions

地 区 Region	毕(结)业生数 Graduates			招生数	
	计 Total	本 科 Normal Courses	专 科 Short-cycle Courses	计 Total	本 科 Normal Courses
总 计 Total	**29751**	**10874**	**18877**	**44291**	**19377**
北 京 Beijing	4778	3932	846	5132	4576
天 津 Tianjin					
河 北 Hebei	917	491	426	1965	1650
山 西 Shanxi	720		720	900	
内蒙古 Inner Mongolia					
辽 宁 Liaoning	1780	1088	692	2584	1723
吉 林 Jilin	746		746	800	
黑龙江 Heilongjiang					
上 海 Shanghai	1806	1486	320	3061	2051
江 苏 Jiangsu	1373		1373	2488	893
浙 江 Zhejiang	991		991	1242	
安 徽 Anhui					
福 建 Fujian	536		536	612	
江 西 Jiangxi	505		505	906	
山 东 Shandong	708		708	993	
河 南 Henan	1758		1758	2257	
湖 北 Hubei	999		999	1605	595
湖 南 Hunan	1199		1199	1755	
广 东 Guangdong	1172		1172	1515	
广 西 Guangxi	556		556	1285	
海 南 Hainan					
重 庆 Chongqing	2573	1927	646	3869	3161
四 川 Sichuan	2958		2958	1961	
贵 州 Guizhou					
云 南 Yunnan	1095		1095	1977	353
西 藏 Tibet				270	
陕 西 Shaanxi	1493	1493		3527	2800
甘 肃 Gansu	1088	457	631	2462	1575
青 海 Qinghai					
宁 夏 Ningxia					
新 疆 Xinjiang				1125	

专科生学生数
of Political Science & Law

单位：人
Unit: in Person

Entrants	在校学生数 Enrolment			预计毕业生数 Anticipated Graduates for Next Year		
专科 Short-cycle Courses	计 Total	本科 Normal Courses	专科 Short-cycle Courses	计 Total	本科 Normal Courses	专科 Short-cycle Courses
24914	**127015**	**59791**	**67224**	**32518**	**12819**	**19699**
556	17705	16180	1525	4712	4001	711
315	5541	4806	735	1418	998	420
900	2495		2495	745		745
861	7721	5006	2715	2044	1141	903
800	2201		2201	584		584
1010	7587	6262	1325	1902	1587	315
1595	6500	1713	4787	1842		1842
1242	2817		2817	600		600
612	1952		1952	622		622
906	2648		2648	859		859
993	2699		2699	695		695
2257	8440		8440	2915		2915
1010	4636	1362	3274	1176	135	1041
1755	4747		4747	1130		1130
1515	4382		4382	1298		1298
1285	3813		3813	1161		1161
708	11701	10485	1216	2178	2178	
1961	4243		4243	910		910
1624	4632	353	4279	1204		1204
270	319		319	49		49
727	11599	9561	2038	2692	2101	591
887	6348	4063	2285	1335	678	657
1125	2289		2289	447		447

高等体育院校本科、

Data on Students of Institutions

地　区 Region	毕(结)业生数 Graduates 计 Total	本　科 Normal Courses	专　科 Short-cycle Courses	招生数 计 Total	本　科 Normal Courses
总　计 Total	**10224**	**8348**	**1876**	**20942**	**17975**
北　京 Beijing	929	918	11	1928	1928
天　津 Tianjin	896	487	409	2170	1415
河　北 Hebei	674	406	268	913	777
山　西 Shanxi					
内蒙古 Inner Mongolia					
辽　宁 Liaoning	782	782		1530	1530
吉　林 Jilin	473	473		1100	1100
黑龙江 Heilongjiang	569	569		1100	1100
上　海 Shanghai	775	775		993	993
江　苏 Jiangsu	444	295	149	584	458
浙　江 Zhejiang					
安　徽 Anhui					
福　建 Fujian					
江　西 Jiangxi					
山　东 Shandong	409	409		1700	1700
河　南 Henan					
湖　北 Hubei	755	755		2153	2153
湖　南 Hunan					
广　东 Guangdong	890	572	318	1971	1417
广　西 Guangxi	641		641	777	
海　南 Hainan					
重　庆 Chongqing					
四　川 Sichuan	940	940		2429	1900
贵　州 Guizhou					
云　南 Yunnan					
西　藏 Tibet					
陕　西 Shaanxi	1047	967	80	1594	1504
甘　肃 Gansu					
青　海 Qinghai					
宁　夏 Ningxia					
新　疆 Xinjiang					

专科生学生数
of Physical Culture

单位:人
Unit:in Person

Entrants	在校学生数 Enrolment			预计毕业生数 Anticipated Graduates for Next Year		
专科 Short-cycle Courses	计 Total	本科 Normal Courses	专科 Short-cycle Courses	计 Total	本科 Normal Courses	专科 Short-cycle Courses
2967	**61576**	**55853**	**5723**	**13015**	**10604**	**2411**
	6407	6407		1268	1268	
755	5200	3873	1327	1171	653	518
136	3403	2954	449	970	657	313
	4945	4945		952	952	
	3188	3188		527	527	
	3274	3274		601	601	
	3842	3842		884	884	
126	1856	1486	370	450	297	153
	3782	3584	198	694	496	198
	5879	5879		866	866	
554	5288	4213	1075	1186	865	321
777	1556		1556	779		779
529	7481	6952	529	1435	1435	
90	5475	5256	219	1232	1103	129

地 区 Region	毕(结)业生数 Graduates			招生数	
	计 Total	本 科 Normal Courses	专 科 Short-cycle Courses	计 Total	本 科 Normal Courses
总 计 Total	**10893**	**8017**	**2876**	**27776**	**23286**
北 京 Beijing	1287	1055	232	3400	2531
天 津 Tianjin	500	452	48	1455	1444
河 北 Hebei					
山 西 Shanxi					
内蒙古 Inner Mongolia					
辽 宁 Liaoning	694	694		1866	1765
吉 林 Jilin	473	302	171	2806	2453
黑龙江 Heilongjiang					
上 海 Shanghai	379	294	85	721	611
江 苏 Jiangsu	594	465	129	1394	1295
浙 江 Zhejiang	423	253	170	2497	2044
安 徽 Anhui					
福 建 Fujian				170	128
江 西 Jiangxi					
山 东 Shandong	1242	726	516	2442	1723
河 南 Henan					
湖 北 Hubei	573	571	2	1276	1276
湖 南 Hunan					
广 东 Guangdong	835	749	86	1073	1053
广 西 Guangxi	423	233	190	753	753
海 南 Hainan					
重 庆 Chongqing	741	488	253	1026	908
四 川 Sichuan	1082	434	648	2743	1620
贵 州 Guizhou					
云 南 Yunnan	486	415	71	1373	1054
西 藏 Tibet					
陕 西 Shaanxi	1053	793	260	2245	2093
甘 肃 Gansu					
青 海 Qinghai					
宁 夏 Ningxia					
新 疆 Xinjiang	108	93	15	536	535

专科生学生数

Institutions of Art

单位：人
Unit: in Person

Entrants	在校学生数 Enrolment			预计毕业生数 Anticipated Graduates for Next Year		
专科 Short-cycle Courses	计 Total	本科 Normal Courses	专科 Short-cycle Courses	计 Total	本科 Normal Courses	专科 Short-cycle Courses
4490	**82177**	**72292**	**9885**	**15690**	**11579**	**4111**
869	9687	8208	1479	1927	1345	582
11	4412	4182	230	772	580	192
101	4989	4687	302	796	728	68
353	8085	7146	939	1208	754	454
110	2172	1793	379	548	341	207
99	4814	4549	265	843	797	46
453	6177	5306	871	649	448	201
42	294	213	81	50	26	24
719	6432	5224	1208	1470	1006	464
	3828	3828		706	706	
20	4070	3854	216	1051	855	196
	2830	2600	230	626	396	230
118	3842	3239	603	1076	710	366
1123	7532	5654	1878	1611	856	755
319	3622	3037	585	602	538	64
152	7609	6993	616	1448	1188	260
1	1782	1779	3	307	305	2

高等民族院校本科、
Data on Students of

地 区 Region	毕(结)业生数 Graduates			招生数	
	计 Total	本 科 Normal Courses	专 科 Short-cycle Courses	计 Total	本 科 Normal Courses
总 计 Total	**15003**	**12067**	**2936**	**32366**	**29243**
北 京 Beijing	864	864		2602	2602
天 津 Tianjin					
河 北 Hebei					
山 西 Shanxi					
内蒙古 Inner Mongolia					
辽 宁 Liaoning	872	872		2300	2300
吉 林 Jilin					
黑龙江 Heilongjiang					
上 海 Shanghai					
江 苏 Jiangsu					
浙 江 Zhejiang					
安 徽 Anhui					
福 建 Fujian					
江 西 Jiangxi					
山 东 Shandong					
河 南 Henan					
湖 北 Hubei	3445	3215	230	6544	6144
湖 南 Hunan					
广 东 Guangdong					
广 西 Guangxi	1914	1256	658	2936	2831
海 南 Hainan					
重 庆 Chongqing					
四 川 Sichuan	1208	1179	29	4200	3800
贵 州 Guizhou	1283	1139	144	2684	2684
云 南 Yunnan	1307	1162	145	2413	1900
西 藏 Tibet	529	264	265	1755	1050
陕 西 Shaanxi					
甘 肃 Gansu	1067	887	180	3380	2980
青 海 Qinghai	1697	414	1283	1742	1142
宁 夏 Ningxia	817	815	2	1810	1810
新 疆 Xinjiang					

专科生学生数
Institutions of Art

单位：人
Unit: in Person

Entrants	在校学生数 Enrolment			预计毕业生数 Anticipated Graduates for Next Year		
专科 Short-cycle Courses	计 Total	本科 Normal Courses	专科 Short-cycle Courses	计 Total	本科 Normal Courses	专科 Short-cycle Courses
3123	**102781**	**93923**	**8858**	**19249**	**16690**	**2559**
	8100	8100		1191	1191	
	7238	7238		1003	1003	
400	21589	20554	1035	4137	3994	143
105	9996	8850	1146	2116	1630	486
400	12871	12444	427	2179	2152	27
	8791	8606	185	1619	1546	73
513	7993	6761	1232	1662	1550	112
705	3781	2412	1369	541	282	259
400	9484	8624	860	1748	1387	361
600	6655	4131	2524	1846	748	1098
	6283	6203	80	1207	1207	

职业技术学院本科、

Data on Students of Short-cycle

地区 Region	毕(结)业生数 Graduates 计 Total	本科 Normal Courses	专科 Short-cycle Courses	招生数 计 Total	本科 Normal Courses
总计 Total	**232878**	**167**	**232711**	**883848**	**913**
北京 Beijing	3130		3130	14038	
天津 Tianjin	5253		5253	28747	
河北 Hebei	16346		16346	48871	
山西 Shanxi	3494		3494	15050	
内蒙古 Inner Mongolia	2129		2129	11921	
辽宁 Liaoning	11810		11810	21568	
吉林 Jilin	2275		2275	7606	
黑龙江 Heilongjiang	3952		3952	22745	
上海 Shanghai	7388		7388	29840	
江苏 Jiangsu	22317	132	22185	78549	564
浙江 Zhejiang	20588		20588	57186	
安徽 Anhui	9238		9238	39968	
福建 Fujian	5382		5382	21150	349
江西 Jiangxi	3119		3119	35219	
山东 Shandong	10418		10418	67492	
河南 Henan	16425		16425	40167	
湖北 Hubei	24916		24916	79292	
湖南 Hunan	15954		15954	63413	
广东 Guangdong	19644		19644	67029	
广西 Guangxi	5193		5193	19173	
海南 Hainan	1091		1091	5085	
重庆 Chongqing	1433		1433	11318	
四川 Sichuan	2961		2961	24922	
贵州 Guizhou	1732		1732	10584	
云南 Yunnan	2066		2066	7122	
西藏 Tibet					
陕西 Shaanxi	7987		7987	35270	
甘肃 Gansu	3631		3631	9179	
青海 Qinghai	188		188	2421	
宁夏 Ningxia	100		100	2525	
新疆 Xinjiang	2718	35	2683	6398	

专科生学生数

Vocational Colleges

单位：人

Unit: in Person

Entrants	在校学生数 Enrolment			预计毕业生数 Anticipated Graduates for Next Year		
专科 Short-cycle Courses	计 Total	本科 Normal Courses	专科 Short-cycle Courses	计 Total	本科 Normal Courses	专科 Short-cycle Courses
882935	**1897859**	**1906**	**1895953**	**395486**	**236**	**395250**
14038	25413		25413	4317		4317
28747	64045		64045	11040		11040
48871	104341		104341	26139		26139
15050	35356		35356	4896		4896
11921	21475		21475	3843		3843
21568	56735		56735	14398		14398
7606	14354		14354	2948		2948
22745	45207		45207	8893		8893
29840	71067		71067	15964		15964
77985	214382	1381	213001	59420	176	59244
57186	133606		133606	32290		32290
39968	86780		86780	16506		16506
20801	36916	349	36567	5968		5968
35219	57630		57630	6128		6128
67492	131790		131790	27271		27271
40167	89648		89648	20443		20443
79292	164317		164317	30907		30907
63413	138626		138626	26808		26808
67029	141355		141355	28487		28487
19173	36727		36727	7240		7240
5085	9327		9327	1553		1553
11318	21991		21991	4477		4477
24922	42063		42063	5038		5038
10584	18995		18995	3473		3473
7122	14429	116	14313	3247		3247
35270	80545		80545	15427		15427
9179	18146		18146	3698		3698
2421	3905		3905	552		552
2525	4678		4678	1185		1185
6398	14010	60	13950	2930	60	2870

广播电视大学本、

Number of Students in Radio/TV

地　　区 Region	毕业生数 Graduates			招生数	
	合　计 Total	本　科 Normal Courses	专　科 Short-cycle Courses	合　计 Total	本　科 Normal Courses
合　计 Total	**152691**	**539**	**152152**	**0**	**0**
北　京 Beijing	1334	0	1334	0	0
天　津 Tianjin	2192	0	2192	0	0
河　北 Hebei	8808	0	8808	0	0
山　西 Shanxi	2333	0	2333	0	0
内蒙古 Inner Mongolia	3348	0	3348	0	0
辽　宁 Liaoning	4865	0	4865	0	0
吉　林 Jilin	6838	0	6838	0	0
黑龙江 Heilongjiang	5912	0	5912	0	0
上　海 Shanghai	1043	0	1043	0	0
江　苏 Jiangsu	2379	132	2247	0	0
浙　江 Zhejiang	4595	0	4595	0	0
安　徽 Anhui	800	0	800	0	0
福　建 Fujian	2499	0	2499	0	0
江　西 Jiangxi	4927	0	4927	0	0
山　东 Shandong	4174	9	4165	0	0
河　南 henan	1494	0	1494	0	0
湖　北 Hubei	6819	112	6707	0	0
湖　南 Hunan	11774	0	11774	0	0
广　东 Guangdong	5765	0	5765	0	0
广　西 Guangxi	4322	192	4130	0	0
海　南 Hainan	960	0	960	0	0
重　庆 Chongqing	10320	0	10320	0	0
四　川 Sichuan	23987	94	23893	0	0
贵　州 guizhou	7004	0	7004	0	0
云　南 Yunnan	1144	0	1144	0	0
西　藏 Tibet	0	0	0	0	0
陕　西 Shaanxi	9724	0	9724	0	0
甘　肃 Gansu	4230	0	4230	0	0
青　海 Qinghai	2316	0	2316	0	0
宁　夏 Ningxia	2789	0	2789	0	0
新　疆 Xinjiang	3996	0	3996	0	0

专科学生数

Universities by Type of Courses

单位:人

Unit:in Person

Entrants	在校学生数 Enrolment			毕业班学生数 Graduates for Next Year		
专科 Short-cycle Courses	合计 Total	本科 Normal Courses	专科 Short-cycle Courses	合计 Total	本科 Normal Courses	专科 Short-cycle Courses
0	**385130**	**2432**	**382698**	**159500**	**1044**	**158456**
0	4264	0	4264	1343	0	1343
0	10230	0	10230	4233	0	4233
0	27841	0	27841	11549	0	11549
0	4515	0	4515	1607	0	1607
0	6443	0	6443	2629	0	2629
0	9684	0	9684	3921	0	3921
0	13053	0	13053	6884	0	6884
0	11822	0	11822	4652	0	4652
0	2125	0	2125	679	0	679
0	4830	300	4530	1427	155	1272
0	13708	0	13708	5345	0	5345
0	1606	0	1606	518	0	518
0	6624	0	6624	2444	0	2444
0	13686	0	13686	4295	0	4295
0	10609	66	10543	3959	0	3959
0	5983	0	5983	3157	0	3157
0	22729	425	22304	8543	287	8256
0	27492	0	27492	10706	0	10706
0	23570	0	23570	6202	0	6202
0	12053	1093	10960	4544	482	4062
0	2059	0	2059	614	0	614
0	23608	142	23466	7519	5	7514
0	52668	406	52262	31268	115	31153
0	11638	0	11638	5729	0	5729
0	5714	0	5714	1747	0	1747
0	0	0	0	0	0	0
0	22779	0	22779	10423	0	10423
0	9392	0	9392	3268	0	3268
0	3885	0	3885	1179	0	1179
0	11274	0	11274	4820	0	4820
0	9246	0	9246	4296	0	4296

职工高等学校本、

Number of Students in Workers'

地区 Region	毕业生数 Graduates			招生数	
	合计 Total	本科 Normal Courses	专科 Short-cycle Courses	合计 Total	本科 Normal Courses
合计 Total	**101192**	**1754**	**99438**	**0**	**0**
北京 Beijing	6274	477	5797	0	0
天津 Tianjin	5969	0	5969	0	0
河北 Hebei	3667	387	3280	0	0
山西 Shanxi	3427	130	3297	0	0
内蒙古 Inner Mongolia	1890	0	1890	0	0
辽宁 Liaoning	5829	0	5829	0	0
吉林 Jilin	3307	511	2796	0	0
黑龙江 Heilongjiang	7821	44	7777	0	0
上海 Shanghai	4232	0	4232	0	0
江苏 Jiangsu	4881	0	4881	0	0
浙江 Zhejiang	2851	0	2851	0	0
安徽 Anhui	1388	0	1388	0	0
福建 Fujian	1359	0	1359	0	0
江西 Jiangxi	3444	0	3444	0	0
山东 Shandong	1871	0	1871	0	0
河南 henan	4837	0	4837	0	0
湖北 Hubei	2467	0	2467	0	0
湖南 Hunan	10613	0	10613	0	0
广东 Guangdong	5253	0	5253	0	0
广西 Guangxi	984	0	984	0	0
海南 Hainan	0	0	0	0	0
重庆 Chongqing	1472	0	1472	0	0
四川 Sichuan	6958	167	6791	0	0
贵州 guizhou	1481	0	1481	0	0
云南 Yunnan	373	0	373	0	0
西藏 Tibet	0	0	0	0	0
陕西 Shaanxi	3658	38	3620	0	0
甘肃 Gansu	1760	0	1760	0	0
青海 Qinghai	1259	0	1259	0	0
宁夏 Ningxia	0	0	0	0	0
新疆 Xinjiang	1867	0	1867	0	0

专科学生数

Colleges by Type of Courses

单位:人

Unit: in Person

Entrants	在校学生数 Enrolment			毕业班学生数 Graduates for Next Year		
专 科 Short-cycle Courses	合 计 Total	本 科 Normal Courses	专 科 Short-cycle Courses	合 计 Total	本 科 Normal Courses	专 科 Short-cycle Courses
0	**367280**	**6121**	**361159**	**131180**	**2390**	**128790**
0	22779	1369	21410	8322	834	7488
0	18613	0	18613	9869	0	9869
0	9939	1052	8887	3609	653	2956
0	10626	450	10176	4268	242	4026
0	10032	0	10032	4587	0	4587
0	21499	59	21440	8008	15	7993
0	10372	886	9486	3684	375	3309
0	27999	219	27780	9767	175	9592
0	19847	0	19847	4910	0	4910
0	17047	0	17047	5655	0	5655
0	18152	0	18152	7192	0	7192
0	9205	0	9205	1665	0	1665
0	3634	0	3634	1436	0	1436
0	10654	0	10654	3399	0	3399
0	7583	61	7522	1429	0	1429
0	19618	0	19618	6064	0	6064
0	14442	1726	12716	2072	0	2072
0	25024	0	25024	12824	0	12824
0	22717	0	22717	7643	0	7643
0	3148	0	3148	1094	0	1094
0	0	0	0	0	0	0
0	5493	0	5493	2281	0	2281
0	20207	240	19967	7904	77	7827
0	4225	0	4225	1653	0	1653
0	1028	0	1028	179	0	179
0	0	0	0	0	0	0
0	12566	59	12507	4076	19	4057
0	5466	0	5466	2403	0	2403
0	5411	0	5411	2018	0	2018
0	0	0	0	0	0	0
0	9954	0	9954	3169	0	3169

农民高等学校本、

Number of Students in

地　区 Region	毕业生数 Graduates				招生数
	合　计 Total	本　科 Normal Courses	专　科 Short-cycle Courses	合　计 Total	本　科 Normal Courses
合　计 Total	**316**	**0**	**316**	**0**	**0**
北　京 Beijing	0	0	0	0	0
天　津 Tianjin	0	0	0	0	0
河　北 Hebei	0	0	0	0	0
山　西 Shanxi	0	0	0	0	0
内蒙古 Inner Mongolia	0	0	0	0	0
辽　宁 Liaoning	0	0	0	0	0
吉　林 Jilin	316	0	316	0	0
黑龙江 Heilongjiang	0	0	0	0	0
上　海 Shanghai	0	0	0	0	0
江　苏 Jiangsu	0	0	0	0	0
浙　江 Zhejiang	0	0	0	0	0
安　徽 Anhui	0	0	0	0	0
福　建 Fujian	0	0	0	0	0
江　西 Jiangxi	0	0	0	0	0
山　东 Shandong	0	0	0	0	0
河　南 henan	0	0	0	0	0
湖　北 Hubei	0	0	0	0	0
湖　南 Hunan	0	0	0	0	0
广　东 Guangdong	0	0	0	0	0
广　西 Guangxi	0	0	0	0	0
海　南 Hainan	0	0	0	0	0
重　庆 Chongqing	0	0	0	0	0
四　川 Sichuan	0	0	0	0	0
贵　州 guizhou	0	0	0	0	0
云　南 Yunnan	0	0	0	0	0
西　藏 Tibet	0	0	0	0	0
陕　西 Shaanxi	0	0	0	0	0
甘　肃 Gansu	0	0	0	0	0
青　海 Qinghai	0	0	0	0	0
宁　夏 Ningxia	0	0	0	0	0
新　疆 Xinjiang	0	0	0	0	0

专科学生数

Peasants Colleges

单位:人

Unit:in Person

Entrants	在校学生数 Enrolment			毕业班学生数 Graduates for Next Year		
专科 Short-cycle Courses	合计 Total	本科 Normal Courses	专科 Short-cycle Courses	合计 Total	本科 Normal Courses	专科 Short-cycle Courses
0	**1008**	**0**	**1008**	**552**	**0**	**552**
0	0	0	0	0	0	0
0	0	0	0	0	0	0
0	0	0	0	0	0	0
0	0	0	0	0	0	0
0	0	0	0	0	0	0
0	0	0	0	0	0	0
0	1008	0	1008	552	0	552
0	0	0	0	0	0	0
0	0	0	0	0	0	0
0	0	0	0	0	0	0
0	0	0	0	0	0	0
0	0	0	0	0	0	0
0	0	0	0	0	0	0
0	0	0	0	0	0	0
0	0	0	0	0	0	0
0	0	0	0	0	0	0
0	0	0	0	0	0	0
0	0	0	0	0	0	0
0	0	0	0	0	0	0
0	0	0	0	0	0	0
0	0	0	0	0	0	0
0	0	0	0	0	0	0
0	0	0	0	0	0	0
0	0	0	0	0	0	0
0	0	0	0	0	0	0
0	0	0	0	0	0	0
0	0	0	0	0	0	0
0	0	0	0	0	0	0
0	0	0	0	0	0	0
0	0	0	0	0	0	0
0	0	0	0	0	0	0

独立函授学院本、

Number of Students in Independent

地　区 Region	毕业生数 Graduates			招生数	
	合　计 Total	本　科 Normal Courses	专　科 Short-cycle Courses	合　计 Total	本　科 Normal Courses
合　计 Total	**4672**	**556**	**4116**	**0**	**0**
北　京 Beijing	0	0	0	0	0
天　津 Tianjin	0	0	0	0	0
河　北 Hebei	0	0	0	0	0
山　西 Shanxi	0	0	0	0	0
内蒙古 Inner Mongolia	0	0	0	0	0
辽　宁 Liaoning	0	0	0	0	0
吉　林 Jilin	0	0	0	0	0
黑龙江 Heilongjiang	0	0	0	0	0
上　海 Shanghai	0	0	0	0	0
江　苏 Jiangsu	0	0	0	0	0
浙　江 Zhejiang	0	0	0	0	0
安　徽 Anhui	0	0	0	0	0
福　建 Fujian	0	0	0	0	0
江　西 Jiangxi	0	0	0	0	0
山　东 Shandong	0	0	0	0	0
河　南 henan	0	0	0	0	0
湖　北 Hubei	0	0	0	0	0
湖　南 Hunan	0	0	0	0	0
广　东 Guangdong	0	0	0	0	0
广　西 Guangxi	0	0	0	0	0
海　南 Hainan	0	0	0	0	0
重　庆 Chongqing	0	0	0	0	0
四　川 Sichuan	4672	556	4116	0	0
贵　州 guizhou	0	0	0	0	0
云　南 Yunnan	0	0	0	0	0
西　藏 Tibet	0	0	0	0	0
陕　西 Shaanxi	0	0	0	0	0
甘　肃 Gansu	0	0	0	0	0
青　海 Qinghai	0	0	0	0	0
宁　夏 Ningxia	0	0	0	0	0
新　疆 Xinjiang	0	0	0	0	0

专科学生数

Correspondence Colleges

单位:人

Unit:in Person

Entrants	在校学生数 Enrolment			毕业班学生数 Graduates for Next Year		
专科 Short-cycle Courses	合计 Total	本科 Normal Courses	专科 Short-cycle Courses	合计 Total	本科 Normal Courses	专科 Short-cycle Courses
0	**10032**	**0**	**10032**	**5326**	**831**	**4495**
0	0	0	0	0	0	0
0	0	0	0	0	0	0
0	0	0	0	0	0	0
0	0	0	0	0	0	0
0	0	0	0	0	0	0
0	0	0	0	0	0	0
0	0	0	0	0	0	0
0	0	0	0	0	0	0
0	0	0	0	0	0	0
0	0	0	0	0	0	0
0	0	0	0	0	0	0
0	0	0	0	0	0	0
0	0	0	0	0	0	0
0	0	0	0	0	0	0
0	0	0	0	0	0	0
0	0	0	0	0	0	0
0	0	0	0	0	0	0
0	0	0	0	0	0	0
0	0	0	0	0	0	0
0	0	0	0	0	0	0
0	0	0	0	0	0	0
0	0	0	0	0	0	0
0	10032	0	10032	5326	831	4495
0	0	0	0	0	0	0
0	0	0	0	0	0	0
0	0	0	0	0	0	0
0	0	0	0	0	0	0
0	0	0	0	0	0	0
0	0	0	0	0	0	0
0	0	0	0	0	0	0
0	0	0	0	0	0	0

教育学院本、

Number of Students in Educational

地 区 Region	毕业生数 Graduates			招生数	
	合 计 Total	本 科 Normal Courses	专 科 Short-cycle Courses	合 计 Total	本 科 Normal Courses
合 计 Total	**109602**	**39224**	**70378**	**0**	**0**
北 京 Beijing	4181	1580	2601	0	0
天 津 Tianjin	0	0	0	0	0
河 北 Hebei	314	0	314	0	0
山 西 Shanxi	590	0	590	0	0
内蒙古 Inner Mongolia	1029	0	1029	0	0
辽 宁 Liaoning	608	298	310	0	0
吉 林 Jilin	2770	1936	834	0	0
黑龙江 Heilongjiang	4900	2199	2701	0	0
上 海 Shanghai	0	0	0	0	0
江 苏 Jiangsu	3677	1926	1751	0	0
浙 江 Zhejiang	8768	5490	3278	0	0
安 徽 Anhui	5544	1769	3775	0	0
福 建 Fujian	3476	1994	1482	0	0
江 西 Jiangxi	5017	2457	2560	0	0
山 东 Shandong	6421	2021	4400	0	0
河 南 henan	5950	1384	4566	0	0
湖 北 Hubei	5275	1977	3298	0	0
湖 南 Hunan	7030	0	7030	0	0
广 东 Guangdong	5884	2638	3246	0	0
广 西 Guangxi	2619	466	2153	0	0
海 南 Hainan	0	0	0	0	0
重 庆 Chongqing	1094	434	660	0	0
四 川 Sichuan	12873	4883	7990	0	0
贵 州 guizhou	7973	2959	5014	0	0
云 南 Yunnan	258	0	258	0	0
西 藏 Tibet	0	0	0	0	0
陕 西 Shaanxi	5246	1817	3429	0	0
甘 肃 Gansu	910	0	910	0	0
青 海 Qinghai	0	0	0	0	0
宁 夏 Ningxia	0	0	0	0	0
新 疆 Xinjiang	7195	996	6199	0	0

专科学生数

Colleges by Type of Courses

单位:人
Unit:in Person

Entrants	在校学生数 Enrolment			毕业班学生数 Graduates for Next Year		
专科 Short-cycle Courses	合计 Total	本科 Normal Courses	专科 Short-cycle Courses	合计 Total	本科 Normal Courses	专科 Short-cycle Courses
0	**326380**	**119489**	**206891**	**116558**	**46816**	**69742**
0	14979	6120	8859	5873	2692	3181
0	0	0	0	0	0	0
0	1362	0	1362	250	0	250
0	3621	0	3621	2080	0	2080
0	6576	0	6576	1039	0	1039
0	2466	1648	818	891	726	165
0	8757	6199	2558	2696	1745	951
0	15137	5497	9640	4765	1683	3082
0	0	0	0	0	0	0
0	11541	6442	5099	4499	2824	1675
0	24660	16611	8049	9071	6271	2800
0	15144	5054	10090	5707	2685	3022
0	12710	7025	5685	3779	2316	1463
0	12449	5607	6842	4638	2168	2470
0	23005	10050	12955	9942	5281	4661
0	20715	4242	16473	9039	1618	7421
0	10832	3669	7163	3520	866	2654
0	11231	0	11231	4744	0	4744
0	18093	9233	8860	6038	3393	2645
0	11252	2688	8564	4098	1289	2809
0	0	0	0	0	0	0
0	6275	3382	2893	2555	1383	1172
0	38406	9091	29315	11559	3549	8010
0	16703	5819	10884	5933	1891	4042
0	1025	0	1025	161	0	161
0	0	0	0	0	0	0
0	12856	4931	7925	3941	1426	2515
0	4161	0	4161	1301	0	1301
0	0	0	0	0	0	0
0	0	0	0	0	0	0
0	22424	6181	16243	8439	3010	5429

管理干部学院本、

Number of Students in Institutes for

地　区 Region	毕业生数 Graduates			招生数	
	合　计 Total	本　科 Normal Courses	专　科 Short-cycle Courses	合　计 Total	本　科 Normal Courses
合　计 Total	**50878**	**4340**	**46538**	**0**	**0**
北　京 Beijing	3018	182	2836	0	0
天　津 Tianjin	2107	0	2107	0	0
河　北 Hebei	1399	0	1399	0	0
山　西 Shanxi	3774	0	3774	0	0
内蒙古 Inner Mongolia	0	0	0	0	0
辽　宁 Liaoning	599	63	536	0	0
吉　林 Jilin	1061	338	723	0	0
黑龙江 Heilongjiang	1535	244	1291	0	0
上　海 Shanghai	1430	0	1430	0	0
江　苏 Jiangsu	1043	40	1003	0	0
浙　江 Zhejiang	0	0	0	0	0
安　徽 Anhui	1000	0	1000	0	0
福　建 Fujian	2284	367	1917	0	0
江　西 Jiangxi	943	246	697	0	0
山　东 Shandong	6117	1059	5058	0	0
河　南 henan	1388	381	1007	0	0
湖　北 Hubei	3810	740	3070	0	0
湖　南 Hunan	1052	169	883	0	0
广　东 Guangdong	5566	95	5471	0	0
广　西 Guangxi	4376	96	4280	0	0
海　南 Hainan	0	0	0	0	0
重　庆 Chongqing	204	0	204	0	0
四　川 Sichuan	5976	286	5690	0	0
贵　州 guizhou	0	0	0	0	0
云　南 Yunnan	0	0	0	0	0
西　藏 Tibet	0	0	0	0	0
陕　西 Shaanxi	2196	34	2162	0	0
甘　肃 Gansu	0	0	0	0	0
青　海 Qinghai	0	0	0	0	0
宁　夏 Ningxia	0	0	0	0	0
新　疆 Xinjiang	0	0	0	0	0

专科学生数

Administration by Type of Courses

单位：人

Unit：in Person

Entrants	在校学生数 Enrolment			毕业班学生数 Graduates for Next Year		
专　科 Short-cycle Courses	合　计 Total	本　科 Normal Courses	专　科 Short-cycle Courses	合　计 Total	本　科 Normal Courses	专　科 Short-cycle Courses
0	**155538**	**12852**	**142686**	**54823**	**5841**	**48982**
0	13053	982	12071	3882	262	3620
0	6029	15	6014	3105	0	3105
0	4912	53	4859	1123	0	1123
0	10098	0	10098	2968	0	2968
0	1562	0	1562	0	0	0
0	1038	277	761	496	179	317
0	3979	584	3395	683	246	437
0	1159	0	1159	2052	227	1825
0	3677	0	3677	1510	0	1510
0	3917	151	3766	504	0	504
0	0	0	0	0	0	0
0	2235	0	2235	637	0	637
0	6873	1396	5477	2473	540	1933
0	2081	624	1457	841	335	506
0	16600	2744	13856	6095	1212	4883
0	2491	770	1721	1390	281	1109
0	13239	2577	10662	4647	1281	3366
0	2669	866	1803	758	311	447
0	22495	269	22226	7817	151	7666
0	16662	629	16033	5255	260	4995
0	0	0	0	0	0	0
0	440	0	440	236	0	236
0	16169	782	15387	6482	457	6025
0	0	0	0	0	0	0
0	0	0	0	0	0	0
0	0	0	0	0	0	0
0	4160	133	4027	1869	99	1770
0	0	0	0	0	0	0
0	0	0	0	0	0	0
0	0	0	0	0	0	0
0	0	0	0	0	0	0

其他机构本、

地　区 Region	毕业生数 Graduates			招生数	
	合　计 Total	本　科 Normal Courses	专　科 Short-cycle Courses	合　计 Total	本　科 Normal Courses
合　计 Total	**4024**	**352**	**3672**	**0**	**0**
北　京 Beijing	265	0	265	0	0
天　津 Tianjin	0	0	0	0	0
河　北 Hebei	0	0	0	0	0
山　西 Shanxi	0	0	0	0	0
内蒙古 Inner Mongolia	0	0	0	0	0
辽　宁 Liaoning	0	0	0	0	0
吉　林 Jilin	607	0	607	0	0
黑龙江 Heilongjiang	0	0	0	0	0
上　海 Shanghai	70	0	70	0	0
江　苏 Jiangsu	0	0	0	0	0
浙　江 Zhejiang	0	0	0	0	0
安　徽 Anhui	0	0	0	0	0
福　建 Fujian	0	0	0	0	0
江　西 Jiangxi	0	0	0	0	0
山　东 Shandong	0	0	0	0	0
河　南 henan	1318	352	966	0	0
湖　北 Hubei	0	0	0	0	0
湖　南 Hunan	1356	0	1356	0	0
广　东 Guangdong	0	0	0	0	0
广　西 Guangxi	266	0	266	0	0
海　南 Hainan	0	0	0	0	0
重　庆 Chongqing	0	0	0	0	0
四　川 Sichuan	0	0	0	0	0
贵　州 guizhou	0	0	0	0	0
云　南 Yunnan	0	0	0	0	0
西　藏 Tibet	0	0	0	0	0
陕　西 Shaanxi	142	0	142	0	0
甘　肃 Gansu	0	0	0	0	0
青　海 Qinghai	0	0	0	0	0
宁　夏 Ningxia	0	0	0	0	0
新　疆 Xinjiang	0	0	0	0	0

专科学生数

单位：人
Unit:in Person

Entrants	在校学生数 Enrolment			毕业班学生数 Graduates for Next Year		
专科 Short-cycle Courses	合计 Total	本科 Normal Courses	专科 Short-cycle Courses	合计 Total	本科 Normal Courses	专科 Short-cycle Courses
0	**16421**	**1111**	**15310**	**5078**	**232**	**4846**
0	1259	0	1259	502	0	502
0	0	0	0	0	0	0
0	0	0	0	0	0	0
0	0	0	0	0	0	0
0	0	0	0	0	0	0
0	368	0	368	0	0	0
0	40	0	40	602	0	602
0	0	0	0	0	0	0
0	19	0	19	0	0	0
0	0	0	0	0	0	0
0	49	0	49	24	0	24
0	0	0	0	0	0	0
0	0	0	0	0	0	0
0	0	0	0	0	0	0
0	14	0	14	0	0	0
0	3925	997	2928	1350	232	1118
0	0	0	0	0	0	0
0	7029	114	6915	1441	0	1441
0	0	0	0	0	0	0
0	0	0	0	266	0	266
0	0	0	0	0	0	0
0	2294	0	2294	0	0	0
0	0	0	0	0	0	0
0	0	0	0	0	0	0
0	0	0	0	0	0	0
0	0	0	0	0	0	0
0	1424	0	1424	893	0	893
0	0	0	0	0	0	0
0	0	0	0	0	0	0
0	0	0	0	0	0	0
0	0	0	0	0	0	0

普通高等学校举办函授、业余、

Number of Students by Type of Courses in Correspondence Courses for Adults run by Regular Institu

地 区 Region	函授、业余 Divisions of Correspondence and Sparetime Schools							
	毕业生数 Graduates			招生数 Entrants			在校学生 Enrolm	
	合 计 Total	本 科 Normal Courses	专 科 Short-cycle Courses	合 计 Total	本 科 Normal Courses	专 科 Short-cycle Courses	合 计 Total	本 科 Normal Courses
合 计 Total	**636345**	**207331**	**429014**	**0**	**0**	**0**	**2472060**	**864379**
北 京 Beijing	42043	17057	24986	0	0	0	154304	65061
天 津 Tianjin	4699	1792	2907	0	0	0	16753	7250
河 北 Hebei	36099	7556	28543	0	0	0	145776	36506
山 西 Shanxi	18946	4585	14361	0	0	0	80744	17421
内蒙古 Inner Mongolia	12352	7702	4650	0	0	0	47282	27937
辽 宁 Liaoning	20018	7470	12548	0	0	0	75937	36785
吉 林 Jilin	22013	10503	11510	0	0	0	77783	39921
黑龙江 Heilongjiang	17422	8734	8688	0	0	0	65404	36604
上 海 Shanghai	7552	3486	4066	0	0	0	29627	14243
江 苏 Jiangsu	37141	13936	23205	0	0	0	151703	64027
浙 江 Zhejiang	39325	20155	19170	0	0	0	150606	69159
安 徽 Anhui	25237	3619	21618	0	0	0	78547	16455
福 建 Fujian	6992	3315	3677	0	0	0	37212	17976
江 西 Jiangxi	14090	6275	7815	0	0	0	61890	27791
山 东 Shandong	43742	11338	32404	0	0	0	178898	61641
河 南 henan	22879	5321	17558	0	0	0	112125	22480
湖 北 Hubei	42306	16007	26299	0	0	0	147814	55989
湖 南 Hunan	39662	11341	28321	0	0	0	155838	43737
广 东 Guangdong	21117	5393	15724	0	0	0	107301	30663
广 西 Guangxi	25165	3514	21651	0	0	0	103222	17188
海 南 Hainan	3891	710	3181	0	0	0	14511	3518
重 庆 Chongqing	12109	4482	7627	0	0	0	50064	21122
四 川 Sichuan	49469	11666	37803	0	0	0	119249	32729
贵 州 guizhou	5695	2186	3509	0	0	0	27861	7155
云 南 Yunnan	13212	3427	9785	0	0	0	71234	22040
西 藏 Tibet	485	91	394	0	0	0	3830	299
陕 西 Shaanxi	26774	8203	18571	0	0	0	102757	33517
甘 肃 Gansu	8381	2962	5319	0	0	0	41215	14657
青 海 Qinghai	611	84	527	0	0	0	3639	1258
宁 夏 Ningxia	3371	1269	2102	0	0	0	11958	4233
新 疆 Xinjiang	13647	3152	10495	0	0	0	46976	15017

脱产分本专科学生数

Divisions、Sparetime Schools & Short-cycle tions of Higher Education

单位:人

Unit:in Person

数 ent	脱产 Short-cycle courses for Adults								
	毕业生数 Graduates			招生数 Entrants			在校学生数 Enrolment		
专科 Short-cycle Courses	合计 Total	本科 Normal Courses	专科 Short-cycle Courses	合计 Total	本科 Normal Courses	专科 Short-cycle Courses	合计 Total	本科 Normal Courses	专科 Short-cycle Courses
1607681	**334145**	**69463**	**264682**	**0**	**0**	**0**	**996742**	**272505**	**724237**
89243	22147	7059	15088	0	0	0	66663	29290	37373
9503	4123	873	3250	0	0	0	12020	3731	8289
109270	18275	2614	15661	0	0	0	54693	10329	44364
63323	6893	1123	5770	0	0	0	21255	3253	18002
19345	5971	732	5239	0	0	0	16864	3693	13171
39152	21422	8179	13243	0	0	0	53634	25032	28602
37862	7200	1653	5547	0	0	0	28131	7944	20187
28800	14441	4465	9976	0	0	0	36511	11429	25082
15384	3025	320	2705	0	0	0	11626	3957	7669
87676	23732	3686	20046	0	0	0	73628	17003	56625
81447	8844	389	8455	0	0	0	29700	5678	24022
62092	11581	2776	8805	0	0	0	34422	9800	24622
19236	4357	134	4223	0	0	0	10030	971	9059
34099	4375	270	4105	0	0	0	17234	2349	14885
117257	4779	991	3788	0	0	0	14682	3039	11643
898645	20470	944	19526	0	0	0	61635	5652	55983
91825	23964	10561	13403	0	0	0	81926	40848	41078
112101	18643	3389	15254	0	0	0	60601	11891	48710
76638	9845	546	9299	0	0	0	18831	1342	17489
86034	2098	138	1960	0	0	0	5229	420	4809
10993	1394	152	1242	0	0	0	5036	1099	3937
28942	10612	2105	8507	0	0	0	27952	11166	16786
86520	31943	4735	27208	0	0	0	91226	21692	69534
20706	16124	2801	13323	0	0	0	43417	8862	34555
49194	6924	1177	5747	0	0	0	30849	4357	26492
3531	528	44	484	0	0	0	1281	59	1222
69240	11793	3643	8150	0	0	0	36255	15071	21184
26558	9120	2033	7087	0	0	0	26004	6532	19472
2381	1872	383	1489	0	0	0	4551	1136	3415
7725	1138	100	1038	0	0	0	3597	487	3110
31959	6512	1448	5064	0	0	0	17259	4393	12866

在职人员攻读博士、硕士

Number of Postgraduate Students

	授予学位数 Degrees Awarded		
	计 Total	博士 Doctor's Degrees	硕士 Master's Degrees
总计 Total	**17663**	**640**	**17023**
北京 Beijing	2984	164	2820
天津 Tianjin	418	34	384
河北 Hebei			
山西 Shanxi	430	10	420
内蒙古 Inner Mongolia	157		157
辽宁 Liaoning	1441	119	1322
吉林 Jilin	672	1	671
黑龙江 Heilongjiang	1454	3	1451
上海 Shanghai	1722	45	1677
江苏 Jiangsu	1054	14	1040
浙江 Zhejiang	501		501
安徽 Anhui	444	12	432
福建 Fujian	315		315
江西 Jiangxi	27		27
山东 Shandong	435	21	414
河南 Henan	121		121
湖北 Hubei	1139	64	1075
湖南 Hunan	381	5	376
广东 Guangdong	639	11	628
广西 Guangxi	64		64
海南 Hainan			
重庆 Chongqing	187	1	186
四川 Sichuan	644		644
贵州 Guizhou	31		31
云南 Yunnan	92	12	80
西藏 Tibet	18		18
陕西 Shaanxi	1289		1289
甘肃 Gansu	945	113	832
青海 Qinghai	15	5	10
宁夏 Ningxia			
新疆 Xinjiang	44	6	38

学位学生数

Studying Without Leaving Their Jobs

单位:人

Unit: in Person

招生数 Entrants			在校学生数 Enrolment		
计 Total	博　士 Doctor's Degrees	硕　士 Master's Degrees	计 Total	博　士 Doctor's Degrees	硕　士 Master's Degrees
59747	1687	58060	149695	4729	144966
8345	456	7889	23531	1263	22268
1667	115	1552	5056	492	4564
1399	45	1354	2580	125	2455
816		816	2301		2301
4391	273	4118	10231	757	9474
2026		2026	3998		3998
2502		2502	6800		6800
6086	314	5772	12798	943	11855
5137	84	5053	13053	237	12816
1458	1	1457	4235	5	4230
2475	25	2450	4908	57	4851
977		977	2835		2835
577		577	1321		1321
1526		1526	3596		3596
1474		1474	2579		2579
4416	145	4271	8687	239	8448
1778		1778	5614		5614
2666	1	2665	5913	6	5907
105		105	582		582
17	9	8	44	17	27
1592	184	1408	4393	504	3889
2578		2578	6603		6603
275		275	364		364
657	15	642	2555	24	2531
15		15	41		41
3893		3893	12737		12737
710	5	705	1999	17	1982
16	6	10	40	15	25
173	9	164	301	28	273

高等教育非学历

Data on Students Enrolled in Non-formal

	毕(结)业生数 Corupleters										
				证书教育 Programs Awarding Certificates on Completion of Courses		岗位培训 Job-related Training		进修及培训 In-service Training			
	研究生课程进修班 Postgraduate Courses	自考助学班 Classes run by Non-state/private HEIs for Students Preparing for State-administered Examinations for Self-directed Leacners	普通预科生 College-preparatory Classes	单科班 Programs Awarding Certificateson Completion of Courses	专业证书班	资格性培训 Job-related Training	适应性培训	一周至三个月以下 In-service Training: a week to 3 months under	三个月至半年以下 3 months to half year under	半年至一年以下 half year to one year under	一年以上 One year and over
合　计 Total	**104355**	**220554**	**12169**	**172949**	**118973**	**1100242**	**673226**	**737394**	**180506**	**152545**	**59620**
北　京 Beijing	18390	24841	384	8439	13470	174277	36955	62930	24296	60347	8451
天　津 Tianjin	2134	10765	25	1838	870	41790	9310	23842	6468	4733	680
河　北 Hebei	1047	7897	0	304	2593	15873	7147	13935	1368	4147	536
山　西 Shanxi	2486	4840	0	32732	447	12919	15476	9077	2863	1509	490
内蒙古 Inner Mongolia	0	1546	287	2677	1895	7870	1743	6107	562	767	1372
辽　宁 Liaoning	3378	4660	342	663	1570	16738	13130	8983	7734	457	2669
吉　林 Jilin	6489	6936	29	142	324	39105	10629	2831	1054	317	231
黑龙江 Heilongjiang	1296	7711	488	2991	3285	31683	7741	13406	1497	1137	923
上　海 Shanghai	5801	33501	121	18183	5249	94709	117813	101737	77052	31225	3945
江　苏 Jiangsu	6567	117	87	1413	16800	38108	23637	18714	3405	2087	1250
浙　江 Zhejiang	6032	2319	0	24051	5899	38427	14628	51329	2825	5101	788
安　徽 Anhui	2878	1309	0	16652	3734	35360	16208	3438	326	844	243
福　建 Fujian	1216	2028	1589	646	641	32878	17833	9715	1240	595	120
江　西 Jiangxi	437	5035	0	1196	1663	12203	3396	9594	1069	1876	21285
山　东 Shandong	8864	4953	105	5125	7600	105898	179200	43713	6311	3971	4129
河　南 henan	2584	25135	0	21347	13784	48176	11271	27363	3070	1826	626
湖　北 Hubei	9398	9891	200	13342	9629	36658	13115	76679	4180	1352	381
湖　南 Hunan	1858	9536	725	1120	7881	49295	23536	25708	1557	7600	399
广　东 Guangdong	3919	10203	647	10127	6433	70431	50907	51391	16396	6875	3169
广　西 Guangxi	3354	2207	195	55	1481	10011	13648	15664	424	8667	456
海　南 Hainan	90	327	39	105	75	711	248	405	47	0	0
重　庆 Chongqing	1827	10792	556	669	1260	12261	5119	24581	2018	1201	95
四　川 Sichuan	6512	10760	2314	4672	5324	28299	20437	15577	3192	1392	2103
贵　州 guizhou	496	1517	673	0	35	8465	5895	2714	32	0	0
云　南 Yunnan	2332	2024	0	0	0	4524	1614	69795	825	216	68
西　藏 Tibet	0	0	0	0	0	0	0	58	783	0	0
陕　西 Shaanxi	1398	15972	122	1360	3144	56029	23388	14930	1762	3170	2602
甘　肃 Gansu	2580	3717	1347	1744	141	14105	17450	15180	6849	896	575
青　海 Qinghai	0	15	889	546	565	5919	2320	999	634	0	0
宁　夏 Ningxia	40	0	1005	130	2236	18305	2847	5032	267	0	934
新　疆 Xinjiang	952	0	0	680	945	39215	6585	11967	400	237	1100

教育学生情况(总计)

Programmes of HEIS(Total)

单位:人

Unit: in Person

注册学生数 Total Enrolment										
研究生课程进修班 Postgraduate Courses	自考助学班 Classes run by Non-state/private HEIs for Students Preparing for State-administered Examinations for Self-directed Leacners	普通预科生 College-preparatory Classes	证书教育 Programs Awarding Certificates on Completion of Courses		岗位培训 Job-related Training		进修及培训 In-service Training			
			单科班 Programs Awarding Certificateson Completion of Courses	专业证书班	资格性培训 Job-related Training	适应性培训	一周至三个月以下 In-service Training: a week to 3 months under	三个月至半年以下 3 months to half year under	半年至一年以下 half year to one year under	一年以上 One year and over
172169	**764010**	**22151**	**79298**	**139752**	**349214**	**271299**	**290190**	**91966**	**101694**	**113443**
29445	145901	565	7353	24587	119606	5424	12128	8104	38280	23603
3065	21653	60	687	2266	4848	1640	5749	1095	6155	1797
1956	51738	47	305	3310	4364	485	1090	733	677	1417
2217	10010	74	25324	27	3251	6673	5810	2965	2122	683
150	4984	1108	1947	1984	1054	40	185	0	584	3350
9333	12729	301	461	4628	4253	1	3883	9098	56	801
7565	20796	226	0	455	1485	4001	1041	79	191	257
2456	16865	2868	44	1541	7271	4448	1580	1014	497	1621
10890	63541	259	7196	5825	47686	169919	31188	42739	20227	10043
14480	13801	312	3043	37770	7696	3550	2182	451	1882	6995
10526	10832	66	10616	7615	8884	9596	10030	797	583	4729
5449	4583	79	0	3453	1362	1091	529	138	1422	241
2685	8874	827	1382	1052	17281	7228	1911	278	1364	545
1152	12184	0	14	711	1653	70	5812	110	1626	24691
14795	20923	172	1864	6672	10594	8967	10387	5585	3720	9084
5466	55453	1317	1634	4287	8506	1727	4805	987	3261	924
15011	53563	646	2623	522	6124	2436	7451	677	971	821
3786	38525	917	1734	3711	23745	822	3699	893	3136	690
7180	26241	656	2744	3374	14230	14547	14159	6145	3804	4737
809	11750	324	0	1052	971	1373	756	67	4627	0
11	361	75	0	230	0	0	0	57	0	0
1264	23651	746	808	3365	13668	8072	148686	1941	704	49
5398	39739	2477	2596	5822	7403	3941	2085	943	2539	4718
738	4797	1579	0	16	0	288	24	0	0	0
5335	945	2333	0	0	447	220	624	228	0	439
0	0	136	0	0	0	0	0	0	0	100
3844	76181	190	3363	9385	14941	3668	7989	3607	2362	8350
5227	10962	1273	2740	4679	5699	7443	632	1751	504	476
0	2428	929	140	350	135	0	0	78	0	0
106	0	1405	0	0	3652	773	4425	0	0	0
1830	0	184	680	1063	8405	2858	1350	1406	400	2282

高等教育非学历

Data on Students Enrolled in Non-formal

	毕(结)业生数 Corupleters										
	研究生课程进修班 Postgra-duate Courses	自考助学班 Classes run by Non-state/private HEIs for Students Preparing for State-administered Examinations for Self-directed Leacners	普通预科生 College-preparatory Classes	证书教育 Programs Awarding Certificates on Completion of Courses		岗位培训 Job-related Training		进修及培训 In-service Training			
				单科班 Programs Awarding Certificateson Completion of Courses	专业证书班	资格性培训 Job-related Training	适应性培训	一周至三个月以下 In-service Training: a week to 3 months under	三个月至半年以下 3 months to half year under	半年至一年以下 half year to one year under	一年以上 One year and over
合　计 Total	**104007**	**77964**	**12169**	**30951**	**31217**	**378048**	**98773**	**336159**	**54754**	**26778**	**13091**
北　京 Beijing	18042	11887	384	1957	1297	115286	8057	38682	16499	6415	3107
天　津 Tianjin	2134	2328	25	198	98	10742	0	7562	155	189	78
河　北 Hebei	1047	235	0	0	1800	12021	4996	12357	833	0	302
山　西 Shanxi	2486	260	0	0	81	0	0	3	0	0	3
内蒙古 Inner Mongolia	0	0	287	2647	1895	4915	1026	5221	0	12	0
辽　宁 Liaoning	3378	803	342	36	986	1406	5510	4545	7661	410	121
吉　林 Jilin	6489	4023	29	0	211	7263	10269	2715	993	190	171
黑龙江 Heilongjiang	1296	835	488	0	302	18440	2105	1134	144	306	387
上　海 Shanghai	5801	3212	121	3914	1259	37392	4678	20527	9911	3600	78
江　苏 Jiangsu	6567	104	87	265	11771	18860	2902	12740	1454	1059	1176
浙　江 Zhejiang	6032	795	0	120	2001	22371	2678	29223	2528	1425	712
安　徽 Anhui	2878	1258	0	0	0	8651	6250	729	0	15	0
福　建 Fujian	1216	1649	1589	400	0	5877	1014	4033	566	412	95
江　西 Jiangxi	437	3458	0	1159	1253	6538	3051	3359	875	283	1515
山　东 Shandong	8864	1422	105	306	578	6711	479	1632	364	477	54
河　南 henan	2584	163	0	16221	0	4304	1713	2391	779	3	147
湖　北 Hubei	9398	7047	200	2975	138	20066	9792	27578	2780	1132	381
湖　南 Hunan	1858	1192	725	10	1089	6134	7690	17526	726	2673	85
广　东 Guangdong	3919	7318	647	14	1207	9142	9224	15180	2479	683	236
广　西 Guangxi	3354	1933	195	55	1432	7281	8306	6396	200	4867	160
海　南 Hainan	90	252	39	105	0	246	248	405	0	0	0
重　庆 Chongqing	1827	4648	556	244	932	3902	654	23416	2018	371	50
四　川 Sichuan	6512	7726	2314	0	0	3326	305	9378	727	1329	1112
贵　州 guizhou	496	209	673	0	35	7429	0	1907	0	0	0
云　南 Yunnan	2332	1772	0	0	0	3024	410	69425	825	216	68
西　藏 Tibet	0	0	0	0	0	0	0	58	783	0	0
陕　西 Shaanxi	1398	11638	122	195	406	5389	270	6343	469	474	1019
甘　肃 Gansu	2580	1782	1347	0	0	64	1120	1874	42	0	0
青　海 Qinghai	0	15	889	0	0	1692	0	889	533	0	0
宁　夏 Ningxia	40	0	1005	130	2236	18305	2847	5032	267	0	934
新　疆 Xinjiang	952	0	0	0	210	11271	3179	3899	143	237	1100

教育学生情况(普通高校)

Programmes of HEIS(Regular HEIs)

单位：人

Unit: in Person

注册学生数 Total Enrolment										
研究生课程进修班 Postgraduate Courses	自考助学班 Classes run by Non-state/private HEIs for Students Preparing for State-administered Examinations for Self-directed Leacners	普通预科生 College-preparatory Classes	证书教育 Programs Awarding Certiticates on Completion of Courses		岗位培训 Job-related Training		进修及培训 In-service Training			
			单科班 Programs Awarding Certificateson Completion of Courses	专业证书班	资格性培训 Job-related Training	适应性培训	一周至三个月以下 In-service Training: a week to 3 months under	三个月至半年以下 3 months to half year under	半年至一年以下 half year to one year under	一年以上 One year and over
171509	**341778**	**22151**	**9517**	**27995**	**156061**	**23813**	**46720**	**34195**	**22544**	**32586**
28981	37485	565	2165	823	101374	989	3605	5645	5021	8625
3065	9414	60	60	301	2673	0	390	0	81	84
1956	10696	47	0	1487	2789	116	0	179	0	1106
2217	579	74	0	0	0	0	132	0	0	195
150	0	1108	1947	1691	179	0	185	0	4	17
9333	3620	301	164	3191	451	0	3883	7528	56	510
7565	13346	226	0	0	16	4000	900	32	150	131
2456	6536	2868	44	352	4200	3860	800	411	0	301
10890	9230	259	748	2575	13104	5581	2573	12510	6351	1525
14480	13717	312	176	9780	2936	777	1536	291	1432	1788
10526	4179	66	96	3344	4818	1268	4828	519	583	4106
5449	2245	79	0	0	483	0	219	0	12	70
2685	7528	827	1150	0	1204	0	159	0	1014	545
1152	8359	0	0	13	75	0	4718	0	0	2396
14600	7988	172	366	954	612	0	894	296	927	530
5466	553	1317	0	0	2553	668	813	0	1	291
15011	43819	646	1704	48	5568	2076	7451	677	971	821
3786	28996	917	0	125	992	40	1404	454	1394	278
7180	16810	656	0	217	1456	2140	3802	325	585	185
809	10554	324	0	982	497	893	270	17	627	0
11	81	75	0	0	0	0	0	0	0	0
1264	14153	746	245	782	1392	120	686	1941	574	49
5397	30142	2477	0	0	50	0	1096	653	2509	2916
738	3352	1579	0	16	0	0	0	0	0	0
5335	463	2333	0	0	447	220	254	228	0	439
0	0	136	0	0	0	0	0	0	0	100
3844	47472	190	652	793	3022	292	1548	2288	131	4121
5227	8316	1273	0	0	4	0	0	68	0	115
0	2145	929	0	0	135	0	0	0	0	0
106	0	1405	0	0	3652	773	4425	0	0	0
1830	0	184	0	521	1379	0	149	133	121	1342

高等教育非学历

Data on Students Enrolled in Non-formal

	毕(结)业生数 Corupleters										
	研究生课程进修班 Postgraduate Courses	自考助学班 Classes run by Non-state/private HEIs for Students Preparing for State-administered Examinations for Self-directed Leacners	普通预科生 College-preparatory Classes	证书教育 Programs Awarding Certiticates on Completion of Courses		岗位培训 Job-related Training		进修及培训 In-service Training			
				单科班 Programs Awarding Certificateson Completion of Courses	专业证书班	资格性培训 Job-related Training	适应性培训	一周至三个月以下 In-service Training: a week to 3 months under	三个月至半年以下 3 months to half year under	半年至一年以下 half year to one year under	一年以上 One year and over
合　计 Total	**0**	**6762**	**0**	**108620**	**42764**	**565100**	**535112**	**274246**	**30899**	**18856**	**5083**
北　京 Beijing	0	1479	0	1353	1354	37527	27216	10271	6246	3927	295
天　津 Tianjin	0	752	0	757	341	25354	9072	7995	5369	16	0
河　北 Hebei	0	0	0	0	0	2254	60	168	0	0	0
山　西 Shanxi	0	0	0	32237	305	10965	15348	7213	1932	112	0
内蒙古 Inner Mongolia	0	0	0	30	0	121	0	600	540	170	0
辽　宁 Liaoning	0	197	0	627	584	15282	7620	4438	73	47	2548
吉　林 Jilin	0	0	0	142	0	31436	150	0	0	0	0
黑龙江 Heilongjiang	0	0	0	991	1484	12210	5559	9846	271	0	0
上　海 Shanghai	0	2392	0	7265	899	17330	101823	15324	4248	3806	1009
江　苏 Jiangsu	0	0	0	1032	5029	19248	20735	5974	1951	1028	74
浙　江 Zhejiang	0	158	0	22850	3898	11438	11950	19243	0	94	25
安　徽 Anhui	0	51	0	16652	1814	26709	9958	2149	0	99	0
福　建 Fujian	0	379	0	246	641	27001	16819	5682	674	183	25
江　西 Jiangxi	0	0	0	0	0	3615	277	6122	0	379	0
山　东 Shandong	0	0	0	3448	3416	86970	169803	29660	707	32	0
河　南 henan	0	0	0	3737	3940	39493	8276	21018	1230	1313	22
湖　北 Hubei	0	0	0	4103	7027	8834	2802	49101	1400	220	0
湖　南 Hunan	0	0	0	406	1807	23244	15726	7245	620	37	200
广　东 Guangdong	0	0	0	4645	2956	49426	32323	29944	2806	1242	524
广　西 Guangxi	0	220	0	0	0	2705	5315	9268	224	3800	296
海　南 Hainan	0	0	0	0	0	465	0	0	0	0	0
重　庆 Chongqing	0	0	0	425	294	7916	4430	0	0	830	45
四　川 Sichuan	0	150	0	4568	4564	18330	18579	5033	987	31	0
贵　州 guizhou	0	984	0	0	0	1036	5895	807	32	0	0
云　南 Yunnan	0	0	0	0	0	1500	1204	370	0	0	0
西　藏 Tibet	0	0	0	556	970	47568	22905	7459	968	1490	0
陕　西 Shaanxi	0	0	0	1324	141	4952	15541	11138	263	0	20
甘　肃 Gansu	0	0	0	546	565	4227	2320	110	101	0	0
青　海 Qinghai	0	0	0	0	0	0	0	0	0	0	0
宁　夏 Ningxia	0	0	0	680	735	27944	3406	8068	257	0	0
新　疆 Xinjiang	952	0	0	0	210	11271	3179	3899	143	237	1100

教育学生情况(成人高校)

Programmes of HEIS(HEIs for Adults)

单位:人

Unit: in Person

注册学生数 Total Enrolment										
研究生课程进修班 Postgraduate Courses	自考助学班 Classes run by Non-state/private HEIs for Students Preparing for State-administered Examinations for Self-directed Leacners	普通预科生 College-preparatory Classes	证书教育 Programs Awarding Certiticates on Completion of Courses		岗位培训 Job-related Training		进修及培训 In-service Training			
			单科班 Programs Awarding Certificateson Completion of Courses	专业证书班	资格性培训 Job-related Training	适应性培训	一周至三个月以下 In-service Training: a week to 3 months under	三个月至半年以下 3 months to half year under	半年至一年以下 half year to one year under	一年以上 One year and over
0	**15172**	**0**	**51113**	**59735**	**124929**	**231599**	**204321**	**12451**	**12004**	**11597**
0	1227	0	1233	3923	10658	2149	2746	1140	2328	397
0	2077	0	114	159	1453	1560	4470	739	169	0
0	0	0	0	0	283	0	89	0	0	0
0	0	0	25249	27	1344	6442	4097	1940	118	0
0	0	0	0	0	237	0	0	0	300	0
0	236	0	297	1410	3802	0	0	1570	0	291
0	0	0	0	0	1375	0	119	0	0	0
0	24	0	0	62	1416	580	270	0	0	0
0	7380	0	705	126	26948	163804	10911	3033	918	395
0	0	0	2732	27990	4760	2773	646	160	450	5207
0	746	0	9820	4271	3306	8328	4611	0	0	0
0	203	0	0	1003	749	1091	0	0	0	0
0	1315	0	232	1052	16077	7228	1752	278	350	0
0	0	0	0	0	556	70	1050	0	379	0
0	0	0	0	0	3870	6150	6308	556	0	3720
0	0	0	239	1980	3310	70	268	0	50	44
0	0	0	919	474	556	360	0	0	0	0
0	0	0	111	2499	5218	538	1806	333	1702	134
0	0	0	910	408	6757	8619	8523	228	286	290
0	337	0	0	0	474	450	486	50	4000	0
0	0	0	0	0	0	0	0	0	0	0
0	0	0	563	2583	6078	4169	148000	0	130	0
0	1083	0	2542	4274	6611	3796	560	120	0	0
0	544	0	0	0	0	288	24	0	0	0
0	0	0	0	0	0	0	370	0	0	0
0	0	0	2007	1997	7328	3069	5768	750	510	46
0	0	0	2620	4605	4737	7207	246	203	35	133
0	0	0	140	350	0	0	0	78	0	0
0	0	0	0	0	0	0	0	0	0	0
0	0	0	680	542	7026	2858	1201	1273	279	940
1830	0	184	0	521	1379	0	149	133	121	1342

高等教育非学历

Data on Students Enrolled in Non-formal

	毕(结)业生数 Corupleters										
	研究生课程进修班 Postgra-duate Courses	自考助学班 Classes run by Non-state/private HEIs for Students Preparing for State-administered Examinations for Self-directed Leacners	普通预科生 College-preparatory Classes	证书教育 Programs Awarding Certiticates on Completion of Courses		岗位培训 Job-related Training		进修及培训 In-service Training			
				单科班 Programs Awarding Certificateson Completion of Courses	专业证书班	资格性培训 Job-related Training	适应性培训	一周至三个月以下 In-service Training: a week to 3 months under	三个月至半年以下 3 months to half year under	半年至一年以下 half year to one year under	一年以上 One year and over
合　计 Total	**0**	**135828**	**0**	**33378**	**44992**	**156818**	**37385**	**126853**	**94837**	**106792**	**41446**
北　京 Beijing	0	11475	0	5129	10819	21458	1682	13977	1551	49886	5049
天　津 Tianjin	0	7685	0	883	431	5694	238	8285	944	4528	602
河　北 Hebei	0	7662	0	304	793	1377	180	1410	535	4147	234
山　西 Shanxi	0	4580	0	495	61	1954	128	1861	931	1397	487
内蒙古 Inner Mongolia	0	1546	0	0	0	2834	717	286	22	585	1372
辽　宁 Liaoning	0	3660	0	0	0	50	0	0	0	0	0
吉　林 Jilin	0	2913	0	0	113	406	210	116	61	127	60
黑龙江 Heilongjiang	0	6876	0	2000	1499	1033	77	2426	1082	831	536
上　海 Shanghai	0	27897	0	7004	3091	39987	11312	65886	62893	23819	2858
江　苏 Jiangsu	0	13	0	116	0	0	0	0	0	0	0
浙　江 Zhejiang	0	1366	0	1081	0	4618	0	2863	297	3582	51
安　徽 Anhui	0	0	0	0	1920	0	0	560	326	730	243
福　建 Fujian	0	0	0	0	0	0	0	0	0	0	0
江　西 Jiangxi	0	1577	0	37	410	2050	68	113	194	1214	19770
山　东 Shandong	0	3531	0	1371	3606	12217	8918	12421	5240	3462	4075
河　南 henan	0	24972	0	1389	9844	4379	1282	3954	1061	510	457
湖　北 Hubei	0	2844	0	6264	2464	7758	521	0	0	0	0
湖　南 Hunan	0	8344	0	704	4985	19917	120	937	211	4890	114
广　东 Guangdong	0	2885	0	5468	2270	11863	9360	6267	11111	4950	2409
广　西 Guangxi	0	54	0	0	49	25	27	0	0	0	0
海　南 Hainan	0	75	0	0	75	0	0	0	47	0	0
重　庆 Chongqing	0	6144	0	0	34	443	35	1165	0	0	0
四　川 Sichuan	0	2884	0	104	760	6643	1553	1166	1478	32	991
贵　州 guizhou	0	324	0	0	0	0	0	0	0	0	0
云　南 Yunnan	0	252	0	0	0	0	0	0	0	0	0
西　藏 Tibet											
陕　西 Shaanxi	0	4334	0	609	1768	3023	168	992	309	1206	1583
甘　肃 Gansu	0	1935	0	420	0	9089	789	2168	6544	896	555
青　海 Qinghai	0	0	0	0	0	0	0	0	0	0	0
宁　夏 Ningxia											
新　疆 Xinjiang											

教育学生情况(民办的其他高等教育机构)

Programmes of HEIS(Non-state/Private HEIs)

单位:人

Unit: in Person

注册学生数 Total Enrolment										
研究生课程进修班 Postgraduate Courses	自考助学班 Classes run by Non-state/private HEIs for Students Preparing for State-administered Examinations for Self-directed Leacners	普通预科生 College-preparatory Classes	证书教育 Programs Awarding Certificates on Completion of Courses		岗位培训 Job-related Training		进修及培训 In-service Training			
			单科班 Programs Awarding Certificateson Completion of Courses	专业证书班	资格性培训 Job-related Training	适应性培训	一周至三个月以下 In-service Training: a week to 3 months under	三个月至半年以下 3 months to half year under	半年至一年以下 half year to one year under	一年以上 One year and over
0	**407060**	**0**	**18668**	**52022**	**68224**	**15887**	**39149**	**45320**	**67098**	**69260**
0	107189	0	3955	19841	7574	2286	5777	1319	30883	14581
0	10162	0	513	1806	722	80	889	356	5905	1713
0	41042	0	305	1823	1292	369	1001	554	677	311
0	9431	0	75	0	1907	231	1581	1025	2004	488
0	4984	0	0	293	638	40	0	0	280	3333
0	8873	0	0	27	0	0	0	0	0	0
0	7450	0	0	455	94	0	22	47	41	126
0	10305	0	0	1127	1655	8	510	603	497	1320
0	46931	0	5743	3124	7634	534	17704	27196	12958	8123
0	84	0	135	0	0	0	0	0	0	0
0	5907	0	700	0	760	0	591	278	0	623
0	2135	0	0	2450	130	0	310	138	1410	171
0	31	0	0	0	0	0	0	0	0	0
0	3825	0	14	698	1022	0	44	110	1247	22295
0	12935	0	1498	5718	6112	2817	3185	4733	2793	4834
0	54900	0	1395	2307	2643	989	3724	987	3210	589
0	9744	0	0	0	0	0	0	0	0	0
0	9529	0	1623	1087	17535	244	489	106	40	278
0	9431	0	1834	2749	6017	3788	1834	5592	2933	4262
0	859	0	0	70	0	30	0	0	0	0
0	280	0	0	230	0	0	0	57	0	0
0	9498	0	0	0	6198	3783	0	0	0	0
0	8514	0	54	1548	742	145	429	170	30	1802
0	901	0	0	0	0	0	0	0	0	0
0	482	0	0	0	0	0	0	0	0	0
0	28709	0	704	6595	4591	307	673	569	1721	4183
0	2646	0	120	74	958	236	386	1480	469	228
0	283	0	0	0	0	0	0	0	0	0

高等教育非学历

Data on Students Enrolled in Non-formal

	毕(结)业生数 Corupleters										
	研究生课程进修班 Postgra-duate Courses	自考助学班 Classes run by Non-state/private HEIs for Students Preparing for State-administered Examinations for Self-directed Leacners	普通预科生 College-preparatory Classes	证书教育 Programs Awarding Certiticates on Completion of Courses		岗位培训 Job-related Training		进修及培训 In-service Training			
				单科班 Programs Awarding Certificateson Completion of Courses	专业证书班	资格性培训 Job-related Training	适应性培训	一周至三个月以下 In-service Training: a week to 3 months under	三个月至半年以下 3 months to half year under	半年至一年以下 half year to one year under	一年以上 One year and over
合　计 Total	**348**	**0**	**0**	**0**	**0**	**276**	**1956**	**136**	**16**	**119**	**0**
北　京 Beijing	348	0	0	0	0	6	0	0	0	119	0
天　津 Tianjin	0	0	0	0	0	0	0	0	0	0	0
河　北 Hebei	0	0	0	0	0	221	1911	0	0	0	0
山　西 Shanxi	0	0	0	0	0	0	0	0	0	0	0
内蒙古 Inner Mongolia	0	0	0	0	0	0	0	0	0	0	0
辽　宁 Liaoning	0	0	0	0	0	0	0	0	0	0	0
吉　林 Jilin	0	0	0	0	0	0	0	0	0	0	0
黑龙江 Heilongjiang	0	0	0	0	0	0	0	0	0	0	0
上　海 Shanghai	0	0	0	0	0	0	0	0	0	0	0
江　苏 Jiangsu	0	0	0	0	0	0	0	0	0	0	0
浙　江 Zhejiang	0	0	0	0	0	0	0	0	0	0	0
安　徽 Anhui	0	0	0	0	0	0	0	0	0	0	0
福　建 Fujian	0	0	0	0	0	0	0	0	0	0	0
江　西 Jiangxi	0	0	0	0	0	0	0	0	0	0	0
山　东 Shandong	0	0	0	0	0	0	0	0	0	0	0
河　南 henan	0	0	0	0	0	0	0	0	0	0	0
湖　北 Hubei	0	0	0	0	0	0	0	0	0	0	0
湖　南 Hunan	0	0	0	0	0	0	0	0	0	0	0
广　东 Guangdong	0	0	0	0	0	0	0	0	0	0	0
广　西 Guangxi	0	0	0	0	0	0	0	0	0	0	0
海　南 Hainan	0	0	0	0	0	0	0	0	0	0	0
重　庆 Chongqing	0	0	0	0	0	0	0	0	0	0	0
四　川 Sichuan	0	0	0	0	0	0	0	0	0	0	0
贵　州 guizhou	0	0	0	0	0	0	0	0	0	0	0
云　南 Yunnan	0	0	0	0	0	0	0	0	0	0	0
西　藏 Tibet	0	0	0	0	0	0	0	0	0	0	0
陕　西 Shaanxi	0	0	0	0	0	49	45	136	16	0	0
甘　肃 Gansu	0	0	0	0	0	0	0	0	0	0	0
青　海 Qinghai	0	0	0	0	0	0	0	0	0	0	0
宁　夏 Ningxia	0	0	0	0	0	0	0	0	0	0	0
新　疆 Xinjiang	0	0	0	0	0	0	0	0	0	0	0

教育学生情况(科研机构)

Programmes of HEIS (Research Institutes)

单位:人

Unit: in Person

注册学生数 Total Enrolment										
研究生课程进修班 Postgraduate Courses	自考助学班 Classes run by Non-state/private HEIs for Students Preparing for State-administered Examinations for Self-directed Leacners	普通预科生 College-preparatory Classes	证书教育 Programs Awarding Certificates on Completion of Courses		岗位培训 Job-related Training		进修及培训 In-service Training			
			单科班 Programs Awarding Certificateson Completion of Courses	专业证书班	资格性培训 Job-related Training	适应性培训	一周至三个月以下 In-service Training: a week to 3 months under	三个月至半年以下 3 months to half year under	半年至一年以下 half year to one year under	一年以上 One year and over
660	**0**	**0**	**0**	**0**	**0**	**0**	**0**	**0**	**48**	**0**
464	0	0	0	0	0	0	0	0	48	0
0	0	0	0	0	0	0	0	0	0	0
0	0	0	0	0	0	0	0	0	0	0
0	0	0	0	0	0	0	0	0	0	0
0	0	0	0	0	0	0	0	0	0	0
0	0	0	0	0	0	0	0	0	0	0
0	0	0	0	0	0	0	0	0	0	0
0	0	0	0	0	0	0	0	0	0	0
0	0	0	0	0	0	0	0	0	0	0
0	0	0	0	0	0	0	0	0	0	0
0	0	0	0	0	0	0	0	0	0	0
0	0	0	0	0	0	0	0	0	0	0
0	0	0	0	0	0	0	0	0	0	0
0	0	0	0	0	0	0	0	0	0	0
195	0	0	0	0	0	0	0	0	0	0
0	0	0	0	0	0	0	0	0	0	0
0	0	0	0	0	0	0	0	0	0	0
0	0	0	0	0	0	0	0	0	0	0
0	0	0	0	0	0	0	0	0	0	0
0	0	0	0	0	0	0	0	0	0	0
0	0	0	0	0	0	0	0	0	0	0
0	0	0	0	0	0	0	0	0	0	0
1	0	0	0	0	0	0	0	0	0	0
0	0	0	0	0	0	0	0	0	0	0
0	0	0	0	0	0	0	0	0	0	0
0	0	0	0	0	0	0	0	0	0	0
0	0	0	0	0	0	0	0	0	0	0
0	0	0	0	0	0	0	0	0	0	0
0	0	0	0	0	0	0	0	0	0	0
0	0	0	0	0	0	0	0	0	0	0
0	0	0	0	0	0	0	0	0	0	0

外国留

Information on

地　区 Region	毕(结)业生数 Graduates	授予学位数 Degrees Awarded	招生数 Entrants 计 Total	其中:春季招生 Of Which:Spring term
合　计 Total	**34349**	**2901**	**40165**	**13913**
北　京 Beijing	15775	1307	13896	4159
天　津 Tianjin	2053	204	2431	1106
河　北 Hebei	155	11	149	56
山　西 Shanxi	18	0	38	0
内蒙古 Inner Mongolia	75	14	126	37
辽　宁 Liaoning	1623	128	1946	939
吉　林 Jilin	653	121	1213	489
黑龙江 Heilongjiang	1265	74	1158	418
上　海 Shanghai	3812	275	7015	2875
江　苏 Jiangsu	838	222	1314	363
浙　江 Zhejiang	1016	42	1341	731
安　徽 Anhui	253	3	313	71
福　建 Fujian	507	31	515	230
江　西 Jiangxi	24	2	60	16
山　东 Shandong	1478	73	1860	706
河　南 henan	449	50	547	180
湖　北 Hubei	394	120	592	125
湖　南 Hunan	88	29	141	31
广　东 Guangdong	1163	88	1034	304
广　西 Guangxi	515	26	1171	349
海　南 Hainan	36	0	104	36
重　庆 Chongqing	115	5	115	54
四　川 Sichuan	392	15	536	148
贵　州 guizhou	25	0	33	7
云　南 Yunnan	1085	5	1287	0
西　藏 Tibet	0	0	0	0
陕　西 Shaanxi	392	56	830	411
甘　肃 Gansu	35	0	48	25
青　海 Qinghai	29	0	67	10
宁　夏 Ningxia	11	0	7	4
新　疆 Xinjiang	75	0	278	33

学生情况

Foreign Students

单位:人

Unit: in Person

在校学生数 Enrolment					
计 Total	第一年 1st year	第二年 2st year	第三年 3st year	第四年 4st year	第五年 5st year
53461	**35069**	**10379**	**4530**	**2592**	**891**
17031	11332	3234	1370	839	256
3389	2196	633	288	221	51
341	247	60	11	19	4
50	38	9	3	0	0
202	148	32	13	5	4
3080	2099	616	248	91	26
2227	987	529	310	264	137
1507	770	451	143	94	49
8589	5947	1483	685	353	121
2262	1329	574	214	117	28
1350	954	230	92	37	37
361	256	67	21	17	0
647	278	226	101	41	1
99	61	5	3	28	2
2443	1793	359	191	84	16
935	542	190	101	64	38
1186	560	372	137	74	43
313	156	81	47	19	10
1463	1060	190	132	66	15
1171	847	202	68	45	9
106	102	4	0	0	0
227	135	47	41	4	0
843	591	176	47	20	9
33	30	1	2	0	0
1881	1561	239	75	5	1
39	27	12	0	0	0
1082	668	222	87	71	34
89	67	17	2	3	0
82	67	15	0	0	0
19	7	8	4	0	0
414	214	95	94	11	0

高等教育学校(机构)
Aggregate Data on Staff

地区 Region	计 Total	教职 Teacher, staff				
		校本部 Teacher, staff & Workers				
		计 Total	专任教师 Full-time Teachers			
			计 Total	正高级 Senior	副高级 Sub-senior	中级 Middle
合　计 Total	**1663557**	**1475680**	**834342**	**75636**	**245795**	**285286**
北　京 Beijing	120929	97818	44984	8256	15488	14622
天　津 Tianjin	40323	36195	18987	2295	6636	5961
河　北 Hebei	76313	68404	38844	3521	11999	12200
山　西 Shanxi	45193	41707	23608	1628	6399	8275
内蒙古 Inner Mongolia	25750	24218	13516	722	3999	4796
辽　宁 Liaoning	83267	74925	42023	3899	13970	14487
吉　林 Jilin	53489	48479	25228	2736	7590	8322
黑龙江 Heilongjiang	72611	62633	34659	3355	11712	10532
上　海 Shanghai	68559	54079	26761	3567	8038	10249
江　苏 Jiangsu	112981	98695	57073	4920	15339	18805
浙　江 Zhejiang	61956	56267	34407	2690	9314	11329
安　徽 Anhui	49099	45505	27376	1775	7519	8762
福　建 Fujian	35497	32086	18796	1733	5331	6211
江　西 Jiangxi	46978	41792	24346	1700	6835	7595
山　东 Shandong	100655	92295	54357	5447	16614	16658
河　南 henan	70973	65116	39811	2138	11028	14095
湖　北 Hubei	101733	89441	50948	5144	16227	17449
湖　南 Hunan	73831	64952	37367	3219	11147	13301
广　东 Guangdong	87348	79548	49798	3814	13338	18982
广　西 Guangxi	27955	26055	15789	908	4029	6528
海　南 Hainan	5283	4845	2784	244	769	844
重　庆 Chongqing	35662	31927	18500	1515	5264	6995
四　川 Sichuan	72402	64262	36721	3125	10678	12697
贵　州 guizhou	22152	20751	12750	714	3293	4697
云　南 Yunnan	26171	24347	13677	999	3811	5097
西　藏 Tibet	1794	1749	972	21	162	434
陕　西 Shaanxi	78569	67405	35716	3800	10318	11751
甘　肃 Gansu	24802	22244	13347	879	3313	4775
青　海 Qinghai	6847	5903	3551	108	832	1683
宁　夏 Ningxia	6383	5866	3415	223	1008	1189
新　疆 Xinjiang	28052	26171	14231	541	3795	5965

教职工情况(总计)

and Workers in HEIs(Total)

单位:人

Unit:in Person

工　数 & Workers							
教职工 in College or Uni. Proper					科研机构人员 Personnel in Affiliated Research Org.	校办企业职工 Employees in School-run Factories & Farms	其他附设机构人员 Personnel in Others Subsidiary Units
初　级 Junior	无职称 No Rank	行政人员 Adm. Personnel	教辅人员 Supporting Staff	工勤人员 Workers			
168943	**58682**	**271139**	**184163**	**186036**	**42971**	**60385**	**84521**
4601	2017	21602	16908	14324	12369	4904	5838
3307	788	7335	5067	4806	1250	1556	1322
7955	3169	11859	7513	10188	459	2828	4622
5258	2048	7398	4924	5777	506	1296	1684
3184	815	4690	3276	2736	150	429	953
7326	2341	13685	9909	9308	1720	2467	4155
5123	1457	9345	6458	7448	1074	1166	2770
6814	2246	10810	7416	9748	1301	3098	5579
3779	1128	10402	8769	8147	2879	4312	7289
13832	4177	17606	12158	11858	2912	4248	7126
7921	3153	9611	6866	5383	1229	1671	2789
6843	2477	7082	5273	5774	970	668	1956
4163	1358	6351	3575	3364	600	1745	1066
6145	2071	7813	4183	5450	470	2978	1738
11112	4526	17358	10881	9699	1433	3873	3054
9549	3001	10965	7182	7158	611	2581	2665
8577	3551	16715	11211	10567	2017	3940	6335
6852	2848	11747	8284	7554	1292	2778	4809
10210	3454	13939	9152	6659	1465	2665	3670
3228	1096	4214	3150	2902	302	879	719
595	332	946	481	634	54	115	269
3748	978	5628	3777	4022	915	895	1925
7581	2640	11235	7776	8530	1805	2644	3691
3057	989	3600	2163	2238	333	760	308
2619	1151	4720	2966	2984	422	795	607
302	53	353	194	230	26	5	14
7210	2637	13420	8005	10264	3083	3269	4812
3374	1006	3646	2441	2810	666	910	982
764	164	1019	743	590	503	178	263
768	227	1107	491	853	51	21	445
3146	784	4938	2971	4031	104	711	1066

高等教育学校(机构)

Aggregate Data on Female Staff

地区 Region	教职 Teacher, staff					
	计 Total	校本部 Teacher, staff & Workers				
		计 Total	专任教师 Full-time Teachers			
			计 Total	正高级 Senior	副高级 Sub-senior	中级 Middle
合　计 Total	**709412**	**632560**	**351618**	**13745**	**90481**	**130086**
北　京 Beijing	58089	47741	20608	1689	6804	8148
天　津 Tianjin	18103	16655	8749	459	2905	3096
河　北 Hebei	34218	30944	18465	916	5186	6343
山　西 Shanxi	20697	19192	11255	393	2618	4160
内蒙古 Inner Mongolia	11818	11193	6702	133	1730	2567
辽　宁 Liaoning	38261	35138	20844	930	6494	7887
吉　林 Jilin	23258	21299	11812	688	3431	4157
黑龙江 Heilongjiang	32398	27929	16075	829	5201	5127
上　海 Shanghai	29680	23731	10738	394	2615	4859
江　苏 Jiangsu	45982	40148	22634	569	4692	7980
浙　江 Zhejiang	26678	24464	14388	363	3107	4880
安　徽 Anhui	18031	16654	9660	237	2205	3052
福　建 Fujian	14557	13299	7586	238	1764	2663
江　西 Jiangxi	18352	16285	9141	232	2166	2968
山　东 Shandong	41923	38552	23471	1241	6256	7775
河　南 henan	27738	25621	15826	441	3699	5912
湖　北 Hubei	41786	36338	19148	772	5159	7305
湖　南 Hunan	30610	27074	14323	437	3674	5559
广　东 Guangdong	38236	34297	19945	522	4481	8362
广　西 Guangxi	12047	11206	6276	108	1296	2810
海　南 Hainan	2215	2027	1121	49	234	399
重　庆 Chongqing	14284	12718	7099	208	1690	2906
四　川 Sichuan	28618	25626	14041	573	3505	5035
贵　州 guizhou	10071	9536	5666	162	1228	2175
云　南 Yunnan	12031	11222	6286	220	1599	2407
西　藏 Tibet	711	696	402	3	49	173
陕　西 Shaanxi	31354	27519	14349	594	3337	5295
甘　肃 Gansu	9491	8646	5094	145	970	1887
青　海 Qinghai	2869	2560	1660	30	379	758
宁　夏 Ningxia	2905	2703	1629	54	431	576
新　疆 Xinjiang	12401	11547	6625	116	1576	2865

女教职工情况(总计)

and Workers in HEIs(Total)

单位:人
Unit:in Person

工数 & Workers							
教职工 in College or Uni. Proper					科研机构人员 Personnel in Affiliated Research Org.	校办企业职工 Employees in School-run Factories & Farms	其他附设机构人员 Personnel in Others Subsidiary Units
初级 Junior	无职称 No Rank	行政人员 Adm. Personnel	教辅人员 Supporting Staff	工勤人员 Workers			
86102	**31204**	**116105**	**96751**	**68086**	**15404**	**19745**	**41703**
2832	1135	11311	10178	5644	5729	1684	2935
1851	438	3466	2767	1673	338	422	688
4226	1794	4612	4144	3723	141	995	2138
2915	1169	3159	2740	2038	182	531	792
1839	433	1858	1740	893	41	141	443
4251	1282	6178	5344	2772	665	658	1800
2735	801	3713	3426	2348	303	325	1331
3613	1305	4660	3616	3578	574	1023	2872
2216	654	4927	4533	3533	1015	1654	3280
7088	2305	7175	5792	4547	747	1291	3796
4222	1816	4290	3605	2181	376	538	1300
3026	1140	2566	2526	1902	256	151	970
2188	733	2638	1745	1330	182	536	540
2771	1004	2958	2088	2098	123	1118	826
5781	2418	6337	5444	3300	571	1207	1593
4345	1429	4063	3521	2211	180	701	1236
4143	1769	7205	5936	4049	566	1332	3550
3226	1427	5128	4510	3113	424	936	2176
4845	1735	6558	4961	2833	517	980	2442
1485	577	1924	1788	1218	103	315	423
286	153	364	268	274	15	23	150
1760	535	2519	1692	1408	311	312	943
3637	1291	4972	3796	2817	569	788	1635
1562	539	1726	1296	848	102	275	158
1440	620	2047	1592	1297	157	262	390
149	28	121	104	69	3	1	11
3647	1476	5454	4086	3630	806	967	2062
1577	515	1319	1173	1060	178	244	423
397	96	347	388	165	171	51	87
427	141	438	291	345	16	8	178
1622	446	2072	1661	1189	43	276	535

高等教育学校(机构)

Aggregate Data on Staff

地区 Region	教职 Teacher, staff 计 Total	校本部 Teacher, staff & Workers 计 Total	专任教师 Full-time Teachers 计 Total	正高级 Senior	副高级 Sub-senior	中级 Middle
合计 Total	**1452623**	**1271567**	**724658**	**70063**	**216161**	**240555**
北京 Beijing	103220	80488	38007	6973	13137	12293
天津 Tianjin	33371	29348	15553	2171	5388	4625
河北 Hebei	67962	60255	34542	3124	10618	10733
山西 Shanxi	38358	35317	20224	1457	5339	6983
内蒙古 Inner Mongolia	22592	21068	12153	713	3591	4179
辽宁 Liaoning	75632	67425	38086	3780	12697	12828
吉林 Jilin	46950	42028	21824	2544	6626	6898
黑龙江 Heilongjiang	60609	51053	28525	3128	9470	8073
上海 Shanghai	63138	48782	24387	3492	7458	9037
江苏 Jiangsu	100789	86720	49826	4759	13881	15932
浙江 Zhejiang	54331	48691	29945	2585	8426	9506
安徽 Anhui	44395	41022	24744	1728	6813	7815
福建 Fujian	30699	27430	16171	1654	4707	5214
江西 Jiangxi	41621	36918	21938	1588	6121	6724
山东 Shandong	84393	76842	45457	4752	14280	13588
河南 henan	59680	54157	33344	1890	9304	11451
湖北 Hubei	94215	82089	46947	5036	15145	15626
湖南 Hunan	66084	57484	33229	3019	10089	11356
广东 Guangdong	70394	63080	40192	3444	11249	14612
广西 Guangxi	24746	22943	14106	885	3615	5661
海南 Hainan	5157	4719	2699	239	755	813
重庆 Chongqing	31070	27468	16013	1353	4700	6041
四川 Sichuan	62457	54734	31372	2855	9207	10353
贵州 guizhou	20400	19020	11775	699	3061	4249
云南 Yunnan	23662	21929	12236	991	3522	4449
西藏 Tibet	1794	1749	972	21	162	434
陕西 Shaanxi	67527	57077	30696	3491	8936	9729
甘肃 Gansu	23012	20520	12274	846	3003	4285
青海 Qinghai	5589	4684	2769	102	702	1231
宁夏 Ningxia	6383	5866	3415	223	1008	1189
新疆 Xinjiang	22393	20661	11237	521	3151	4648

教职工情况(普通高校)

and Workers in HEIs(Regular HEIs)

单位:人

Unit:in Person

工　　数

& Workers

教职工 in College or Uni. Proper					科研机构人员 Personnel in Affiliated Research Org.	校办企业职工 Employees in School-run Factories & Farms	其他附设机构人员 Personnel in Others Subsidiary Units
初　级 Junior	无职称 No Rank	行政人员 Adm. Personnel	教辅人员 Supporting Staff	工勤人员 Workers			
146092	**51787**	**225725**	**160180**	**161004**	**42240**	**57166**	**81650**
3892	1712	16128	14564	11789	12289	4827	5616
2727	642	5657	4107	4031	1238	1484	1301
7197	2870	10151	6596	8966	444	2729	4534
4578	1867	6010	4194	4889	486	936	1619
2877	793	3830	2871	2214	150	421	953
6671	2110	11934	9093	8312	1715	2430	4062
4440	1316	7870	5708	6626	1058	1130	2734
5913	1941	8410	6092	8026	1222	3016	5318
3333	1067	9163	7959	7273	2867	4243	7246
11687	3567	15550	10715	10629	2833	4146	7090
6647	2781	8250	5883	4613	1228	1638	2774
6213	2175	6092	4815	5371	961	600	1812
3480	1116	5189	3176	2894	591	1662	1016
5623	1882	6776	3504	4700	433	2573	1697
9052	3785	14076	9282	8027	1352	3362	2837
8156	2543	8654	6056	6103	566	2514	2443
7784	3356	15099	10226	9817	2010	3839	6277
6138	2627	10093	7459	6703	1276	2576	4748
8030	2857	10718	7457	4713	1427	2575	3312
2894	1051	3508	2810	2519	277	823	703
576	316	919	476	625	54	115	269
3093	826	4806	3077	3572	912	803	1887
6583	2374	8979	6953	7430	1775	2569	3379
2820	946	3163	1977	2105	333	749	298
2284	990	4261	2718	2714	422	720	591
302	53	353	194	230	26	5	14
6300	2240	10953	6564	8864	3021	2897	4532
3166	974	3285	2311	2650	659	879	954
586	148	823	600	492	472	175	258
768	227	1107	491	853	51	21	445
2282	635	3918	2252	3254	92	709	931

高等教育学校(机构)

Aggregate Data on Female Staff

地　区 Region	教　职 Teacher, staff					
	计 Total	校本部 Teacher, staff & Workers				
		计 Total	专任教师 Full-time Teachers			
			计 Total	正高级 Senior	副高级 Sub-senior	中级 Middle
合　计 Total	**616825**	**542967**	**302257**	**12332**	**78922**	**108809**
北　京 Beijing	50098	39906	17372	1377	5812	6789
天　津 Tianjin	14702	13297	6925	431	2271	2324
河　北 Hebei	30346	27156	16245	780	4559	5507
山　西 Shanxi	17589	16325	9695	349	2168	3527
内蒙古 Inner Mongolia	10315	9691	5949	133	1533	2207
辽　宁 Liaoning	34461	31417	18677	888	5867	6939
吉　林 Jilin	20109	18202	10022	610	2968	3377
黑龙江 Heilongjiang	26886	22638	13033	760	4152	3853
上　海 Shanghai	27200	21307	9718	386	2435	4318
江　苏 Jiangsu	40474	34712	19307	537	4204	6655
浙　江 Zhejiang	23295	21092	12407	348	2832	4063
安　徽 Anhui	16206	14918	8713	227	1979	2705
福　建 Fujian	12395	11227	6402	232	1531	2177
江　西 Jiangxi	16283	14438	8291	213	1963	2605
山　东 Shandong	35081	32052	19542	1029	5348	6385
河　南 henan	22900	20921	12966	363	3044	4677
湖　北 Hubei	38880	33480	17675	754	4846	6588
湖　南 Hunan	27443	23980	12565	401	3315	4658
广　东 Guangdong	30986	27352	16064	447	3743	6562
广　西 Guangxi	10624	9811	5525	100	1159	2410
海　南 Hainan	2156	1968	1082	47	228	379
重　庆 Chongqing	12514	10989	6043	185	1487	2480
四　川 Sichuan	24376	21556	11884	507	2940	4059
贵　州 guizhou	9274	8749	5222	159	1144	1964
云　南 Yunnan	10897	10130	5645	219	1495	2115
西　藏 Tibet	711	696	402	3	49	173
陕　西 Shaanxi	26835	23275	12188	512	2878	4361
甘　肃 Gansu	8770	7951	4662	139	885	1650
青　海 Qinghai	2376	2078	1311	30	345	547
宁　夏 Ningxia	2905	2703	1629	54	431	576
新　疆 Xinjiang	9738	8950	5096	112	1311	2179

女教职工情况(普通高校)

and Workers in HEIs(Regular HEIs)

单位:人

Unit:in Person

工 数 & Workers							
教职工 in College or Uni. Proper					科研机构人员 Personnel in Affiliated Research Org.	校办企业职工 Employees in School-run Factories & Farms	其他附设机构人员 Personnel in Others Subsidiary Units
初级 Junior	无职称 No Rank	行政人员 Adm. Personnel	教辅人员 Supporting Staff	工勤人员 Workers			
74568	**27626**	**96853**	**84582**	**59275**	**15165**	**18411**	**40282**
2411	983	8848	8984	4702	5695	1657	2840
1543	356	2673	2277	1422	332	394	679
3797	1602	3935	3655	3321	140	948	2102
2568	1083	2570	2360	1700	173	327	764
1654	422	1490	1536	716	41	140	443
3862	1121	5355	4923	2462	662	640	1742
2341	726	3065	2999	2116	296	307	1304
3136	1132	3615	2988	3002	547	992	2709
1964	615	4336	4080	3173	1011	1620	3262
5937	1974	6317	5003	4085	721	1266	3775
3573	1591	3746	3104	1835	376	531	1296
2781	1021	2158	2298	1749	251	119	918
1855	607	2126	1561	1138	180	490	498
2580	930	2563	1782	1802	111	919	815
4770	2010	4988	4738	2784	546	1015	1468
3683	1199	3143	2938	1874	172	675	1132
3803	1684	6581	5424	3800	564	1313	3523
2876	1315	4482	4084	2849	421	876	2166
3821	1491	5204	4051	2033	504	924	2206
1304	552	1633	1587	1066	96	304	413
279	149	349	265	272	15	23	150
1430	461	2231	1453	1262	311	280	934
3207	1171	3897	3351	2424	554	752	1514
1447	508	1541	1183	803	102	272	151
1267	549	1856	1449	1180	157	225	385
149	28	121	104	69	3	1	11
3177	1260	4493	3416	3178	791	836	1933
1494	494	1168	1114	1007	176	231	412
299	90	311	326	130	161	50	87
427	141	438	291	345	16	8	178
1133	361	1620	1258	976	40	276	472

高等教育学校(机构)

Aggregate Data on Staff

地 区 Region	计 Total	教职 Teacher, staff					
		校本部 Teacher, staff & Workers					
		计 Total	专任教师 Full-time Teachers				
			计 Total	正高级 Senior	副高级 Sub-senior	中级 Middle
合 计 Total	**158397**	**153504**	**85141**	**2050**	**22758**	**36795**
北 京 Beijing	8804	8533	3537	234	1049	1523
天 津 Tianjin	5624	5523	2922	57	1058	1233
河 北 Hebei	4112	3999	2118	70	588	820
山 西 Shanxi	4584	4439	2382	35	795	928
内蒙古 Inner Mongolia	2558	2552	1363	9	408	617
辽 宁 Liaoning	6467	6336	3412	66	1168	1534
吉 林 Jilin	5591	5534	2878	87	819	1246
黑龙江 Heilongjiang	10342	9974	5360	146	2071	2168
上 海 Shanghai	4499	4375	2147	62	521	1136
江 苏 Jiangsu	11715	11509	7103	145	1409	2830
浙 江 Zhejiang	5735	5707	3475	72	714	1521
安 徽 Anhui	3997	3834	2234	24	587	834
福 建 Fujian	3863	3723	2133	22	541	896
江 西 Jiangxi	3797	3351	1773	64	538	677
山 东 Shandong	9877	9423	5300	206	1368	1867
河 南 henan	8076	7963	4764	59	1263	1967
湖 北 Hubei	6697	6551	3657	62	987	1698
湖 南 Hunan	4614	4487	2551	44	656	1248
广 东 Guangdong	12673	12207	7259	150	1542	3444
广 西 Guangxi	3061	2964	1587	22	373	817
海 南 Hainan	105	105	66	2	12	24
重 庆 Chongqing	3177	3048	1730	119	411	766
四 川 Sichuan	8676	8282	4730	153	1300	2128
贵 州 guizhou	1714	1693	973	14	231	448
云 南 Yunnan	2470	2379	1422	5	285	642
西 藏 Tibet						
陕 西 Shaanxi	7362	7035	3661	93	1048	1608
甘 肃 Gansu	1302	1261	831	2	242	409
青 海 Qinghai	1246	1207	779	6	130	449
宁 夏 Ningxia						
新 疆 Xinjiang	5659	5510	2994	20	644	1317

教职工情况(成人高校)

and Workers in HEIs(HEIs for Adults)

单位:人
Unit:in Person

工　数
& Workers

教职工 in College or Uni. Proper					科研机构人员 Personnel in Affiliated Research Org.	校办企业职工 Employees in School-run Factories & Farms	其他附设机构人员 Personnel in Others Subsidiary Units
初级 Junior	无职称 No Rank	行政人员 Adm. Personnel	教辅人员 Supporting Staff	工勤人员 Workers			
18917	**4621**	**32151**	**18308**	**17904**	**525**	**2101**	**2267**
549	182	2448	1285	1263	29	57	185
456	118	1169	847	585	12	68	21
511	129	784	497	600	5	37	71
520	104	948	526	583	6	84	55
307	22	505	323	361		6	
541	103	1396	737	791	5	37	89
605	121	1281	651	724	12	10	35
797	178	2009	1150	1455	63	64	241
405	23	847	621	760	12	69	43
2126	593	1911	1341	1154	79	102	25
962	206	971	734	527	1	26	1
577	212	842	417	341	3	17	143
541	133	891	337	362	9	83	48
390	104	624	479	475	37	402	7
1422	437	2105	1035	983	21	253	180
1115	360	1559	886	754	44	59	10
724	186	1416	863	615	7	81	58
474	129	975	487	474	5	110	12
1757	366	2378	1296	1274	33	82	351
330	45	664	334	379	25	56	16
19	9	27	5	7			
375	59	606	453	259	3	92	34
934	215	1967	661	924	30	60	304
237	43	424	174	122		11	10
333	157	447	244	266		75	16
717	195	1510	982	882	34	124	169
151	27	240	81	109	7	31	3
178	16	187	143	98	31	3	5
864	149	1020	719	777	12	2	135

高等教育学校(机构)
Aggregate Data on Female Staff

地区 Region	计 Total	教职 Teacher, staff 校本部 Teacher, staff & Workers 计 Total	专任教师 Full-time Teachers 计 Total	正高级 Senior	副高级 Sub-senior	中级 Middle
合计 Total	**70573**	**68421**	**39089**	**510**	**9074**	**17603**
北京 Beijing	4322	4196	1964	78	532	932
天津 Tianjin	2738	2696	1595	14	540	718
河北 Hebei	2021	1980	1168	31	291	482
山西 Shanxi	2153	2097	1176	9	349	479
内蒙古 Inner Mongolia	1244	1244	753		197	360
辽宁 Liaoning	3227	3149	1912	30	596	903
吉林 Jilin	2700	2662	1517	36	387	673
黑龙江 Heilongjiang	4715	4511	2655	44	973	1122
上海 Shanghai	1985	1929	911	5	161	508
江苏 Jiangsu	5263	5197	3254	24	464	1305
浙江 Zhejiang	2460	2455	1494	11	213	697
安徽 Anhui	1616	1554	853	3	207	321
福建 Fujian	1813	1725	1007		213	442
江西 Jiangxi	1540	1328	678	7	172	305
山东 Shandong	4069	3898	2245	55	514	780
河南 henan	3593	3558	2173	28	513	917
湖北 Hubei	2599	2556	1340	10	278	657
湖南 Hunan	1839	1804	1052	12	222	540
广东 Guangdong	5667	5367	3057	29	573	1477
广西 Guangxi	1363	1335	710	8	123	375
海南 Hainan	47	47	27		5	15
重庆 Chongqing	1146	1107	710	19	150	336
四川 Sichuan	3700	3536	1912	28	492	896
贵州 guizhou	783	773	443	3	83	211
云南 Yunnan	1115	1073	632		101	291
西藏 Tibet						
陕西 Shaanxi	3149	3031	1615	22	355	757
甘肃 Gansu	555	539	361		71	210
青海 Qinghai	488	477	346		34	208
宁夏 Ningxia						
新疆 Xinjiang	2663	2597	1529	4	265	686

女教职工情况(成人高校)

and Workers in HEIs(HEIs for Adults)

单位:人

Unit:in Person

工　数

& Workers

教职工 in College or Uni. Proper					科研机构人员 Personnel in Affiliated Research Org.	校办企业职工 Employees in School-run Factories & Farms	其他附设机构人员 Personnel in Others Subsidiary Units
初级 Junior	无职称 No Rank	行政人员 Adm. Personnel	教辅人员 Supporting Staff	工勤人员 Workers			
9518	**2384**	**13642**	**9442**	**6248**	**174**	**794**	**1184**
330	92	1130	642	460	11	27	88
255	68	524	422	155	6	27	9
288	76	322	277	213		16	25
282	57	424	287	210	5	27	24
185	11	205	160	126			
319	64	648	363	226	3	18	57
350	71	553	391	201	7	4	27
421	95	852	551	453	21	25	158
228	9	375	333	310	4	34	18
1140	321	789	720	434	26	25	15
460	113	366	352	243		5	
233	89	356	217	128	3	7	52
284	68	397	160	161	2	46	40
155	39	228	226	196	12	198	2
651	245	871	470	312	9	51	111
516	199	642	489	254	7	22	6
312	83	547	450	219	2	14	27
216	62	355	257	140		34	1
824	154	1034	720	556	12	52	236
179	25	276	198	151	7	11	10
7		15	3	2			
184	21	194	131	72		32	7
394	102	946	371	307	15	30	119
115	31	183	106	41		3	7
172	68	187	141	113		37	5
370	111	632	500	284	7	35	76
61	19	105	40	33	2	13	1
98	6	34	62	35	10	1	
489	85	452	403	213	3		63

高等教育学校(机构)

Aggregate Data on Female Staff

地区 Region	教职 Teacher, staff					
	计 Total	校本部 Teacher, staff & Workers				
		计 Total	专任教师 Full-time Teachers			
			计 Total	正高级 Senior	副高级 Sub-senior	中级 Middle
合 计 Total	**52537**	**50609**	**24543**	**3523**	**6876**	**7936**
北 京 Beijing	8905	8797	3440	1049	1302	806
天 津 Tianjin	1328	1324	512	67	190	103
河 北 Hebei	4239	4150	2184	327	793	647
山 西 Shanxi	2251	1951	1002	136	265	364
内蒙古 Inner Mongolia	600	598				
辽 宁 Liaoning	1168	1164	525	53	105	125
吉 林 Jilin	948	917	526	105	145	178
黑龙江 Heilongjiang	1660	1606	774	81	171	291
上 海 Shanghai	922	922	227	13	59	76
江 苏 Jiangsu	477	466	144	16	49	43
浙 江 Zhejiang	1890	1869	987	33	174	302
安 徽 Anhui	707	649	398	23	119	113
福 建 Fujian	935	933	492	57	83	101
江 西 Jiangxi	1560	1523	635	48	176	194
山 东 Shandong	6385	6030	3600	489	966	1203
河 南 Henan	3217	2996	1703	189	461	677
湖 北 Hubei	821	801	344	46	95	125
湖 南 Hunan	3133	2981	1587	156	402	697
广 东 Guangdong	4281	4261	2347	220	547	926
广 西 Guangxi	148	148	96	1	41	50
海 南 Hainan	21	21	19	3	2	7
重 庆 Chongqing	1415	1411	757	43	153	188
四 川 Sichuan	1269	1246	619	117	171	216
贵 州 Guizhou	38	38	2	1	1	
云 南 Yunnan	39	39	19	3	4	6
西 藏 Tibet						
陕 西 Shaanxi	3680	3293	1359	216	334	414
甘 肃 Gansu	488	463	242	31	68	81
青 海 Qinghai	12	12	3			3
宁 夏 Ningxia						
新 疆 Xinjiang						

教职工情况(民办的其他高等教育机构)

and Workers in HEIs(Non-state/private HEIs)

单位:人

Unit:in Person

工　数 & Workers							
教职工 in College or Uni. Proper					科研机构人员 Personnel in Affiliated Research Org.	校办企业职工 Employees in School-run Factories & Farms	其他附设机构人员 Personnel in Others Subsidiary Units
		行政人员 Adm. Personnel	教辅人员 Supporting Staff	工勤人员 Workers			
初　级 Junior	无职称 No Rank						
3934	**2274**	**13263**	**5675**	**7128**	**206**	**1118**	**604**
160	123	3026	1059	1272	51	20	37
124	28	509	113	190		4	
247	170	924	420	622	10	62	17
160	77	440	204	305	14	276	10
		355	82	161		2	
114	128	355	79	205			4
78	20	194	99	98	4	26	1
104	127	391	174	267	16	18	20
41	38	392	189	114			
19	17	145	102	75			11
312	166	390	249	243		7	14
53	90	148	41	62	6	51	1
142	109	271	62	108			2
132	85	413	200	275		3	34
638	304	1177	564	689	60	258	37
278	98	752	240	301	1	8	212
69	9	200	122	135		20	
240	92	679	338	377	11	92	49
423	231	843	399	672	5	8	7
4		42	6	4			
	7			2			
280	93	216	247	191			4
64	51	289	162	176		15	8
		13	12	11			
2	4	12	4	4			
193	202	957	459	518	28	248	111
57	5	121	49	51			25
		9					

高等教育学校(机构)

Aggregate Data on Female Staff

地区 Region	计 Total	教职 Teacher, staff 校本部 Teacher, staff & Workers 计 Total	专任教师 Full-time Teachers 计 Total	正高级 Senior	副高级 Sub-senior	中级 Middle
合　计 Total	**22014**	**21172**	**10272**	**903**	**2485**	**3674**
北　京 Beijing	3669	3639	1272	234	460	427
天　津 Tianjin	663	662	229	14	94	54
河　北 Hebei	1851	1808	1052	105	336	354
山　西 Shanxi	955	770	384	35	101	154
内蒙古 Inner Mongolia	259	258				
辽　宁 Liaoning	573	572	255	12	31	45
吉　林 Jilin	449	435	273	42	76	107
黑龙江 Heilongjiang	797	780	387	25	76	152
上　海 Shanghai	495	495	109	3	19	33
江　苏 Jiangsu	245	239	73	8	24	20
浙　江 Zhejiang	923	917	487	4	62	120
安　徽 Anhui	209	182	94	7	19	26
福　建 Fujian	349	347	177	6	20	44
江　西 Jiangxi	529	519	172	12	31	58
山　东 Shandong	2773	2602	1684	157	394	610
河　南 Henan	1245	1142	687	50	142	318
湖　北 Hubei	307	302	133	8	35	60
湖　南 Hunan	1328	1290	706	24	137	361
广　东 Guangdong	1583	1578	824	46	165	323
广　西 Guangxi	60	60	41		14	25
海　南 Hainan	12	12	12	2	1	5
重　庆 Chongqing	624	622	346	4	53	90
四　川 Sichuan	542	534	245	38	73	80
贵　州 Guizhou	14	14	1		1	
云　南 Yunnan	19	19	9	1	3	1
西　藏 Tibet						
陕　西 Shanxi	1370	1213	546	60	104	177
甘　肃 Gansu	166	156	71	6	14	27
青　海 Qinghai	5	5	3			3
宁　夏 Ningxia						
新　疆 Xinjiang						

女教职工情况(民办的其他高等教育机构)

and Workers in HEIs(Non-state/private HEIs)

单位:人

Unit:in Person

工数 & Workers							
教职工 in College or Uni. Proper					科研机构人员 Personnel in Affiliated Research Org.	校办企业职工 Employees in School-run Factories & Farms	其他附设机构人员 Personnel in Others Subsidiary Units
初级 Junior	无职称 No Rank	行政人员 Adm. Personnel	教辅人员 Supporting Staff	工勤人员 Workers			
2016	**1194**	**5610**	**2727**	**2563**	**65**	**540**	**237**
91	60	1333	552	482	23		7
53	14	269	68	96		1	
141	116	355	212	189	1	31	11
65	29	165	93	128	4	177	4
		163	44	51		1	
70	97	175	58	84			1
44	4	95	36	31		14	
56	78	193	77	123	6	6	5
24	30	216	120	50			
11	10	69	69	28			6
189	112	178	149	103		2	4
12	30	52	11	25	2	25	
49	58	115	24	31			2
36	35	167	80	100		1	9
360	163	478	236	204	16	141	14
146	31	278	94	83	1	4	98
28	2	77	62	30		5	
134	50	291	169	124	3	26	9
200	90	320	190	244	1	4	
2		15	3	1			
	4						
146	53	94	108	74			2
36	18	129	74	86		6	2
		2	7	4			
1	3	4	2	4			
100	105	329	170	168	8	96	53
22	2	46	19	20			10
		2					

专任教师学历、职称情况(总计)

Data on Academic Qualifications、Rank of Full-time Teacher (Total)

单位:人

Unit: in Person

地区 Region	计 Total	按学历分 By Educational Attainment				按职称分 By Rank				
		博士 Doctor's Degrees	硕士 Master's Degrees	本科 Normal Courses	专科及以下 Short-cycle Courses and Under	正高级 Senior	副高级 Sub-Senior	中级 Middle	初级 Junior	无职称 No Rank
合计 Total	**834342**	**54790**	**192123**	**544083**	**43346**	**75636**	**245795**	**285286**	**168943**	**58682**
北京 Beijing	44984	8704	15595	19090	1595	8256	15488	14622	4601	2017
天津 Tianjin	18987	1839	4192	11754	1202	2295	6636	5961	3307	788
河北 Hebei	38844	1340	8025	27671	1808	3521	11999	12200	7955	3169
山西 Shanxi	23608	846	4587	16336	1839	1628	6399	8275	5258	2048
内蒙古 Inner Mongolia	13516	326	2051	10168	971	722	3999	4796	3184	815
辽宁 Liaoning	42023	2504	11430	26581	1508	3899	13970	14487	7326	2341
吉林 Jilin	25228	1592	5736	16986	914	2736	7590	8322	5123	1457
黑龙江 Heilongjiang	34659	1884	7173	23878	1724	3355	11712	10532	6814	2246
上海 Shanghai	26761	4600	8373	12348	1440	3567	8038	10249	3779	1128
江苏 Jiangsu	57073	4885	14355	35943	1890	4920	15339	18805	13832	4177
浙江 Zhejiang	34407	2208	8131	22451	1617	2690	9314	11329	7921	3153
安徽 Anhui	27376	1091	4995	19831	1459	1775	7519	8762	6843	2477
福建 Fujian	18796	1447	4205	12182	962	1733	5331	6211	4163	1358
江西 Jiangxi	24346	523	3344	18700	1779	1700	6835	7595	6145	2071
山东 Shandong	54357	2817	12536	36448	2556	5447	16614	16658	11112	4526
河南 henan	39811	1267	7579	29783	1182	2138	11028	14095	9549	3001
湖北 Hubei	50948	3616	13495	30921	2916	5144	16227	17449	8577	3551
湖南 Hunan	37367	1972	7832	25875	1688	3219	11147	13301	6852	2848
广东 Guangdong	49798	3726	13233	30551	2288	3814	13338	18982	10210	3454
广西 Guangxi	15789	508	3205	11331	745	908	4029	6528	3228	1096
海南 Hainan	2784	106	557	1971	150	244	769	844	595	332
重庆 Chongqing	18500	1083	4517	11459	1441	1515	5264	6995	3748	978
四川 Sichuan	36721	2130	9154	22575	2862	3125	10678	12697	7581	2640
贵州 guizhou	12750	120	1286	10268	1076	714	3293	4697	3057	989
云南 Yunnan	13677	454	2734	9695	794	999	3811	5097	2619	1151
西藏 Tibet	972	10	86	726	150	21	162	434	302	53
陕西 Shaanxi	35716	2391	8797	22685	1843	3800	10318	11751	7210	2637
甘肃 Gansu	13347	548	2705	9443	651	879	3313	4775	3374	1006
青海 Qinghai	3551	10	210	2638	693	108	832	1683	764	164
宁夏 Ningxia	3415	57	551	2575	232	223	1008	1189	768	227
新疆 Xinjiang	14231	186	1454	11220	1371	541	3795	5965	3146	784

专任教师学历、职称情况(普通高校)

Data on Academic Qualifications、Rank of Full-time Teacher (Regular HEIs)

单位:人

Unit:in Person

地 区 Region	计 Total	按学历分 By Educational Attainment				按职称分 By Rank				
		博 士 Doctor's Degrees	硕 士 Master's Degrees	本 科 Normal Courses	专科及以下 Short-cycle Courses and Under	正高级 Senior	副高级 Sub-Senior	中 级 Middle	初 级 Junior	无职称 No Rank
合 计 Total	**724658**	**53612**	**182517**	**458522**	**30007**	**70063**	**216161**	**240555**	**146092**	**51787**
北 京 Beijing	38007	8205	14025	14568	1209	6973	13137	12293	3892	1712
天 津 Tianjin	15553	1830	3981	8921	821	2171	5388	4625	2727	642
河 北 Hebei	34542	1313	7667	24213	1349	3124	10618	10733	7197	2870
山 西 Shanxi	20224	832	4352	13701	1339	1457	5339	6983	4578	1867
内蒙古 Inner Mongolia	12153	326	2025	9077	725	713	3591	4179	2877	793
辽 宁 Liaoning	38086	2493	11204	23364	1025	3780	12697	12828	6671	2110
吉 林 Jilin	21824	1568	5516	14165	575	2544	6626	6898	4440	1316
黑龙江 Heilongjiang	28525	1859	6935	18812	919	3128	9470	8073	5913	1941
上 海 Shanghai	24387	4573	8016	10710	1088	3492	7458	9037	3333	1067
江 苏 Jiangsu	49826	4835	13877	29969	1145	4759	13881	15932	11687	3567
浙 江 Zhejiang	29945	2182	7798	18729	1236	2585	8426	9506	6647	2781
安 徽 Anhui	24744	1081	4829	17611	1223	1728	6813	7815	6213	2175
福 建 Fujian	16171	1440	3980	10022	729	1654	4707	5214	3480	1116
江 西 Jiangxi	21938	516	3207	16821	1394	1588	6121	6724	5623	1882
山 东 Shandong	45457	2734	11762	29503	1458	4752	14280	13588	9052	3785
河 南 henan	33344	1213	7099	24656	376	1890	9304	11451	8156	2543
湖 北 Hubei	46947	3584	13156	27726	2481	5036	15145	15626	7784	3356
湖 南 Hunan	33229	1933	7430	22824	1042	3019	10089	11356	6138	2627
广 东 Guangdong	40192	3609	11858	23424	1301	3444	11249	14612	8030	2857
广 西 Guangxi	14106	503	3060	9893	650	885	3615	5661	2894	1051
海 南 Hainan	2699	106	550	1902	141	239	755	813	576	316
重 庆 Chongqing	16013	1066	4366	9514	1067	1353	4700	6041	3093	826
四 川 Sichuan	31372	2087	8656	18735	1894	2855	9207	10353	6583	2374
贵 州 guizhou	11775	118	1247	9490	920	699	3061	4249	2820	946
云 南 Yunnan	12236	454	2675	8421	686	991	3522	4449	2284	990
西 藏 Tibet	972	10	86	726	150	21	162	434	302	53
陕 西 Shaanxi	30696	2351	8434	18976	935	3491	8936	9729	6300	2240
甘 肃 Gansu	12274	542	2608	8682	442	846	3003	4285	3166	974
青 海 Qinghai	2769	10	197	2050	512	102	702	1231	586	148
宁 夏 Ningxia	3415	57	551	2575	232	223	1008	1189	768	227
新 疆 Xinjiang	11237	182	1370	8742	943	521	3151	4648	2282	635

专任教师学历、职称情况(成人高校)

Data on Academic Qualifications、Rank of Full-time Teacher (HEIs for Adults)

单位:人

Unit:in Person

地 区 Region	计 Total	按学历分 By Educational Attainment				按职称分 By Rank				
		博 士 Doctor's Degrees	硕 士 Master's Degrees	本 科 Normal Courses	专科及以下 Short-cycle Courses and Under	正高级 Senior	副高级 Sub-Senior	中 级 Middle	初 级 Junior	无职称 No Rank
合 计 Total	**85141**	**514**	**6453**	**68761**	**9413**	**2050**	**22758**	**36795**	**18917**	**4621**
北 京 Beijing	3537	177	732	2370	258	234	1049	1523	549	182
天 津 Tianjin	2922	7	175	2421	319	57	1058	1233	456	118
河 北 Hebei	2118	6	118	1908	86	70	588	820	511	129
山 西 Shanxi	2382	4	155	1898	325	35	795	928	520	104
内蒙古 Inner Mongolia	1363		26	1091	246	9	408	617	307	22
辽 宁 Liaoning	3412	3	166	2880	363	66	1168	1534	541	103
吉 林 Jilin	2878	18	165	2406	289	87	819	1246	605	121
黑龙江 Heilongjiang	5360	13	193	4584	570	146	2071	2168	797	178
上 海 Shanghai	2147	25	319	1481	322	62	521	1136	405	23
江 苏 Jiangsu	7103	49	472	5849	733	145	1409	2830	2126	593
浙 江 Zhejiang	3475	19	258	2914	284	72	714	1521	962	206
安 徽 Anhui	2234	7	151	1898	178	24	587	834	577	212
福 建 Fujian	2133	2	170	1767	194	22	541	896	541	133
江 西 Jiangxi	1773	7	123	1422	221	64	538	677	390	104
山 东 Shandong	5300	24	422	4410	444	206	1368	1867	1422	437
河 南 henan	4764	14	346	4033	371	59	1263	1967	1115	360
湖 北 Hubei	3657	6	208	3010	433	62	987	1698	724	186
湖 南 Hunan	2551	7	136	2029	379	44	656	1248	474	129
广 东 Guangdong	7259	75	1036	5430	718	150	1542	3444	1757	366
广 西 Guangxi	1587	5	136	1358	88	22	373	817	330	45
海 南 Hainan	66		4	56	6	2	12	24	19	9
重 庆 Chongqing	1730	12	117	1305	296	119	411	766	375	59
四 川 Sichuan	4730	19	388	3457	866	153	1300	2128	934	215
贵 州 guizhou	973	2	39	776	156	14	231	448	237	43
云 南 Yunnan	1422		57	1257	108	5	285	642	333	157
西 藏 Tibet										
陕 西 Shaanxi	3661	8	204	3060	389	93	1048	1608	717	195
甘 肃 Gansu	831	1	40	627	163	2	242	409	151	27
青 海 Qinghai	779		13	586	180	6	130	449	178	16
宁 夏 Ningxia										
新 疆 Xinjiang	2994	4	84	2478	428	20	644	1317	864	149

专任教师学历、职称情况(民办的其他高等教育机构)

Data on Academic Qualifications、Rank of Full-time Teacher (Non-state/private HEIs)

单位:人

Unit:in Person

地区 Region	计 Total	按学历分 By Educational Attainment				按职称分 By Rank				
		博士 Doctor's Degrees	硕士 Master's Degrees	本科 Normal Courses	专科及以下 Short-cycle Courses and Under	正高级 Senior	副高级 Sub-Senior	中级 Middle	初级 Junior	无职称 No Rank
合计 Total	**24543**	**664**	**3153**	**16800**	**3926**	**3523**	**6876**	**7936**	**3934**	**2274**
北京 Beijing	3440	322	838	2152	128	1049	1302	806	160	123
天津 Tianjin	512	2	36	412	62	67	190	103	124	28
河北 Hebei	2184	21	240	1550	373	327	793	647	247	170
山西 Shanxi	1002	10	80	737	175	136	265	364	160	77
内蒙古 Inner Mongolia										
辽宁 Liaoning	525	8	60	337	120	53	105	125	114	128
吉林 Jilin	526	6	55	415	50	105	145	178	78	20
黑龙江 Heilongjiang	774	12	45	482	235	81	171	291	104	127
上海 Shanghai	227	2	38	157	30	13	59	76	41	38
江苏 Jiangsu	144	1	6	125	12	16	49	43	19	17
浙江 Zhejiang	987	7	75	808	97	33	174	302	312	166
安徽 Anhui	398	3	15	322	58	23	119	113	53	90
福建 Fujian	492	5	55	393	39	57	83	101	142	109
江西 Jiangxi	635		14	457	164	48	176	194	132	85
山东 Shandong	3600	59	352	2535	654	489	966	1203	638	304
河南 Henan	1703	40	134	1094	435	189	461	677	278	98
湖北 Hubei	344	26	131	185	2	46	95	125	69	9
湖南 Hunan	1587	32	266	1022	267	156	402	697	240	92
广东 Guangdong	2347	42	339	1697	269	220	547	926	423	231
广西 Guangxi	96		9	80	7	1	41	50	4	
海南 Hainan	19		3	13	3	3	2	7		7
重庆 Chongqing	757	5	34	640	78	43	153	188	280	93
四川 Sichuan	619	24	110	383	102	117	171	216	64	51
贵州 Guizhou	2			2		1	1			
云南 Yunnan	19		2	17		3	4	6	2	4
西藏 Tibet										
陕西 Shaanxi	1359	32	159	649	519	216	334	414	193	202
甘肃 Gansu	242	5	57	134	46	31	68	81	57	5
青海 Qinghai	3			2	1			3		
宁夏 Ningxia										
新疆 Xinjiang										

聘请校外教师学历情况(总计)

Aggregate Data on Academic Qualifications of Part-time Teachers in HEIs (Total)

单位:人

Unit:in Person

地　区 Region	计 Total	博　士 Doctor's Degrees	硕　士 Master's Degrees	本　科 Normal Courses	专科及以下 Short-cycle Courses and Under
合　计 Total	**229257**	**12811**	**50121**	**149369**	**16956**
北　京 Beijing	27558	1822	5364	12929	7443
天　津 Tianjin	5228	229	946	3890	163
河　北 Hebei	14131	485	3362	9678	606
山　西 Shanxi	4806	132	796	3582	296
内蒙古 Inner Mongolia	2448	59	250	1983	156
辽　宁 Liaoning	8682	534	2451	5532	165
吉　林 Jilin	3265	274	734	2105	152
黑龙江 Heilongjiang	8358	221	1327	6334	476
上　海 Shanghai	16085	1446	3487	10309	843
江　苏 Jiangsu	9007	597	2409	5654	347
浙　江 Zhejiang	10345	450	2187	6741	967
安　徽 Anhui	6129	229	1221	4458	221
福　建 Fujian	6564	465	1087	4594	418
江　西 Jiangxi	6201	75	699	4918	509
山　东 Shandong	17457	1114	5105	10725	513
河　南 henan	9536	425	1949	6824	338
湖　北 Hubei	8067	827	2744	4390	106
湖　南 Hunan	8826	592	2039	5797	398
广　东 Guangdong	10611	469	2483	7083	576
广　西 Guangxi	4061	82	560	3208	211
海　南 Hainan	437	13	37	333	54
重　庆 Chongqing	4100	137	769	2953	241
四　川 Sichuan	13746	782	3235	8930	799
贵　州 guizhou	1748	50	154	1424	120
云　南 Yunnan	2081	85	522	1382	92
西　藏 Tibet	43	2	2	37	2
陕　西 Shaanxi	12638	918	2778	8410	532
甘　肃 Gansu	3345	208	955	2141	41
青　海 Qinghai	451		39	391	21
宁　夏 Ningxia	646	1	72	542	31
新　疆 Xinjiang	2657	88	358	2092	119

聘请校外教师学历情况(普通高校)

Aggregate Data on Academic Qualifications of Part-time Teachers (Regular HEIs)

单位:人

Unit:in Person

地　　区 Region	计 Total	博　士 Doctor's Degrees	硕　士 Master's Degrees	本　科 Normal Courses	专科及以下 Short-cycle Courses and Under
合　计 Total	**134250**	**9815**	**33123**	**85505**	**5807**
北　京 Beijing	8055	1067	2344	4434	210
天　津 Tianjin	2227	157	455	1546	69
河　北 Hebei	11089	431	2816	7359	483
山　西 Shanxi	2668	69	413	2042	144
内蒙古 Inner Mongolia	793	52	107	579	55
辽　宁 Liaoning	6214	465	1983	3652	114
吉　林 Jilin	2205	223	555	1347	80
黑龙江 Heilongjiang	5505	172	1028	4030	275
上　海 Shanghai	6908	899	1679	3993	337
江　苏 Jiangsu	5637	434	1550	3437	216
浙　江 Zhejiang	7089	372	1503	4375	839
安　徽 Anhui	3791	199	940	2544	108
福　建 Fujian	4465	436	755	2896	378
江　西 Jiangxi	4244	60	449	3338	397
山　东 Shandong	13747	985	4157	8246	359
河　南 henan	5540	343	1368	3755	74
湖　北 Hubei	6402	756	2215	3348	83
湖　南 Hunan	5146	524	1288	3132	202
广　东 Guangdong	4242	275	987	2726	254
广　西 Guangxi	2927	77	462	2219	169
海　南 Hainan	337	13	27	246	51
重　庆 Chongqing	1752	115	465	1097	75
四　川 Sichuan	7959	629	2094	4835	401
贵　州 guizhou	1037	49	106	779	103
云　南 Yunnan	1661	77	432	1065	87
西　藏 Tibet	43	2	2	37	2
陕　西 Shaanxi	7690	663	1788	5120	119
甘　肃 Gansu	2656	186	812	1650	8
青　海 Qinghai	49		6	40	3
宁　夏 Ningxia	646	1	72	542	31
新　疆 Xinjiang	1526	84	265	1096	81

聘请校外教师学历情况(成人高校)

Aggregate Data on Academic Qualifications of Part-time Teachers (HEIs for Adults)

单位:人

Unit:in Person

地　区 Region	计 Total	博　士 Doctor's Degrees	硕　士 Master's Degrees	本　科 Normal Courses	专科及以下 Short-cycle Courses and Under
合　计 Total	**44437**	**852**	**7516**	**34132**	**1937**
北　京 Beijing	3066	142	706	2141	77
天　津 Tianjin	1523	16	225	1227	55
河　北 Hebei	857	10	136	695	16
山　西 Shanxi	766	11	129	602	24
内蒙古 Inner Mongolia	454		17	365	72
辽　宁 Liaoning	1406	2	219	1167	18
吉　林 Jilin	406	8	51	329	18
黑龙江 Heilongjiang	1933	26	152	1629	126
上　海 Shanghai	1215	60	243	877	35
江　苏 Jiangsu	2600	43	601	1839	117
浙　江 Zhejiang	2230	33	342	1743	112
安　徽 Anhui	1881	14	223	1587	57
福　建 Fujian	1602	10	244	1311	37
江　西 Jiangxi	1121	5	109	964	43
山　东 Shandong	1126	12	315	775	24
河　南 henan	1171	9	120	985	57
湖　北 Hubei	923	25	147	729	22
湖　南 Hunan	1760	12	274	1387	87
广　东 Guangdong	4923	125	1086	3480	232
广　西 Guangxi	1009	5	87	877	40
海　南 Hainan	100		10	87	3
重　庆 Chongqing	2099	12	218	1719	150
四　川 Sichuan	4766	126	971	3297	372
贵　州 guizhou	631	1	45	568	17
云　南 Yunnan	406	8	86	308	4
西　藏 Tibet					
陕　西 Shaanxi	2658	127	568	1913	50
甘　肃 Gansu	286	6	67	197	16
青　海 Qinghai	388		32	338	18
宁　夏 Ningxia					
新　疆 Xinjiang	1131	4	93	996	38

聘请校外教师学历情况(民办的其他高等教育机构)

Aggregate Data on Academic Qualifications of Part-time Teachers (Non-state/private HEIs)

单位:人

Unit:in Person

地区 Region	计 Total	博士 Doctor's Degrees	硕士 Master's Degrees	本科 Normal Courses	专科及以下 Short-cycle Courses and Under
合计 Total	**50570**	**2144**	**9482**	**29732**	**9212**
北京 Beijing	16437	613	2314	6354	7156
天津 Tianjin	1478	56	266	1117	39
河北 Hebei	2185	44	410	1624	107
山西 Shanxi	1372	52	254	938	128
内蒙古 Inner Mongolia	1201	7	126	1039	29
辽宁 Liaoning	1062	67	249	713	33
吉林 Jilin	654	43	128	429	54
黑龙江 Heilongjiang	920	23	147	675	75
上海 Shanghai	7962	487	1565	5439	471
江苏 Jiangsu	770	120	258	378	14
浙江 Zhejiang	1026	45	342	623	16
安徽 Anhui	457	16	58	327	56
福建 Fujian	497	19	88	387	3
江西 Jiangxi	836	10	141	616	69
山东 Shandong	2584	117	633	1704	130
河南 Henan	2825	73	461	2084	207
湖北 Hubei	742	46	382	313	1
湖南 Hunan	1920	56	477	1278	109
广东 Guangdong	1446	69	410	877	90
广西 Guangxi	125		11	112	2
海南 Hainan					
重庆 Chongqing	249	10	86	137	16
四川 Sichuan	1021	27	170	798	26
贵州 Guizhou	80		3	77	
云南 Yunnan	14		4	9	1
西藏 Tibet					
陕西 Shaanxi	2290	128	422	1377	363
甘肃 Gansu	403	16	76	294	17
青海 Qinghai	14		1	13	
宁夏 Ningxia					
新疆 Xinjiang					

地区 Region	学校占地面积(平方米) Area of School sites (m^2)			图书音像 Audio-visual	
				一般图书(万册) Books & Magazines in Libraries(10 Thouand Volume)	
	计 Total	其中:绿化用地面积 Of Which: Green Arens	其中:运动场地面积 Of Which: Sports Areas	计 Total	当年新增 New Floor Space Added in Current Year
合 计 Total	**1132873054**	**256248743**	**79379123**	**97919.11**	**9725.46**
北 京 Beijing	44688597	13336816	2708481	5908.27	274.94
天 津 Tianjin	18149502	2762547	1164401	2122.71	191.68
河 北 Hebei	42425052	7368070	3882021	3993.60	349.50
山 西 Shanxi	18691634	3973284	2108910	3040.53	500.15
内蒙古 Inner Mongolia	12582671	2933314	1416406	1300.75	51.85
辽 宁 Liaoning	47062213	8730004	3847404	4434.10	302.74
吉 林 Jilin	40783965	4612155	2628165	2596.93	110.00
黑龙江 Heilongjiang	51104108	6549728	3131329	3578.19	352.35
上 海 Shanghai	24924143	6983509	1886940	4356.58	126.50
江 苏 Jiangsu	91616956	23268214	5889848	6458.75	459.82
浙 江 Zhejiang	45563881	13871253	3741883	3846.43	484.73
安 徽 Anhui	41031766	8139164	2722466	3067.39	264.73
福 建 Fujian	27087655	6560674	1567777	2172.50	175.15
江 西 Jiangxi	46914469	12538815	2900001	2712.91	385.23
山 东 Shandong	90998650	19484092	6706540	5719.16	685.90
河 南 henan	58687661	10265334	4547705	4866.74	607.04
湖 北 Hubei	67124252	17963386	4381354	5720.56	367.34
湖 南 Hunan	51312256	15269947	3535237	4360.45	397.23
广 东 Guangdong	72494659	18630090	4656916	5797.95	809.22
广 西 Guangxi	21905285	5315549	1652140	2049.76	135.54
海 南 Hainan	6569239	1976620	469272	336.79	32.20
重 庆 Chongqing	27862659	9461843	1365010	1993.91	177.05
四 川 Sichuan	59002050	12513638	3686591	4242.87	293.62
贵 州 guizhou	20536841	3312508	1048601	1472.25	65.08
云 南 Yunnan	15291965	3218477	1162131	1537.45	90.10
西 藏 Tibet	2729729	460557	118742	111.53	5.33
陕 西 Shaanxi	38579553	7232422	3367505	5243.44	995.92
甘 肃 Gansu	14537110	2272649	1231277	2076.92	68.18
青 海 Qinghai	4060770	385388	296803	363.96	24.26
宁 夏 Ningxia	7677296	1065365	321348	318.23	17.02
新 疆 Xinjiang	20876467	5793331	1235919	2117.50	925.06

(学校产权)(总计)

Resources (Owned by HEIs) (Total)

资料情况 ed. Resources		拥有教学用计算机(台) No. of computers used for Instruction	语音实验室座位数(个) No. of Seats in Audio-Labs	多媒体教室座位数(个) No. of Seats in Multimedia Class rooms	网上教学课程数(种) No. of Web-Based Courses	固定资产值(万元) Fixed Assets (in 10000 yuan)		
电子图书(片) Electronic Books & Magazines in Libraries(Disk)						合　计 Total	其中:教学、科研仪器设备资产 of which: Teaching Equipment & Instruments	
计 Total	当年新增 New Floor Space Added in Current Year						计 Total	当年新增 New Floor SpaceAdded in Current Year
45546551	**20502002**	**2563538**	**879077**	**4908240**	**52241**	**39756102.04**	**8915882.98**	**1625974.14**
2633479	1143321	157478	43137	367662	5573	3353486.15	887283.68	160542.49
1189790	166993	58452	19803	104095	636	870824.20	262233.45	41143.48
4338464	1738776	108208	37692	217026	1802	1702909.33	314109.15	48998.27
414982	145340	55194	19860	96452	580	698803.01	162938.23	36060.56
35076	13990	27264	7464	32343	208	421236.66	85751.84	13841.29
147191	39539	119363	54059	204245	3247	1855476.52	420222.33	76153.56
1290310	825182	67369	20958	83211	812	1205142.96	247988.87	42303.01
2779967	1338839	93089	41468	170825	1112	1641691.93	328666.86	77927.48
464552	212453	119405	27453	208711	1297	2074518.55	542119.76	88515.40
2198469	342906	207795	56917	437489	1708	3037499.39	678216.85	117196.10
2541973	1756100	144273	44270	289840	5765	2146736.56	397659.49	97858.94
609850	437300	70041	30113	130632	1339	1027422.61	268440.94	50272.49
303181	167447	61109	22699	130948	846	921962.38	213461.91	44007.52
4166765	2086369	88447	36555	172530	3077	1061095.10	228337.28	51652.78
235577	75307	151056	55978	326331	2008	2651695.79	497279.76	111230.39
3784823	2629831	116082	41302	193936	1456	1578630.12	355544.64	70103.58
2844432	890678	143892	52029	325791	2070	2413547.35	511475.19	87701.18
4573202	1523816	118493	40474	208240	7319	1544025.78	345819.86	59137.29
1401672	475444	167398	60372	371802	3243	2621444.14	559469.74	102472.96
1032705	459608	45113	19120	92364	483	485710.04	148172.69	25220.83
93565	9842	9715	4424	18618	7	119111.07	27534.26	4804.61
1858166	1623410	58531	17067	100189	411	820424.78	159884.15	32282.03
2034671	856185	112332	39318	255294	2323	1602234.42	397325.42	47329.46
35850	11212	28354	11505	33886	403	407378.34	86314.91	12640.83
52119	21482	33003	13151	48671	0	583638.82	129677.66	21214.87
5983	2036	1001	406	978	87	24777.76	3414.96	651.00
2043697	813897	130234	35405	168455	1369	1704675.53	409966.68	69501.87
2331109	653669	30165	9065	44566	267	568910.91	106533.59	15306.60
8196	429	5774	1628	5134	218	79523.68	22745.78	1197.23
18903	4368	8561	2418	16188	100	91958.80	24286.32	4134.91
77832	36233	26347	12967	51788	2475	439609.36	93006.73	14571.13

资产情况(学校

Condition of Fixed Assets and

地　区 Region	学校占地面积(平方米) Area of School sites (m^2) 计 Total	其中:绿化用地面积 Of Which:Green Arens	其中:运动场地面积 Of Which:Sports Areas	图书音像 Audio-visual 一般图书(万册) Books & Magazines in Libraries(10 Thouand Volume) 计 Total	当年新增 New Floor Space Added in Current Year
合　计 Total	**1035638801**	**235175170**	**69633469**	**83649.02**	**6936.20**
北　京 Beijing	34372854	9119967	2311406	5186.90	207.52
天　津 Tianjin	16583375	2675308	1065098	1840.65	179.86
河　北 Hebei	38910065	6866850	3544209	3588.37	314.44
山　西 Shanxi	16248931	3621942	1792080	1978.35	177.21
内蒙古 Inner Mongolia	11396363	2778945	1228283	1177.46	39.81
辽　宁 Liaoning	44347324	8444370	3377791	4034.51	280.06
吉　林 Jilin	39143973	4310895	2337210	2356.54	103.47
黑龙江 Heilongjiang	47407834	6027911	2596380	3036.77	325.85
上　海 Shanghai	23424497	6672554	1755246	3538.95	117.60
江　苏 Jiangsu	86025041	21970411	5176166	5846.20	408.67
浙　江 Zhejiang	42222328	13044118	3369129	3330.66	438.24
安　徽 Anhui	37840851	7747563	2468578	2788.64	250.43
福　建 Fujian	25684640	6287485	1465887	1917.32	155.51
江　西 Jiangxi	43550200	11874390	2642522	2375.42	360.86
山　东 Shandong	81432485	17735387	5435618	4882.03	573.3
河　南 henan	51238449	8679658	3740473	4139.84	532.73
湖　北 Hubei	63042272	16927023	4097421	5204.63	339.16
湖　南 Hunan	48434326	14794039	3305679	3950.87	360.54
广　东 Guangdong	62824157	16151814	3620270	4558.97	590.83
广　西 Guangxi	20565563	5009822	1588771	1837.67	123.49
海　南 Hainan	6480419	1925259	454472	329.06	31.81
重　庆 Chongqing	26005450	9028096	1185745	1758.37	162.45
四　川 Sichuan	55208313	11869333	3300264	3701.11	255.11
贵　州 guizhou	19891064	3166553	1001193	1297.76	60.63
云　南 Yunnan	14149415	3049736	1026893	1424.63	65.37
西　藏 Tibet	2729729	460557	118742	111.53	5.33
陕　西 Shaanxi	34276988	6640964	2932946	3886.08	326.71
甘　肃 Gansu	13754394	2045403	1134221	1973.13	65.08
青　海 Qinghai	2974294	302932	231821	319.07	20.57
宁　夏 Ningxia	7677296	1065365	321348	318.23	17.02
新　疆 Xinjiang	17795911	4880520	1007607	959.3	46.54

产权)(普通高校)

Teaching Resources (Owned by HEIs)(Regular HEIs)

资料情况 ed. Resources		拥有教学用计算机(台) No. of computers used for Instruction	语音实验室座位数(个) No. of Seats in Audio-Labs	多媒体教室座位数(个) No. of Seats in Multimedia Classrooms	网上教学课程数(种) No. of Web-Based Courses	固定资产值(万元) Fixed Assets (in 10000 yuan)		
电子图书(片) Electronic Books & Magazines in Libraries(Disk)						合计 Total	其中:教学、科研仪器设备资产 of which: Teaching Equipment & Instruments	
计 Total	当年新增 New Floor Space Added in Current Year						计 Total	当年新增 New Floor SpaceAdded in Current Year
42790841	**19142440**	**2158221**	**737531**	**4393919**	**17171**	**35798177.75**	**8116128.04**	**1481045.74**
2057679	926743	123420	33569	326118	3816	3056814.95	833615.83	148276.48
1131728	162907	45414	15959	91589	167	792539.87	238180.92	37898.70
3630692	1131846	96326	32718	202878	356	1537835.77	286572.96	46037.14
331441	131202	44248	16466	86549	156	584996.13	140105.24	30640.16
29528	13169	23785	6180	29999	82	389936.64	79991.54	13280.59
133467	36823	106306	47785	189131	1297	1760475.88	398670.94	73324.13
1276877	823327	60089	18153	77411	401	1134811.85	235949.71	41093.70
2686399	1328845	79021	34636	158136	600	1494603.65	298185.34	73471.66
459728	212012	103836	22587	188549	735	1775940.66	498458.89	73885.00
2150800	326336	180669	49149	403633	850	2768986.64	630469.65	107352.56
2496621	1738587	120677	37855	240200	698	1970913.31	350111.13	92292.97
434951	282982	60947	26525	120508	358	936772.06	251111.52	47694.65
275694	162535	49770	19009	111963	632	826353.92	192878.25	40127.71
4147004	2077850	76959	31660	159940	315	998015.38	213255.87	48732.49
182248	64869	123228	45222	299259	931	2355152.65	436793.62	99128.81
3709854	2595507	95252	33946	171023	518	1339604.11	311772.51	63220.46
2713424	784087	130755	47268	305706	1228	2271659.97	477173.96	84165.04
4504476	1515391	100474	32914	188785	826	1431920.26	321288.63	55350.95
1153463	393715	117120	42313	278922	1410	2166447.19	451369.6	81688.96
979243	459380	38475	16643	84933	0	427655.62	134323.83	23597.73
93565	9842	9289	4330	18043	2	117900	26823.7	4796
1853862	1620588	48858	14852	87977	411	749313.08	141997.92	29471.53
1915264	847684	95499	33147	234740	403	1439653.09	368915.64	42808.7
27312	7484	25078	10512	30072	5	267963.97	75575.25	10910.82
42451	20900	29567	12011	45102	0	549599.62	122053.13	17975.03
5983	2036	1001	406	978	87	24777.76	3414.96	651
1975407	804668	112831	29808	156590	468	1536619.04	377370.7	60768.54
2327268	652321	27276	8227	41868	15	548769.17	100291.39	14904
4145	220	4272	1234	3674	45	71768.38	20443.62	1079.13
18903	4368	8561	2418	16188	100	91958.8	24286.32	4134.91
41364	4216	19218	10029	43455	259	378418.33	74675.47	12286.19

资产情况(学校

Condition of Fixed Assets and Teaching

地 区 Region	学校占地面积(平方米) Area of School sites (m^2)			图书音像 Audio-visual	
				一般图书(万册) Books & Magazines in Libraries(10 Thouand Volume)	
	计 Total	其中:绿化用地面积 Of Which: Green Arens	其中:运动场地面积 Of Which: Sports Areas	计 Total	当年新增 New Floor Space Added in Current Year
合 计 Total	**72093070**	**15699337**	**6922975**	**10135.88**	**1560.32**
北 京 Beijing	6510074	3415296	231049	516.32	25.16
天 津 Tianjin	1508226	81639	90903	262.76	9.71
河 北 Hebei	1668100	239541	140932	232.47	11.64
山 西 Shanxi	1576140	199547	210002	194.20	16.71
内蒙古 Inner Mongolia	1127446	139138	174834	108.54	9.53
辽 宁 Liaoning	1804782	139828	326844	334.53	15.57
吉 林 Jilin	1416444	266480	225555	210.29	4.63
黑龙江 Heilongjiang	3204566	427556	317549	465.56	19.61
上 海 Shanghai	1331311	261535	106438	271.41	5.57
江 苏 Jiangsu	5304302	1146981	689582	588.21	49.85
浙 江 Zhejiang	2412252	592877	283374	433.92	38.29
安 徽 Anhui	2380235	307751	183478	236.95	12.15
福 建 Fujian	1281452	240162	76890	230.53	13.10
江 西 Jiangxi	2064968	431372	145631	219.73	11.05
山 东 Shandong	4747758	953995	827813	539.28	48.73
河 南 henan	5123402	1049288	475624	547.95	50.87
湖 北 Hubei	4034680	1003163	273733	500.13	25.97
湖 南 Hunan	2285609	357798	164748	293.18	15.80
广 东 Guangdong	7124940	1489318	645634	1074.19	178.11
广 西 Guangxi	1333114	305377	61119	208.79	11.85
海 南 Hainan	88820	51361	14800	7.73	0.39
重 庆 Chongqing	1333438	267003	110550	188.48	5.15
四 川 Sichuan	3290334	487180	310957	478.63	17.97
贵 州 guizhou	645777	145955	47408	168.49	4.45
云 南 Yunnan	1097153	149266	127638	111.32	24.73
西 藏 Tibet	0	0	0	0.00	0.00
陕 西 Shaanxi	2451651	327417	269540	421.00	50.51
甘 肃 Gansu	779864	227246	97056	90.00	1.21
青 海 Qinghai	1085676	82456	64982	43.09	3.49
宁 夏 Ningxia	0	0	0	0.00	0.00
新 疆 Xinjiang	3080556	912811	228312	1158.20	878.52

产权)(成人高校)

Resources (Owned by HEIs)(HEIs for Adults)

资料情况 ed. Resources: 电子图书(片) Electronic Books & Magazines in Libraries(Disk): 计 Total	资料情况 ed. Resources: 电子图书(片) Electronic Books & Magazines in Libraries(Disk): 当年新增 New Floor Space Added in Current Year	拥有教学用计算机(台) No. of computers used for Instruction	语音实验室座位数(个) No. of Seats in Audio-Labs	多媒体教室座位数(个) No. of Seats in Multimedia Class rooms	网上教学课程数(种) No. of Web-Based Courses	固定资产值(万元) Fixed Assets (in 10000 yuan): 合计 Total	固定资产值(万元) Fixed Assets (in 10000 yuan): 其中:教学、科研仪器设备资产 of which: Teaching Equipment & Instruments: 计 Total	固定资产值(万元) Fixed Assets (in 10000 yuan): 其中:教学、科研仪器设备资产 of which: Teaching Equipment & Instruments: 当年新增 New Floor SpaceAdded in Current Year
1716508	**814644**	**297903**	**94835**	**407923**	**29592**	**2901143.60**	**604961.71**	**92181.34**
28566	6614	21003	3948	25709	1599	197953.52	32676.15	3774.00
57310	3564	11464	3213	11118	460	70607.15	20419.03	3180.31
685554	601270	5286	2151	10931	1411	74127.06	15603.94	1313.18
74531	11307	6421	1656	6641	316	67774.33	14495.96	2601.10
5266	795	2744	880	1950	126	22703.02	4484.20	359.26
12974	2500	10317	3799	10017	1317	68106.96	16764.86	1942.06
7776	1221	5632	2131	4791	377	58241.28	9683.46	1117.61
70375	6187	10308	5311	10870	451	122924.59	25382.98	3775.46
3813	357	9382	2586	14138	557	96912.14	24077.28	2267.88
47669	16570	25733	6973	32025	853	264290.40	46789.03	9467.54
39322	11895	18891	4605	43130	4927	127756.03	40387.77	4326.60
14533	4168	7315	2808	9378	974	64554.60	14558.45	2151.84
17949	3782	9067	2732	17427	201	70949.59	16562.19	2215.34
13352	6548	6698	2900	9102	638	38153.12	9646.25	2018.09
44596	7411	17225	5227	16090	499	181808.48	40137.35	6292.56
57227	28074	14306	5187	16973	600	167865.00	30882.04	5150.56
30816	6569	11617	3933	18098	832	134051.86	28540.63	2724.44
44871	2601	9823	3164	14798	5631	75310.17	17614.38	1609.14
176482	38026	38774	13456	75841	1648	370717.93	82215.03	14667.51
53462	228	6455	2381	7431	483	55333.42	13585.86	1616.10
0	0	380	48	575	0	1181.07	710.56	8.61
3581	2718	6550	1599	8992	0	47645.70	10927.02	1659.50
116985	8235	14062	4924	15079	1916	142544.60	21795.38	2973.29
8538	3728	3225	945	3784	398	138862.37	10654.66	1730.01
9176	90	2876	1140	3289	0	31666.20	7336.53	3194.84
0	0	0	0	0	0	0.00	0.00	0.00
48114	7152	11233	3193	7847	811	121194.71	22781.20	7360.07
3151	808	2541	669	2186	186	19064.97	5712.10	281.40
4051	209	1446	338	1380	165	7652.30	2206.16	118.10
0	0	0	0	0	0	0.00	0.00	0.00
36468	32017	7129	2938	8333	2216	61191.03	18331.26	2284.94

资产情况(学校产权)

Condition of Fixed Assets and Teaching Resources (Owned by HEIs)

地区 Region	学校占地面积(平方米) Area of School sites (m^2) 计 Total	其中:绿化用地面积 Of Which: Green Arens	其中:运动场地面积 Of Which: Sports Areas	图书音像 Audio-visual 一般图书(万册) Books & Magazines in Libraries(10 Thouand Volume) 计 Total	当年新增 New Floor Space Added in Current Year
合 计 Total	**25141183**	**5374236**	**2822679**	**4134.21**	**1228.94**
北 京 Beijing	3805669	801553	166026	205.05	42.26
天 津 Tianjin	57901	5600	8400	19.30	2.11
河 北 Hebei	1846887	261679	196880	172.76	23.42
山 西 Shanxi	866563	151795	106828	867.98	306.23
内蒙古 Inner Mongolia	58862	15231	13289	14.75	2.51
辽 宁 Liaoning	910107	145806	142769	65.06	7.11
吉 林 Jilin	223548	34780	65400	30.10	1.90
黑龙江 Heilongjiang	491708	94261	217400	75.86	6.89
上 海 Shanghai	168335	49420	25256	546.22	3.33
江 苏 Jiangsu	287613	150822	24100	24.34	1.30
浙 江 Zhejiang	929301	234258	89380	81.85	8.20
安 徽 Anhui	810680	83850	70410	41.80	2.15
福 建 Fujian	121563	33027	25000	24.65	6.54
江 西 Jiangxi	1299301	233053	111848	117.76	13.32
山 东 Shandong	4818407	794710	443109	297.85	63.87
河 南 Henan	2325810	536388	331608	178.95	23.44
湖 北 Hubei	47300	33200	10200	15.80	2.21
湖 南 Hunan	592321	118110	64810	116.40	20.89
广 东 Guangdong	2545562	988958	391012	164.79	40.28
广 西 Guangxi	6608	350	2250	3.30	0.20
海 南 Hainan	0	0	0	0.00	0.00
重 庆 Chongqing	523771	166744	68715	47.06	9.45
四 川 Sichuan	503403	157125	75370	63.13	20.54
贵 州 Guizhou	0	0	0	6.00	0.00
云 南 Yunnan	45397	19475	7600	1.50	0.00
西 藏 Tibet	0	0	0	0.00	0.00
陕 西 Shaanxi	1850914	264041	165019	936.36	618.70
甘 肃 Gansu	2852	0	0	13.79	1.89
青 海 Qinghai	800	0	0	1.80	0.20
宁 夏 Ningxia	0	0	0	0.00	0.00
新 疆 Xinjiang	0	0	0	0.00	0.00

(民办的其他高等教育机构)

(Non-state/private HEIs)

资料情况 ed. Resources		拥有教学用计算机(台) No. of computers used for Instruction	语音实验室座位数(个) No. of Seats in Audio-Labs	多媒体教室座位数(个) No. of Seats in Multimedia Class rooms	网上教学课程数(种) No. of Web-Based Courses	固定资产值(万元) Fixed Assets (in 10000 yuan)		
电子图书(片) Electronic Books & Magazines in Libraries(Disk)						合　计 Total	其中:教学、科研仪器设备资产 of which: Teaching Equipment & Instruments	
计 Total	当年新增 New Floor Space Added in Current Year						计 Total	当年新增 New Floor SpaceAdded in Current Year
1039202	**544918**	**107414**	**46711**	**106398**	**5478**	**1056780.69**	**194793.23**	**52747.06**
547234	209964	13055	5620	15835	158	98717.68	20991.70	8492.01
752	522	1574	631	1388	9	7677.18	3633.50	64.47
22218	5660	6596	2823	3217	35	90946.50	11932.25	1647.95
9010	2831	4525	1738	3262	108	46032.55	8337.03	2819.30
282	26	735	404	394	0	8597.00	1276.10	201.44
750	216	2740	2475	5097	633	26893.68	4786.53	887.37
5657	634	1648	674	1009	34	12089.83	2355.70	91.70
23193	3807	3760	1521	1819	61	24163.69	5098.54	680.36
1011	84	6187	2280	6024	5	201665.75	19583.59	12362.52
0	0	1393	795	1831	5	4222.35	958.17	376.00
6030	5618	4705	1810	6510	140	48067.22	7160.59	1239.37
160366	150150	1779	780	746	7	26095.95	2770.97	426.00
9538	1130	2272	958	1558	13	24658.87	4021.47	1664.47
6409	1971	4790	1995	3488	2124	24926.60	5435.16	902.20
8733	3027	10603	5529	10982	578	114734.66	20348.79	5809.02
17742	6250	6524	2169	5940	338	71161.01	12890.09	1732.56
100192	100022	1520	828	1987	10	7835.52	5760.60	811.70
23855	5824	8196	4396	4657	862	36795.35	6916.85	2177.20
71727	43703	11504	4603	17039	185	84279.02	25885.11	6116.49
0	0	183	96	0	0	2721.00	263.00	7.00
0	0	46	46	0	5	30.00	0.00	0.00
723	104	3123	616	3220	0	23466.00	6959.21	1151.00
2422	266	2771	1247	5475	4	20036.73	6614.40	1547.47
0	0	51	48	30	0	552.00	85.00	0.00
492	492	560	0	280	0	2373.00	288.00	45.00
0	0	0	0	0	0	0.00	0.00	0.00
20176	2077	6170	2404	4018	90	46861.78	9814.78	1373.26
690	540	348	169	512	66	1076.77	530.10	121.20
0	0	56	56	80	8	103.00	96.00	0.00
0	0	0	0	0	0	0.00	0.00	0.00
0	0	0	0	0	0	0.00	0.00	0.00

资产情况

Condition of Fixed Assets and Teaching Resources

总计 Total	学校占地面积(平方米) Area of School sites (m^2) 计 Total	其中:绿化用地面积 Of Which: Green Arens	其中:运动场地面积 Of Which: Sports Areas	图书音像 Audio-visual 一般图书(万册) Books & Magazines in Libraries(10 Thouand Volume) 计 Total	当年新增 New Floor Space Added in Current Year
合 计 Total	**59939206**	**11770732**	**5658170**	**46915.44**	**21381.44**
北 京 Beijing	3429726	907198	494061	73.61	16.79
天 津 Tianjin	820319	84220	41354	35.15	7.73
河 北 Hebei	5629638	910935	475655	11482.00	1042.83
山 西 Shanxi	2245642	399715	312916	186.71	15.00
内蒙古 Inner Mongolia	1622657	75010	86101	59.71	1.83
辽 宁 Liaoning	2216880	397148	313850	35.50	1.02
吉 林 Jilin	2072627	226687	142188	22037.18	10010.23
黑龙江 Heilongjiang	1770981	117339	120354	143.49	2.56
上 海 Shanghai	1986496	501600	151235	295.44	0.78
江 苏 Jiangsu	2590262	801793	182287	43.40	6.48
浙 江 Zhejiang	1392201	290961	103491	17.20	0.00
安 徽 Anhui	1409173	204300	91175	215.87	10.55
福 建 Fujian	3823392	266964	158616	77.68	41.35
江 西 Jiangxi	1773954	180635	131025	4.19	1.34
山 东 Shandong	4883415	1683697	512613	141.23	36.00
河 南 henan	1889264	247731	188363	10084.60	10005.97
湖 北 Hubei	2629451	558388	239222	87.50	9.60
湖 南 Hunan	1762044	410769	244140	71.22	23.73
广 东 Guangdong	5220899	1456454	662403	365.15	68.64
广 西 Guangxi	314046	38500	78787	37.08	20.47
海 南 Hainan	0	0	0	3.00	0.00
重 庆 Chongqing	1653715	308354	77815	96.11	23.60
四 川 Sichuan	3082423	771080	367237	1055.14	8.57
贵 州 guizhou	325079	118787	41311	8.00	0.15
云 南 Yunnan	512783	9400	10050	0.00	0.00
西 藏 Tibet	950000	1550	17355	6.29	2.00
陕 西 Shaanxi	3088344	765868	361795	227.53	22.92
甘 肃 Gansu	192459	26039	30730	19.66	0.10
青 海 Qinghai	5838	0	1500	1.80	0.20
宁 夏 Ningxia	33300	0	0	0.00	0.00
新 疆 Xinjiang	612198	9610	20541	4.00	1.00

(非学校产权)(总计)

(Not Owned by HEIs)(Total)

资料情况 ed. Resources		拥有教学用计算机(台) No. of computers used for Instruction	语音实验室座位数(个) No. of Seats in Audio-Labs	多媒体教室座位数(个) No. of Seats in Multimedia Class rooms	网上教学课程数(种) No. of Web-Based Courses	固定资产值(万元) Fixed Assets (in 10000 yuan)		
电子图书(片) Electronic Books & Magazines in Libraries(Disk)						合计 Total	其中:教学、科研仪器设备资产 of which: Teaching Equipment & Instruments	
计 Total	当年新增 New Floor Space Added in Current Year						计 Total	当年新增 New Floor SpaceAdded in Current Year
734431	**179148**	**94654**	**45753**	**150620**	**2345**	**1434370.81**	**344914.30**	**56948.03**
14348	3867	5787	4258	13898	173	30009.66	10448.26	6032.26
12277	1670	3178	779	3486	22	87181.11	60775.84	4774.92
50742	2535	11145	7427	17522	471	191353.28	38806.25	5680.43
48791	1739	4024	1516	6482	5	47323.84	8527.70	1500.20
6525	6525	2060	676	1085	0	44468.30	9679.22	119.40
800	0	1352	715	1910	0	62329.00	6087.00	0.00
51551	50836	1952	1166	5952	127	69443.19	4980.56	2077.87
136782	8958	2497	1150	3609	38	45414.72	14322.06	6946.15
673	170	3758	2013	11102	1	22998.00	3360.00	134.40
9810	3109	3958	2040	12424	49	77951.42	11601.71	1963.10
30	30	313	100	350	0	19974.90	1972.18	30.00
17846	1830	3864	1581	3914	0	41094.84	22332.00	422.00
1806	908	3083	708	5350	12	73856.35	11560.75	2368.57
2803	2803	120	80	0	0	11868.47	1917.73	0.00
4073	255	2984	1260	4231	6	40478.56	12820.70	2024.00
17013	2264	4347	858	2881	0	8053.42	3212.16	397.40
140000	40000	1758	1082	3632	35	34758.00	10819.30	2421.21
62300	22200	3114	1002	2376	764	33594.00	5709.10	1052.00
27997	9537	11750	7093	21814	176	229801.87	44079.41	7137.85
445	61	634	367	4166	0	61828.02	17736.72	4469.22
1000	0	400	200	1200	0	220.00	220.00	0.00
92686	16865	9001	1064	3170	107	52441.50	14372.00	939.00
17236	722	5649	3368	12757	39	51998.51	11429.00	2735.00
0	0	446	166	170	0	14701.00	7481.00	1420.00
3560	0	296	384	360	0	170.00	48.00	2.00
0	0	122	42	250	0	3590.00	477.00	0.00
12218	2264	5847	4340	5998	244	70199.45	7746.85	1905.45
1119	0	747	45	151	33	5794.40	1128.80	36.60
0	0	238	143	160	43	206.00	199.00	0.00
0	0	0	0	0	0	0.00	0.00	0.00
0	0	230	130	220	0	1269.00	1064.00	359.00

资产情况

Condition of Fixed Assets and Teaching Resources

地 区 Region	学校占地面积(平方米) Area of School sites (m²)			图书音像 Audio-visual	
				一般图书(万册) Books & Magazines in Libraries(10 Thouand Volume)	
	计 Total	其中:绿化用地面积 Of Which: Green Arens	其中:运动场地面积 Of Which: Sports Areas	计 Total	当年新增 New Floor Space Added in Current Year
合 计 Total	**44685738**	**8155877**	**3459639**	**2192.34**	**324.62**
北 京 Beijing	1245035	228138	103853	33.29	11.51
天 津 Tianjin	716328	79370	34264	23.95	6.13
河 北 Hebei	4894842	715342	401075	462.01	41.33
山 西 Shanxi	1948915	374892	269143	166.71	14.00
内蒙古 Inner Mongolia	956569	66360	58013	31.11	1.45
辽 宁 Liaoning	2050694	384262	241640	34.80	1.02
吉 林 Jilin	1979493	211057	123666	34.38	10.23
黑龙江 Heilongjiang	1444510	70397	42073	138.49	2.56
上 海 Shanghai	1587298	441087	103476	58.72	0.50
江 苏 Jiangsu	2091873	583436	143410	42.23	6.48
浙 江 Zhejiang	1142285	246324	57831	15.00	0.00
安 徽 Anhui	1190547	187514	61958	196.58	10.55
福 建 Fujian	3405301	168964	97099	66.02	39.15
江 西 Jiangxi	1344100	88637	78980	4.19	1.34
山 东 Shandong	2449800	1015153	130147	71.2	17.1
河 南 henan	1408745	209000	119334	68.1	5.3
湖 北 Hubei	2358495	495293	187954	57.5	9.6
湖 南 Hunan	626743	106801	26300	44.07	23.03
广 东 Guangdong	2945226	920245	457822	247.14	62.61
广 西 Guangxi	299723	37500	77987	35.28	20.47
海 南 Hainan	0	0	0	3	0
重 庆 Chongqing	1444279	255360	71208	93.31	23.6
四 川 Sichuan	2743492	698502	272943	47.25	7.85
贵 州 guizhou	284909	114487	32511	8	0.15
云 南 Yunnan	477905	0	0	0	0
西 藏 Tibet	950000	1550	17355	6.29	2
陕 西 Shaanxi	1984843	447596	225689	184.16	5.66
甘 肃 Gansu	81890	0	8667	15.56	0
青 海 Qinghai	0	0	0	0	0
宁 夏 Ningxia	33300	0	0	0	0
新 疆 Xinjiang	598598	8610	15241	4	1

(非学校产权)(普通高校)
(Not Owned by HEIs)(HEIs)

资料情况 ed. Resources		拥有教学用计算机(台) No. of computers used for Instruction	语音实验室座位数(个) No. of Seats in Audio-Labs	多媒体教室座位数(个) No. of Seats in Multimedia Class rooms	网上教学课程数(种) No. of Web-Based Courses	固定资产值(万元) Fixed Assets (in 10000 yuan)		
电子图书(片) Electronic Books & Magazines in Libraries(Disk)						合计 Total	其中:教学、科研仪器设备资产 of which: Teaching Equipment & Instruments	
计 Total	当年新增 New Floor Space Added in Current Year						计 Total	当年新增 New Floor SpaceAdded in Current Year
634914	**164415**	**72377**	**36684**	**127979**	**267**	**1282006.61**	**306390.39**	**45545.01**
6652	2740	2399	2606	8814	20	16741.77	1994.00	392.70
5657	140	2286	514	3008	11	86470.81	60288.51	4506.09
40392	2335	10493	7189	17009	0	187267.50	36917.60	5450.43
47091	739	2957	1060	5812	0	35147.30	7339.70	1224.20
6525	6525	1071	372	734	0	43610.80	9308.02	70.00
0	0	1054	615	1210	0	56849.00	4710.00	0.00
50511	50336	1714	946	5538	1	67908.69	4812.44	2001.87
136782	8958	2191	950	3469	38	44426.41	13588.06	6946.15
653	170	2961	1511	10049	1	22998.00	3360.00	134.40
9780	3109	3888	1990	12194	49	76007.24	11495.32	1930.42
0	0	163	0	0	0	18507.20	1792.18	0.00
17746	1830	2102	940	2673	0	28589.6	18218	372
1286	887	2328	598	5010	0	57795.91	10201.04	2364.67
2803	2803	120	80	0	0	10367.73	1917.73	0
3625	235	2313	766	3097	0	27238	10485.1	1364
1350	420	3555	790	2760	0	5616.28	2578.28	275
140000	40000	1243	910	2386	35	31836	9957.3	1946.21
50000	20000	1418	578	980	0	22945	3221	700
11655	3682	8028	5280	17359	5	192893.34	36854.79	4938.65
445	61	563	319	4154	0	61447.02	17540.72	4469.22
1000	0	400	200	1200	0	220	220	0
92686	16865	8821	982	3050	107	52281.5	14322	939
2116	662	4843	3013	11240	0	50190.51	10531	2545
0	0	446	166	170	0	12431	7481	1420
0	0	240	384	240	0	0	0	0
0	0	122	42	250	0	3590	477	0
5040	1918	3867	3753	5353	0	64661	5315.6	1196
1119	0	561	0	0	0	2700	400	0
0	0	0	0	0	0	0	0	0
0	0	0	0	0	0	0	0	0
0	0	230	130	220	0	1269	1064	359

地区 Region	学校占地面积(平方米) Area of School sites (m^2) 计 Total	其中:绿化用地面积 Of Which: Green Arens	其中:运动场地面积 Of Which: Sports Areas	图书音像 Audio-visual 一般图书(万册) Books & Magazines in Libraries(10 Thouand Volume) 计 Total	当年新增 New Floor Space Added in Current Year
合　计 Total	**3429334**	**815288**	**487302**	**246.90**	**18.75**
北　京 Beijing	225812	25082	3618	15.37	0.12
天　津 Tianjin	14479	200	2400	0.00	0.00
河　北 Hebei	102895	38033	8300	12.46	0.00
山　西 Shanxi	93000	2036	6000	12.90	0.00
内蒙古 Inner Mongolia	0	0	0	0.00	0.00
辽　宁 Liaoning	57497	5886	32341	0.70	0.00
吉　林 Jilin	4501	60	110	2.80	0.00
黑龙江 Heilongjiang	46474	1200	5800	4.00	0.00
上　海 Shanghai	174425	12102	7069	0.00	0.00
江　苏 Jiangsu	160959	73502	20010	0.07	0.00
浙　江 Zhejiang	50890	6707	8660	0.00	0.00
安　徽 Anhui	182226	13882	24517	19.29	0.00
福　建 Fujian	36391	6000	12347	6.66	0.20
江　西 Jiangxi	374	0	0	0.00	0.00
山　东 Shandong	437065	211100	176835	0.00	0.00
河　南 henan	113550	3300	0	0.00	0.00
湖　北 Hubei	60000	1325	7624	27.80	0.00
湖　南 Hunan	133825	52574	30	12.25	0.15
广　东 Guangdong	778398	156771	48485	97.99	1.98
广　西 Guangxi	13373	1000	800	0.50	0.00
海　南 Hainan	0	0	0	0.00	0.00
重　庆 Chongqing	12752	1213	2000	2.80	0.00
四　川 Sichuan	101811	21005	30526	1.70	0.00
贵　州 guizhou	8000	1300	800	0.00	0.00
云　南 Yunnan	34878	9400	10050	0.00	0.00
西　藏 Tibet	0	0	0	0.00	0.00
陕　西 Shaanxi	472612	151011	53797	27.11	16.30
甘　肃 Gansu	93709	19599	18383	2.50	0.00
青　海 Qinghai	5838	0	1500	0.00	0.00
宁　夏 Ningxia	0	0	0	0.00	0.00
新　疆 Xinjiang	13600	1000	5300	0.00	0.00

(非学校产权)(成人高校)
(Not Owned by HEIs)(HEIs for Adults)

资料情况 ed. Resources		拥有教学用计算机(台) No. of computers used for Instruction	语音实验室座位数(个) No. of Seats in Audio-Labs	多媒体教室座位数(个) No. of Seats in Multimedia Class rooms	网上教学课程数(种) No. of Web-Based Courses	固定资产值(万元) Fixed Assets (in 10000 yuan)		
电子图书(片) Electronic Books & Magazines in Libraries(Disk)						合计 Total	其中:教学、科研仪器设备资产 of which: Teaching Equipment & Instruments	
计 Total	当年新增 New Floor Space Added in Current Year						计 Total	当年新增 New Floor Space Added in Current Year
32046	**452**	**9504**	**3700**	**9302**	**993**	**67099.10**	**17580.10**	**2210.41**
1030	0	1123	316	1748	78	3266.37	1511.76	110.56
0	0	0	0	0	0	0.00	0.00	0.00
120	0	160	99	418	468	1066.78	448.65	0.00
0	0	579	306	320	0	600.00	136.00	23.00
0	0	0	0	0	0	0.00	0.00	0.00
150	0	40	0	0	0	1860.00	60.00	0.00
40	0	50	51	74	0	161.00	7.12	0.00
0	0	306	200	140	0	886.31	734.00	0.00
0	0	241	62	0	0	0.00	0.00	0.00
30	0	40	50	230	0	874.18	11.39	2.68
0	0	0	0	0	0	1287.70	0.00	0.00
100	0	1062	641	1229	0	12155.24	3914.00	0.00
420	21	555	60	140	0	1690.39	344.71	3.90
0	0	0	0	0	0	0.00	0.00	0.00
0	0	260	250	200	0	2997.56	767.60	0.00
7686	0	400	0	0	0	767.28	17.28	0.00
0	0	245	80	396	0	2750.00	690.00	470.00
0	0	914	104	862	100	5021.00	1698.10	264.00
1732	85	1880	952	2541	30	24584.24	4399.24	679.82
0	0	0	0	0	0	200.00	15.00	0.00
0	0	0	0	0	0	0.00	0.00	0.00
0	0	180	82	120	0	160.00	50.00	0.00
15000	0	179	109	159	39	60.00	23.00	5.00
0	0	0	0	0	0	0.00	0.00	0.00
3560	0	56	0	120	0	170.00	48.00	2.00
0	0	0	0	0	0	0.00	0.00	0.00
2178	346	990	251	445	243	3962.45	2111.25	649.45
0	0	62	0	80	0	2475.60	490.00	0.00
0	0	182	87	80	35	103.00	103.00	0.00
0	0	0	0	0	0	0.00	0.00	0.00
0	0	0	0	0	0	0.00	0.00	0.00

资产情况

Condition of Fixed Assets and Teaching Resources

总　计 Total	学校占地面积(平方米) Area of School sites (m^2)			图书音像 Audio-visual	
				一般图书(万册) Books & Magazines in Libraries(10 Thouand Volume)	
	计 Total	其中:绿化用地面积 Of Which: Green Arens	其中:运动场地面积 Of Which: Sports Areas	计 Total	当年新增 New Floor Space Added in Current Year
合　计 Total	**11824134**	**2799567**	**1711229**	**44476.20**	**21038.07**
北　京 Beijing	1958879	653978	386590	24.95	5.16
天　津 Tianjin	89512	4650	4690	11.20	1.60
河　北 Hebei	631901	157560	66280	11007.53	1001.50
山　西 Shanxi	203727	22787	37773	7.10	1.00
内蒙古 Inner Mongolia	666088	8650	28088	28.60	0.38
辽　宁 Liaoning	108689	7000	39869	0.00	0.00
吉　林 Jilin	88633	15570	18412	22000.00	10000.00
黑龙江 Heilongjiang	279997	45742	72481	1.00	0.00
上　海 Shanghai	224773	48411	40690	236.72	0.28
江　苏 Jiangsu	337430	144855	18867	1.10	0.00
浙　江 Zhejiang	199026	37930	37000	2.20	0.00
安　徽 Anhui	36400	2904	4700	0.00	0.00
福　建 Fujian	381700	92000	49170	5.00	2.00
江　西 Jiangxi	429480	91998	52045	0.00	0.00
山　东 Shandong	1996550	457444	205631	70.03	18.90
河　南 Henan	366969	35431	69029	10016.50	10000.67
湖　北 Hubei	210956	61770	43644	2.20	0.00
湖　南 Hunan	1001476	251394	217810	14.90	0.55
广　东 Guangdong	1497275	379438	156096	20.02	4.05
广　西 Guangxi	950	0	0	1.30	0.00
海　南 Hainan	0	0	0	0.00	0.00
重　庆 Chongqing	196684	51781	4607	0.00	0.00
四　川 Sichuan	237120	51573	63768	1006.19	0.72
贵　州 Guizhou	32170	3000	8000	0.00	0.00
云　南 Yunnan	0	0	0	0.00	0.00
西　藏 Tibet	0	0	0	0.00	0.00
陕　西 Shaanxi	630889	167261	82309	16.26	0.96
甘　肃 Gansu	16860	6440	3680	1.60	0.10
青　海 Qinghai	0	0	0	1.80	0.20
宁　夏 Ningxia	0	0	0	0.00	0.00
新　疆 Xinjiang	0	0	0	0.00	0.00

(非学校产权)(民办的其他高等教育机构)

(Not Owned by HEIs)(Non-state/private HEIs)

资料情况 ed. Resources		拥有教学用计算机(台) No. of computers used for Instruction	语音实验室座位数(个) No. of Seats in Audio-Labs	多媒体教室座位数(个) No. of Seats in Multimedia Class rooms	网上教学课程数(种) No. of Web-Based Courses	固定资产值(万元) Fixed Assets (in 10000 yuan)		
电子图书(片) Electronic Books & Magazines in Libraries(Disk)						合计 Total	其中:教学、科研仪器设备资产 of which: Teaching Equipment & Instruments	
计 Total	当年新增 New Floor Space Added in Current Year						计 Total	当年新增 New Floor Space Added in Current Year
67471	**14281**	**12773**	**5369**	**13339**	**1085**	**85265.10**	**20943.81**	**9192.61**
6666	1127	2265	1336	3336	75	10001.52	6942.50	5529.00
6620	1530	892	265	478	11	710.30	487.33	268.83
10230	200	492	139	95	3	3019.00	1440.00	230.00
1700	1000	488	150	350	5	11576.54	1052.00	253.00
0	0	989	304	351	0	857.50	371.20	49.40
650	0	258	100	700	0	3620.00	1317.00	0.00
1000	500	188	169	340	126	1373.50	161.00	76.00
0	0	0	0	0	0	102.00	0.00	0.00
20	0	556	440	1053	0	0.00	0.00	0.00
0	0	30	0	0	0	1070.00	95.00	30.00
30	30	150	100	350	0	180.00	180.00	30.00
0	0	700	0	12	0	350.00	200.00	50.00
100	0	200	50	200	12	14370.05	1015.00	0.00
0	0	0	0	0	0	1500.74	0.00	0.00
448	20	411	244	934	6	10243.00	1568.00	660.00
7977	1844	392	68	121	0	1669.86	616.60	122.40
0	0	270	92	850	0	172.00	172.00	5.00
12300	2200	782	320	534	664	5628.00	790.00	88.00
14610	5770	1842	861	1914	141	12324.29	2825.38	1519.38
0	0	71	48	12	0	181.00	181.00	0.00
0	0	0	0	0	0	0.00	0.00	0.00
0	0	0	0	0	0	0.00	0.00	0.00
120	60	627	246	1358	0	1748.00	875.00	185.00
0	0	0	0	0	0	2270.00	0.00	0.00
0	0	0	0	0	0	0.00	0.00	0.00
0	0	0	0	0	0	0.00	0.00	0.00
5000	0	990	336	200	1	1576.00	320.00	60.00
0	0	124	45	71	33	618.80	238.80	36.60
0	0	56	56	80	8	103.00	96.00	0.00
0	0	0	0	0	0	0.00	0.00	0.00
0	0	0	0	0	0	0.00	0.00	0.00

校舍情况(总计)
Conditions of School Buidings (Total)

单位:平方米
Unit: m^2

总　计 Total	学校产权建筑面积 Floor Area of School Building Owned by HEIs				正在施工面积 Floor Area Under Construction	独立使用非学校产权建筑面积 Floor Area of School Building Not Owned by HEIs
	计 Subtotal	其中:危房 Of Which: Dilapidated Buildings	其中:当年新增 Of Which: Newly Added in Current Year	其中:被外单位借用 Of Which: Floor Space Hired by Other Schools or Units		
合　计 Total	**426007768**	**1965975**	**54392904**	**1260003**	**47624638**	**41815149**
北　京 Beijing	23869834	223129	1750904	191432	2364921	2422125
天　津 Tianjin	8736682	20291	969692	4583	1148031	1655147
河　北 Hebei	18356753	27965	1204381	24027	1436546	3931705
山　西 Shanxi	10645527	27339	1203701	299747	982928	912436
内蒙古 Inner Mongolia	5557838	87165	396484	7673	755759	799098
辽　宁 Liaoning	16534385	85387	1825738	28053	2013436	2024424
吉　林 Jilin	12458241	125399	1109776	54944	600661	1278877
黑龙江 Heilongjiang	17351477	118361	2672807	88901	879768	983694
上　海 Shanghai	12894477	19498	1144567	91591	1438526	2286485
江　苏 Jiangsu	31145603	104813	4027397	28512	4897682	1359648
浙　江 Zhejiang	17205670	37497	3645093	54208	2744591	1548239
安　徽 Anhui	13561338	60773	2144439	27065	1961851	1603690
福　建 Fujian	9478833	48205	1553194	5150	1418681	1537718
江　西 Jiangxi	14855355	54642	3208445	52053	1615868	529707
山　东 Shandong	29470804	102556	5039932	37944	3634467	1448249
河　南 henan	22861254	56695	3631611	7431	2833780	1461789
湖　北 Hubei	27937498	81595	3320670	126795	2076985	2789233
湖　南 Hunan	19130039	60591	2383743	9268	2265657	2715551
广　东 Guangdong	23877028	29019	2424936	74501	3592099	3617318
广　西 Guangxi	8449696	8037	948907	11535	650011	320886
海　南 Hainan	1621181	5990	378526	0	85406	197573
重　庆 Chongqing	9744879	176797	1055590	550	1134010	943436
四　川 Sichuan	19980800	71190	2457470	8784	2813930	2015645
贵　州 guizhou	6214817	33293	708448	2637	586976	417607
云　南 Yunnan	6212469	61351	848034	4506	226546	204316
西　藏 Tibet	384454	26287	0	0	28396	0
陕　西 Shaanxi	21697443	87902	2919802	8805	2395708	2173217
甘　肃 Gansu	6258756	20467	798087	450	692039	406210
青　海 Qinghai	1333685	5827	60970	0	27681	58880
宁　夏 Ningxia	1348792	10842	41516	0	132860	68690
新　疆 Xinjiang	6832160	87072	518044	8858	188838	103556

校舍情况(普通高校)

Conditions of School Buidings (Regular HEIs)

单位:平方米

Unit: m^2

地　区 Region	学校产权建筑面积 Floor Area of School Building Owned by HEIs				正在施工面积 Floor Area Under Construction	独立使用非学校产权建筑面积 Floor Area of School Building Not Owned by HEIs
	计 Subtotal	其中:危房 Of Which: Dilapidated Buildings	其中:当年新增 Of Which: Newly Added in Current Year	其中:被外单位借用 Of Which: Floor Space Hired by Other Schools or Units		
合　计 Total	**382017582**	**1857033**	**50655732**	**1114358**	**44019739**	**34542433**
北　京 Beijing	21242040	222552	1576316	190708	1966999	1412737
天　津 Tianjin	8104294	14208	925349	4319	1065591	1471239
河　北 Hebei	16478409	26480	1028601	22852	1282598	3693245
山　西 Shanxi	9315958	26989	1053853	298848	956354	751398
内蒙古 Inner Mongolia	5085253	87165	381645	7673	743359	709859
辽　宁 Liaoning	15419712	84922	1735111	27535	1970296	1867998
吉　林 Jilin	11546570	123547	1096512	50673	538653	1178812
黑龙江 Heilongjiang	15664914	115157	2550099	73111	831868	696980
上　海 Shanghai	11986475	19498	1067484	83444	1375974	1922284
江　苏 Jiangsu	28479152	104303	3898909	28466	4736098	1252407
浙　江 Zhejiang	15521772	1097	3525895	43797	2639103	1380336
安　徽 Anhui	12594531	59052	2075339	25547	1797780	1476259
福　建 Fujian	8540271	48205	1433474	2238	1335709	1065867
江　西 Jiangxi	13737545	47065	3111545	51773	1467137	396910
山　东 Shandong	25118385	99912	4567176	37724	3191323	1100318
河　南 henan	19448836	56695	3455661	0	2569885	1312106
湖　北 Hubei	26019356	80173	2985430	44028	2041823	2434133
湖　南 Hunan	17662604	58178	2283815	7768	2152718	1979761
广　东 Guangdong	19276174	20273	2153304	73901	3098924	2442786
广　西 Guangxi	7740884	8037	939836	11535	610174	297619
海　南 Hainan	1598522	5990	378526	0	85406	196373
重　庆 Chongqing	8745786	176797	950239	550	1093219	864301
四　川 Sichuan	17586443	63434	2380803	8534	2761026	1778252
贵　州 guizhou	5828379	33293	687132	2637	562976	356886
云　南 Yunnan	5593714	55083	644601	4506	194375	204316
西　藏 Tibet	384454	26287	0	0	28396	0
陕　西 Shaanxi	19101602	78167	2420914	3543	1905103	1752644
甘　肃 Gansu	5972543	18760	774067	0	673393	316161
青　海 Qinghai	1141757	1237	59070	0	27681	58200
宁　夏 Ningxia	1348792	10842	41516	0	132860	68690
新　疆 Xinjiang	5732455	83635	473510	8648	182938	103556

校舍情况(成人高校)

Conditions of School Buidings (HEIs for Adults)

单位:平方米

Unit: m²

地区 Region	学校产权建筑面积 Floor Area of School Building Owned by HEIs				正在施工面积 Floor Area Under Construction	独立使用非学校产权建筑面积 Floor Area of School Building Not Owned by HEIs
	计 Subtotal	其中:危房 Of Which: Dilapidated Buildings	其中:当年新增 Of Which: Newly Added in Current Year	其中:被外单位借用 Of Which: Floor Space Hired by Other Schools or Units		
合 计 Total	**34738545**	**72542**	**2372703**	**127177**	**2036111**	**2207072**
北 京 Beijing	1828462	577	3070	724	11481	148839
天 津 Tianjin	581402	6083	42343	264	82440	22987
河 北 Hebei	906258	1485	49474	185	138388	95294
山 西 Shanxi	974378	350	88565	899	24174	33387
内蒙古 Inner Mongolia	400471	0	9422	0	12400	0
辽 宁 Liaoning	781988	465	34127	518	14300	66171
吉 林 Jilin	808448	1852	7254	4271	62008	33682
黑龙江 Heilongjiang	1505982	3204	111514	15415	9900	86801
上 海 Shanghai	844290	0	77083	5668	62552	95268
江 苏 Jiangsu	2610610	510	117488	46	53529	34875
浙 江 Zhejiang	1211498	0	46590	6811	105488	18191
安 徽 Anhui	815086	1721	44540	1518	164071	110651
福 建 Fujian	838562	0	113401	2912	59102	302061
江 西 Jiangxi	801103	7577	55938	280	9200	2294
山 东 Shandong	2422809	2644	242570	220	60268	2179
河 南 henan	2516089	0	97675	7341	185550	34832
湖 北 Hubei	1893128	1422	324306	71833	14962	108480
湖 南 Hunan	1181413	2413	48818	1500	68900	110636
广 东 Guangdong	3602672	8746	115539	600	418815	564267
广 西 Guangxi	702070	0	9071	0	39837	22317
海 南 Hainan	22659	0	0	0	0	0
重 庆 Chongqing	754405	0	105351	0	37885	7910
四 川 Sichuan	2143145	7756	41950	250	40904	83001
贵 州 guizhou	386438	0	21316	0	24000	37095
云 南 Yunnan	585960	6268	200433	0	32171	0
西 藏 Tibet	0	0	0	0	0	0
陕 西 Shaanxi	2046793	9735	294411	5262	279240	122425
甘 肃 Gansu	280793	1707	24020	450	18646	63429
青 海 Qinghai	191928	4590	1900	0	0	0
宁 夏 Ningxia	0	0	0	0	0	0
新 疆 Xinjiang	1099705	3437	44534	210	5900	0

校舍情况(民办的其他高等教育机构)

Conditions of School Buidings (Non-state/private HEIs)

单位:平方米

Unit: m^2

地　　区 Region	学校产权建筑面积 Floor Area of School Building Owned by HEIs				正在施工面积 Floor Area Under Construction	独立使用非学校产权建筑面积 Floor Area of School Building Not Owned by HEIs
	计 Subtotal	其中:危房 Of Which: Dilapidated Buildings	其中:当年新增 Of Which: Newly Added in Current Year	其中:被外单位借用 Of Which: Floor Space Hired by Other Schools or Units		
合　计 Total	**9251641**	**36400**	**1364469**	**18468**	**1568788**	**5065644**
北　京 Beijing	799332	0	171518	0	386441	860549
天　津 Tianjin	50986	0	2000	0	0	160921
河　北 Hebei	972086	0	126306	990	15560	143166
山　西 Shanxi	355191	0	61283	0	2400	127651
内蒙古 Inner Mongolia	72114	0	5417	0	0	89239
辽　宁 Liaoning	332685	0	56500	0	28840	90255
吉　林 Jilin	103223	0	6010	0	0	66383
黑龙江 Heilongjiang	180581	0	11194	375	38000	199913
上　海 Shanghai	63712	0	0	2479	0	268933
江　苏 Jiangsu	55841	0	11000	0	108055	72366
浙　江 Zhejiang	472400	36400	72608	3600	0	149712
安　徽 Anhui	151721	0	24560	0	0	16780
福　建 Fujian	100000	0	6319	0	23870	169790
江　西 Jiangxi	316707	0	40962	0	139531	130503
山　东 Shandong	1929610	0	230186	0	382876	345752
河　南 henan	896329	0	78275	90	78345	114851
湖　北 Hubei	25014	0	10934	10934	20200	246620
湖　南 Hunan	286022	0	51110	0	44039	625154
广　东 Guangdong	998182	0	156093	0	74360	610265
广　西 Guangxi	6742	0	0	0	0	950
海　南 Hainan	0	0	0	0	0	1200
重　庆 Chongqing	244688	0	0	0	2906	71225
四　川 Sichuan	251212	0	34717	0	12000	154392
贵　州 guizhou	0	0	0	0	0	23626
云　南 Yunnan	32795	0	3000	0	0	0
西　藏 Tibet	0	0	0	0	0	0
陕　西 Shaanxi	549048	0	204477	0	211365	298148
甘　肃 Gansu	5420	0	0	0	0	26620
青　海 Qinghai	0	0	0	0	0	680
宁　夏 Ningxia	0	0	0	0	0	0
新　疆 Xinjiang	0	0	0	0	0	0

普通高中校数、班数(总计)

Number of Senior Secondary Schools and Classes (Regional Aggregates)

总　计 Total	学校数(所) Schools 合　计 Total	 高级中学 Senior Sec. Schools	 完全中学 Complete Sec. Schools	班数(个) Classes 计 Total	 一年级 Grade 1	 二年级 Grade 2	 三年级 Grade 3
合　计 Total	**15779**	**5868**	**9911**	**344059**	**129584**	**114038**	**100437**
北　京 Beijing	329	66	263	5855	2178	1960	1717
天　津 Tianjin	222	77	145	3914	1443	1265	1206
河　北 Hebei	810	394	416	18608	7174	5977	5457
山　西 Shanxi	531	220	311	10070	3793	3310	2967
内蒙古 Inner Mongolia	381	140	241	7447	2858	2424	2165
辽　宁 Liaoning	456	333	123	10814	4129	3590	3095
吉　林 Jilin	297	172	125	6726	2541	2229	1956
黑龙江 Heilongjiang	481	258	223	8838	3261	2891	2686
上　海 Shanghai	343	154	189	6474	2259	2217	1998
江　苏 Jiangsu	845	297	548	22584	8352	7627	6605
浙　江 Zhejiang	614	409	205	15393	5858	5167	4368
安　徽 Anhui	741	155	586	15584	5754	5258	4572
福　建 Fujian	592	98	494	12944	4697	4433	3814
江　西 Jiangxi	629	175	454	12639	4783	4217	3639
山　东 Shandong	845	529	316	26860	10020	8927	7913
河　南 Henan	888	600	288	21302	8034	7027	6241
湖　北 Hubei	626	399	227	16431	5999	5370	5062
湖　南 Hunan	765	327	438	21158	7980	7030	6148
广　东 Guangdong	995	206	789	20574	7921	6714	5939
广　西 Guangxi	519	191	328	9761	3630	3260	2871
海　南 Hainan	105	6	99	1544	581	506	457
重　庆 Chongqing	293	14	279	7118	2706	2488	1924
四　川 Sichuan	785	96	689	18414	7208	6192	5014
贵　州 Guizhou	420	99	321	6724	2720	2146	1858
云　南 Yunnan	421	43	378	6442	2428	2118	1896
西　藏 Tibet	17	9	8	416	162	128	126
陕　西 Shaanxi	624	232	392	12262	4576	3990	3696
甘　肃 Gansu	453	73	380	7074	2716	2259	2099
青　海 Qinghai	148	16	132	1521	589	496	436
宁　夏 Ningxia	104	22	82	1877	688	612	577
新　疆 Xinjiang	500	58	442	6691	2546	2210	1935

普通高中校数、班数(城市)

Number of Senior Secondary Schools and Classes (Urban)

总计 Total	学校数(所) Schools 合计 Total	高级中学 Senior Sec. Schools	完全中学 Complete Sec. Schools	班数(个) Classes 计 Total	一年级 Grade 1	二年级 Grade 2	三年级 Grade 3
合计 Total	**6300**	**2142**	**4158**	**135188**	**50665**	**45027**	**39496**
北京 Beijing	209	30	179	3677	1315	1230	1132
天津 Tianjin	134	27	107	2323	859	753	711
河北 Hebei	293	80	213	6226	2466	2015	1745
山西 Shanxi	246	67	179	4406	1674	1444	1288
内蒙古 Inner Mongolia	193	67	126	3741	1440	1226	1075
辽宁 Liaoning	285	194	91	6233	2373	2057	1803
吉林 Jilin	104	52	52	2460	951	805	704
黑龙江 Heilongjiang	206	101	105	3805	1418	1265	1122
上海 Shanghai	209	112	97	4266	1446	1461	1359
江苏 Jiangsu	255	70	185	6103	2245	2063	1795
浙江 Zhejiang	270	162	108	6865	2663	2321	1881
安徽 Anhui	245	47	198	5529	1954	1940	1635
福建 Fujian	194	44	150	3630	1376	1182	1072
江西 Jiangxi	188	51	137	3823	1352	1287	1184
山东 Shandong	380	219	161	12129	4555	4064	3510
河南 Henan	348	167	181	7055	2645	2390	2020
湖北 Hubei	347	201	146	8806	3260	2890	2656
湖南 Hunan	275	63	212	9165	3358	3053	2754
广东 Guangdong	389	83	306	7736	2957	2512	2267
广西 Guangxi	166	73	93	3059	1117	1050	892
海南 Hainan	32	3	29	539	197	180	162
重庆 Chongqing	158	10	148	3256	1210	1149	897
四川 Sichuan	224	30	194	5149	1982	1764	1403
贵州 Guizhou	148	30	118	2348	941	751	656
云南 Yunnan	92	13	79	1559	595	499	465
西藏 Tibet	10	6	4	246	93	77	76
陕西 Shaanxi	269	61	208	4410	1653	1453	1304
甘肃 Gansu	149	30	119	2210	865	691	654
青海 Qinghai	42	6	36	392	155	127	110
宁夏 Ningxia	37	13	24	694	266	230	198
新疆 Xinjiang	203	30	173	3348	1284	1098	966

普通高中校数、班数(县镇)

Number of Senior Secondary Schools and Classes (County Seats & Towns)

总　计 Total	学校数(所) Schools 合　计 Total	 高级中学 Senior Sec. Schools	 完全中学 Complete Sec. Schools	班数(个) Classes 计 Total	 一年级 Grade 1	 二年级 Grade 2	 三年级 Grade 3
合　计 Total	**7191**	**3013**	**4178**	**173161**	**65521**	**57136**	**50504**
北　京 Beijing	103	31	72	2018	790	687	541
天　津 Tianjin	72	34	38	1195	433	382	380
河　北 Hebei	428	273	155	10979	4130	3525	3324
山　西 Shanxi	222	129	93	4961	1848	1631	1482
内蒙古 Inner Mongolia	169	68	101	3486	1333	1126	1027
辽　宁 Liaoning	128	108	20	3821	1458	1281	1082
吉　林 Jilin	178	116	62	4121	1535	1379	1207
黑龙江 Heilongjiang	190	129	61	4056	1486	1305	1265
上　海 Shanghai	128	40	88	2139	786	734	619
江　苏 Jiangsu	292	120	172	9690	3661	3244	2785
浙　江 Zhejiang	342	245	97	8490	3182	2834	2474
安　徽 Anhui	307	75	232	7379	2825	2429	2125
福　建 Fujian	332	50	282	8364	2957	2943	2464
江　西 Jiangxi	353	112	241	7786	3052	2557	2177
山　东 Shandong	415	277	138	13590	5035	4490	4065
河　南 Henan	411	340	71	12366	4672	4000	3694
湖　北 Hubei	188	140	48	5662	2029	1823	1810
湖　南 Hunan	358	186	172	9258	3583	3076	2599
广　东 Guangdong	396	90	306	9476	3689	3080	2707
广　西 Guangxi	329	114	215	6427	2404	2120	1903
海　南 Hainan	56	2	54	893	342	290	261
重　庆 Chongqing	123	4	119	3458	1352	1200	906
四　川 Sichuan	478	49	429	11660	4589	3884	3187
贵　州 Guizhou	210	64	146	3899	1577	1250	1072
云　南 Yunnan	278	27	251	4347	1637	1436	1274
西　藏 Tibet	7	3	4	170	69	51	50
陕　西 Shaanxi	206	103	103	5390	2002	1750	1638
甘　肃 Gansu	196	40	156	3811	1450	1237	1124
青　海 Qinghai	93	10	83	1008	387	329	292
宁　夏 Ningxia	41	8	33	881	324	277	280
新　疆 Xinjiang	162	26	136	2380	904	786	690

普通高中校数、班数(农村)

Number of Senior Secondary Schools and Classes (Rural)

总　计 Total	学校数(所) Schools			班数(个) Classes			
	合　计 Total	高级中学 Senior Sec. Schools	完全中学 Complete Sec. Schools	计 Total	一年级 Grade 1	二年级 Grade 2	三年级 Grade 3
合　计 Total	**2288**	**713**	**1575**	**35710**	**13398**	**11875**	**10437**
北　京 Beijing	17	5	12	160	73	43	44
天　津 Tianjin	16	16	0	396	151	130	115
河　北 Hebei	89	41	48	1403	578	437	388
山　西 Shanxi	63	24	39	703	271	235	197
内蒙古 Inner Mongolia	19	5	14	220	85	72	63
辽　宁 Liaoning	43	31	12	760	298	252	210
吉　林 Jilin	15	4	11	145	55	45	45
黑龙江 Heilongjiang	85	28	57	977	357	321	299
上　海 Shanghai	6	2	4	69	27	22	20
江　苏 Jiangsu	298	107	191	6791	2446	2320	2025
浙　江 Zhejiang	2	2	0	38	13	12	13
安　徽 Anhui	189	33	156	2676	975	889	812
福　建 Fujian	66	4	62	950	364	308	278
江　西 Jiangxi	88	12	76	1030	379	373	278
山　东 Shandong	50	33	17	1141	430	373	338
河　南 Henan	129	93	36	1881	717	637	527
湖　北 Hubei	91	58	33	1963	710	657	596
湖　南 Hunan	132	78	54	2735	1039	901	795
广　东 Guangdong	210	33	177	3362	1275	1122	965
广　西 Guangxi	24	4	20	275	109	90	76
海　南 Hainan	17	1	16	112	42	36	34
重　庆 Chongqing	12	0	12	404	144	139	121
四　川 Sichuan	83	17	66	1605	637	544	424
贵　州 Guizhou	62	5	57	477	202	145	130
云　南 Yunnan	51	3	48	536	196	183	157
西　藏 Tibet	0	0	0	0	0	0	0
陕　西 Shaanxi	149	68	81	2462	921	787	754
甘　肃 Gansu	108	3	105	1053	401	331	321
青　海 Qinghai	13	0	13	121	47	40	34
宁　夏 Ningxia	26	1	25	302	98	105	99
新　疆 Xinjiang	135	2	133	963	358	326	279

普通高中学生数(总计)

Number of Students in Senior Secondary Schools (Regional Aggregates)

单位:人

Unit: in Person

地　区 Region	毕业生数 Graduates	招生数 Students Admitted	在校学生数 Enrolment 合　计 Total	其中女 Of Which: Female	一年级 Grade 1	二年级 Grade 2	三年级 Grade 3	毕业班学生数 Graduates for Next Year
合　计 Total	**4581235**	**7521264**	**19648261**	**8857158**	**7528644**	**6574860**	**5544757**	**5544757**
北　京 Beijing	56601	94894	250959	132808	95464	85661	69834	69834
天　津 Tianjin	44968	69875	182529	93728	69978	58938	53613	53613
河　北 Hebei	264873	449334	1142264	570554	449446	370717	322101	322101
山　西 Shanxi	138440	217394	573639	271589	217488	190609	165542	165542
内蒙古 Inner Mongolia	102500	165772	420138	210927	165868	137289	116981	116981
辽　宁 Liaoning	148501	232730	602442	299517	232978	200611	168853	168853
吉　林 Jilin	92934	146132	381362	191428	146272	130830	104260	104260
黑龙江 Heilongjiang	115778	187643	486096	245021	187677	157918	140501	140501
上　海 Shanghai	78270	104030	299095	155439	104573	103127	91395	91395
江　苏 Jiangsu	291593	462352	1240038	529171	462519	424407	353112	353112
浙　江 Zhejiang	196142	302695	787249	368920	303058	267116	217075	217075
安　徽 Anhui	209603	344862	899943	360698	345376	301160	253407	253407
福　建 Fujian	139457	218414	575152	259781	218930	190925	165297	165297
江　西 Jiangxi	155520	278808	724053	277972	279927	245761	198365	198365
山　东 Shandong	413708	638087	1690657	739477	638125	569940	482592	482592
河　南 Henan	363787	537749	1464205	637070	538330	494695	431180	431180
湖　北 Hubei	272741	396137	1072914	456258	396407	355334	321173	321173
湖　南 Hunan	233929	422322	1065740	466620	422410	355833	287497	287497
广　东 Guangdong	274956	442596	1137234	499992	442683	375373	319178	319178
广　西 Guangxi	140988	216817	585085	270949	216953	198316	169816	169816
海　南 Hainan	22299	32620	88946	33778	32667	29902	26377	26377
重　庆 Chongqing	74895	157825	407905	186447	157971	143212	106722	106722
四　川 Sichuan	201256	458577	1130813	506688	458827	385730	286256	286256
贵　州 Guizhou	75141	156515	383052	152596	156734	124142	102176	102176
云　南 Yunnan	84456	138369	363368	168851	138633	121039	103696	103696
西　藏 Tibet	6022	9024	22076	11159	9024	6543	6509	6509
陕　西 Shaanxi	178276	273499	741329	333440	273928	247763	219638	219638
甘　肃 Gansu	89040	168181	427011	167358	168200	137745	121066	121066
青　海 Qinghai	17626	32785	80310	39731	32902	26133	21275	21275
宁　夏 Ningxia	26111	39063	107479	50777	39066	34739	33674	33674
新　疆 Xinjiang	70824	126163	315178	168414	126230	103352	85596	85596

普通高中学生数(城市)

Number of Students in Senior Secondary Schools (Urban)

单位:人

Unit: in Person

地区 Region	毕业生数 Graduates	招生数 Students Admitted	在校学生数 Enrolment 合计 Total	其中女 Of Which: Female	一年级 Grade 1	二年级 Grade 2	三年级 Grade 3	毕业班学生数 Graduates for Next Year
合 计 Total	**1691793**	**2698002**	**7090958**	**3362427**	**2700048**	**2379140**	**2011770**	**2011770**
北 京 Beijing	37025	55937	151836	80378	56328	51448	44060	44060
天 津 Tianjin	25999	38697	102462	52854	38764	33100	30598	30598
河 北 Hebei	80732	136972	345193	173501	136976	113738	94479	94479
山 西 Shanxi	60681	90477	240485	116047	90483	80020	69982	69982
内蒙古 Inner Mongolia	51002	81897	207192	105081	81942	68098	57152	57152
辽 宁 Liaoning	84931	125733	326624	167237	125787	107300	93537	93537
吉 林 Jilin	33008	51026	132027	67041	51070	43599	37358	37358
黑龙江 Heilongjiang	48435	76736	198826	101959	76760	65895	56171	56171
上 海 Shanghai	52757	66194	195145	101383	66449	67449	61247	61247
江 苏 Jiangsu	75089	111490	301756	138898	111511	103237	87008	87008
浙 江 Zhejiang	83985	135833	346043	164269	135997	118133	91913	91913
安 徽 Anhui	60902	98150	259075	113092	98197	87081	73797	73797
福 建 Fujian	43693	66496	174268	83445	66588	56675	51005	51005
江 西 Jiangxi	42876	74574	198138	83804	74661	67683	55794	55794
山 东 Shandong	175982	274652	723618	327419	274668	245178	203772	203772
河 南 Henan	99886	159412	429028	197180	159611	147613	121804	121804
湖 北 Hubei	136620	198287	532077	237724	198399	176928	156750	156750
湖 南 Hunan	69725	125865	321099	148573	125904	106373	88822	88822
广 东 Guangdong	99910	158378	410738	191683	158437	134827	117474	117474
广 西 Guangxi	40890	61449	171475	82131	61490	59475	50510	50510
海 南 Hainan	6993	10054	28153	12023	10082	9704	8367	8367
重 庆 Chongqing	34148	63389	169355	82005	63447	59949	45959	45959
四 川 Sichuan	58969	117863	303761	142245	117926	105541	80294	80294
贵 州 Guizhou	25684	50038	124431	55451	50102	41395	32934	32934
云 南 Yunnan	21550	32503	86869	43152	32505	27991	26373	26373
西 藏 Tibet	3679	5343	13372	6791	5343	4042	3987	3987
陕 西 Shaanxi	58835	92170	248261	117454	92201	83083	72977	72977
甘 肃 Gansu	28050	49920	126523	55315	49928	40257	36338	36338
青 海 Qinghai	4329	8218	20089	10240	8222	6458	5409	5409
宁 夏 Ningxia	8560	14563	38921	18822	14566	12785	11570	11570
新 疆 Xinjiang	36868	65686	164118	85230	65704	54085	44329	44329

普通高中学生数(县镇)

Number of Students in Senior Secondary Schools (County Seats & Towns)

单位:人

Unit: in Person

地区 Region	毕业生数 Graduates	招生数 Students Admitted	在校学生数 Enrolment 合计 Total	其中女 Of Which: Female	一年级 Grade 1	二年级 Grade 2	三年级 Grade 3	毕业班学生数 Graduates for Next Year
合　计 Total	**2411586**	**4009038**	**10453499**	**4583972**	**4013730**	**3488144**	**2951625**	**2951625**
北　京 Beijing	18639	35994	92914	49381	36169	32519	24226	24226
天　津 Tianjin	14412	22711	58348	30118	22747	18489	17112	17112
河　北 Hebei	164835	273725	706745	350454	273831	228900	204014	204014
山　西 Shanxi	69425	111489	294989	138154	111559	98192	85238	85238
内蒙古 Inner Mongolia	49009	79563	201814	100123	79614	65483	56717	56717
辽　宁 Liaoning	53422	88629	230106	110557	88817	77700	63589	63589
吉　林 Jilin	58055	91793	241230	120337	91889	84396	64945	64945
黑龙江 Heilongjiang	56845	91780	238039	117872	91790	76071	70178	70178
上　海 Shanghai	24748	36587	100798	52550	36873	34673	29252	29252
江　苏 Jiangsu	123148	208602	547957	228141	208668	185413	153876	153876
浙　江 Zhejiang	111492	166195	439309	203915	166394	148426	124489	124489
安　徽 Anhui	108306	183658	472320	180071	184021	157266	131033	131033
福　建 Fujian	83276	132990	350378	154395	133384	117643	99351	99351
江　西 Jiangxi	100817	182731	469541	173375	183731	157354	128456	128456
山　东 Shandong	222229	337280	899861	383025	337298	302174	260389	260389
河　南 Henan	229910	329832	909020	385988	330178	303146	275696	275696
湖　北 Hubei	102923	146255	403795	161950	146379	132467	124949	124949
湖　南 Hunan	126834	228435	573563	246364	228465	192352	152746	152746
广　东 Guangdong	129874	209992	536832	227115	210009	177801	149022	149022
广　西 Guangxi	96799	148696	397450	181735	148791	133661	114998	114998
海　南 Hainan	14070	20012	54827	19505	20031	18428	16368	16368
重　庆 Chongqing	37550	85497	214390	93798	85585	74804	54001	54001
四　川 Sichuan	127066	299812	731226	320738	299998	246850	184378	184378
贵　州 Guizhou	44872	93617	231103	86544	93772	74580	62751	62751
云　南 Yunnan	57065	94938	247934	112198	95161	83226	69547	69547
西　藏 Tibet	2343	3681	8704	4368	3681	2501	2522	2522
陕　西 Shaanxi	82436	125588	341865	148066	125846	114826	101193	101193
甘　肃 Gansu	50315	92873	238892	90044	92884	78165	67843	67843
青　海 Qinghai	12104	21811	53868	26607	21864	17611	14393	14393
宁　夏 Ningxia	13285	19108	52461	24595	19108	16380	16973	16973
新　疆 Xinjiang	25482	45164	113220	61889	45193	36647	31380	31380

普通高中学生数(农村)

Number of Students in Senior Secondary Schools (Rural)

单位:人
Unit:in Person

地区 Region	毕业生数 Graduates	招生数 Students Admitted	在校学生数 Enrolment 合计 Total	其中女 Of Which: Female	一年级 Grade 1	二年级 Grade 2	三年级 Grade 3	毕业班学生数 Graduates for Next Year
合计 Total	**477856**	**814224**	**2103804**	**910759**	**814866**	**707576**	**581362**	**581362**
北京 Beijing	937	2963	6209	3049	2967	1694	1548	1548
天津 Tianjin	4557	8467	21719	10756	8467	7349	5903	5903
河北 Hebei	19306	38637	90326	46599	38639	28079	23608	23608
山西 Shanxi	8334	15428	38165	17388	15446	12397	10322	10322
内蒙古 Inner Mongolia	2489	4312	11132	5723	4312	3708	3112	3112
辽宁 Liaoning	10148	18368	45712	21723	18374	15611	11727	11727
吉林 Jilin	1871	3313	8105	4050	3313	2835	1957	1957
黑龙江 Heilongjiang	10498	19127	49231	25190	19127	15952	14152	14152
上海 Shanghai	765	1249	3152	1506	1251	1005	896	896
江苏 Jiangsu	93356	142260	390325	162132	142340	135757	112228	112228
浙江 Zhejiang	665	667	1897	736	667	557	673	673
安徽 Anhui	40395	63054	168548	67535	63158	56813	48577	48577
福建 Fujian	12488	18928	50506	21941	18958	16607	14941	14941
江西 Jiangxi	11827	21503	56374	20793	21535	20724	14115	14115
山东 Shandong	15497	26155	67178	29033	26159	22588	18431	18431
河南 Henan	33991	48505	126157	53902	48541	43936	33680	33680
湖北 Hubei	33198	51595	137042	56584	51629	45939	39474	39474
湖南 Hunan	37370	68022	171078	71683	68041	57108	45929	45929
广东 Guangdong	45172	74226	189664	81194	74237	62745	52682	52682
广西 Guangxi	3299	6672	16160	7083	6672	5180	4308	4308
海南 Hainan	1236	2554	5966	2250	2554	1770	1642	1642
重庆 Chongqing	3197	8939	24160	10644	8939	8459	6762	6762
四川 Sichuan	15221	40902	95826	43705	40903	33339	21584	21584
贵州 Guizhou	4585	12860	27518	10601	12860	8167	6491	6491
云南 Yunnan	5841	10928	28565	13501	10967	9822	7776	7776
西藏 Tibet	0	0	0	0	0	0	0	0
陕西 Shaanxi	37005	55741	151203	67920	55881	49854	45468	45468
甘肃 Gansu	10675	25388	61596	21999	25388	19323	16885	16885
青海 Qinghai	1193	2756	6353	2884	2816	2064	1473	1473
宁夏 Ningxia	4266	5392	16097	7360	5392	5574	5131	5131
新疆 Xinjiang	8474	15313	37840	21295	15333	12620	9887	9887

普通高中女学生数

Number of Female Students in Senior Secondary Schools

单位：人

Unit: in Person

地 区 Region	毕业生数 Graduates	招生数 Students Admitted	在校学生数 Enrolment 合计 Total	一年级 Grade 1	二年级 Grade 2	三年级 Grade 3	毕业班学生数 Graduates for Next Year
合 计 Total	**1978861**	**3448819**	**8857158**	**3450778**	**2955553**	**2450827**	**2450827**
北 京 Beijing	30306	51170	132808	51335	45053	36420	36420
天 津 Tianjin	22848	36077	93728	36101	30494	27133	27133
河 北 Hebei	125393	230835	570554	230876	183533	156145	156145
山 西 Shanxi	61215	107610	271589	107644	88350	75595	75595
内蒙古 Inner Mongolia	50418	84855	210927	84896	68195	57836	57836
辽 宁 Liaoning	72238	115926	299517	116007	99529	83981	83981
吉 林 Jilin	44823	76329	191428	76370	63463	51595	51595
黑龙江 Heilongjiang	57096	95772	245021	95780	79918	69323	69323
上 海 Shanghai	41383	54121	155439	54237	53788	47414	47414
江 苏 Jiangsu	118984	199486	529171	199531	180750	148890	148890
浙 江 Zhejiang	88414	143518	368920	143591	124870	100459	100459
安 徽 Anhui	78654	142709	360698	142837	119876	97985	97985
福 建 Fujian	60331	101850	259781	101936	85267	72578	72578
江 西 Jiangxi	56432	109404	277972	109684	94567	73721	73721
山 东 Shandong	172004	284665	739477	284674	247893	206910	206910
河 南 Henan	146693	239201	637070	239402	216070	181598	181598
湖 北 Hubei	112138	172640	456258	172720	150460	133078	133078
湖 南 Hunan	95505	186422	466620	186434	155534	124652	124652
广 东 Guangdong	113310	199465	499992	199479	164843	135670	135670
广 西 Guangxi	61043	101451	270949	101494	92491	76964	76964
海 南 Hainan	8137	12848	33778	12854	11225	9699	9699
重 庆 Chongqing	34005	71601	186447	71647	65552	49248	49248
四 川 Sichuan	88623	205268	506688	205343	172638	128707	128707
贵 州 Guizhou	28485	63093	152596	63143	50253	39200	39200
云 南 Yunnan	38446	64112	168851	64164	56638	48049	48049
西 藏 Tibet	3153	4655	11159	4655	3289	3215	3215
陕 西 Shaanxi	77906	124280	333440	124419	111127	97894	97894
甘 肃 Gansu	33688	67396	167358	67403	54810	45145	45145
青 海 Qinghai	8885	16022	39731	16053	12946	10732	10732
宁 夏 Ningxia	11596	18651	50777	18653	16654	15470	15470
新 疆 Xinjiang	36709	67387	168414	67416	55477	45521	45521

普通中学教职工数(总计)

Number of Teachers, Staff & Workers in General Secondary Schools (Regional Aggregates)

单位:人
Unit:in Person

地区 Region	教职工数 Teachers, Staff & Workers						代课教师 Substitute Teachers	兼任教师 Part-time Teachers
	合计 Total	专任教师 Full-time Teachers	行政人员 Adm. Personnel	教辅人员 Supporting Staff	工勤人员 Workers	校办工厂、农(林)场职工 Employees in School-run Factories & Farms		
合计 Total	**5496535**	**4537310**	**360888**	**227448**	**356318**	**14571**	**119041**	**36532**
北京 Beijing	76484	51448	11231	6625	6533	647	1397	734
天津 Tianjin	55107	41422	6687	3299	3287	412	581	600
河北 Hebei	339848	285865	20506	12401	20007	1069	5551	1226
山西 Shanxi	180083	147347	9962	8367	13484	923	9309	1402
内蒙古 Inner Mongolia	118311	89935	10157	6869	11034	316	3461	1037
辽宁 Liaoning	179521	144016	26173	952	8218	162	1098	1453
吉林 Jilin	122120	92338	13773	9570	6228	211	1409	899
黑龙江 Heilongjiang	186384	149629	16165	6975	13115	500	1221	864
上海 Shanghai	76853	51455	7795	9310	7442	851	2169	1963
江苏 Jiangsu	318703	259817	18622	15678	23574	1012	7508	1725
浙江 Zhejiang	187820	158305	10208	7014	11514	779	0	2410
安徽 Anhui	210197	179529	10892	6728	12732	316	7358	3074
福建 Fujian	160212	135778	11551	4327	8311	245	2974	1461
江西 Jiangxi	176175	155764	6299	4380	9421	311	2808	1592
山东 Shandong	468627	374811	30460	29179	32831	1346	4584	1082
河南 Henan	417707	358840	21517	15219	21412	719	6905	1977
湖北 Hubei	263879	223751	11556	11180	16199	1193	7766	1103
湖南 Hunan	301306	259281	13407	10124	17679	815	4400	1065
广东 Guangdong	323075	271589	21626	10690	18767	403	11679	976
广西 Guangxi	187457	144975	15058	9188	17972	264	9998	1752
海南 Hainan	31537	24903	1614	1105	3874	41	502	169
重庆 Chongqing	110133	89560	7546	4884	7815	328	2366	610
四川 Sichuan	297743	247098	18629	10712	20633	671	5621	2441
贵州 Guizhou	123132	107312	6890	3150	5636	144	3648	1596
云南 Yunnan	143290	120221	5644	4239	13063	123	2420	303
西藏 Tibet	7334	6461	259	32	582	0	129	70
陕西 Shaanxi	178330	148437	14498	7054	8075	266	4307	1257
甘肃 Gansu	100004	87753	4441	2866	4770	174	3555	704
青海 Qinghai	21257	18613	799	479	1346	20	170	111
宁夏 Ningxia	25549	21725	871	1098	1778	77	1009	136
新疆 Xinjiang	108357	89332	6052	3754	8986	233	3138	740

普通中学教职工数(城市)

Number of Teachers, Staff & Workers in General Secondary Schools (Urban)

单位:人

Unit: in Person

地区 Region	教职工数 Teachers, Staff & Workers						代课教师 Substitute Teachers	兼任教师 Part-time Teachers
	合计 Total	专任教师 Full-time Teachers	行政人员 Adm. Personnel	教辅人员 Supporting Staff	工勤人员 Workers	校办工厂、农(林)场职工 Employees in School-run Factories & Farms		
合计 Total	**1416121**	**1096706**	**129601**	**79817**	**102675**	**7322**	**31246**	**19116**
北京 Beijing	39385	25551	6565	3356	3399	514	755	587
天津 Tianjin	26794	18549	4176	1703	2050	316	487	465
河北 Hebei	71432	55527	6057	3899	5292	657	1293	702
山西 Shanxi	50285	37808	4418	3027	4729	303	2555	836
内蒙古 Inner Mongolia	39980	29762	4751	2505	2809	153	1966	599
辽宁 Liaoning	75169	59992	11515	482	3114	66	228	905
吉林 Jilin	32177	23894	3898	2455	1816	114	536	613
黑龙江 Heilongjiang	55332	43645	5464	2543	3519	161	386	728
上海 Shanghai	45611	30192	4532	6144	4213	530	1605	1784
江苏 Jiangsu	72186	56408	6178	3865	5494	241	1096	845
浙江 Zhejiang	64938	52389	3988	3031	4944	586	0	1175
安徽 Anhui	44727	35859	3255	2300	3210	103	1847	1247
福建 Fujian	35214	28739	2741	1490	2100	144	419	590
江西 Jiangxi	30809	25748	2066	979	1926	90	425	781
山东 Shandong	137135	104520	11536	10266	10073	740	1315	585
河南 Henan	78503	61379	7364	4349	5171	240	2094	681
湖北 Hubei	90790	72929	6347	5247	5728	539	2953	900
湖南 Hunan	52913	42081	3381	3001	3937	513	879	578
广东 Guangdong	95493	75100	8024	5378	6777	214	4880	605
广西 Guangxi	30801	23380	2785	1846	2704	86	643	910
海南 Hainan	6719	5080	427	290	915	7	247	46
重庆 Chongqing	41877	32961	3233	2022	3416	245	540	352
四川 Sichuan	51854	40423	4040	2765	4386	240	916	611
贵州 Guizhou	24115	19415	2035	929	1615	121	536	295
云南 Yunnan	16351	12700	1172	824	1599	56	101	112
西藏 Tibet	2364	2009	142	20	193	0	49	12
陕西 Shaanxi	38267	29589	4643	1822	2045	168	823	556
甘肃 Gansu	20901	16710	1617	1064	1427	83	495	439
青海 Qinghai	4979	4057	376	175	371	0	27	50
宁夏 Ningxia	6856	5551	352	334	595	24	335	80
新疆 Xinjiang	32164	24759	2523	1706	3108	68	815	447

普通中学教职工数(县镇)

Number of Teachers, Staff & Workers in General Secondary Schools (County Seats & Towns)

单位:人

Unit:in Person

地区 Region	教职工数 Teachers,Staff & Workers						代课教师 Substitute Teachers	兼任教师 Part－time Teachers
	合计 Total	专任教师 Full－time Teachers	行政人员 Adm. Personnel	教辅人员 Supporting Staff	工勤人员 Workers	校办工厂、农(林)场职工 Employees in School－run Factories & Farms		
合计 Total	**2134433**	**1748178**	**126652**	**99930**	**154396**	**5277**	**35960**	**10401**
北京 Beijing	28589	19977	3724	2497	2269	122	491	98
天津 Tianjin	18250	14002	1859	1359	940	90	12	121
河北 Hebei	143660	119179	7939	6131	10044	367	1914	231
山西 Shanxi	58265	46422	2738	3374	5132	599	2414	179
内蒙古 Inner Mongolia	49416	37449	3473	3103	5270	121	694	92
辽宁 Liaoning	37258	28661	5505	262	2797	33	36	28
吉林 Jilin	57765	43457	6072	4932	3229	75	533	223
黑龙江 Heilongjiang	53252	41523	4982	2391	4184	172	234	60
上海 Shanghai	29592	20061	3089	3074	3060	308	490	176
江苏 Jiangsu	85504	68079	4714	4999	7236	476	1204	393
浙江 Zhejiang	112222	96401	5609	3840	6194	178	0	1128
安徽 Anhui	66912	55617	3333	2924	4899	139	2170	1299
福建 Fujian	79032	67385	5364	1975	4213	95	1123	603
江西 Jiangxi	83244	73156	2513	2634	4828	113	1143	582
山东 Shandong	221155	177167	13554	13711	16263	460	2293	309
河南 Henan	143460	121068	6585	6657	8848	302	2255	862
湖北 Hubei	65713	56286	2011	2949	4136	331	1155	75
湖南 Hunan	116370	97869	5009	5090	8168	234	1218	355
广东 Guangdong	125999	107396	7145	3465	7890	103	3357	213
广西 Guangxi	109415	84213	7966	5887	11200	149	5992	478
海南 Hainan	17459	14091	621	609	2121	17	168	115
重庆 Chongqing	48334	39376	3168	2359	3356	75	931	213
四川 Sichuan	135255	110801	7576	6153	10347	378	2057	947
贵州 Guizhou	54208	46319	3019	1815	3034	21	741	703
云南 Yunnan	62084	51014	2319	2361	6338	52	770	77
西藏 Tibet	4939	4422	116	12	389	0	80	58
陕西 Shaanxi	54003	45053	3714	2560	2609	67	799	387
甘肃 Gansu	31925	27389	1268	1333	1854	81	879	173
青海 Qinghai	9781	8402	325	269	773	12	68	52
宁夏 Ningxia	9107	7524	326	474	730	53	482	43
新疆 Xinjiang	22265	18419	1016	731	2045	54	257	128

普通中学教职工数(农村)

Number of Teachers, Staff & Workers in General Secondary Schools (Rural)

单位:人
Unit:in Person

地区 Region	教职工数 Teachers, Staff & Workers						代课教师 Substitute Teachers	兼任教师 Part-time Teachers
	合计 Total	专任教师 Full-time Teachers	行政人员 Adm. Personnel	教辅人员 Supporting Staff	工勤人员 Workers	校办工厂、农(林)场职工 Employees in School-run Factories & Farms		
合计 Total	**1945981**	**1692426**	**104635**	**47701**	**99247**	**1972**	**51835**	**7015**
北京 Beijing	8510	5920	942	772	865	11	151	49
天津 Tianjin	10063	8871	652	237	297	6	82	14
河北 Hebei	124756	111159	6510	2371	4671	45	2344	293
山西 Shanxi	71533	63117	2806	1966	3623	21	4340	387
内蒙古 Inner Mongolia	28915	22724	1933	1261	2955	42	801	346
辽宁 Liaoning	67094	55363	9153	208	2307	63	834	520
吉林 Jilin	32178	24987	3803	2183	1183	22	340	63
黑龙江 Heilongjiang	77800	64461	5719	2041	5412	167	601	76
上海 Shanghai	1650	1202	174	92	169	13	74	3
江苏 Jiangsu	161013	135330	7730	6814	10844	295	5208	487
浙江 Zhejiang	10660	9515	611	143	376	15	0	107
安徽 Anhui	98558	88053	4304	1504	4623	74	3341	528
福建 Fujian	45966	39654	3446	862	1998	6	1432	268
江西 Jiangxi	62122	56860	1720	767	2667	108	1240	229
山东 Shandong	110337	93124	5370	5202	6495	146	976	188
河南 Henan	195744	176393	7568	4213	7393	177	2556	434
湖北 Hubei	107376	94536	3198	2984	6335	323	3658	128
湖南 Hunan	132023	119331	5017	2033	5574	68	2303	132
广东 Guangdong	101583	89093	6457	1847	4100	86	3442	158
广西 Guangxi	47241	37382	4307	1455	4068	29	3363	364
海南 Hainan	7359	5732	566	206	838	17	87	8
重庆 Chongqing	19922	17223	1145	503	1043	8	895	45
四川 Sichuan	110634	95874	7013	1794	5900	53	2648	883
贵州 Guizhou	44809	41578	1836	406	987	2	2371	598
云南 Yunnan	64855	56507	2153	1054	5126	15	1549	114
西藏 Tibet	31	30	1	0	0	0	0	0
陕西 Shaanxi	86060	73795	6141	2672	3421	31	2685	314
甘肃 Gansu	47178	43654	1556	469	1489	10	2181	92
青海 Qinghai	6497	6154	98	35	202	8	75	9
宁夏 Ningxia	9586	8650	193	290	453	0	192	13
新疆 Xinjiang	53928	46154	2513	1317	3833	111	2066	165

普通中学女教职工数

Number of Female Teachers, Staff & Workers in General Secondary Schools

单位:人

Unit:in Person

地区 Region	教职工数 Teachers, Staff & Workers						代课教师 Substitute Teachers	兼任教师 Part-time Teachers
	合计 Total	专任教师 Full-time Teachers	行政人员 Adm. Personnel	教辅人员 Supporting Staff	工勤人员 Workers	校办工厂、农(林)场职工 Employees in School-run Factories & Farms		
合计 Total	**2308993**	**2000679**	**77040**	**103285**	**122764**	**5225**	**56420**	**12359**
北京 Beijing	48331	35941	5481	3873	2758	278	941	352
天津 Tianjin	31345	25489	2706	1829	1181	140	343	245
河北 Hebei	184577	168585	3463	5874	6175	480	3099	632
山西 Shanxi	90399	79791	1990	4145	4146	327	5106	553
内蒙古 Inner Mongolia	58600	49266	2715	3328	3201	90	1791	426
辽宁 Liaoning	98475	86119	9279	559	2478	40	684	742
吉林 Jilin	66304	55487	3979	4798	1954	86	770	459
黑龙江 Heilongjiang	101459	87761	5280	3492	4738	188	626	468
上海 Shanghai	43115	31017	2963	5526	3320	289	1272	1027
江苏 Jiangsu	121341	104023	3005	6451	7512	350	3781	486
浙江 Zhejiang	85304	74352	2145	3474	5018	315	0	1008
安徽 Anhui	58454	50242	1426	3024	3651	111	2670	780
福建 Fujian	58171	50660	1841	2216	3370	84	1381	335
江西 Jiangxi	52117	46167	998	1705	3150	97	1244	457
山东 Shandong	187012	163160	4707	10739	7928	478	1770	235
河南 Henan	177972	161595	3717	6483	5941	236	3197	642
湖北 Hubei	86131	74202	2067	4296	5213	353	3372	322
湖南 Hunan	111894	100402	1440	4075	5659	318	2015	227
广东 Guangdong	137711	118766	3714	5916	9144	171	5688	263
广西 Guangxi	75579	60515	2005	4141	8809	109	5038	572
海南 Hainan	11381	8479	324	621	1934	23	272	51
重庆 Chongqing	39794	34440	1180	2061	2026	87	942	168
四川 Sichuan	103199	89815	2899	4494	5821	170	2334	434
贵州 Guizhou	39141	34201	1217	1362	2308	53	1135	347
云南 Yunnan	57921	47971	1100	1996	6809	45	1313	105
西藏 Tibet	2723	2379	97	20	227	0	54	14
陕西 Shaanxi	75058	67517	2478	2820	2158	85	1974	438
甘肃 Gansu	30097	26808	581	1164	1476	68	1554	161
青海 Qinghai	9288	8216	209	267	591	5	73	29
宁夏 Ningxia	10054	8766	125	460	656	47	270	57
新疆 Xinjiang	56046	48547	1909	2076	3412	102	1711	324

普通中学教职工总数中

Number of General Secondary Schools Teachers,

教职工数 Teachers, Staff

地区 Region	合计 Total	专任教师 Full - time Teachers	行政人员 Adm. Personnel	教辅人员 Supporting Staff
合计 Total	**291604**	**201421**	**25175**	**15633**
北京 Beijing	3169	1924	465	266
天津 Tianjin	2542	1429	399	268
河北 Hebei	23793	16851	1764	909
山西 Shanxi	17896	12167	1212	891
内蒙古 Inner Mongolia	5240	3530	595	258
辽宁 Liaoning	4497	3594	680	105
吉林 Jilin	4322	2640	473	221
黑龙江 Heilongjiang	8448	6289	821	330
上海 Shanghai	8465	5723	845	941
江苏 Jiangsu	23301	16534	1646	1108
浙江 Zhejiang	19990	14353	1146	1017
安徽 Anhui	10560	6750	935	678
福建 Fujian	6523	4604	701	332
江西 Jiangxi	14226	10006	1125	691
山东 Shandong	26982	18937	2360	1639
河南 Henan	21043	14902	1697	1082
湖19北 Henan	7386	4779	569	401
湖南 Hunan	14283	10356	1062	729
广东 Guangdong	17426	11740	1569	1029
广西 Guangxi	10871	7344	1163	440
海南 Hainan	2807	1671	292	181
重庆 Chongqing	3564	2352	318	194
四川 Sichuan	9398	6297	684	667
贵州 Guizhou	5905	3971	557	206
云南 Yunnan	2881	1825	272	222
西藏 Tibet	175	144	14	4
陕西 Shaanxi	10187	7118	1257	477
甘肃 Gansu	1633	1140	179	74
青海 Qinghai	386	244	40	28
宁夏 Ningxia	418	241	37	25
新疆 Xinjiang	3287	1966	298	220

社会力量办教职工数

Staff & Workers Maintained by the Communities

单位：人

Unit: in Person

& Workers			
工勤人员 Workers	校办工厂、农（林）场职工 Employees in School－run Factories & Farms	代课教师 Substitute Teachers	兼任教师 Part－time Teachers
15560	48601	774	14933
513	1	185	163
446	0	146	165
4258	11	711	522
3621	5	1267	749
846	11	496	684
118	0	128	495
988	0	213	579
931	77	90	559
837	119	1463	1562
3992	21	830	571
3447	27	0	1486
2190	7	1573	1490
879	7	146	453
2382	22	202	671
3978	68	1583	476
3814	3214	148	1381
1619	18	421	303
2126	10	193	395
3042	46	629	297
1835	89	737	791
652	11	26	60
699	1	445	182
1706	44	501	455
1171	0	388	378
560	2	22	81
13	0	0	0
1327	8	658	644
233	7	386	396
66	8	10	0
110	5	69	53
802	1	34	87

普通高中专任教师

Breakdown of Senior Secondary Schools Heads and Teachers by

地　区 Region	合计 Total	其中女 `Of Which: Female	按学历分 By Educational Attainment			
			研究生毕业 Graduate	本科毕业 Under－graduate	专科毕业 Associate Bachelor	高中阶段毕业 High School Graduate
合　计 Total	**1070575**	**430638**	**9244**	**801276**	**254026**	**5837**
北　京 Beijing	17179	11495	449	15576	1106	47
天　津 Tianjin	12024	7369	154	9737	2056	75
河　北 Hebei	61285	33308	422	44255	16251	350
山　西 Shanxi	32500	15925	389	23608	8188	310
内蒙古 Inner Mongolia	22472	11109	115	15217	6875	260
辽　宁 Liaoning	32668	19358	142	28643	3628	238
吉　林 Jilin	20903	11808	427	18286	2109	80
黑龙江 Heilongjiang	29728	16599	263	23057	6299	106
上　海 Shanghai	17252	9470	381	16328	526	14
江　苏 Jiangsu	74635	27893	322	59805	14206	294
浙　江 Zhejiang	48770	20694	402	42995	5211	155
安　徽 Anhui	40980	10334	210	32094	8539	135
福　建 Fujian	35853	13070	126	24080	11490	153
江　西 Jiangxi	39160	10954	350	23071	15408	323
山　东 Shandong	91629	37224	794	71272	19313	246
河　南 henan	67217	25195	971	51719	14151	355
湖　北 Hubei	56540	16718	716	42718	12568	520
湖　南 Hunan	56185	17812	422	40622	14922	215
广　东 Guangdong	66190	26420	668	49524	15658	334
广　西 Guangxi	29258	10999	233	19786	9068	166
海　南 Hainan	4768	1547	27	3629	1101	11
重　庆 Chongqing	21561	7190	128	15846	5459	123
四　川 Sichuan	58600	18842	399	39001	18880	307
贵　州 guizhou	19413	6265	70	14223	4958	144
云　南 Yunnan	21497	7779	181	16119	5081	113
西　藏 Tibet	1488	519	3	1114	331	38
陕　西 Shaanxi	36823	14515	251	24907	11356	302
甘　肃 Gansu	21754	5713	63	12442	9093	154
青　海 Qinghai	5360	2172	18	3206	2087	49
宁　夏 Ningxia	5907	2199	28	4457	1393	29
新　疆 Xinjiang	20976	10143	120	13939	6715	191

学历、职称情况(总计)

Educational Attainment (Regional Aggregates)

单位:人

Unit: in Person

	按职称分 By Rank				
高中阶段毕业以下 Below High School Graduate	中学高级 Senior Secondary	中学一级 1st Grade	中学二级 2st Grade	中学三级 3st Grade	未评职称 Rank Undecided
192	**191670**	**377317**	**350104**	**33982**	**117502**
1	4301	6128	4960	58	1732
2	2982	4121	3656	313	952
7	8427	19265	22609	2132	8852
5	4804	10606	11777	1438	3875
5	4049	9287	6158	775	2203
17	8861	11094	8460	344	3909
1	3813	8889	6813	502	886
3	7253	11975	6760	891	2849
3	3986	7344	4591	70	1261
8	12012	25066	24348	1613	11596
7	8083	15415	17939	693	6640
2	9253	14868	11693	1392	3774
4	5656	11291	15300	950	2656
8	8151	13933	11671	1249	4156
4	13491	25539	35558	3727	13314
21	11466	20381	23442	4262	7666
18	12360	22936	14477	2122	4645
4	10824	23007	16725	1129	4500
6	8953	26341	21893	1420	7583
5	5015	10390	9656	1367	2830
0	1181	1810	1382	29	366
5	3318	7251	8140	753	2099
13	10877	20478	19094	2365	5786
18	3701	6440	6827	603	1842
3	3856	8939	6404	503	1795
2	75	367	598	92	356
7	6409	12020	11687	1666	5041
2	2803	7941	8201	951	1858
0	632	2531	1827	71	299
0	1377	2498	1449	123	460
11	3701	9166	6009	379	1721

普通高中专任教师

Breakdown of Senior Secondary Schools Heads and

地 区 Region	合计 Total	其中女 Of Which: Female	按学历分 By Educational Attainment 研究生毕业 Graduate	本科毕业 Under-graduate	专科毕业 Associate Bachelor	高中阶段毕业 High School Graduate
合 计 Total	**407063**	**191997**	**5346**	**347549**	**52639**	**1460**
北 京 Beijing	10400	7280	378	9447	553	21
天 津 Tianjin	6671	4358	132	5970	548	20
河 北 Hebei	19479	11461	163	16430	2833	52
山 西 Shanxi	13759	7383	223	11453	2026	55
内蒙古 Inner Mongolia	11181	5970	61	8761	2276	81
辽 宁 Liaoning	18200	11702	107	16837	1163	81
吉 林 Jilin	7128	4302	301	6414	390	23
黑龙江 Heilongjiang	12825	7910	149	11517	1139	19
上 海 Shanghai	10667	6119	327	10049	281	9
江 苏 Jiangsu	19997	9109	101	17769	2051	70
浙 江 Zhejiang	21935	9903	151	20178	1541	63
安 徽 Anhui	13205	4452	97	11506	1549	51
福 建 Fujian	11866	5377	105	9827	1888	44
江 西 Jiangxi	11486	4110	96	8319	2971	98
山 东 Shandong	42030	19336	305	36993	4639	89
河 南 henan	22151	9424	540	19098	2464	47
湖 北 Hubei	29262	10029	632	24300	4156	168
湖 南 Hunan	17120	6226	186	14277	2627	29
广 东 Guangdong	24410	11672	447	20482	3400	79
广 西 Guangxi	8785	3990	184	7080	1486	31
海 南 Hainan	1663	678	14	1463	181	5
重 庆 Chongqing	9704	3834	65	8077	1528	32
四 川 Sichuan	17033	6435	115	14364	2477	71
贵 州 guizhou	6630	2894	38	5620	931	39
云 南 Yunnan	5261	2415	62	4563	615	20
西 藏 Tibet	905	346	2	697	186	19
陕 西 Shaanxi	12549	5712	189	10277	2003	78
甘 肃 Gansu	6911	2559	50	5410	1440	11
青 海 Qinghai	1451	749	8	981	452	10
宁 夏 Ningxia	2020	869	21	1633	359	7
新 疆 Xinjiang	10379	5393	97	7757	2486	38

学历、职称情况(城市)

Teachers by Educational Attainment (Urban)

单位:人

Unit: in Person

	按职称分 By Rank				
高中阶段毕业以下 Below High School Graduate	中学高级 Senior Secondary	中学一级 1st Grade	中学二级 2st Grade	中学三级 3st Grade	未评职称 Rank Undecided
69	**101982**	**146295**	**113952**	**6227**	**38607**
1	3073	4033	2832	13	449
1	2031	2231	1858	29	522
1	4434	6671	5861	341	2172
2	2921	4826	4193	311	1508
2	2723	4458	2755	264	981
12	5144	5631	4908	92	2425
0	1923	2655	2040	116	394
1	4024	4418	2871	222	1290
1	2742	4434	2818	12	661
6	5030	6601	6210	110	2046
2	4896	7123	7146	133	2637
2	3973	4648	3131	205	1248
2	2969	3869	3917	135	976
2	3433	4182	2509	262	1100
4	7720	11912	15950	920	5528
2	5354	7105	6771	641	2280
6	7815	11234	7273	681	2259
1	5052	7650	3297	168	953
2	5197	10176	6662	167	2208
4	2391	3055	2388	158	793
0	581	626	383	12	61
2	1979	3484	3178	286	777
6	4771	6517	3983	231	1531
2	1856	2426	1621	97	630
1	1467	2283	1124	34	353
1	62	251	386	52	154
2	3413	4766	3004	183	1183
0	1578	2929	1809	154	441
0	356	760	264	6	65
0	677	923	327	20	73
1	2397	4418	2483	172	909

普通高中专任教师

Breakdown of Senior Secondary Schools Heads and Teachers

地　区 Region	合计 Total	其中女 Of Which: Female	按学历分 By Educational Attainment			
			研究生毕业 Graduate	本科毕业 Under-graduate	专科毕业 Associate Bachelor	高中阶段毕业 High School Graduate
合　计 Total	**549200**	**201309**	**3251**	**386407**	**156211**	**3241**
北　京 Beijing	6277	3939	64	5723	481	9
天　津 Tianjin	4067	2317	12	2991	1010	53
河　北 Hebei	36977	19406	257	25024	11441	249
山　西 Shanxi	16600	7607	158	10950	5263	228
内蒙古 Inner Mongolia	10687	4868	54	6120	4344	166
辽　宁 Liaoning	11972	6496	35	9864	1943	127
吉　林 Jilin	13264	7243	126	11507	1578	52
黑龙江 Heilongjiang	13630	7134	41	9554	3971	62
上　海 Shanghai	6352	3255	54	6071	221	4
江　苏 Jiangsu	32015	11433	142	26865	4961	47
浙　江 Zhejiang	26693	10735	251	22724	3624	89
安　徽 Anhui	20349	4479	69	16081	4147	52
福　建 Fujian	21202	6901	20	12692	8392	96
江　西 Jiangxi	24484	6165	108	13450	10731	190
山　东 Shandong	45670	16373	471	31827	13256	116
河　南 henan	38986	13845	416	29044	9272	246
湖　北 Hubei	20846	5239	64	14835	5714	225
湖　南 Hunan	30549	8843	229	21084	9104	129
广　东 Guangdong	30876	10998	61	22114	8591	109
广　西 Guangxi	19598	6737	48	12304	7117	128
海　南 Hainan	2784	785	13	1943	825	3
重　庆 Chongqing	10625	3026	62	7169	3305	86
四　川 Sichuan	36467	10975	267	22335	13661	198
贵　州 guizhou	11376	3086	28	7968	3266	98
云　南 Yunnan	14449	4777	111	10402	3846	88
西　藏 Tibet	583	173	1	417	145	19
陕　西 Shaanxi	16527	6065	55	10770	5561	137
甘　肃 Gansu	11562	2620	12	5961	5471	116
青　海 Qinghai	3501	1315	10	1998	1459	34
宁　夏 Ningxia	2831	1016	7	2147	664	13
新　疆 Xinjiang	7401	3458	5	4473	2847	72

学历、职称情况(县镇)

by Educational Attainment (County Seats & Towns)

单位:人

Unit: in Person

	按职称分 By Rank				
高中阶段毕业以下 Below High School Graduate	中学高级 Senior Secondary	中学一级 1st Grade	中学二级 2nd Grade	中学三级 3st Grade	未评职称 Rank Undecided
90	**78556**	**194525**	**192382**	**20585**	**63152**
0	1135	1916	1974	42	1210
1	842	1481	1303	150	291
6	3613	11361	14761	1474	5768
1	1730	5236	6708	885	2041
3	1241	4604	3208	490	1144
3	3113	4522	2867	218	1252
1	1837	5981	4617	352	477
2	2605	6190	3215	530	1090
2	1211	2770	1724	55	592
0	5083	11550	9847	516	5019
5	3182	8246	10727	548	3990
0	4417	7506	5930	688	1808
2	2510	6819	9797	665	1411
5	4241	8637	8034	822	2750
0	5406	12727	17827	2441	7269
8	5595	11870	14350	2776	4395
8	3848	9022	5108	859	2009
3	5052	12390	9697	737	2673
1	2994	12380	10896	854	3752
1	2548	7079	6949	1089	1933
0	562	1080	866	11	265
3	1261	3448	4342	381	1193
6	5585	12350	12925	1723	3884
16	1678	3624	4624	397	1053
2	2180	5999	4673	365	1232
1	13	116	212	40	202
4	2204	5157	5938	740	2488
2	1064	4071	4910	493	1024
0	273	1665	1341	52	170
0	549	1231	744	64	243
4	984	3497	2268	128	524

普通高中专任教师

Breakdown of Senior Secondary Schools Heads and Teachers

地　区 Region	合计 Total	其中女 Of Which: Female	按学历分 By Educational Attainment			
			研究生毕业 Graduate	本科毕业 Under-graduate	专科毕业 Associate Bachelor	高中阶段毕业 High School Graduate
合　计 Total	**114312**	**37332**	**647**	**67320**	**45176**	**1136**
北　京 Beijing	502	276	7	406	72	17
天　津 Tianjin	1286	694	10	776	498	2
河　北 Hebei	4829	2441	2	2801	1977	49
山　西 Shanxi	2141	935	8	1205	899	27
内蒙古 Inner Mongolia	604	271	0	336	255	13
辽　宁 Liaoning	2496	1160	0	1942	522	30
吉　林 Jilin	511	263	0	365	141	5
黑龙江 Heilongjiang	3273	1555	73	1986	1189	25
上　海 Shanghai	233	96	0	208	24	1
江　苏 Jiangsu	22623	7351	79	15171	7194	177
浙　江 Zhejiang	142	56	0	93	46	3
安　徽 Anhui	7426	1403	44	4507	2843	32
福　建 Fujian	2785	792	1	1561	1210	13
江　西 Jiangxi	3190	679	146	1302	1706	35
山　东 Shandong	3929	1515	18	2452	1418	41
河　南 henan	6080	1926	15	3577	2415	62
湖　北 Hubei	6432	1450	20	3583	2698	127
湖　南 Hunan	8516	2743	7	5261	3191	57
广　东 Guangdong	10904	3750	160	6928	3667	146
广　西 Guangxi	875	272	1	402	465	7
海　南 Hainan	321	84	0	223	95	3
重　庆 Chongqing	1232	330	1	600	626	5
四　川 Sichuan	5100	1432	17	2302	2742	38
贵　州 guizhou	1407	285	4	635	761	7
云　南 Yunnan	1787	587	8	1154	620	5
西　藏 Tibet	0	0	0	0	0	0
陕　西 Shaanxi	7747	2738	7	3860	3792	87
甘　肃 Gansu	3281	534	1	1071	2182	27
青　海 Qinghai	408	108	0	227	176	5
宁　夏 Ningxia	1056	314	0	677	370	9
新　疆 Xinjiang	3196	1292	18	1709	1382	81

学历、职称情况（农村）
by Educational Attainment (Rural)

单位：人

Unit: in Person

	按职称分 By Rank				
高中阶段毕业以下 Below High School Graduate	中学高级 Senior Secondary	中学一级 1st Grade	中学二级 2st Grade	中学三级 3st Grade	未评职称 Rank Undecided
33	**11132**	**36497**	**43770**	**7170**	**15743**
0	93	179	154	3	73
0	109	409	495	134	139
0	380	1233	1987	317	912
2	153	544	876	242	326
0	85	225	195	21	78
2	604	941	685	34	232
0	53	253	156	34	15
0	624	1367	674	139	469
0	33	140	49	3	8
2	1899	6915	8291	987	4531
0	5	46	66	12	13
0	863	2714	2632	499	718
0	177	603	1586	150	269
1	477	1114	1128	165	306
0	365	900	1781	366	517
11	517	1406	2321	845	991
4	697	2680	2096	582	377
0	720	2967	3731	224	874
3	762	3785	4335	399	1623
0	76	256	319	120	104
0	38	104	133	6	40
0	78	319	620	86	129
1	521	1611	2186	411	371
0	167	390	582	109	159
0	209	657	607	104	210
0	0	0	0	0	0
1	792	2097	2745	743	1370
0	161	941	1482	304	393
0	3	106	222	13	64
0	151	344	378	39	144
6	320	1251	1258	79	288

普通高中办学

Condition of School Buildings in Senior

地 区 Region	学校占地面积 Areas Occupied	校舍建筑面积 Floor Space	教学及辅 Teaching & Assistant 计 Total	其中 普通教室 classroom	实验室 Laboratory	图书室 Library
合 计 Total	**766396702**	**273613355**	**107640441**	**66428898**	**17644795**	**7604951**
北 京 Beijing	13395967	5968791	2219761	1146739	399210	190393
天 津 Tianjin	7250734	3001160	1284254	648156	220833	101160
河 北 Hebei	39812519	13744609	5612663	3564697	1112855	382235
山 西 Shanxi	21786174	7750514	2876562	1848062	420280	214825
内蒙古 Inner Mongolia	21770335	4763580	1929714	1242933	318725	112512
辽 宁 Liaoning	17726643	6373913	2660741	1473653	364874	181329
吉 林 Jilin	13383771	4032368	1828268	1128193	232013	101673
黑龙江 Heilongjiang	20268040	5187215	2505650	1542048	378517	140910
上 海 Shanghai	9240748	5175834	2224608	998489	399589	186337
江 苏 Jiangsu	51884398	20590835	8575385	5037204	1435341	731359
浙 江 Zhejiang	34768722	14875608	6019708	2927876	1150623	656782
安 徽 Anhui	37146364	11191742	4500095	3019362	774797	305420
福 建 Fujian	27133300	10450293	4443144	2489189	902086	392996
江 西 Jiangxi	31159565	9963284	3968402	2726003	557836	265167
山 东 Shandong	57453270	21444509	7857293	4956042	1187302	532903
河 南 Henan	41214090	15036314	5316795	3554352	770646	358336
湖 北 Hubei	33550498	13456058	4476949	2781069	792220	294447
湖 南 Hunan	40982448	15561419	5895090	3663383	943864	441201
广 东 Guangdong	58736938	22414029	9016071	5107647	1605787	631637
广 西 Guangxi	27008110	8616598	2807598	1964747	360225	193227
海 南 Hainan	7762092	1934658	682810	435384	119746	66814
重 庆 Chongqing	13444013	6480405	2422176	1592439	357431	119302
四 川 Sichuan	35164691	15768729	5539556	3747915	823584	308698
贵 州 Guizhou	13448736	4192839	1751996	1163002	268144	90230
云 南 Yunnan	19024151	6019559	2332955	1538917	419436	151881
西 藏 Tibet	1222332	293065	100819	70430	11571	4530
陕 西 Shaanxi	19638045	7431337	3327471	2274388	510502	191607
甘 肃 Gansu	14661235	4409084	2052621	1469931	253762	107814
青 海 Qinghai	5468950	1157207	511361	368969	73544	18617
宁 夏 Ningxia	4704620	1278463	552220	356396	98066	23684
新 疆 Xinjiang	26185203	5049336	2347705	1591283	381386	106925

条件(一)(总计)

Secondary Schools (1) (Total)

单位:平方米

Unit: m^2

助用房 Buildings Of Which 微机室 PC-room	语音室 Linguistic	行政办公用房 Administritive 计 Total	其中教师办公室 Of Which: for Teachers	生活用房 Residential and Welfare	其他用房 Rooms for Other Purposes	校舍面积中 Of the Floor Space 危房面积 Floor Space of Dilapidated Buildings	当年新增 New Floor Space Added in Current Year
3885833	**2112256**	**27508583**	**16109548**	**107418962**	**31045369**	**5371839**	**19464077**
88986	36782	689882	388024	1457679	1601469	16362	418934
52799	31041	398204	214032	753319	565383	2378	182005
217609	129259	1491845	994883	5188395	1451706	161030	882222
94797	63842	1020772	614485	2988434	864746	120687	318481
80427	48827	697483	392719	1572139	564244	241259	413237
86905	65969	873015	443158	1820119	1020038	41423	443504
68683	44057	533944	324154	1118717	551439	42375	426804
88038	56879	795919	474201	1293916	591730	119921	324597
90623	48454	524004	270179	1253064	1174158	0	376738
298856	133793	1961250	1168339	7895229	2158971	1153	1514695
222099	136320	1313811	760106	5841653	1700436	7697	1576668
171726	83666	979266	574995	4734056	978325	471538	672259
139335	83756	880992	432182	4053813	1072344	190454	689102
147333	93372	932174	602572	4198371	864337	199124	846273
281589	163752	2324450	1431983	9498169	1764597	188630	1707209
196191	95260	1913396	1267096	6332706	1473417	288337	1049761
166606	92161	1311483	705020	6134046	1533580	181536	449509
200920	104869	1162545	633871	6807753	1696031	259212	956125
297611	154832	1928840	953204	8593509	2875609	281066	1060310
100849	50172	566181	328886	4291508	951311	298796	698783
27602	13008	102682	54836	929154	220012	63874	210897
92454	40732	492844	268503	2777522	787863	153153	325188
198059	101007	1166811	639791	7777941	1284421	358360	1199649
75886	30559	387419	195823	1580277	473147	100372	298570
72410	43986	447169	225790	2622290	617145	422996	747692
2483	2142	40859	22517	128605	22782	4051	8554
128060	74098	1070902	742973	2317846	715118	288144	723931
77778	33811	631376	439638	1206441	518646	416172	366735
16751	10589	158581	94422	360462	126803	72150	88398
25421	10385	136182	106041	440197	149864	50024	95299
76947	34876	574302	345125	1451632	675697	329565	391948

普通高中办学

Condition of School Buildings in Senior

地　区 Region	学校占地面积 Areas Occupied	校舍建筑面积 Floor Space	教学及辅 Teaching & Assistant 计 Total	其中 普通教室 classroom	 实验室 Laboratory	 图书室 Library
合　计 Total	**275515752**	**116544856**	**48369871**	**27649671**	**8287027**	**3871151**
北　京 Beijing	6392278	3826792	1347984	698334	244162	122418
天　津 Tianjin	3822904	1906154	828615	413819	142025	71371
河　北 Hebei	12693135	5256605	2317553	1415597	496128	180828
山　西 Shanxi	9182911	4211851	1567664	920103	242808	125828
内蒙古 Inner Mongolia	9180628	2692303	1117528	670624	202893	74376
辽　宁 Liaoning	9930588	3903150	1673453	862742	226578	124629
吉　林 Jilin	3970741	1603123	746389	450173	77198	45305
黑龙江 Heilongjiang	7082504	2357848	1202484	661830	177986	75901
上　海 Shanghai	4159919	2915105	1280780	531601	235278	113542
江　苏 Jiangsu	13305348	5817439	2771475	1556281	462869	272083
浙　江 Zhejiang	17330561	7949938	3291763	1555358	620775	381356
安　徽 Anhui	10632408	3875879	1729669	1064163	341612	138287
福　建 Fujian	7241597	3419799	1576443	771147	349654	166843
江　西 Jiangxi	7708538	3117110	1344359	856599	217679	99051
山　东 Shandong	26097588	10784254	4183213	2465329	663417	344097
河　南 Henan	14726540	6134568	2241531	1379083	361702	176796
湖　北 Hubei	18774452	7519338	2735396	1645774	494277	189978
湖　南 Hunan	13257623	5893949	2455860	1387765	419345	199321
广　东 Guangdong	17788069	8023417	3638795	1802772	666869	274436
广　西 Guangxi	7050999	2797760	964461	638430	140503	79362
海　南 Hainan	1908573	825316	264136	149253	55053	35205
重　庆 Chongqing	6476843	3452029	1305681	816493	207368	73709
四　川 Sichuan	11624986	5709641	2136699	1368908	323589	141315
贵　州 Guizhou	4283340	1703818	688854	425771	117115	43442
云　南 Yunnan	4313371	1804863	742470	460258	137682	62892
西　藏 Tibet	716527	170359	59518	34958	8063	3566
陕　西 Shaanxi	6783572	3230882	1560133	977980	239372	110784
甘　肃 Gansu	4961277	1829376	863961	569147	128445	58101
青　海 Qinghai	1288592	398783	182795	123225	34407	7273
宁　夏 Ningxia	2014203	570061	254315	146587	45884	11614
新　疆 Xinjiang	10815137	2843346	1295894	829567	206291	67442

条件(一)(城市)

Secondary Schools (1) (Urban)

单位:平方米

Unit:m^2

助用房 Buildings		行政办公用房 Administritive		生活用房 Residential and Welfare	其他用房 Rooms for Other Purposes	校舍面积中 Of the Floor Space	
Of Which							
微机室 PC-room	语音室 Linguistic	计 Total	其中教师办公室 Of Which: for Teachers			危房面积 Floor Space of Dilapidated Buildings	当年新增 New Floor Space Added in Current Year
1889175	**999978**	**12552060**	**7067798**	**39475644**	**16147281**	**1046979**	**8236462**
59213	24169	450079	250573	805213	1223516	15590	186983
33934	20836	261592	137327	366743	449204	0	132765
92814	53432	601126	362924	1754593	583333	32625	354144
53327	36319	554028	299738	1529151	561008	29308	168113
49440	27683	398426	199277	790412	385937	80445	219548
56322	44655	521085	273926	978898	729714	22902	181544
34881	18782	195050	123935	390351	271333	0	113846
39494	24130	369910	196135	516715	268739	31927	115564
50268	28490	317058	154708	579213	738054	0	30815
98495	35657	574277	351377	1717151	754536	663	308232
132840	83931	687042	421392	2897885	1073248	3438	1081938
67529	33547	422456	244064	1296638	427116	58861	252465
56142	30182	360072	164821	1030159	453125	42241	248540
56632	35125	334852	213120	1158678	279221	33810	222221
160867	96074	1155672	708491	4262573	1182796	36843	781524
84114	39595	787618	548672	2565520	539899	40895	300025
110729	56505	792309	416207	3059675	931958	54660	295869
93197	48067	502691	248794	2187291	748107	52540	340055
129352	63481	820555	389636	2254068	1309999	33448	366868
43310	17195	197528	112718	1225869	409902	20100	311707
14510	5315	40797	21838	413012	107371	10131	113918
51806	18109	279059	138434	1355822	511467	72700	144739
85831	42946	480556	253714	2556211	536175	21622	685820
36239	13017	193840	89625	560479	260645	22478	103265
28651	15226	136387	74192	642316	283690	37677	350473
1819	1449	18472	6033	77038	15331	642	8554
66886	39098	395418	261711	881842	393489	42025	354367
33720	16767	254921	150441	464048	246446	73166	152661
6691	4611	68002	32249	95646	52340	26902	38007
11035	4515	55243	38931	191701	68802	4784	48972
49087	21070	325939	182795	870733	350780	144556	222920

普通高中办学

Condition of School Buildings in Senior

地 区 Region	学校占地面积 Areas Occupied	校舍建筑面积 Floor Space	教学及辅 Teaching & Assistant			
			计 Total	其中		
				普通教室 classroom	实验室 Laboratory	图书室 Library
合 计 Total	**381506400**	**127158950**	**48138785**	**31083557**	**7790242**	**3180888**
北 京 Beijing	6345951	1969726	811314	413652	140704	63228
天 津 Tianjin	2761307	890501	389537	201129	69468	26356
河 北 Hebei	23175677	7383910	2841613	1818406	544010	176821
山 西 Shanxi	9758746	3004043	1113683	799011	147672	70781
内蒙古 Inner Mongolia	11149651	1900454	761253	540872	106189	35425
辽 宁 Liaoning	6106029	2025063	817324	503129	118220	49812
吉 林 Jilin	8657148	2316090	1020922	637368	145387	54505
黑龙江 Heilongjiang	8739449	2105822	959646	635025	150973	49573
上 海 Shanghai	4697692	2202845	908856	450301	154230	69916
江 苏 Jiangsu	20454617	8671811	3444405	2026645	574096	310302
浙 江 Zhejiang	17314467	6903760	2719520	1364719	529558	275243
安 徽 Anhui	16941396	5184276	1973256	1327228	346319	135773
福 建 Fujian	16636340	5970457	2428729	1445233	478338	200309
江 西 Jiangxi	20004824	5901973	2293759	1629445	303698	146626
山 东 Shandong	27792516	9563018	3251756	2165155	492471	177087
河 南 Henan	22619154	7897714	2720549	1894074	372377	170219
湖 北 Hubei	10622529	4548328	1353476	844647	251805	90423
湖 南 Hunan	21917447	7629892	2798947	1836209	437685	211617
广 东 Guangdong	27504713	9599846	3744936	2283530	692062	260513
广 西 Guangxi	18613521	5514855	1766503	1269750	213087	111504
海 南 Hainan	4797267	945062	361152	246251	58105	28397
重 庆 Chongqing	6273279	2710700	1027014	702637	141932	43039
四 川 Sichuan	20771270	9038749	3064682	2115127	456964	157449
贵 州 Guizhou	7108601	2126787	873421	592913	134151	39104
云 南 Yunnan	12406401	3610862	1378866	933877	245387	80711
西 藏 Tibet	505805	122706	41301	35472	3508	964
陕 西 Shaanxi	7877763	2855108	1235984	890876	204171	61287
甘 肃 Gansu	6632862	1970695	904924	664226	100912	40595
青 海 Qinghai	3606435	698187	303009	223278	37584	10985
宁 夏 Ningxia	1699283	505487	212256	143525	40835	9076
新 疆 Xinjiang	8014260	1390223	616192	449847	98344	23248

条件(一)(县镇)

Secondary Schools (1) (County Seats & Towns)

单位:平方米

Unit: m^2

助用房 Buildings		行政办公用房 Administritive		生活用房 Residential and Welfare	其他用房 Rooms for Other Purposes	校舍面积中 Of the Floor Space	
Of Which							
微机室 PC-room	语音室 Linguistic	计 Total	其中教师办公室 Of Which: for Teachers			危房面积 Floor Space of Dilapidated Buildings	当年新增 New Floor Space Added in Current Year
1646772	**939947**	**12149070**	**7281923**	**54803021**	**12068074**	**3165245**	**9540073**
27163	11851	212729	126253	589303	356380	736	209950
14471	8371	117029	64247	286177	97758	2378	14892
111316	68925	770459	538708	3008795	763043	110801	501029
34228	23054	398604	270558	1243604	248152	74522	132346
28848	19546	269715	179924	705810	163676	149251	179954
25175	17344	306405	144091	674481	226853	14891	235824
32090	23976	323916	189066	701848	269404	33611	303994
36089	25129	331381	216668	599934	214861	61755	148195
38654	18579	197123	111369	667473	429393	0	345752
121416	65423	855072	511684	3516941	855393	0	773912
89106	52389	624422	337964	2932965	626853	4259	485206
76879	39085	406914	233120	2406076	398030	237351	259891
72080	47949	449717	236666	2554298	537713	96687	392935
78740	48420	494110	327596	2669228	444876	128516	558795
109953	61250	981769	610148	4807971	521522	120808	890092
98628	51120	1011053	624319	3318177	847935	194281	698031
45686	30344	390787	218904	2339024	465041	76289	126581
86250	44759	533371	310499	3597650	699924	137775	522912
121993	66884	784801	383350	3963116	1106993	146959	515297
55957	32234	358222	208648	2881137	508993	264351	372916
10929	6736	52693	27303	433344	97873	48472	96603
37816	21245	189355	110391	1236997	257334	75370	159793
103221	55021	610231	349177	4703522	660314	266283	446103
31881	14518	166921	91554	897047	189398	64421	171939
37967	25301	272224	130082	1665260	294512	332036	344096
664	693	22387	16484	51567	7451	3409	0
45209	26822	431253	300549	954579	233292	132976	257384
35500	14553	280029	204763	580822	204920	232430	172906
9494	5531	85353	57444	240203	69622	38788	50161
11664	5028	62375	50107	181164	49692	18925	34180
17705	7867	158650	100287	394508	220873	96914	138404

普通高中办学

Condition of School Buildings in Senior

地 区 Region	学校占地面积 Areas Occupied	校舍建筑面积 Floor Space	教学及辅 Teaching & Assistant			
			计 Total	其中 普通教室 classroom	实验室 Laboratory	图书室 Library
合 计 Total	**109374550**	**29909549**	**11131785**	**7695670**	**1567526**	**552912**
北 京 Beijing	657738	172273	60463	34753	14344	4747
天 津 Tianjin	666523	204505	66102	33208	9340	3433
河 北 Hebei	3943707	1104094	453497	330694	72717	24586
山 西 Shanxi	2844517	534620	195215	128948	29800	18216
内蒙古 Inner Mongolia	1440056	170823	50933	31437	9643	2711
辽 宁 Liaoning	1690026	445700	169964	107782	20076	6888
吉 林 Jilin	755882	113155	60957	40652	9428	1863
黑龙江 Heilongjiang	4446087	723545	343520	245193	49558	15436
上 海 Shanghai	383137	57884	34972	16587	10081	2879
江 苏 Jiangsu	18124433	6101585	2359505	1454278	398376	148974
浙 江 Zhejiang	123694	21910	8425	7799	290	183
安 徽 Anhui	9572560	2131587	797170	627971	86866	31360
福 建 Fujian	3255363	1060037	437972	272809	74094	25844
江 西 Jiangxi	3446203	944201	330284	239959	36459	19490
山 东 Shandong	3563166	1097237	422324	325558	31414	11719
河 南 Henan	3868396	1004032	354715	281195	36567	11321
湖 北 Hubei	4153517	1388392	388077	290648	46138	14046
湖 南 Hunan	5807378	2037578	640283	439409	86834	30263
广 东 Guangdong	13444156	4790766	1632340	1021345	246856	96688
广 西 Guangxi	1343590	303983	76634	56567	6635	2361
海 南 Hainan	1056252	164280	57522	39880	6588	3212
重 庆 Chongqing	693891	317676	89481	73309	8131	2554
四 川 Sichuan	2768435	1020339	338175	263880	43031	9934
贵 州 Guizhou	2056795	362234	189721	144318	16878	7684
云 南 Yunnan	2304379	603834	211619	144782	36367	8278
西 藏 Tibet	0	0	0	0	0	0
陕 西 Shaanxi	4976710	1345347	531354	405532	66959	19536
甘 肃 Gansu	3067096	609013	283736	236558	24405	9118
青 海 Qinghai	573923	60237	25557	22466	1553	359
宁 夏 Ningxia	991134	202915	85649	66284	11347	2994
新 疆 Xinjiang	7355806	815767	435619	311869	76751	16235

条件(一)(农村)

Secondary Schools (1) (Rural)

单位:平方米

Unit: m^2

助用房 Buildings Of Which 微机室 PC-room	语音室 Linguistic	行政办公用房 Administritive 计 Total	其中教师办公室 Of Which: for Teachers	生活用房 Residential and Welfare	其他用房 Rooms for Other Purposes	校舍面积中 Of the Floor Space 危房面积 Floor Space of Dilapidated Buildings	当年新增 New Floor Space Added in Current Year
349886	**172331**	**2807453**	**1759827**	**13140297**	**2830014**	**1159615**	**1687542**
2610	762	27074	11198	63163	21573	36	22001
4394	1834	19583	12458	100399	18421	0	34348
13479	6902	120260	93251	425007	105330	17604	27049
7242	4469	68140	44189	215679	55586	16857	18022
2139	1598	29342	13518	75917	14631	11563	13735
5408	3970	45525	25141	166740	63471	3630	26136
1712	1299	14978	11153	26518	10702	8764	8964
12455	7620	94628	61398	177267	108130	26239	60838
1701	1385	9823	4102	6378	6711	0	171
78945	32713	531901	305278	2661137	549042	490	432551
153	0	2347	750	10803	335	0	9524
27318	11034	149896	97811	1031342	153179	175326	159903
11113	5625	71203	30695	469356	81506	51526	47627
11961	9827	103212	61856	370465	140240	36798	65257
10769	6428	187009	113344	427625	60279	30979	35593
13449	4545	114725	94105	449009	85583	53161	51705
10191	5312	128387	69909	735347	136581	50587	27059
21473	12043	126483	74578	1022812	248000	68897	93158
46266	24467	323484	180218	2376325	458617	100659	178145
1582	743	10431	7520	184502	32416	14345	14160
2163	957	9192	5695	82798	14768	5271	376
2832	1378	24430	19678	184703	19062	5083	20656
9007	3040	76024	36900	518208	87932	70455	67726
7766	3024	26658	14644	122751	23104	13473	23366
5792	3459	38558	21516	314714	38943	53283	53123
0	0	0	0	0	0	0	0
15965	8178	244231	180713	481425	88337	113143	112180
8558	2491	96426	84434	161571	67280	110576	41168
566	447	5226	4729	24613	4841	6460	230
2722	842	18564	17003	67332	31370	26315	12147
10155	5939	89713	62043	186391	104044	88095	30624

普通高中办

Condition of School Buildings in Senior

地　区 Region	体育运动场(馆) 面　积 (平方米) Sports Areas (m^2)	计　算　机 (台) PC (set)	图书藏量 (册) Books & Magazines in Libraries (Volume)
合　计 Total	**182625764**	**1813251**	**444803404**
北　京 Beijing	3464867	55789	14810748
天　津 Tianjin	2182095	27664	5795969
河　北 Hebei	11026852	89206	21943097
山　西 Shanxi	5066068	46482	11862134
内蒙古 Inner Mongolia	5733999	32107	7816225
辽　宁 Liaoning	5027149	53718	9345788
吉　林 Jilin	3864768	36291	6525519
黑龙江 Heilongjiang	6311130	49072	7567705
上　海 Shanghai	2843340	58919	11925073
江　苏 Jiangsu	12014423	144679	37516790
浙　江 Zhejiang	9317355	102296	23980174
安　徽 Anhui	8181068	80130	20469972
福　建 Fujian	6515836	72026	25274963
江　西 Jiangxi	6723917	56110	13164713
山　东 Shandong	12507320	132289	25282056
河　南 Henan	9949970	76615	21211668
湖　北 Hubei	7329113	58744	16463963
湖　南 Hunan	8385000	88823	21856152
广　东 Guangdong	13527928	162334	46039335
广　西 Guangxi	5252893	48112	14418323
海　南 Hainan	1517377	11381	2772406
重　庆 Chongqing	2917775	39290	7020650
四　川 Sichuan	8056867	79958	20121892
贵　州 Guizhou	2970969	30125	6836740
云　南 Yunnan	3471692	27857	9649065
西　藏 Tibet	190446	1588	320313
陕　西 Shaanxi	5554392	61653	14903033
甘　肃 Gansu	3810940	35065	8614232
青　海 Qinghai	1388185	8110	1817750
宁　夏 Ningxia	1147589	11969	2061967
新　疆 Xinjiang	6374441	34849	7414989

学条件(二)(总计)
Secondary Schools (2) (Regional Aggregates)

电子图书藏量(片) Electronic Books & Magazines in Libraries (disk)	固定资产总值(万元) Total Volue of Fixed Asset (in 10 thousand yuan)			
	合计 Total	其中:仪器设备总值(万元) Of Which: Total Volue of Equip & Instru. (in 10 thousand yuan)		
		小计 SubTotal	专业实验设备 For Prefession	专业实习设备 For Practice
8808254	**21524438.56**	**2401690.83**	**1526799.76**	**302713.52**
413160	558883.76	60223.04	39498.50	5758.76
78779	228707.21	41415.60	17332.86	2591.47
667543	1006040.40	115175.87	65888.01	14190.19
300566	509246.23	65446.68	47208.75	6969.45
94968	283841.34	29079.76	19254.46	3388.92
22808	413296.00	58979.00	33360.00	3927.00
68194	445002.47	55703.49	34902.89	7158.32
152284	611539.58	67827.17	47196.81	11327.43
211369	829156.58	115162.50	77687.53	5139.93
739396	2029542.33	205417.05	127230.68	17271.06
211220	1587455.00	134208.54	69079.15	0.00
226737	937894.35	77078.46	49773.49	15249.11
189512	750879.00	94037.00	75858.00	18179.00
205596	701298.13	90877.84	35746.22	11446.96
265601	1704391.22	145705.41	79671.63	21061.74
444446	919687.73	117201.23	86462.20	15644.57
179798	939873.69	94778.71	62227.60	15559.52
425019	940809.86	117957.54	74629.15	15877.50
2197635	2064281.86	266127.55	217433.69	44997.14
103134	370050.73	40855.04	27268.13	7265.34
60705	197645.94	18746.00	13448.59	4092.10
232596	471652.30	43308.40	22891.78	10452.37
560755	1108265.01	112936.82	63058.94	12420.29
91264	246998.47	29196.70	19450.87	5639.05
49511	351193.51	31178.55	18046.40	3141.21
630	29948.58	1924.95	1601.65	94.00
398040	574294.42	82858.38	49021.31	12874.73
92286	242096.06	31515.16	21953.30	5175.76
8279	52239.38	5092.51	4052.52	648.02
10035	81275.22	13584.08	4672.89	1117.44
106388	336952.20	38091.80	20891.76	4055.14

普通高中办

Condition of School Buildings in Senior

地　区 Region	体育运动场(馆) 面　积 (平方米) Sports Areas (m^2)	计　算　机 (台) PC (set)	图书藏量 (册) Books & Magazines in Libraries (Volume)
合　计 Total	**70726957**	**925855**	**201338080**
北　京 Beijing	1836331	39755	10711864
天　津 Tianjin	1186622	18826	4228435
河　北 Hebei	3479889	40334	8280947
山　西 Shanxi	2511839	26540	6920871
内蒙古 Inner Mongolia	2634704	19246	4436614
辽　宁 Liaoning	2809275	38444	6623807
吉　林 Jilin	1152944	17234	2637461
黑龙江 Heilongjiang	2417083	24715	3659955
上　海 Shanghai	1429194	39574	7768786
江　苏 Jiangsu	3120674	57447	12206825
浙　江 Zhejiang	4579474	59259	12229937
安　徽 Anhui	2493747	32411	7066233
福　建 Fujian	1732663	31102	8623028
江　西 Jiangxi	2010346	22804	4508389
山　东 Shandong	5636956	77188	13766270
河　南 Henan	4431530	38209	9609425
湖　北 Hubei	4295534	38489	10355219
湖　南 Hunan	2912833	39312	9066060
广　东 Guangdong	4596538	81017	17557649
广　西 Guangxi	1658328	19858	5000142
海　南 Hainan	394352	4919	941195
重　庆 Chongqing	1393956	22248	3496932
四　川 Sichuan	2592120	32975	7876780
贵　州 Guizhou	1009483	13851	3056926
云　南 Yunnan	865167	10949	3277580
西　藏 Tibet	165463	1067	252621
陕　西 Shaanxi	2370456	31954	7697234
甘　肃 Gansu	1264514	16343	3996577
青　海 Qinghai	310985	3294	676030
宁　夏 Ningxia	402988	5336	805898
新　疆 Xinjiang	3030969	21155	4002390

学条件(二)(城市)

Secondary Schools (2) (Urban)

电子图书藏量(片) Electronic Books & Magazines in Libraries (disk)	固定资产总值(万元) Total Value of Fixed Asset (in 10 thousand yuan)			
	计 Total	其中:仪器设备总值(万元) Of Which: Total Value of Equip & Instru. (in 10 thousand yuan)		
		计 SubTotal	专业实验设备 For Prefession	专业实习设备 For Practice
4943639	**10625443.73**	**1354080.41**	**858037.96**	**145423.43**
258183	304029.20	39655.20	25499.24	3742.45
53428	129943.72	27194.59	10117.66	1175.80
375801	417447.26	53914.40	31131.10	7216.34
200256	327833.29	48262.63	36638.55	3753.70
64864	147168.44	18544.68	11667.62	1557.58
17778	260374.00	42301.00	23603.00	1414.00
49943	232636.95	29794.78	18911.60	3665.70
123552	417714.96	40708.30	30122.34	4947.20
155544	487588.36	83536.41	56637.16	1627.44
313164	729523.18	80744.98	44179.68	4068.13
119054	933573.65	88721.52	42846.06	0.00
113066	462963.42	34121.52	21922.40	6327.47
126674	377603.00	60178.00	48311.00	11867.00
82211	253390.35	59550.92	16859.90	5641.08
158481	939131.49	79773.62	46493.60	11376.31
177234	385220.13	72521.96	58599.88	5531.75
117339	565272.46	59834.75	41089.30	9301.38
132026	398133.50	57081.32	38566.26	6670.90
1330175	893911.55	130730.52	107333.63	20386.17
38653	122571.78	17593.00	12013.01	2594.47
25613	85511.63	10202.27	7305.07	1771.20
160092	330500.66	29832.49	15805.66	8044.20
304171	459690.21	52524.51	31411.09	4474.91
43054	115480.83	14010.83	8622.02	3265.65
34785	116158.25	13903.11	9376.64	700.77
390	17460.07	1480.00	1166.00	94.00
214970	314007.14	57576.05	31144.01	8974.75
54469	126847.69	17420.17	12808.13	2720.35
1528	17719.79	2008.93	1903.83	95.10
3911	44300.82	8280.29	1855.60	196.52
93230	211735.95	22077.66	14096.92	2221.11

普通高中办

Condition of School Buildings in Senior

地　区 Region	体育运动场(馆) 面　积 (平方米) Sports Areas (m^2)	计　算　机 (台) PC (set)	图书藏量 (册) Books & Magazines in Libraries (Volume)
合　计 Total	**86451604**	**725155**	**195164121**
北　京 Beijing	1469024	14413	3692950
天　津 Tianjin	828591	7544	1365350
河　北 Hebei	6364309	43547	11717688
山　西 Shanxi	2052530	16758	4286223
内蒙古 Inner Mongolia	2752133	11631	3069527
辽　宁 Liaoning	1753890	13054	2319272
吉　林 Jilin	2468834	18195	3637777
黑龙江 Heilongjiang	2525409	18607	2755838
上　海 Shanghai	1355763	18716	4018259
江　苏 Jiangsu	4440533	52713	14116292
浙　江 Zhejiang	4729952	42952	11727406
安　徽 Anhui	3548469	34935	9698194
福　建 Fujian	3976470	35633	14471625
江　西 Jiangxi	3909281	28565	7372799
山　东 Shandong	5985877	48941	10444841
河　南 Henan	4730622	33580	10493737
湖　北 Hubei	2191798	16035	4678051
湖　南 Hunan	4402148	39652	10396421
广　东 Guangdong	6176207	56338	19008994
广　西 Guangxi	3260041	27327	8995773
海　南 Hainan	882489	5592	1601305
重　庆 Chongqing	1363597	15226	3098420
四　川 Sichuan	4820583	42565	11210609
贵　州 Guizhou	1564957	14056	3125311
云　南 Yunnan	2065868	14930	5575319
西　藏 Tibet	24983	521	67692
陕　西 Shaanxi	2020402	20421	4991803
甘　肃 Gansu	1720976	14475	3518794
青　海 Qinghai	919361	4377	1022162
宁　夏 Ningxia	510071	4811	830701
新　疆 Xinjiang	1636436	9045	1854988

学条件(二)(县镇)

Secondary Schools (2) (County Seats & Towns)

电子图书藏量 (片) Electronic Books & Magazines in Libraries (disk)	固定资产总值(万元) Total Value of Fixed Asset (in 10 thousand yuan)			
	计 Total	其中:仪器设备总值(万元) Of Which: Total Value of Equip & Instru. (in 10 thousand yuan)		
		计 Sub Total	专业实验设备 For Prefession	专业实习设备 For Practice
3425279	**9078184.97**	**853343.68**	**546772.90**	**127123.60**
144173	237370.30	17804.28	12246.49	1886.67
24911	79448.42	13042.13	6281.76	1170.40
271851	534680.97	55712.76	30921.09	5971.79
92065	149614.53	13849.18	8854.70	2255.11
28392	128026.40	9838.24	7107.84	1688.33
3397	127151.00	13798.00	7963.00	1725.00
14811	205798.52	25500.71	15746.29	3397.62
25039	155677.68	21011.93	13343.52	5034.61
54889	334624.82	30316.17	20541.15	3338.49
255671	888953.54	89504.19	56934.15	10097.23
92045	652785.76	45428.15	26174.22	0.00
88189	342400.78	33947.20	22786.36	5949.55
53390	324227.00	31045.00	25268.00	5777.00
116480	393163.30	26437.39	16533.80	4995.66
98044	657021.88	44879.02	29619.63	9130.49
256141	491687.71	40366.07	24852.31	9080.98
51845	308402.88	29790.08	17448.95	5247.58
288057	439534.75	50745.08	29706.15	7567.22
798736	800417.22	87985.12	72300.93	15498.19
64181	238460.57	22695.75	14814.04	4570.66
34922	100906.33	6976.59	4851.18	2086.70
71296	128520.69	12523.51	6508.92	2262.17
250957	599919.47	57358.82	29579.95	7331.92
47046	114784.30	12591.70	8964.20	2051.54
13604	207500.21	15033.60	7820.56	2044.24
240	12488.51	444.95	435.65	0.00
133325	199940.41	20573.42	14848.38	3010.77
30817	91061.52	10683.05	6611.18	1899.23
6035	29998.69	2852.07	2017.32	534.52
5515	28754.63	4043.79	1978.65	661.40
9215	74862.18	6565.73	3712.53	858.53

地　区 Region	体育运动场(馆)面积(平方米) Sports Areas (m^2)	计算机(台) PC (set)	图书藏量(册) Books & Magazines in Libraries (Volume)
合　计 Total	**25447203**	**162241**	**48301203**
北　京 Beijing	159512	1621	405934
天　津 Tianjin	166882	1294	202184
河　北 Hebei	1182654	5325	1944462
山　西 Shanxi	501699	3184	655040
内蒙古 Inner Mongolia	347162	1230	310084
辽　宁 Liaoning	463984	2220	402709
吉　林 Jilin	242990	862	250281
黑龙江 Heilongjiang	1368638	5750	1151912
上　海 Shanghai	58383	629	138028
江　苏 Jiangsu	4453216	34519	11193673
浙　江 Zhejiang	7929	85	22831
安　徽 Anhui	2138852	12784	3705545
福　建 Fujian	806703	5291	2180310
江　西 Jiangxi	804290	4741	1283525
山　东 Shandong	884487	6160	1070945
河　南 Henan	787818	4826	1108506
湖　北 Hubei	841781	4220	1430693
湖　南 Hunan	1070019	9859	2393671
广　东 Guangdong	2755183	24979	9472692
广　西 Guangxi	334524	927	422408
海　南 Hainan	240536	870	229906
重　庆 Chongqing	160222	1816	425298
四　川 Sichuan	644164	4418	1034503
贵　州 Guizhou	396529	2218	654503
云　南 Yunnan	540657	1978	796166
西　藏 Tibet	0	0	0
陕　西 Shaanxi	1163534	9278	2213996
甘　肃 Gansu	825450	4247	1098861
青　海 Qinghai	157839	439	119558
宁　夏 Ningxia	234530	1822	425368
新　疆 Xinjiang	1707036	4649	1557611

学条件(二)(农村)

Senior Secondary Schools (2) (Rural)

电子图书藏量(片) Electronic Books & Magazines in Libraries (disk)	固定资产总值(万元) Total Value of Fixed Asset (in 10 thousand yuan)			
	计 Total	其中:仪器设备总值(万元) Of Which: Total Value of Equip & Instru. (in 10 thousand yuan)		
		计 Sub Total	专业实验设备 For Prefession	专业实习设备 For Practice
439336	**1820809.86**	**194266.74**	**121988.90**	**30166.49**
10804	17484.26	2763.56	1752.77	129.64
440	19315.07	1178.88	933.44	245.27
19891	53912.17	5548.71	3835.82	1002.06
8245	31798.41	3334.87	1715.50	960.64
1712	8646.50	696.84	479.00	143.01
1633	25771.00	2880.00	1794.00	788.00
3440	6567.00	408.00	245.00	95.00
3693	38146.94	6106.94	3730.95	1345.62
936	6943.40	1309.92	509.22	174.00
170561	411065.61	35167.88	26116.85	3105.70
121	1095.59	58.87	58.87	0.00
25482	132530.15	9009.74	5064.73	2972.09
9448	49049.00	2814.00	2279.00	535.00
6905	54744.48	4889.53	2352.52	810.22
9076	108237.85	21052.77	3558.40	554.94
11071	42779.89	4313.20	3010.01	1031.84
10614	66198.35	5153.88	3689.35	1010.56
4936	103141.61	10131.14	6356.74	1639.38
68724	369953.09	47411.91	37799.13	9112.78
300	9018.38	566.29	441.08	100.21
170	11227.98	1567.14	1292.34	234.20
1208	12630.95	952.40	577.20	146.00
5627	48655.33	3053.49	2067.90	613.46
1164	16733.34	2594.17	1864.65	321.86
1122	27535.05	2241.84	849.20	396.20
0	0.00	0.00	0.00	0.00
49745	60346.87	4708.91	3028.92	889.21
7000	24186.85	3411.94	2533.99	556.18
716	4520.90	231.51	131.37	18.40
609	8219.77	1260.00	838.64	259.52
3943	50354.07	9448.41	3082.31	975.50

中等职业学

Number of Secondary

地 区 Region	中等职业学校 Secondary Vocational Schools				普通中等专业学校 Reg. Specialized Sec. Schools			
	计 Total	中央部门 HEIs under Central Ministries & Agencies	地方部门 HEIs under Local Auth.	民 办 Non-state/private	计 Total	中央部门 HEIs under Central Ministries & Agencies	地方部门 HEIs under Local Auth.	民 办 Non-state/private
合 计 Total	**11712**	**98**	**10232**	**1382**	**3065**	**65**	**2811**	**189**
北 京 Beijing	177	10	148	19	63	8	54	1
天 津 Tianjin	183		175	8	51		50	1
河 北 Hebei	623	3	530	90	133	2	84	47
山 西 Shanxi	446	3	426	17	79	1	78	
内蒙古 Inner Mongolia	258	1	252	5	58	1	57	
辽 宁 Liaoning	416	4	339	73	130	4	117	9
吉 林 Jilin	268	1	261	6	57	1	56	
黑龙江 Heilongjiang	331	2	323	6	51	2	49	
上 海 Shanghai	184	7	167	10	83	4	77	2
江 苏 Jiangsu	558	3	536	19	144	2	136	6
浙 江 Zhejiang	572	5	417	150	57	3	50	4
安 徽 Anhui	521		460	61	103		94	9
福 建 Fujian	355	2	299	54	355	2	299	54
江 西 Jiangxi	367	4	278	85	58	2	51	5
山 东 Shandong	751		681	70	154		153	1
河 南 henan	821	9	776	36	137	5	132	
湖 北 Hubei	390		365	25	174		168	6
湖 南 Hunan	668	3	444	221	81	3	78	
广 东 Guangdong	717	5	627	85	248	3	225	20
广 西 Guangxi	424	1	350	73	106	1	104	1
海 南 Hainan	89		76	13	30		30	
重 庆 Chongqing	295		229	66	39		38	1
四 川 Sichuan	619	1	561	57	126	1	114	11
贵 州 guizhou	223		197	26	97		97	
云 南 Yunnan	418	11	387	20	113	4	99	10
西 藏 Tibet	10		10		9		9	
陕 西 Shaanxi	465	8	378	79	89	4	85	
甘 肃 Gansu	287	9	273	5	125	6	118	1
青 海 Qinghai	53	1	51	1	26	1	25	
宁 夏 Ningxia	39		38	1	11		11	
新 疆 Xinjiang	184	5	178	1	78	5	73	

校(机构)数

Vocational Schools

单位:人
Unit:in Person

成人中等专业学校 Specialized Sec. Schools for Adults				职业高中学校 Vocational High Schools			
计 Total	中央部门 HEIs under Central Ministries& Agencies	地方部门 HEIs under Local Auth.	民办 Non-state/private	计 Total	中央部门 HEIs under Central Ministries& Agencies	地方部门 HEIs under Local Auth.	民办 Non-state/private
2823	**27**	**2673**	**123**	**5824**	**6**	**4748**	**1070**
17	2	15		97		79	18
29		28	1	103		97	6
194		181	13	296	1	265	30
160	2	158		207		190	17
79		79		121		116	5
1		1		285		221	64
98		98		113		107	6
127		127		153		147	6
49	3	41	5	52		49	3
156	1	155		258		245	13
98	2	95	1	417		272	145
114		103	11	304		263	41
100	1	98	1	209	1	129	79
197		180	17	400		348	52
233	1	220	12	451	3	424	24
72		72		144		125	19
134		112	22	453		254	199
190	1	182	7	279	1	220	58
115		112	3	203		134	69
14		14		45		32	13
91		77	14	165		114	51
215		204	11	278		243	35
21		18	3	105		82	23
138	7	131		167		157	10
1		1					
83	4	79		293		214	79
54	3	50	1	108		105	3
10		9	1	17		17	
5		5		23		22	1
28		28		78		77	1

中等职业学校(机构)

Number of students in Secondary

地　区 Region	毕业生数 Graduates		招生数 Entrants		
	计 Total	其中:获得职业资格证书 Of which: Recitpents of Vocational qualifications	计 Total	其中:初中毕业 of which: Junior Sec. School Graduates	
				计 Total	应届毕业生 Autumn Session
合　计 Total	**3011438**	**1393781**	**4241166**	**3927843**	**3706506**
北　京 Beijing	57865	28331	64937	61711	58337
天　津 Tianjin	55146	25947	46366	43731	41786
河　北 Hebei	188101	81271	231496	205715	192048
山　西 Shanxi	115778	46444	117786	98958	90038
内蒙古 Inner Mongolia	57099	17089	64010	57752	53223
辽　宁 Liaoning	106024	40780	149217	135065	129323
吉　林 Jilin	47381	19378	53386	51389	45425
黑龙江 Heilongjiang	77915	45989	78604	74446	66060
上　海 Shanghai	64342	33433	69431	64742	64366
江　苏 Jiangsu	159366	74508	313486	305905	303486
浙　江 Zhejiang	158053	90897	289429	277164	270027
安　徽 Anhui	109605	35362	177494	162097	151430
福　建 Fujian	111221	56632	145067	135618	123959
江　西 Jiangxi	97487	42786	138076	128433	119556
山　东 Shandong	250720	119600	369584	340942	321346
河　南 henan	253814	111765	362219	310014	290314
湖　北 Hubei	108936	44433	151838	145322	139972
湖　南 Hunan	144185	80596	277140	264963	249124
广　东 Guangdong	176492	101017	233281	229637	224998
广　西 Guangxi	97743	46973	128236	120984	111630
海　南 Hainan	12665	4283	17109	16681	16013
重　庆 Chongqing	66548	35049	122306	113408	108737
四　川 Sichuan	133117	70947	216172	201253	191004
贵　州 guizhou	56261	21907	59000	54596	45302
云　南 Yunnan	85911	31388	83647	81620	74829
西　藏 Tibet	1973	1123	2203	1977	1394
陕　西 Shaanxi	105283	47114	163066	142685	132197
甘　肃 Gansu	51903	17132	58659	52725	47417
青　海 Qinghai	6835	2378	5485	4450	3721
宁　夏 Ningxia	14726	8269	18014	14637	13648
新　疆 Xinjiang	38943	10960	34422	29223	25796

学生数

Vocational Schools (Institutions)

单位：人

Unit: in Person

在校学生数 Enrolment					预计毕业生数 Graduates for Next Year
计 Total	一年级 Grade 1	二年级 Grade 2	三年级 Grade 3	四年级及以上 Over Grade 4	
10635841	**4254287**	**3530848**	**2567389**	**283317**	**3029702**
216981	65843	65805	62363	22970	68918
142288	46415	42307	38915	14651	52924
598362	233519	193028	157706	14109	185255
320724	117959	103716	80229	18820	105832
174291	64747	55995	47489	6060	56702
376622	149702	120204	96051	10665	102883
135873	53395	46450	34074	1954	39489
220641	78604	80172	56220	5645	71194
226557	69902	70867	64101	21687	66342
742908	314029	243091	171507	14281	164912
695996	289710	235285	166300	4701	178196
413157	177631	143392	85707	6427	106933
377640	145569	119633	97747	14691	117192
323244	138402	112520	70450	1872	83416
901892	370663	312711	204824	13694	256492
892472	362261	299491	218244	12476	252262
364276	154057	121181	81468	7570	103362
574141	277283	180355	108366	8137	137475
630818	234030	201037	172863	22888	196111
324129	128314	108296	77943	9576	89014
44616	17111	13726	11260	2519	13057
287626	122354	104582	60172	518	77441
504905	216872	176817	104425	6791	134275
160616	59186	53772	43221	4437	52890
270436	83670	93629	84063	9074	91588
6718	2203	2243	2004	268	2596
378974	163288	126387	78278	11021	113259
171424	58730	55813	49465	7416	53029
17558	5485	5756	5013	1304	6729
45017	18023	13488	9909	3597	15744
94939	35330	29099	27012	3498	34190

中等职业学校(机

Number of Female Students in

地区 Region	毕业生数 Graduates		招生数 Entrants		
	计 Total	其中:获得职业资格证书 Of which: Recipients of Vocational qualifications	计 Total	其中:初中毕业 of which: Junior Sec. School Graduates	
				计 Total	应届毕业生 Autumn Session
合　计 Total	**1587363**	**701644**	**2138863**	**1990870**	**1882504**
北　京 Beijing	30265	14715	31661	29763	28539
天　津 Tianjin	29531	13168	23843	22600	21713
河　北 Hebei	105290	43759	122514	108385	102103
山　西 Shanxi	68930	26213	67003	54325	50471
内蒙古 Inner Mongolia	30141	8347	31637	28456	26039
辽　宁 Liaoning	55592	20286	73841	71225	68382
吉　林 Jilin	27162	11333	27107	26133	24013
黑龙江 Heilongjiang	39503	22096	39828	37742	33792
上　海 Shanghai	32648	15986	34600	32489	32274
江　苏 Jiangsu	82906	35864	160343	156185	155145
浙　江 Zhejiang	84431	45463	145432	137184	132826
安　徽 Anhui	54975	16357	86727	79944	74505
福　建 Fujian	59199	29049	68309	63711	58392
江　西 Jiangxi	50724	20462	68124	63708	59304
山　东 Shandong	122297	54096	183886	170863	161132
河　南 henan	136533	56219	181053	159847	149222
湖　北 Hubei	54959	21875	72948	69980	66788
湖　南 Hunan	77824	43748	144735	139633	130781
广　东 Guangdong	94283	51217	121524	119551	116313
广　西 Guangxi	52577	23246	62680	58870	54224
海　南 Hainan	7558	2171	9145	8895	8586
重　庆 Chongqing	34678	18477	62143	58157	55871
四　川 Sichuan	68024	35015	105876	99102	93272
贵　州 guizhou	25918	9805	27673	25168	22211
云　南 Yunnan	42548	15953	42782	41578	38550
西　藏 Tibet	1195	677	1200	1078	784
陕　西 Shaanxi	58488	25626	83261	72986	68956
甘　肃 Gansu	25048	8509	30969	28810	26052
青　海 Qinghai	3234	995	2641	2289	1897
宁　夏 Ningxia	8626	4850	8190	6587	6234
新　疆 Xinjiang	22276	6067	17188	15626	14133

构)女学生数

Secondary Vocational Schools (Institutions)

单位:人

Unit: in Person

在校学生数 Enrolment					预计毕业生数 Graduates for Next Year
计 Total	一年级 Grade 1	二年级 Grade 2	三年级 Grade 3	四年级及以上 Over Grade 4	
5518321	**2149509**	**1837743**	**1361612**	**169457**	**1556694**
111482	32338	34484	32131	12529	34348
74612	24010	22555	20637	7410	27996
330222	124441	107561	89014	9206	101517
185632	67289	60007	47149	11187	62449
89680	32150	29235	24363	3932	29095
197231	74218	65477	50881	6655	53103
72764	27204	25647	18817	1096	20891
115416	39838	40248	31069	4261	36362
115076	34764	36145	32923	11244	33485
383796	160891	126111	88369	8425	81662
355493	145639	121882	85371	2601	89958
206321	86840	70601	44073	4807	52304
184111	68420	59038	48772	7881	57008
162100	68384	54446	37971	1299	42840
449808	184706	154020	101751	9331	126467
461856	181486	155772	117231	7367	133798
179008	74319	59082	41335	4272	48310
302273	144861	93322	58454	5636	71343
337099	121974	109073	93703	12349	103330
170823	62790	56894	43173	7966	50238
25168	9158	7679	6640	1691	7240
148978	62301	54904	31372	401	38574
256870	106151	91141	54812	4766	64629
76595	27736	26067	21038	1754	24399
140648	42783	48529	43955	5381	46712
3567	1226	1161	1019	161	1246
207434	83608	70963	46421	6442	61217
92636	31187	31076	26170	4203	27731
9027	2662	3222	2406	737	3155
22689	8193	6363	5639	2494	8650
49906	17942	15038	14953	1973	16637

普通中等专业

Number of Students in Reg.

地　区 Region	毕业生数 Graduates		招生数 Entrants		
	计 Total	其中：获得职业资格证书 Of which: Recieptents of Vocational qualifications	计 Total	其中：初中毕业 of which: Junior Sec. School Graduates	
				计 Total	应届毕业生 Autumn Session
合　计 Total	**1484471**	**603232**	**1838777**	**1764773**	**1669399**
北　京 Beijing	29248	12435	35271	34364	33508
天　津 Tianjin	23071	11103	23844	23411	22185
河　北 Hebei	75276	28076	85235	79437	72398
山　西 Shanxi	73444	27671	57295	55022	51494
内蒙古 Inner Mongolia	33516	6071	30102	29102	26147
辽　宁 Liaoning	47479	14632	73948	61919	58622
吉　林 Jilin	25373	9244	27261	26242	24961
黑龙江 Heilongjiang	45279	22500	36258	34886	29379
上　海 Shanghai	33929	17803	43439	43176	43165
江　苏 Jiangsu	92456	40955	189064	186387	185209
浙　江 Zhejiang	41198	15108	46666	46280	45219
安　徽 Anhui	46134	11067	47872	44855	40272
福　建 Fujian	105747	55962	136465	131315	121851
江　西 Jiangxi	56174	18280	66391	62133	56805
山　东 Shandong	89550	34325	122832	120181	118273
河　南 henan	100630	34107	134915	127789	118596
湖　北 Hubei	71978	28129	89749	85461	82902
湖　南 Hunan	60664	21951	92245	88031	81891
广　东 Guangdong	83871	44677	111574	111308	110195
广　西 Guangxi	57941	28534	63742	61201	55644
海　南 Hainan	9637	3149	13180	12942	12658
重　庆 Chongqing	23414	11253	34621	34560	33037
四　川 Sichuan	57536	27224	74308	71933	68223
贵　州 guizhou	43248	18029	41592	38722	31978
云　南 Yunnan	39355	16025	45394	44750	42255
西　藏 Tibet	1938	1123	2093	1947	1364
陕　西 Shaanxi	40195	17446	39463	37560	36089
甘　肃 Gansu	30383	10095	38215	36748	33915
青　海 Qinghai	4596	1618	2691	2348	2295
宁　夏 Ningxia	9907	5725	9036	8521	8146
新　疆 Xinjiang	31304	8915	24016	22242	20723

学校学生数

Specialized Sec. Schools

单位:人

Unit: in Person

在校学生数 Enrolment					预计毕业生数 Graduates for Next Year
计 Total	一年级 Grade 1	二年级 Grade 2	三年级 Grade 3	四年级及以上 Over Grade 4	
5023708	**1844565**	**1626312**	**1285290**	**267541**	**1419617**
116725	35327	31313	29478	20607	35404
73254	23847	20732	16972	11703	27224
246956	85523	80816	66704	13913	75286
191902	57295	62039	53795	18773	64546
90415	30649	28294	25412	6060	28790
173347	73955	54750	34499	10143	38959
77955	27261	28104	20709	1881	21421
111540	36258	40419	29218	5645	35087
136879	43780	39636	33530	19933	32482
461328	189170	147820	110367	13971	90581
120658	46683	39925	29813	4237	32595
122450	48000	38244	29827	6379	34421
358575	136967	113816	93101	14691	110482
155084	66395	50744	36151	1794	35587
336691	122841	114765	85677	13408	91385
364252	134925	121184	96218	11925	107822
222006	91489	72366	51439	6712	61982
226487	92359	71915	54765	7448	61668
306714	112282	94466	79851	20115	95947
173173	63760	57410	42477	9526	50215
36427	13182	10749	9999	2497	10517
95057	34637	34280	25622	518	25697
198979	74400	70109	48068	6402	52562
120635	41730	39921	34625	4359	38299
148407	45417	49224	45322	8444	48469
6519	2093	2180	1978	268	2570
125825	39478	40542	35229	10576	37460
116439	38257	38789	32158	7235	33654
10184	2691	2879	3331	1283	4446
27346	9036	7896	6817	3597	9420
71499	24878	20985	22138	3498	24639

普通中等专业

Number of Female Students in

地　区 Region	毕业生数 Graduates		招生数 Entrants		
	计 Total	其中：获得职业资格证书 Of which: Reciptents of Vocational qualifications	计 Total	其中：初中毕业 of which: Junior Sec. School Graduates	
				计 Total	应届毕业生 Autumn Session
合　计 Total	**835780**	**318628**	**996449**	**961620**	**911965**
北　京 Beijing	14707	5988	18359	17624	17397
天　津 Tianjin	12363	5338	12054	11902	11472
河　北 Hebei	44955	17017	47528	44537	41704
山　西 Shanxi	45053	16494	32869	31227	29960
内蒙古 Inner Mongolia	18375	3005	14426	14062	12520
辽　宁 Liaoning	27165	7870	36401	34437	32621
吉　林 Jilin	15784	5642	14565	14120	13609
黑龙江 Heilongjiang	25168	12460	19936	19264	16295
上　海 Shanghai	17015	8537	22716	22553	22546
江　苏 Jiangsu	49740	20585	101861	100553	100092
浙　江 Zhejiang	24808	8078	26702	26405	25708
安　徽 Anhui	25378	5228	28156	26873	24243
福　建 Fujian	57039	28773	65439	63182	58365
江　西 Jiangxi	32819	9726	36841	34033	31063
山　东 Shandong	52756	18436	71387	70166	68880
河　南 henan	61551	18814	76175	72138	66746
湖　北 Hubei	37754	13870	45561	43160	41188
湖　南 Hunan	33797	12452	50576	48847	45469
广　东 Guangdong	46001	22700	61339	61051	60154
广　西 Guangxi	32964	14569	34710	33331	30303
海　南 Hainan	5953	1523	7385	7220	7053
重　庆 Chongqing	13382	6559	19472	19424	18820
四　川 Sichuan	31753	13998	41105	39853	37514
贵　州 guizhou	20375	8153	21278	19305	16867
云　南 Yunnan	20408	8141	25749	25078	23635
西　藏 Tibet	1183	677	1187	1065	771
陕　西 Shaanxi	24661	10141	22211	21344	20586
甘　肃 Gansu	15918	4917	21802	21207	19611
青　海 Qinghai	2260	716	1452	1307	1260
宁　夏 Ningxia	5733	3212	4328	4090	3988
新　疆 Xinjiang	18962	5009	12879	12262	11525

学校女学生数

Reg. Specialized Sec. Schools

单位：人

Unit: in Person

在校学生数 Enrolment					
计 Total	一年级 Grade 1	二年级 Grade 2	三年级 Grade 3	四年级及以上 Over Grade 4	预计毕业生数 Graduates for Next Year
2811533	**1000768**	**914664**	**735629**	**160472**	**788219**
62504	18381	17470	15482	11171	17408
37794	12154	10596	9149	5895	14246
144837	48124	47425	40187	9101	43511
115374	32879	37322	34021	11152	39547
46662	14826	14922	12982	3932	14967
93457	36402	31208	19572	6275	20938
43245	14646	15811	11727	1061	11799
62943	19936	21996	16750	4261	19921
71126	22812	20606	17527	10181	17352
252306	101960	81418	60660	8268	47504
70431	26714	23529	17746	2442	18431
74598	28207	23084	18512	4795	20410
177554	65507	57102	47064	7881	54293
89764	36928	28688	22877	1271	21984
199437	71407	67651	51257	9122	55434
213434	76175	71224	59065	6970	63937
115968	46648	37778	27700	3842	31094
126195	50621	39488	30973	5113	32556
171124	61733	53637	44945	10809	51201
101816	34731	32957	26169	7959	32009
21117	7398	6135	5907	1677	5989
53499	19472	19100	14526	401	14434
114878	41155	41334	27825	4564	30244
61476	21329	20704	17717	1726	18999
83358	25750	27718	24859	5031	26094
3490	1187	1136	1006	161	1233
75511	22341	24642	22361	6167	21963
66859	21956	22599	18246	4058	18888
5819	1471	1785	1844	719	2312
14940	4328	4034	4084	2494	5848
40017	13590	11565	12889	1973	13673

成人中等专业

Number of Students in Specialized

地　区 Region	毕业生数 Graduates		招生数 Entrants		
	计 Total	其中:获得职业资格证书 Of which: Reciptents of Vocational qualifications	计 Total	其中:初中毕业 of which: Junior Sec. School Graduates	
				计 Total	应届毕业生 Autumn Session
合　计 Total	**400315**	**158417**	**429818**	**284395**	**240683**
北　京 Beijing	5356	2829	3720	2896	934
天　津 Tianjin	8010	3125	2291	953	631
河　北 Hebei	28300	14623	22098	11119	8255
山　西 Shanxi	16538	4239	13752	628	552
内蒙古 Inner Mongolia	5486	2243	4473	1497	649
辽　宁 Liaoning	10651	3718	3220	3037	2228
吉　林 Jilin					
黑龙江 Heilongjiang	14989	10656	12567	11369	9324
上　海 Shanghai	8759	1508	5033	607	244
江　苏 Jiangsu	19323	5720	16238	12552	11560
浙　江 Zhejiang	20540	3700	29351	17582	13841
安　徽 Anhui	11398	3013	10615	9382	8355
福　建 Fujian	5474	670	8602	4303	2108
江　西 Jiangxi	6092	2553	9360	6736	6207
山　东 Shandong	37752	16542	48997	36522	33094
河　南 henan	39488	20075	60970	18990	16696
湖　北 Hubei	7172	2968	11356	10237	8700
湖　南 Hunan	14959	10089	25124	21580	19904
广　东 Guangdong	35435	17516	44072	40784	37426
广　西 Guangxi	14610	3520	13030	10978	8502
海　南 Hainan	702	80	421	382	217
重　庆 Chongqing	13260	4438	25083	22756	21700
四　川 Sichuan	28052	14918	28836	21684	18548
贵　州 guizhou	5129	494	5299	4939	2924
云　南 Yunnan	13797	2481			
西　藏 Tibet	35		110	30	30
陕　西 Shaanxi	11570	2601	11012	6843	4472
甘　肃 Gansu	10761	1655	5884	2561	1441
青　海 Qinghai	1160	460	1395	703	288
宁　夏 Ningxia	2169	1624	3709	1661	1454
新　疆 Xinjiang	3348	359	3200	1084	399

学校学生数

Sec. Schools for Adults

单位：人

Unit: in Person

在校学生数 Enrolment					
计 Total	一年级 Grade 1	二年级 Grade 2	三年级 Grade 3	四年级及以上 Over Grade 4	预计毕业生数 Graduates for Next Year
1054511	**433258**	**374697**	**241277**	**5279**	**389185**
15994	4493	5891	5610		7129
7619	2314	2719	2400	186	4499
59723	23598	21793	14222	110	25181
20751	13752	4282	2717		11709
11326	4652	3444	3230		7764
17731	3220	2653	11858		12654
33217	12567	13870	6780		14573
20243	5042	6930	8177	94	10983
45704	16672	17043	11736	253	15667
72560	29426	25850	16950	334	21969
26348	10617	10137	5546	48	9132
19065	8602	5817	4646		6710
24152	9360	10958	3834		6737
100988	49213	36345	15398	32	36518
113262	60970	37393	14388	511	32320
27772	11376	12215	4181		11494
51716	25124	17980	8476	136	13357
120096	44078	38909	34336	2773	39077
39666	13031	14706	11893	36	12677
1117	421	562	134		534
57216	25095	22274	9847		14553
68450	28932	26506	12801	211	23433
17164	5347	6296	5443	78	7723
18955		7493	11184	278	12300
199	110	63	26		26
27319	11012	12054	4075	178	11392
18892	5884	5449	7559		8763
3315	1395	975	924	21	1184
5799	3709	1559	531		3522
8152	3246	2531	2375		5605

成人中等专业

Number of Female Students in

地 区 Region	毕业生数 Graduates		招生数 Entrants		
	计 Total	其中:获得职业资格证书 Of which: Reciptents of Vocational qualifications	计 Total	其中:初中毕业 of which:Junior Sec. School Graduates	
				计 Total	应届毕业生 Autumn Session
合 计 Total	**205117**	**77600**	**209126**	**139283**	**118915**
北 京 Beijing	3912	2277	1643	1194	445
天 津 Tianjin	3938	1379	1282	582	415
河 北 Hebei	16109	7643	12747	6206	4595
山 西 Shanxi	10625	2395	9599	443	407
内蒙古 Inner Mongolia	2696	977	2538	929	424
辽 宁 Liaoning	5054	1721	1308	1240	942
吉 林 Jilin					
黑龙江 Heilongjiang	4954	2684	4405	3794	3246
上 海 Shanghai	4677	327	2276	328	120
江 苏 Jiangsu	11757	2719	8577	5956	5468
浙 江 Zhejiang	13281	2617	18442	10536	7979
安 徽 Anhui	5050	1337	4763	4216	3952
福 建 Fujian	2160	276	2870	529	27
江 西 Jiangxi	2664	1072	3490	3117	2893
山 东 Shandong	17335	6916	24463	17715	15761
河 南 henan	20344	10883	25583	10142	9216
湖 北 Hubei	2959	1411	4572	4400	3975
湖 南 Hunan	7468	4929	12544	11004	9805
广 东 Guangdong	19857	9379	23274	21693	19504
广 西 Guangxi	8730	1976	6433	5528	4330
海 南 Hainan	345	44	207	184	136
重 庆 Chongqing	6103	1877	12741	11747	11222
四 川 Sichuan	13572	7358	13559	10666	8808
贵 州 guizhou	2297	158	1677	1627	1300
云 南 Yunnan	6552	1311			
西 藏 Tibet	12		13	13	13
陕 西 Shaanxi	5631	1436	5388	3593	2789
甘 肃 Gansu	3811	983	2047	952	592
青 海 Qinghai	478	172	505	298	124
宁 夏 Ningxia	1508	1150	1298	239	160
新 疆 Xinjiang	1238	193	882	412	267

学校女学生数

Specialized Sec. Schools for Adults

单位:人

Unit: in Person

在校学生数 Enrolment					预计毕业生数 Graduates for Next Year
计 Total	一年级 Grade 1	二年级 Grade 2	三年级 Grade 3	四年级及以上 Over Grade 4	
523450	**212614**	**184958**	**123067**	**2811**	**187855**
8067	2274	2948	2845		3855
4067	1315	1618	1028	106	2330
35620	14078	12670	8812	60	14709
13950	9599	2677	1674		8205
6154	2648	1924	1582		3826
8324	1308	1162	5854		6155
12220	4415	4590	3215		4614
10193	2324	3519	4294	56	4909
23045	8862	8724	5342	117	7941
45615	18511	16935	10114	55	12669
12181	4785	4676	2708	12	3924
6557	2913	1936	1708		2715
9476	3490	4185	1801		2867
49124	24653	17244	7205	22	17873
50691	25934	16788	7609	360	17346
10962	4640	4372	1950		3501
25204	12544	8150	4415	95	6933
66949	23310	22267	19832	1540	22011
20271	6434	7740	6093	4	6515
609	207	286	116		264
29266	12878	12016	4372		6258
32943	13601	12685	6555	102	7849
5727	1687	2029	1983	28	2713
8906		3394	5359	153	5800
77	39	25	13		13
14309	5388	6513	2325	83	5856
7390	2047	2353	2990		3294
1095	507	339	231	18	331
1895	1298	334	263		1435
2563	925	859	779		1144

职业高中学

Number of Students in

地　区 Region	毕业生数 Graduates 计 Total	其中:获得职业资格证书 Of which: Reciptents of Vocational qualifications	招生数 Entrants 计 Total	其中:初中毕业 of which: Junior Sec. School Graduates 计 Total	应届毕业生 Autumn Session
合　计 Total	**1126652**	**632132**	**1972571**	**1878675**	**1796424**
北　京 Beijing	23261	13067	25946	24451	23895
天　津 Tianjin	24065	11719	20231	19367	18970
河　北 Hebei	84525	38572	124163	115159	111395
山　西 Shanxi	25796	14534	46739	43308	37992
内蒙古 Inner Mongolia	18097	8775	29435	27153	26427
辽　宁 Liaoning	47894	22430	72049	70109	68473
吉　林 Jilin	22008	10134	26125	25147	20464
黑龙江 Heilongjiang	17647	12833	29779	28191	27357
上　海 Shanghai	21654	14122	20959	20959	20957
江　苏 Jiangsu	47587	27833	108184	106966	106717
浙　江 Zhejiang	96315	72089	213412	213302	210967
安　徽 Anhui	52073	21282	119007	107860	102803
福　建 Fujian					
江　西 Jiangxi	35221	21953	62325	59564	56544
山　东 Shandong	123418	68733	197755	184239	169979
河　南 henan	113696	57583	166334	163235	155022
湖　北 Hubei	29786	13336	50733	49624	48370
湖　南 Hunan	68562	48556	159771	155352	147329
广　东 Guangdong	57186	38824	77635	77545	77377
广　西 Guangxi	25192	14919	51464	48805	47484
海　南 Hainan	2326	1054	3508	3357	3138
重　庆 Chongqing	29874	19358	62602	56092	54000
四　川 Sichuan	47529	28805	113028	107636	104233
贵　州 guizhou	7884	3384	12109	10935	10400
云　南 Yunnan	32759	12882	38253	36870	32574
西　藏 Tibet					
陕　西 Shaanxi	53518	27067	112591	98282	91636
甘　肃 Gansu	10759	5382	14560	13416	12061
青　海 Qinghai	1079	300	1399	1399	1138
宁　夏 Ningxia	2650	920	5269	4455	4048
新　疆 Xinjiang	4291	1686	7206	5897	4674

校学生数

Vocational High Schools

单位:人

Unit: in Person

在校学生数 Enrolment					预计毕业生数 Graduates for Next Year
计 Total	一年级 Grade 1	二年级 Grade 2	三年级 Grade 3	四年级及以上 Over Grade 4	
4557622	**1976464**	**1529839**	**1040822**	**10497**	**1220900**
84262	26023	28601	27275	2363	26385
61415	20254	18856	19543	2762	21201
291683	124398	90419	76780	86	84788
108071	46912	37395	23717	47	29577
72550	29446	24257	18847		20148
185544	72527	62801	49694	522	51270
57918	26134	18346	13365	73	18068
75884	29779	25883	20222		21534
69435	21080	24301	22394	1660	22877
235876	108187	78228	49404	57	58664
502778	213601	169510	119537	130	123632
264359	119014	95011	50334		63380
144008	62647	50818	30465	78	41092
464213	198609	161601	103749	254	128589
414958	166366	140914	107638	40	112120
114498	51192	36600	25848	858	29886
295938	159800	90460	45125	553	62450
204008	77670	67662	58676		61087
111290	51523	36180	23573	14	26122
7072	3508	2415	1127	22	2006
135353	62622	48028	24703		37191
237476	113540	80202	43556	178	58280
22817	12109	7555	3153		6868
103074	38253	36912	27557	352	30819
225830	112798	73791	38974	267	64407
36093	14589	11575	9748	181	10612
4059	1399	1902	758		1099
11872	5278	4033	2561		2802
15288	7206	5583	2499		3946

职业高中学

Number of Female Students in

地 区 Region	毕业生数 Graduates 计 Total	其中:获得职业资格证书 Of which: Reciptents of Vocational qualifications	招生数 Entrants 计 Total	其中:初中毕业 of which: Junior Sec. School Graduates 计 Total	应届毕业生 Autumn Session
合 计 Total	**546466**	**305416**	**933288**	**889967**	**851624**
北 京 Beijing	11646	6450	11659	10945	10697
天 津 Tianjin	13230	6451	10507	10116	9826
河 北 Hebei	44226	19099	62239	57642	55804
山 西 Shanxi	13252	7324	24535	22655	20104
内蒙古 Inner Mongolia	9070	4365	14673	13465	13095
辽 宁 Liaoning	23373	10695	36132	35548	34819
吉 林 Jilin	11378	5691	12542	12013	10404
黑龙江 Heilongjiang	9381	6952	15487	14684	14251
上 海 Shanghai	10956	7122	9608	9608	9608
江 苏 Jiangsu	21409	12560	49905	49676	49585
浙 江 Zhejiang	46342	34768	100288	100243	99139
安 徽 Anhui	24547	9792	53808	48855	46310
福 建 Fujian					
江 西 Jiangxi	15241	9664	27793	26558	25348
山 东 Shandong	52206	28744	88036	82982	76491
河 南 henan	54638	26522	79295	77567	73260
湖 北 Hubei	14246	6594	22815	22420	21625
湖 南 Hunan	36559	26367	81615	79782	75507
广 东 Guangdong	28425	19138	36911	36807	36655
广 西 Guangxi	10883	6701	21537	20011	19591
海 南 Hainan	1260	604	1553	1491	1397
重 庆 Chongqing	15193	10041	29930	26986	25829
四 川 Sichuan	22699	13659	51212	48583	46950
贵 州 guizhou	3246	1494	4718	4236	4044
云 南 Yunnan	15588	6501	17033	16500	14915
西 藏 Tibet					
陕 西 Shaanxi	28196	14049	55662	48049	45581
甘 肃 Gansu	5319	2609	7120	6651	5849
青 海 Qinghai	496	107	684	684	513
宁 夏 Ningxia	1385	488	2564	2258	2086
新 疆 Xinjiang	2076	865	3427	2952	2341

校女学生数

Vocational High Schools

单位:人

Unit: in Person

在校学生数 Enrolment					预计毕业生数
计 Total	一年级 Grade 1	二年级 Grade 2	三年级 Grade 3	四年级及以上 Over Grade 4	Graduates for Next Year
2183338	**936127**	**738121**	**502916**	**6174**	**580620**
40911	11683	14066	13804	1358	13085
32751	10541	10341	10460	1409	11420
149765	62239	47466	40015	45	43297
56308	24811	20008	11454	35	14697
36864	14676	12389	9799		10302
95450	36508	33107	25455	380	26010
29519	12558	9836	7090	35	9092
40253	15487	13662	11104		11827
33757	9628	12020	11102	1007	11224
108445	50069	35969	22367	40	26217
239447	100414	81418	57511	104	58858
119542	53848	42841	22853		27970
62860	27966	21573	13293	28	17989
201247	88646	69125	43289	187	53160
197731	79377	67760	50557	37	52515
52078	23031	16932	11685	430	13715
150874	81696	45684	23066	428	31854
99026	36931	33169	28926		30118
48736	21625	16197	10911	3	11714
3442	1553	1258	617	14	987
66213	29951	23788	12474		17882
109049	51395	37122	20432	100	26536
9392	4720	3334	1338		2687
48384	17033	17417	13737	197	14818
117614	55879	39808	21735	192	33398
18387	7184	6124	4934	145	5549
2113	684	1098	331		512
5854	2567	1995	1292		1367
7326	3427	2614	1285		1820

中等职业学校(机

Number of Students by age in Secondary

地　区 Region	计 Total	14岁及以下 14 years and under	15岁 15 years	16岁 16 years	17岁 17 years
合　计 Total	**10635841**	**173193**	**1299001**	**2914114**	**2891838**
北　京 Beijing	216981	3969	35117	56671	55595
天　津 Tianjin	142288	183	8955	35814	40630
河　北 Hebei	598362	2993	25317	136577	163931
山　西 Shanxi	320724	4227	42405	81396	83825
内蒙古 Inner Mongolia	174291	2595	12455	36792	49102
辽　宁 Liaoning	376622	5706	22726	91845	115374
吉　林 Jilin	135873	1165	7495	30281	42747
黑龙江 Heilongjiang	220641	916	8317	43309	60987
上　海 Shanghai	226557	1370	30285	54624	58492
江　苏 Jiangsu	742908	6465	76946	213743	228321
浙　江 Zhejiang	695996	11462	84403	202876	197008
安　徽 Anhui	413157	9635	84378	124220	107304
福　建 Fujian	377640	6082	46201	95076	100782
江　西 Jiangxi	323244	21408	87369	97236	68068
山　东 Shandong	901892	13180	124502	267427	257561
河　南 henan	892472	22570	150729	253325	220968
湖　北 Hubei	364276	9643	74419	111031	90476
湖　南 Hunan	574141	8971	117363	199144	136160
广　东 Guangdong	630818	3258	29195	157760	185288
广　西 Guangxi	324129	1990	18148	78334	93796
海　南 Hainan	44616	330	2895	9170	12120
重　庆 Chongqing	287626	12075	44869	94696	75404
四　川 Sichuan	504905	8060	59358	168089	149488
贵　州 guizhou	160616	2047	16480	37859	39983
云　南 Yunnan	270436	2771	24669	60984	71738
西　藏 Tibet	6718	163	405	1239	1376
陕　西 Shaanxi	378974	3510	30944	97090	104536
甘　肃 Gansu	171424	3522	14732	41328	44053
青　海 Qinghai	17558	777	1774	3515	4148
宁　夏 Ningxia	45017	491	5056	10549	10365
新　疆 Xinjiang	94939	1659	11094	22114	22212

构)分年龄学生数

Vocational Schools (Institutions)

单位:人

Unit: in Person

18 岁 18 years	19 岁 19 years	20 岁 20years	21 岁 21 years	22 岁及以上 22 years and over
1877682	**753323**	**252692**	**106285**	**367713**
37301	14662	3541	1332	8793
34157	15553	3405	833	2758
129626	63620	22354	11137	42807
57804	22883	6793	2298	19093
36700	19469	6527	2567	8084
84925	33073	9020	4521	9432
33076	15161	3775	1636	537
52898	23401	15685	4225	10903
42069	18086	6581	1054	13996
138121	49274	13026	3100	13912
116016	39536	10582	6565	27548
55800	19925	5083	1785	5027
68857	29187	9253	3100	19102
32483	8341	2174	578	5587
149372	52799	16896	5871	14284
124572	45701	22516	20159	31932
48113	15562	4268	1885	8879
69992	24434	6044	2524	9509
154937	62000	17989	6023	14368
72313	32376	10648	3586	12938
10376	6049	2723	588	365
40241	8486	2308	1329	8218
75632	25713	7275	2797	8493
27136	15031	6554	3779	11747
52549	28113	11032	3541	15039
1312	916	396	236	675
70950	35284	14832	4905	16923
31020	14330	5956	2117	14366
3122	1687	818	360	1357
7872	4802	2456	627	2799
18340	7869	2182	1227	8242

中等职业学校(机构)

Number of Female Students by age in

地　区 Region	计 Total	14岁及以下 14 years and under	15岁 15 years	16岁 16 years
合计 Total	**5518321**	**96594**	**683379**	**1526153**
北　京 Beijing	111482	2768	18106	28456
天　津 Tianjin	74612	119	4654	19257
河　北 Hebei	330222	1598	13432	72591
山　西 Shanxi	185632	2505	24355	46251
内蒙古 Inner Mongolia	89680	1500	6335	18389
辽　宁 Liaoning	197231	3818	12500	49794
吉　林 Jilin	72764	710	3525	16252
黑龙江 Heilongjiang	115416	550	4534	24712
上　海 Shanghai	115076	832	15500	28906
江　苏 Jiangsu	383796	3696	40794	110790
浙　江 Zhejiang	355493	5916	42784	100548
安　徽 Anhui	206321	4696	42830	62810
福　建 Fujian	184111	3205	22741	47620
江　西 Jiangxi	162100	12250	47625	49840
山　东 Shandong	449808	6948	62123	134656
河　南 henan	461856	12104	79872	133953
湖　北 Hubei	179008	5135	38135	54703
湖　南 Hunan	302273	5403	63570	105879
广　东 Guangdong	337099	2101	15809	86460
广　西 Guangxi	170823	1228	10148	42243
海　南 Hainan	25168	246	1393	5063
重　庆 Chongqing	148978	5776	23490	49878
四　川 Sichuan	256870	4927	30170	86286
贵　州 guizhou	76595	1066	8563	18735
云　南 Yunnan	140648	1540	14087	32516
西　藏 Tibet	3567	66	266	734
陕　西 Shaanxi	207434	2116	17896	55235
甘　肃 Gansu	92636	1937	8172	23703
青　海 Qinghai	9027	628	1060	2016
宁　夏 Ningxia	22689	243	2690	5789
新　疆 Xinjiang	49906	967	6220	12088

分年龄女学生数

Secondary Vocational Schools (Institutions)

单位:人

Unit: in Person

17岁 17 years	18岁 18 years	19岁 19 years	20岁 20years	21岁 21 years	22岁及以上 22 years and over
1519343	**973953**	**385225**	**120449**	**44532**	**168693**
28776	18936	7560	2334	749	3797
21672	17645	7795	1684	416	1370
90216	72747	36010	12685	6012	24931
49346	32053	13273	3787	1136	12926
24558	19924	10191	3592	1220	3971
63611	44309	16149	4033	1300	1717
23232	17973	8118	1914	827	213
35163	26768	12390	5354	1571	4374
28819	21618	8816	3234	523	6828
119555	70849	24087	5434	1390	7201
99791	58904	19804	5556	4463	17727
53152	27808	9591	2365	907	2162
49885	34190	14282	3775	1231	7182
32864	14195	3339	925	232	830
128159	73253	26461	9259	2970	5979
117218	65050	23739	11317	4503	14100
44506	24087	6840	1552	863	3187
71278	35753	12163	2683	1151	4393
99640	82068	32139	8272	2895	7715
49106	37398	17430	5760	1647	5863
7023	6224	3345	1478	240	156
40339	20779	4165	878	567	3106
78129	37115	12496	3051	1106	3590
20460	13721	6934	2225	1328	3563
38040	27021	14455	5322	1474	6193
860	694	394	176	92	285
59406	39507	18063	7055	2120	6036
24691	17321	7570	2860	816	5566
2207	1483	739	330	123	441
5469	3994	2489	508	197	1310
12172	10566	4398	1051	463	1981

中等职业学校(机

Data on Training Students of Graduation

地 区 Region	合 计 Total	其中:女 Of Which: Female	其中:少数民族 Of Which: Minority	按时间分:by training time 一周至一个月以下 from one week to a month under	一个月至半年以下 from one month to half yera under	半年以上 over half a year
合 计 Total	**5646046**	**2511467**	**314491**	**3321071**	**1643031**	**681944**
北 京 Beijing	65612	35352	2283	30347	29356	5909
天 津 Tianjin	84315	51702	264	33298	42927	8090
河 北 Hebei	331044	172801	13075	153339	127834	49871
山 西 Shanxi	164179	95238	110	127602	23314	13263
内蒙古 Inner Mongolia	89452	39747	20583	70549	16167	2736
辽 宁 Liaoning	109922	41404	10935	45664	30177	34081
吉 林 Jilin	40203	21811	1632	24619	13401	2183
黑龙江 Heilongjiang	89165	38540	1136	56874	20064	12227
上 海 Shanghai	176721	76510	0	81226	82315	13180
江 苏 Jiangsu	554401	290426	201	345357	132628	76416
浙 江 Zhejiang	255336	113351	199	167947	62296	25093
安 徽 Anhui	147038	55228	652	105282	23791	17965
福 建 Fujian	252892	95262	1842	168337	28449	56106
江 西 Jiangxi	86072	38300	88	49686	29550	6836
山 东 Shandong	230107	95795	1504	124791	80630	24686
河 南 henan	526590	195363	1949	300811	162117	63662
湖 北 Hubei	190631	44312	7514	105268	58991	26372
湖 南 Hunan	138953	67554	16544	67537	43877	27539
广 东 Guangdong	404952	218537	281	198855	136427	69670
广 西 Guangxi	135899	57976	51129	72042	33881	29976
海 南 Hainan	12186	5290	1053	8853	1110	2223
重 庆 Chongqing	59701	26989	4043	44387	12159	3155
四 川 Sichuan	271132	134116	8578	166332	67208	37592
贵 州 guizhou	100138	34197	26498	78387	16419	5332
云 南 Yunnan	402036	200622	92655	259095	132770	10171
西 藏 Tibet	1353	324	541	825	453	75
陕 西 Shaanxi	424452	119818	1380	290714	83359	50379
甘 肃 Gansu	104117	49084	4597	69933	29647	4537
青 海 Qinghai	15306	5637	4225	12503	2709	94
宁 夏 Ningxia	111871	39738	26465	12029	98657	1185
新 疆 Xinjiang	70270	50443	12535	48582	20348	1340

构)培训学生结业情况

in Secondary Vocational Schools (Institutions)

单位:人次
Unit: in Person

按类型分:by training type		按内容分:by content			
资格证书培训	岗位证书培训 Job-related Training	外语 Foreign language	会计 Accountant	计算机 Computer	农业技术 Agriculture Technology
1663205	**1425562**	**187751**	**562465**	**1011251**	**979239**
27018	12042	11734	6440	12540	333
17577	13014	26997	1124	19637	240
94807	90093	29238	13618	75076	39053
57973	24048	2096	5147	57229	5209
29466	31390	1525	1520	26939	3401
27148	45623	2096	5036	16146	13812
13338	12333	262	970	14709	2158
28791	41567	2210	5090	10417	6435
38794	62320	5912	20192	23966	22926
151238	124556	16258	175742	81616	64545
88924	74910	12704	12067	38615	4885
34236	57910	3541	5104	20275	29135
83690	22601	3088	9845	32788	52233
23107	38011	1743	4378	17104	3829
69024	56983	11591	22454	67331	14742
121327	95408	2738	7721	89741	199177
42816	69100	2548	11101	25189	81033
52895	33465	9554	2652	43845	6662
116271	110439	16691	45924	105165	4653
43723	29461	1632	3306	24022	27989
2014	5448	185	2358	1529	929
16940	21659	3632	3348	18902	2958
75089	87541	8949	35481	35847	16675
30734	16142	696	3575	15969	32910
116422	123067	3769	64902	61603	24528
440	0	17	28	180	355
104289	52266	3023	34543	47131	214498
19852	44738	2697	14136	16604	4955
3625	2913	321	110	3880	111
100331	6611	100	2556	2414	93097
31303	19903	204	41997	4842	5773

中等职业学校(机

Data on Training Students of Enrolment in Secondary

地 区 Region	计 Total	其中:女 Of Which: Female	其中:少数民族 Of Which: Minority	按类型分:by training type 其中:资格证书培训 Of Which:	其中:岗位证书培训 Of Which:Job-related Traininguage
合 计 Total	**2972650**	**1299506**	**194311**	**837250**	**657081**
北 京 Beijing	45357	21968	2350	18518	6290
天 津 Tianjin	49136	33445	91	9151	10720
河 北 Hebei	185403	101073	5966	54396	34674
山 西 Shanxi	83704	44151	48	27597	9756
内蒙古 Inner Mongolia	22945	11057	3853	6814	7861
辽 宁 Liaoning	62587	21626	8013	10338	32927
吉 林 Jilin	22114	11506	1767	10292	7790
黑龙江 Heilongjiang	60435	23800	751	13430	27402
上 海 Shanghai	126577	60360	16	23384	48107
江 苏 Jiangsu	166264	85330	135	37452	40168
浙 江 Zhejiang	120064	55314	140	49864	22867
安 徽 Anhui	48547	20971	259	8794	15578
福 建 Fujian	230699	80842	1951	82511	15479
江 西 Jiangxi	76316	34616	616	12715	44534
山 东 Shandong	102444	48689	893	36326	16928
河 南 Henan	269549	102462	2368	63772	39185
湖 北 Hubei	177462	29937	9819	18562	76548
湖 南 Hunan	96890	48876	9992	29003	15105
广 东 Guangdong	206067	112357	190	64528	44645
广 西 Guangxi	89219	34717	34079	33383	13905
海 南 Hainan	4096	1617	231	1065	2120
重 庆 Chongqing	34178	17273	3363	10804	6014
四 川 Sichuan	133771	69611	3194	31114	30461
贵 州 Guizhou	57644	18598	15169	11546	7603
云 南 Yunnan	165401	68759	50437	21206	20594
西 藏 Tibet	2923	1374	1733	1218	0
陕 西 Shaanxi	124505	47459	403	29165	23671
甘 肃 Gansu	64589	30116	1414	11879	19201
青 海 Qinghai	5843	2293	2322	1157	983
宁 夏 Ningxia	109093	40232	26448	100774	2994
新 疆 Xinjiang	28828	19077	6300	6492	12971

构)注册生培训情况

Vocational Schools (Institutions)

单位:人次

Unit: in Person

按内容分:by content				按时间分:by training time		
外语 Foreign language	其中:会计 Of Which: Accountant	其中:计算机 Of Which: Computer	其中:农业技术 Of Which: Agriculture Technology	一周至一个月以下 from one week to a month under	一个月至半年以下 from one month to half year under	半年以上 over half a year
187751	**154806**	**546811**	**488802**	**1381863**	**895596**	**695191**
11734	2964	10228	0	16792	23275	5290
22997	216	10871	646	8743	30583	9810
29238	4742	38540	11917	72871	52387	60145
2096	4167	33190	3653	50538	14822	18344
1525	368	5640	2942	14656	3151	5138
2096	1424	9179	8772	18253	13009	31325
262	1021	8386	864	7493	9664	4957
2210	4127	7096	6352	38732	6399	15304
5912	14530	13324	22926	60978	55566	10033
16258	12437	44563	2366	65156	48642	52466
12704	3069	20075	3474	58433	36737	24894
3541	1770	10467	7075	27886	9181	11480
3088	5110	22336	62817	138143	20740	71816
1743	610	9388	3174	49386	15887	11043
11591	7168	26535	906	43023	33719	25702
2738	2509	47603	23393	128961	74879	65709
2548	4570	7529	112606	92081	50759	34622
9554	1713	32820	1268	24091	27964	44835
16691	18923	63813	1921	84588	60273	61206
1632	1268	15528	23490	50205	16886	22128
185	0	706	432	1213	636	2247
3632	3114	8707	241	16645	4544	12989
8949	30407	18566	11492	68618	36774	28379
696	2229	9418	27621	44687	8812	4145
3769	2526	19877	10197	72679	78895	13827
17	28	0	247	770	275	1878
3023	1090	30024	36595	60655	27112	36738
2697	6733	14589	2720	35302	23839	5448
100	100	2643	33	3981	1692	170
204	2133	2666	94492	9576	98873	644
13740	2504	4170	16728	9621	2479	

中等职业学校(机构)

Changes of Enrolment in Secondary

	上学年初报表在校学生数 Total enrolment at beginning of previous academic year	增加学生数 Factors of Increase			
		计 Total	招生 No. of Students Admitted	复学 Students Resuming Studies	转入 Transfers from Other Inst.
甲	1	2	3	4	5
总计 Total	**9894205**	**4696097**	**4241166**	**7846**	**180704**
北京 Beijing	213775	67600	64937	91	1776
天津 Tianjin	151980	49836	46366	45	1974
河北 Hebei	570194	251518	231496	515	8621
山西 Shanxi	328654	127666	117786	80	5314
内蒙古 Inner Mongolia	183057	73530	64010	175	7018
辽宁 Liaoning	335984	160185	149217	70	2145
吉林 Jilin	142782	62402	53386	189	2310
黑龙江 Heilongjiang	227982	82485	78604	47	1457
上海 Shanghai	228001	73377	69431	79	1433
江苏 Jiangsu	674223	363672	313486	315	40341
浙江 Zhejiang	600838	303980	289429	159	7485
安徽 Anhui	350179	204872	177494	313	5234
福建 Fujian	355383	156136	145067	315	1952
江西 Jiangxi	285517	166270	138076	286	4515
山东 Shandong	801562	413395	369584	195	16567
河南 Henan	806407	421621	362219	222	14816
湖北 Hubei	336772	172665	151838	174	7653
湖南 Hunan	490736	302388	277140	739	19026
广东 Guangdong	611961	250760	233281	673	5863
广西 Guangxi	306585	135866	128236	408	2697
海南 Hainan	41703	17627	17109	50	271
重庆 Chongqing	237360	134299	122306	237	4420
四川 Sichuan	450834	240057	216172	1355	5094
贵州 Guizhou	171984	65064	59000	139	622
云南 Yunnan	289956	91428	83647	32	1981
西藏 Tibet	6611	2452	2203	23	174
陕西 Shaanxi	349105	175239	163066	258	6584
甘肃 Gansu	169735	65881	58659	28	2056
青海 Qinghai	19583	5707	5485	8	20
宁夏 Ningxia	42625	19798	18014	10	209
新疆 Xinjiang	112137	38321	34422	616	1076

学生变动情况

Vocational Schools (Institutions)

单位:人

Unit:in Person

	减少学生数 Factors of Decrease									本学年初报表在校学生数 Tota lenrolmentat beginning of academic year
其他 Others	计 Total	毕业 Graduates	结业 Completers of Courses without formal awards	休学 Suspended	退学 Quitting	开除 Expelled	死亡 Dead	转出 Transfer to Other Inst.	其他 Others	
6	7	8	9	10	11	12	13	14	15	16
266381	**3954461**	**3011438**	**81977**	**19096**	**193855**	**7873**	**549**	**324871**	**314802**	**10635841**
796	64394	57865	160	186	2575	48	18	1663	1879	216981
1451	59528	55146	105	144	1745	20	9	1472	887	142288
10886	223350	188101	6311	358	6194	204	20	14169	7993	598362
4486	135596	115778	2236	214	1944	106	14	4311	10993	320724
2327	82296	57099	2587	258	3449	147	7	13626	5123	174291
8753	119547	106024	221	392	5541	343	12	1826	5188	376622
6517	69311	47381	1153	224	2298	122	3	8013	10117	135873
2377	89826	77915	778	367	1944	97	3	5279	3443	220641
2434	74821	64342	1111	318	2507	15	17	5326	1185	226557
9530	294987	159366	3378	794	11408	238	17	103786	16000	742908
6907	208822	158053	1660	1754	22487	482	30	14224	10132	695996
21831	141894	109605	5382	567	6454	139	8	5980	13759	413157
8802	133879	111221	3573	1041	7757	261	21	4531	5474	377640
23393	128543	97487	1323	614	4747	277	10	2101	21984	323244
27049	313065	250720	847	432	8248	278	12	34261	18267	901892
44364	335556	253814	9771	1492	10755	665	9	12185	46865	892472
13000	145161	108936	3293	379	6543	314	31	8731	16934	364276
5483	218983	144185	9359	2664	20402	1034	33	23868	17438	574141
10943	231903	176492	4744	928	14656	247	33	15405	19398	630818
4525	118322	97743	1331	836	6592	430	23	5212	6155	324129
197	14714	12665	70	143	736	57	4	122	917	44616
7336	84033	66548	2060	488	6155	359	48	2986	5389	287626
17436	185986	133117	5625	1986	18064	658	64	10601	15871	504905
5303	76432	56261	415	452	3562	243	24	2335	13140	160616
5768	110948	85911	495	947	5031	322	27	3094	15121	270436
52	2345	1973	66	0	92	12	1	180	21	6718
5331	145370	105283	11602	658	5164	290	24	10182	12167	378974
5138	64192	51903	1306	264	3555	131	14	2830	4189	171424
194	7732	6835	84	9	302	12	4	99	387	17558
1565	17406	14726	159	17	373	38	1	479	1613	45017
2207	55519	38943	772	170	2575	284	8	5994	6773	94939

中等职业学校(机构)

Changes of Female Enrolment in

甲	上学年初报表在校学生数 Total enrolment at beginning of previous academic year	增加学生数 Factors of Increase			
		计 Total	招生 No. of Students Admitted	复学 Students Resuming Studies	转入 Transfers from Other Inst.
甲	1	2	3	4	5
总计 Total	**5152382**	**2364058**	**2138863**	**3448**	**92786**
北京 Beijing	111293	32571	31661	33	400
天津 Tianjin	80722	25460	23843	9	938
河北 Hebei	320251	133387	122514	382	4487
山西 Shanxi	192376	72123	67003	68	2590
内蒙古 Inner Mongolia	93311	36912	31637	75	3841
辽宁 Liaoning	180283	78786	73841	20	1276
吉林 Jilin	80024	32040	27107	15	1056
黑龙江 Heilongjiang	118870	41402	39828	8	873
上海 Shanghai	115295	36871	34600	26	683
江苏 Jiangsu	342852	192242	160343	121	24867
浙江 Zhejiang	308223	152225	145432	51	3024
安徽 Anhui	175562	100319	86727	131	2338
福建 Fujian	178398	73138	68309	123	867
江西 Jiangxi	145618	79688	68124	125	1973
山东 Shandong	394697	206791	183886	111	8504
河南 Henan	429143	204975	181053	96	7304
湖北 Hubei	164199	82234	72948	53	3721
湖南 Hunan	257426	157639	144735	406	9822
广东 Guangdong	315924	131242	121524	236	3202
广西 Guangxi	164592	66656	62680	191	1067
海南 Hainan	24105	9347	9145	10	90
重庆 Chongqing	124033	67628	62143	118	1795
四川 Sichuan	231427	116925	105876	572	2241
贵州 Guizhou	82205	30033	27673	36	203
云南 Yunnan	147334	46822	42782	12	916
西藏 Tibet	3529	1384	1200	12	134
陕西 Shaanxi	192014	90248	83261	129	2956
甘肃 Gansu	88182	34496	30969	24	1142
青海 Qinghai	9881	2795	2641	3	9
宁夏 Ningxia	22841	9248	8190	4	83
新疆 Xinjiang	57772	18431	17188	248	384

学生变动情况

Secondary Vocational Schools (Institutions)

单位:人

Unit:in Person

	减少学生数 Factors of Decrease									本学年初报表在校学生数 Tota lenrolmentat beginning of academic year
其 他 Others	计 Total	毕 业 Graduates	结 业 Completers of Courses without formal awards	休 学 Suspended	退 学 Quitting	开 除 Expelled	死 亡 Dead	转 出 Transfer to Other Inst.	其 他 Others	
6	7	8	9	10	11	12	13	14	15	16
128961	**1998119**	**1587363**	**35757**	**8013**	**80744**	**1719**	**190**	**150705**	**133628**	**5518321**
477	32382	30265	14	72	868	8	7	406	742	111482
670	31570	29531	97	84	686	3	4	718	447	74612
6004	123416	105290	3129	128	2511	34	8	7736	4580	330222
2462	78867	68930	1201	101	1039	20	6	1857	5713	185632
1359	40543	30141	1159	120	1719	30	2	4961	2411	89680
3649	61838	55592	70	200	2489	75	5	871	2536	197231
3862	39300	27162	673	92	929	29	0	4881	5534	72764
693	44856	39503	347	137	950	5	0	2264	1650	115416
1562	37090	32648	417	145	813	0	7	2568	492	115076
6911	151298	82906	1099	340	4661	29	9	56994	5260	383796
3718	104955	84431	546	814	7872	106	8	5972	5206	355493
11123	69560	54975	2946	221	3188	53	1	2879	5297	206321
3839	67425	59199	1343	331	2439	43	8	1924	2138	184111
9466	63206	50724	624	245	2033	42	3	790	8745	162100
14290	151680	122297	530	155	3215	63	5	16157	9258	449808
16522	172262	136533	4109	780	5101	201	2	6028	19508	461856
5512	67425	54959	664	134	2530	29	7	3421	5681	179008
2676	112792	77824	4994	1153	9355	235	10	11133	8088	302273
6280	110067	94283	929	349	5501	23	9	2541	6432	337099
2718	60425	52577	477	366	2364	53	6	2123	2459	170823
102	8284	7558	17	45	267	3	3	38	353	25168
3572	42683	34678	1225	232	3035	132	18	1591	1772	148978
8236	91482	68024	2756	731	8307	179	32	4494	6959	256870
2121	35643	25918	157	170	1298	62	5	1057	6976	76595
3112	53508	42548	90	373	2126	89	9	1433	6840	140648
38	1346	1195	27	0	24	3	0	88	9	3567
3902	74828	58488	5532	284	2536	62	7	3682	4237	207434
2361	30042	25048	295	143	1602	24	3	1183	1744	92636
142	3649	3234	24	1	156	0	1	44	189	9027
971	9400	8626	111	13	150	7	1	245	247	22689
611	26297	22276	155	54	980	77	4	626	2125	49906

中等职业学校(机

Information on foreign Students in

地　区 Region	计 Total	其中:女 Of Which: Female	结业生数 分时间 一周至一个月以下 from one week to a month under	一个月至半年以下 from one month to half year under
合　计 Total	**2652**	**1111**	**178**	**2209**
北　京 Beijing	223	84	115	55
天　津 Tianjin	69	17	0	0
河　北 Hebei	0	0	0	0
山　西 Shanxi	0	0	0	0
内蒙古 Inner Mongolia	0	0	0	0
辽　宁 Liaoning	38	20	0	0
吉　林 Jilin	4	2	0	4
黑龙江 Heilongjiang	168	0	56	112
上　海 Shanghai	39	34	0	38
江　苏 Jiangsu	0	0	0	0
浙　江 Zhejiang	0	0	0	0
安　徽 Anhui	2000	890	0	2000
福　建 Fujian	4	1	0	0
江　西 Jiangxi	0	0	0	0
山　东 Shandong	16	6	0	0
河　南 henan	0	0	0	0
湖　北 Hubei	0	0	0	0
湖　南 Hunan	0	0	0	0
广　东 Guangdong	7	2	7	0
广　西 Guangxi	15	5	0	0
海　南 Hainan	1	0	0	0
重　庆 Chongqing	31	31	0	0
四　川 Sichuan	9	6	0	0
贵　州 guizhou	0	0	0	0
云　南 Yunnan	28	13	0	0
西　藏 Tibet	0	0	0	0
陕　西 Shaanxi	0	0	0	0
甘　肃 Gansu	0	0	0	0
青　海 Qinghai	0	0	0	0
宁　夏 Ningxia	0	0	0	0
新　疆 Xinjiang	0	0	0	0

构)外国留学生情况

Secondary Vocational Schools (Institutions)

单位:人次

Unit: in Person

Graduates by time 半年以上 half year and over	分地区 by continent 亚洲 Asia	非洲 Africa	欧洲 Europe	北美洲 North America	南美洲 South America	澳洲 Australia
265	**2449**	**40**	**129**	**25**	**2**	**7**
53	129	2	66	22	2	2
69	30	38	0	0	0	1
0	0	0	0	0	0	0
0	0	0	0	0	0	0
0	0	0	0	0	0	0
38	38	0	0	0	0	0
0	4	0	0	0	0	0
0	168	0	0	0	0	0
1	1	0	38	0	0	0
0	0	0	0	0	0	0
0	0	0	0	0	0	0
0	2000	0	0	0	0	0
4	4	0	0	0	0	0
0	0	0	0	0	0	0
16	16	0	0	0	0	0
0	0	0	0	0	0	0
0	0	0	0	0	0	0
0	0	0	0	0	0	0
0	0	0	7	0	0	0
15	15	0	0	0	0	0
1	0	0	0	0	0	1
31	28	0	0	3	0	0
9	3	0	3	0	0	3
0	0	0	0	0	0	0
28	13	0	15	0	0	0
0	0	0	0	0	0	0
0	0	0	0	0	0	0
0	0	0	0	0	0	0
0	0	0	0	0	0	0
0	0	0	0	0	0	0
0	0	0	0	0	0	0

地　区 Region	教职工数 Teachers,		
	合　计 Total	校本部教职工 Teacher,	
		小　计 Total	专任教师 Full-time Teachers
合　计 Total	**880772**	**854035**	**559952**
北　京 Beijing	20465	19852	10980
天　津 Tianjin	16201	15745	9360
河　北 Hebei	54767	53551	34539
山　西 Shanxi	29590	28779	18793
内蒙古 Inner Mongolia	18956	18637	12451
辽　宁 Liaoning	36238	35117	22287
吉　林 Jilin	25774	24874	15264
黑龙江 Heilongjiang	23315	22783	14347
上　海 Shanghai	19349	18235	9551
江　苏 Jiangsu	50405	49581	34365
浙　江 Zhejiang	39503	38722	29109
安　徽 Anhui	28011	27282	18441
福　建 Fujian	25104	24874	17357
江　西 Jiangxi	20648	19323	13402
山　东 Shandong	76420	74333	49266
河　南 henan	67904	63673	43532
湖　北 Hubei	32750	31768	20263
湖　南 Hunan	42388	40780	26609
广　东 Guangdong	49556	48752	33700
广　西 Guangxi	30441	28830	18084
海　南 Hainan	5091	4894	3046
重　庆 Chongqing	19402	18650	12257
四　川 Sichuan	38505	37877	25011
贵　州 guizhou	12763	12584	8008
云　南 Yunnan	25837	25339	16464
西　藏 Tibet	1108	1108	715
陕　西 Shaanxi	32365	30886	19504
甘　肃 Gansu	18656	18233	11440
青　海 Qinghai	2400	2314	1624
宁　夏 Ningxia	2956	2923	1863
新　疆 Xinjiang	13904	13736	8320

(机构)教职工数

Secondary Vocational Schools (Institutions)

单位:人次

Unit: in Person

Staff & Workers					
staff & Workers in College or Uni. Proper			校办企业职工 Employees in School-run Factories & Farms	其他附设机构人员 Personnel in Others Subsidiary Units	聘请校外教师 Part-time Teachers
行政人员 Adm. Personnel	教辅人员 Supporting Staff	工勤人员 Workers			
120985	**66811**	**106287**	**13468**	**13269**	**78888**
4315	1823	2734	148	465	1932
3287	1091	2007	243	213	1444
7480	4271	7261	695	521	3664
4007	2252	3727	456	355	1486
2487	1659	2040	195	124	787
5607	2778	4445	699	422	3336
4567	2568	2475	706	194	645
3599	1785	3052	154	378	904
3236	2168	3280	834	280	3897
5463	3847	5906	479	345	5500
3648	2195	3770	468	313	5304
3584	1983	3274	304	425	3125
3433	1569	2515	94	136	3853
2355	1223	2343	1162	163	1717
10560	5849	8658	1538	549	3684
7812	5118	7211	1124	3107	5197
4990	2696	3819	349	633	3076
5676	3042	5453	971	637	3191
6448	3439	5165	289	515	5189
3906	2524	4316	390	1221	2894
745	318	785	16	181	469
2606	1643	2144	315	437	2593
5078	2771	5017	345	283	2973
2306	881	1389	33	146	1450
3103	1747	4025	199	299	2388
152	56	185	0	0	33
5280	2611	3491	912	567	4909
2497	1523	2773	159	264	1727
274	110	306	48	38	112
400	209	451	30	3	371
2084	1062	2270	113	55	1038

中等职业学校(机

Number of Female Teachers, Staff & Workers

地　区 Region	教职工数 Teachers,		
	合　计 Total	校本部教职工 Teacher,	
		小　计 Total	专任教师 Full-time Teachers
合　计 Total	**385493**	**373266**	**258413**
北　京 Beijing	11820	11567	7180
天　津 Tianjin	8479	8255	5489
河　北 Hebei	26745	26291	19327
山　西 Shanxi	14366	14017	10047
内蒙古 Inner Mongolia	8940	8808	6403
辽　宁 Liaoning	19295	18768	13285
吉　林 Jilin	13137	12611	8746
黑龙江 Heilongjiang	11638	11359	8034
上　海 Shanghai	9342	8978	4921
江　苏 Jiangsu	20864	20537	14946
浙　江 Zhejiang	17910	17525	13589
安　徽 Anhui	9221	8866	5958
福　建 Fujian	10338	10228	7237
江　西 Jiangxi	7485	6919	4714
山　东 Shandong	31396	30591	22471
河　南 Henan	29059	26562	19254
湖　北 Hubei	12896	12481	7827
湖　南 Hunan	16527	15914	10758
广　东 Guangdong	21888	21597	14860
广　西 Guangxi	13146	12223	7477
海　南 Hainan	2000	1891	1086
重　庆 Chongqing	8182	7778	5321
四　川 Sichuan	14880	14624	9995
贵　州 Guizhou	5255	5193	3289
云　南 Yunnan	11347	11140	7168
西　藏 Tibet	478	478	300
陕　西 Shaanxi	13027	12495	8456
甘　肃 Gansu	6887	6724	4374
青　海 Qinghai	1027	988	709
宁　夏 Ningxia	1232	1223	806
新　疆 Xinjiang	6686	6635	4386

构)女教职工数

in Secondary Vocational Schools (Institutions)

单位:人

Unit: in Person

Staff & Workers						
staff & Workers in College or Uni. Proper			校办企业职工 Employees in School-run Factories & Farms	其他附设机构人员 Personnel in Others Subsidiary Units	聘请校外教师 Part-time Teachers
行政人员 Adm. Personnel	教辅人员 Supporting Staff	工勤人员 Workers			
42283	**35027**	**37543**	**5161**	**7066**	**30297**
2332	1021	1034	54	199	953
1452	652	662	93	131	653
2254	2150	2560	235	219	1764
1409	1360	1201	152	197	748
867	896	642	82	50	345
2488	1544	1451	341	186	1625
1822	1400	643	414	112	320
1426	971	928	25	254	473
1460	1207	1390	248	116	1592
1702	1912	1977	167	160	2061
1172	1158	1606	242	143	1919
1053	928	927	117	238	986
1155	791	1045	33	77	1054
744	604	857	519	47	554
2775	2903	2442	495	310	1490
2437	2580	2291	567	1930	1885
1841	1345	1468	120	295	997
1584	1480	2092	355	258	1156
2441	1924	2372	121	170	1948
1415	1375	1956	161	762	1041
266	185	354	4	105	200
952	810	695	100	304	982
1742	1386	1501	108	148	1120
911	464	529	7	55	445
1105	958	1909	63	144	811
57	38	83	0	0	11
1632	1295	1112	226	306	1897
688	807	855	68	95	714
105	68	106	19	20	31
127	127	163	8	1	167
869	688	692	17	34	355

普通中等专业学

Number of Teachers, Staff & Workers

地 区 Region	教职工数 Teachers,			
	合 计 Total	校本部教职工 Teacher, staff & Workers		
		小 计 Total	专任教师 Full-time Teachers	行政人民 Adm. Personnel
合 计 Total	**347013**	**330934**	**198550**	**55932**
北 京 Beijing	8001	7474	3775	1673
天 津 Tianjin	6814	6539	3600	1379
河 北 Hebei	14890	14399	7816	2631
山 西 Shanxi	10907	10480	5983	1945
内蒙古 Inner Mongolia	7391	7265	4386	1115
辽 宁 Liaoning	15615	15092	8521	2770
吉 林 Jilin	7558	7089	3966	1448
黑龙江 Heilongjiang	6592	6320	3302	1224
上 海 Shanghai	11912	11003	5286	2197
江 苏 Jiangsu	17655	17223	11134	2524
浙 江 Zhejiang	6030	5760	3636	832
安 徽 Anhui	10193	9771	5983	1519
福 建 Fujian	22684	22512	15769	3086
江 西 Jiangxi	7396	7094	4374	1116
山 东 Shandong	23630	22789	13761	4192
河 南 Henan	23697	20202	12200	3283
湖 北 Hubei	17402	16638	10317	2911
湖 南 Hunan	11471	10662	6377	1864
广 东 Guangdong	22769	22320	14381	3445
广 西 Guangxi	14057	12774	7969	1762
海 南 Hainan	2627	2526	1480	431
重 庆 Chongqing	5022	4600	2656	858
四 川 Sichuan	14629	14252	8290	2563
贵 州 Guizhou	8058	7985	5045	1557
云 南 Yunnan	12443	12121	7262	1838
西 藏 Tibet	933	933	621	122
陕 西 Shaanxi	12723	11740	6646	2270
甘 肃 Gansu	12320	11957	7201	1634
青 海 Qinghai	1536	1496	1015	186
宁 夏 Ningxia	1219	1195	641	194
新 疆 Xinjiang	8839	8723	5157	1363

校教职工数

in Reg. Specialized Sec. Schools

单位:人

Unit: in Person

Staff & Workers in College or Uni. Proper		校办企业职工 Employees in School-run Factories & Farms	其他附设机构人员 Personnel in Others Subsidiary Units	聘请校外教师 Part-time Teachers
教辅人员 Supporting Staff	工勤人员 Workers			
28314	**48138**	**6429**	**9650**	**27986**
699	1327	119	408	968
450	1110	153	122	492
1381	2571	281	210	1552
898	1654	208	219	555
762	1002	53	73	501
1488	2313	250	273	1369
694	981	407	62	116
647	1147	31	241	224
1229	2291	682	227	2503
1287	2278	256	176	1702
538	754	114	156	669
798	1471	171	251	662
1421	2236	82	90	3784
606	998	287	15	685
2072	2764	480	361	1091
1765	2954	627	2868	1196
1339	2071	273	491	1264
889	1532	462	347	948
1887	2607	224	225	1862
1173	1870	123	1160	967
200	415	2	99	344
454	632	64	358	522
1247	2152	183	194	1133
513	870	8	65	321
955	2066	174	148	521
39	151	0	0	33
1112	1712	515	468	1342
926	2196	113	250	339
63	232	4	36	47
94	266	22	2	49
688	1515	61	55	225

普通中等专业学

Number of Female Teachers, Staff &

地　区 Region	合　计 Total	小　计 Total	专任教师 Full-time Teachers	行政人民 Adm. Personnel
		教职工数 Teachers,		
		校本部教职工 Teacher, staff &		
合　计 Total	**155050**	**146931**	**92629**	**21972**
北　京 Beijing	4229	4009	2304	863
天　津 Tianjin	3360	3211	1990	572
河　北 Hebei	7151	6936	4240	993
山　西 Shanxi	5428	5254	3350	791
内蒙古 Inner Mongolia	3700	3647	2369	493
辽　宁 Liaoning	7851	7668	4897	1199
吉　林 Jilin	3800	3510	2275	626
黑龙江 Heilongjiang	3214	3053	1846	525
上　海 Shanghai	5567	5260	2658	1004
江　苏 Jiangsu	7840	7666	5232	956
浙　江 Zhejiang	2757	2639	1757	338
安　徽 Anhui	3793	3551	2226	552
福　建 Fujian	9222	9156	6479	1029
江　西 Jiangxi	3045	2909	1771	449
山　东 Shandong	10373	9929	6675	1297
河　南 Henan	10867	8713	5583	1219
湖　北 Hubei	6971	6626	4020	1100
湖　南 Hunan	4693	4317	2651	659
广　东 Guangdong	10453	10218	6632	1443
广　西 Guangxi	6473	5679	3458	729
海　南 Hainan	1090	1044	568	166
重　庆 Chongqing	2279	1982	1184	371
四　川 Sichuan	6211	6023	3596	1072
贵　州 Guizhou	3576	3536	2225	677
云　南 Yunnan	5567	5457	3326	766
西　藏 Tibet	393	393	252	44
陕　西 Shaanxi	5163	4771	2880	784
甘　肃 Gansu	4508	4376	2745	499
青　海 Qinghai	671	648	454	78
宁　夏 Ningxia	542	535	302	66
新　疆 Xinjiang	4263	4215	2684	612

校女教职工数

Workers in Reg. Specialized Sec. Schools

单位:人

Unit: in Person

Staff & Workers				聘请校外教师 Part-time Teachers
Workers in College or Uni. Proper		校办企业职工 Employees in School-run Factories & Farms	其他附设机构人员 Personnel in Others Subsidiary Units	
教辅人员 Supporting Staff	工勤人员 Workers			
15752	**16578**	**2552**	**5567**	**11281**
402	440	45	175	468
266	383	66	83	246
761	942	114	101	698
568	545	60	114	342
450	335	21	32	218
886	686	86	97	711
361	248	269	21	69
351	331	7	154	115
625	973	208	99	1052
691	787	91	83	649
291	253	44	74	258
379	394	77	165	226
706	942	29	37	1027
322	367	127	9	251
1184	773	183	261	513
954	957	326	1828	486
734	772	95	250	450
507	500	209	167	378
1048	1095	109	126	786
683	809	53	741	349
127	183	1	45	150
240	187	27	270	209
696	659	63	125	455
303	331	3	37	114
536	829	55	55	237
30	67	0	0	11
600	507	119	273	573
476	656	41	91	84
36	80	4	19	16
70	97	6	1	20
469	450	14	34	120

成人中等专业学校教

Number of Teachers, Staff & Workers

地　区 Region	合　计 Total	小　计 Total	专任教师 Full-time Teachers	行政人民 Adm. Personnel
		教职工数 Teachers,		
		校本部教职工 Teacher, staff &		
合　计 Total	**126113**	**123465**	**75341**	**20064**
北　京 Beijing	1008	1005	414	344
天　津 Tianjin	1192	1187	705	242
河　北 Hebei	8233	8132	5078	1305
山　西 Shanxi	4507	4406	2761	722
内蒙古 Inner Mongolia	3438	3335	2143	521
辽　宁 Liaoning	581	557	371	94
吉　林 Jilin	6571	6489	4231	981
黑龙江 Heilongjiang	6139	6105	4028	922
上　海 Shanghai	1597	1553	742	353
江　苏 Jiangsu	7950	7829	4349	1093
浙　江 Zhejiang	2878	2869	1849	469
安　徽 Anhui	3158	3130	1606	680
福　建 Fujian				
江　西 Jiangxi	3280	2726	1838	422
山　东 Shandong	10817	10608	6712	1782
河　南 Henan	13785	13611	8545	1926
湖　北 Hubei	5083	5020	2889	866
湖　南 Hunan	5771	5556	3565	719
广　东 Guangdong	8691	8484	5461	1320
广　西 Guangxi	5857	5604	3124	912
海　南 Hainan	416	405	229	62
重　庆 Chongqing	4313	4186	2443	726
四　川 Sichuan	6802	6724	4141	1045
贵　州 Guizhou	1529	1500	818	312
云　南 Yunnan	3875	3874	2346	644
西　藏 Tibet	59	59	35	13
陕　西 Shaanxi	3956	3942	2265	765
甘　肃 Gansu	2326	2310	1218	483
青　海 Qinghai	358	316	215	44
宁　夏 Ningxia	336	336	197	67
新　疆 Xinjiang	1607	1607	1023	230

职工数

Specialized Sec. Schools for Adults

单位：人

Unit: in Person

Staff & Workers				聘请校外教师 Part-time Teachers
Workers in College or Uni. Proper		校办企业职工 Employees in School-run Factories & Farms	其他附设机构人员 Personnel in Others Subsidiary Units	
教辅人员 Supporting Staff	工勤人员 Workers			
12806	**15254**	**1781**	**867**	**26477**
129	118	3	0	405
89	151	5	0	402
769	980	36	65	652
437	486	40	61	257
306	365	87	16	144
65	27	24	0	714
820	457	54	28	74
449	706	26	8	264
210	248	22	22	722
1077	1310	62	59	2556
281	270	4	5	2366
380	464	12	16	808
159	307	537	17	328
913	1201	180	29	1455
1559	1581	74	100	2316
644	621	20	43	1168
478	794	141	74	476
609	1094	17	190	2141
603	965	217	36	937
24	90	11	0	6
493	524	94	33	1222
659	879	57	21	998
181	189	0	29	837
371	513	0	1	1438
0	11	0	0	0
532	380	7	7	1819
366	243	11	5	1081
26	31	40	2	42
26	46	0	0	206
151	203	0	0	643

成人中等专业学校女

Number of Female Teachers, Staff & Workers

地　区 Region	教职工数 Teachers,			
	合　计 Total	校本部教职工 Teacher, staff &		
		小　计 Total	专任教师 Full-time Teachers	行政人民 Adm. Personnel
合　计 Total	**52681**	**51662**	**32970**	**6389**
北　京 Beijing	542	541	220	201
天　津 Tianjin	617	614	370	132
河　北 Hebei	3756	3727	2712	282
山　西 Shanxi	2213	2157	1472	224
内蒙古 Inner Mongolia	1547	1499	1034	156
辽　宁 Liaoning	266	254	182	39
吉　林 Jilin	3183	3155	2240	341
黑龙江 Heilongjiang	2894	2888	2068	364
上　海 Shanghai	712	696	303	159
江　苏 Jiangsu	3076	3031	1783	331
浙　江 Zhejiang	1268	1264	849	162
安　徽 Anhui	1006	998	485	203
福　建 Fujian				
江　西 Jiangxi	1174	873	584	98
山　东 Shandong	4565	4464	3160	477
河　南 Henan	5737	5659	3752	553
湖　北 Hubei	1865	1830	1009	298
湖　南 Hunan	2031	1984	1275	162
广　东 Guangdong	3569	3556	2142	537
广　西 Guangxi	2273	2175	1158	301
海　南 Hainan	137	134	50	19
重　庆 Chongqing	1779	1743	1029	269
四　川 Sichuan	2534	2507	1573	316
贵　州 Guizhou	608	608	320	124
云　南 Yunnan	1648	1647	978	171
西　藏 Tibet	21	21	9	7
陕　西 Shaanxi	1608	1607	972	214
甘　肃 Gansu	977	970	519	134
青　海 Qinghai	144	129	78	20
宁　夏 Ningxia	133	133	83	20
新　疆 Xinjiang	798	798	561	75

教职工数

in Specialized Sec. Schools for Adults

单位：人

Unit: in Person

Staff & Workers					
Workers in College or Uni. Proper		校办企业职工 Employees in School-run Factories & Farms	其他附设机构人员 Personnel in Others Subsidiary Units		聘请校外教师 Part-time Teachers
教辅人员 Supporting Staff	工勤人员 Workers				
6621	**5682**	**729**	**290**		**9111**
71	49	1	0		195
56	56	3	0		145
365	368	6	23		307
256	205	16	40		99
183	126	47	1		70
31	2	12	0		298
452	122	17	11		29
242	214	6	0		85
121	113	5	11		246
503	414	19	26		946
148	105	2	2		807
168	142	2	6		201
87	104	292	9		105
486	341	87	14		549
799	555	32	46		708
272	251	10	25		307
203	344	22	25		154
340	537	3	10		751
310	406	83	15		287
10	55	3	0		0
249	196	24	12		374
340	278	18	9		369
85	79	0	0		241
210	288	0	1		439
0	5	0	0		0
268	153	0	1		596
230	87	5	2		524
21	10	14	1		9
15	15	0	0		98
100	62	0	0		172

职业高中学

Number of Teachers, Staff &

地区 Region	合计 Total	教职工数 Teachers, 校本部教职工 Teacher, staff & 小计 Total	专任教师 Full-time Teachers	行政人民 Adm. Personnel
合计 Total	**363312**	**356506**	**257945**	**38621**
北京 Beijing	11244	11161	6634	2282
天津 Tianjin	7559	7385	4637	1559
河北 Hebei	24267	24033	17670	2307
山西 Shanxi	11170	10965	8183	948
内蒙古 Inner Mongolia	7847	7767	5714	817
辽宁 Liaoning	19662	19088	13015	2743
吉林 Jilin	7566	7359	4754	1377
黑龙江 Heilongjiang	9979	9875	6759	1369
上海 Shanghai	5459	5314	3293	637
江苏 Jiangsu	21527	21257	16509	1470
浙江 Zhejiang	26859	26383	20638	2048
安徽 Anhui	13280	13040	9943	1209
福建 Fujian				
江西 Jiangxi	9372	8965	6841	695
山东 Shandong	39541	38577	27259	4390
河南 henan	28784	28239	21776	2337
湖北 Hubei	7977	7870	5717	801
湖南 Hunan	23504	22945	15633	2850
广东 Guangdong	15715	15570	12135	1398
广西 Guangxi	9719	9644	6537	1066
海南 Hainan	1260	1243	858	145
重庆 Chongqing	9190	8995	6502	933
四川 Sichuan	17074	16901	12580	1470
贵州 guizhou	2829	2752	1875	396
云南 Yunnan	9186	9021	6652	552
西藏 Tibet				
陕西 Shaanxi	14872	14390	10087	2081
甘肃 Gansu	3644	3606	2801	324
青海 Qinghai	506	502	394	44
宁夏 Ningxia	1001	992	800	57
新疆 Xinjiang	2719	2667	1749	316

校教职工数

Workers in Vocational High Schools

单位:人

Unit: in Person

Staff & Workers					
Workers in College or Uni. Proper		校办企业职工 Employees in School-run Factories & Farms	其他附设机构人员 Personnel in Others Subsidiary Units	聘请校外教师 Part-time Teachers
教辅人员 Supporting Staff	工勤人员 Workers			
22442	**37498**	**4768**	**2038**	**20134**
962	1283	26	57	557
523	666	85	89	435
1469	2587	192	42	1021
678	1156	178	27	551
577	659	55	25	142
1225	2105	425	149	1233
687	541	141	66	297
638	1109	92	12	146
679	705	114	31	620
1282	1996	161	109	810
1176	2521	346	130	1715
724	1164	116	124	1375
433	996	319	88	655
2734	4194	818	146	1087
1667	2459	416	129	1406
551	801	41	66	422
1515	2947	346	213	1600
761	1276	45	100	816
646	1395	50	25	913
52	188	3	14	85
649	911	157	38	748
865	1986	105	68	842
170	311	25	52	281
404	1413	25	140	302
913	1309	390	92	1615
188	293	33	5	268
21	43	4	0	23
70	65	8	1	83
183	419	52	0	86

职业高中学校女

Number of Female Teachers, Staff

地区 Region	教职工数 Teachers,			
		校本部教职工 Teacher, staff &		
	合计 Total	小计 Total	专任教师 Full-time Teachers	行政人民 Adm. Personnel
合计 Total	**158334**	**155814**	**119817**	**11706**
北京 Beijing	6927	6895	4556	1257
天津 Tianjin	4170	4100	2899	697
河北 Hebei	12495	12417	10271	563
山西 Shanxi	5373	5307	4310	276
内蒙古 Inner Mongolia	3574	3549	2908	209
辽宁 Liaoning	10938	10606	7966	1250
吉林 Jilin	4074	3949	2882	553
黑龙江 Heilongjiang	5176	5162	3975	484
上海 Shanghai	2862	2825	1822	278
江苏 Jiangsu	8588	8480	6912	320
浙江 Zhejiang	12338	12086	9706	612
安徽 Anhui	3945	3853	2959	232
福建 Fujian				
江西 Jiangxi	3017	2907	2211	148
山东 Shandong	15476	15227	12001	942
河南 Henan	11828	11571	9501	571
湖北 Hubei	3080	3057	2212	273
湖南 Hunan	9176	8995	6455	686
广东 Guangdong	6837	6796	5355	373
广西 Guangxi	4038	4007	2653	306
海南 Hainan	455	448	284	53
重庆 Chongqing	3812	3745	2889	272
四川 Sichuan	6135	6094	4826	354
贵州 Guizhou	894	872	605	90
云南 Yunnan	4016	3922	2796	141
西藏 Tibet				
陕西 Shaanxi	5958	5819	4420	586
甘肃 Gansu	1289	1268	1031	47
青海 Qinghai	212	211	177	7
宁夏 Ningxia	389	387	321	10
新疆 Xinjiang	1262	1259	914	116

教职工数

& Workers in Vocational High Schools

单位：人

Unit: in Person

Staff & Workers				
Workers in College or Uni. Proper		校办企业职工 Employees in School-run Factories & Farms	其他附设机构人员 Personnel in Others Subsidiary Units	聘请校外教师 Part-time Teachers
教辅人员 Supporting Staff	工勤人员 Workers			
10912	**13379**	**1707**	**813**	**8205**
538	544	8	24	288
310	194	24	46	223
678	905	59	19	546
388	333	58	8	239
257	175	14	11	57
627	763	243	89	600
364	150	77	48	141
348	355	11	3	76
435	290	31	6	274
604	644	57	51	292
608	1160	196	56	677
338	324	35	57	481
186	362	90	20	183
1180	1104	214	35	411
773	726	206	51	585
264	308	12	11	183
693	1161	118	63	571
416	652	7	34	298
339	709	25	6	358
21	90	0	7	35
298	286	49	18	351
350	564	27	14	296
65	112	4	18	85
201	784	8	86	93
409	404	107	32	694
90	100	21	0	86
11	16	1	0	6
33	23	2	0	31
88	141	3	0	45

Number of Teachers, Staff &

地 区 Rogion	教职工数 Teachers,			
	合 计 Total	校本部教职工 Teacher, staff & Workers		
		小 计 Total	专任教师 Full-time Teachers	行政人民 Adm. Personnel
合 计 Total	**44334**	**43130**	**28116**	**6368**
北 京 Beijing	212	212	157	16
天 津 Tianjin	636	634	418	107
河 北 Hebei	7377	6987	3975	1237
山 西 Shanxi	3006	2928	1866	392
内蒙古 Inner Mongolia	280	270	208	34
辽 宁 Liaoning	380	380	380	0
吉 林 Jilin	4079	3937	2313	761
黑龙江 Heilongjiang	605	483	258	84
上 海 Shanghai	381	365	230	49
江 苏 Jiangsu	3273	3272	2373	376
浙 江 Zhejiang	3736	3710	2986	299
安 徽 Anhui	1380	1341	909	176
福 建 Fujian	2420	2362	1588	347
江 西 Jiangxi	600	538	349	122
山 东 Shandong	2432	2359	1534	196
河 南 Henan	1638	1621	1011	266
湖 北 Hubei	2288	2240	1340	412
湖 南 Hunan	1642	1617	1034	243
广 东 Guangdong	2381	2378	1723	285
广 西 Guangxi	808	808	454	166
海 南 Hainan	788	720	479	107
重 庆 Chongqing	877	869	656	89
四 川 Sichuan	0	0	0	0
贵 州 Guizhou	347	347	270	41
云 南 Yunnan	333	323	204	69
西 藏 Tibet	116	116	59	17
陕 西 Shaanxi	814	814	506	164
甘 肃 Gansu	366	360	220	56
青 海 Qinghai				
宁 夏 Ningxia	400	400	225	82
新 疆 Xinjiang	739	739	391	175

教职工数

Workers in Other Institutions

单位:人

Unit: in Person

Staff & Workers in College or Uni. Proper		校办企业职工 Employees in School-run Factories & Farms	其他附设机构人员 Personnel in Others Subsidiary Units	聘请校外教师 Part-time Teachers
教辅人员 Supporting Staff	工勤人员 Workers			
3249	**5397**	**490**	**714**	**4291**
33	6	0	0	2
29	80	0	2	115
652	1123	186	204	439
239	431	30	48	123
14	14	0	10	0
0	0	0	0	20
367	496	104	38	158
51	90	5	117	270
50	36	16	0	52
201	322	0	1	432
200	225	4	22	554
81	175	5	34	280
148	279	12	46	69
25	42	19	43	49
130	499	60	13	51
127	217	7	10	279
162	326	15	33	222
160	180	22	3	167
182	188	3	0	370
102	86	0	0	77
42	92	0	68	34
47	77	0	8	101
0	0	0	0	0
17	19	0	0	11
17	33	0	10	127
17	23	0	0	0
54	90	0	0	133
43	41	2	4	39
19	74	0	0	33
40	133	0	0	84

其他机构女

Number of Female Teachers, Staff

地　区 Region	合 计 Total	教职工数 Teachers,		
		校本部教职工 Teacher, staff & Workers		
		小 计 Total	专任教师 Full-time Teachers	行政人民 Adm. Personnel
合　计 Total	**19428**	**18859**	**12997**	**2216**
北　京 Beijing	122	122	100	11
天　津 Tianjin	332	330	230	51
河　北 Hebei	3343	3211	2104	416
山　西 Shanxi	1352	1299	915	118
内蒙古 Inner Mongolia	119	113	92	9
辽　宁 Liaoning	240	240	240	0
吉　林 Jilin	2080	1997	1349	302
黑龙江 Heilongjiang	354	256	145	53
上　海 Shanghai	201	197	138	19
江　苏 Jiangsu	1360	1360	1019	95
浙　江 Zhejiang	1547	1536	1277	60
安　徽 Anhui	477	464	288	66
福　建 Fujian	1116	1072	758	126
江　西 Jiangxi	249	230	148	49
山　东 Shandong	982	971	635	59
河　南 Henan	627	619	418	94
湖　北 Hubei	980	968	586	170
湖　南 Hunan	627	618	377	77
广　东 Guangdong	1029	1027	731	88
广　西 Guangxi	362	362	208	79
海　南 Hainan	318	265	184	28
重　庆 Chongqing	312	308	219	40
四　川 Sichuan	0	0	0	0
贵　州 Guizhou	177	177	139	20
云　南 Yunnan	116	114	68	27
西　藏 Tibet	64	64	39	6
陕　西 Shaanxi	298	298	184	48
甘　肃 Gansu	113	110	79	8
青　海 Qinghai				
宁　夏 Ningxia	168	168	100	31
新　疆 Xinjiang	363	363	227	66

教职工数

& Workers in Other Institutions

单位：人

Unit: in Person

Staff & Workers in College or Uni. Proper		校办企业职工 Employees in School-run Factories & Farms	其他附设机构人员 Personnel in Others Subsidiary Units	聘请校外教师 Part-time Teachers
教辅人员 Supporting Staff	工勤人员 Workers			
1742	**1904**	**173**	**396**	**1700**
10	1	0	0	2
20	29	0	2	39
346	345	56	76	213
148	118	18	35	68
6	6	0	6	0
0	0	0	0	16
223	123	51	32	81
30	28	1	97	197
26	14	4	0	20
114	132	0	0	174
111	88	0	11	177
43	67	3	10	78
85	103	4	40	27
9	24	10	9	15
53	224	11	0	17
54	53	3	5	106
75	137	3	9	57
77	87	6	3	53
120	88	2	0	113
43	32	0	0	47
27	26	0	53	15
23	26	0	4	48
0	0	0	0	0
11	7	0	0	5
11	8	0	2	42
8	11	0	0	0
18	48	0	0	34
11	12	1	2	20
9	28	0	0	18
31	39	0	0	18

中等职业学校(机构)专

Data on Rank、Academic Qualifications of Full-time

地　区 Region	合　计 Total	职称 Rank 正高级 Senior	副高级 Sub-Senior	中级 Middle
合　计 Total	**559952**	**4732**	**90536**	**227281**
北　京 Beijing	10980	137	1981	4246
天　津 Tianjin	9360	97	2650	3805
河　北 Hebei	34539	321	5456	13721
山　西 Shanxi	18793	3	2730	7071
内蒙古 Inner Mongolia	12451	37	1728	5299
辽　宁 Liaoning	22287	280	6100	9030
吉　林 Jilin	15264	82	2954	7329
黑龙江 Heilongjiang	14347	130	3750	6243
上　海 Shanghai	9551	58	1374	5122
江　苏 Jiangsu	34365	177	4785	13331
浙　江 Zhejiang	29109	47	2684	9850
安　徽 Anhui	18441	241	3434	7521
福　建 Fujian	17357	204	2281	6611
江　西 Jiangxi	13402	118	2582	5384
山　东 Shandong	49266	332	9274	17369
河　南 Henan	43532	331	6042	16389
湖　北 Hubei	20263	149	4213	9751
湖　南 Hunan	26609	477	3823	11038
广　东 Guangdong	33700	333	3620	14939
广　西 Guangxi	18084	143	2514	8202
海　南 Hainan	3046	72	526	1152
重　庆 Chongqing	12257	180	1719	4720
四　川 Sichuan	25011	343	4023	10847
贵　州 Guizhou	8008	0	1278	3458
云　南 Yunnan	16464	76	2443	7354
西　藏 Tibet	715	0	25	224
陕　西 Shaanxi	19504	312	2866	7125
甘　肃 Gansu	11440	34	1786	4758
青　海 Qinghai	1624	2	186	771
宁　夏 Ningxia	1863	1	425	714
新　疆 Xinjiang	8320	15	1284	3907

任教师职称、学历情况

Teachers in Secondary Vocational Schools (Institutions)

单位:人

Unit: in Person

初级 Junior	无职称 No Rank	学历 Academic Qualificafions 博士 Doctor's Degrees	硕士 Master's Degrees	本科 Normal Courses	专科 Short-cycle Courses	高中阶段及以下 Below High School Graduate
190089	**47314**	**179**	**5870**	**366529**	**169043**	**18331**
3553	1063	2	235	8666	1780	297
2363	445	1	67	6209	2672	411
12074	2967	17	290	24310	8901	1021
7397	1592	3	98	11396	6345	951
4391	996	1	77	7092	4758	523
5169	1708	3	242	16068	5313	661
4405	494	4	120	11207	3619	314
3456	768	0	45	8894	4997	411
2481	516	3	237	7463	1473	375
12205	3867	13	335	24503	8563	951
10839	5689	1	97	20767	7558	686
5880	1365	8	176	11894	5912	451
6996	1265	9	153	9708	6797	690
4172	1146	1	124	7425	5273	579
18333	3958	27	818	33494	13657	1270
18078	2692	14	421	29132	12794	1171
5276	874	2	310	13364	5895	692
8086	3185	4	331	15862	9576	836
11710	3098	21	532	23573	8760	814
5828	1397	3	296	11080	6032	673
1003	293	0	34	2137	785	90
4392	1246	8	79	7598	4181	391
8314	1484	6	165	14531	9230	1079
2908	364	0	23	5272	2403	310
5712	879	3	98	9998	5639	726
343	123	0	18	483	194	20
6864	2337	17	222	10094	8060	1111
4092	770	8	88	6815	4100	429
509	156	0	31	760	664	169
610	113	0	7	1191	605	60
2650	464	0	101	5543	2507	169

普通中等专业学校专任

Data on Rank、Academic Qualifications of Full-

地 区 Region	合 计 Total	正高级 Senior	副高级 Sub-Senior	中级 Middle
		职称 Rank		
合 计 Total	**198550**	**1395**	**43269**	**84165**
北 京 Beijing	3775	38	798	1636
天 津 Tianjin	3600	3	1162	1513
河 北 Hebei	7816	189	2096	2974
山 西 Shanxi	5983	1	1392	2505
内蒙古 Inner Mongolia	4386	12	926	2028
辽 宁 Liaoning	8521	166	2571	3479
吉 林 Jilin	3966	8	1012	1788
黑龙江 Heilongjiang	3302	25	1361	1133
上 海 Shanghai	5286	29	927	2794
江 苏 Jiangsu	11134	63	2081	4371
浙 江 Zhejiang	3636	4	549	1522
安 徽 Anhui	5983	106	1532	2224
福 建 Fujian	15769	186	2016	6003
江 西 Jiangxi	4374	37	1138	1752
山 东 Shandong	13761	12	4153	5082
河 南 Henan	12200	68	2858	4997
湖 北 Hubei	10317	74	2452	4840
湖 南 Hunan	6377	24	1651	2725
广 东 Guangdong	14381	125	2018	6799
广 西 Guangxi	7969	9	1336	3890
海 南 Hainan	1480	6	303	616
重 庆 Chongqing	2656	18	584	1097
四 川 Sichuan	8290	102	1833	3680
贵 州 Guizhou	5045	0	903	2168
云 南 Yunnan	7262	42	1649	3360
西 藏 Tibet	621	0	14	186
陕 西 Shaanxi	6646	32	1539	2728
甘 肃 Gansu	7201	10	1326	3082
青 海 Qinghai	1015	1	122	512
宁 夏 Ningxia	641	0	160	243
新 疆 Xinjiang	5157	5	807	2438

教师职称、学历情况

time Teachers in Reg. Specialized Sec. Schools

单位:人

Unit: in Person

初级 Junior	无职称 No Rank	学历 Academic Qualificafions 博士 Doctor's Degrees	硕士 Master's Degrees	本科 Normal Courses	专科 Short-cycle Courses	高中阶段及以下 Below High School Graduate
56797	**12924**	**56**	**3272**	**148082**	**40932**	**6208**
1056	247	1	177	2988	467	142
792	130	1	21	2690	784	104
1838	719	2	91	5861	1520	342
1646	439	0	55	4489	1069	370
1217	203	1	53	2980	1136	216
1736	569	3	116	6721	1423	258
1046	112	2	57	3195	649	63
605	178	0	33	2852	377	40
1291	245	3	190	4006	803	284
3488	1131	2	198	8782	1749	403
1150	411	0	22	2935	566	113
1683	438	1	103	4573	1188	118
6402	1162	9	127	8600	6365	668
1085	362	0	102	3200	1017	55
3772	742	3	355	11151	2006	246
3635	642	3	286	10060	1520	331
2496	455	2	201	7356	2472	286
1525	452	0	96	5129	1014	138
4415	1024	15	329	10742	2935	360
2337	397	0	177	5920	1646	226
482	73	0	7	1175	244	54
795	162	0	13	2117	476	50
2214	461	3	74	6087	1810	316
1753	221	0	8	3712	1147	178
1826	385	2	71	5787	1220	182
302	119	0	7	427	167	20
1813	534	2	127	4932	1414	171
2321	462	1	53	4839	2090	218
277	103	0	27	491	387	110
204	34	0	3	456	149	33
1595	312	0	93	3829	1122	113

成人中等专业学校专任

Data on Rank、Academic Qualifications of Full-time

地　区 Region	合计 Total	职称 Rank		
		正高级 Senior	副高级 Sub-Senior	中级 Middle
合　计 Total	**75341**	**1021**	**13497**	**36217**
北　京 Beijing	414	6	106	177
天　津 Tianjin	705	0	242	281
河　北 Hebei	5078	93	829	2403
山　西 Shanxi	2761	2	455	1242
内蒙古 Inner Mongolia	2143	13	312	1072
辽　宁 Liaoning	371	3	78	172
吉　林 Jilin	4231	33	970	2344
黑龙江 Heilongjiang	4028	56	1269	1944
上　海 Shanghai	742	9	124	447
江　苏 Jiangsu	4349	27	734	2073
浙　江 Zhejiang	1849	3	349	870
安　徽 Anhui	1606	45	287	772
福　建 Fujian	0	0	0	0
江　西 Jiangxi	1838	8	464	823
山　东 Shandong	6712	202	1511	2920
河　南 Henan	8545	86	1160	3886
湖　北 Hubei	2889	26	627	1518
湖　南 Hunan	3565	113	524	1670
广　东 Guangdong	5461	84	575	2554
广　西 Guangxi	3124	14	316	1650
海　南 Hainan	229	1	24	107
重　庆 Chongqing	2443	80	582	1090
四　川 Sichuan	4141	79	833	2178
贵　州 Guizhou	818	0	102	487
云　南 Yunnan	2346	16	255	1291
西　藏 Tibet	35	0	1	13
陕　西 Shaanxi	2265	12	305	946
甘　肃 Gansu	1218	10	248	584
青　海 Qinghai	215	0	36	91
宁　夏 Ningxia	197	0	51	92
新　疆 Xinjiang	1023	0	128	520

教师职称、学历情况

Teachers in Specialized Sec. Schools for Adults

单位:人

Unit: in Person

		学历 Academic Qualificafions				
初级 Junior	无职称 No Rank	博士 Doctor's Degrees	硕士 Master's Degrees	本科 Normal Courses	专科 Short-cycle Courses	高中阶段及以下 Below High School Graduate
20653	**3953**	**58**	**972**	**46199**	**24862**	**3250**
93	32	0	8	319	77	10
133	49	0	15	409	229	52
1528	225	13	61	3302	1523	179
990	72	0	6	1474	1103	178
663	83	0	11	1282	753	97
112	6	0	5	168	188	10
850	34	2	18	2797	1305	109
678	81	0	7	2200	1629	192
134	28	0	14	550	151	27
1180	335	0	17	3036	1147	149
494	133	0	20	1429	339	61
411	91	7	19	945	593	42
0	0	0	4	917	712	205
421	122	21	343	4352	1757	239
1714	365	1	73	5606	2560	305
2978	435	0	28	1595	1087	179
625	93	0	55	1982	1415	113
815	443	4	86	3556	1609	206
1905	343	0	34	1647	1314	129
970	174	0	0	130	90	9
87	10	0	19	1708	600	116
558	133	3	59	2520	1353	206
937	114	0	9	511	277	21
205	24	0	1	1168	984	193
707	77	0	0	23	12	0
21	0	0	26	1041	1057	141
639	363	7	29	708	438	36
313	63	0	3	97	87	28
78	10	0	1	110	73	13
48	6	0	1	617	400	5
366	9					

职业高中学校专任教

Data on Rank、Academic Qualifications of Full-

地 区 Region	合 计 Total	职称 Rank 正高级 Senior	副高级 Sub-Senior	中级 Middle
合 计 Total	**257945**	**2013**	**28496**	**95931**
北 京 Beijing	6634	90	1052	2368
天 津 Tianjin	4637	88	1111	1826
河 北 Hebei	17670	25	1499	6893
山 西 Shanxi	8183	0	466	2688
内蒙古 Inner Mongolia	5714	10	482	2109
辽 宁 Liaoning	13015	110	3355	5211
吉 林 Jilin	4754	23	420	2225
黑龙江 Heilongjiang	6759	49	1014	3056
上 海 Shanghai	3293	20	312	1745
江 苏 Jiangsu	16509	42	1677	6009
浙 江 Zhejiang	20638	36	1575	6426
安 徽 Anhui	9943	90	1393	4136
福 建 Fujian	0	0	0	0
江 西 Jiangxi	6841	71	900	2660
山 东 Shandong	27259	118	3354	8807
河 南 Henan	21776	119	1842	7167
湖 北 Hubei	5717	37	765	2779
湖 南 Hunan	15633	320	1461	6231
广 东 Guangdong	12135	114	837	4840
广 西 Guangxi	6537	120	733	2434
海 南 Hainan	858	36	106	291
重 庆 Chongqing	6502	74	495	2301
四 川 Sichuan	12580	162	1357	4989
贵 州 Guizhou	1875	0	215	677
云 南 Yunnan	6652	8	504	2613
西 藏 Tibet	0	0	0	0
陕 西 Shaanxi	10087	239	957	3221
甘 肃 Gansu	2801	0	169	1011
青 海 Qinghai	394	1	28	168
宁 夏 Ningxia	800	1	173	289
新 疆 Xinjiang	1749	10	244	761

师职称、学历情况

time Teachers in Vocational High Schools

单位：人

Unit: in Person

初级 Junior	无职称 No Rank	学历 Academic Qualificafions				
		博士 Doctor's Degrees	硕士 Master's Degrees	本科 Normal Courses	专科 Short-cycle Courses	高中阶段及以下 Below High School Graduate
104123	**27382**	**44**	**1053**	**152092**	**96644**	**8112**
2353	771	1	50	5234	1215	134
1365	247	0	26	2885	1562	164
7671	1582	0	29	11837	5397	407
4190	839	3	29	3923	3855	373
2414	699	0	13	2746	2753	202
3219	1120	0	119	8890	3623	383
1930	156	0	8	3449	1203	94
2134	506	0	2	3636	2942	179
981	235	0	32	2720	487	54
6727	2054	0	38	11159	4989	323
8010	4591	0	41	14335	5803	459
3555	769	0	46	5677	3938	282
0	0					
2588	622	1	14	3151	3369	306
12200	2780	3	106	16976	9435	739
11130	1518	9	52	12696	8513	506
1859	277	0	39	3504	2002	172
5461	2160	4	136	8011	6910	572
4841	1503	0	63	8021	3834	217
2449	801	3	46	3135	3036	317
320	105	0	10	421	402	25
2811	821	5	32	3517	2757	191
5163	909	0	32	5924	6067	557
874	109	0	6	868	896	105
3126	401	0	7	2912	3385	348
0	0					
4337	1333	15	67	3911	5344	750
1378	243	0	2	1111	1518	170
154	43	0	1	172	190	31
287	50	0	2	467	317	14
596	138	0	5	804	902	38

其他机构专任教师

Data on Rank、Academic Qualifications of

地 区 Region	合 计 Total	职称 Rank		
		正高级 Senior	副高级 Sub-Senior	中级 Middle
合 计 Total	**28116**	**303**	**5274**	**10968**
北 京 Beijing	157	3	25	65
天 津 Tianjin	418	6	135	185
河 北 Hebei	3975	14	1032	1451
山 西 Shanxi	1866	0	417	636
内蒙古 Inner Mongolia	208	2	8	90
辽 宁 Liaoning	380	1	96	168
吉 林 Jilin	2313	18	552	972
黑龙江 Heilongjiang	258	0	106	110
上 海 Shanghai	230	0	11	136
江 苏 Jiangsu	2373	45	293	878
浙 江 Zhejiang	2986	4	211	1032
安 徽 Anhui	909	0	222	389
福 建 Fujian	1588	18	265	608
江 西 Jiangxi	349	2	80	149
山 东 Shandong	1534	0	256	560
河 南 Henan	1011	58	182	339
湖 北 Hubei	1340	12	369	614
湖 南 Hunan	1034	20	187	412
广 东 Guangdong	1723	10	190	746
广 西 Guangxi	454	0	129	228
海 南 Hainan	479	29	93	138
重 庆 Chongqing	656	8	58	232
四 川 Sichuan	0	0	0	0
贵 州 Guizhou	270	0	58	126
云 南 Yunnan	204	10	35	90
西 藏 Tibet	59	0	10	25
陕 西 Shaanxi	506	29	65	230
甘 肃 Gansu	220	14	43	81
青 海 Qinghai	0	0	0	0
宁 夏 Ningxia	225	0	41	90
新 疆 Xinjiang	391	0	105	188

职称、学历情况

Full-time Teachers in Other Institutions

单位：人

Unit: in Person

		学历 Academic Qualificafions				
初级 Junior	无职称 No Rank	博士 Doctor's Degrees	硕士 Master's Degrees	本科 Normal Courses	专科 Short-cycle Courses	高中阶段及以下 Below High School Graduate
8516	**3055**	**21**	**573**	**20156**	**6605**	**761**
51	13	0	0	125	21	11
73	19	0	5	225	97	91
1037	441	2	109	3310	461	93
571	242	0	8	1510	318	30
97	11	0	0	84	116	8
102	13	0	2	289	79	10
579	192	0	37	1766	462	48
39	3	0	3	206	49	0
75	8	0	1	187	32	10
810	347	11	82	1526	678	76
1185	554	1	14	2068	850	53
231	67	0	8	699	193	9
594	103	0	26	1108	432	22
78	40	0	4	157	175	13
647	71	0	14	1015	459	46
335	97	1	10	770	201	29
296	49	0	42	909	334	55
285	130	0	44	740	237	13
549	228	2	54	1254	382	31
72	25	0	39	378	36	1
114	105	0	17	411	49	2
228	130	3	15	256	348	34
0	0	0	0	0	0	0
76	10	0	0	181	83	6
53	16	1	19	131	50	3
20	4	0	11	33	15	0
75	107	0	2	210	245	49
80	2	0	4	157	54	5
0	0					
71	23	0	1	158	66	0
93	5	0	2	293	83	13

中等职业学校(机构)

Condition of Fixed Assets and Teaching Resources in Secondary

地　区 Region	学校占地面积(平方米) Area of School sites (m²)			图书音像 Audio-visul ed.		
	计 Total	其中:绿化用地面积 Of Which: Green Arens	其中:运动场地面积 Of Which: Sports Areas	一般图书(万册) Books & Magazines in Libraries(10 Thouand Volume) 计 Total	当年新增 New Floor Space Added in Current Year	电子图书 Electronic Books in Libraries 计 Total
合　计 Total	**488927373**	**91670027**	**73222352**	**301304013**	**19543197**	**12952879**
北　京 Beijing	7237474	1657842	1483715	5886963	271285	723558
天　津 Tianjin	5918827	806093	933870	5263180	356996	77900
河　北 Hebei	32637287	4227654	4933684	15667338	939205	663584
山　西 Shanxi	12074027	2006207	1670075	7873996	309907	121808
内蒙古 Inner Mongolia	12653832	1227311	1730471	5471249	243614	121608
辽　宁 Liaoning	11039795	1306311	2556005	9534508	962581	13041
吉　林 Jilin	9370310	1904945	1830604	6929039	214432	98763
黑龙江 Heilongjiang	9369243	1524850	1627289	5078099	107793	61084
上　海 Shanghai	3913396	1086902	813404	5669120	361133	689500
江　苏 Jiangsu	27992246	6679205	4379937	18954943	1128930	389823
浙　江 Zhejiang	18614036	4329101	3661586	12011412	1546728	152761
安　徽 Anhui	23655503	4060079	3643892	11701073	810360	551357
福　建 Fujian	19692957	3209819	2086699	9235603	740985	725666
江　西 Jiangxi	25920725	7002767	1795299	7815642	558014	272929
山　东 Shandong	38659188	7874770	6067850	22058306	1737460	985955
河　南 Henan	35924404	4964429	4817695	24105582	1577016	1162476
湖　北 Hubei	17717117	3703003	2829664	12815436	690318	563858
湖　南 Hunan	27994327	6950618	3351250	15809000	1023915	378880
广　东 Guangdong	29480586	6619342	5114269	25394281	1732329	1437260
广　西 Guangxi	23361936	4173138	3974527	13667972	1119353	736054
海　南 Hainan	3988729	922458	480268	2285102	228459	86296
重　庆 Chongqing	7209447	1395583	1200283	5784831	493387	622630
四　川 Sichuan	14140816	3026928	2669533	14261663	512323	752906
贵　州 Guizhou	7031283	1677354	979303	4081890	320533	197338
云　南 Yunnan	15190775	2819302	1787587	11011942	508887	46351
西　藏 Tibet	2205284	169353	1300602	367711	59821	3852
陕　西 Shaanxi	12674193	1726956	2045573	10330826	587617	501698
甘　肃 Gansu	11460618	1819112	1805020	6647883	222424	499577
青　海 Qinghai	2039027	275286	190830	601918	14075	5433
宁　夏 Ningxia	2563258	357355	299408	918918	59445	70981
新　疆 Xinjiang	17196727	2165954	1162160	4068587	103872	237952

资产情况(学校产权)

Vocational Schools (Institutions) (Owned by HEIs)

单位:人

Unit: in Person

资料情况 Resources (片) & Magazines (Disk) 当年新增 New Floor Space Added in Current Year	拥有教学用计算机(台) No. of computers used for Instruction	语音实验室座位数(个) No. of Seats in Audio-Labs	多媒体教室座位数(个) No. of Seats in Multimedia Class rooms	网上教学课程数(种) No. of Web-Based Courses	固定资产值(万元) Fixed Assets (in 10000 yuan) 合计 Total	其中:教学、科研仪器设备资产 of which: Teaching Equipment & Instruments 小计 Total	当年新增 New Floor Space Added in Current Year
4520551	**1380820**	**404771**	**1201176**	**44230**	**13319121.04**	**3120588.01**	**329421.14**
468243	33706	8945	22806	659	234108.65	62298.14	8184.77
8496	27597	7165	14596	383	157850.40	48075.34	3759.34
177236	74296	30482	75133	4016	750646.03	118338.34	13798.65
24585	24369	7515	17898	0	462166.70	93594.76	7227.71
16856	19371	6971	16195	488	155682.61	28478.45	5312.19
4264	50706	15741	35368	565	322468.27	75331.44	10823.87
35955	28714	8958	19494	961	368009.07	58673.86	6219.18
7890	26783	8308	19765	572	186720.27	40663.52	3092.84
372698	36997	10360	48421	116	350771.78	99195.70	10098.90
120923	81118	22022	71448	4004	866643.90	161507.82	19179.03
70872	82352	15371	74458	1221	657470.14	116647.55	22016.68
296659	47062	13506	38709	1635	744070.26	350750.71	9829.94
364857	52499	21670	46548	810	655667.71	341371.46	25342.22
172194	36515	11951	26641	649	552473.45	56183.64	7831.15
194528	107398	33966	98348	3140	933973.71	155562.44	25101.84
297173	91537	25123	76810	1995	1021948.66	155335.06	22241.83
86800	44254	15407	46135	1503	427005.09	78407.23	8497.24
118127	91885	24156	58580	6619	901350.27	356591.98	16791.94
741085	129388	35924	148973	8696	1076644.45	230939.74	34638.06
143349	49995	14510	51704	882	349116.60	88328.99	13106.22
70785	9456	3120	12268	132	103433.52	19359.49	2165.11
197283	34732	8111	24042	454	266258.36	42870.16	6573.64
167842	61550	14444	38848	1554	492241.52	82436.73	10831.76
7332	17434	4671	17009	289	141859.47	30582.02	4647.05
15824	37439	9896	29840	0	356852.61	61426.36	8012.34
3012	842	319	976	126	18695.63	2452.90	255.00
160221	37619	10158	29067	1001	328455.33	67002.17	8014.02
80346	24278	7064	20975	1061	206278.21	48031.58	5859.47
184	2479	530	2855	28	23798.95	4958.71	244.52
40578	4973	951	3565	68	35230.57	13085.59	991.79
54354	13476	7456	13701	603	171228.85	32106.13	8732.84

中等职业学校(机构)资产情况

Condition of Fixed Assets and Teaching Resources in Secondary

地 区 Region	学校占地面积(平方米) Area of School sites (m^2)			图书音像 Audio-visual ed.		
				一般图书(万册) Books & Magazines in Libraries(10 Thouand Volume)		电子图书 Electronic Books in Libraries
	计 Total	其中:绿化用地面积 Of Which: Green Arens	其中:运动场地面积 Of Which: Sports Areas	计 Total	当年新增 New Floor Space Added in Current Year	计 Total
合 计 Total	**24916634**	**4308027**	**4242666**	**26524797**	**497723**	**170944**
北 京 Beijing	539611	95272	107107	222558	1805	37230
天 津 Tianjin	293263	18040	63146	191077	4920	3139
河 北 Hebei	2579279	811063	375673	600549	27327	2868
山 西 Shanxi	323733	44290	84936	68929	5630	700
内蒙古 Inner Mongolia	245320	14258	69918	97663	11662	2105
辽 宁 Liaoning	880159	107260	273123	377848	10912	1411
吉 林 Jilin	192084	30780	25408	54921	1300	0
黑龙江 Heilongjiang	157229	33220	72811	20325932	656	0
上 海 Shanghai	284221	89600	49412	152700	10321	780
江 苏 Jiangsu	429587	126731	115121	70650	15800	400
浙 江 Zhejiang	1222694	156192	239883	227255	34863	1300
安 徽 Anhui	248323	34691	49286	196734	19103	4635
福 建 Fujian	626092	152437	96927	105096	10820	360
江 西 Jiangxi	1177357	294396	207031	468200	35750	10366
山 东 Shandong	1903113	237111	354200	587963	29933	3043
河 南 Henan	1262840	192033	198303	284942	36892	10025
湖 北 Hubei	355794	44326	56792	107784	41913	13377
湖 南 Hunan	2247644	402356	380528	330981	14620	5770
广 东 Guangdong	2812635	322756	349897	667233	60259	11311
广 西 Guangxi	535060	74134	107944	169394	19950	11628
海 南 Hainan	320255	144410	38838	20543	2587	800
重 庆 Chongqing	771045	138592	116617	258061	45636	6291
四 川 Sichuan	1595833	169433	221469	147300	7066	0
贵 州 Guizhou	425503	128574	76903	58703	7502	48
云 南 Yunnan	415307	108443	51403	71157	7890	159
西 藏 Tibet	1285	0	0	0	0	0
陕 西 Shaanxi	1249746	226588	360500	302436	29070	43068
甘 肃 Gansu	219018	35300	57658	182376	3300	100
青 海 Qinghai	0	0	0	0	0	0
宁 夏 Ningxia	1363307	10000	5000	0	0	0
新 疆 Xinjiang	239297	65741	36832	175812	236	30

(非学校产权中独立使用)

Vocational Schools (Institutions) (Not Owned by HEIs)

单位:人

Unit: in Person

资料情况 Resources (片) & Magazines (Disk) 当年新增 New Floor Space Added in Current Year	拥有教学用计算机(台) No. of computers used for Instruction	语音实验室座位数(个) No. of Seats in Audio-Labs	多媒体教室座位数(个) No. of Seats in Multimedia Class rooms	网上教学课程数(种) No. of Web-Based Courses	固定资产值(万元) Fixed Assets (in 10000 yuan) 合计 Total	其中:教学、科研仪器设备资产 of which: Teaching Equipment & Instruments 计 Total	当年新增 New Floor Space Added in Current Year
48701	**41031**	**13067**	**26385**	**1465**	**9131438.33**	**8361517.57**	**362147.65**
86	1289	424	693	17	17739.11	3879.34	112.00
125	965	481	293	16	4685.94	1456.00	238.00
668	2081	1175	958	64	24829.40	4095.28	265.87
200	494	36	85	0	3727.90	706.20	119.60
1970	422	15	56	22	1334.32	76.28	19.58
186	2398	1125	1577	229	12772.09	4295.33	497.22
0	435	152	121	1	2019.38	321.62	2.60
0	674	124	632	15	2100.40	1891.10	38.60
600	1740	646	764	0	2937048.50	2513631.70	338727.00
150	1073	266	484	2	5376.19	1773.19	61.19
486	2152	385	2366	6	16253.98	2209.50	457.00
4295	1205	165	925	19	4153.05	854.00	175.00
30	1480	319	852	17	5946543.46	5791740.34	15067.30
3683	3204	1070	3169	108	20178.10	4058.30	1542.00
706	4679	1361	3201	110	25016.19	4096.99	718.07
4190	1318	429	876	17	7561.00	1367.92	310.92
77	475	369	347	20	7678.77	800.60	431.00
1955	2866	1001	1548	37	16691.08	3367.56	272.60
391	3746	662	2506	420	16860.23	5097.00	709.88
1050	663	249	352	45	598.88	375.28	66.60
200	371	1	146	20	1629.00	210.00	48.00
380	1674	712	1021	44	16728.83	2445.86	224.10
0	1369	406	530	56	7788.56	1245.00	31.00
48	501	160	271	0	5608.25	1428.00	774.00
65	483	210	150	0	6205.72	5316.48	22.97
0	0	0	0	0	0.00	0.00	0.00
27110	2012	456	1696	168	8973.95	2919.25	872.05
50	576	116	428	12	4692.05	772.95	212.00
0	0	0	0	0	0.00	0.00	0.00
0	0	0	0	0	50.00	0.00	0.00
0	686	552	338	0	6594.00	1086.50	131.50

普通中专学校资产情

Condition of Fixed Assets and Teaching

地　区 Region	学校占地面积(平方米) Area of School sites (m^2)			图书音像 Audio-visual ed.		
	合　计 Total	其中:绿化用地面积 Of Which: Green Arens	其中:运动场地面积 Of Which: SportsAreas	一般图书(万册) Books & Magazines in Libraries(10 Thouand Volume) 小　计 Total	当年新增 New Floor Space Added in Current Year	电子图书 Electronic Books in Libraries 小　计 Total
合　计 Total	**205915959**	**38731111**	**30454339**	**155830843**	**8006780**	**7313340**
北　京 Beijing	2417010	421097	425297	2664275	81592	268172
天　津 Tianjin	3383617	563258	421399	2317242	96734	37429
河　北 Hebei	7357083	1021694	1244754	4468553	393272	201173
山　西 Shanxi	5290682	708476	640703	4510425	147653	101501
内蒙古 Inner Mongolia	6664935	559796	582007	2656385	95640	78092
辽　宁 Liaoning	5188916	830285	1198364	5336978	530681	4996
吉　林 Jilin	3326431	830936	491021	2258921	119719	48413
黑龙江 Heilongjiang	3840627	576058	451854	2635328	60465	48214
上　海 Shanghai	2726613	788910	522201	3736314	140207	643651
江　苏 Jiangsu	10030710	2333066	1507936	9179581	449633	110477
浙　江 Zhejiang	3383207	1137748	689394	2445188	260789	35502
安　徽 Anhui	8752096	1401815	1217392	4635154	252870	385874
福　建 Fujian	18839119	3023124	1996084	8408891	719034	704093
江　西 Jiangxi	6220256	2146518	634699	4257350	232008	216192
山　东 Shandong	13164375	1947552	1772614	9673559	414207	245809
河　南 Henan	11881020	1979353	1565669	11500361	565135	649620
湖　北 Hubei	11011767	2340257	1629564	8548728	435254	460953
湖　南 Hunan	6719999	1932669	1069465	6894990	289733	170804
广　东 Guangdong	14694883	2794749	2618171	14234322	765198	857826
广　西 Guangxi	10717598	2220479	2445289	8479553	698311	460970
海　南 Hainan	1502154	481651	219789	1180504	56864	57190
重　庆 Chongqing	2066838	548529	340365	2374692	59794	233884
四　川 Sichuan	5745042	1373547	932432	8321068	151307	270611
贵　州 Guizhou	5026123	1251060	661764	3136565	240316	137745
云　南 Yunnan	6727722	1528869	1050502	7849971	264227	26291
西　藏 Tibet	2126438	153138	1248902	340711	57821	3852
陕　西 Shaanxi	5612190	912832	782496	5512703	177254	308379
甘　肃 Gansu	8354093	1389750	1226545	4931022	149924	488078
青　海 Qinghai	1448323	191602	102379	384630	9800	4909
宁　夏 Ningxia	1409334	175590	108961	467308	12524	41735
新　疆 Xinjiang	10286758	1166703	656327	2489571	78814	10905

况(学校产权)

Resources in SSSs (Owned by HEIs)

单位:人
Unit: in Person

资料情况 Resources (片) & Magazines (Disk) 当年新增 New Floor Space Added in Current Year	拥有教学用计算机(台) No. of computers used for Instruction	语音实验室座位数(个) No. of Seats in Audio-Labs	多媒体教室座位数(个) No. of Seats in Multimedia Class rooms	网上教学课程数(种) No. of Web-Based Courses	固定资产值(万元) Fixed Assets (in 10000 yuan) 合计 Total	其中:教学、科研仪器设备资产 of which: Teaching Equipment & Instruments 小计 Total	当年新增 New Floor Space Added in Current Year
2625953	**547360**	**168718**	**561043**	**22588**	**6190272.73**	**1453967.19**	**167299.05**
192827	13269	2481	10814	159	120005.56	33576.62	5936.96
4456	11184	2704	6801	177	94429.92	28868.67	1660.77
54047	20401	6845	17017	938	351893.59	42290.74	5224.66
17962	9869	3347	9504	0	131057.22	35332.11	1791.36
2480	7276	2373	8282	288	95494.37	15020.62	2974.53
2085	21731	6964	19630	330	171729.29	41928.26	6260.19
33298	9769	2949	7259	347	197382.24	26210.30	2057.14
5975	9714	3541	8697	112	92812.90	20649.80	1716.58
358254	17831	6488	24233	87	204288.97	66536.36	7115.11
37468	29776	9622	30380	541	340544.20	70986.09	9121.52
22351	12876	3183	12387	143	140012.46	24360.72	4801.40
223492	14405	4335	12350	207	148936.77	41015.75	3214.28
352688	50026	20830	43428	807	624944.32	335247.07	24770.83
161341	13472	5102	11687	184	122682.57	26006.66	3554.48
50423	38418	10607	41892	1205	356684.08	62458.55	5460.03
142119	36091	9866	40617	715	565354.86	84748.27	13058.87
55860	22539	8614	26645	733	274667.21	49703.99	5465.53
87901	19990	5285	20078	4715	286671.52	36092.58	4083.05
410932	55947	16566	71579	7720	595296.04	120627.82	19319.96
75688	21827	6535	29916	382	191835.47	52742.38	8225.39
54838	4839	1227	6800	89	49086.06	12189.95	871.54
42183	8440	2147	9482	61	63545.34	13536.64	1381.95
16515	22875	5536	17276	677	200110.12	40083.48	3443.71
2322	11772	3085	11166	173	108631.92	22708.89	3513.78
9677	20455	5176	16172	0	179006.12	42169.47	4913.86
3012	757	289	926	68	18208.63	2439.90	255.00
106049	15498	4283	17002	510	176466.20	41103.55	4699.01
77053	16058	4971	15269	824	152006.44	37340.92	3975.69
10	1313	251	1655	8	15850.60	3045.56	137.50
21180	1635	531	1806	12	13325.30	4351.20	347.70
1467	7307	2985	10293	376	107312.44	20594.27	7946.67

普通中专学校资产情况(非

Condition of Fixed Assets and Teaching

地区 Region	学校占地面积(平方米) Area of School sites (m^2) 小计 Total	其中:绿化用地面积 Of Which: Green Arens	其中:运动场地面积 Of Which: SportsAreas	图书音像 Audio-visual ed. 一般图书(万册) Books & Magazines in Libraries(10 Thouand Volume) 小计 Total	当年新增 New Floor Space Added in Current Year	电子图书 Electronic Books in Libraries 小计 Total
合　计 Total	**7703655**	**1258837**	**1041561**	**2110099**	**170484**	**54389**
北　京 Beijing	211105	13742	46545	26110	885	540
天　津 Tianjin	118200	10420	8400	10000	0	0
河　北 Hebei	689790	173550	126340	52279	3457	530
山　西 Shanxi	70938	31000	20840	0	0	0
内蒙古 Inner Mongolia	1200	800	200	500	0	0
辽　宁 Liaoning	313836	29920	63056	244333	1000	0
吉　林 Jilin	72128	0	4128	0	0	0
黑龙江 Heilongjiang	40000	30000	10000	61000	0	0
上　海 Shanghai	138496	27696	16784	125700	9621	500
江　苏 Jiangsu	62509	7500	18057	12000	0	0
浙　江 Zhejiang	280249	69960	38295	0	0	0
安　徽 Anhui	45673	6014	10000	11011	3	120
福　建 Fujian	597186	143699	78359	104846	10720	360
江　西 Jiangxi	187339	74500	33451	179000	4000	0
山　东 Shandong	256279	29364	45023	168958	5178	0
河　南 Henan	208624	91114	19125	104000	0	0
湖　北 Hubei	179322	29073	32384	68574	41000	377
湖　南 Hunan	167484	32651	16121	91100	0	0
广　东 Guangdong	885274	109578	166101	256688	52620	10698
广　西 Guangxi	47758	600	450	0	0	0
海　南 Hainan	52247	12830	15021	0	0	0
重　庆 Chongqing	165325	19864	10991	119000	11100	0
四　川 Sichuan	728341	62033	55603	66000	1000	0
贵　州 Guizhou	53335	4000	10000	0	0	0
云　南 Yunnan	207747	56162	13832	15000	5000	0
西　藏 Tibet	1285	0	0	0	0	0
陕　西 Shaanxi	468705	152867	163780	189000	23900	41264
甘　肃 Gansu	71330	23000	10800	85000	1000	0
青　海 Qinghai	0	0	0	0	0	0
宁　夏 Ningxia	1332000	0	0	0	0	0
新　疆 Xinjiang	49950	16900	7875	120000	0	0

学校产权中独立使用)

Resources in SSSs (Not Owned by HEIs)

单位:人
Unit: in Person

资料情况 sources (片) & Magazines (Disk) 当年新增 New Floor Space Added in Current Year	拥有教学用计算机(台) No. of computers used for Instruction	语音实验室座位数(个) No. of Seats in Audio-Labs	多媒体教室座位数(个) No. of Seats in Multimedia Class rooms	网上教学课程数(种) No. of Web-Based Courses	固定资产值(万元) Fixed Assets (in 10000 yuan) 合计 Total	其中:教学、科研仪器设备资产 of which: Teaching Equipment & Instruments 小计 Total	当年新增 New Floor Space Added in Current Year
27440	**11829**	**3413**	**10358**	**412**	**8899252.89**	**8319442.67**	**355349.31**
80	233	130	287	1	4957.80	538	2.00
0	46	0	45	0	433.00	178.00	16.00
50	457	130	32	0	3645.76	309.11	34.00
0	55	0	0	0	0.00	0.00	0.00
0	0	0	0	0	0.00	0.00	0.00
0	1274	478	937	161	6518.89	2550.03	247.22
0	175	48	0	0	0.00	0.00	0.00
0	108	42	320	0	1465.60	1430.00	35.60
500	1300	482	572	0	2887245.00	2513454.00	338727.00
0	473	100	300	0	3400.19	933.19	8.19
0	0	0	0	0	0.00	0.00	0.00
30	439	120	600	15	1638.39	346.00	17.00
30	1480	319	852	17	5946543.46	5791740.34	15067.30
0	197	64	1950	0	7593.00	1246.00	12.00
0	797	250	1650	0	4857.00	704.00	5.00
0	230	100	260	0	1573.00	529.00	29.00
77	290	208	210	20	3999.00	489.00	409.00
0	622	260	535	1	3616.00	191.00	5.00
10	1206	0	157	19	3685.00	2037.00	222.00
0	145	0	65	32	0.00	0.00	0.00
0	200	0	0	0	0.00	0.00	0.00
0	450	164	344	1	8367.20	736.00	49.00
0	330	184	52	5	2051.60	237.00	13.00
0	0	0	0	0	0.00	0.00	0.00
0	80	60	0	0	415.00	415.00	5.00
0	0	0	0	0	0.00	0.00	0.00
26663	887	98	978	140	3500.00	1020.00	434.00
0	100	96	140	0	1800.00	287.00	12.00
0	0	0	0	0	0.00	0.00	0.00
0	0	0	0	0	0.00	0.00	0.00
0	255	80	72	0	1948.00	73.00	0.00

成人中专学校资产情
Condition of Fixed Assets and Teaching

地　区 Region	学校占地面积(平方米) Area of School sites (m^2)			图书音像 Audio-visual ed.		
	小　计 Total	其中:绿化用地面积 Of Which: Green Arens	其中:运动场地面积 Of Which: Sports Areas	一般图书(万册) Books & Magazines in Libraries(10 Thouand Volume)		电子图书 Electronic Books in Libraries
				小　计 Total	当年新增 New Floor Space Added in Current Year	小　计 Total
合　计 Total	**47834298**	**8002007**	**5906533**	**35685726**	**2107232**	**1520828**
北　京 Beijing	616708	61125	29135	248446	41000	21695
天　津 Tianjin	102322	9930	12087	250045	6610	220
河　北 Hebei	2594789	355162	395635	2264356	127632	101086
山　西 Shanxi	835279	106126	129829	933332	41010	5068
内蒙古 Inner Mongolia	1215476	203743	221205	897869	59991	24930
辽　宁 Liaoning	35721	970	6018	134650	5157	0
吉　林 Jilin	1075464	107676	160330	1641580	22943	12660
黑龙江 Heilongjiang	1072844	187597	268507	886071	17274	5339
上　海 Shanghai	133395	32680	16010	347214	50806	2412
江　苏 Jiangsu	3661122	619132	314760	2483904	100478	39818
浙　江 Zhejiang	1421457	262153	191745	1312402	72187	12225
安　徽 Anhui	1234496	175831	140310	1041026	52211	43752
福　建 Fujian	0	0	0	0	0	0
江　西 Jiangxi	1207317	206693	143432	1109786	33884	3756
山　东 Shandong	3625650	716586	549910	2742769	238768	151612
河　南 Henan	7733473	643389	634409	4222726	403717	222727
湖　北 Hubei	2517323	424059	415612	1305018	111205	12637
湖　南 Hunan	3887632	1148996	364152	1594149	105446	25233
广　东 Guangdong	3784740	1165389	570175	3840526	174957	221116
广　西 Guangxi	4711655	478739	422802	1961198	117046	186680
海　南 Hainan	120559	26640	14840	69490	1950	800
重　庆 Chongqing	1463672	229271	208304	1248415	135517	185217
四　川 Sichuan	1391639	315218	227107	2239186	73086	10962
贵　州 Guizhou	246972	22902	54462	278673	12900	35580
云　南 Yunnan	1033572	186385	99986	972886	38957	11756
西　藏 Tibet	8810	0	1700	25000	0	0
陕　西 Shaanxi	581217	49240	98300	727883	33727	9913
甘　肃 Gansu	630818	91422	106017	421247	13538	1522
青　海 Qinghai	292539	41531	34023	157800	2700	0
宁　夏 Ningxia	86202	17109	20547	75411	10675	14636
新　疆 Xinjiang	511435	116313	55184	252668	1860	157476

况(学校产权)

Resources in Adult SSSs(Owned by HEIs)

单位:人

Unit: in Person

资料情况 Resources / (片) & Magazines (Disk) / 当年新增 New Floor Space Added in Current Year	拥有教学用计算机(台) No. of computers used for Instruction	语音实验室座位数(个) No. of Seats in Audio-Labs	多媒体教室座位数(个) No. of Seats in Multimedia Class rooms	网上教学课程数(种) No. of Web-Based Courses	固定资产值(万元) Fixed Assets (in 10000 yuan) 合计 Total	其中:教学、科研仪器设备资产 of which: Teaching Equipment & Instruments 小计 Total	当年新增 New Floor Space Added in Current Year
405653	**182647**	**56781**	**182915**	**6192**	**1910961.66**	**527189.04**	**33009.59**
433	2329	1646	2127	18	24349.13	2755.40	353.60
125	1625	486	1277	60	8530.28	3206.08	475.12
7029	12003	6053	18716	505	66906.89	13591.33	1517.79
1014	4319	1182	2927	0	51358.75	5550.03	352.54
9470	3803	1616	3171	109	15936.41	5614.17	1010.10
0	410	140	256	6	3491.20	787.10	72.00
1364	4500	1705	5585	467	29992.59	9370.56	309.46
884	4042	1308	4645	169	33080.15	6490.06	354.20
5	3468	1021	6619	12	18709.12	6880.91	223.18
1797	12631	3762	11057	136	132157.63	19230.27	1941.13
1296	7522	1967	15781	286	47256.92	10271.53	1889.48
3423	5401	1668	6553	936	305128.63	273704.74	771.49
0	0	0	0	0	0.00	0.00	0.00
759	3515	1430	4758	237	67786.24	7886.17	588.66
67075	18302	6279	15289	376	141212.72	21096.07	6185.20
121785	18454	4870	13204	766	245262.81	23183.44	2110.73
2010	5430	1923	5469	305	51420.62	10821.05	742.81
10730	10557	4739	6495	597	45765.00	9846.01	1148.82
109365	24766	5990	26779	178	160344.81	40712.26	4836.25
24041	7807	2247	6848	123	47671.73	11831.64	1606.92
0	261	250	225	0	3012.10	292.50	11.20
21780	7414	1582	5939	258	63895.13	11111.50	2040.75
1825	10228	2263	7623	272	164362.33	11694.42	2211.42
4220	1283	253	1065	80	15279.60	3977.40	314.00
3534	5408	1091	5115	0	93892.32	5785.65	596.74
0	25	0	0	0	487.00	13.00	0.00
1554	2447	454	1905	117	36572.30	2891.74	237.50
906	2358	394	2270	66	19319.12	4712.68	782.58
0	463	230	321	0	4135.72	984.49	60.12
8660	698	0	320	0	2078.50	588.00	93.30
569	1178	232	576	113	11565.91	2308.84	172.50

成人中专学校资产情况(非

Condition of Fixed Assets and Teaching

地 区 Region	学校占地面积(平方米) Area of School sites (m^2) 计 Total	其中:绿化用地面积 Of Which: Green Arens	其中:运动场地面积 Of Which: SportsAreas	图书音像 Audio-visual ed. 一般图书(万册) Books & Magazines in Libraries(10 Thouand Volume) 小计 Total	当年新增 New Floor Space Added in Current Year	电子图书 Electronic Books in Libraries 小计 Total
合 计 Total	**3581377**	**522558**	**681196**	**21271006**	**91975**	**9256**
北 京 Beijing	46014	50	140	13343	0	0
天 津 Tianjin	12584	500	1780	1045	0	0
河 北 Hebei	158120	44203	60725	15300	2100	150
山 西 Shanxi	20789	500	3672	35700	3230	200
内蒙古 Inner Mongolia	13816	0	0	8100	0	0
辽 宁 Liaoning	9070	0	0	0	0	0
吉 林 Jilin	20963	403	3080	34621	0	0
黑龙江 Heilongjiang	14625	20	10690	20200000	0	0
上 海 Shanghai	67423	15232	23412	16000	500	180
江 苏 Jiangsu	162468	59299	35797	38650	15000	400
浙 江 Zhejiang	33015	5800	4200	37804	0	0
安 徽 Anhui	97723	1200	8600	62300	0	165
福 建 Fujian	0	0	0	0	0	0
江 西 Jiangxi	79262	11342	27926	66400	2500	20
山 东 Shandong	677107	31548	106256	96977	2000	1174
河 南 Henan	511014	24819	40417	32000	16000	3147
湖 北 Hubei	16141	632	2718	0	0	0
湖 南 Hunan	633234	163865	153956	52296	320	125
广 东 Guangdong	125170	8089	19435	292139	1633	400
广 西 Guangxi	77933	11533	3715	70722	4450	200
海 南 Hainan	6670	1000	1500	0	0	0
重 庆 Chongqing	242339	80166	53049	83228	30450	2900
四 川 Sichuan	393099	34017	87979	39134	3000	0
贵 州 Guizhou	102648	24756	25633	47903	7502	0
云 南 Yunnan	22507	2034	1200	11376	1390	139
西 藏 Tibet	0	0	0	0	0	0
陕 西 Shaanxi	23446	0	4666	5900	1400	56
甘 肃 Gansu	11490	800	0	10068	500	0
青 海 Qinghai	0	0	0	0	0	0
宁 夏 Ningxia	1307	0	0	0	0	0
新 疆 Xinjiang	1400	750	650	0	0	0

学校产权中独立使用)

Resources in Adult SSSs (Not Owned by HEIs)

单位:人

Unit: in Person

资料情况 Resources (片) & Magazines (Disk) 当年新增 New Floor Space Added in Current Year	拥有教学用计算机(台) No. of computers used for Instruction	语音实验室座位数(个) No. of Seats in Audio-Labs	多媒体教室座位数(个) No. of Seats in Multimedia Class rooms	网上教学课程数(种) No. of Web-Based Courses	固定资产值(万元) Fixed Assets (in 10000 yuan) 合计 Total	其中:教学、科研仪器设备资产 of which: Teaching Equipment & Instruments 小计 Total	当年新增 New Floor Space Added in Current Year
3142	**7419**	**2251**	**6289**	**232**	**91891.32**	**6463.70**	**815.06**
0	177	48	87	0	7209.55	156.84	0.00
0	44	48	80	0	6.00	5.00	1.00
20	58	54	201	0	1019.20	167.20	7.00
100	200	0	85	0	834.80	162.80	17.90
0	12	0	0	0	69.00	10.00	0.00
0	0	0	0	0	0.00	0.00	0.00
0	125	48	41	1	955.00	146.00	0.00
0	38	0	200	0	0.00	0.00	0.00
100	342	114	192	0	49636.50	57.70	0.00
150	357	166	184	2	1059.00	546.00	40.00
0	180	50	1500	0	510.00	332.00	10.00
165	66	0	220	0	95.83	0.00	0.00
0	0	0	0	0	0.00	0.00	0.00
0	263	270	420	40	386.90	102.00	40.00
220	2279	510	490	100	7159.00	963.00	148.00
1627	322	40	60	0	2837.00	358.00	109.00
0	0	0	0	0	665.55	0.00	0.00
50	312	284	146	4	5186.00	480.00	35.00
349	902	233	1353	7	3150.47	1202.00	215.64
100	221	80	80	1	210.80	90.80	20.00
0	0	0	0	0	0.00	0.00	0.00
200	524	98	152	40	3816.99	514.50	54.10
0	409	50	278	1	2451.00	326.00	1.00
0	290	56	100	0	2357.00	339.00	24.00
45	50	50	50	0	222.23	121.81	8.97
0	0	0	0	0	0.00	0.00	0.00
16	108	32	270	24	243.45	138.45	83.45
0	140	20	100	12	1768.05	229.60	0.00
0	0	0	0	0	0.00	0.00	0.00
0	0	0	0	0	0.00	0.00	0.00
0	0	0	0	0	42.00	15.00	0.00

职业高中学校资产情
Condition of Fixed Assets and Teaching Resources

地　区 Region	学校占地面积(平方米) Area of School sites (m^2)			一般图书(万册) Books & Magazines in Libraries(10 Thouand Volume)		图书音像 Audio-visual ed. 电子图书 Electronic Books in Libraries
	小　计 Total	其中:绿化用地面积 Of Which: Green Arens	其中:运动场地面积 Of Which: Sports Areas	小　计 Total	当年新增 New Floor Space Added in Current Year	小　计 Total
合　计 Total	**21526994**	**39762169**	**33939944**	**94656674**	**8562305**	**3871545**
北　京 Beijing	3958964	1175620	1029283	2908442	148693	433691
天　津 Tianjin	2353841	228705	494734	2571593	240052	36851
河　北 Hebei	18417641	2250281	2873739	6337126	316320	285850
山　西 Shanxi	5818906	1151955	854243	2357739	119244	15239
内蒙古 Inner Mongolia	4487477	457616	891951	1842345	87983	18576
辽　宁 Liaoning	5815158	475056	1351623	4062880	426743	8045
吉　林 Jilin	3143637	558851	884732	1475467	43415	35220
黑龙江 Heilongjiang	4438012	758395	905828	1552590	29054	7514
上　海 Shanghai	1010847	258952	259748	1478187	152563	43437
江　苏 Jiangsu	12678104	3441459	2290391	6368658	518935	232220
浙　江 Zhejiang	12936076	2819989	2637441	7662376	1178378	101955
安　徽 Anhui	12575543	2243415	2088743	5241824	458839	117193
福　建 Fujian	0	0	0	0	0	0
江　西 Jiangxi	18176413	4553056	995063	2115006	272022	52381
山　东 Shandong	20088422	4761030	3586994	9035102	1017291	566089
河　南 Henan	15301811	1790413	2506257	7908005	582692	288819
湖　北 Hubei	3677363	834947	666319	2431152	128589	85478
湖　南 Hunan	14253052	2985894	1607267	5849860	589766	151285
广　东 Guangdong	9657231	2371426	1635298	5985771	574664	345476
广　西 Guangxi	7632009	1368428	1047116	2736916	285507	57017
海　南 Hainan	1306926	269140	175586	428205	113320	26356
重　庆 Chongqing	3438346	604368	631484	2069448	292528	203173
四　川 Sichuan	7004135	1338163	1509994	3701409	287930	471333
贵　州 Guizhou	1686052	392292	248337	597489	67317	24013
云　南 Yunnan	7429481	1104048	637099	2170385	194653	8254
西　藏 Tibet	0	0	0	0	0	0
陕　西 Shaanxi	6302483	731074	1158914	3969110	364056	179836
甘　肃 Gansu	2254634	320627	440958	1008414	38962	7927
青　海 Qinghai	298165	42153	54428	59488	1575	524
宁　夏 Ningxia	592082	58035	114650	182199	18246	14530
新　疆 Xinjiang	4794183	416781	361724	549488	12968	53263

况(学校产权)

in High Vocational Schools(Owned by HEIs)

单位:人

Unit: in Person

资料情况 Resources (片) & Magazines (Disk) 当年新增 New Floor Space Added in Current Year	拥有教学用计算机(台) No. of computers used for Instruction	语音实验室座位数(个) No. of Seats in Audio-Labs	多媒体教室座位数(个) No. of Seats in Multimedia Class rooms	网上教学课程数(种) No. of Web-Based Courses	固定资产值(万元) Fixed Assets (in 10000 yuan) 合 计 Total	其中:教学、科研仪器设备资产 of which: Teaching Equipment & Instruments 小 计 Total	 当年新增 New Floor Space Added in Current Year
1390885	**583307**	**154996**	**401019**	**12366**	**4211802.92**	**758625.10**	**109414.96**
274983	18076	4782	9834	482	89662.77	25902.90	1893.03
3115	14225	3693	6294	146	52772.81	15057.59	1541.45
90391	33938	12322	30447	2504	233483.27	44962.24	5554.31
5609	10044	2968	5455	0	274413.13	49032.22	1650.08
4906	8157	2926	4741	91	41227.53	7673.56	1327.56
2179	28565	8637	15482	229	147247.78	32616.08	4491.68
1101	7002	2343	3292	118	49863.24	8064.52	588.42
1031	10381	2953	6223	291	58107.22	12846.26	1018.06
14439	15166	2701	17325	17	124978.59	24702.24	2634.17
80938	33920	7142	24814	1099	290828.91	52600.15	6851.99
45366	57790	9237	40800	783	434911.76	77190.81	14704.09
69026	24732	6622	17742	474	261769.23	31181.66	4904.01
0	0	0	0	0	0.00	0.00	0.00
9975	17358	4775	9552	218	355549.04	20138.01	2964.41
56440	47467	16165	38683	1492	390229.63	61270.58	11316.61
33259	35470	9926	21728	482	192732.62	44408.35	7012.73
28130	11794	4352	11354	325	70342.16	13206.57	1667.50
19211	53674	12848	28143	1060	218192.95	55240.76	10710.37
219830	42825	11012	41977	778	258584.18	57866.67	9611.57
13260	18756	5406	12466	293	96430.53	20498.31	2703.37
15346	1973	589	2197	38	18862.36	3003.04	345.37
133270	17702	4086	8330	115	132906.34	16068.97	2849.44
149502	28447	6645	13949	604	127769.07	30658.83	5176.63
790	4218	1233	4548	36	17436.25	3474.03	815.47
2603	11185	2903	8493	0	83640.67	13202.74	2396.14
0	0	0	0	0	0.00	0.00	0.00
51548	18690	5288	9947	344	110947.33	21277.38	2870.51
2187	5395	1587	3091	169	25754.65	5151.98	1071.20
174	703	49	879	20	3812.63	928.66	46.90
10713	2096	320	1299	50	13532.77	7350.39	320.79
51563	3558	1486	1934	108	35813.50	3049.60	377.10

职业高中学校资产情况(非
Condition of Fixed Assets and Teaching Resources

地 区 Region	学校占地面积(平方米) Area of School sites (m^2)			图书音像 Audio-visual ed.		
	小 计 Total	其中:绿化用地面积 Of Which: Green Arens	其中:运动场地面积 Of Which: Sports Areas	一般图书(万册) Books & Magazines in Libraries(10 Thouand Volume)		电子图书 Electronic Books in Libraries
				小 计 Total	当年新增 New Floor Space Added in Current Year	小 计 Total
合 计 Total	**11855692**	**1845331**	**2294176**	**2689687**	**227414**	**106861**
北 京 Beijing	282492	81480	60422	183105	920	36690
天 津 Tianjin	157559	7120	52966	180032	4920	3139
河 北 Hebei	882625	91534	153608	232970	19770	1988
山 西 Shanxi	219806	11690	56124	20229	2400	500
内蒙古 Inner Mongolia	195881	7458	68718	85663	11662	2105
辽 宁 Liaoning	557253	77340	210067	133515	9912	1411
吉 林 Jilin	98993	30377	18200	20300	1300	0
黑龙江 Heilongjiang	102604	3200	52121	64932	656	0
上 海 Shanghai	78302	46672	9216	11000	200	100
江 苏 Jiangsu	154529	56282	57107	7000	600	0
浙 江 Zhejiang	815051	57986	179835	189451	34863	1300
安 徽 Anhui	104927	27477	30686	123423	19100	4350
福 建 Fujian	0	0	0	0	0	0
江 西 Jiangxi	880756	205554	138654	220800	29250	10346
山 东 Shandong	937274	170482	194621	314028	22755	1869
河 南 Henan	393025	29900	97246	148942	20892	6878
湖 北 Hubei	115481	6211	19070	30710	413	13000
湖 南 Hunan	1436214	204840	207451	182585	14300	5645
广 东 Guangdong	1791742	203618	161999	110811	5756	213
广 西 Guangxi	409369	62001	103779	98672	15500	11428
海 南 Hainan	261338	130580	22317	20543	2587	800
重 庆 Chongqing	235941	35076	46733	52833	1086	3391
四 川 Sichuan	474393	73383	77887	42166	3066	0
贵 州 Guizhou	248120	97818	22670	10800	0	48
云 南 Yunnan	66957	12857	27471	38781	500	0
西 藏 Tibet	0	0	0	0	0	0
陕 西 Shaanxi	658461	55306	159345	98876	2970	1530
甘 肃 Gansu	120286	10500	38858	42308	1800	100
青 海 Qinghai	0	0	0	0	0	0
宁 夏 Ningxia	30000	10000	5000	0	0	0
新 疆 Xinjiang	146313	38589	22005	25212	236	30

学校产权中独立使用)
in High Vocational Schools (Not Owned by HEIs)

单位:人
Unit: in Person

资料情况 Resources (片) & Magazines (Disk) 当年新增 New Floor Space Added in Current Year	拥有教学用计算机(台) No. of computers used for Instruction	语音实验室座位数(个) No. of Seats in Audio-Labs	多媒体教室座位数(个) No. of Seats in Multimedia Class rooms	网上教学课程数(种) No. of Web-Based Courses	固定资产值(万元) Fixed Assets (in 10000 yuan) 合计 Total	其中:教学、科研仪器设备资产 of which: Teaching Equipment & Instruments 小计 Total	当年新增 New Floor Space Added in Current Year
18038	**19936**	**6772**	**8755**	**758**	**117237.95**	**30941.40**	**5646.18**
6	879	246	319	16	5571.76	3184.50	110.00
125	875	433	168	16	4246.94	1273.00	221.00
598	995	725	431	4	8916.57	1556.97	174.87
100	224	36	0	0	2673.10	343.40	81.70
1970	386	15	56	22	1197.52	65.78	19.58
186	1124	647	640	68	6253.20	1745.30	250.00
0	135	56	80	0	1064.38	175.62	2.60
0	528	82	112	15	634.80	461.10	3.00
0	98	50	0	0	167.00	120.00	0.00
0	131	0	0	0	153.00	31.00	13.00
486	1972	335	866	6	15743.98	1877.50	447.00
4100	700	45	105	4	2418.83	508.00	158.00
0	0	0	0	0	0.00	0.00	0.00
3683	2644	736	619	68	10698.20	2673.30	1490.00
486	1587	601	1061	10	11929.19	2344.29	556.07
2563	766	289	556	17	3151.00	480.92	172.92
0	175	161	137	0	1434.22	179.60	2.00
1905	1902	457	867	32	7089.08	2696.56	232.60
32	1608	429	995	394	9435.76	1758.00	262.24
950	297	169	207	12	388.08	284.48	46.60
200	171	1	146	20	1629.00	210.00	48.00
180	650	350	460	3	4054.64	1137.36	71.00
0	630	172	200	50	3285.96	682.00	17.00
48	171	104	171	0	3018.25	1065.00	750.00
0	230	0	0	0	5168.49	4729.67	9.00
0	0	0	0	0	0.00	0.00	0.00
370	651	241	385	1	3077.00	843.20	226.50
50	216	0	68	0	1124.00	256.35	200.00
0	0	0	0	0	0.00	0.00	0.00
0	0	0	0	0	50.00	0.00	0.00
0	191	392	106	0	2664.00	258.50	81.50

其他机构资产情

Condition of Fixed Assets and Teaching Resources

地 区 Region	学校占地面积(平方米) Area of School sites (m^2)			图书音像 Audio-visual ed.		
				一般图书(万册) Books & Magazines in Libraries(10 Thouand Volume)		电子图书 Electronic Books in Libraries
	小 计 Total	其中:绿化用地面积 Of Which: Green Arens	其中:运动场地面积 Of Which: Sports Areas	小 计 Total	当年新增 New Floor Space Added in Current Year	小 计 Total
合 计 Total	**23650122**	**5174740**	**2921536**	**15130770**	**866880**	**247166**
北 京 Beijing	244792	0	0	65800	0	0
天 津 Tianjin	79047	4200	5650	124300	13600	3400
河 北 Hebei	4267774	600517	419556	2597303	101981	75475
山 西 Shanxi	129160	39650	45300	72500	2000	0
内蒙古 Inner Mongolia	285944	6156	35308	74650	0	10
辽 宁 Liaoning	0	0	0	0	0	0
吉 林 Jilin	1824778	407482	294521	1553071	28355	2470
黑龙江 Heilongjiang	17760	2800	1100	4110	1000	17
上 海 Shanghai	42541	6360	15445	107405	17557	0
江 苏 Jiangsu	1622310	285548	266850	922800	59884	7308
浙 江 Zhejiang	873296	109211	143006	591446	35374	3079
安 徽 Anhui	1093368	239018	197447	783069	46440	4538
福 建 Fujian	853838	186695	90615	826712	21951	21573
江 西 Jiangxi	316739	96500	22105	333500	20100	600
山 东 Shandong	1780741	449602	158332	606876	67194	22445
河 南 Henan	1008100	551274	111360	474490	25472	1310
湖 北 Hubei	510664	103740	118169	530538	15270	4790
湖 南 Hunan	3133644	883059	310366	1470001	38970	31558
广 东 Guangdong	1343732	287778	290625	1333662	217510	12842
广 西 Guangxi	300674	105492	59320	490305	18489	31387
海 南 Hainan	1059090	145027	70053	606903	56325	1950
重 庆 Chongqing	240591	13415	20130	92276	5548	356
四 川 Sichuan	0	0	0	0	0	0
贵 州 Guizhou	72136	11100	14740	69163	0	0
云 南 Yunnan	0	0	0	18700	11050	50
西 藏 Tibet	70036	16215	50000	2000	2000	0
陕 西 Shaanxi	178303	33810	5863	121130	12580	3570
甘 肃 Gansu	221073	17313	31500	287200	20000	2050
青 海 Qinghai	0	0	0	0	0	0
宁 夏 Ningxia	475640	106621	55250	194000	18000	80
新 疆 Xinjiang	1604351	466157	88925	776860	10230	16308

况(学校产权)

in Other Institutions(Owned by HEIs)

单位:人

Unit: in Person

资料情况 Resources (片) & Magazines (Disk) 当年新增 New Floor Space Added in Current Year	拥有教学用计算机(台) No. of computers used for Instruction	语音实验室座位数(个) No. of Seats in Audio-Labs	多媒体教室座位数(个) No. of Seats in Multimedia Class rooms	网上教学课程数(种) No. of Web-Based Courses	固定资产值(万元) Fixed Assets (in 10000 yuan) 合计 Total	其中:教学、科研仪器设备资产 of which: Teaching Equipment & Instruments 小计 Total	当年新增 New Floor Space Added in Current Year
98060	**67506**	**24276**	**56199**	**3084**	**1006083.73**	**380806.68**	**19697.54**
0	32	36	31	0	91.19	63.22	1.18
800	563	282	224	0	2117.39	943.00	82.00
25769	7954	5262	8953	69	98362.28	17494.03	1501.89
0	137	18	12	0	5337.60	3680.40	3433.73
0	135	56	1	0	3024.30	170.10	0.00
0	0	0	0	0	0.00	0.00	0.00
192	7443	1961	3358	29	90771.00	15028.48	3264.16
0	2646	506	200	0	2720.00	677.40	4.00
0	532	150	244	0	2795.10	1076.19	126.44
720	4791	1496	5197	2228	103113.16	18691.31	1264.39
1859	4164	984	5490	9	35289.00	4824.49	621.71
718	2524	881	2064	18	28235.63	4848.56	940.16
12169	2473	840	3120	3	30723.39	6124.39	571.39
119	2170	644	644	10	6455.60	2152.80	723.60
20590	3211	915	2484	67	45847.28	10737.24	2140.00
10	1522	461	1261	32	18598.37	2995.00	59.50
800	4491	518	2667	140	30575.10	4675.62	621.40
285	7664	1284	3864	247	350720.80	255412.63	849.70
958	5850	2356	8638	20	62419.42	11732.99	870.28
30360	1605	322	2474	84	13178.87	3256.66	570.54
601	2383	1054	3046	5	32473.00	3874.00	937.00
50	1176	296	291	20	5911.55	2153.05	301.50
0	0	0	0	1	0.00	0.00	0.00
0	161	100	230	0	511.70	421.70	3.80
10	391	726	60	0	313.50	268.50	105.60
0	60	30	50	58	0.00	0.00	0.00
1070	984	133	213	30	4469.50	1729.50	207.00
200	467	112	345	2	9198.00	826.00	30.00
0	0	0	0	0	0.00	0.00	0.00
25	544	100	140	6	6294.00	796.00	230.00
755	1433	2753	898	6	16537.00	6153.42	236.57

其他机构资产情况(非学

Condition of Fixed Assets and Teaching Resources

地　区 Region	学校占地面积(平方米) Area of School sites (m^2) 小　计 Total	其中:绿化用地面积 Of Which: Green Arens	其中:运动场地面积 Of Which: Sports Areas	图书音像 Audio-visual ed. 一般图书(万册) Books & Magazines in Libraries(10 Thouand Volume) 小　计 Total	当年新增 New Floor Space Added in Current Year	电子图书 Electronic Books in Libraries 小　计 Total
合　计 Total	**1775910**	**681301**	**225733**	**454005**	**7850**	**438**
北　京 Beijing	0	0	0	0	0	0
天　津 Tianjin	4920	0	0	0	0	0
河　北 Hebei	848744	501776	35000	300000	2000	200
山　西 Shanxi	12200	1100	4300	13000	0	0
内蒙古 Inner Mongolia	34423	6000	1000	3400	0	0
辽　宁 Liaoning	0	0	0	0	0	0
吉　林 Jilin	0	0	0	0	0	0
黑龙江 Heilongjiang	0	0	0	0	0	0
上　海 Shanghai	0	0	0	0	0	0
江　苏 Jiangsu	50081	3650	4160	13000	200	0
浙　江 Zhejiang	94379	22446	17553	0	0	0
安　徽 Anhui	0	0	0	0	0	0
福　建 Fujian	28906	8738	18568	250	100	0
江　西 Jiangxi	30000	3000	7000	2000	0	0
山　东 Shandong	32453	5717	8300	8000	0	0
河　南 Henan	150177	46200	41515	0	0	0
湖　北 Hubei	44850	8410	2620	8500	500	0
湖　南 Hunan	10712	1000	3000	5000	0	0
广　东 Guangdong	10449	1471	2362	7595	250	0
广　西 Guangxi	0	0	0	0	0	0
海　南 Hainan	0	0	0	0	0	0
重　庆 Chongqing	127440	3486	5844	3000	3000	0
四　川 Sichuan	0	0	0	0	0	0
贵　州 Guizhou	21400	2000	18600	0	0	0
云　南 Yunnan	118096	37390	8900	6000	1000	20
西　藏 Tibet	0	0	0	0	0	0
陕　西 Shaanxi	99134	18415	32709	8660	800	218
甘　肃 Gansu	15912	1000	8000	45000	0	0
青　海 Qinghai	0	0	0	0	0	0
宁　夏 Ningxia	0	0	0	0	0	0
新　疆 Xinjiang	41634	9502	6302	30600	0	0

校产权中独立使用)
in Other Institutions (Not Owned by HEIs)

单位:人

Unit: in Person

资料情况 Resources (片) & Magazines (Disk) 当年新增 New Floor Space Added in Current Year	拥有教学用计算机(台) No. of computers used for Instruction	语音实验室座位数(个) No. of Seats in Audio-Labs	多媒体教室座位数(个) No. of Seats in Multimedia Class rooms	网上教学课程数(种) No. of Web-Based Courses	固定资产值(万元) Fixed Assets (in 10000 yuan) 合计 Total	其中:教学、科研仪器设备资产 of which: Teaching Equipment & Instruments 小计 Total	当年新增 New Floor Space Added in Current Year
81	**1847**	**631**	**983**	**63**	**23056.17**	**4669.80**	**337.10**
0	0	0	0	0	0.00	0.00	0.00
0	0	0	0	0	0.00	0.00	0.00
0	571	266	294	60	11247.87	2062.00	50.00
0	15	0	0	0	220.00	200.00	20.00
0	24	0	0	0	67.80	0.50	0.00
0	0	0	0	0	0.00	0.00	0.00
0	0	0	0	0	0.00	0.00	0.00
0	0	0	0	0	0.00	0.00	0.00
0	0	0	0	0	0.00	0.00	0.00
0	112	0	0	0	764.00	263.00	0.00
0	0	0	0	0	0.00	0.00	0.00
0	0	0	0	0	0.00	0.00	0.00
0	0	0	0	0	0.00	0.00	0.00
0	100	0	180	0	1500.00	37.00	0.00
0	16	0	0	0	1071.00	85.70	9.00
0	0	0	0	0	0.00	0.00	0.00
0	10	0	0	0	1580.00	132.00	20.00
0	30	0	0	0	800.00	0.00	0.00
0	30	0	1	0	589.00	100.00	10.00
0	0	0	0	0	0.00	0.00	0.00
0	0	0	0	0	0.00	0.00	0.00
0	50	100	65	0	490.00	58.00	50.00
0	0	0	0	0	0.00	0.00	0.00
0	40	0	0	0	233.00	24.00	0.00
20	123	100	100	0	400.00	50.00	0.00
0	0	0	0	0	0.00	0.00	0.00
61	366	85	63	3	2153.50	917.60	128.10
0	120	0	120	0	0.00	0.00	0.00
0	0	0	0	0	0.00	0.00	0.00
0	0	0	0	0	0.00	0.00	0.00
0	240	80	160	0	1940.00	740.00	50.00

中等职业学校(机构)校舍情况(总计)

Conditions of School Buidings in Secondary Vocational Schools (Regional Aggregates)

单位:平方米

Unit:m^2

地　区 Region	学校产权建筑面积 Floor Area of School Building Owned by HEIs				正在施工面积 Floor Area Under Construction	独立使用非学校产权建筑面积 Floor Area of School Building Not Owned by HEIs
	合　计 Subtotal	其中:危房 Of Which: Dilapidated Buildings	其中:当年新增 Of Which: Newly Added in Current Year	其中:被外单位借用 Of Which: Floor Space Hired by Other Schools or Units		
合　计 Total	**161490486**	**1579309**	**8487882**	**610543**	**5545278**	**7841276**
北　京 Beijing	2641833	4689	78334	19007	58217	229034
天　津 Tianjin	2189582	862	136623	15753	57892	155561
河　北 Hebei	9961348	38675	377898	29293	216648	451580
山　西 Shanxi	4216169	62227	205707	20061	187291	88963
内蒙古 Inner Mongolia	2491919	96145	89730	9085	53386	60303
辽　宁 Liaoning	4544026	9960	250140	9030	222571	499639
吉　林 Jilin	3096834	17209	62954	3952	111928	123584
黑龙江 Heilongjiang	2684503	16739	77308	99468	26407	45691
上　海 Shanghai	2771668	772	129401	33621	67002	299233
江　苏 Jiangsu	9544945	8577	523880	69145	331231	153311
浙　江 Zhejiang	7270218	3861	923808	17145	393196	528450
安　徽 Anhui	6641886	210793	323286	43160	203953	100452
福　建 Fujian	5104170	22475	279351	1630	276020	280151
江　西 Jiangxi	3954080	43724	282669	7980	303443	212687
山　东 Shandong	13348455	71657	680751	26086	650143	448266
河　南 Henan	11944338	167831	520346	16827	346593	407165
湖　北 Hubei	7342663	46975	352040	33273	63903	162094
湖　南 Hunan	9052580	57713	372480	5515	284534	1074324
广　东 Guangdong	11968787	46411	612399	43997	305471	632636
广　西 Guangxi	6650944	77709	244681	5350	208780	238460
海　南 Hainan	1323887	17383	122145	1797	41283	57078
重　庆 Chongqing	4110076	47749	332128	3461	248299	320097
四　川 Sichuan	8005843	81889	358521	26561	209878	617700
贵　州 Guizhou	2700478	32830	98107	29224	75224	81171
云　南 Yunnan	4600401	135778	256638	5828	114992	155687
西　藏 Tibet	208222	6608	6712	0	18098	1285
陕　西 Shaanxi	5798939	87672	418094	21316	307455	356841
甘　肃 Gansu	3655417	96783	162831	2554	121231	49400
青　海 Qinghai	405121	18501	5616	24	1229	920
宁　夏 Ningxia	547133	936	81545	0	4444	1307
新　疆 Xinjiang	2714021	48176	121759	10400	34536	8206

普通中专学校校舍情况

Conditions of School Buidings in Specialized Sec. Schools

单位:平方米

Unit:m^2

地 区 Region	学校产权建筑面积 Floor Area of School Building Owned by HEIs				正在施工面积 Floor Area Under Construction	独立使用非学校产权建筑面积 Floor Area of School Building Not Owned by HEIs
	合 计 Subtotal	其中:危房 Of Which: Dilapidated Buildings	其中:当年新增 Of Which: Newly Added in Current Year	其中:被外单位借用 Of Which: Floor Space Hired by Other Schools or Units		
合 计 Total	**77693422**	**435867**	**3446001**	**294927**	**2916091**	**2408806**
北 京 Beijing	1260688	0	56379	1402	17193	115456
天 津 Tianjin	1140555	562	115258	15453	48612	48401
河 北 Hebei	3232549	4489	177385	6618	128739	181217
山 西 Shanxi	2323815	27587	51837	5767	99354	36574
内蒙古 Inner Mongolia	1380860	7334	34521	8715	23830	2610
辽 宁 Liaoning	2301106	5486	128052	0	105654	195986
吉 林 Jilin	1209175	9867	18584	0	12162	47934
黑龙江 Heilongjiang	1290481	3297	62367	96717	18269	0
上 海 Shanghai	1816966	365	108790	19222	61302	235786
江 苏 Jiangsu	3915545	3881	229716	17589	170772	28295
浙 江 Zhejiang	1454199	0	59741	1240	149997	130855
安 徽 Anhui	2826549	37455	156895	21888	75700	29740
福 建 Fujian	4686240	22275	272626	1498	273978	278551
江 西 Jiangxi	1818364	2667	56660	145	188063	22699
山 东 Shandong	5161870	15530	152789	19736	309416	82720
河 南 Henan	5739789	20257	228254	11003	232373	109326
湖 北 Hubei	4641653	18970	272435	2098	48949	83195
湖 南 Hunan	2996311	7619	83783	0	101807	67585
广 东 Guangdong	6505624	15137	292571	16599	140056	316671
广 西 Guangxi	3681982	18064	156369	1624	133369	23824
海 南 Hainan	703587	4684	32345	684	11523	23909
重 庆 Chongqing	1129183	14176	51814	0	8126	35852
四 川 Sichuan	3654751	22038	169806	21697	126470	154632
贵 州 Guizhou	2059468	24932	47400	6435	56577	16361
云 南 Yunnan	2680159	46320	118271	2717	39751	73924
西 藏 Tibet	187976	6608	6712	0	18098	1285
陕 西 Shaanxi	2928838	12957	124691	10121	176755	60842
甘 肃 Gansu	2728817	43103	119242	1735	115117	4576
青 海 Qinghai	270877	15652	3388	24	0	0
宁 夏 Ningxia	260694	0	9043	0	1944	0
新 疆 Xinjiang	1704751	24555	48277	4200	22135	0

成人中专学校校舍情况

Conditions of School Buidings in Specialized Sec. Schools for Adults

单位：平方米

Unit：m²

地　区 Rgion	学校产权建筑面积 Floor Area of School Building Owned by HEIs				正在施工面积 Floor Area Under Construction	独立使用非学校产权建筑面积 Floor Area of School Building Not Owned by HEIs
	合　计 Subtotal	其中：危房 Of Which: Dilapidated Buildings	其中：当年新增 Of Which: Newly Added in Current Year	其中：被外单位借用 Of Which: Floor Space Hired by Other Schools or Units		
合　计 Total	**19071998**	**131941**	**745278**	**89751**	**478689**	**1660792**
北　京 Beijing	135629	0	0	12840	0	31238
天　津 Tianjin	72045	0	0	0	0	6404
河　北 Hebei	1113963	1637	21497	965	9867	41794
山　西 Shanxi	453587	9632	1190	8563	8284	10448
内蒙古 Inner Mongolia	257173	7477	2251	370	1200	2662
辽　宁 Liaoning	28276	0	840	750	100	5558
吉　林 Jilin	394276	0	522	3952	4224	31832
黑龙江 Heilongjiang	500565	840	4149	1886	5418	10046
上　海 Shanghai	197889	0	458	0	0	30408
江　苏 Jiangsu	1501859	0	20188	15107	8744	68432
浙　江 Zhejiang	620167	0	74824	3976	24515	8838
安　徽 Anhui	517869	2056	8859	7520	8330	23155
福　建 Fujian	0	0	0	0	0	0
江　西 Jiangxi	412519	770	36473	354	19262	13688
山　东 Shandong	1885136	6148	142591	5495	182072	128039
河　南 Henan	1867627	14755	82187	2814	21551	200437
湖　北 Hubei	891494	2210	20980	2657	2079	16441
湖　南 Hunan	897294	741	13915	480	6380	325818
广　东 Guangdong	1684169	7420	67388	7831	33468	143445
广　西 Guangxi	1103295	21958	21781	3631	21089	14953
海　南 Hainan	67569	860	3085	1113	2500	1582
重　庆 Chongqing	994210	8457	134105	1300	80017	158007
四　川 Sichuan	1322076	10454	6753	2883	15613	315186
贵　州 Guizhou	178346	0	5900	0	8000	34113
云　南 Yunnan	519495	12084	50020	1511	5847	9548
西　藏 Tibet	9928	0	0	0	0	0
陕　西 Shaanxi	823530	11611	8160	2274	8800	10648
甘　肃 Gansu	314481	8808	13736	819	0	15845
青　海 Qinghai	78169	260	0	0	1229	920
宁　夏 Ningxia	44893	0	199	0	100	1307
新　疆 Xinjiang	184469	3763	3227	660	0	0

职业高中学校校舍情况

Conditions of School Buidings in Vocational High Schools

单位:平方米

Unit:m²

地　区 Region	学校产权建筑面积 Floor Area of School Building Owned by HEIs				正在施工面积 Floor Area Under Construction	独立使用非学校产权建筑面积 Floor Area of School Building Not Owned by HEIs
	计 Subtotal	其中:危房 Of Which: Dilapidated Buildings	其中:当年新增 Of Which: Newly Added in Current Year	其中:被外单位借用 Of Which: Floor Space Hired by Other Schools or Units		
合　计 Total	**56005517**	**975124**	**3694603**	**173613**	**1849582**	**3325895**
北　京 Beijing	1202650	4122	21955	4765	41024	78594
天　津 Tianjin	890204	300	21365	100	9280	95346
河　北 Hebei	3993128	32289	156450	19660	52812	78038
山　西 Shanxi	1392457	25008	137080	5731	57653	40671
内蒙古 Inner Mongolia	794312	78664	52958	0	28356	55031
辽　宁 Liaoning	2214644	4474	121248	8280	116817	298095
吉　林 Jilin	640344	7342	3638	0	11984	19118
黑龙江 Heilongjiang	882817	12602	10792	865	2720	35645
上　海 Shanghai	728581	407	20153	8694	5700	33039
江　苏 Jiangsu	3592406	4696	259827	22293	135090	47060
浙　江 Zhejiang	4860002	3861	774404	11929	218684	355850
安　徽 Anhui	2926223	165183	120675	12842	98888	47487
福　建 Fujian	0	0	0	0	0	0
江　西 Jiangxi	1544517	40287	182142	7481	96118	163020
山　东 Shandong	5902721	48307	329140	855	153995	224368
河　南 Henan	4039225	131698	204375	2000	92669	96440
湖　北 Hubei	1408951	15638	43037	1929	10075	46668
湖　南 Hunan	4219008	45118	160140	3535	153477	653301
广　东 Guangdong	3128737	23854	215992	19567	117637	161877
广　西 Guangxi	1643854	37687	62459	95	28323	199683
海　南 Hainan	263129	11839	3669	0	0	28747
重　庆 Chongqing	1779209	25116	137027	2161	150929	103635
四　川 Sichuan	3029016	49397	181962	1981	67795	147882
贵　州 Guizhou	415465	7898	44807	22789	10647	28937
云　南 Yunnan	1392563	77374	88347	1600	69394	31615
西　藏 Tibet	0	0	0	0	0	0
陕　西 Shaanxi	1979847	63104	285123	8921	98600	238596
甘　肃 Gansu	549777	44872	29853	0	6114	17002
青　海 Qinghai	56075	2589	2228	0	0	0
宁　夏 Ningxia	125658	936	5403	0	2400	0
新　疆 Xinjiang	409997	10462	18354	5540	12401	150

其他机构

Conditions of School Buidings

	学校产权 Floor Area of School	
地区 Region	合计 Subtotal	其中:危房 Of Which: Dilapidated Buildings
合计 Total	**8719549**	**36377**
北京 Beijing	42866	567
天津 Tianjin	86778	0
河北 Hebei	1621708	260
山西 Shanxi	46310	0
内蒙古 Inner Mongolia	59574	2670
辽宁 Liaoning	0	0
吉林 Jilin	853039	0
黑龙江 Heilongjiang	10640	0
上海 Shanghai	28232	0
江苏 Jiangsu	535135	0
浙江 Zhejiang	335850	0
安徽 Anhui	371245	6099
福建 Fujian	417930	200
江西 Jiangxi	178680	0
山东 Shandong	398728	1672
河南 Henan	297697	1121
湖北 Hubei	400565	10157
湖南 Hunan	939967	4235
广东 Guangdong	650257	0
广西 Guangxi	221813	0
海南 Hainan	289602	0
重庆 Chongqing	207474	0
四川 Sichuan	0	0
贵州 Guizhou	47199	0
云南 Yunnan	8184	0
西藏 Tibet	10318	0
陕西 Shaanxi	66724	0
甘肃 Gansu	62342	0
青海 Qinghai	0	0
宁夏 Ningxia	115888	0
新疆 Xinjiang	414804	9396

校舍情况
in Other Institutions

单位：平方米

Unit：m²

建筑面积 Buiding Owned by HEIs 其中：当年新增 Of Which：Newly Added in CurrentYear	其中：被外单位借用 Of Which：Floor Space Hired by OtherSchools or Units	正在施工面积 Floor AreaUnder Construction	独立使用非学校产权建筑面积 FloorArea of School Building Not Owned by HEIs
602000	**52252**	**300916**	**445783**
0	0	0	3746
0	200	0	5410
22566	2050	25230	150531
15600	0	22000	1270
0	0	0	0
0	0	0	0
40210	0	83558	24700
0	0	0	0
0	5705	0	0
14149	14156	16625	9524
14839	0	0	32907
36857	910	21035	70
6725	132	2042	1600
7394	0	0	13280
56231	0	4660	13139
5530	1010	0	962
15588	26589	2800	15790
114642	1500	22870	27620
36448	0	14310	10643
4072	0	25999	0
83046	0	27260	2840
9182	0	9227	22603
0	0	0	0
0	0	0	1760
0	0	0	40600
0	0	0	0
120	0	23300	46755
0	0	0	1197
0	0	0	0
66900	0	0	0
51901	0	0	8056

职业技术培训

Basic Statistics of Vocational

地　区 Region	学校数(所) Schools	教学班(点) (个)External Teaching Sites (classes)	结业生数 Graduates 计 Total	其中:女 Of which: Female
合　计 Total	**230667**	**668538**	**66774722**	**29521906**
北　京 Beijing	3360	23124	2725030	1353825
天　津 Tianjin	2638	10617	721822	314481
河　北 Hebei	9871	33295	3903119	1748190
山　西 Shanxi	9479	20599	1828684	740295
内蒙古 Inner Mongolia	5439	6002	525043	224229
辽　宁 Liaoning	3791	14245	1708147	628218
吉　林 Jilin	1972	3507	661083	229017
黑龙江 Heilongjiang	5397	14144	2190906	914288
上　海 Shanghai	726	20404	1159963	580911
江　苏 Jiangsu	13313	87250	6363936	3042433
浙　江 Zhejiang	12337	57124	4946107	2065382
安　徽 Anhui	3960	11029	1606897	591120
福　建 Fujian	7446	19331	1957393	930563
江　西 Jiangxi	5823	7968	860230	395892
山　东 Shandong	22455	47968	5054865	2377786
河　南 Henan	26408	45899	5380540	2448606
湖　北 Hubei	4155	12019	955303	376584
湖　南 Hunan	1402	4715	230219	105478
广　东 Guangdong	2247	19106	1698605	730874
广　西 Guangxi	6049	23845	2779466	1171160
海　南 Hainan	1289	3272	217846	96949
重　庆 Chongqing	9802	29795	3076506	1132885
四　川 Sichuan	17926	42602	4065056	1919858
贵　州 Guizhou	12511	18271	2248044	960634
云　南 Yunnan	12033	44105	5464759	2588698
西　藏 Tibet	0	0	0	0
陕　西 Shaanxi	16711	22822	1914477	831984
甘　肃 Gansu	8139	14422	1290446	547953
青　海 Qinghai	2246	4566	415508	155735
宁　夏 Ningxia	516	559	39718	17115
新　疆 Xinjiang	1226	5933	785004	300763

机构基本情况(总计)

Technical Training Institutions (Total)

注册学生数 Enrolment		教职工数 Teachers, Staff & Workers		聘请校外教师 Part-time Teachers
小 计 total	其中:女 Of which: Female	小 计 Total	其中:专任教师 Of which: Full-time Teacher	
53799582	**24107405**	**457157**	**205952**	**458585**
1797288	971480	44963	19469	23107
414944	190452	5534	2326	7836
2960695	1333784	17353	8126	19265
1494018	602909	20429	7187	16015
518259	234095	6361	2881	6318
1012212	455541	11247	6813	8661
734952	256785	3745	2560	1748
1728139	694233	23216	12560	10173
1118109	571594	15462	5460	13044
5705527	2627803	31724	15921	35140
4899884	2032703	19887	9472	34908
1302463	518896	7114	1855	12578
1801654	837038	8360	4446	15945
750282	349571	6557	1945	10883
4213670	2001581	55248	32284	35670
4467015	2004158	28957	16713	31953
531722	245455	8532	4863	7887
192193	89441	5684	2756	2925
1436924	638397	21248	12096	12077
2051113	877505	16025	4086	14956
205126	100021	2551	616	2844
2313563	937330	8601	2828	14552
3144776	1573581	15819	8888	28033
2152480	930866	24237	2402	16847
3062474	1381513	5945	468	24671
0	0	0	0	0
1603534	755205	20536	9757	30937
1161540	509929	17780	5903	14539
259506	80835	1157	164	1650
41788	16466	358	164	281
723732	288238	2527	943	3142

职工技术培训

Basic Statistics of Vocational

地区 Region	学校数(所) Schools	教学班(点)(个)External Teaching Sites (classes)	结业生数 Graduates	
			小计 Total	其中:女 Of which: Female
合 计 Total	**4944**	**42828**	**3164059**	**1323552**
北 京 Beijing	38	557	38108	17671
天 津 Tianjin	45	708	23996	11250
河 北 Hebei	481	6394	256269	159543
山 西 Shanxi	152	3610	322927	115295
内蒙古 Inner Mongolia	13	83	9069	4636
辽 宁 Liaoning	549	2656	374473	93217
吉 林 Jilin	87	85	12691	6280
黑龙江 Heilongjiang	159	1551	95420	24550
上 海 Shanghai	105	2855	202380	58873
江 苏 Jiangsu	701	10268	544313	243951
浙 江 Zhejiang	426	3031	262542	114130
安 徽 Anhui	7	53	2597	1033
福 建 Fujian	375	2263	172962	73931
江 西 Jiangxi	349	369	81609	33328
山 东 Shandong	110	477	81704	38171
河 南 Henan	416	1260	126990	64357
湖 北 Hubei	157	2201	50723	26188
湖 南 Hunan	36	664	26532	14128
广 东 Guangdong	116	717	58825	27275
广 西 Guangxi	90	453	84166	35831
海 南 Hainan	24	117	4333	2148
重 庆 Chongqing	7	27	3660	2743
四 川 Sichuan	218	1128	226618	110804
贵 州 Guizhou	18	163	7477	3223
云 南 Yunnan	4	8	165	84
西 藏 Tibet	0	0	0	0
陕 西 Shaanxi	125	303	30383	15040
甘 肃 Gansu	68	593	42792	17212
青 海 Qinghai	43	22	943	359
宁 夏 Ningxia	9	39	10294	3997
新 疆 Xinjiang	16	173	9098	4304

学校基本情况
Technical Training Schools

注册学生数 Enrolment		教职工数 Teachers, Staff & Workers		聘请校外教师 Part-time Teachers
小　计 total	其中:女 Of which: Female	小　计 Total	其中:专任教师 Of which: Full-time Teacher	
2812372	**1256456**	**44899**	**28507**	**24916**
35751	15190	592	304	153
12522	6135	703	530	514
252957	147873	2179	1087	1212
309111	108475	3247	1447	1118
7102	3437	253	159	41
200389	102404	1578	840	2700
44753	18620	1085	824	117
22552	8610	2333	1722	560
181146	48972	2854	1599	1428
578347	265817	7179	4012	6683
315213	133353	3381	2253	2400
969	530	174	127	32
128217	54624	2175	1591	1172
86067	28008	325	289	1454
45831	22494	2306	1556	643
122390	64474	2312	1622	1015
22136	10746	1706	1125	425
17741	10667	628	386	203
66622	31842	2584	2356	343
39129	17664	834	438	533
3933	1912	194	174	98
3787	2807	92	20	75
208785	106452	2891	1803	881
8757	3721	182	48	66
284	162	3	2	7
0	0	0	0	0
41869	19548	1153	736	420
35322	14050	1451	1133	481
331	139	19	0	6
11300	3346	131	121	8
9059	4384	355	203	128

农村成人文化技术

Basic Statistics of Technical

地　区 Region	学校数(所) Schools	教学班(点)(个)External Teaching Sites (classes)	结业生数 Graduates 小　计 Total	 其中:女 Of which: Female
合　计 Total	**214529**	**535023**	**57654793**	**25301441**
北　京 Beijing	1581	5859	852187	413474
天　津 Tianjin	2318	6303	543657	232715
河　北 Hebei	9139	26250	3510754	1509214
山　西 Shanxi	8727	14948	1422136	590286
内蒙古 Inner Mongolia	5390	5837	512065	217601
辽　宁 Liaoning	2637	8207	1190466	487107
吉　林 Jilin	1789	3111	637728	217255
黑龙江 Heilongjiang	4088	8762	1842260	758464
上　海 Shanghai	120	3670	267726	148278
江　苏 Jiangsu	11464	61576	5127803	2474260
浙　江 Zhejiang	10998	42289	4046056	1683255
安　徽 Anhui	3844	10822	1574308	579126
福　建 Fujian	6857	15348	1684080	800251
江　西 Jiangxi	5458	7563	772700	359610
山　东 Shandong	21460	45273	4704388	2199996
河　南 Henan	25719	44057	5213099	2366349
湖　北 Hubei	3907	9430	880703	337485
湖　南 Hunan	1247	3269	149876	61811
广　东 Guangdong	1252	11444	1178805	486952
广　西 Guangxi	5835	22501	2658093	1118745
海　南 Hainan	1213	2552	196065	86003
重　庆 Chongqing	9768	29514	3066230	1126991
四　川 Sichuan	17543	40405	3791644	1785743
贵　州 Guizhou	12443	17566	2229646	950736
云　南 Yunnan	11952	43389	5379022	2550972
西　藏 Tibet	0	0	0	0
陕　西 Shaanxi	15948	21126	1814211	786521
甘　肃 Gansu	7963	13279	1202508	513368
青　海 Qinghai	2166	4421	409119	152281
宁　夏 Ningxia	500	508	22473	10694
新　疆 Xinjiang	1203	5744	774985	295898

培训学校基本情况

Training Schools for Peasants

注册学生数 Enrolment		教职工数 Teachers, Staff & Workers		聘请校外教师 Part-time Teachers
小计 total	其中:女 Of which: Female	小计 Total	其中:专任教师 Of which: Full-time Teacher	
45494316	**20122905**	**277559**	**109941**	**366158**
475629	268012	1742	301	2851
274142	125647	1687	625	4831
2580653	1112323	13263	5652	17683
1098244	451689	13487	4058	13493
506408	228167	6065	2689	6237
647053	291079	2199	1158	4227
671040	228951	2074	1433	1502
1477705	564907	11569	4035	6213
208453	112989	906	549	2146
4288449	1966857	11979	6128	25030
3936437	1624776	10291	3898	26600
1269463	506167	6505	1494	12120
1593711	743181	3284	1052	13634
658106	318608	6183	1620	9368
3964188	1868351	43272	25286	30978
4299502	1918547	25744	14583	30108
492251	225248	6066	3231	7110
141398	62192	3300	1301	1899
898440	393796	7128	3292	5183
1963134	839052	13981	3045	14140
145517	68494	1399	136	2286
2308182	933766	8298	2657	14469
2864272	1432726	11802	6211	25338
2126625	916456	23653	2157	16639
3028819	1362133	5942	466	24131
0	0	0	0	0
1487036	701825	16642	7664	29254
1101090	485975	15750	4402	13775
253779	77400	1017	84	1644
20946	10373	199	25	259
713644	283218	2132	709	3010

地　区 Region	学校数(所) Schools	教学班(点)(个) External Teaching Sites (classes)	结业生数 Graduates 小计 Total	其中:女 Of which: Female
合　计 Total	**11194**	**90687**	**5955870**	**2896913**
北　京 Beijing	1741	16708	1834735	922680
天　津 Tianjin	275	3606	154169	70516
河　北 Hebei	251	651	136096	79433
山　西 Shanxi	600	2041	83621	34714
内蒙古 Inner Mongolia	36	82	3909	1992
辽　宁 Liaoning	605	3382	143208	47894
吉　林 Jilin	96	311	10664	5482
黑龙江 Heilongjiang	1150	3831	253226	131274
上　海 Shanghai	501	13879	689857	373760
江　苏 Jiangsu	1148	15406	691820	324222
浙　江 Zhejiang	913	11804	637509	267997
安　徽 Anhui	109	154	29992	10961
福　建 Fujian	214	1720	100351	56381
江　西 Jiangxi	16	36	5921	2954
山　东 Shandong	885	2218	268773	139619
河　南 Henan	273	582	40451	17900
湖　北 Hubei	91	388	23877	12911
湖　南 Hunan	119	782	53811	29539
广　东 Guangdong	879	6945	460975	216647
广　西 Guangxi	124	891	37207	16584
海　南 Hainan	52	603	17448	8798
重　庆 Chongqing	27	254	6616	3151
四　川 Sichuan	165	1069	46794	23311
贵　州 Guizhou	50	542	10921	6675
云　南 Yunnan	77	708	85572	37642
西　藏 Tibet	0	0	0	0
陕　西 Shaanxi	638	1393	69883	30423
甘　肃 Gansu	108	550	45146	17373
青　海 Qinghai	37	123	5446	3095
宁　夏 Ningxia	7	12	6951	2424
新　疆 Xinjiang	7	16	921	561

构基本情况
of Others

注册学生数 Enrolment		教职工数 Teachers, Staff & Workers		聘请校外教师 Part-time Teachers
小计 total	其中:女 Of which: Female	小计 Total	其中:专任教师 Of which: Full-time Teacher	
5492894	**2728044**	**134699**	**67504**	**67511**
1285908	688278	42629	18864	20103
128280	58670	3144	1171	2491
127085	73588	1911	1387	370
86663	42745	3695	1682	1404
4749	2491	43	33	40
164770	62058	7470	4815	1734
19159	9214	586	303	129
227882	120716	9314	6803	3400
728510	409633	11702	3312	9470
838731	395129	12566	5781	3427
648234	274574	6215	3321	5908
32031	12199	435	234	426
79726	39233	2901	1803	1139
6109	2955	49	36	61
203651	110736	9670	5442	4049
45123	21137	901	508	830
17335	9461	760	507	352
33054	16582	1756	1069	823
471862	212759	11536	6448	6551
48850	20789	1210	603	283
55676	29615	958	306	460
1594	757	211	151	8
71719	34403	1126	874	1814
17098	10689	402	197	142
33371	19218	0	0	533
0	0	0	0	0
74629	33832	2741	1357	1263
25128	9904	579	368	283
5396	3296	121	80	0
9542	2747	28	18	14
1029	636	40	31	4

Condition of Fixed Assets and Teaching Resources

地　区 Region	占地面积(平方米) Area of School sites (m^2)	教学行政用房 建筑面积(平方米) Administritive (m^2)	图书藏量(册) Books (Volume)
合　计 Total	**117339904**	**33593632**	**95731304**
北　京 Beijing	5450903	2102370	23861790
天　津 Tianjin	1762568	1697204	2790671
河　北 Hebei	7481574	1161782	4863090
山　西 Shanxi	2379432	738348	3201869
内蒙古 Inner Mongolia	1667642	239465	645889
辽　宁 Liaoning	1347983	535352	835240
吉　林 Jilin	1729488	341798	345427
黑龙江 Heilongjiang	4465607	1042472	2187881
上　海 Shanghai	2067289	688276	1591540
江　苏 Jiangsu	8972115	4191161	4380184
浙　江 Zhejiang	8523348	2449261	4758578
安　徽 Anhui	1885494	334544	388060
福　建 Fujian	998907	591807	1897518
江　西 Jiangxi	717413	369211	1021255
山　东 Shandong	24405931	3761254	12389491
河　南 Henan	7740901	1873135	5246887
湖　北 Hubei	9164054	3773655	1573893
湖　南 Hunan	1213050	340816	1209835
广　东 Guangdong	5481512	2172860	10471657
广　西 Guangxi	2491611	513519	1635719
海　南 Hainan	890131	135947	337204
重　庆 Chongqing	485297	266454	426971
四　川 Sichuan	2292824	1042698	1789503
贵　州 Guizhou	1489535	416370	546964
云　南 Yunnan	1793151	426729	1097594
西　藏 Tibet	0	0	0
陕　西 Shaanxi	3352295	972057	2696056
甘　肃 Gansu	5105652	1171306	2059800
青　海 Qinghai	594248	54713	143256
宁　夏 Ningxia	28634	7927	45424
新　疆 Xinjiang	1361315	181141	1292058

构资产情况

in Vocational Technical Training Institutions

教学用计算机(台)No. of computers used for Instruction	语音实验室座位数(个) No. of Seats in Audio-Labs	多媒体教室座位数(个) No. of Seats in Multimedia Class rooms	固定资产总值(万元) Fixed Assets (in 10000 yuan) 计 Total	其中:教学、实习仪器设备资产值 of which: Teaching Equipment & Instruments
364646	**104127**	**262660**	**239032806.80**	**108552038.20**
18435	5423	17256	222412799.20	102998436.50
19613	4122	4124	395073.31	30077.60
14669	3180	11222	57633.67	12268.78
6944	2037	2342	44437.99	13687.26
1562	250	990	28045.31	2075.71
8013	4618	2041	61915.85	13244.00
2995	779	476	48102.00	29685.66
19590	4651	9370	77321.58	18468.08
20578	5266	26172	115023.13	78246.37
34696	4695	28805	196434.39	51837.03
29736	12634	23002	231141.88	31570.75
1561	374	762	1220775.13	145325.66
11302	1503	13319	41659.41	13902.94
1250	1	23733	282722.88	272268.28
73869	11644	21748	8426508.37	3510573.54
9985	9592	13272	177322.91	20229.20
7293	3134	6078	1883721.28	74607.38
6218	1334	4069	357440.50	343828.69
43895	10189	26628	438971.93	179204.34
3541	1727	2230	15160.69	2819.96
583	545	618	4096.91	1221.00
1647	580	908	23688.32	18336.58
11905	4441	5596	927509.88	351762.65
1390	210	702	9657.48	894.72
1769	1065	2372	19579.88	2089.45
0	0	0	0.00	0.00
5425	3379	1332	1310970.06	164170.21
4686	735	3841	214962.67	167628.96
540	43	2	1675.20	336.60
267	0	0	297.30	80.86
689	5976	9650	8157.73	3159.41

Condition of Fixed Assets and Teaching

地　区 Region	占地面积(平方米) Area of School sites (m^2)	教学行政用房建筑面积(平方米) Administritive (m^2)	图书藏量(册) Books (Volume)
合　计 Total	**14791082**	**4900248**	**10217319**
北　京 Beijing	84770	29727	61188
天　津 Tianjin	141632	64363	89781
河　北 Hebei	213558	138865	232517
山　西 Shanxi	409961	262620	1450488
内蒙古 Inner Mongolia	362292	38298	97842
辽　宁 Liaoning	91943	35763	68500
吉　林 Jilin	181690	16069	38280
黑龙江 Heilongjiang	276270	99777	212954
上　海 Shanghai	317194	185172	637876
江　苏 Jiangsu	1257029	1307213	878728
浙　江 Zhejiang	761974	586760	920118
安　徽 Anhui	164521	9196	52844
福　建 Fujian	279184	153119	750743
江　西 Jiangxi	130284	41895	75553
山　东 Shandong	5927232	456357	1303563
河　南 Henan	938770	262462	701293
湖　北 Hubei	510508	183203	672530
湖　南 Hunan	246019	85015	310971
广　东 Guangdong	342272	381710	236500
广　西 Guangxi	491356	42884	170230
海　南 Hainan	30385	24350	46070
重　庆 Chongqing	14631	10091	13443
四　川 Sichuan	242136	116213	234679
贵　州 Guizhou	21447	6305	23804
云　南 Yunnan	1300	360	410
西　藏 Tibet	0	0	0
陕　西 Shaanxi	521776	138964	440422
甘　肃 Gansu	628895	160042	378332
青　海 Qinghai	6500	1240	500
宁　夏 Ningxia	7546	5418	10120
新　疆 Xinjiang	188007	56797	107040

校资产情况

Resources in Technical Training Schools

教学用计算机(台)No. of computers used for Instruction	语音实验室座位数(个) No. of Seats in Audio-Labs	多媒体教室座位数(个) No. of Seats in Multimedia Class rooms	固定资产总值(万元) Fixed Assets (in 10000 yuan)	
			计 Total	其中:教学、实习仪器设备资产值 of which: Teaching Equipment & Instruments
65002	**17232**	**46295**	**1758263.03**	**114272.16**
645	75	137	4994.58	976.00
1608	393	436	10116.16	2041.40
1834	643	1201	10018.25	2552.40
2576	436	1483	18094.13	5657.49
803	250	384	2559.00	529.80
592	50	81	2639.00	814.00
504	56	120	745.05	54.90
2218	420	724	30974.38	8779.00
3542	1059	6394	22638.73	9661.66
10142	1098	9182	57631.08	15812.95
7184	6767	6244	41480.06	6431.15
352	65	431	983.60	172.60
3619	65	5552	15083.59	5413.85
220	0	30	919.36	111.63
7993	1308	2235	154146.60	12747.23
4240	1850	3927	31166.22	6624.18
2551	504	1756	364441.70	18882.40
1874	325	1300	4079.40	1066.00
5749	329	1831	35217.64	7946.14
727	235	323	1054.38	204.69
80	0	0	495.00	100.00
202	0	40	264.70	76.30
1688	170	613	18546.40	1333.50
125	0	0	360.00	66.00
20	0	0	94.00	88.20
0	0	0	0.00	0.00
1596	242	334	911195.42	1723.62
1567	686	1095	15417.60	3274.77
0	0	0	2.00	0.00
217	0	0	275.00	74.00
534	206	442	2630.00	1056.30

农村成人文化技术培

Condition of Fixed Assets and Teaching Resources

地　区 Region	占地面积(平方米) Area of School sites (m^2)	教学行政用房 建筑面积(平方米) Administritive (m^2)	图书藏量(册) Books (Volume)
合　计 Total	**80471559**	**19456915**	**38638244**
北　京 Beijing	1361816	203943	1619066
天　津 Tianjin	483223	99527	283882
河　北 Hebei	6405467	814193	4417926
山　西 Shanxi	1893870	406020	1500941
内蒙古 Inner Mongolia	1298725	199155	544399
辽　宁 Liaoning	567428	106372	338087
吉　林 Jilin	1452320	268927	196197
黑龙江 Heilongjiang	3373755	707818	1424692
上　海 Shanghai	319174	148293	152601
江　苏 Jiangsu	5382488	2049656	2170138
浙　江 Zhejiang	6859257	1298948	2411352
安　徽 Anhui	1485673	258277	300115
福　建 Fujian	296122	200292	460461
江　西 Jiangxi	577709	323121	939502
山　东 Shandong	15357880	2223376	5499134
河　南 Henan	6726236	1557566	4388316
湖　北 Hubei	8398833	3478619	727415
湖　南 Hunan	610590	119692	412466
广　东 Guangdong	2077475	1013619	1301314
广　西 Guangxi	1809167	412897	1385657
海　南 Hainan	774014	61045	103634
重　庆 Chongqing	394729	230927	383262
四　川 Sichuan	1442223	710579	1321525
贵　州 Guizhou	977418	343077	434618
云　南 Yunnan	1699814	378376	998565
西　藏 Tibet	0	0	0
陕　西 Shaanxi	2520872	717694	2067761
甘　肃 Gansu	4289625	962872	1602054
青　海 Qinghai	502819	41868	75093
宁　夏 Ningxia	20488	2169	35304
新　疆 Xinjiang	1112349	117997	1142767

训学校资产情况

in Technical Training Schools for Peasants

教学用计算机（台）No. of computers used for Instruction	语音实验室座位数（个）No. of Seats in Audio-Labs	多媒体教室座位数（个）No. of Seats in Multimedia Class rooms	固定资产总值（万元）Fixed Assets (in 10000 yuan) 计 Total	其中：教学、实习仪器设备资产值 of which: Teaching Equipment & Instruments
112582	**37108**	**103579**	**5418115.55**	**1335153.70**
2515	684	2993	20070.62	7106.68
692	180	220	5422.62	856.20
5298	1888	7468	41709.96	7400.19
1588	921	502	20751.57	6610.68
659	0	426	25424.31	1543.31
989	204	213	8562.85	1744.00
278	50	42	11788.95	511.06
6850	1010	5559	21204.30	2531.38
3277	393	1182	10475.06	3027.07
10173	1547	8269	73450.35	16542.17
11897	3220	10346	95629.08	11211.80
377	93	30	1217531.43	144533.76
1384	236	4509	9679.22	1738.54
910	0	23701	281637.92	272116.35
37385	3994	4496	96246.13	22105.44
3773	5362	6142	143151.29	12963.92
1705	2469	3241	1512806.10	53385.80
259	72	231	3304.80	751.34
11820	4447	7967	266668.49	72362.30
1313	243	344	12281.89	1558.75
16	0	0	2406.80	402.00
522	377	378	22010.32	17694.06
4098	3619	2650	895821.83	348301.86
897	50	228	5741.68	401.38
507	230	950	18320.27	1372.93
0	0	0	0.00	0.00
611	0	486	393610.97	160824.17
2307	49	2713	197557.31	163472.19
373	0	2	339.00	100.00
50	0	0	18.20	4.76
59	5770	8291	4492.23	1979.61

地　区 Region	占地面积(平方米) Area of School sites (m^2)	教学行政用房 建筑面积(平方米) Administritive (m^2)	图书藏量(册) Books (Volume)
合　计 Total	**22077263**	**9236469**	**46875741**
北　京 Beijing	4004317	1868700	22181536
天　津 Tianjin	1137713	1533314	2417008
河　北 Hebei	862549	208724	212647
山　西 Shanxi	75601	69708	250440
内蒙古 Inner Mongolia	6625	2012	3648
辽　宁 Liaoning	688612	393217	428653
吉　林 Jilin	95478	56802	110950
黑龙江 Heilongjiang	815582	234877	550235
上　海 Shanghai	1430921	354811	801063
江　苏 Jiangsu	2332598	834292	1331318
浙　江 Zhejiang	902117	563553	1427108
安　徽 Anhui	235300	67071	35101
福　建 Fujian	423601	238396	686314
江　西 Jiangxi	9420	4195	6200
山　东 Shandong	3120819	1081521	5586794
河　南 Henan	75895	53107	157278
湖　北 Hubei	254713	111833	173948
湖　南 Hunan	356441	136109	486398
广　东 Guangdong	3061765	777531	8933843
广　西 Guangxi	191088	57738	79832
海　南 Hainan	85732	50552	187500
重　庆 Chongqing	75937	25436	30266
四　川 Sichuan	608465	215906	233299
贵　州 Guizhou	490670	66988	88542
云　南 Yunnan	92037	47993	98619
西　藏 Tibet	0	0	0
陕　西 Shaanxi	309647	115399	187873
甘　肃 Gansu	187132	48392	79414
青　海 Qinghai	84929	11605	67663
宁　夏 Ningxia	600	340	0
新　疆 Xinjiang	60959	6347	42251

资产情况
Teaching Resources in Others

教学用计算机(台)No. of computers used for Instruction	语音实验室座位数(个) No. of Seats in Audio-Labs	多媒体教室座位数(个)No. of Seats in Multimedia Class rooms	固定资产总值(万元) Fixed Assets (in 10000 yuan)	
			计 Total	其中:教学、实习仪器设备资产值 of which: Teaching Equipment & Instruments
187062	**49787**	**112786**	**231856428.20**	**107102612.40**
15275	4664	14126	222387734.00	102990353.90
17313	3549	3468	379534.53	27180.00
7537	649	2553	5905.46	2316.19
2780	680	357	5592.29	1419.09
100	0	180	62.00	2.60
6432	4364	1747	50714.00	10686.00
2213	673	314	35568.00	29119.70
10522	3221	3087	25142.90	7157.70
13759	3814	18596	81909.34	65557.64
14381	2050	11354	65352.96	19481.91
10655	2647	6412	94032.74	13927.80
832	216	301	2260.10	619.30
6299	1202	3258	16896.60	6750.55
120	1	2	165.60	40.30
28491	6342	15017	8176115.64	3475720.87
1972	2380	3203	3005.40	641.10
3037	161	1081	6473.48	2339.18
4085	937	2538	350056.30	342011.35
26326	5413	16830	137085.80	98895.90
1501	1249	1563	1824.42	1056.52
487	545	618	1195.11	719.00
923	203	490	1413.30	566.22
6119	652	2333	13141.65	2127.29
368	160	474	3555.80	427.34
1242	835	1422	1165.61	628.32
0	0	0	0.00	0.00
3218	3137	512	6163.67	1622.42
812	0	33	1987.76	882.00
167	43	0	1334.20	236.60
0	0	0	4.10	2.10
96	0	917	1035.50	123.50

普通初中校数、班数(总计)

Number of Junior Schools and Classes (Regional Aggregates)

地 区 Region	学校数(所) Schools			班数(个) Classes				
	合 计 Total	初级中学 Junior Sec. Schools	九年一贯制学校 9-Year Sec. Schools	合 计 Total	一年级 Grade 1	二年级 Grade 2	三年级 Grade 3	四年级 Grade 4
合 计 Total	**63711**	**55327**	**8384**	**1165041**	**390110**	**384723**	**369305**	**20903**
北 京 Beijing	434	401	33	12064	3596	4111	4313	44
天 津 Tianjin	442	415	27	9816	3021	3103	3153	539
河 北 Hebei	4214	3863	351	74011	24984	24513	23479	1035
山 西 Shanxi	2848	2566	282	37071	12430	12375	11910	356
内蒙古 Inner Mongolia	1362	1119	243	22503	7109	7185	6811	1398
辽 宁 Liaoning	1885	1774	111	34790	11620	11384	11207	579
吉 林 Jilin	1401	1246	155	25636	8767	8631	8077	161
黑龙江 Heilongjiang	2238	1893	345	37679	8680	10510	10836	7653
上 海 Shanghai	515	382	133	10665	3114	3655	3873	23
江 苏 Jiangsu	2357	2158	199	66059	23028	22371	20651	9
浙 江 Zhejiang	2081	1814	267	39273	12711	13148	13378	36
安 徽 Anhui	3079	2893	186	52284	17937	17594	16745	8
福 建 Fujian	1414	1357	57	36339	12528	11923	11888	0
江 西 Jiangxi	2219	1945	274	38413	12906	13146	12358	3
山 东 Shandong	3761	3482	279	81873	22839	24157	27378	7499
河 南 Henan	5475	5231	244	91812	31260	30648	29467	437
湖 北 Hubei	2679	2403	276	51373	17867	17402	15581	523
湖 南 Hunan	3924	3347	577	64009	21558	22096	20355	0
广 东 Guangdong	3181	2877	304	76142	27157	25407	23577	1
广 西 Guangxi	2471	2304	167	42235	14912	14059	13264	0
海 南 Hainan	437	324	113	7145	2738	2386	2021	0
重 庆 Chongqing	1271	1121	150	22792	7911	7666	7210	5
四 川 Sichuan	4215	2778	1437	65399	22382	22109	20788	120
贵 州 Guizhou	2068	1622	446	34094	12973	11295	9826	0
云 南 Yunnan	1854	1749	105	34380	12076	11369	10648	287
西 藏 Tibet	88	88	0	1745	722	561	462	0
陕 西 Shaanxi	2090	1792	298	37123	12993	12559	11569	2
甘 肃 Gansu	1578	1194	384	23199	7907	7649	7492	151
青 海 Qinghai	356	171	185	4245	1512	1410	1304	19
宁 夏 Ningxia	342	259	83	4983	1675	1647	1658	3
新 疆 Xinjiang	1432	759	673	25889	9197	8654	8026	12

普通初中校数、班数(城市)

Number of Junior Schools and Classes (Urban)

地 区 Region	学校数(所) Schools 合 计 Total	初级中学 Junior Sec. Schools	九年一贯制学校 9-Year Sec. Schools	班数(个) Classes 小 计 Total	一年级 Grade 1	二年级 Grade 2	三年级 Grade 3	四年级 Grade 4
合 计 Total	**8989**	**6850**	**2139**	**222960**	**71750**	**72730**	**72085**	**6395**
北 京 Beijing	138	125	13	5484	1646	1856	1964	18
天 津 Tianjin	177	158	19	4065	1160	1334	1461	110
河 北 Hebei	437	272	165	11240	3662	3648	3654	276
山 西 Shanxi	331	255	76	9325	3117	3123	3026	59
内蒙古 Inner Mongolia	235	177	58	6263	1933	1961	1847	522
辽 宁 Liaoning	523	478	45	12461	3849	3935	4106	571
吉 林 Jilin	201	186	15	5094	1644	1652	1717	81
黑龙江 Heilongjiang	425	362	63	9109	2359	2458	2547	1745
上 海 Shanghai	291	234	57	6217	1765	2145	2307	0
江 苏 Jiangsu	386	335	51	11662	3756	3941	3956	9
浙 江 Zhejiang	427	364	63	10531	3475	3522	3498	36
安 徽 Anhui	307	224	83	7679	2603	2566	2510	0
福 建 Fujian	137	120	17	5657	1966	1874	1817	0
江 西 Jiangxi	182	125	57	4287	1331	1480	1476	0
山 东 Shandong	696	564	132	17443	4760	5090	5573	2020
河 南 Henan	561	456	105	12908	4315	4283	4088	222
湖 北 Hubei	696	525	171	13524	4334	4411	4267	512
湖 南 Hunan	332	200	132	7852	2603	2670	2579	0
广 东 Guangdong	703	502	201	18401	6689	6104	5607	1
广 西 Guangxi	243	165	78	5129	1734	1732	1663	0
海 南 Hainan	44	20	24	1159	425	384	350	0
重 庆 Chongqing	372	330	42	7414	2504	2499	2406	5
四 川 Sichuan	246	154	92	7210	2431	2412	2258	109
贵 州 Guizhou	242	142	100	4369	1517	1479	1373	0
云 南 Yunnan	80	61	19	2437	804	805	777	51
西 藏 Tibet	15	15	0	307	107	105	95	0
陕 西 Shaanxi	208	140	68	6005	1973	2023	2007	2
甘 肃 Gansu	118	59	59	3155	1050	1025	1041	39
青 海 Qinghai	28	13	15	790	278	259	250	3
宁 夏 Ningxia	51	35	16	1119	371	374	374	0
新 疆 Xinjiang	157	54	103	4664	1589	1580	1491	4

普通初中校数、班数(县镇)

Number of Junior Schools and Classes (County Seats & Towns)

地区 Region	学校数(所) Schools 合计 Total	初级中学 Junior Sec. Schools	九年一贯制学校 9-Year Sec. Schools	班数(个) Classes 小计 Total	一年级 Grade 1	二年级 Grade 2	三年级 Grade 3	四年级 Grade 4
合 计 Total	**17471**	**15889**	**1582**	**397249**	**133835**	**130718**	**126541**	**6155**
北 京 Beijing	176	163	13	4715	1403	1616	1670	26
天 津 Tianjin	144	142	2	3273	1047	994	977	255
河 北 Hebei	1246	1163	83	26656	9136	8808	8393	319
山 西 Shanxi	523	464	59	9011	3048	2983	2888	92
内蒙古 Inner Mongolia	415	345	70	8814	2788	2800	2721	505
辽 宁 Liaoning	216	201	15	4766	1636	1563	1567	0
吉 林 Jilin	488	443	45	12174	4111	4144	3859	60
黑龙江 Heilongjiang	362	314	48	7761	1773	2181	2297	1510
上 海 Shanghai	199	135	64	4134	1263	1406	1456	9
江 苏 Jiangsu	358	320	38	12647	4542	4248	3857	0
浙 江 Zhejiang	1296	1200	96	25258	8135	8466	8657	0
安 徽 Anhui	550	527	23	12810	4368	4269	4170	3
福 建 Fujian	483	475	8	17097	5902	5594	5601	0
江 西 Jiangxi	714	640	74	15749	5355	5336	5058	0
山 东 Shandong	1550	1471	79	38305	10895	11437	12786	3187
河 南 Henan	1241	1173	68	25283	8671	8400	8132	80
湖 北 Hubei	451	415	36	9786	3554	3372	2857	3
湖 南 Hunan	1008	914	94	20610	7067	7089	6454	0
广 东 Guangdong	1044	994	50	27730	9830	9251	8649	0
广 西 Guangxi	1123	1089	34	23354	8266	7768	7320	0
海 南 Hainan	185	161	24	3945	1519	1308	1118	0
重 庆 Chongqing	474	419	55	9673	3427	3252	2994	0
四 川 Sichuan	1153	934	219	25043	8629	8385	8020	9
贵 州 Guizhou	622	552	70	13483	5287	4328	3868	0
云 南 Yunnan	500	466	34	12355	4271	4103	3911	70
西 藏 Tibet	72	72	0	1425	607	453	365	0
陕 西 Shaanxi	417	381	36	9454	3222	3180	3052	0
甘 肃 Gansu	198	158	40	5225	1771	1735	1718	1
青 海 Qinghai	77	34	43	1519	524	503	476	16
宁 夏 Ningxia	68	52	16	1363	454	444	462	3
新 疆 Xinjiang	118	72	46	3831	1334	1302	1188	7

普通初中校数、班数(农村)

Number of Junior Schools and Classes (Rural)

地区 Region	学校数(所) Schools			班数(个) Classes				
	小计 Total	初级中学 Junior Sec. Schools	九年一贯制学校 9-Year Sec. Schools	小计 Total	一年级 Grade 1	二年级 Grade 2	三年级 Grade 3	四年级 Grade 4
合计 Total	**37251**	**32588**	**4663**	**544832**	**184525**	**181275**	**170679**	**8353**
北京 Beijing	120	113	7	1865	547	639	679	0
天津 Tianjin	121	115	6	2478	814	775	715	174
河北 Hebei	2531	2428	103	36115	12186	12057	11432	440
山西 Shanxi	1994	1847	147	18735	6265	6269	5996	205
内蒙古 Inner Mongolia	712	597	115	7426	2388	2424	2243	371
辽宁 Liaoning	1146	1095	51	17563	6135	5886	5534	8
吉林 Jilin	712	617	95	8368	3012	2835	2501	20
黑龙江 Heilongjiang	1451	1217	234	20809	4548	5871	5992	4398
上海 Shanghai	25	13	12	314	86	104	110	14
江苏 Jiangsu	1613	1503	110	41750	14730	14182	12838	0
浙江 Zhejiang	358	250	108	3484	1101	1160	1223	0
安徽 Anhui	2222	2142	80	31795	10966	10759	10065	5
福建 Fujian	794	762	32	13585	4660	4455	4470	0
江西 Jiangxi	1323	1180	143	18377	6220	6330	5824	3
山东 Shandong	1515	1447	68	26125	7184	7630	9019	2292
河南 Henan	3673	3602	71	53621	18274	17965	17247	135
湖北 Hubei	1532	1463	69	28063	9979	9619	8457	8
湖南 Hunan	2584	2233	351	35547	11888	12337	11322	0
广东 Guangdong	1434	1381	53	30011	10638	10052	9321	0
广西 Guangxi	1105	1050	55	13752	4912	4559	4281	0
海南 Hainan	208	143	65	2041	794	694	553	0
重庆 Chongqing	425	372	53	5705	1980	1915	1810	0
四川 Sichuan	2816	1690	1126	33146	11322	11312	10510	2
贵州 Guizhou	1204	928	276	16242	6169	5488	4585	0
云南 Yunnan	1274	1222	52	19588	7001	6461	5960	166
西藏 Tibet	1	1	0	13	8	3	2	0
陕西 Shaanxi	1465	1271	194	21664	7798	7356	6510	0
甘肃 Gansu	1262	977	285	14819	5086	4889	4733	111
青海 Qinghai	251	124	127	1936	710	648	578	0
宁夏 Ningxia	223	172	51	2501	850	829	822	0
新疆 Xinjiang	1157	633	524	17394	6274	5772	5347	1

职业初中校数、班数(总计)

Number of Schools, Classes Admitted in Vocational Schools (Regional Aggregates)

地 区 Region	学校数 (所) Schools	班数(个) Classes 小计 Total	一年级 Grade 1	二年级 Grade 2	三年级 Grade 3	四年级 Grade 4
合 计 Total	**1019**	**12415**	**4187**	**4076**	**3788**	**364**
北 京 Beijing	2	12	3	4	5	0
天 津 Tianjin	0	0	0	0	0	0
河 北 Hebei	59	749	252	248	249	0
山 西 Shanxi	96	581	185	191	203	2
内蒙古 Inner Mongolia	190	2288	692	704	657	235
辽 宁 Liaoning	13	44	17	15	12	0
吉 林 Jilin	34	706	295	198	176	37
黑龙江 Heilongjiang	14	227	32	56	74	65
上 海 Shanghai	3	36	7	12	6	11
江 苏 Jiangsu	0	0	0	0	0	0
浙 江 Zhejiang	0	10	0	5	5	0
安 徽 Anhui	363	4319	1555	1460	1299	5
福 建 Fujian	1	8	2	3	3	0
江 西 Jiangxi	11	90	31	33	26	0
山 东 Shandong	6	71	17	25	27	2
河 南 Henan	11	136	35	52	48	1
湖 北 Hubei	43	506	188	173	141	4
湖 南 Hunan	11	60	14	23	23	0
广 东 Guangdong	0	29	9	9	11	0
广 西 Guangxi	18	223	73	83	67	0
海 南 Hainan	0	0	0	0	0	0
重 庆 Chongqing	3	10	4	4	2	0
四 川 Sichuan	11	144	45	53	46	0
贵 州 Guizhou	84	765	276	260	229	0
云 南 Yunnan	14	452	183	148	121	0
西 藏 Tibet	2	57	20	23	14	0
陕 西 Shaanxi	11	79	32	25	21	1
甘 肃 Gansu	9	40	2	19	19	0
青 海 Qinghai	2	21	9	7	5	0
宁 夏 Ningxia	0	55	22	19	14	0
新 疆 Xinjiang	8	697	187	224	285	1

职业初中校数、班数(城市)

Number of Schools, Classes Admitted in Vocational Schools (Urban)

地 区 Region	学校数(所) Schools	班数(个) Classes 小 计 Total	一年级 Grade 1	二年级 Grade 2	三年级 Grade 3	四年级 Grade 4
合 计 Total	**48**	**455**	**147**	**155**	**140**	**13**
北 京 Beijing	0	0	0	0	0	0
天 津 Tianjin	0	0	0	0	0	0
河 北 Hebei	5	41	13	14	14	0
山 西 Shanxi	8	112	41	34	37	0
内蒙古 Inner Mongolia	0	7	2	2	3	0
辽 宁 Liaoning	2	12	4	4	4	0
吉 林 Jilin	2	23	8	8	7	0
黑龙江 Heilongjiang	1	4	1	1	1	1
上 海 Shanghai	3	36	7	12	6	11
江 苏 Jiangsu	0	0	0	0	0	0
浙 江 Zhejiang	0	2	0	1	1	0
安 徽 Anhui	5	72	23	26	23	0
福 建 Fujian	0	0	0	0	0	0
江 西 Jiangxi	0	0	0	0	0	0
山 东 Shandong	1	10	3	3	3	1
河 南 Henan	3	5	2	2	1	0
湖 北 Hubei	6	28	8	9	11	0
湖 南 Hunan	1	5	2	2	1	0
广 东 Guangdong	0	0	0	0	0	0
广 西 Guangxi	1	29	9	10	10	0
海 南 Hainan	0	0	0	0	0	0
重 庆 Chongqing	2	10	4	4	2	0
四 川 Sichuan	0	7	2	3	2	0
贵 州 Guizhou	2	11	4	4	3	0
云 南 Yunnan	0	24	9	8	7	0
西 藏 Tibet	0	0	0	0	0	0
陕 西 Shaanxi	2	6	2	2	2	0
甘 肃 Gansu	1	0	0	0	0	0
青 海 Qinghai	1	3	1	1	1	0
宁 夏 Ningxia	0	0	0	0	0	0
新 疆 Xinjiang	2	8	2	5	1	0

职业初中校数、班数(县镇)

Number of Schools, Classes Admitted in Vocational Schools (County Seats & Towns)

地 区 Region	学校数(所) Schools	班数(个) Classes 小 计 Total	一年级 Grade 1	二年级 Grade 2	三年级 Grade 3	四年级 Grade 4
合 计 Total	**231**	**3207**	**1099**	**1064**	**976**	**68**
北 京 Beijing	1	4	1	1	2	0
天 津 Tianjin	0	0	0	0	0	0
河 北 Hebei	26	436	153	142	141	0
山 西 Shanxi	34	211	64	73	74	0
内蒙古 Inner Mongolia	47	766	239	238	227	62
辽 宁 Liaoning	1	0	0	0	0	0
吉 林 Jilin	12	159	76	44	35	4
黑龙江 Heilongjiang	3	8	1	1	6	0
上 海 Shanghai	0	0	0	0	0	0
江 苏 Jiangsu	0	0	0	0	0	0
浙 江 Zhejiang	0	5	0	3	2	0
安 徽 Anhui	31	578	210	192	176	0
福 建 Fujian	0	0	0	0	0	0
江 西 Jiangxi	3	23	7	9	7	0
山 东 Shandong	3	42	9	14	19	0
河 南 Henan	1	7	2	3	2	0
湖 北 Hubei	7	85	34	32	19	0
湖 南 Hunan	8	52	12	21	19	0
广 东 Guangdong	0	29	9	9	11	0
广 西 Guangxi	17	173	57	65	51	0
海 南 Hainan	0	0	0	0	0	0
重 庆 Chongqing	1	0	0	0	0	0
四 川 Sichuan	3	40	9	17	14	0
贵 州 Guizhou	18	189	70	61	58	0
云 南 Yunnan	3	187	67	69	51	0
西 藏 Tibet	2	57	20	23	14	0
陕 西 Shaanxi	2	27	12	9	5	1
甘 肃 Gansu	4	3	1	1	1	0
青 海 Qinghai	1	0	0	0	0	0
宁 夏 Ningxia	0	36	16	13	7	0
新 疆 Xinjiang	3	90	30	24	35	1

职业初中校数、班数(农村)

Number of Schools, Classes Admitted in Vocational Schools (Rural)

地 区 Region	学校数(所) Schools	班数(个) Classes 小计 Total	一年级 Grade 1	二年级 Grade 2	三年级 Grade 3	四年级 Grade 4
合 计 Total	**740**	**8753**	**2941**	**2857**	**2672**	**283**
北 京 Beijing	1	8	2	3	3	0
天 津 Tianjin	0	0	0	0	0	0
河 北 Hebei	28	272	86	92	94	0
山 西 Shanxi	54	258	80	84	92	2
内蒙古 Inner Mongolia	143	1515	451	464	427	173
辽 宁 Liaoning	10	32	13	11	8	0
吉 林 Jilin	20	524	211	146	134	33
黑龙江 Heilongjiang	10	215	30	54	67	64
上 海 Shanghai	0	0	0	0	0	0
江 苏 Jiangsu	0	0	0	0	0	0
浙 江 Zhejiang	0	3	0	1	2	0
安 徽 Anhui	327	3669	1322	1242	1100	5
福 建 Fujian	1	8	2	3	3	0
江 西 Jiangxi	8	67	24	24	19	0
山 东 Shandong	2	19	5	8	5	1
河 南 Henan	7	124	31	47	45	1
湖 北 Hubei	30	393	146	132	111	4
湖 南 Hunan	2	3	0	0	3	0
广 东 Guangdong	0	0	0	0	0	0
广 西 Guangxi	0	21	7	8	6	0
海 南 Hainan	0	0	0	0	0	0
重 庆 Chongqing	0	0	0	0	0	0
四 川 Sichuan	8	97	34	33	30	0
贵 州 Guizhou	64	565	202	195	168	0
云 南 Yunnan	11	241	107	71	63	0
西 藏 Tibet	0	0	0	0	0	0
陕 西 Shaanxi	7	46	18	14	14	0
甘 肃 Gansu	4	37	1	18	18	0
青 海 Qinghai	0	18	8	6	4	0
宁 夏 Ningxia	0	19	6	6	7	0
新 疆 Xinjiang	3	599	155	195	249	0

普通初中学生数(总计)

Number of Students in Junior Secondary Schools (Regional Aggregates)

单位:人

Unit:in Person

地　区 Region	毕业生数 Graduates	招生数 Students Admitted	在校学生数 Enrolment 合　计 Total	其中女 Of Which: Female	一年级 Grade 1	二年级 Grade 2	三年级 Grade 3	四年级 Grade 4	毕业班学生数 Graduates for Next Yesr
合　计 Total	**19955825**	**21953113**	**66184186**	**31381370**	**22010411**	**22135558**	**20906121**	**1132096**	**20854262**
北　京 Beijing	177606	123666	453446	219089	124381	158196	169250	1619	169314
天　津 Tianjin	139271	128428	432505	212630	128643	137024	142237	24601	139532
河　北 Hebei	1366057	1429717	4294874	2113107	1430000	1432568	1380815	51491	1394015
山　西 Shanxi	451365	585139	1932486	937921	595026	707728	613353	16379	612084
内蒙古 Inner Mongolia	299694	353320	1123586	542026	353835	368236	338880	62635	321764
辽　宁 Liaoning	592493	587450	1808303	877202	587882	593980	597007	29434	595943
吉　林 Jilin	376752	412773	1196226	580882	413604	397768	377339	7515	372344
黑龙江 Heilongjiang	543199	431234	1987827	973971	431434	550846	582147	423400	554018
上　海 Shanghai	182041	128565	463261	224886	129124	160924	172387	826	172359
江　苏 Jiangsu	1030282	1283001	3703519	1719089	1285097	1267689	1150401	332	1150471
浙　江 Zhejiang	684726	607199	1919386	900694	607545	654490	655794	1557	655549
安　徽 Anhui	962287	1169847	3383157	1594471	1173490	1151937	1057260	470	1057090
福　建 Fujian	593799	656411	1896759	902575	657358	619439	619962	0	619962
江　西 Jiangxi	684057	757786	2286573	1038141	763734	795968	726846	25	726830
山　东 Shandong	1814459	1291354	4852715	2296084	1291945	1442166	1687817	430787	1681557
河　南 Henan	1887770	1994221	6040927	2898571	2006644	2035570	1971477	27236	1969029
湖　北 Hubei	916054	1164538	3341801	1551074	1165640	1156088	993830	26243	995243
湖　南 Hunan	1091623	1291864	3822026	1836153	1292152	1346731	1183143	0	1183143
广　东 Guangdong	1282353	1548622	4321843	2030480	1548988	1444756	1328048	51	1328049
广　西 Guangxi	747437	876348	2449891	1144969	877623	819768	752500	0	752500
海　南 Hainan	119122	156650	418940	190070	157176	140375	121389	0	121389
重　庆 Chongqing	400171	445833	1255823	591941	446365	426211	383062	185	383053
四　川 Sichuan	1098454	1288174	3679899	1740068	1292168	1256311	1126613	4807	1126912
贵　州 Guizhou	502251	728959	1969955	880474	730180	665073	574702	0	574702
云　南 Yunnan	554903	677495	1921251	894689	679155	638994	588342	14760	587012
西　藏 Tibet	15268	37911	92060	41648	37951	28556	25553	0	25553
陕　西 Shaanxi	626847	768009	2212732	1062273	771482	761496	679664	90	679620
甘　肃 Gansu	367004	453109	1306024	601129	455380	433934	410455	6255	409546
青　海 Qinghai	57795	77540	214090	99276	77672	71427	64152	839	64087
宁　夏 Ningxia	82240	91126	268948	125090	91403	89234	88231	80	88268
新　疆 Xinjiang	308445	406824	1133353	560697	407334	382075	343465	479	343324

普通初中学生数(城市)

Number of Students in Junior Secondary Schools (Urban)

单位:人

Unit:in Person

地　区 Region	毕业生数 Graduates	招生数 Students Admitted	在校学生数 Enrolment						毕业班学生数 Graduates for Next Yesr
			合　计 Total	其中女 Of Which: Female	一年级 Grade 1	二年级 Grade 2	三年级 Grade 3	四年级 Grade 4	
合　计 Total	**3488014**	**3591798**	**11439364**	**5458427**	**3599294**	**3798285**	**3709604**	**332181**	**3690684**
北　京 Beijing	78458	52680	194361	94844	52792	67064	73828	677	73819
天　津 Tianjin	61882	47906	170378	84004	47968	57151	61147	4112	61016
河　北 Hebei	189116	195839	617514	300354	195983	205416	203026	13089	202442
山　西 Shanxi	86951	112038	398003	192416	117059	151835	126195	2914	126461
内蒙古 Inner Mongolia	88194	100736	335100	162863	100816	108214	100768	25302	97312
辽　宁 Liaoning	216066	186825	636569	309897	186860	203141	217505	29063	216824
吉　林 Jilin	82879	80698	255665	124480	80711	84072	87192	3690	83820
黑龙江 Heilongjiang	122130	113719	460852	227682	113747	125839	132135	89131	125019
上　海 Shanghai	109851	70671	265999	129328	70980	93444	101575	0	101575
江　苏 Jiangsu	181418	173942	555660	265620	173958	189667	191703	332	191773
浙　江 Zhejiang	173341	164346	517234	238182	164401	177087	174189	1557	173944
安　徽 Anhui	125655	148502	440221	208402	148623	150067	141531	0	141531
福　建 Fujian	84229	98535	285322	132292	98568	94605	92149	0	92149
江　西 Jiangxi	71287	70561	230189	105024	70756	81136	78297	0	78297
山　东 Shandong	317252	246589	957234	450204	246636	282321	313352	114925	309721
河　南 Henan	197840	220486	679775	325631	220742	226370	220197	12466	219032
湖　北 Hubei	218953	239231	753752	357829	239361	252099	236499	25793	238021
湖　南 Hunan	131495	149730	451255	214962	149733	156677	144845	0	144845
广　东 Guangdong	267736	361294	989058	455755	361452	330553	297002	51	297003
广　西 Guangxi	81374	90492	267371	123664	90528	91006	85837	0	85837
海　南 Hainan	19320	23640	63469	27778	23656	21062	18751	0	18751
重　庆 Chongqing	125857	122905	355149	171748	123017	120057	111890	185	111881
四　川 Sichuan	112030	124172	373908	180165	124393	127153	118075	4287	118368
贵　州 Guizhou	62881	78799	225619	107598	78835	75559	71225	0	71225
云　南 Yunnan	38310	41092	128334	63964	41097	43394	41090	2753	40945
西　藏 Tibet	3475	5161	14689	7038	5168	5024	4497	0	4497
陕　西 Shaanxi	99195	102618	319638	153949	102730	110578	106240	90	106196
甘　肃 Gansu	50928	56750	170850	82521	56863	56518	55965	1504	55780
青　海 Qinghai	11261	14821	42098	20409	14830	14342	12827	99	12691
宁　夏 Ningxia	17991	19343	59813	29152	19348	20037	20428	0	20428
新　疆 Xinjiang	60659	77677	224285	110672	77683	76797	69644	161	69481

普通初中学生数(县镇)

Number of Students in Junior Secondary Schools (County Seats & Towns)

单位:人

Unit: in Person

地　区 Region	毕业生数 Graduates	招生数 Students Admitted	在校学生数 Enrolment 合　计 Total	其中女 Of Which: Female	一年级 Grade 1	二年级 Grade 2	三年级 Grade 3	四年级 Grade 4	毕业班学生数 Graduates for Next Yesr
合　计 Total	**7093950**	**7725374**	**23140839**	**10924001**	**7744497**	**7713589**	**7343162**	**339591**	**7322121**
北　京 Beijing	70927	52036	190352	91499	52509	66975	69926	942	69999
天　津 Tianjin	45867	45708	150999	74059	45829	45649	47216	12305	44888
河　北 Hebei	491192	542818	1606001	787200	542902	535958	510386	16755	514325
山　西 Shanxi	144117	169217	528450	253944	171195	185450	167618	4187	167042
内蒙古 Inner Mongolia	119764	143438	454505	218960	143726	149255	138774	22750	130386
辽　宁 Liaoning	88401	90143	268570	130572	90226	89102	89242	0	88846
吉　林 Jilin	162530	181433	526133	255212	181937	176083	164919	3194	163352
黑龙江 Heilongjiang	111258	94142	424147	208631	94168	120779	126777	82423	118027
上　海 Shanghai	67564	54550	184758	89560	54754	63307	66355	342	66342
江　苏 Jiangsu	185364	257459	722714	330591	259372	245453	217889	0	217889
浙　江 Zhejiang	451394	393992	1245451	586497	394222	424514	426715	0	426715
安　徽 Anhui	242916	288442	839595	390714	289876	282033	267548	138	267541
福　建 Fujian	279416	306212	882984	421180	306782	287872	288330	0	288330
江　西 Jiangxi	299546	325008	970950	438773	327853	334828	308269	0	308269
山　东 Shandong	880273	640403	2344651	1106177	640697	704208	813510	186236	810517
河　南 Henan	526902	567642	1721238	823720	571216	580802	564046	5174	564287
湖　北 Hubei	186793	256894	700641	318136	257011	245084	198386	160	198320
湖　南 Hunan	357323	447001	1291483	618101	447137	452283	392063	0	392063
广　东 Guangdong	485122	567501	1593417	749862	567601	533325	492491	0	492491
广　西 Guangxi	431094	505228	1414026	657452	505646	474866	433514	0	433514
海　南 Hainan	70194	90768	244352	110976	91184	81746	71422	0	71422
重　庆 Chongqing	177828	209521	583234	273221	209679	198997	174558	0	174558
四　川 Sichuan	440698	524114	1479824	696049	525306	500014	454049	455	454083
贵　州 Guizhou	206775	278707	772910	344568	279125	261902	231883	0	231883
云　南 Yunnan	206796	245013	702287	333170	245349	235299	218240	3399	217950
西　藏 Tibet	11728	32368	76698	34310	32401	23430	20867	0	20867
陕　西 Shaanxi	169034	194797	580492	275263	195456	198215	186821	0	186821
甘　肃 Gansu	89118	107520	312670	145352	107903	104500	100229	38	100239
青　海 Qinghai	20393	26208	74340	34553	26246	24944	22410	740	22481
宁　夏 Ningxia	24321	25160	76062	35895	25210	25483	25289	80	25244
新　疆 Xinjiang	49302	61931	176905	89804	61979	61233	53420	273	53430

普通初中学生数(农村)

Number of Students in Junior Secondary Schools (Rural)

单位:人

Unit:in Person

地 区 Region	毕业生数 Graduates	招生数 Students Admitted	在校学生数 Enrolment						毕业班学生数 Graduates for Next Yesr
			合 计 Total	其中女 Of Which: Female	一年级 Grade 1	二年级 Grade 2	三年级 Grade 3	四年级 Grade 4	
合 计 Total	**9373861**	**10635941**	**31603983**	**14998942**	**10666620**	**10623684**	**9853355**	**460324**	**9841457**
北 京 Beijing	28221	18950	68733	32746	19080	24157	25496	0	25496
天 津 Tianjin	31522	34814	111128	54567	34846	34224	33874	8184	33628
河 北 Hebei	685749	691060	2071359	1025553	691115	691194	667403	21647	677248
山 西 Shanxi	220297	303884	1006033	491561	306772	370443	319540	9278	318581
内蒙古 Inner Mongolia	91736	109146	333981	160203	109293	110767	99338	14583	94066
辽 宁 Liaoning	288026	310482	903164	436733	310796	301737	290260	371	290273
吉 林 Jilin	131343	150642	414428	201190	150956	137613	125228	631	125172
黑龙江 Heilongjiang	309811	223373	1102828	537658	223519	304228	323235	251846	310972
上 海 Shanghai	4626	3344	12504	5998	3390	4173	4457	484	4442
江 苏 Jiangsu	663500	851600	2425145	1122878	851767	832569	740809	0	740809
浙 江 Zhejiang	59991	48861	156701	76015	48922	52889	54890	0	54890
安 徽 Anhui	593716	732903	2103341	995355	734991	719837	648181	332	648018
福 建 Fujian	230154	251664	728453	349103	252008	236962	239483	0	239483
江 西 Jiangxi	313224	362217	1085434	494344	365125	380004	340280	25	340264
山 东 Shandong	616934	404362	1550830	739703	404612	455637	560955	129626	561319
河 南 Henan	1163028	1206093	3639914	1749220	1214686	1228398	1187234	9596	1185710
湖 北 Hubei	510308	668413	1887408	875109	669268	658905	558945	290	558902
湖 南 Hunan	602805	695133	2079288	1003090	695282	737771	646235	0	646235
广 东 Guangdong	529495	619827	1739368	824863	619935	580878	538555	0	538555
广 西 Guangxi	234969	280628	768494	363853	281449	253896	233149	0	233149
海 南 Hainan	29608	42242	111119	51316	42336	37567	31216	0	31216
重 庆 Chongqing	96486	113407	317440	146972	113669	107157	96614	0	96614
四 川 Sichuan	545726	639888	1826167	863854	642469	629144	554489	65	554461
贵 州 Guizhou	232595	371453	971426	428308	372220	327612	271594	0	271594
云 南 Yunnan	309797	391390	1090630	497555	392709	360301	329012	8608	328117
西 藏 Tibet	65	382	673	300	382	102	189	0	189
陕 西 Shaanxi	358618	470594	1312602	633061	473296	452703	386603	0	386603
甘 肃 Gansu	226958	288839	822504	373256	290614	272916	254261	4713	253527
青 海 Qinghai	26141	36511	97652	44314	36596	32141	28915	0	28915
宁 夏 Ningxia	39928	46623	133073	60043	46845	43714	42514	0	42596
新 疆 Xinjiang	198484	267216	732163	360221	267672	244045	220401	45	220413

普通初中女学生数

Number of Female Students in Junior Secondary Schools

单位:人

Unit:in Person

地　区 Region	毕业生数 Graduates	招生数 Students Admitted	在校学生数 Enrolment 合　计 Total	一年级 Grade 1	二年级 Grade 2	三年级 Grade 3	四年级 Grade 4	毕业班学生数 Graduates for Next Yesr
合　计 Total	**9504902**	**10382894**	**31381370**	**10401189**	**10466292**	**9961821**	**552068**	**9852206**
北　京 Beijing	87656	59533	219089	59667	76085	82589	748	81114
天　津 Tianjin	68994	62804	212630	62848	67485	70555	11742	68695
河　北 Hebei	675180	698049	2113107	698191	704848	684860	25208	680310
山　西 Shanxi	232667	297496	937921	299672	331329	299061	7859	295073
内蒙古 Inner Mongolia	150095	168163	542026	168355	176654	165581	31436	156809
辽　宁 Liaoning	292593	283463	877202	283599	288125	290946	14532	290627
吉　林 Jilin	184496	198785	580882	199147	192446	185560	3729	182808
黑龙江 Heilongjiang	268864	209269	973971	209346	269620	286044	208961	272168
上　海 Shanghai	89845	62159	224886	62281	77849	84361	395	83258
江　苏 Jiangsu	478151	595238	1719089	595866	587063	535982	178	533464
浙　江 Zhejiang	326536	283616	900694	283710	306202	310108	674	310072
安　徽 Anhui	448924	553482	1594471	554992	543207	496055	217	491736
福　建 Fujian	286069	309594	902575	309837	295554	297184	0	297184
江　西 Jiangxi	310635	345215	1038141	346870	359716	331550	5	315763
山　东 Shandong	857791	607279	2296084	607475	680780	800821	207008	798500
河　南 Henan	902358	956431	2898571	961526	976923	946841	13281	941723
湖　北 Hubei	420155	546780	1551074	547077	532672	458458	12867	451099
湖　南 Hunan	526279	616816	1836153	616873	645892	573388	0	571267
广　东 Guangdong	601058	725747	2030480	725829	678582	626037	32	612161
广　西 Guangxi	352686	403270	1144969	403551	382030	359388	0	359388
海　南 Hainan	54599	71004	190070	71140	64116	54814	0	54814
重　庆 Chongqing	189329	210173	591941	210280	200392	181169	100	172881
四　川 Sichuan	522688	609545	1740068	610999	593208	533533	2328	530675
贵　州 Guizhou	220541	326935	880474	327302	296230	256942	0	256942
云　南 Yunnan	259583	314125	894689	314704	297971	275056	6958	274452
西　藏 Tibet	7186	16848	41648	16856	13077	11715	0	11507
陕　西 Shaanxi	301705	366687	1062273	367763	365071	329391	48	329290
甘　肃 Gansu	167599	207728	601129	208524	200157	189408	3040	184783
青　海 Qinghai	27285	35531	99276	35574	33144	30143	415	29862
宁　夏 Ningxia	38368	41721	125090	41776	41365	41899	50	41804
新　疆 Xinjiang	154987	199408	560697	199559	188499	172382	257	171977

职业初中学生数(总计)

Number of Students in Junior Secondary Schools (Regional Aggregates)

单位:人

Unit: in Person

地　区 Region	毕业生数 Graduates	招生数 Students Admitted	在校学生数 Enrolment 合　计 Total	其中女 Of Which: Female	一年级 Grade 1	二年级 Grade 2	三年级 Grade 3	四年级 Grade 4	毕业班学生数 Graduates for Next Yesr
合　计 Total	**228816**	**248172**	**724087**	**337287**	**249085**	**240953**	**216738**	**17311**	**218345**
北　京 Beijing	0	0	0	0	0	0	0	0	0
天　津 Tianjin	0	0	0	0	0	0	0	0	0
河　北 Hebei	12555	14516	43031	21181	14581	14611	13839	0	13839
山　西 Shanxi	10067	10106	30240	14018	10304	9628	10228	80	10384
内蒙古 Inner Mongolia	25615	32199	104229	50325	32305	33031	29152	9741	27618
辽　宁 Liaoning	711	459	1273	561	459	441	373	0	373
吉　林 Jilin	12855	16483	41604	20533	16501	11680	11247	2176	11400
黑龙江 Heilongjiang	7468	1561	13032	6351	1594	3109	4188	4141	6429
上　海 Shanghai	338	162	979	372	162	301	137	379	516
江　苏 Jiangsu	0	0	0	0	0	0	0	0	0
浙　江 Zhejiang	236	0	403	61	0	200	203	0	203
安　徽 Anhui	85930	109238	300923	139484	109251	102868	88519	285	88529
福　建 Fujian	108	57	261	116	57	108	96	0	96
江　西 Jiangxi	2585	1859	5394	2328	1873	2003	1518	0	1518
山　东 Shandong	1124	813	4027	1869	813	1547	1575	92	1555
河　南 Henan	3057	2184	8214	3693	2184	3018	2964	48	3012
湖　北 Hubei	11682	13789	37227	16901	13790	13086	10106	245	10228
湖　南 Hunan	926	733	3207	1542	733	1293	1181	0	1181
广　东 Guangdong	707	583	1792	853	583	586	623	0	623
广　西 Guangxi	12664	3798	11740	5255	3821	4319	3600	0	3600
海　南 Hainan	0	0	0	0	0	0	0	0	0
重　庆 Chongqing	191	129	308	166	129	124	55	0	55
四　川 Sichuan	2399	2393	7219	3193	2397	2662	2160	0	2160
贵　州 Guizhou	11583	15855	43493	18997	15860	14794	12839	0	12839
云　南 Yunnan	10264	9014	22116	9990	9211	7470	5435	0	5435
西　藏 Tibet	335	394	2337	1001	614	759	964	0	964
陕　西 Shaanxi	1411	1882	4676	2282	1896	1470	1248	62	1310
甘　肃 Gansu	1453	85	2378	1078	85	1117	1176	0	1176
青　海 Qinghai	304	468	981	417	469	298	214	0	214
宁　夏 Ningxia	849	1239	2950	1185	1239	1015	696	0	696
新　疆 Xinjiang	11394	8172	30042	13524	8173	9409	12398	62	12388

职业初中学生数(城市)

Number of Students in Junior Secondary Schools (Urban)

单位:人

Unit: in Person

地 区 Region	毕业生数 Graduates	招生数 Students Admitted	在校学生数 Enrolment 合 计 Total	其中女 Of Which: Female	一年级 Grade 1	二年级 Grade 2	三年级 Grade 3	四年级 Grade 4	毕业班学生数 Graduates for Next Yesr
合 计 Total	**6893**	**7270**	**21825**	**9336**	**7323**	**7495**	**6538**	**469**	**6963**
北 京 Beijing	0	0	0	0	0	0	0	0	0
天 津 Tianjin	0	0	0	0	0	0	0	0	0
河 北 Hebei	556	731	2269	1061	731	818	720	0	720
山 西 Shanxi	1619	2531	6754	2857	2580	2133	2041	0	2090
内蒙古 Inner Mongolia	84	86	261	91	86	93	82	0	82
辽 宁 Liaoning	147	80	313	108	80	94	139	0	139
吉 林 Jilin	321	210	748	400	210	259	279	0	279
黑龙江 Heilongjiang	12	7	83	36	7	13	28	35	35
上 海 Shanghai	338	162	979	372	162	301	137	379	516
江 苏 Jiangsu	0	0	0	0	0	0	0	0	0
浙 江 Zhejiang	43	0	98	15	0	40	58	0	58
安 徽 Anhui	985	1239	3643	1758	1239	1311	1093	0	1093
福 建 Fujian	0	0	0	0	0	0	0	0	0
江 西 Jiangxi	0	0	0	0	0	0	0	0	0
山 东 Shandong	105	78	358	145	78	133	92	55	82
河 南 Henan	121	70	201	77	70	72	59	0	59
湖 北 Hubei	224	431	1270	325	431	371	468	0	468
湖 南 Hunan	67	63	176	76	63	84	29	0	29
广 东 Guangdong	0	0	0	0	0	0	0	0	0
广 西 Guangxi	710	406	1428	495	409	494	525	0	525
海 南 Hainan	0	0	0	0	0	0	0	0	0
重 庆 Chongqing	151	129	308	166	129	124	55	0	55
四 川 Sichuan	117	47	228	82	48	115	65	0	65
贵 州 Guizhou	192	228	656	318	228	246	182	0	182
云 南 Yunnan	446	549	1294	561	549	431	314	0	314
西 藏 Tibet	0	0	0	0	0	0	0	0	0
陕 西 Shaanxi	295	131	328	169	131	97	100	0	100
甘 肃 Gansu	89	0	0	0	0	0	0	0	0
青 海 Qinghai	14	37	80	30	37	21	22	0	22
宁 夏 Ningxia	0	0	0	0	0	0	0	0	0
新 疆 Xinjiang	257	55	350	194	55	245	50	0	50

职业初中学生数(县镇)

Number of Students in Junior Secondary Schools (County Seats & Towns)

单位:人

Unit:in Person

地 区 Region	毕业生数 Graduates	招生数 Students Admitted	在校学生数 Enrolment 合 计 Total	其中女 Of Which: Female	一年级 Grade 1	二年级 Grade 2	三年级 Grade 3	四年级 Grade 4	毕业班学生数 Graduates for Next Yesr
合 计 Total	**65120**	**61334**	**179138**	**83642**	**61984**	**59095**	**54987**	**3072**	**55801**
北 京 Beijing	0	0	0	0	0	0	0	0	0
天 津 Tianjin	0	0	0	0	0	0	0	0	0
河 北 Hebei	6896	9061	25787	13003	9126	8623	8038	0	8038
山 西 Shanxi	4460	3315	11044	5168	3448	3401	4195	0	4286
内蒙古 Inner Mongolia	10020	11881	37199	18062	11881	11985	10557	2776	11056
辽 宁 Liaoning	0	0	0	0	0	0	0	0	0
吉 林 Jilin	2229	4265	9448	4529	4265	2747	2245	191	2436
黑龙江 Heilongjiang	16	29	413	323	29	41	343	0	343
上 海 Shanghai	0	0	0	0	0	0	0	0	0
江 苏 Jiangsu	0	0	0	0	0	0	0	0	0
浙 江 Zhejiang	117	0	184	41	0	112	72	0	72
安 徽 Anhui	15929	13970	39538	17242	13980	13066	12492	0	12492
福 建 Fujian	0	0	0	0	0	0	0	0	0
江 西 Jiangxi	369	309	1131	471	309	473	349	0	349
山 东 Shandong	720	454	2523	1177	454	889	1180	0	1180
河 南 Henan	342	78	306	129	78	122	106	0	106
湖 北 Hubei	1377	2374	6314	2839	2374	2133	1807	0	1807
湖 南 Hunan	768	670	2881	1401	670	1209	1002	0	1002
广 东 Guangdong	707	583	1792	853	583	586	623	0	623
广 西 Guangxi	11638	2956	9125	4219	2976	3367	2782	0	2782
海 南 Hainan	0	0	0	0	0	0	0	0	0
重 庆 Chongqing	0	0	0	0	0	0	0	0	0
四 川 Sichuan	790	436	2042	904	436	858	748	0	748
贵 州 Guizhou	2707	4119	10480	4510	4120	3335	3025	0	3025
云 南 Yunnan	3659	3340	8788	4163	3527	3153	2108	0	2108
西 藏 Tibet	335	394	2337	1001	614	759	964	0	964
陕 西 Shaanxi	417	760	1743	885	774	542	384	43	427
甘 肃 Gansu	155	11	45	25	11	17	17	0	17
青 海 Qinghai	0	0	0	0	0	0	0	0	0
宁 夏 Ningxia	519	949	1947	880	949	628	370	0	370
新 疆 Xinjiang	950	1379	4065	1811	1379	1045	1579	62	1569

职业初中学生数(农村)

Number of Students in Junior Secondary Schools (Rural)

单位:人

Unit:in Person

地 区 Region	毕业生数 Graduates	招生数 Students Admitted	在校学生数 Enrolment						毕业班学生数 Graduates for Next Yesr
			合 计 Total	其中女 Of Which: Female	一年级 Grade 1	二年级 Grade 2	三年级 Grade 3	四年级 Grade 4	
合 计 Total	**156803**	**179568**	**523124**	**244309**	**179778**	**174363**	**155213**	**13770**	**155581**
北 京 Beijing	0	0	0	0	0	0	0	0	0
天 津 Tianjin	0	0	0	0	0	0	0	0	0
河 北 Hebei	5103	4724	14975	7117	4724	5170	5081	0	5081
山 西 Shanxi	3988	4260	12442	5993	4276	4094	3992	80	4008
内蒙古 Inner Mongolia	15511	20232	66769	32172	20338	20953	18513	6965	16480
辽 宁 Liaoning	564	379	960	453	379	347	234	0	234
吉 林 Jilin	10305	12008	31408	15604	12026	8674	8723	1985	8685
黑龙江 Heilongjiang	7440	1525	12536	5992	1558	3055	3817	4106	6051
上 海 Shanghai	0	0	0	0	0	0	0	0	0
江 苏 Jiangsu	0	0	0	0	0	0	0	0	0
浙 江 Zhejiang	76	0	121	5	0	48	73	0	73
安 徽 Anhui	69016	94029	257742	120484	94032	88491	74934	285	74944
福 建 Fujian	108	57	261	116	57	108	96	0	96
江 西 Jiangxi	2216	1550	4263	1857	1564	1530	1169	0	1169
山 东 Shandong	299	281	1146	547	281	525	303	37	293
河 南 Henan	2594	2036	7707	3487	2036	2824	2799	48	2847
湖 北 Hubei	10081	10984	29643	13737	10985	10582	7831	245	7953
湖 南 Hunan	91	0	150	65	0	0	150	0	150
广 东 Guangdong	0	0	0	0	0	0	0	0	0
广 西 Guangxi	316	436	1187	541	436	458	293	0	293
海 南 Hainan	0	0	0	0	0	0	0	0	0
重 庆 Chongqing	40	0	0	0	0	0	0	0	0
四 川 Sichuan	1492	1910	4949	2207	1913	1689	1347	0	1347
贵 州 Guizhou	8684	11508	32357	14169	11512	11213	9632	0	9632
云 南 Yunnan	6159	5125	12034	5266	5135	3886	3013	0	3013
西 藏 Tibet	0	0	0	0	0	0	0	0	0
陕 西 Shaanxi	699	991	2605	1228	991	831	764	19	783
甘 肃 Gansu	1209	74	2333	1053	74	1100	1159	0	1159
青 海 Qinghai	290	431	901	387	432	277	192	0	192
宁 夏 Ningxia	330	290	1003	305	290	387	326	0	326
新 疆 Xinjiang	10187	6738	25627	11519	6739	8119	10769	0	10769

职业初中女学生数

Number of Female Students in Junior Secondary Schools

单位:人

Unit:in Person

地 区 Region	毕业生数 Graduates	招生数 Students Admitted	在校学生数 Enrolment					毕业班学生数 Graduates for Next Yesr
			合 计 Total	一年级 Grade 1	二年级 Grade 2	三年级 Grade 3	四年级 Grade 4	
合 计 Total	**105244**	**115157**	**337287**	**115489**	**112632**	**100997**	**8169**	**99693**
北 京 Beijing	0	0	0	0	0	0	0	0
天 津 Tianjin	0	0	0	0	0	0	0	0
河 北 Hebei	6165	7136	21181	7168	7088	6925	0	6617
山 西 Shanxi	4919	4545	14018	4545	4567	4853	53	4728
内蒙古 Inner Mongolia	12711	15356	50325	15404	15948	14084	4889	13520
辽 宁 Liaoning	346	213	561	213	208	140	0	140
吉 林 Jilin	5873	7931	20533	7936	6001	5713	883	5596
黑龙江 Heilongjiang	3468	785	6351	795	1558	2143	1855	2587
上 海 Shanghai	118	58	372	58	123	44	147	191
江 苏 Jiangsu	0	0	0	0	0	0	0	0
浙 江 Zhejiang	25	0	61	0	41	20	0	20
安 徽 Anhui	38558	50902	139484	50905	47896	40553	130	40373
福 建 Fujian	54	18	116	18	53	45	0	45
江 西 Jiangxi	1059	815	2328	828	865	635	0	631
山 东 Shandong	516	403	1869	403	768	665	33	670
河 南 Henan	1399	927	3693	927	1294	1453	19	1472
湖 北 Hubei	4999	6449	16901	6449	5805	4557	90	4123
湖 南 Hunan	411	336	1542	336	609	597	0	537
广 东 Guangdong	307	285	853	285	282	286	0	286
广 西 Guangxi	5806	1662	5255	1672	1999	1584	0	1584
海 南 Hainan	0	0	0	0	0	0	0	0
重 庆 Chongqing	106	64	166	64	68	34	0	13
四 川 Sichuan	1220	983	3193	983	1214	996	0	850
贵 州 Guizhou	4916	6991	18997	6993	6411	5593	0	5593
云 南 Yunnan	4720	4093	9990	4178	3368	2444	0	2444
西 藏 Tibet	159	191	1001	313	270	418	0	425
陕 西 Shaanxi	643	881	2282	881	729	636	36	672
甘 肃 Gansu	689	38	1078	38	515	525	0	525
青 海 Qinghai	117	211	417	212	125	80	0	80
宁 夏 Ningxia	515	450	1185	450	449	286	0	286
新 疆 Xinjiang	5420	3433	13524	3434	4372	5684	34	5681

职业初中教职工数(总计)

Number of Teachers, Staff & Workers in Vocational Schools (Regional Aggregates)

单位:人
Unit:in Person

地区 Region	教职工数 Teachers, Staff & Workers						代课教师 Substitute Teachers	兼任教师 Part-time Teachers
	合计 Total	专任教师 Full-time Teachers	行政人员 Adm. Personnel	教辅人员 Supporting Staff	工勤人员 Workers	校办工厂、农(林)场职工 Employees in School-run Factories & Farms		
合计 Total	**36300**	**30788**	**1945**	**1112**	**2310**	**145**	**1311**	**777**
北京 Beijing	0	0	0	0	0	0	0	0
天津 Tianjin	0	0	0	0	0	0	0	0
河北 Hebei	2743	2320	184	96	123	20	128	9
山西 Shanxi	2231	1818	173	86	138	16	193	89
内蒙古 Inner Mongolia	8880	6929	444	442	1002	63	243	17
辽宁 Liaoning	81	58	20	0	3	0	0	0
吉林 Jilin	1911	1477	223	135	74	2	12	10
黑龙江 Heilongjiang	448	418	23	2	5	0	0	24
上海 Shanghai	90	39	13	24	14	0	2	0
江苏 Jiangsu	0	0	0	0	0	0	0	0
浙江 Zhejiang	30	25	1	3	1	0	0	8
安徽 Anhui	11584	10452	484	164	476	8	421	146
福建 Fujian	29	23	5	0	1	0	0	0
江西 Jiangxi	286	261	7	0	18	0	3	2
山东 Shandong	303	243	18	7	28	7	0	0
河南 Henan	333	292	8	5	28	0	23	0
湖北 Hubei	1973	1749	62	58	100	4	65	0
湖南 Hunan	198	181	9	2	6	0	3	4
广东 Guangdong	148	132	8	0	4	4	4	0
广西 Guangxi	692	506	68	26	92	0	9	27
海南 Hainan	0	0	0	0	0	0	0	0
重庆 Chongqing	53	40	5	3	5	0	0	0
四川 Sichuan	458	383	36	6	28	5	35	40
贵州 Guizhou	2302	2078	109	37	66	12	66	46
云南 Yunnan	585	515	11	7	50	2	12	337
西藏 Tibet	13	10	2	0	1	0	18	5
陕西 Shaanxi	300	270	20	3	7	0	10	6
甘肃 Gansu	104	100	0	0	4	0	4	0
青海 Qinghai	30	22	4	0	4	0	0	0
宁夏 Ningxia	99	99	0	0	0	0	0	0
新疆 Xinjiang	396	348	8	6	32	2	60	7

职业初中教职工数(城市)

Number of Teachers, Staff & Workers in Vocational Schools (Urban)

单位:人

Unit:in Person

地 区 Region	教职工数 Teachers, Staff & Workers 合 计 Total	专任教师 Full-time Teachers	行政人员 Adm. Personnel	教辅人员 Supporting Staff	工勤人员 Workers	校办工厂、农(林)场职工 Employees in School-run Factories & Farms	代课教师 Substitute Teachers	兼任教师 Part-time Teachers
合 计 Total	**1631**	**1177**	**186**	**77**	**182**	**9**	**60**	**39**
北 京 Beijing	0	0	0	0	0	0	0	0
天 津 Tianjin	0	0	0	0	0	0	0	0
河 北 Hebei	117	116	1	0	0	0	0	0
山 西 Shanxi	537	381	60	23	64	9	30	28
内蒙古 Inner Mongolia	34	34	0	0	0	0	0	0
辽 宁 Liaoning	34	23	8	0	3	0	0	0
吉 林 Jilin	71	49	18	0	4	0	0	0
黑龙江 Heilongjiang	11	10	1	0	0	0	0	0
上 海 Shanghai	90	39	13	24	14	0	2	0
江 苏 Jiangsu	0	0	0	0	0	0	0	0
浙 江 Zhejiang	11	6	1	3	1	0	0	0
安 徽 Anhui	178	114	34	4	26	0	14	0
福 建 Fujian	0	0	0	0	0	0	0	0
江 西 Jiangxi	0	0	0	0	0	0	0	0
山 东 Shandong	33	18	5	0	10	0	0	0
河 南 Henan	50	26	5	5	14	0	0	0
湖 北 Hubei	104	79	6	6	13	0	0	0
湖 南 Hunan	21	14	5	0	2	0	3	4
广 东 Guangdong	0	0	0	0	0	0	0	0
广 西 Guangxi	125	92	11	5	17	0	7	7
海 南 Hainan	0	0	0	0	0	0	0	0
重 庆 Chongqing	53	40	5	3	5	0	0	0
四 川 Sichuan	31	27	1	1	2	0	0	0
贵 州 Guizhou	38	31	6	0	1	0	4	0
云 南 Yunnan	0	0	0	0	0	0	0	0
西 藏 Tibet	0	0	0	0	0	0	0	0
陕 西 Shaanxi	48	42	2	3	1	0	0	0
甘 肃 Gansu	0	0	0	0	0	0	0	0
青 海 Qinghai	22	15	3	0	4	0	0	0
宁 夏 Ningxia	0	0	0	0	0	0	0	0
新 疆 Xinjiang	23	21	1	0	1	0	0	0

职业初中教职工数(县镇)

Number of Teachers, Staff & Workers in Vocational Schools (County Seats & Towns)

单位:人

Unit:in Person

地区 Region	教职工数 Teachers, Staff & Workers 合计 Total	专任教师 Full-time Teachers	行政人员 Adm. Personnel	教辅人员 Supporting Staff	工勤人员 Workers	校办工厂、农(林)场职工 Employees in School-run Factories & Farms	代课教师 Substitute Teachers	兼任教师 Part-time Teachers
合计 Total	**10155**	**8432**	**620**	**342**	**666**	**95**	**303**	**254**
北京 Beijing	0	0	0	0	0	0	0	0
天津 Tianjin	0	0	0	0	0	0	0	0
河北 Hebei	1521	1253	115	70	64	19	70	0
山西 Shanxi	822	686	53	41	40	2	81	20
内蒙古 Inner Mongolia	2834	2270	149	97	264	54	36	8
辽宁 Liaoning	8	5	3	0	0	0	0	0
吉林 Jilin	588	452	77	42	17	0	0	0
黑龙江 Heilongjiang	14	13	1	0	0	0	0	0
上海 Shanghai	0	0	0	0	0	0	0	0
江苏 Jiangsu	0	0	0	0	0	0	0	0
浙江 Zhejiang	19	19	0	0	0	0	0	8
安徽 Anhui	1812	1587	90	34	96	5	49	0
福建 Fujian	0	0	0	0	0	0	0	0
江西 Jiangxi	78	64	3	0	11	0	3	2
山东 Shandong	153	130	9	7	7	0	0	0
河南 Henan	17	12	0	0	5	0	0	0
湖北 Hubei	313	298	7	1	7	0	6	0
湖南 Hunan	159	153	2	1	3	0	0	0
广东 Guangdong	148	132	8	0	4	4	4	0
广西 Guangxi	493	356	50	21	66	0	2	20
海南 Hainan	0	0	0	0	0	0	0	0
重庆 Chongqing	0	0	0	0	0	0	0	0
四川 Sichuan	91	68	11	1	6	5	6	38
贵州 Guizhou	600	504	31	25	38	2	18	19
云南 Yunnan	171	153	1	0	15	2	5	134
西藏 Tibet	13	10	2	0	1	0	18	5
陕西 Shaanxi	99	95	4	0	0	0	1	0
甘肃 Gansu	11	7	0	0	4	0	0	0
青海 Qinghai	4	3	1	0	0	0	0	0
宁夏 Ningxia	51	51	0	0	0	0	0	0
新疆 Xinjiang	136	111	3	2	18	2	4	0

职业初中教职工数(农村)

Number of Teachers, Staff & Workers in Vocational Schools (Rural)

单位:人

Unit: in Person

地区 Region	教职工数 Teachers, Staff & Workers						代课教师 Substitute Teachers	兼任教师 Part-time Teachers
	合计 Total	专任教师 Full-time Teachers	行政人员 Adm. Personnel	教辅人员 Supporting Staff	工勤人员 Workers	校办工厂、农(林)场职工 Employees in School-run Factories & Farms		
合计 Total	**24514**	**21179**	**1139**	**693**	**1462**	**41**	**948**	**484**
北京 Beijing	0	0	0	0	0	0	0	0
天津 Tianjin	0	0	0	0	0	0	0	0
河北 Hebei	1105	951	68	26	59	1	58	9
山西 Shanxi	872	751	60	22	34	5	82	41
内蒙古 Inner Mongolia	6012	4625	295	345	738	9	207	9
辽宁 Liaoning	39	30	9	0	0	0	0	0
吉林 Jilin	1252	976	128	93	53	2	12	10
黑龙江 Heilongjiang	423	395	21	2	5	0	0	24
上海 Shanghai	0	0	0	0	0	0	0	0
江苏 Jiangsu	0	0	0	0	0	0	0	0
浙江 Zhejiang	0	0	0	0	0	0	0	0
安徽 Anhui	9594	8751	360	126	354	3	358	146
福建 Fujian	29	23	5	0	1	0	0	0
江西 Jiangxi	208	197	4	0	7	0	0	0
山东 Shandong	117	95	4	0	11	7	0	0
河南 Henan	266	254	3	0	9	0	23	0
湖北 Hubei	1556	1372	49	51	80	4	59	0
湖南 Hunan	18	14	2	1	1	0	0	0
广东 Guangdong	0	0	0	0	0	0	0	0
广西 Guangxi	74	58	7	0	9	0	0	0
海南 Hainan	0	0	0	0	0	0	0	0
重庆 Chongqing	0	0	0	0	0	0	0	0
四川 Sichuan	336	288	24	4	20	0	29	2
贵州 Guizhou	1664	1543	72	12	27	10	44	27
云南 Yunnan	414	362	10	7	35	0	7	203
西藏 Tibet	0	0	0	0	0	0	0	0
陕西 Shaanxi	153	133	14	0	6	0	9	6
甘肃 Gansu	93	93	0	0	0	0	4	0
青海 Qinghai	4	4	0	0	0	0	0	0
宁夏 Ningxia	48	48	0	0	0	0	0	0
新疆 Xinjiang	237	216	4	4	13	0	56	7

职业初中女教职工数

Number of Female Teachers, Staff & Workers in Vocational Schools

单位:人
Unit:in Person

地　区 Region	教职工数 Teachers,Staff & Workers						代课教师 Substitute Teachers	兼任教师 Part-time Teachers
	合　计 Total	专任教师 Full-time Teachers	行政人员 Adm. Personnel	教辅人员 Supporting Staff	工勤人员 Workers	校办工厂、农(林)场职工 Employees in School-run Factories & Farms		
合　计 Total	**12164**	**10995**	**169**	**410**	**571**	**19**	**556**	**227**
北　京 Beijing	0	0	0	0	0	0	0	0
天　津 Tianjin	0	0	0	0	0	0	0	0
河　北 Hebei	1441	1341	11	41	42	6	83	2
山　西 Shanxi	997	909	14	41	32	1	92	22
内蒙古 Inner Mongolia	3461	3102	17	126	208	8	121	3
辽　宁 Liaoning	30	24	6	0	0	0	0	0
吉　林 Jilin	922	814	36	56	16	0	6	0
黑龙江 Heilongjiang	132	127	4	0	1	0	0	9
上　海 Shanghai	64	27	10	17	10	0	2	0
江　苏 Jiangsu	0	0	0	0	0	0	0	0
浙　江 Zhejiang	11	10	0	0	1	0	0	1
安　徽 Anhui	2490	2286	30	65	109	0	116	34
福　建 Fujian	5	4	0	0	1	0	0	0
江　西 Jiangxi	61	53	0	0	8	0	2	1
山　东 Shandong	130	116	3	3	8	0	0	0
河　南 Henan	119	110	1	3	5	0	19	0
湖　北 Hubei	544	514	2	9	19	0	35	0
湖　南 Hunan	77	71	4	0	2	0	0	2
广　东 Guangdong	43	41	1	0	1	0	0	0
广　西 Guangxi	266	198	11	15	42	0	3	12
海　南 Hainan	0	0	0	0	0	0	0	0
重　庆 Chongqing	34	27	2	2	3	0	0	0
四　川 Sichuan	147	134	5	2	6	0	19	14
贵　州 Guizhou	609	559	5	19	23	3	15	14
云　南 Yunnan	200	171	1	4	23	1	5	106
西　藏 Tibet	5	4	1	0	0	0	7	1
陕　西 Shaanxi	134	127	2	3	2	0	7	5
甘　肃 Gansu	22	21	0	0	1	0	2	0
青　海 Qinghai	11	9	0	0	2	0	0	0
宁　夏 Ningxia	47	47	0	0	0	0	0	0
新　疆 Xinjiang	162	149	3	4	6	0	22	1

职业初中教职工总数中社会力量办教职工数

Number of General Secondary Schools Teachers, Staff & Workers Maintained by the Communities

单位:人

Unit:in Person

地区 Region	教职工数 Teachers,Staff & Workers						代课教师 Substitute Teachers	兼任教师 Part－time Teachers
	合计 Total	专任教师 Full－time Teachers	行政人员 Adm. Personnel	教辅人员 Supporting Staff	工勤人员 Workers	校办工厂、农(林)场职工 Employees in School－run Factories & Farms		
合计 Total	**1253**	**879**	**149**	**44**	**178**	**3**	**180**	**61**
北京 Beijing	0	0	0	0	0	0	0	0
天津 Tianjin	0	0	0	0	0	0	0	0
河北 Hebei	50	42	3	0	5	0	0	0
山西 Shanxi	52	30	9	0	13	0	4	12
内蒙古 Inner Mongolia	0	0	0	0	0	0	43	2
辽宁 Liaoning	13	8	5	0	0	0	0	0
吉林 Jilin	0	0	0	0	0	0	0	0
黑龙江 Heilongjiang	0	0	0	0	0	0	0	0
上海 Shanghai	0	0	0	0	0	0	0	0
江苏 Jiangsu	0	0	0	0	0	0	0	0
浙江 Zhejiang	30	25	1	3	1	0	0	8
安徽 Anhui	777	539	95	31	109	3	108	24
福建 Fujian	0	0	0	0	0	0	0	0
江西 Jiangxi	43	33	3	0	7	0	0	2
山东 Shandong	51	36	5	0	10	0	0	0
河南 Henan	0	0	0	0	0	0	22	0
湖北 Hubei	66	48	4	5	9	0	0	0
湖南 Hunan	18	11	5	0	2	0	3	0
广东 Guangdong	0	0	0	0	0	0	0	0
广西 Guangxi	52	28	9	2	13	0	0	4
海南 Hainan	0	0	0	0	0	0	0	0
重庆 Chongqing	33	20	5	3	5	0	0	0
四川 Sichuan	14	14	0	0	0	0	0	0
贵州 Guizhou	32	29	1	0	2	0	0	3
云南 Yunnan	0	0	0	0	0	0	0	0
西藏 Tibet	0	0	0	0	0	0	0	0
陕西 Shaanxi	22	16	4	0	2	0	0	6
甘肃 Gansu	0	0	0	0	0	0	0	0
青海 Qinghai	0	0	0	0	0	0	0	0
宁夏 Ningxia	0	0	0	0	0	0	0	0
新疆 Xinjiang	0	0	0	0	0	0	0	0

普通初中专任教师学

Breakdown of Junior Secondary Schools Heads and Teachers

地　区 Region	合计 Total	其中女 Of Which: Female	按学历分 By Educational Attainment			
			研究生毕业 Graduate	本科毕业 Under-graduate	专科毕业 Associate Bachelor	高中阶段毕业 High School Graduate
合　计 Total	**3466735**	**1570041**	**4991**	**821025**	**2364815**	**269273**
北　京 Beijing	34269	24446	257	19696	13447	848
天　津 Tianjin	29398	18120	78	9626	16429	3214
河　北 Hebei	224580	135277	155	45548	164101	14623
山　西 Shanxi	114847	63866	207	21612	80220	12566
内蒙古 Inner Mongolia	67463	38157	139	14390	45970	6792
辽　宁 Liaoning	111348	66761	112	30729	73881	6153
吉　林 Jilin	71435	43679	509	33531	35422	1892
黑龙江 Heilongjiang	119901	71162	257	31819	79199	8217
上　海 Shanghai	34203	21547	117	24350	9314	341
江　苏 Jiangsu	185182	76130	88	57496	114708	12586
浙　江 Zhejiang	109535	53658	65	43505	62490	3355
安　徽 Anhui	138549	39908	229	34377	94011	9694
福　建 Fujian	99925	37590	30	15683	80716	3351
江　西 Jiangxi	116604	35213	67	23219	81341	11681
山　东 Shandong	283182	125936	395	71066	192100	19275
河　南 henan	291623	136400	411	54600	212601	23552
湖　北 Hubei	167211	57484	206	43457	106547	16526
湖　南 Hunan	203096	82590	169	36521	149554	16446
广　东 Guangdong	205399	92346	477	53749	134807	16181
广　西 Guangxi	115717	49516	170	11318	93248	10763
海　南 Hainan	20135	6932	22	5906	13063	1109
重　庆 Chongqing	67999	27250	164	20510	42810	4379
四　川 Sichuan	188498	70973	250	35263	133457	19052
贵　州 guizhou	87899	27936	70	11828	66759	8958
云　南 Yunnan	98724	40192	38	16587	74537	7397
西　藏 Tibet	4973	1860	1	1989	2610	340
陕　西 Shaanxi	111614	53002	99	17812	77624	15765
甘　肃 Gansu	65999	21095	49	8728	49024	8038
青　海 Qinghai	13253	6044	39	3206	8895	1086
宁　夏 Ningxia	15818	6567	10	4740	10214	839
新　疆 Xinjiang	68356	38404	111	18164	45716	4254

历、职称情况(总计)

by Educational Attainment (Regional Aggregates)

单位:人

Unit: in Person

高中阶段毕业以下 Below High School Graduate	按职称分 By Rank				
	中学高级 Senior Secondary	中学一级 1st Grade	中学二级 2st Grade	中学三级 3st Grade	未评职称 Rank Undecided
6631	**169283**	**1119241**	**1477150**	**358052**	**343009**
21	4115	12214	13473	790	3677
51	4237	11759	9811	2113	1478
153	7601	56464	106282	21944	32289
242	2866	32550	53174	14022	12235
172	3740	23494	26053	6550	7626
473	20086	50771	28415	4957	7119
81	4905	29309	29646	5064	2511
409	10000	50129	38826	11331	9615
81	1862	19373	11005	171	1792
304	9739	67545	70950	13116	23832
120	4161	40961	46260	7135	11018
238	6793	48083	59763	12627	11283
145	4357	21695	56975	10600	6298
296	6162	34323	54104	12032	9983
346	15932	85742	136094	24690	20724
459	14646	78807	130875	46917	20378
475	8962	78392	56183	15894	7780
406	6089	79646	85535	13667	18159
185	5751	67471	83309	16499	32369
218	3500	33442	45229	21270	12276
35	1061	5578	9609	1121	2766
136	1866	16791	34624	7321	7397
476	5422	58180	93206	18085	13605
284	2529	15764	40672	16520	12414
165	2783	29222	42566	15145	9008
33	15	602	1718	443	2195
314	3509	24319	43186	19580	21020
160	1313	16567	27836	10093	10190
27	444	4321	5760	965	1763
15	1671	5719	5668	1304	1456
111	3166	20008	30343	6086	8753

普通初中专任教师学

Breakdown of Junior Secondary Schools Heads and Teachers

地　区 Reion	合计 Total	其中女 Of Which: Female	按学历分 By Educational Attainment 研究生毕业 Graduate	本科毕业 Under-graduate	专科毕业 Associate Bachelor	高中阶段毕业 High School Graduate
合　计 Total	**689643**	**421190**	**2991**	**332505**	**334106**	**19424**
北　京 Beijing	15151	11819	174	11119	3580	263
天　津 Tianjin	11878	8652	66	6121	5248	423
河　北 Hebei	36048	25680	92	15692	19451	801
山　西 Shanxi	24049	16587	133	10576	12637	671
内蒙古 Inner Mongolia	18581	12522	134	6851	10935	649
辽　宁 Liaoning	41792	30813	106	21204	19589	850
吉　林 Jilin	16766	12467	391	11273	4885	212
黑龙江 Heilongjiang	30820	22506	69	14938	15039	767
上　海 Shanghai	19525	13299	104	14064	5247	104
江　苏 Jiangsu	36411	20581	36	19083	15960	1282
浙　江 Zhejiang	30454	18055	26	17285	12689	435
安　徽 Anhui	22654	10509	124	9592	12353	559
福　建 Fujian	16873	9338	22	6979	9598	270
江　西 Jiangxi	14262	7416	26	5592	8033	595
山　东 Shandong	62490	37035	203	30125	30656	1461
河　南 henan	39228	23593	228	17420	20813	747
湖　北 Hubei	43667	20112	179	19313	22021	2087
湖　南 Hunan	24961	14362	93	10697	13523	633
广　东 Guangdong	50690	29596	333	25143	22740	2449
广　西 Guangxi	14595	8574	51	4730	9389	408
海　南 Hainan	3417	1796	20	2038	1310	46
重　庆 Chongqing	23257	11167	86	10584	11401	1134
四　川 Sichuan	23390	13094	64	11753	10790	741
贵　州 guizhou	12785	7041	21	4908	7401	438
云　南 Yunnan	7439	4483	21	3846	3445	121
西　藏 Tibet	1104	530	1	479	555	61
陕　西 Shaanxi	17040	10703	68	8098	8378	486
甘　肃 Gansu	9799	5218	24	3557	5903	301
青　海 Qinghai	2606	1676	20	1159	1349	75
宁　夏 Ningxia	3531	2136	8	1598	1846	77
新　疆 Xinjiang	14380	9830	68	6688	7342	278

历、职称情况(城市)

by Educational Attainment (Urban)

单位:人

Unit: in Person

高中阶段毕业以下 Below High School Graduate	按职称分 By Rank				
	中学高级 Senior Secondary	中学一级 1st Grade	中学二级 2nd Grade	中学三级 3st Grade	未评职称 Rank Undecided
617	**85260**	**283446**	**235839**	**30519**	**54579**
15	3004	6096	5229	44	778
20	3058	4610	3274	328	608
12	4523	13971	13068	1482	3004
32	1863	10020	9043	1158	1965
12	2285	7575	5658	1109	1954
43	7671	18065	11526	1121	3409
5	2975	7350	4785	831	825
7	5334	13494	7343	2226	2423
6	1217	11218	6412	75	603
50	4817	14074	12496	965	4059
19	2683	14031	10847	685	2208
26	3187	9341	7190	1122	1814
4	1894	5323	7659	805	1192
16	2433	5913	4401	658	857
45	6562	22189	27043	2677	4019
20	5945	14560	13556	2691	2476
67	5799	20826	12384	2581	2077
15	3100	12627	6864	579	1791
25	3502	20257	18180	1894	6857
17	1694	5703	4660	1279	1259
3	410	1143	1417	80	367
52	1111	7228	11203	2150	1565
42	2557	10069	8384	785	1595
17	1421	4233	4738	1033	1360
6	827	3497	2507	192	416
8	11	335	393	104	261
10	1798	6385	6248	708	1901
14	752	4401	3230	499	917
3	288	1293	689	52	284
2	714	1676	892	95	154
4	1825	5943	4520	511	1581

普通初中专任教师学

Breakdown of Junior Secondary Schools Heads and Teachers

地 区 Reion	合计 Total	其中女 Of Which: Female	按学历分 By Educational Attainment			
			研究生毕业 Graduate	本科毕业 Under-graduate	专科毕业 Associate Bachelor	高中阶段毕业 High School Graduate
合 计 Total	**1198978**	**546871**	**1271**	**263952**	**855552**	**76348**
北 京 Beijing	13700	9271	68	6359	6852	417
天 津 Tianjin	9935	5839	12	2547	5982	1377
河 北 Hebei	82202	51246	39	16047	60966	5090
山 西 Shanxi	29822	17063	43	4908	22478	2350
内蒙古 Inner Mongolia	26762	15362	5	5125	19488	2066
辽 宁 Liaoning	16689	10861	5	3560	12324	770
吉 林 Jilin	30193	19174	89	13626	15760	681
黑龙江 Heilongjiang	27893	18745	159	7320	19166	1196
上 海 Shanghai	13709	7814	13	9821	3602	204
江 苏 Jiangsu	36064	16823	14	15244	19851	941
浙 江 Zhejiang	69708	31977	29	24181	43190	2235
安 徽 Anhui	35268	10694	34	9664	23730	1755
福 建 Fujian	46183	17178	4	5555	39067	1510
江 西 Jiangxi	48672	14918	13	10025	34373	4140
山 东 Shandong	131497	55309	127	27049	94927	9217
河 南 henan	82082	41309	80	14706	62057	5160
湖 北 Hubei	35440	12196	11	7689	24531	3095
湖 南 Hunan	67320	27742	41	11566	51144	4448
广 东 Guangdong	76520	32641	104	14950	55284	6131
广 西 Guangxi	64615	27624	117	4857	53285	6225
海 南 Hainan	11307	3605	2	2909	7821	556
重 庆 Chongqing	28751	11019	54	7264	19872	1513
四 川 Sichuan	74334	29344	129	14203	54304	5541
贵 州 guizhou	34943	11308	25	4493	27878	2473
云 南 Yunnan	36565	16004	13	6802	27648	2054
西 藏 Tibet	3839	1325	0	1493	2043	278
陕 西 Shaanxi	28526	13477	18	4320	21624	2520
甘 肃 Gansu	15827	5574	8	2085	12229	1488
青 海 Qinghai	4901	2372	12	1111	3433	331
宁 夏 Ningxia	4693	2087	1	1519	2997	175
新 疆 Xinjiang	11018	6970	2	2954	7646	411

历、职称情况(县镇)

by Educational Attainment (County Seats & Towns)

单位:人

Unit: in Person

高中阶段毕业以下 Below High School Graduate	按职称分 By Rank 中学高级 Senior Secondary	中学一级 1st Grade	中学二级 2st Grade	中学三级 3st Grade	未评职称 Rank Undecided
1855	**47236**	**395361**	**531112**	**114239**	**111030**
4	883	4521	5740	488	2068
17	892	4293	3289	741	720
60	2019	21433	39259	7454	12037
43	545	8608	14375	2924	3370
78	1136	9847	10625	2458	2696
30	3374	8085	3994	613	623
37	1401	13626	12555	1796	815
52	2665	13786	8247	1665	1530
69	604	7608	4314	65	1118
14	2136	15483	13174	1641	3630
73	1426	24421	30973	5171	7717
85	1865	12972	15523	2518	2390
47	1759	10224	27142	4517	2541
121	2459	15157	23392	4106	3558
177	6063	37944	64912	12444	10134
79	4077	23493	37528	11375	5609
114	1589	19348	9900	2918	1685
121	1843	27626	28072	4693	5086
51	1346	25607	31446	6536	11585
131	1523	19351	25299	12298	6144
19	512	3011	5689	602	1493
48	633	6921	15316	2818	3063
157	2099	24483	36559	6292	4901
74	849	6542	17618	5767	4167
48	1306	12659	15616	4276	2708
25	4	267	1319	339	1910
44	823	6535	12707	4474	3987
17	317	4031	7673	1933	1873
14	124	1691	2309	350	427
1	435	1770	1820	316	352
5	529	4018	4727	651	1093

普通初中专任教师学

Breakdown of Junior Secondary Schools Heads and Teachers

地 区 Reion	合计 Total	其中女 Of Which: Female	按学历分 By Educational Attainment 研究生毕业 Graduate	本科毕业 Under-graduate	专科毕业 Associate Bachelor	高中阶段毕业 High School Graduate
合 计 Total	**1578114**	**601980**	**729**	**224568**	**1175157**	**173501**
北 京 Beijing	5418	3356	15	2218	3015	168
天 津 Tianjin	7585	3629	0	958	5199	1414
河 北 Hebei	106330	58351	24	13809	83684	8732
山 西 Shanxi	60976	30216	31	6128	45105	9545
内蒙古 Inner Mongolia	22120	10273	0	2414	15547	4077
辽 宁 Liaoning	52867	25087	1	5965	41968	4533
吉 林 Jilin	24476	12038	29	8632	14777	999
黑龙江 Heilongjiang	61188	29911	29	9561	44994	6254
上 海 Shanghai	969	434	0	465	465	33
江 苏 Jiangsu	112707	38726	38	23169	78897	10363
浙 江 Zhejiang	9373	3626	10	2039	6611	685
安 徽 Anhui	80627	18705	71	15121	57928	7380
福 建 Fujian	36869	11074	4	3149	32051	1571
江 西 Jiangxi	53670	12879	28	7602	38935	6946
山 东 Shandong	89195	33592	65	13892	66517	8597
河 南 henan	170313	71498	103	22474	129731	17645
湖 北 Hubei	88104	25176	16	16455	59995	11344
湖 南 Hunan	110815	40486	35	14258	84887	11365
广 东 Guangdong	78189	30109	40	13656	56783	7601
广 西 Guangxi	36507	13318	2	1731	30574	4130
海 南 Hainan	5411	1531	0	959	3932	507
重 庆 Chongqing	15991	5064	24	2662	11537	1732
四 川 Sichuan	90774	28535	57	9307	68363	12770
贵 州 guizhou	40171	9587	24	2427	31480	6047
云 南 Yunnan	54720	19705	4	5939	43444	5222
西 藏 Tibet	30	5	0	17	12	1
陕 西 Shaanxi	66048	28822	13	5394	47622	12759
甘 肃 Gansu	40373	10303	17	3086	30892	6249
青 海 Qinghai	5746	1996	7	936	4113	680
宁 夏 Ningxia	7594	2344	1	1623	5371	587
新 疆 Xinjiang	42958	21604	41	8522	30728	3565

历、职称情况（农村）
by Educational Attainment (Rural)

单位：人

Unit: in Person

	按职称分 By Rank				
高中阶段毕业以下 Below High School Graduate	中学高级 Senior Secondary	中学一级 1st Grade	中学二级 2st Grade	中学三级 3st Grade	未评职称 Rank Undecided
4159	**36787**	**440434**	**710199**	**213294**	**177400**
2	228	1597	2504	258	831
14	287	2856	3248	1044	150
81	1059	21060	53955	13008	17248
167	458	13922	29756	9940	6900
82	319	6072	9770	2983	2976
400	9041	24621	12895	3223	3087
39	529	8333	12306	2437	871
350	2001	22849	23236	7440	5662
6	41	547	279	31	71
240	2786	37988	45280	10510	16143
28	52	2509	4440	1279	1093
127	1741	25770	37050	8987	7079
94	704	6148	22174	5278	2565
159	1270	13253	26311	7268	5568
124	3307	25609	44139	9569	6571
360	4624	40754	79791	32851	12293
294	1574	38218	33899	10395	4018
270	1146	39393	50599	8395	11282
109	903	21607	33683	8069	13927
70	283	8388	15270	7693	4873
13	139	1424	2503	439	906
36	122	2642	8105	2353	2769
277	766	23628	48263	11008	7109
193	259	4989	18316	9720	6887
111	650	13066	24443	10677	5884
0	0	0	6	0	24
260	888	11399	24231	14398	15132
129	244	8135	16933	7661	7400
10	32	1337	2762	563	1052
12	522	2273	2956	893	950
102	812	10047	21096	4924	6079

职业初中专任教师学

Breakdown of Vocational Junior Secondary Schools Heads and Teachers

地 区 Reion	合计 Total	其中女 Of Which: Female	按学历分 By Educational Attainment			
			研究生毕业 Graduate	本科毕业 Under-graduate	专科毕业 Associate Bachelor	高中阶段毕业 High School Graduate
合 计 Total	**30788**	**10995**	**34**	**5277**	**20838**	**4542**
北 京 Beijing	0	0	0	0	0	0
天 津 Tianjin	0	0	0	0	0	0
河 北 Hebei	2320	1341	1	725	1483	109
山 西 Shanxi	1818	909	26	518	1107	162
内蒙古 Inner Mongolia	6929	3102	1	794	4823	1299
辽 宁 Liaoning	58	24	0	5	37	16
吉 林 Jilin	1477	814	1	615	844	17
黑龙江 Heilongjiang	418	127	0	30	296	90
上 海 Shanghai	39	27	0	15	18	3
江 苏 Jiangsu	0	0	0	0	0	0
浙 江 Zhejiang	25	10	0	3	12	9
安 徽 Anhui	10452	2286	3	1562	6959	1899
福 建 Fujian	23	4	0	2	19	2
江 西 Jiangxi	261	53	0	36	157	65
山 东 Shandong	243	116	0	70	149	24
河 南 henan	292	110	0	69	195	28
湖 北 Hubei	1749	514	2	243	1260	232
湖 南 Hunan	181	71	0	40	133	8
广 东 Guangdong	132	41	0	7	119	5
广 西 Guangxi	506	198	0	91	388	27
海 南 Hainan	0	0	0	0	0	0
重 庆 Chongqing	40	27	0	10	20	10
四 川 Sichuan	383	134	0	69	285	29
贵 州 guizhou	2078	559	0	176	1596	291
云 南 Yunnan	515	171	0	41	384	89
西 藏 Tibet	10	4	0	4	2	4
陕 西 Shaanxi	270	127	0	28	188	46
甘 肃 Gansu	100	21	0	10	84	6
青 海 Qinghai	22	9	0	2	17	3
宁 夏 Ningxia	99	47	0	28	69	2
新 疆 Xinjiang	348	149	0	84	194	67

历、职称情况(总计)

by Educational Attainment (Regional Aggregates)

单位:人

Unit: in Person

	按职称分 By Rank				
高中阶段毕业以下 Below High School Graduate	中学高级 Senior Secondary	中学一级 1st Grade	中学二级 2st Grade	中学三级 3st Grade	未评职称 Rank Undecided
97	**540**	**8214**	**14250**	**4345**	**3439**
0	0	0	0	0	0
0	0	0	0	0	0
2	16	524	1277	183	320
5	65	517	856	201	179
12	81	1898	2731	1169	1050
0	6	24	13	4	11
0	25	280	994	133	45
2	3	192	177	27	19
3	0	17	21	0	1
0	0	0	0	0	0
1	0	3	1	0	21
29	216	2977	4821	1405	1033
0	0	2	18	2	1
3	5	47	121	48	40
0	6	54	119	39	25
0	13	86	110	76	7
12	26	662	678	271	112
0	3	63	76	24	15
1	2	58	55	4	13
0	11	123	281	67	24
0	0	0	0	0	0
0	3	13	13	7	4
0	11	82	215	25	50
15	15	312	1115	344	292
1	3	116	206	138	52
0	0	1	0	1	8
8	9	60	99	57	45
0	6	25	56	8	5
0	0	7	13	1	1
0	12	11	36	24	16
3	3	60	148	87	50

职业初中专任教师学

Breakdown of Vocational Junior Secondary Schools Heads and Teachers

地 区 Reion	合计 Total	其中女 Of Which: Female	按学历分 By Educational Attainment			
			研究生毕业 Graduate	本科毕业 Under-graduate	专科毕业 Associate Bachelor	高中阶段毕业 High School Graduate
合 计 Total	**1177**	**629**	**5**	**494**	**569**	**97**
北 京 Beijing	0	0	0	0	0	0
天 津 Tianjin	0	0	0	0	0	0
河 北 Hebei	116	79	0	91	24	1
山 西 Shanxi	381	207	4	219	153	5
内蒙古 Inner Mongolia	34	18	0	13	21	0
辽 宁 Liaoning	23	11	0	3	16	4
吉 林 Jilin	49	34	1	41	6	1
黑龙江 Heilongjiang	10	9	0	6	4	0
上 海 Shanghai	39	27	0	15	18	3
江 苏 Jiangsu	0	0	0	0	0	0
浙 江 Zhejiang	6	3	0	0	4	1
安 徽 Anhui	114	24	0	26	79	9
福 建 Fujian	0	0	0	0	0	0
江 西 Jiangxi	0	0	0	0	0	0
山 东 Shandong	18	9	0	7	7	4
河 南 henan	26	20	0	6	14	6
湖 北 Hubei	79	34	0	9	33	37
湖 南 Hunan	14	9	0	7	4	3
广 东 Guangdong	0	0	0	0	0	0
广 西 Guangxi	92	46	0	18	73	1
海 南 Hainan	0	0	0	0	0	0
重 庆 Chongqing	40	27	0	10	20	10
四 川 Sichuan	27	11	0	12	15	0
贵 州 guizhou	31	12	0	2	18	9
云 南 Yunnan	0	0	0	0	0	0
西 藏 Tibet	0	0	0	0	0	0
陕 西 Shaanxi	42	31	0	8	28	0
甘 肃 Gansu	0	0	0	0	0	0
青 海 Qinghai	15	8	0	1	14	0
宁 夏 Ningxia	0	0	0	0	0	0
新 疆 Xinjiang	21	10	0	0	18	3

历、职称情况（城市）

by Educational Attainment (Urban)

单位：人

Unit: in Person

	按职称分 By Rank				
高中阶段毕业以下 Below High School Graduate	中学高级 Senior Secondary	中学一级 1st Grade	中学二级 2st Grade	中学三级 3st Grade	未评职称 Rank Undecided
12	**78**	**386**	**448**	**114**	**151**
0	0	0	0	0	0
0	0	0	0	0	0
0	2	38	68	1	7
0	28	125	124	40	64
0	3	14	17	0	0
0	2	9	2	1	9
0	11	21	11	4	2
0	0	6	4	0	0
3	0	17	21	0	1
0	0	0	0	0	0
1	0	2	0	0	4
0	3	53	38	10	10
0	0	0	0	0	0
0	0	0	0	0	0
0	2	4	3	5	4
0	2	9	10	5	0
0	5	19	25	6	24
0	0	6	2	2	4
0	0	0	0	0	0
0	8	22	38	17	7
0	0	0	0	0	0
0	3	13	13	7	4
0	6	1	10	5	5
2	0	0	21	4	6
0	0	0	0	0	0
0	0	0	0	0	0
6	3	17	22	0	0
0	0	0	0	0	0
0	0	3	11	1	0
0	0	0	0	0	0
0	0	7	8	6	0

职业初中专任教师学

Breakdown of Vocational Junior Secondary Schools Heads and Teachers

地 区 Region	合计 Total	其中女 Of Which: Female	按学历分 By Educational Attainment 研究生毕业 Graduate	本科毕业 Under-graduate	专科毕业 Associate Bachelor	高中阶段毕业 High School Graduate
合 计 Total	**8432**	**3734**	**10**	**1748**	**5933**	**721**
北 京 Beijing	0	0	0	0	0	0
天 津 Tianjin	0	0	0	0	0	0
河 北 Hebei	1253	725	0	393	808	51
山 西 Shanxi	686	390	10	191	430	54
内蒙古 Inner Mongolia	2270	1161	0	290	1661	315
辽 宁 Liaoning	5	3	0	1	1	3
吉 林 Jilin	452	238	0	134	306	12
黑龙江 Heilongjiang	13	6	0	1	11	1
上 海 Shanghai	0	0	0	0	0	0
江 苏 Jiangsu	0	0	0	0	0	0
浙 江 Zhejiang	19	7	0	3	8	8
安 徽 Anhui	1587	447	0	346	1122	113
福 建 Fujian	0	0	0	0	0	0
江 西 Jiangxi	64	20	0	17	45	2
山 东 Shandong	130	64	0	39	89	2
河 南 henan	12	8	0	3	5	4
湖 北 Hubei	298	73	0	46	220	26
湖 南 Hunan	153	58	0	29	119	5
广 东 Guangdong	132	41	0	7	119	5
广 西 Guangxi	356	129	0	69	264	23
海 南 Hainan	0	0	0	0	0	0
重 庆 Chongqing	0	0	0	0	0	0
四 川 Sichuan	68	22	0	5	58	5
贵 州 guizhou	504	152	0	70	384	50
云 南 Yunnan	153	60	0	22	117	14
西 藏 Tibet	10	4	0	4	2	4
陕 西 Shaanxi	95	42	0	17	68	9
甘 肃 Gansu	7	0	0	2	3	2
青 海 Qinghai	3	1	0	0	0	3
宁 夏 Ningxia	51	32	0	21	30	0
新 疆 Xinjiang	111	51	0	38	63	10

历、职称情况(县镇)

by Educational Attainment (County Seats & Towns)

单位:人

Unit: in Person

	按职称分 By Rank				
高中阶段毕业以下 Below High School Graduate	中学高级 Senior Secondary	中学一级 1st Grade	中学二级 2st Grade	中学三级 3st Grade	未评职称 Rank Undecided
20	**198**	**2356**	**4062**	**933**	**883**
0	0	0	0	0	0
0	0	0	0	0	0
1	12	295	700	87	159
1	20	198	360	73	35
4	34	645	971	333	287
0	0	2	3	0	0
0	6	97	315	21	13
0	0	12	1	0	0
0	0	0	0	0	0
0	0	0	0	0	0
0	0	1	1	0	17
6	74	477	668	176	192
0	0	0	0	0	0
0	3	17	38	4	2
0	3	21	72	30	4
0	0	5	5	2	0
6	6	156	113	14	9
0	3	50	68	22	10
1	2	58	55	4	13
0	3	89	217	30	17
0	0	0	0	0	0
0	0	0	0	0	0
0	3	15	47	3	0
0	9	103	254	74	64
0	2	53	67	21	10
0	0	1	0	1	8
1	4	23	31	18	19
0	5	2	0	0	0
0	0	2	0	0	1
0	7	7	22	4	11
0	2	27	54	16	12

职业初中专任教师学

Breakdown of Vocational Junior Secondary Schools Heads and Teachers

地　区 Region	合计 Total	其中女 Of Which: Female	按学历分 By Educational Attainment			
			研究生毕业 Graduate	本科毕业 Under-graduate	专科毕业 Associate Bachelor	高中阶段毕业 High School Graduate
合　计 Total	**21179**	**10995**	**19**	**3035**	**14336**	**3724**
北　京 Beijing	0	0	0	0	0	0
天　津 Tianjin	0	0	0	0	0	0
河　北 Hebei	951	1341	1	241	651	57
山　西 Shanxi	751	909	12	108	524	103
内蒙古 Inner Mongolia	4625	3102	1	491	3141	984
辽　宁 Liaoning	30	24	0	1	20	9
吉　林 Jilin	976	814	0	440	532	4
黑龙江 Heilongjiang	395	127	0	23	281	89
上　海 Shanghai	0	27	0	0	0	0
江　苏 Jiangsu	0	0	0	0	0	0
浙　江 Zhejiang	0	10	0	0	0	0
安　徽 Anhui	8751	2286	3	1190	5758	1777
福　建 Fujian	23	4	0	2	19	2
江　西 Jiangxi	197	53	0	19	112	63
山　东 Shandong	95	116	0	24	53	18
河　南 henan	254	110	0	60	176	18
湖　北 Hubei	1372	514	2	188	1007	169
湖　南 Hunan	14	71	0	4	10	0
广　东 Guangdong	0	41	0	0	0	0
广　西 Guangxi	58	198	0	4	51	3
海　南 Hainan	0	0	0	0	0	0
重　庆 Chongqing	0	27	0	0	0	0
四　川 Sichuan	288	134	0	52	212	24
贵　州 guizhou	1543	559	0	104	1194	232
云　南 Yunnan	362	171	0	19	267	75
西　藏 Tibet	0	4	0	0	0	0
陕　西 Shaanxi	133	127	0	3	92	37
甘　肃 Gansu	93	21	0	8	81	4
青　海 Qinghai	4	9	0	1	3	0
宁　夏 Ningxia	48	47	0	7	39	2
新　疆 Xinjiang	216	149	0	46	113	54

历、职称情况(农村)

by Educational Attainment (Rural)

单位:人

Unit: in Person

高中阶段毕业以下 Below High School Graduate	按职称分 By Rank				
	中学高级 Senior Secondary	中学一级 1st Grade	中学二级 2st Grade	中学三级 3st Grade	未评职称 Rank Undecided
65	**264**	**5472**	**9740**	**3298**	**2405**
0	0	0	0	0	0
0	0	0	0	0	0
1	2	191	509	95	154
4	17	194	372	88	80
8	44	1239	1743	836	763
0	4	13	8	3	2
0	8	162	668	108	30
2	3	174	172	27	19
0	0	0	0	0	0
0	0	0	0	0	0
0	0	0	0	0	0
23	139	2447	4115	1219	831
0	0	2	18	2	1
3	2	30	83	44	38
0	1	29	44	4	17
0	11	72	95	69	7
6	15	487	540	251	79
0	0	7	6	0	1
0	0	0	0	0	0
0	0	12	26	20	0
0	0	0	0	0	0
0	0	0	0	0	0
0	2	66	158	17	45
13	6	209	840	266	222
1	1	63	139	117	42
0	0	0	0	0	0
1	2	20	46	39	26
0	1	23	56	8	5
0	0	2	2	0	0
0	5	4	14	20	5
3	1	26	86	65	38

普通初中办

Condition of School Buildings in Junior Secondary

地区 Region	学校占地面积 Areas Occupied	校舍建筑面积 Floor Space	教学及辅 Teaching & Assistant			
			计 Total	其中		
				普通教室 classroom	实验室 Laboratory	图书室 Library
合 计 Total	**1422218450**	**334730429**	**152832033**	**109677136**	**19558728**	**6556132**
北 京 Beijing	10486795	2643664	1161922	651252	183963	54614
天 津 Tianjin	7751499	1872463	1039161	656336	142005	40778
河 北 Hebei	99645025	18762013	10209573	7242315	1749126	443712
山 西 Shanxi	41851186	9127936	3928366	2939161	449888	192715
内蒙古 Inner Mongolia	46182217	5129934	2494419	1778821	317625	122329
辽 宁 Liaoning	48038008	8863296	4985874	2973289	661681	196473
吉 林 Jilin	35639910	5119615	2984178	1955685	398547	127673
黑龙江 Heilongjiang	54390582	8449585	5221727	3769548	587585	189611
上 海 Shanghai	8453035	4358336	2024968	1110809	393288	138658
江 苏 Jiangsu	75028272	18891408	9090424	6351993	1244060	438294
浙 江 Zhejiang	46832649	15617473	7564125	4521255	1168541	362126
安 徽 Anhui	67523351	12305669	5904244	4662459	649329	276981
福 建 Fujian	30417347	8926810	3866008	2545989	537238	205718
江 西 Jiangxi	46924849	11362145	4719081	3686650	480928	183397
山 东 Shandong	137674390	27362884	12920539	9006098	1855935	530395
河 南 Henan	115634596	29593519	13097883	9916053	1441392	576263
湖 北 Hubei	66662947	21265329	7473753	5465567	968631	325893
湖 南 Hunan	82842050	21597500	9502985	7354202	919599	358607
广 东 Guangdong	85621920	25916452	11019314	7530415	1515741	523479
广 西 Guangxi	55385673	15146533	5380535	4207381	493560	192907
海 南 Hainan	16121293	1900400	780035	561019	86941	46658
重 庆 Chongqing	15499047	6785241	2636799	1922447	281332	90341
四 川 Sichuan	47213676	17201536	7480126	5595292	880630	256750
贵 州 Guizhou	24738200	6300833	3403837	2647106	336930	116466
云 南 Yunnan	41971383	10492853	3895217	2932251	588004	159235
西 藏 Tibet	3931220	708909	273722	220422	29555	9265
陕 西 Shaanxi	32680515	8861749	4374500	3305607	558480	171600
甘 肃 Gansu	23318708	4144809	2128506	1714366	201469	87421
青 海 Qinghai	4708478	765979	394192	324798	23769	12909
宁 夏 Ningxia	6927543	1112344	577606	419063	86440	27490
新 疆 Xinjiang	42122086	4143212	2298414	1709487	326516	97374

学条件(一)(总计)

Schools (1) (Regional Aggregates)

单位:平方米

Unit: m^2

助用房 Buildings		行政办公用房 Administritive		生活用房 Residential and Welfare	其他用房 Rooms for Other Purposes	校舍面积中 Of the Floor Space	
Of Which							
微机室 PC-room	语音室 Linguistic	计 Total	其中教师办公室 Of Which: for Teachers			危房面积 Floor Space of Dilapidated Buildings	当年新增 New Floor Space Added in Current Year
4688197	**2017740**	**37430396**	**25807112**	**110412789**	**34055211**	**15625863**	**12084968**
45840	19281	421972	223847	455303	604467	6402	45933
36087	23799	312562	202974	216181	304559	2016	11408
370415	177457	2698683	2122990	3993824	1859933	421418	701368
120616	57188	1599885	1231484	2640281	959404	385378	393817
87651	44903	794550	593134	1367884	473081	741950	232103
161960	112892	1485313	875300	1129434	1262675	190493	175685
112859	79993	923599	627922	620135	591703	464730	216122
161562	78761	1324593	977893	1014936	888329	442852	200483
95046	46613	519365	279665	654769	1159234	0	131150
294119	107723	2025999	1218209	5787274	1987711	7932	1041604
233978	117520	1443184	874980	4981420	1628744	21595	828755
121573	45848	1245033	847969	4309045	847347	1428419	469959
102425	35587	658450	366977	3673202	729150	208763	186149
139437	56666	870520	567796	4885789	886755	670456	430216
384696	225079	3650795	2410459	8478166	2313384	924971	506887
403148	127474	5027159	3939838	8445757	3022720	1475226	930751
229741	85308	1667456	1068159	9968539	2155581	840109	352168
266826	99205	1823988	1304112	7605098	2665429	1172117	492773
320823	169556	1972844	1146922	9601800	3322494	650246	942136
147300	45188	739472	466825	7754892	1271634	901928	543966
23834	9221	114555	67145	855616	150194	91730	94943
94757	21778	488047	289496	2968967	691428	403452	206611
249732	52096	1144409	725876	7273693	1303308	902927	586522
107321	23692	464818	294771	1812694	619484	180603	574452
57196	24990	543287	310247	5478661	575688	1128508	852761
3552	2346	49072	40061	330871	55244	43249	114943
148617	73805	1881032	1535345	1966591	639626	753149	292655
70351	14512	750555	633084	854503	411245	557239	215157
12688	3746	74239	64253	239551	57997	77259	36131
26382	8471	166334	127787	253756	114648	111691	42896
57665	27042	548626	371592	794157	502015	419055	234464

普通初中办

Condition of School Buildings in Junior

地区 Region	学校占地面积 Areas Occupied	校舍建筑面积 Floor Space	教学及辅 Teaching & Assistant			
			计 Total	其中 普通教室 classroom	实验室 Laboratory	图书室 Library
合计 Total	**173209444**	**61055332**	**30301984**	**19102894**	**4261819**	**1494536**
北京 Beijing	1845235	946441	391255	204005	60244	19399
天津 Tianjin	1608218	675866	348729	186796	48934	16678
河北 Hebei	9088886	2943387	1546866	1034389	257656	73951
山西 Shanxi	5253088	1565647	750686	517355	109896	36138
内蒙古 Inner Mongolia	5850491	1236424	670662	456103	79066	32734
辽宁 Liaoning	11344374	3616980	1953760	1051852	225107	80009
吉林 Jilin	4120095	1335181	748090	464269	84981	26242
黑龙江 Heilongjiang	8078584	2182437	1267663	778503	149889	48105
上海 Shanghai	3175777	2437621	1108873	598482	195703	81778
江苏 Jiangsu	9359361	3404591	1811113	1056555	299041	117430
浙江 Zhejiang	10370843	4268330	2187239	1138474	329181	141279
安徽 Anhui	5109864	1494988	814551	564340	119484	39139
福建 Fujian	2704038	1138999	548548	309806	101439	38340
江西 Jiangxi	2640739	924835	451840	349048	42900	17409
山东 Shandong	19888319	5898413	2988229	1924683	418779	124585
河南 Henan	11069491	4108898	1893155	1297203	301395	95465
湖北 Hubei	13825142	4945739	2156560	1442455	314381	96146
湖南 Hunan	6869092	1967337	1015371	731521	114531	47241
广东 Guangdong	13791552	6184276	2964355	1787434	422922	162775
广西 Guangxi	4322979	1373924	633602	420576	80578	27295
海南 Hainan	979774	290372	128699	79627	12450	8886
重庆 Chongqing	4492700	2138769	845833	610573	99028	30848
四川 Sichuan	3223108	1685196	819921	547462	100284	32369
贵州 Guizhou	2334997	919555	502307	348983	53440	18366
云南 Yunnan	1311474	452926	226008	144537	37053	12095
西藏 Tibet	557125	116696	44132	34470	5090	2214
陕西 Shaanxi	2515645	1048571	557517	377537	74588	22962
甘肃 Gansu	2104620	531434	278865	203151	33301	13514
青海 Qinghai	534774	117220	63905	47861	5531	2611
宁夏 Ningxia	1288302	248522	142862	94413	22801	7549
新疆 Xinjiang	3550757	855757	440788	300431	62146	20984

学条件(一)(城市)

Secondary Schools (1) (Urban)

单位:平方米

Unit: m^2

助用房 Buildings		行政办公用房 Administritive		生活用房 Residential and Welfare	其他用房 Rooms for Other Purposes	校舍面积中 Of the Floor Space	
Of Which							
微机室 PC-room	语音室 Linguistic	计 Total	其中教师办公室 Of Which: for Teachers			危房面积 Floor Space of Dilapidated Buildings	当年新增 New Floor Space Added in Current Year
1123326	**575535**	**8180481**	**5000829**	**13349742**	**9223125**	**1031100**	**2427064**
16369	7672	162709	83765	102371	290106	1799	23982
13397	8775	113046	71092	60529	153562	500	3959
59140	29936	441544	312586	574309	380668	36085	111036
25304	14712	294898	189761	326501	193562	21735	26118
24623	15858	217824	145688	197814	150124	114052	67913
63043	42139	591963	299441	353569	717688	22728	75542
32328	18215	229075	146383	143160	214856	35137	91707
40575	23743	374037	242091	206764	333973	35879	60195
54653	28844	297677	159451	282185	748886	0	53403
70341	27524	441428	244814	636069	515981	2713	150038
76484	40892	454968	267341	1062316	563807	5959	301989
28604	14798	225318	144192	283103	172016	65367	49525
20225	11117	105902	60610	283362	201187	7687	29533
15242	7907	90745	65304	274775	107475	24456	60335
110225	65792	959847	569729	1276391	673946	84775	131642
72136	34915	670828	466242	1034405	510510	56333	126945
76878	33585	574724	345102	1591563	622892	68230	148291
35144	22050	192594	133166	521116	238256	55476	75419
109085	51438	592576	346436	1377849	1249496	26937	332373
27389	10804	118718	79365	447092	174512	25333	92206
4361	1811	23115	15485	98925	39633	1630	9922
32062	11022	189043	105210	816068	287825	150078	77206
29720	14171	192078	115256	490210	182987	34590	106422
21057	5387	101434	64254	207276	108538	9612	26585
6714	3509	39176	22783	149346	38396	27698	91836
828	389	9217	7370	51461	11886	1968	2345
19530	11350	188926	123450	211261	90867	20443	18874
11596	5310	89120	53128	85284	78165	25160	18977
3186	1301	17374	13329	26245	9696	14337	8621
7993	3432	41735	28779	32322	31603	1697	4216
15094	7137	138842	79226	146101	130026	52706	49909

Condition of School Buildings in Junior Secondary

地　区 Region	学校占地面积 Areas Occupied	校舍建筑面积 Floor Space	教学及辅 Teaching & Assistant 计 Total	其中 普通教室 classroom	其中 实验室 Laboratory	其中 图书室 Library
合　计 Total	**460096404**	**115015174**	**51011788**	**36820224**	**6526906**	**2088227**
北　京 Beijing	5548485	1083256	516224	297407	74980	21717
天　津 Tianjin	3117157	686515	377692	237489	51379	13082
河　北 Hebei	34949814	6824738	3606920	2637547	561125	143910
山　西 Shanxi	9398496	2433683	998807	751545	113117	45075
内蒙古 Inner Mongolia	16506320	1921686	923801	664156	116424	41474
辽　宁 Liaoning	4815584	1204979	691489	431663	82430	25266
吉　林 Jilin	13552868	2106583	1204349	795498	153408	50893
黑龙江 Heilongjiang	9889980	1891664	1200111	876394	130557	38888
上　海 Shanghai	4693382	1778525	846941	473669	181839	51062
江　苏 Jiangsu	11049296	3628764	1728815	1199095	230930	92137
浙　江 Zhejiang	31836623	9951321	4732910	2939096	747576	199395
安　徽 Anhui	13953811	2780751	1302815	1027325	142668	59321
福　建 Fujian	11431481	3395806	1445478	984706	181845	71515
江　西 Jiangxi	18519551	4660586	1857494	1442502	185562	77806
山　东 Shandong	65640257	12848305	5898498	4205604	850301	229310
河　南 Henan	28383045	8160810	3572090	2709889	375808	147092
湖　北 Hubei	12335036	4131897	1439241	1068792	184224	62630
湖　南 Hunan	26818271	7343220	3075434	2354707	315332	115987
广　东 Guangdong	30291273	8951188	3761108	2677128	512800	174881
广　西 Guangxi	30856382	8554987	2889803	2303386	253894	99394
海　南 Hainan	7671395	866806	339781	265151	33129	17821
重　庆 Chongqing	6718707	2916486	1121050	802518	113019	36319
四　川 Sichuan	17403174	6423474	2668229	1980104	330576	93427
贵　州 Guizhou	10457968	2559915	1250500	973207	139246	42885
云　南 Yunnan	13689069	3429815	1298977	978635	193933	51378
西　藏 Tibet	3354752	588106	228252	184794	24405	6991
陕　西 Shaanxi	6936764	2200957	1145756	871346	144455	45665
甘　肃 Gansu	3349205	723284	384530	313048	34062	14220
青　海 Qinghai	1190158	209558	106079	81882	7659	3659
宁　夏 Ningxia	1657553	285973	150406	109928	22953	6524
新　疆 Xinjiang	4080547	471536	248208	182013	37270	8503

学条件(一)(县镇)

Schools (1) (County Seats & Towns)

单位:平方米

Unit:m[2]

助用房 Buildings		行政办公用房 Administritive		生活用房 Residential and Welfare	其他用房 Rooms for Other Purposes	校舍面积中 Of the Floor Space	
Of Which		计 Total	其中教师办公室 Of Which: for Teachers			危房面积 Floor Space of Dilapidated Buildings	当年新增 New Floor Space Added in Current Year
微机室 PC-room	语音室 Linguistic						
1556518	**721203**	**11917062**	**8076637**	**41241628**	**10844696**	**4545619**	**4719890**
19871	7900	166411	84790	210739	189882	3209	14039
13498	8651	120098	70443	93868	94857	273	5189
128197	64292	899037	697280	1656622	662159	168531	344507
32341	16341	414958	323990	733840	286078	93576	183139
32952	18064	295882	221199	538594	163409	307181	101122
20153	14605	204022	128041	184987	124481	5538	29163
43816	42448	389242	247871	286475	226517	160839	85248
40912	21439	339447	249527	179366	172740	101743	47171
36768	15598	202189	107060	340263	389132	0	73959
55782	22152	403832	260343	1093973	402144	975	356923
140697	71235	880258	538764	3376248	961905	10696	477321
31757	12229	267300	181000	1022170	188466	288259	133389
34867	12949	241111	128982	1459603	249614	79045	68727
55921	24330	361812	224275	2075705	365575	209351	221221
157348	96174	1601468	1085671	4356899	991440	424199	240508
117034	38225	1350198	1021174	2431304	807218	336136	315658
45964	23246	317459	212483	1943512	431685	147553	40595
87759	38510	586942	407621	2736246	944598	309704	171022
99064	62086	682640	384453	3539609	967831	262266	281519
84909	23748	384397	245915	4593513	687274	443427	311869
9226	3125	44098	27568	433142	49785	56245	63155
38890	6766	205028	126356	1354826	235582	156683	92792
88174	22822	404934	266967	2923681	426630	238449	214228
40431	10764	185410	115531	853463	270542	77834	237458
23472	9895	219388	126182	1712024	199426	333391	272508
2664	1957	39735	32571	276881	43238	40677	112598
43271	20056	436942	346943	477625	140634	127112	104084
12451	3741	138498	121427	123886	76370	87838	55422
2785	1031	18825	17217	68882	15772	20725	7586
7290	2574	49965	36687	58426	27176	13856	17057
8254	4250	65536	38306	105256	52536	40308	40713

普通初中办

Condition of School Buildings in Junior

地 区 Region	学校占地面积 Areas Occupied	校舍建筑面积 Floor Space	计 Total	普通教室 classroom	实验室 Laboratory	图书室 Library
			教学及辅 Teaching & Assistant			
				其中		
合 计 Total	**788912602**	**158659923**	**71518261**	**53754018**	**8770003**	**2973369**
北 京 Beijing	3093075	613967	254443	149840	48739	13498
天 津 Tianjin	3026124	510082	312740	232051	41692	11018
河 北 Hebei	55606325.	8993888	5055787	3570379	930345	225851
山 西 Shanxi	27199602	5128606	2178873	1670261	226875	111502
内蒙古 Inner Mongolia	23825406	1971824	899956	658562	122135	48121
辽 宁 Liaoning	31878050	4041337	2340625	1489774	354144	91198
吉 林 Jilin	17966947	1677851	1031739	695918	160158	50538
黑龙江 Heilongjiang	36422018	4375484	2753953	2114651	307139	102618
上 海 Shanghai	583876	142190	69154	38658	15746	5818
江 苏 Jiangsu	54619615	11858053	5550496	4096343	714089	228727
浙 江 Zhejiang	4625183	1397822	643976	443685	91784	21452
安 徽 Anhui	48459676	8029930	3786878	3070794	387177	178521
福 建 Fujian	16281828	4392005	1871982	1251477	253954	95863
江 西 Jiangxi	25764559	5776724	2409747	1895100	252466	88182
山 东 Shandong	52145814	8616166	4033812	2875811	586855	176500
河 南 Henan	76182060	17323811	7632638	5908961	764189	333706
湖 北 Hubei	40502769	12187693	3877952	2954320	470026	167117
湖 南 Hunan	49154687	12286943	5412180	4267974	489736	195379
广 东 Guangdong	41539095	10780988	4293851	3065853	580019	185823
广 西 Guangxi	20206312	5217622	1857130	1483419	159088	66218
海 南 Hainan	7470124	743222	311555	216241	41362	19951
重 庆 Chongqing	4287640	1729986	669916	509356	69285	23174
四 川 Sichuan	26587394	9092866	3991976	3067726	449770	130954
贵 州 Guizhou	11945235	2821363	1651030	1324916	144244	55215
云 南 Yunnan	26970840	6610112	2370232	1809079	357018	95762
西 藏 Tibet	19343	4107	1338	1158	60	60
陕 西 Shaanxi	23228106	5612221	2671227	2056724	339437	102973
甘 肃 Gansu	17864883	2890091	1465111	1198167	134106	59687
青 海 Qinghai	2983546	439201	224208	195055	10579	6639
宁 夏 Ningxia	3981688	577849	284338	214722	40686	13417
新 疆 Xinjiang	34490782	2815919	1609418	1227043	227100	67887

学条件(一)(农村)

Secondary Schools (1) (Rural)

单位:平方米

Unit: m^2

助用房 Buildings		行政办公用房 Administritive		生活用房 Residential and Welfare	其他用房 Rooms for Other Purposes	校舍面积中 Of the Floor Space	
Of Which							
微机室 PC-room	语音室 Linguistic	计 Total	其中教师办公室 Of Which: for Teachers			危房面积 Floor Space of Dilapidated Buildings	当年新增 New Floor Space Added in Current Year
2008353	**721002**	**17332853**	**12729646**	**55821419**	**13987390**	**10049144**	**4938014**
9600	3709	92852	55292	142193	124479	1394	7912
9192	6373	79418	61439	61784	56140	1243	2260
183078	83229	1358102	1113124	1762893	817106	216802	245825
62971	26135	890029	717733	1579940	479764	270067	184560
30076	10981	280844	226247	631476	159548	320717	63068
78764	56148	689328	447818	590878	420506	162227	70980
36715	19330	305282	233668	190500	150330	268754	39167
80075	33579	611109	486275	628806	381616	305230	93117
3625	2171	19499	13154	32321	21216	0	3788
167996	58047	1180739	713052	4057232	1069586	4244	534643
16797	5393	107958	68875	542856	103032	4940	49445
61212	18821	752415	522777	3003772	486865	1074793	287045
47333	11521	311437	177385	1930237	278349	122031	87889
68274	24429	417963	278217	2535309	413705	436649	148660
117123	63113	1089480	755059	2844876	647998	415997	134737
213978	54334	3006133	2452422	4980048	1704992	1082757	488148
106899	28477	775273	510574	6433464	1101004	624326	163282
143923	38645	1044452	763325	4347736	1482575	806937	246332
112674	56032	697628	416033	4684342	1105167	361043	328244
35002	10636	236357	141545	2714287	409848	433168	139891
10247	4285	47342	24092	323549	60776	33855	21866
23805	3990	93976	57930	798073	168021	96691	36613
131838	15103	547397	343653	3859802	693691	629888	265872
45833	7541	177974	114986	751955	240404	93157	310409
27010	11586	284723	161282	3617291	337866	767419	488417
60	0	120	120	2529	120	604	0
85816	42399	1255164	1064952	1277705	408125	605594	169697
46304	5461	522937	458529	645333	256710	444241	140758
6717	1414	38040	33707	144424	32529	42197	19924
11099	2465	74634	62321	163008	55869	96138	21623
34317	15655	344248	254060	542800	319453	326041	143842

职业初中办

Condition of School Buildings in Vocational Junior

地 区 Region	学校占地面积 Areas Occupied	校舍建筑面积 Floor Space	教学及辅 Teaching & Assistant			
			计 Total	其中		
				普通教室 classroom	实验室 Laboratory	图书室 Library
合 计 Total	**24518236**	**3307053**	**1452978**	**1077849**	**186087**	**81753**
北 京 Beijing	0	0	0	0	0	0
天 津 Tianjin	0	0	0	0	0	0
河 北 Hebei	2472827	500812	220051	139485	49169	17938
山 西 Shanxi	1458196	237019	86675	56269	11865	6158
内蒙古 Inner Mongolia	6253847	581184	235773	169798	31887	13186
辽 宁 Liaoning	72748	9433	3117	2094	258	335
吉 林 Jilin	897754	88590	54321	37880	8261	2665
黑龙江 Heilongjiang	141220	16924	13269	10877	1496	616
上 海 Shanghai	7965	3977	1478	1246	0	44
江 苏 Jiangsu	0	0	0	0	0	0
浙 江 Zhejiang	0	0	0	0	0	0
安 徽 Anhui	8335014	1044901	527214	430296	46009	27325
福 建 Fujian	4735	2663	714	400	120	81
江 西 Jiangxi	138935	29460	11590	9121	978	288
山 东 Shandong	192101	22299	9629	5798	890	220
河 南 Henan	161575	28910	9110	6815	1235	701
湖 北 Hubei	1116977	271041	84493	60296	12918	5215
湖 南 Hunan	287234	66998	26495	15260	3920	1270
广 东 Guangdong	0	0	0	0	0	0
广 西 Guangxi	355061	82594	27213	20021	2348	855
海 南 Hainan	0	0	0	0	0	0
重 庆 Chongqing	10162	7552	3000	1500	1270	30
四 川 Sichuan	235868	38661	15051	12491	1492	394
贵 州 Guizhou	1555850	180499	88443	68476	8954	3258
云 南 Yunnan	303827	50205	17852	15105	1835	573
西 藏 Tibet	45500	1581	753	500	0	0
陕 西 Shaanxi	151748	16742	7056	6203	278	249
甘 肃 Gansu	109750	14373	5386	4317	469	145
青 海 Qinghai	63404	3702	1129	861	175	75
宁 夏 Ningxia	0	0	0	0	0	0
新 疆 Xinjiang	145938	6933	3166	2740	260	132

学条件(一)(总计)

Secondary Schools (1) (Regional Aggregates)

单位:平方米

Unit: m^2

助用房 Buildings Of Which 微机室 PC-room	语音室 Linguistic	行政办公用房 Administritive 计 Total	其中教师办公室 Of Which: for Teachers	生活用房 Residential and Welfare	其他用房 Rooms for Other Purposes	校舍面积中 Of the Floor Space 危房面积 Floor Space of Dilapidated Buildings	当年新增 New Floor Space Added in Current Year	实习工厂(农场)面积
43819	**14143**	**372811**	**276711**	**1181724**	**299540**	**308520**	**97722**	**40405**
0	0	0	0	0	0	0	0	0
0	0	0	0	0	0	0	0	0
7481	3006	60689	41285	168547	51525	6595	6308	2000
5175	2217	29293	20789	91369	29682	7574	14823	14489
10070	2948	77500	63138	208449	59462	117443	24112	5444
190	0	618	358	1778	3920	0	0	0
1839	1138	16905	13690	13179	4185	12687	0	0
280	0	1935	1760	940	780	1344	0	1000
88	0	495	111	213	1791	0	0	0
0	0	0	0	0	0	0	0	0
0	0	0	0	0	0	0	0	0
8507	2472	116306	84669	325919	75462	114899	28543	7721
58	0	134	50	1407	408	0	0	0
271	132	5217	5197	10220	2433	1407	198	0
200	170	5522	4592	6403	745	0	180	0
359	0	7000	6011	11374	1426	5070	1060	0
3212	1257	16530	10366	142971	27047	12575	515	561
900	172	5510	3290	21633	13360	1600	0	2600
0	0	0	0	0	0	0	0	0
1387	0	2310	1794	49758	3313	2791	1810	3720
0	0	0	0	0	0	0	0	0
0	0	400	320	3752	400	0	0	0
225	0	2222	1344	18187	3201	2482	2060	60
2925	311	12571	7816	65300	14185	8328	14600	2374
219	120	1672	1104	26818	3863	7345	0	160
0	0	160	160	643	25	0	278	0
126	0	3325	3031	5658	703	3080	280	276
255	200	5272	4872	3203	512	2305	2780	0
18	0	399	399	1702	472	492	175	0
0	0	0	0	0	0	0	0	0
34	0	826	565	2301	640	503	0	0

职业初中办

Condition of School Buildings in Vocational

地区 Region	学校占地面积 Areas Occupied	校舍建筑面积 Floor Space	教学及辅 Teaching & Assistant			
			计 Total	其中 普通教室 classroom	实验室 Laboratory	图书室 Library
合 计 Total	**649486**	**180969**	**77653**	**46931**	**14249**	**6147**
北 京 Beijing	0	0	0	0	0	0
天 津 Tianjin	0	0	0	0	0	0
河 北 Hebei	71440	37030	13182	7005	2940	1231
山 西 Shanxi	191728	66156	27973	16340	5750	2312
内蒙古 Inner Mongolia	0	0	0	0	0	0
辽 宁 Liaoning	48468	6230	1100	660	90	160
吉 林 Jilin	11115	2322	1998	546	0	14
黑龙江 Heilongjiang	12000	4198	3798	3386	300	72
上 海 Shanghai	7965	3977	1478	1246	0	44
江 苏 Jiangsu	0	0	0	0	0	0
浙 江 Zhejiang	0	0	0	0	0	0
安 徽 Anhui	64323	12682	3976	3160	384	252
福 建 Fujian	0	0	0	0	0	0
江 西 Jiangxi	0	0	0	0	0	0
山 东 Shandong	0	0	0	0	0	0
河 南 Henan	53333	1929	582	387	65	65
湖 北 Hubei	56935	26989	15317	8559	3080	1668
湖 南 Hunan	2200	2300	1500	1200	100	100
广 东 Guangdong	0	0	0	0	0	0
广 西 Guangxi	39872	1912	826	487	95	124
海 南 Hainan	0	0	0	0	0	0
重 庆 Chongqing	10162	7552	3000	1500	1270	30
四 川 Sichuan	0	0	0	0	0	0
贵 州 Guizhou	43480	5058	1730	1730	0	0
云 南 Yunnan	0	0	0	0	0	0
西 藏 Tibet	0	0	0	0	0	0
陕 西 Shaanxi	8122	200	200	0	0	0
甘 肃 Gansu	0	0	0	0	0	0
青 海 Qinghai	25346	2099	833	565	175	75
宁 夏 Ningxia	0	0	0	0	0	0
新 疆 Xinjiang	2997	335	160	160	0	0

学条件(一)(城市)

Junior Secondary Schools (1) (Urban)

单位:平方米

Unit: m^2

助用房 Buildings		行政办公用房 Administritive		生活用房 Residential and Welfare	其他用房 Rooms for Other Purposes	校舍面积中 Of the Floor Space		
Of Which								
微机室 PC-room	语音室 Linguistic	计 Total	其中教师办公室 Of Which: for Teachers			危房面积 Floor Space of Dilapidated Buildings	当年新增 New Floor Space Added in Current Year	实习工厂(农场)面积
4981	**1833**	**22764**	**11798**	**63203**	**17349**	**5527**	**295**	**8145**
0	0	0	0	0	0	0	0	0
0	0	0	0	0	0	0	0	0
1698	308	6699	2900	10515	6634	0	0	0
1996	1415	9968	4675	26645	1570	0	0	8145
0	0	0	0	0	0	0	0	0
150	0	260	140	1150	3720	0	0	0
0	0	204	30	120	0	600	0	0
40	0	400	400	0	0	0	0	0
88	0	495	111	213	1791	0	0	0
0	0	0	0	0	0	0	0	0
0	0	0	0	0	0	0	0	0
120	60	1340	720	6674	692	417	0	0
0	0	0	0	0	0	0	0	0
0	0	0	0	0	0	0	0	0
0	0	0	0	0	0	0	0	0
65	0	220	155	1127	0	0	0	0
610	50	2256	1870	7181	2235	4175	120	0
100	0	100	100	500	200	0	0	0
0	0	0	0	0	0	0	0	0
96	0	157	112	856	73	0	0	0
0	0	0	0	0	0	0	0	0
0	0	400	320	3752	400	0	0	0
0	0	0	0	0	0	0	0	0
0	0	40	40	3288	0	0	0	0
0	0	0	0	0	0	0	0	0
0	0	0	0	0	0	0	0	0
0	0	0	0	0	0	0	0	0
0	0	0	0	0	0	0	0	0
18	0	120	120	1112	34	0	175	0
0	0	0	0	0	0	0	0	0
0	0	105	105	70	0	335	0	0

职业初中办

Condition of School Buildings in Vocational Junior

地　区 Region	学校占地面积 Areas Occupied	校舍建筑面积 Floor Space	教学及辅 Teaching & Assistant			
			计 Total	其中		
				普通教室 classroom	实验室 Laboratory	图书室 Library
合　计 Total	**6613063**	**1036605**	**440684**	**302121**	**67993**	**28019**
北　京 Beijing	0	0	0	0	0	0
天　津 Tianjin	0	0	0	0	0	0
河　北 Hebei	1578729	358762	158928	98100	38209	14451
山　西 Shanxi	528418	91885	32071	21100	3386	2026
内蒙古 Inner Mongolia	2005906	171250	68414	49565	9133	3937
辽　宁 Liaoning	0	0	0	0	0	0
吉　林 Jilin	290105	27759	16490	10772	2738	1024
黑龙江 Heilongjiang	20500	1000	336	336	0	0
上　海 Shanghai	0	0	0	0	0	0
江　苏 Jiangsu	0	0	0	0	0	0
浙　江 Zhejiang	0	0	0	0	0	0
安　徽 Anhui	787003	118339	64410	52120	4603	2719
福　建 Fujian	0	0	0	0	0	0
江　西 Jiangxi	60700	10917	3665	2905	454	90
山　东 Shandong	84390	13511	7451	4150	450	160
河　南 Henan	2931	455	238	238	0	0
湖　北 Hubei	172553	44511	11625	8557	1763	647
湖　南 Hunan	164974	44280	14545	8755	2000	650
广　东 Guangdong	0	0	0	0	0	0
广　西 Guangxi	315189	80682	26387	19534	2253	731
海　南 Hainan	0	0	0	0	0	0
重　庆 Chongqing	0	0	0	0	0	0
四　川 Sichuan	58225	3308	1102	653	0	0
贵　州 Guizhou	391144	50500	25686	17298	2659	1318
云　南 Yunnan	16720	5200	2351	2051	110	190
西　藏 Tibet	45500	1581	753	500	0	0
陕　西 Shaanxi	5000	2500	2500	2500	0	0
甘　肃 Gansu	18404	3487	1396	947	49	0
青　海 Qinghai	38058	1603	296	296	0	0
宁　夏 Ningxia	0	0	0	0	0	0
新　疆 Xinjiang	28614	5075	2040	1744	186	76

学条件(一)(县镇)

Secondary Schools (1) (County Seats & Towns)

单位:平方米

Unit: m^2

助用房 Buildings Of Which 微机室 PC-room	语音室 Linguistic	行政办公用房 Administritive 计 Total	其中教师办公室 Of Which: for Teachers	生活用房 Residential and Welfare	其他用房 Rooms for Other Purposes	校舍面积中 Of the Floor Space 危房面积 Floor Space of Dilapidated Buildings	当年新增 New Floor Space Added in Current Year	实习工厂(农场)面积
13724	**5067**	**109205**	**83496**	**376492**	**110224**	**69152**	**39990**	**8084**
0	0	0	0	0	0	0	0	0
0	0	0	0	0	0	0	0	0
3878	1775	39852	28775	125672	34310	2924	2473	0
2380	732	9862	8768	37714	12238	3646	12674	0
2034	816	23702	19892	56859	22275	36427	11300	1494
0	0	0	0	0	0	0	0	0
538	418	4355	3742	3930	2984	3088	0	0
0	0	64	64	0	600	0	0	0
0	0	0	0	0	0	0	0	0
0	0	0	0	0	0	0	0	0
0	0	0	0	0	0	0	0	0
1396	328	11685	9229	33073	9171	10784	7171	1070
0	0	0	0	0	0	0	0	0
108	108	1844	1824	3639	1769	788	0	0
170	170	4415	3665	900	745	0	180	0
0	0	185	185	0	32	0	0	0
486	172	2014	1488	26937	3935	1708	208	0
300	72	2890	870	14685	12160	0	0	1800
0	0	0	0	0	0	0	0	0
1291	0	2153	1682	48902	3240	2791	1810	3720
0	0	0	0	0	0	0	0	0
0	0	0	0	0	0	0	0	0
0	0	420	192	450	1336	0	0	0
909	276	4226	2203	16448	4140	5137	2096	0
0	0	118	118	2427	304	1213	0	0
0	0	160	160	643	25	0	278	0
0	0	0	0	0	0	0	0	0
200	200	630	230	1461	0	154	1800	0
0	0	279	279	590	438	492	0	0
0	0	0	0	0	0	0	0	0
34	0	351	130	2162	522	0	0	0

职业初中办

Condition of School Buildings in Vocational

地区 Region	学校占地面积 Areas Occupied	校舍建筑面积 Floor Space	教学及辅 Teaching & Assistant			
			计 Total	其中 普通教室 classroom	实验室 Laboratory	图书室 Library
合计 Total	**17255687**	**2089479**	**934641**	**728797**	**103845**	**47587**
北京 Beijing	0	0	0	0	0	0
天津 Tianjin	0	0	0	0	0	0
河北 Hebei	822658	105020	47941	34380	8020	2256
山西 Shanxi	738050	78978	26631	18829	2729	1820
内蒙古 Inner Mongolia	4247941	409934	167359	120233	22754	9249
辽宁 Liaoning	24280	3203	2017	1434	168	175
吉林 Jilin	596534	58509	35833	26562	5523	1627
黑龙江 Heilongjiang	108720	11726	9135	7155	1196	544
上海 Shanghai	0	0	0	0	0	0
江苏 Jiangsu	0	0	0	0	0	0
浙江 Zhejiang	0	0	0	0	0	0
安徽 Anhui	7483688	913880	458828	375016	41022	24354
福建 Fujian	4735	2663	714	400	120	81
江西 Jiangxi	78235	18543	7925	6216	524	198
山东 Shandong	107711	8788	2178	1648	440	60
河南 Henan	105311	26526	8290	6190	1170	636
湖北 Hubei	887489	199541	57551	43180	8075	2900
湖南 Hunan	120060	20418	10450	5305	1820	520
广东 Guangdong	0	0	0	0	0	0
广西 Guangxi	0	0	0	0	0	0
海南 Hainan	0	0	0	0	0	0
重庆 Chongqing	0	0	0	0	0	0
四川 Sichuan	177643	35353	13949	11838	1492	394
贵州 Guizhou	1121226	124941	61027	49448	6295	1940
云南 Yunnan	287107	45005	15501	13054	1725	383
西藏 Tibet	0	0	0	0	0	0
陕西 Shaanxi	138626	14042	4356	3703	278	249
甘肃 Gansu	91346	10886	3990	3370	420	145
青海 Qinghai	0	0	0	0	0	0
宁夏 Ningxia	0	0	0	0	0	0
新疆 Xinjiang	114327	1523	966	836	74	56

学条件(一)(农村)

Junior Secondary Schools (1) (Rural)

单位:平方米

Unit: m^2

助用房 Buildings		行政办公用房 Administritive		生活用房 Residential and Welfare	其他用房 Rooms for Other Purposes	校舍面积中 Of the Floor Space		
Of Which								
微机室 PC-room	语音室 Linguistic	计 Total	其中教师办公室 Of Which: for Teachers			危房面积 Floor Space of Dilapidated Buildings	当年新增 New Floor Space Added in Current Year	实习工厂(农场)面积
25114	**7243**	**240842**	**181417**	**742029**	**171967**	**233841**	**57437**	**24176**
0	0	0	0	0	0	0	0	0
0	0	0	0	0	0	0	0	0
1905	923	14138	9610	32360	10581	3671	3835	2000
799	70	9463	7346	27010	15874	3928	2149	6344
8036	2132	53798	43246	151590	37187	81016	12812	3950
40	0	358	218	628	200	0	0	0
1301	720	12346	9918	9129	1201	8999	0	0
240	0	1471	1296	940	180	1344	0	1000
0	0	0	0	0	0	0	0	0
0	0	0	0	0	0	0	0	0
0	0	0	0	0	0	0	0	0
6991	2084	103281	74720	286172	65599	103698	21372	6651
58	0	134	50	1407	408	0	0	0
163	24	3373	3373	6581	664	619	198	0
30	0	1107	927	5503	0	0	0	0
294	0	6595	5671	10247	1394	5070	1060	0
2116	1035	12260	7008	108853	20877	6692	187	561
500	100	2520	2320	6448	1000	1600	0	800
0	0	0	0	0	0	0	0	0
0	0	0	0	0	0	0	0	0
0	0	0	0	0	0	0	0	0
0	0	0	0	0	0	0	0	0
225	0	1802	1152	17737	1865	2482	2060	60
2016	35	8305	5573	45564	10045	3191	12504	2374
219	120	1554	986	24391	3559	6132	0	160
0	0	0	0	0	0	0	0	0
126	0	3325	3031	5658	703	3080	280	276
55	0	4642	4642	1742	512	2151	980	0
0	0	0	0	0	0	0	0	0
0	0	0	0	0	0	0	0	0
0	0	370	330	69	118	168	0	0

普通初中办

Condition of School Buildings in Junior

地区 Region	体育运动场(馆)面积(平方米) Sports Areas (m^2)	计算机(台) PC (set)	图书藏量(册) Books & Magazines in Libraries (Volume)
合计 Total	**400443980**	**2118469**	**820437062**
北京 Beijing	3497391	23615	9904407
天津 Tianjin	3097340	18773	5646027
河北 Hebei	34879155	157124	83962072
山西 Shanxi	11818852	51787	23613095
内蒙古 Inner Mongolia	14204906	33227	12918433
辽宁 Liaoning	17995423	78131	21207543
吉林 Jilin	13739036	52050	15875666
黑龙江 Heilongjiang	23708899	75918	19357693
上海 Shanghai	2907587	55772	12873681
江苏 Jiangsu	21257593	125879	49183325
浙江 Zhejiang	16092806	113723	37764360
安徽 Anhui	16157378	47219	33448656
福建 Fujian	8151483	56800	17930677
江西 Jiangxi	10540503	49936	20862232
山东 Shandong	40452585	199102	64990417
河南 Henan	30239723	150879	93037929
湖北 Hubei	18187980	93145	40828938
湖南 Hunan	17940004	121681	52607674
广东 Guangdong	21783314	185807	64670358
广西 Guangxi	10631196	60516	23297341
海南 Hainan	3318484	9875	3424208
重庆 Chongqing	4483284	47323	8679100
四川 Sichuan	13518026	107640	26957629
贵州 Guizhou	5641629	42995	13331377
云南 Yunnan	7068383	18577	16337712
西藏 Tibet	382348	1635	555169
陕西 Shaanxi	9676816	70460	24979739
甘肃 Gansu	6468173	29524	9856319
青海 Qinghai	1014189	5166	1419178
宁夏 Ningxia	1948598	10779	2397186
新疆 Xinjiang	9640896	23411	8518921

学条件(二)(总计)

Secondary Schools (2) (Regional Aggregates)

电子图书藏量(片) Electronic Books & Magazines in Libraries (disk)	固定资产总值(万元) Total Value of Fixed Asset (in 10 thousand yuan)			
	计 Total	其中:仪器设备总值(万元) Of Which: Total Value of Equip & Instru. (in 10 thousand yuan)		
		计 Sub Total	专业实验设备 For Prefession	专业实习设备 For Practice
7028617	**20429204.56**	**2096011.52**	**1307276.66**	**279949.93**
27114	194208.46	20211.51	10736.92	976.25
27589	121565.41	18524.70	11012.08	2460.60
713400	1293269.11	279699.17	141581.22	19991.32
199813	468259.28	48830.91	29686.69	7786.31
49494	242706.21	25896.15	17733.15	2876.41
25917	506572.00	73346.00	38987.00	7500.00
110216	402292.49	65568.26	26579.52	6746.63
186778	651052.58	67972.75	45410.71	9136.80
172906	553499.38	85574.99	49849.01	3629.09
776296	1442520.47	123262.87	74497.67	14162.05
159777	1223138.99	104052.54	65345.09	0.00
104747	641658.05	58231.22	46698.89	5744.54
63287	526566.00	35170.00	27768.00	7402.00
194766	574675.03	39225.77	21118.80	7665.08
482165	1551897.62	139602.37	89005.40	20978.92
1098812	1521585.63	132198.26	86514.67	28086.95
174153	1083025.25	109931.26	69675.88	22167.86
304937	944159.89	96436.19	63371.87	13766.69
1264022	2393229.39	204181.74	159042.33	44172.17
38709	614227.95	45554.53	28806.91	8577.27
36749	137770.62	10429.39	5849.00	2138.85
119543	482336.73	34221.42	20232.78	5785.48
144975	813104.41	77095.74	46365.75	11434.51
39458	261106.61	23524.09	13655.32	5033.07
31077	506399.66	27762.02	15872.94	2047.89
147	65528.74	2323.41	662.03	553.20
363905	475455.36	49976.70	30662.12	9649.90
51678	313936.90	54799.76	46279.08	4645.97
8765	38389.45	3353.22	2252.63	375.57
14246	152478.96	7642.99	4199.41	1126.21
43176	232587.93	31411.59	17823.79	3332.34

Condition of School Buildings in Junior

地　区 Region	体育运动场(馆)面积(平方米) Sports Areas (m²)	计算机(台) PC (set)	图书藏量(册) Books & Magazines in Libraries (Volume)
合　计 Total	**56927114**	**582643**	**139857939**
北　京 Beijing	582639	10574	3349983
天　津 Tianjin	652397	8080	2086793
河　北 Hebei	3604399	28375	8437966
山　西 Shanxi	1739175	11775	3639643
内蒙古 Inner Mongolia	2130294	12044	3526564
辽　宁 Liaoning	4431766	36877	8631527
吉　林 Jilin	1776521	17315	3592047
黑龙江 Heilongjiang	3271634	23276	3679509
上　海 Shanghai	1185236	35977	7821504
江　苏 Jiangsu	2947212	33278	8976981
浙　江 Zhejiang	3452245	35723	9681115
安　徽 Anhui	1525174	15941	4108064
福　建 Fujian	677335	10934	2202293
江　西 Jiangxi	643125	7759	1436318
山　东 Shandong	6328116	63279	13319567
河　南 Henan	3322164	34200	9722748
湖　北 Hubei	4215194	33940	10718539
湖　南 Hunan	1689055	16038	4484027
广　东 Guangdong	4145700	58224	12163206
广　西 Guangxi	1388904	13204	2757598
海　南 Hainan	251833	1895	453404
重　庆 Chongqing	1256183	18016	2629244
四　川 Sichuan	1202495	13345	2649324
贵　州 Guizhou	691577	9287	1912019
云　南 Yunnan	358293	2946	743363
西　藏 Tibet	71980	631	68958
陕　西 Shaanxi	867461	11271	3179162
甘　肃 Gansu	841018	5689	1469365
青　海 Qinghai	107457	1136	215398
宁　夏 Ningxia	379309	3877	577900
新　疆 Xinjiang	1191223	7737	1623810

学条件(二)(城市)

Secondary Schools (2) (Urban)

电子图书藏量(片) Electronic Books & Magazines in Libraries (disk)	固定资产总值(万元) Total Volue of Fixed Asset (in 10 thousand yuan)			
	计 Total	其中:仪器设备总值(万元) Of Which: Total Volue of Equip & Instru. (in 10 thousand yuan)		
		计 Sub Total	专业实验设备 For Prefession	专业实习设备 For Practice
2768020	**5118095.10**	**669862.65**	**428491.94**	**68684.81**
14988	65479.16	7244.38	4403.89	287.41
23571	29404.62	10553.85	5674.71	869.48
372246	209433.21	73094.22	64472.07	3479.40
57712	91656.51	14082.58	9162.84	1721.49
22850	71436.52	8444.68	5790.16	888.52
12768	254736.00	38736.00	19191.00	2603.00
55097	149427.83	39077.78	10364.55	2175.52
88622	227386.87	26141.88	18144.50	1701.23
119886	266556.88	49675.13	28339.97	1497.69
404878	340083.98	46705.08	26471.99	3967.32
59033	406708.30	32553.66	19710.31	0.00
39190	110692.54	11723.09	8903.32	1472.22
41740	151070.00	11414.00	8228.00	3186.00
17358	86281.51	5552.39	3517.80	812.55
129072	483353.74	48203.15	30813.81	4121.03
306511	435154.52	27939.06	18936.67	3977.24
61054	263213.71	35408.24	23041.29	3856.13
33890	119705.02	15361.51	10011.17	2352.20
727734	683528.49	88790.64	68213.11	19610.29
11767	70849.15	9003.90	5738.89	1338.49
2056	20941.20	2706.37	1436.69	278.54
45689	174426.52	14970.16	8571.83	2322.95
26475	144783.45	18681.64	9908.30	1298.03
9728	43099.53	6497.56	3314.41	1696.70
2799	32998.10	2499.54	1793.16	105.50
0	9538.30	645.05	159.66	74.06
40878	65042.34	7711.13	5224.74	925.78
10525	39176.27	5274.84	2885.61	732.09
534	6223.89	513.39	389.79	85.40
2874	17193.51	3087.27	1737.43	262.00
26495	48513.43	7570.48	3940.27	986.55

地　区 Region	体育运动场(馆) 面 积 (平方米) Sports Areas (m^2)	计 算 机 (台) PC (set)	图书藏量 (册) Books & Magazines in Libraries (Volume)
合　计 Total	**127028526**	**696135**	**273429015**
北　京 Beijing	1815785	8047	4206770
天　津 Tianjin	1257671	5674	1869981
河　北 Hebei	11671490	55274	29724268
山　西 Shanxi	2516571	13719	6210202
内蒙古 Inner Mongolia	5204207	10874	5074690
辽　宁 Liaoning	2011730	9418	2396363
吉　林 Jilin	5374233	19737	6348224
黑龙江 Heilongjiang	4196076	18650	4022072
上　海 Shanghai	1532183	18498	4611268
江　苏 Jiangsu	2783428	24502	7247878
浙　江 Zhejiang	11132825	69154	24905283
安　徽 Anhui	3163259	12245	7234748
福　建 Fujian	2669387	18891	6716794
江　西 Jiangxi	4285474	19964	8853191
山　东 Shandong	18879191	82355	30154640
河　南 Henan	8140529	41490	25829380
湖　北 Hubei	3311638	17908	8007646
湖　南 Hunan	5802139	36948	17387129
广　东 Guangdong	7661695	57425	24222632
广　西 Guangxi	5862537	35366	12915553
海　南 Hainan	1526129	4350	1634863
重　庆 Chongqing	2074619	18431	3705633
四　川 Sichuan	4734815	36543	8912089
贵　州 Guizhou	2394136	17716	5325474
云　南 Yunnan	2206279	7841	5858885
西　藏 Tibet	309968	985	484211
陕　西 Shaanxi	2093082	21082	6385249
甘　肃 Gansu	969161	5667	1464470
青　海 Qinghai	239352	1353	276767
宁　夏 Ningxia	462979	3049	604456
新　疆 Xinjiang	745958	2979	838206

电子图书藏量(片) Electronic Books & Magazines in Libraries (disk)	固定资产总值(万元) Total Volue of Fixed Asset (in 10 thousand yuan)			
	计 Total	其中:仪器设备总值(万元) Of Which: Total Volue of Equip & Instru. (in 10 thousand yuan)		
		计 Sub Total	专业实验设备 For Prefession	专业实习设备 For Practice
2165951	**6965522.57**	**579778.86**	**375687.88**	**85305.11**
5208	88104.36	6941.82	3665.08	463.05
2661	49039.01	4466.96	3260.11	779.14
250508	399728.40	47590.77	32368.95	6425.78
44316	121100.03	13994.87	8292.17	2112.70
14607	89820.45	9718.35	6941.99	1151.61
3850	71612.00	7848.00	4759.00	1021.00
41383	183982.55	17447.40	10742.49	2637.16
48589	147916.73	16610.75	12289.88	1934.56
49482	275557.55	34388.60	20489.63	1866.13
80317	319886.31	23089.71	14029.46	2915.84
97898	750967.40	64170.73	40972.36	0.00
31738	159177.82	9796.39	5594.90	1686.64
9400	171889.00	10223.00	8306.00	1917.00
127342	205026.47	15214.14	8301.71	2736.65
233823	668115.72	56646.96	37054.93	9567.98
335498	405391.19	34459.53	22778.74	8483.17
37225	243819.70	20210.96	13247.01	3641.10
135611	285658.13	30085.70	18760.24	4183.20
371982	673152.01	48916.16	38111.67	10804.49
20715	351931.11	24186.24	14768.29	5492.22
4721	59266.34	3507.25	2170.60	1017.24
50035	232009.34	12502.79	8002.11	1975.46
45246	323862.68	25442.26	16166.79	4239.08
13014	111701.50	8361.86	5393.81	1779.00
5650	173384.12	8813.23	5138.39	839.62
143	55755.44	1670.36	502.37	471.14
95514	114308.13	14247.30	8031.97	3243.73
5954	81979.89	3545.47	2205.87	1052.33
1652	12232.93	1085.79	676.28	127.02
1389	112896.55	1840.01	976.46	485.47
480	26249.71	2755.50	1688.62	255.60

普通初中办

Condition of School Buildings in Junior

地　　区 Region	体育运动场(馆) 面　积 (平方米) Sports Areas (m^2)	计　算　机 (台) PC (set)	图书藏量 (册) Books & Magazines in Libraries (Volume)
合　计 Total	**216488340**	**839691**	**407150108**
北　京 Beijing	1098967	4994	2347654
天　津 Tianjin	1187272	5019	1689253
河　北 Hebei	19603266	73475	45799838
山　西 Shanxi	7563106	26293	13763250
内蒙古 Inner Mongolia	6870405	10309	4317179
辽　宁 Liaoning	11551927	31836	10179653
吉　林 Jilin	6588282	14998	5935395
黑龙江 Heilongjiang	16241189	33992	11656112
上　海 Shanghai	190168	1297	440909
江　苏 Jiangsu	15526953	68099	32958466
浙　江 Zhejiang	1507736	8846	3177962
安　徽 Anhui	11468945	19033	22105844
福　建 Fujian	4804761	26975	9011590
江　西 Jiangxi	5611904	22213	10572723
山　东 Shandong	15245278	53468	21516210
河　南 Henan	18777030	75189	57485801
湖　北 Hubei	10661148	41297	22102753
湖　南 Hunan	10448810	68695	30736518
广　东 Guangdong	9975919	70158	28284520
广　西 Guangxi	3379755	11946	7624190
海　南 Hainan	1540522	3630	1335941
重　庆 Chongqing	1152482	10876	2344223
四　川 Sichuan	7580716	57752	15396216
贵　州 Guizhou	2555916	15992	6093884
云　南 Yunnan	4503811	7790	9735464
西　藏 Tibet	400	19	2000
陕　西 Shaanxi	6716273	38107	15415328
甘　肃 Gansu	4657994	18168	6922484
青　海 Qinghai	667380	2677	927013
宁　夏 Ningxia	1106310	3853	1214830
新　疆 Xinjiang	7703715	12695	6056905

学条件(二)(农村)

Secondary Schools (2) (Rural)

电子图书藏量(片) Electronic Books & Magazines in Libraries (disk)	固定资产总值(万元) Total Volue of Fixed Asset (in 10 thousand yuan)			
	计 Total	其中:仪器设备总值(万元) Of Which: Total Volue of Equip & Instru. (in 10 thousand yuan)		
		计 Sub Total	专业实验设备 For Prefession	专业实习设备 For Practice
2094646	**8345586.89**	**846370.01**	**503096.84**	**125960.01**
6918	40624.94	6025.31	2667.95	225.79
1357	43121.78	3503.89	2077.26	811.98
90646	684107.50	159014.18	44740.20	10086.14
97785	255502.74	20753.46	12231.68	3952.12
12037	81449.24	7733.12	5001.00	836.28
9299	180224.00	26762.00	15037.00	3876.00
13736	68882.11	9043.08	5472.48	1933.95
49567	275748.98	25220.12	14976.33	5501.01
3538	11384.95	1511.26	1019.41	265.27
291101	782550.18	53468.08	33996.22	7278.89
2846	65463.29	7328.15	4662.42	0.00
33819	371787.69	36711.74	32200.67	2585.68
12147	203607.00	13533.00	11234.00	2299.00
50066	283367.05	18459.24	9299.29	4115.88
119270	400428.16	34752.26	21136.66	7289.91
456803	681039.92	69799.67	44799.26	15626.54
75874	575991.84	54312.06	33387.58	14670.63
135436	538796.74	50988.98	34600.46	7231.29
164306	1036548.89	66474.94	52717.55	13757.39
6227	191447.69	12364.39	8299.73	1746.56
29972	57563.08	4215.77	2241.71	843.07
23819	75900.87	6748.47	3658.84	1487.07
73254	344458.28	32971.84	20290.66	5897.40
16716	106305.58	8664.67	4947.10	1557.37
22628	300017.44	16449.25	8941.39	1102.77
4	235.00	8.00	0.00	8.00
227513	296104.89	28018.27	17405.41	5480.39
35199	192780.74	45979.45	41187.60	2861.55
6579	19932.63	1754.04	1186.56	163.15
9983	22388.90	2715.71	1485.52	378.74
16201	157824.79	21085.61	12194.90	2090.19

职业初中办

Condition of School Buildings in Vocational Junior

地　区 Region	体育运动场(馆) 面　积 (平方米) Sports Areas (m^2)	计　算　机 (台) PC (set)	图书藏量 (册) Books & Magazines in Libraries (Volume)
合　计 Total	**5891546**	**16210**	**7577227**
北　京 Beijing	0	0	0
天　津 Tianjin	0	0	0
河　北 Hebei	686175	3638	1099622
山　西 Shanxi	372913	1486	353209
内蒙古 Inner Mongolia	2184055	3334	1243642
辽　宁 Liaoning	11180	81	26454
吉　林 Jilin	342950	633	368799
黑龙江 Heilongjiang	65100	83	63470
上　海 Shanghai	3955	48	7480
江　苏 Jiangsu	0	0	0
浙　江 Zhejiang	0	0	0
安　徽 Anhui	1577702	2410	2982097
福　建 Fujian	2476	18	6732
江　西 Jiangxi	31731	86	39271
山　东 Shandong	34744	147	32780
河　南 Henan	56587	183	87897
湖　北 Hubei	168685	933	452128
湖　南 Hunan	20819	545	140854
广　东 Guangdong	0	0	0
广　西 Guangxi	71718	664	93933
海　南 Hainan	0	0	0
重　庆 Chongqing	300	150	0
四　川 Sichuan	19507	131	38820
贵　州 Guizhou	140042	1328	404863
云　南 Yunnan	32798	87	67431
西　藏 Tibet	0	17	0
陕　西 Shaanxi	36587	123	33123
甘　肃 Gansu	22992	30	19537
青　海 Qinghai	100	28	2000
宁　夏 Ningxia	0	0	0
新　疆 Xinjiang	8430	27	13085

学条件(二)(总计)

Secondary Schools (2) (Regional Aggregates)

电子图书藏量(片) Electronic Books & Magazines in Libraries (disk)	固定资产总值(万元) Total Value of Fixed Asset (in 10 thousand yuan)			
	计 Total	其中:仪器设备总值(万元) Of Which: Total Volue of Equip & Instru. (in 10 thousand yuan)		
		计 Sub Total	专业实验设备 For Prefession	专业实习设备 For Practice
22683	**144403.80**	**14803.21**	**9479.10**	**2921.45**
0	0.00	0.00	0.00	0.00
0	0.00	0.00	0.00	0.00
5255	24718.96	3037.07	1847.29	702.50
5082	13151.82	1958.44	1207.76	425.99
3302	21098.71	2946.87	2142.35	315.27
0	1078.00	143.00	140.00	1.00
675	3771.75	508.22	368.20	133.02
1000	640.02	100.62	44.32	44.30
0	530.00	131.00	95.00	0.00
0	0.00	0.00	0.00	0.00
0	0.00	0.00	0.00	0.00
3166	47121.64	2440.66	1492.82	333.45
10	139.00	14.00	14.00	0.00
30	835.80	65.10	49.61	13.50
308	1399.00	94.20	46.50	47.70
226	758.20	89.66	68.34	21.32
1284	11207.05	907.53	619.76	130.27
1100	3715.50	731.00	401.00	248.00
0	0.00	0.00	0.00	0.00
847	2698.16	483.87	285.75	192.12
0	0.00	0.00	0.00	0.00
0	150.00	80.00	20.00	60.00
0	946.34	76.38	23.00	2.60
391	6459.79	711.11	457.16	172.74
0	1902.96	70.51	27.89	34.50
7	82.40	16.40	12.10	4.30
0	682.79	54.56	22.56	32.00
0	956.16	42.41	42.36	0.05
0	85.00	76.00	49.00	4.00
0	0.00	0.00	0.00	0.00
0	274.75	24.60	2.33	2.82

职业初中办

Condition of School Buildings in Vocational

地 区 Region	体育运动场(馆) 面 积 (平方米) Sports Areas (m^2)	计 算 机 (台) PC (set)	图书藏量 (册) Books & Magazines in Libraries (Volume)
合 计 Total	**197340**	**1509**	**246688**
北 京 Beijing	0	0	0
天 津 Tianjin	0	0	0
河 北 Hebei	17080	494	84961
山 西 Shanxi	95014	371	85063
内蒙古 Inner Mongolia	0	0	0
辽 宁 Liaoning	2740	70	14500
吉 林 Jilin	4970	18	2468
黑龙江 Heilongjiang	1000	34	2010
上 海 Shanghai	3955	48	7480
江 苏 Jiangsu	0	0	0
浙 江 Zhejiang	0	0	0
安 徽 Anhui	17331	80	11970
福 建 Fujian	0	0	0
江 西 Jiangxi	0	0	0
山 东 Shandong	0	0	0
河 南 Henan	2200	22	4061
湖 北 Hubei	7000	65	20083
湖 南 Hunan	1000	20	300
广 东 Guangdong	0	0	0
广 西 Guangxi	34850	35	952
海 南 Hainan	0	0	0
重 庆 Chongqing	300	150	0
四 川 Sichuan	0	0	0
贵 州 Guizhou	8000	34	7000
云 南 Yunnan	0	0	0
西 藏 Tibet	0	0	0
陕 西 Shaanxi	1500	40	3840
甘 肃 Gansu	0	0	0
青 海 Qinghai	100	28	2000
宁 夏 Ningxia	0	0	0
新 疆 Xinjiang	300	0	0

学条件(二)(城市)

Junior Secondary Schools (2) (Urban)

电子图书藏量(片) Electronic Books & Magazines in Libraries (disk)	固定资产总值(万元) Total Volue of Fixed Asset (in 10 thousand yuan)			
	计 Total	其中:仪器设备总值(万元) Of Which: Total Volue of Equip & Instru. (in 10 thousand yuan)		
		计 Sub Total	专业实验设备 For Prefession	专业实习设备 For Practice
5325	**11250.58**	**2358.03**	**1634.42**	**585.41**
0	0.00	0.00	0.00	0.00
0	0.00	0.00	0.00	0.00
3200	2537.70	545.70	336.70	209.00
1125	4531.41	1133.08	761.97	268.91
0	0.00	0.00	0.00	0.00
0	561.00	100.00	100.00	0.00
0	261.25	66.35	66.35	0.00
0	13.00	13.00	0.00	13.00
0	530.00	131.00	95.00	0.00
0	0.00	0.00	0.00	0.00
0	0.00	0.00	0.00	0.00
0	700.00	39.30	36.30	3.00
0	0.00	0.00	0.00	0.00
0	0.00	0.00	0.00	0.00
0	0.00	0.00	0.00	0.00
0	33.00	5.00	5.00	0.00
0	1573.00	132.00	132.00	0.00
1000	60.00	20.00	10.00	10.00
0	0.00	0.00	0.00	0.00
0	11.90	9.60	2.10	7.50
0	0.00	0.00	0.00	0.00
0	150.00	80.00	20.00	60.00
0	0.00	0.00	0.00	0.00
0	201.27	9.50	9.50	0.00
0	0.00	0.00	0.00	0.00
0	0.00	0.00	0.00	0.00
0	20.00	20.00	10.00	10.00
0	0.00	0.00	0.00	0.00
0	62.00	53.00	49.00	4.00
0	0.00	0.00	0.00	0.00
0	5.05	0.50	0.50	0.00

职业初中办

Condition of School Buildings in Vocational Junior

地区 Region	体育运动场(馆)面积(平方米) Sports Areas (m^2)	计算机(台) PC (set)	图书藏量(册) Books & Magazines in Libraries (Volume)
合计 Total	**1786092**	**6417**	**1926652**
北京 Beijing	0	0	0
天津 Tianjin	0	0	0
河北 Hebei	491525	2335	564596
山西 Shanxi	138598	753	137608
内蒙古 Inner Mongolia	665984	929	386216
辽宁 Liaoning	0	0	0
吉林 Jilin	116480	88	85066
黑龙江 Heilongjiang	16000	0	0
上海 Shanghai	0	0	0
江苏 Jiangsu	0	0	0
浙江 Zhejiang	0	0	0
安徽 Anhui	186194	317	382495
福建 Fujian	0	0	0
江西 Jiangxi	10100	67	8055
山东 Shandong	23940	135	23500
河南 Henan	1941	23	1000
湖北 Hubei	34700	194	85854
湖南 Hunan	13669	353	67244
广东 Guangdong	0	0	0
广西 Guangxi	36868	629	92981
海南 Hainan	0	0	0
重庆 Chongqing	0	0	0
四川 Sichuan	0	0	0
贵州 Guizhou	31739	524	76193
云南 Yunnan	5256	26	3342
西藏 Tibet	0	17	0
陕西 Shaanxi	0	0	0
甘肃 Gansu	6500	0	0
青海 Qinghai	0	0	0
宁夏 Ningxia	0	0	0
新疆 Xinjiang	6598	27	12500

学条件(二)(县镇)

Secondary Schools (2) (County Seats & Towns)

电子图书藏量(片) Electronic Books & Magazines in Libraries (disk)	固定资产总值(万元) Total Volue of Fixed Asset (in 10 thousand yuan)			
	计 Total	其中:仪器设备总值(万元) Of Which: Total Volue of Equip & Instru. (in 10 thousand yuan)		
		计 Sub Total	专业实验设备 For Prefession	专业实习设备 For Practice
4104	**42795.04**	**5349.45**	**3292.65**	**1168.26**
0	0.00	0.00	0.00	0.00
0	0.00	0.00	0.00	0.00
1765	16376.07	1924.05	1189.71	432.44
457	3981.47	506.35	309.02	133.08
645	5392.18	1039.66	681.67	75.09
0	1.00	0.00	0.00	0.00
20	901.21	71.42	47.00	18.42
0	47.40	0.00	0.00	0.00
0	0.00	0.00	0.00	0.00
0	0.00	0.00	0.00	0.00
0	0.00	0.00	0.00	0.00
0	4488.02	356.83	222.83	54.40
0	0.00	0.00	0.00	0.00
0	470.59	38.29	33.30	4.00
308	345.00	83.00	38.00	45.00
0	92.34	0.00	0.00	0.00
0	2732.20	165.60	122.40	25.00
0	2412.90	367.50	149.50	136.00
0	0.00	0.00	0.00	0.00
847	2686.26	474.27	283.65	184.62
0	0.00	0.00	0.00	0.00
0	0.00	0.00	0.00	0.00
0	37.57	0.55	0.00	0.00
55	2145.68	275.72	198.88	54.14
0	139.80	3.20	2.20	1.00
7	82.40	16.40	12.10	4.30
0	50.00	0.00	0.00	0.00
0	163.65	0.61	0.56	0.05
0	23.00	23.00	0.00	0.00
0	0.00	0.00	0.00	0.00
0	226.30	3.00	1.83	0.72

职业初中办

Condition of School Buildings in Vocational

地　区 Region	体育运动场(馆) 面　积 (平方米) Sports Areas (m^2)	计　算　机 (台) PC (set)	图书藏量 (册) Books & Magazines in Libraries (Volume)
合　计 Total	**3908114**	**8284**	**5403887**
北　京 Beijing	0	0	0
天　津 Tianjin	0	0	0
河　北 Hebei	177570	809	450065
山　西 Shanxi	139301	362	130538
内蒙古 Inner Mongolia	1518071	2405	857426
辽　宁 Liaoning	8440	11	11954
吉　林 Jilin	221500	527	281265
黑龙江 Heilongjiang	48100	49	61460
上　海 Shanghai	0	0	0
江　苏 Jiangsu	0	0	0
浙　江 Zhejiang	0	0	0
安　徽 Anhui	1374177	2013	2587632
福　建 Fujian	2476	18	6732
江　西 Jiangxi	21631	19	31216
山　东 Shandong	10804	12	9280
河　南 Henan	52446	138	82836
湖　北 Hubei	126985	674	346191
湖　南 Hunan	6150	172	73310
广　东 Guangdong	0	0	0
广　西 Guangxi	0	0	0
海　南 Hainan	0	0	0
重　庆 Chongqing	0	0	0
四　川 Sichuan	19507	131	38820
贵　州 Guizhou	100303	770	321668
云　南 Yunnan	27542	61	64089
西　藏 Tibet	0	0	0
陕　西 Shaanxi	35087	83	29283
甘　肃 Gansu	16492	30	19537
青　海 Qinghai	0	0	0
宁　夏 Ningxia	0	0	0
新　疆 Xinjiang	1532	0	585

学条件(二)(农村)

Junior Secondary Schools (2) (Rural)

电子图书藏量(片) Electronic Books & Magazines in Libraries (disk)	固定资产总值(万元) Total Volue of Fixed Asset (in 10 thousand yuan)			
	计 Total	其中:仪器设备总值(万元) Of Which: Total Volue of Equip & Instru. (in 10 thousand yuan)		
		计 Sub Total	专业实验设备 For Prefession	专业实习设备 For Practice
13254	**90358.18**	**7095.73**	**4552.03**	**1167.78**
0	0.00	0.00	0.00	0.00
0	0.00	0.00	0.00	0.00
290	5805.19	567.32	320.88	61.06
3500	4638.94	319.01	136.77	24.00
2657	15706.53	1907.21	1460.68	240.18
0	516.00	43.00	40.00	1.00
655	2609.29	370.45	254.85	114.60
1000	579.62	87.62	44.32	31.30
0	0.00	0.00	0.00	0.00
0	0.00	0.00	0.00	0.00
0	0.00	0.00	0.00	0.00
3166	41933.62	2044.53	1233.69	276.05
10	139.00	14.00	14.00	0.00
30	365.21	26.81	16.31	9.50
0	1054.00	11.20	8.50	2.70
226	632.86	84.66	63.34	21.32
1284	6901.85	609.93	365.36	105.27
100	1242.60	343.50	241.50	102.00
0	0.00	0.00	0.00	0.00
0	0.00	0.00	0.00	0.00
0	0.00	0.00	0.00	0.00
0	0.00	0.00	0.00	0.00
0	908.77	75.83	23.00	2.60
336	4112.84	425.89	248.78	118.60
0	1763.16	67.31	25.69	33.50
0	0.00	0.00	0.00	0.00
0	612.79	34.56	12.56	22.00
0	792.51	41.80	41.80	0.00
0	0.00	0.00	0.00	0.00
0	0.00	0.00	0.00	0.00
0	43.40	21.10	0.00	2.10

小学校数、教

Number of Schools, External Teachingsites & Classes

地　区 Region	学校数(所) Schools	教学点数(个) External Teachingsites	班数(个) 计 Total	一年级 Grade 1
合　计 Total	**425846**	**105679**	**3364094**	**577809**
北　京 Beijing	1652	1	21418	3538
天　津 Tianjin	1136	0	17391	2899
河　北 Hebei	25700	3271	192583	27466
山　西 Shanxi	31126	940	131822	21949
内蒙古 Inner Mongolia	7763	3687	65042	12055
辽　宁 Liaoning	11339	556	93300	15185
吉　林 Jilin	8163	664	68654	10849
黑龙江 Heilongjiang	11400	780	87069	15667
上　海 Shanghai	698	23	17876	2998
江　苏 Jiangsu	7845	3697	135723	20302
浙　江 Zhejiang	7712	479	85293	14467
安　徽 Anhui	22328	3329	164188	30783
福　建 Fujian	12406	4030	101644	16400
江　西 Jiangxi	15862	3497	108278	22394
山　东 Shandong	18303	1987	174676	32281
河　南 Henan	36379	3470	274103	48002
湖　北 Hubei	15746	3252	130661	20723
湖　南 Hunan	24673	3039	139018	23944
广　东 Guangdong	22792	2962	249581	43645
广　西 Guangxi	16102	16362	165704	27675
海　南 Hainan	3287	764	30087	5492
重　庆 Chongqing	10966	1016	71195	12155
四　川 Sichuan	24573	13194	201233	35311
贵　州 Guizhou	14504	5324	126957	22999
云　南 Yunnan	20296	19154	153371	26828
西　藏 Tibet	892	2020	12042	2871
陕　西 Shaanxi	24922	2103	135154	20118
甘　肃 Gansu	15635	4004	99641	19016
青　海 Qinghai	2998	491	17984	3623
宁　夏 Ningxia	2816	493	20224	4205
新　疆 Xinjiang	5832	1090	72182	11969

学点数及班数(总计)

in Primary Schools (Regional Aggregates)

Classes

二年级 Grade 2	三年级 Grade 3	四年级 Grade 4	五年级 Grade 5	六年级 Grade 6	复式班 Multiple-grade Classes
573563	**557847**	**547464**	**545526**	**440128**	**121757**
3565	3637	3554	3537	3556	31
2994	2982	2995	3018	2478	25
27603	29649	32045	33076	33554	9190
23685	19456	19082	19243	4622	23785
13331	11475	11236	11416	2230	3299
15580	15699	15972	15584	15145	135
11173	11196	11459	11613	11943	421
15488	15399	15606	15818	7758	1333
2985	2982	2976	2956	2979	0
21224	22175	22398	23371	25430	823
14805	14932	15346	16333	8500	910
31205	30834	29166	28792	8935	4473
16209	16358	16010	16131	17153	3383
20105	19088	18251	18083	6182	4175
31156	28730	27820	29752	24876	61
47945	47680	48458	49951	29187	2880
20587	21211	21612	21727	21360	3441
22818	21990	20389	19696	22474	7707
43222	41716	40848	39552	38776	1822
26249	25596	25253	25793	25449	9689
5322	5094	4835	4609	4531	204
12701	12477	11824	10981	10295	762
36146	34843	32717	30101	28435	3680
22163	20820	19655	18731	18591	3998
25868	23838	22381	21173	20877	12406
2855	2441	1397	1212	1110	156
19737	20271	20277	19924	20059	14768
17836	17122	16083	15285	8441	5858
3576	3012	2697	2580	1075	1421
3731	3443	3269	3244	1901	431
11699	11701	11853	12244	12226	490

小学校数、教

Number of Schools, External Teachingsites

地　区 Region	学校数(所) Schools	教学点数(个) External Teachingsites	班数(个) 计 Total	 一年级 Grade 1
合　计 Total	**25473**	**806**	**404623**	**69702**
北　京 Beijing	482	1	9429	1591
天　津 Tianjin	332	0	5852	968
河　北 Hebei	1098	11	16917	2744
山　西 Shanxi	762	2	14098	2566
内蒙古 Inner Mongolia	522	16	9669	1779
辽　宁 Liaoning	1160	2	20454	3351
吉　林 Jilin	430	0	8294	1382
黑龙江 Heilongjiang	683	1	11303	2070
上　海 Shanghai	412	0	10026	1701
江　苏 Jiangsu	1153	71	21477	3394
浙　江 Zhejiang	1206	40	19733	3494
安　徽 Anhui	1038	10	14434	2372
福　建 Fujian	749	9	10936	1910
江　西 Jiangxi	384	3	6647	1287
山　东 Shandong	1945	34	27696	5310
河　南 Henan	1277	19	20060	3488
湖　北 Hubei	1926	447	26484	4255
湖　南 Hunan	922	17	12200	1993
广　东 Guangdong	2820	0	52557	9394
广　西 Guangxi	815	25	10934	1756
海　南 Hainan	160	0	2813	498
重　庆 Chongqing	2237	41	18658	3072
四　川 Sichuan	587	16	12324	2208
贵　州 Guizhou	519	3	7740	1369
云　南 Yunnan	261	16	4384	774
西　藏 Tibet	27	2	525	93
陕　西 Shaanxi	672	11	10526	1714
甘　肃 Gansu	344	1	5882	1004
青　海 Qinghai	75	0	1469	253
宁　夏 Ningxia	111	0	2130	370
新　疆 Xinjiang	364	8	8972	1542

学点数及班数(城市)

& Classes in Primary Schools (Urban)

Classes

二年级 Grade 2	三年级 Grade 3	四年级 Grade 4	五年级 Grade 5	六年级 Grade 6	复式班 Multiple-grade Classes
70261	**69885**	**69296**	**68322**	**56925**	**232**
1567	1583	1567	1586	1535	0
967	948	964	1012	993	0
2712	2958	2972	2926	2599	6
2933	2506	2400	2339	1337	17
1985	1823	1793	1775	512	2
3453	3511	3662	3587	2890	0
1499	1491	1403	1344	1175	0
2050	2151	2283	2285	464	0
1708	1679	1638	1623	1677	0
3493	3606	3636	3630	3715	3
3510	3427	3423	3496	2363	20
2411	2466	2461	2515	2182	27
1807	1847	1788	1782	1783	19
1263	1303	1277	1228	287	2
5263	4987	4625	4466	3044	1
3436	3573	3481	3520	2562	0
4305	4488	4653	4657	4086	40
1969	2021	2015	2023	2159	20
9244	8939	8779	8293	7903	5
1761	1784	1819	1860	1948	6
494	476	453	433	451	8
3218	3203	3182	3075	2896	12
2149	2095	2091	2023	1758	0
1335	1302	1268	1223	1241	2
765	746	740	732	627	0
96	88	83	84	81	0
1717	1775	1768	1757	1760	35
1014	1013	1001	981	866	3
246	252	246	254	218	0
356	350	346	353	355	0
1535	1494	1479	1460	1458	4

Number of Schools, External Teachingsites & Classes

地　区 Region	学校数(所) Schools	教学点数(个) External Teachingsites	班数(个) 计 Total	一年级 Grade 1
合　计 Total	**40007**	**3199**	**501310**	**83802**
北　京 Beijing	545	0	6641	1091
天　津 Tianjin	421	0	6375	1068
河　北 Hebei	2409	27	26265	3717
山　西 Shanxi	844	9	10977	2214
内蒙古 Inner Mongolia	840	34	11133	2034
辽　宁 Liaoning	572	2	8494	1352
吉　林 Jilin	776	21	12870	2050
黑龙江 Heilongjiang	681	6	10693	1825
上　海 Shanghai	241	7	7167	1190
江　苏 Jiangsu	768	143	17817	2708
浙　江 Zhejiang	5048	288	54774	9172
安　徽 Anhui	1370	31	15558	2685
福　建 Fujian	1896	122	23028	3533
江　西 Jiangxi	4183	747	32436	6497
山　东 Shandong	1915	60	26328	4882
河　南 Henan	2080	51	25123	4299
湖　北 Hubei	585	16	9726	1333
湖　南 Hunan	2222	59	21342	3300
广　东 Guangdong	2215	36	37419	6292
广　西 Guangxi	1271	277	19875	3135
海　南 Hainan	304	0	5011	799
重　庆 Chongqing	1269	121	15201	2437
四　川 Sichuan	1562	157	28499	4512
贵　州 Guizhou	1109	72	15005	2534
云　南 Yunnan	1163	337	14398	2411
西　藏 Tibet	109	118	1722	334
陕　西 Shaanxi	1209	35	12139	1832
甘　肃 Gansu	1377	337	12517	2281
青　海 Qinghai	446	26	3631	687
宁　夏 Ningxia	235	41	2964	539
新　疆 Xinjiang	342	19	6182	1059

学点数及班数(县镇)

in Primary Schools (County seats & Towns)

Classes

二年级 Grade 2	三年级 Grade 3	四年级 Grade 4	五年级 Grade 5	六年级 Grade 6	复式班 Multiple-grade Classes
84357	**84042**	**84635**	**88460**	**72763**	**3251**
1106	1134	1092	1087	1127	4
1099	1106	1112	1107	868	15
3783	4127	4471	4838	5188	141
2463	1960	1919	1977	361	83
2247	2075	2119	2164	473	21
1388	1434	1469	1431	1418	2
2085	2090	2176	2208	2256	5
1863	1912	1984	1973	1134	2
1161	1178	1214	1210	1214	0
2759	2935	3007	3074	3324	10
9508	9623	9918	10724	5415	414
2760	2881	2826	2917	1405	84
3667	3769	3741	3884	4365	69
5954	5736	5506	5670	2111	962
4696	4314	4132	4477	3821	6
4303	4380	4521	4828	2768	24
1372	1519	1685	1847	1935	35
3182	3206	3224	3693	4527	210
6290	6152	6142	6176	6346	21
3127	3153	3216	3489	3695	60
790	820	828	864	910	0
2512	2500	2471	2543	2610	128
4632	4618	4654	4846	5222	15
2516	2461	2433	2465	2528	68
2408	2333	2300	2390	2396	160
338	301	247	250	249	3
1848	1961	2000	2097	2187	214
2251	2245	2155	2137	1117	331
719	605	588	558	320	154
503	508	494	507	409	4
1027	1006	991	1029	1064	6

小学校数、教

Number of Schools, External Teachingsites

地　区 Region	学校数(所) Schools	教学点数(个) External Teachingsites	班数(个) 计 Total	 一年级 Grade 1
合　计 Total	**360366**	**101674**	**2458161**	**424305**
北　京 Beijing	625	0	5348	856
天　津 Tianjin	383	0	5164	863
河　北 Hebei	22193	3233	149401	21005
山　西 Shanxi	29520	929	106747	17169
内蒙古 Inner Mongolia	6401	3637	44240	8242
辽　宁 Liaoning	9607	552	64352	10482
吉　林 Jilin	6957	643	47490	7417
黑龙江 Heilongjiang	10036	773	65073	11772
上　海 Shanghai	45	16	683	107
江　苏 Jiangsu	5924	3483	96429	14200
浙　江 Zhejiang	1458	151	10786	1801
安　徽 Anhui	19920	3288	134196	25726
福　建 Fujian	9761	3899	67680	10957
江　西 Jiangxi	11295	2747	69195	14610
山　东 Shandong	14443	1893	120652	22089
河　南 Henan	33022	3400	228920	40215
湖　北 Hubei	13235	2789	94451	15135
湖　南 Hunan	21529	2963	105476	18651
广　东 Guangdong	17757	2926	159605	27959
广　西 Guangxi	14016	16060	134895	22784
海　南 Hainan	2823	764	22263	4195
重　庆 Chongqing	7460	854	37336	6646
四　川 Sichuan	22424	13021	160410	28591
贵　州 Guizhou	12876	5249	104212	19096
云　南 Yunnan	18872	18801	134589	23643
西　藏 Tibet	756	1900	9795	2444
陕　西 Shaanxi	23041	2057	112489	16572
甘　肃 Gansu	13914	3666	81242	15731
青　海 Qinghai	2477	465	12884	2683
宁　夏 Ningxia	2470	452	15130	3296
新　疆 Xinjiang	5126	1063	57028	9368

学点数及班数(农村)

& Classes in Primary Schools (Rural)

Classes

二年级 Grade 2	三年级 Grade 3	四年级 Grade 4	五年级 Grade 5	六年级 Grade 6	复式班 Multiple-grade Classes
418945	**403920**	**393533**	**388744**	**310440**	**118274**
892	920	895	864	894	27
928	928	919	899	617	10
21108	22564	24602	25312	25767	9043
18289	14990	14763	14927	2924	23685
9099	7577	7324	7477	1245	3276
10739	10754	10841	10566	10837	133
7589	7615	7880	8061	8512	416
11575	11336	11339	11560	6160	1331
116	125	124	123	88	0
14972	15634	15755	16667	18391	810
1787	1882	2005	2113	722	476
26034	25487	23879	23360	5348	4362
10735	10742	10481	10465	11005	3295
12888	12049	11468	11185	3784	3211
21197	19429	19063	20809	18011	54
40206	39727	40456	41603	23857	2856
14910	15204	15274	15223	15339	3366
17667	16763	15150	13980	15788	7477
27688	26625	25927	25083	24527	1796
21361	20659	20218	20444	19806	9623
4038	3798	3554	3312	3170	196
6971	6774	6171	5363	4789	622
29365	28130	25972	23232	21455	3665
18312	17057	15954	15043	14822	3928
22695	20759	19341	18051	17854	12246
2421	2052	1067	878	780	153
16172	16535	16509	16070	16112	14519
14571	13864	12927	12167	6458	5524
2611	2155	1863	1768	537	1267
2872	2585	2429	2384	1137	427
9137	9201	9383	9755	9704	480

小学学生

Number of Students in Primary

地　区 Region	毕业生数 Graduates	招生数 Entrants 计 Total	其中受过学前教育	在校学生数 合　计 Total	其中女 of Which:Female
合　计 Total	**22678857**	**18293875**	**14960487**	**116897395**	**55037589**
北　京 Beijing	123580	82631	76008	546530	263562
天　津 Tianjin	132022	84963	81995	585446	278520
河　北 Hebei	1459161	727434	659465	6065832	2911924
山　西 Shanxi	597477	734901	659000	3635608	1747807
内蒙古 Inner Mongolia	388019	294991	266963	1733702	825517
辽　宁 Liaoning	595278	432650	419769	2891925	1378812
吉　林 Jilin	437518	250000	236830	1833141	879922
黑龙江 Heilongjiang	438212	405337	368829	2401918	1161578
上　海 Shanghai	129623	101633	82358	654844	312036
江　苏 Jiangsu	1300348	742117	714601	5793921	2688934
浙　江 Zhejiang	597818	524509	489032	3402942	1594955
安　徽 Anhui	1271012	1063988	714872	6612171	3123545
福　建 Fujian	669693	402276	338720	3119777	1436157
江　西 Jiangxi	757359	733559	514575	3905386	1805784
山　东 Shandong	1282382	1078606	962563	6427848	3042208
河　南 Henan	2041813	1643456	1512042	10586075	5007467
湖　北 Hubei	1186986	651856	546133	5281177	2436605
湖　南 Hunan	1294814	714944	642928	4686892	2207064
广　东 Guangdong	1586749	1729914	1517304	10253706	4800862
广　西 Guangxi	923669	770795	663921	4918503	2254979
海　南 Hainan	173992	164629	99142	1008860	457289
重　庆 Chongqing	456848	444276	410416	2779441	1325437
四　川 Sichuan	1324117	1223734	1048243	7554308	3581127
贵　州 Guizhou	805694	827264	423977	4768740	2238724
云　南 Yunnan	771499	731132	423576	4418821	2066757
西　藏 Tibet	45695	58913	5462	322060	150221
陕　西 Shaanxi	806239	530089	458857	4014754	1873166
甘　肃 Gansu	481495	572321	331142	3227592	1531429
青　海 Qinghai	81467	94559	53230	506906	237117
宁　夏 Ningxia	96835	128779	75896	669503	318321
新　疆 Xinjiang	421443	347619	162638	2289066	1099763

数(总计)

Schools(Regional Aggregates)

单位:人

Unit:in Person

Enrolment						毕业班学生数
一年级 Grade 1	二年级 Grade 2	三年级 Grade 3	四年级 Grade 4	五年级 Grade 5	六年级 Grade 6	Graduates for Next Year
18560820	**19518737**	**19829825**	**20246141**	**21119095**	**17622777**	**21444969**
83091	85528	91150	92579	95402	98780	99606
85239	94189	100070	105382	108165	92401	115778
728346	800429	953643	1110818	1211664	1260932	1305279
740963	795934	654646	643339	635814	164912	635380
295652	357130	321100	329402	348759	81659	335116
435059	461014	485676	510850	508955	490371	517042
250742	293941	291862	315613	329721	351262	360508
405540	407902	424932	457752	476215	229577	492936
101882	104221	108886	110685	111909	117261	117628
744862	839442	939542	988398	1073035	1208642	1211276
526414	585011	609704	639696	679411	362706	534684
1076042	1239733	1315459	1269215	1295691	416031	1243166
415706	482769	523829	522163	552730	622580	626722
777316	727114	700021	693794	738200	268941	655397
1078875	1070145	1019791	1025933	1177573	1055531	1281710
1664983	1807722	1802385	1943400	2132985	1234600	2000880
655586	706542	841942	954051	1047643	1075413	1104025
716018	703827	717532	709733	811610	1028172	1028172
1729914	1763538	1736263	1719695	1671401	1632895	1632895
779011	791582	793975	810160	869506	874269	894227
167762	167111	167845	166977	168176	170989	170989
447710	487148	479683	466339	455410	443151	443151
1251283	1310506	1298417	1255819	1217626	1220657	1227147
830701	830325	802100	774769	761591	769254	769254
749879	756353	743280	723675	719030	726604	739372
59040	59494	57514	51926	49085	45001	45001
544059	598599	668210	699842	739072	764972	764972
623177	611720	603547	568049	527074	294025	492591
101137	104736	92188	88549	84782	35514	80295
134719	121122	117035	113664	113310	69653	93365
360112	353910	367598	383874	407550	416022	426405

小学学生

Number of Students in

地　区 Region	毕业生数 Graduates	招生数 Entrants 计 Total	其中受过学前教育 Of which:never received the pre-school education	在校学生数 合　计 Total	其中女 Of Which:Female
合　计 Total	**3179926**	**2966115**	**2716715**	**18076855**	**8473273**
北　京 Beijing	49816	39906	35006	258544	126009
天　津 Tianjin	47423	31855	29475	217563	104439
河　北 Hebei	149849	114986	106464	776133	369517
山　西 Shanxi	97897	118529	105436	641349	305847
内蒙古 Inner Mongolia	83978	75833	72906	441295	211422
辽　宁 Liaoning	179055	133169	128590	880270	423864
吉　林 Jilin	68562	54495	51128	348246	168348
黑龙江 Heilongjiang	103800	86264	84604	502950	243399
上　海 Shanghai	70506	53332	42108	340034	163085
江　苏 Jiangsu	168788	133736	130287	904986	420762
浙　江 Zhejiang	139198	143467	134469	871656	401890
安　徽 Anhui	132722	109816	102997	715465	332557
福　建 Fujian	84968	71391	63871	472165	210917
江　西 Jiangxi	55593	65287	58173	341621	154726
山　东 Shandong	206585	233729	225549	1247259	585066
河　南 Henan	179810	158472	150653	942497	442404
湖　北 Hubei	232227	157477	149249	1150591	525709
湖　南 Hunan	123841	94396	83371	603812	281268
广　东 Guangdong	363751	456357	380272	2576086	1186873
广　西 Guangxi	78588	68369	63208	435137	196267
海　南 Hainan	22392	22757	20938	136246	58855
重　庆 Chongqing	120466	114867	110641	730858	353192
四　川 Sichuan	94166	100086	93848	599469	286529
贵　州 Guizhou	58641	65759	55800	359881	170077
云　南 Yunnan	33771	34628	32250	202236	97248
西　藏 Tibet	3786	4279	3168	25077	11972
陕　西 Shaanxi	85517	75719	73590	487511	228058
甘　肃 Gansu	47762	48465	46554	283945	134744
青　海 Qinghai	13628	13886	10780	81153	38323
宁　夏 Ningxia	16566	18834	16897	105797	50429
新　疆 Xinjiang	66274	65969	54433	397023	189477

数(城市)

Primary Schools(Urban)

单位:人

Unit:in Person

Enrolment						毕业班学生数
一年级 Grade 1	二年级 Grade 2	三年级 Grade 3	四年级 Grade 4	五年级 Grade 5	六年级 Grade 6	Graduates for Next Year
2968231	**3048710**	**3136941**	**3164935**	**3143958**	**2614080**	**3075170**
39927	39929	41992	43902	46565	46229	47034
31875	32576	34216	37148	40601	41147	44667
114990	119642	137965	141393	139576	122567	137728
118597	132275	113804	109421	106937	60315	105722
75833	88829	84182	83571	84768	24112	78365
133208	140886	149100	163551	162288	131237	157534
54500	62536	61389	60249	59006	50566	56537
86264	87458	95319	105287	106162	22460	105328
53372	54105	55879	56391	57487	62800	62800
133778	140226	153124	157994	157975	161889	161889
143590	151609	152202	156292	159288	108675	132770
109850	115793	125287	125678	128075	110782	127875
71749	79119	83306	79747	78704	79540	80045
65481	63931	68260	66082	63827	14040	50164
233739	234771	225775	208603	204213	140158	214226
158566	154101	168158	166969	169423	125280	164557
157719	166948	195186	213617	221947	195174	214196
94407	93858	98543	100151	104508	112345	112345
456357	451397	440542	435009	407160	385621	385621
68377	68302	70625	72325	75979	79529	79529
22785	23165	23029	22385	22006	22876	22876
115171	122512	123691	126023	125023	118438	118438
100146	102323	103390	105419	99480	88711	94960
65791	61362	61024	58014	56341	57349	57349
34653	34232	35103	34919	34122	29207	33187
4335	4484	4244	4105	4045	3864	3864
75810	77417	83546	84298	83635	82805	82805
48530	48217	49633	49163	47378	41024	46188
13886	13519	14229	13855	13937	11727	12958
18842	17435	17696	17040	17349	17435	17435
66103	65753	66502	66334	66153	66178	66178

小学学生

Number of Students in Primary

地　区 Region	毕业生数 Graduates	招生数 Entrants 计 Total	其中受过学前教育 of which: never received the pre-school education	在校学生数 合　计 Total	其中女 Of Which: Female
合　计 Total	**4265248**	**3403283**	**3051795**	**21929021**	**10241977**
北　京 Beijing	44143	27394	26335	179021	85662
天　津 Tianjin	42938	30606	30140	206356	99195
河　北 Hebei	242720	128255	123935	1031059	485968
山　西 Shanxi	86218	103889	95921	514855	243516
内蒙古 Inner Mongolia	94547	73903	69693	438077	207107
辽　宁 Liaoning	71135	55816	54863	372214	177847
吉　林 Jilin	111139	71612	69658	503275	241579
黑龙江 Heilongjiang	72586	78154	75612	473140	229552
上　海 Shanghai	54750	44693	37013	290902	137732
江　苏 Jiangsu	176737	118304	115492	869895	395894
浙　江 Zhejiang	392270	333026	313550	2200088	1032842
安　徽 Anhui	151303	120568	101007	794029	366906
福　建 Fujian	191195	124552	108273	928111	426074
江　西 Jiangxi	249657	226291	164712	1265677	581376
山　东 Shandong	222230	197371	180184	1137032	531560
河　南 Henan	240982	208488	195938	1277554	595611
湖　北 Hubei	124185	67009	61538	548735	249878
湖　南 Hunan	279586	134852	126481	973164	455721
广　东 Guangdong	300079	302990	280500	1841902	847936
广　西 Guangxi	151612	119333	115564	782860	350096
海　南 Hainan	44555	34975	24776	229977	100763
重　庆 Chongqing	132909	108127	103170	707496	336538
四　川 Sichuan	284717	229043	212373	1482922	708304
贵　州 Guizhou	126430	114983	92707	708936	329990
云　南 Yunnan	102811	93734	80076	572506	273700
西　藏 Tibet	9709	9884	1797	59252	27888
陕　西 Shaanxi	103676	71470	65888	529964	241154
甘　肃 Gansu	81110	86511	63644	508595	240940
青　海 Qinghai	18524	23701	13584	125005	59386
宁　夏 Ningxia	17507	22630	19570	129914	61523
新　疆 Xinjiang	43288	41119	27801	246508	119739

数(县镇)

Schools(County Seats & Towns)

单位:人

Unit: in Person

Enrolment						毕业班学生数 Graduates for Next Year
一年级 Grade 1	二年级 Grade 2	三年级 Grade 3	四年级 Grade 4	五年级 Grade 5	六年级 Grade 6	
3432963	**3608019**	**3706961**	**3786084**	**4023642**	**3371352**	**4081721**
27610	28348	30347	30208	30278	32230	32251
30715	34166	36326	37780	37794	29575	38662
128386	138829	161369	183953	202846	215676	219940
104588	118034	94006	90804	91173	16250	89550
73956	85965	82815	85428	88327	21586	86318
55866	58785	63441	66368	65058	62696	62991
71757	80382	80968	87859	90008	92301	94267
78166	80634	85493	90520	88423	49904	88357
44867	46236	48742	49879	50029	51149	51516
119156	129287	144777	150355	156808	169512	170635
334209	377865	396010	415911	448501	227592	347803
121448	135683	154125	151207	158118	73448	157637
127871	144188	155639	154129	161445	184839	186339
235976	231425	228421	226212	245796	97847	220937
197376	195294	184462	177455	200472	181973	221711
209584	219074	220149	228959	254940	144848	239223
67110	70022	84947	97483	110458	118715	121292
134982	133392	140410	145625	182628	236127	236127
302990	308516	306772	306235	305240	312149	312149
119689	122199	124551	127860	139386	149175	151543
35513	35109	37217	37734	40671	43733	43733
108545	117006	115739	115343	122041	128822	128822
231314	238262	238633	242626	255519	276568	276568
115185	117386	118174	115847	119021	123323	123323
94259	93743	95065	93661	98285	97493	98981
9885	9866	9770	10154	9890	9687	9687
72211	77813	87707	91171	97637	103425	103425
90167	93237	95901	92232	88435	48623	85098
24138	24826	22583	21984	20510	10964	19297
23481	22353	22372	21964	22321	17423	19840
41963	40094	40030	39138	41584	43699	43699

小学学生

Number of Students in

地　区 Region	毕业生数 Graduates	招生数 Entrants 计 Total	其中受过学前教育 of which: never received the pre-school education	在校学生数 合　计 Total	其中女 Of Which: Female
合　计 Total	**15233683**	**11924477**	**9191977**	**76891519**	**36322339**
北　京 Beijing	29621	15331	14667	108965	51891
天　津 Tianjin	41661	22502	22380	161527	74886
河　北 Hebei	1066592	484193	429066	4258640	2056439
山　西 Shanxi	413362	512483	457643	2479404	1198444
内蒙古 Inner Mongolia	209494	145255	124364	854330	406988
辽　宁 Liaoning	345088	243665	236316	1639441	777101
吉　林 Jilin	257817	123893	116044	981620	469995
黑龙江 Heilongjiang	261826	240919	208613	1425828	688627
上　海 Shanghai	4367	3608	3237	23908	11219
江　苏 Jiangsu	954823	490077	468822	4019040	1872278
浙　江 Zhejiang	66350	48016	41013	331198	160223
安　徽 Anhui	986987	833604	510868	5102677	2424082
福　建 Fujian	393530	206333	166576	1719501	799166
江　西 Jiangxi	452109	441981	291690	2298088	1069682
山　东 Shandong	853567	647506	556830	4043557	1925582
河　南 Henan	1621021	1276496	1165451	8366024	3969452
湖　北 Hubei	830574	427370	335346	3581851	1661018
湖　南 Hunan	891387	485696	433076	3109916	1470075
广　东 Guangdong	922919	970567	856532	5835718	2766053
广　西 Guangxi	693469	583093	485149	3700506	1708616
海　南 Hainan	107045	106897	53428	642637	297671
重　庆 Chongqing	203473	221282	196605	1341087	635707
四　川 Sichuan	945234	894605	742022	5471917	2586294
贵　州 Guizhou	620623	646522	275470	3699923	1738657
云　南 Yunnan	634917	602770	311250	3644079	1695809
西　藏 Tibet	32200	44750	497	237731	110361
陕　西 Shaanxi	617046	382900	319379	2997279	1403954
甘　肃 Gansu	352623	437345	220944	2435052	1155745
青　海 Qinghai	49315	56972	28866	300748	139408
宁　夏 Ningxia	62762	87315	39429	433792	206369
新　疆 Xinjiang	311881	240531	80404	1645535	790547

数(农村)

Primary Schools(Rural)

单位:人

Unit: in Person

Enrolment						毕业班学生数 Graduates for Next Year
一年级 Grade 1	二年级 Grade 2	三年级 Grade 3	四年级 Grade 4	五年级 Grade 5	六年级 Grade 6	
12159626	**12862008**	**12985923**	**13295122**	**13951495**	**11637345**	**14288078**
15554	17251	18811	18469	18559	20321	20321
22649	27447	29528	30454	29770	21679	32449
484970	541958	654309	785472	869242	922689	947611
517778	545625	446836	443114	437704	88347	440108
145863	182336	154103	160403	175664	35961	170433
245985	261343	273135	280931	281609	296438	296517
124485	151023	149505	167505	180707	208395	209704
241110	239810	244120	261945	281630	157213	299251
3643	3880	4265	4415	4393	3312	3312
491928	569929	641641	680049	758252	877241	878752
48615	55537	61492	67493	71622	26439	54111
844744	988257	1036047	992330	1009498	231801	957654
216086	259462	284884	288287	312581	358201	360338
475859	431758	403340	401500	428577	157054	384296
647760	640080	609554	639875	772888	733400	845773
1296833	1434547	1414078	1547472	1708622	964472	1597100
430757	469572	561809	642951	715238	761524	768537
486629	476577	478579	463957	524474	679700	679700
970567	1003625	988949	978451	959001	935125	935125
590945	601081	598799	609975	654141	645565	663155
109464	108837	107599	106858	105499	104380	104380
223994	247630	240253	224973	208346	195891	195891
919823	969921	956394	907774	862627	855378	855619
649725	651577	622902	600908	586229	588582	588582
620967	628378	613112	595095	586623	599904	607204
44820	45144	43500	37667	35150	31450	31450
396038	443369	496957	524373	557800	578742	578742
484480	470266	458013	426654	391261	204378	361305
63113	66391	55376	52710	50335	12823	48040
92396	81334	76967	74660	73640	34795	56090
252046	248063	261066	278402	299813	306145	316528

六年制小

Number of Students in

地 区 Region	毕业生数 Graduates	招生数 Entrants 计 Total	其中受过学前教育 of which: never received the pre-school education	在校学生数 合 计 Total	其中女 Of Which: Female
合 计 Total	**21149172**	**16989890**	**13944899**	**109765576**	**51645581**
北 京 Beijing	122105	81334	74733	539260	260086
天 津 Tianjin	104552	65295	62675	471747	225805
河 北 Hebei	1454098	723160	655664	6043296	2901294
山 西 Shanxi	558369	687568	614590	3439504	1653518
内蒙古 Inner Mongolia	233517	177277	161869	1078932	512801
辽 宁 Liaoning	571707	411495	398847	2768275	1319349
吉 林 Jilin	427611	240924	228958	1783472	855793
黑龙江 Heilongjiang	161102	196379	175316	1220502	592388
上 海 Shanghai	129281	100840	81606	650916	310195
江 苏 Jiangsu	1298599	740681	713165	5784488	2684472
浙 江 Zhejiang	596412	523113	487636	3178993	1492372
安 徽 Anhui	1110043	983201	659830	6125277	2893726
福 建 Fujian	669580	402232	338697	3119483	1436008
江 西 Jiangxi	651222	646560	454538	3464023	1600134
山 东 Shandong	1068931	858880	754775	5380367	2538273
河 南 Henan	1831883	1500808	1380499	9710010	4593115
湖 北 Hubei	1163964	639649	534180	5185622	2392753
湖 南 Hunan	1294814	714944	642928	4686892	2207064
广 东 Guangdong	1586749	1729851	1517257	10253417	4800709
广 西 Guangxi	909380	761821	656386	4860266	2228344
海 南 Hainan	173992	164629	99142	1008860	457289
重 庆 Chongqing	455264	443598	409832	2775519	1323607
四 川 Sichuan	1318063	1215497	1040313	7516377	3562929
贵 州 Guizhou	805694	827264	423977	4768740	2238724
云 南 Yunnan	759118	718786	413051	4355250	2036648
西 藏 Tibet	45673	58544	5462	320402	149465
陕 西 Shaanxi	806208	529990	458760	4014368	1872978
甘 肃 Gansu	328515	365074	249494	2241049	1060871
青 海 Qinghai	35321	53710	22883	280522	130052
宁 夏 Ningxia	66312	87132	65198	495343	236103
新 疆 Xinjiang	411093	339654	162638	2244404	1078716

学学生数

6-year Primary Schools

单位:人

Unit:in Person

Enrolment						毕业班学生数 Graduates for Next Year
一年级 Grade 1	二年级 Grade 2	三年级 Grade 3	四年级 Grade 4	五年级 Grade 5	六年级 Grade 6	
17221736	**18141917**	**18447064**	**18828040**	**19529801**	**17597018**	**19898700**
81793	84228	89615	91043	93801	98780	98801
65461	72368	76891	81083	84195	91749	91830
724120	796233	949203	1105869	1206939	1260932	1301035
693560	757463	618572	606974	599604	163331	599212
177611	227893	189864	194107	207798	81659	197767
413904	437099	460393	484224	482284	490371	490371
241664	284092	281308	305619	319972	350817	350817
196506	185426	191120	205017	212856	229577	229577
101087	103422	108072	109917	111157	117261	117261
743426	837744	937768	986747	1070810	1207993	1207993
524883	583322	600720	599929	507433	362706	362706
994120	1140358	1208564	1168744	1197460	416031	1145325
415654	482712	523759	522118	552694	622546	626688
686529	641295	615489	609204	642800	268706	574505
859123	840178	806044	832346	987145	1055531	1092646
1520414	1652183	1636615	1755694	1922891	1222213	1800805
643378	692498	826495	937935	1013628	1071688	1071688
716018	703827	717532	709733	811610	1028172	1028172
1729851	1763474	1736205	1719636	1671356	1632895	1632895
769518	781302	782263	797158	855756	874269	880477
167762	167111	167845	166977	168176	170989	170989
447031	486491	478974	465771	454815	442437	442437
1243022	1302301	1290685	1248576	1211136	1220657	1220657
830701	830325	802100	774769	761591	769254	769254
737489	743767	730345	710783	706262	726604	726604
58671	59024	57113	51660	48970	44964	44964
543960	598532	668126	699767	739039	764944	764944
393480	401226	403705	386052	367123	289463	336847
59056	54501	48667	43329	39790	35179	35272
89900	85583	83987	82928	83576	69369	70152
352044	345939	359025	374331	397134	415931	416009

小学女

Number of Female Students

地 区 Region	毕业生数 Graduates	招生数 Entrants 计 Total	其中受过 学前教育	在校学生数 合 计 Total
合 计 Total	**10759948**	**8573945**	**6933168**	**55037589**
北 京 Beijing	59398	39850	36555	263562
天 津 Tianjin	63887	40171	38359	278520
河 北 Hebei	709700	345522	311369	2911924
山 西 Shanxi	297583	352969	312986	1747807
内蒙古 Inner Mongolia	184514	138541	124773	825517
辽 宁 Liaoning	284450	204024	196958	1378812
吉 林 Jilin	211146	118673	110666	879922
黑龙江 Heilongjiang	211971	196039	176740	1161578
上 海 Shanghai	62734	47755	38470	312036
江 苏 Jiangsu	611738	339321	324482	2688934
浙 江 Zhejiang	280846	243945	225928	1594955
安 徽 Anhui	606073	496978	326413	3123545
福 建 Fujian	318006	181716	152023	1436157
江 西 Jiangxi	354095	337632	232028	1805784
山 东 Shandong	608428	509879	449249	3042208
河 南 Henan	974925	773168	708447	5007467
湖 北 Hubei	559320	293390	242488	2436605
湖 南 Hunan	615213	335123	297342	2207064
广 东 Guangdong	748348	803494	692993	4800862
广 西 Guangxi	425882	354528	302649	2254979
海 南 Hainan	79143	73528	42705	457289
重 庆 Chongqing	216270	211193	192184	1325437
四 川 Sichuan	627662	580191	495547	3581127
贵 州 Guizhou	372269	392297	196481	2238724
云 南 Yunnan	358174	344345	198903	2066757
西 藏 Tibet	20849	27797	2515	150221
陕 西 Shaanxi	383422	244002	209370	1873166
甘 肃 Gansu	225841	274511	155400	1531429
青 海 Qinghai	38029	44917	25672	237117
宁 夏 Ningxia	45353	61630	35919	318321
新 疆 Xinjiang	204679	166816	77554	1099763

学生数
in Primary Schools

单位：人

Unit: in Person

Enrolment						毕业班学生数 Graduates for Next Year
一年级 Grade 1	二年级 Grade 2	三年级 Grade 3	四年级 Grade 4	五年级 Grade 5	六年级 Grade 6	
8684618	**9171903**	**9334472**	**9558844**	**9961214**	**8326538**	**10086211**
40002	41260	44177	44746	45867	47510	46585
40282	44509	47274	50191	51375	44889	54977
345864	381745	454705	534543	584941	610126	628535
355355	381655	314655	310885	306815	78442	303159
138805	170417	153149	157302	166576	39268	158812
204824	218706	230933	245323	243695	235331	248345
118959	141032	140223	151395	158736	169577	174071
196096	197478	205185	221778	229669	111372	236400
47828	49538	51621	52829	53590	56630	56783
340438	386064	435366	461130	501016	564920	563151
244640	273578	285041	300221	318770	172705	250456
502422	584280	623157	601894	614580	197212	588774
187004	218477	240541	242399	256232	291504	293486
355230	335675	324438	321654	343237	125550	295734
509968	506455	483084	487225	556049	499427	608027
781923	852584	850762	920078	1011146	590974	949750
294900	320953	384274	441965	489713	504800	508244
335498	330560	338157	335044	382627	485178	485178
803494	823395	814107	807020	783434	769412	769412
357741	363446	364756	371035	396450	401551	409849
74742	75897	75947	76005	76922	77776	77772
212503	231868	229044	222823	218109	211090	203910
591311	619204	615042	597667	578312	579591	581830
393781	393962	378434	364084	354266	354197	354197
352298	354798	348277	338618	334998	337768	343801
27857	28070	27290	23868	22779	20357	19677
249629	277886	312057	327468	345265	360861	360861
297090	291328	287078	269752	248518	137663	228099
48224	48829	43083	41330	39348	16303	37259
64387	58153	56235	53694	52719	33133	43165
171523	170101	176380	184878	195460	201421	205912

小学教职工

Number of Teachers, Staff & Workers in

地　区 Region	教职工数		
	合　计 Total	专任教师 Full-time Teachers	行政人员 Adm. Personnel
合　计 Total	**6256185**	**5702750**	**325470**
北　京 Beijing	63174	49843	6967
天　津 Tianjin	52603	43829	5552
河　北 Hebei	352846	329165	15108
山　西 Shanxi	202648	188109	7505
内蒙古 Inner Mongolia	145166	127011	8348
辽　宁 Liaoning	199829	170947	25898
吉　林 Jilin	166592	141363	15110
黑龙江 Heilongjiang	204820	178122	14903
上　海 Shanghai	54157	39408	5270
江　苏 Jiangsu	297083	268436	14446
浙　江 Zhejiang	175366	159127	8155
安　徽 Anhui	279648	266458	9320
福　建 Fujian	189027	177248	8519
江　西 Jiangxi	207306	198513	4245
山　东 Shandong	410968	380066	15694
河　南 Henan	516735	488490	15392
湖　北 Hubei	252645	233902	8329
湖　南 Hunan	275811	260704	6686
广　东 Guangdong	447013	389262	41146
广　西 Guangxi	235014	205142	21924
海　南 Hainan	54869	49367	2428
重　庆 Chongqing	129140	115212	8492
四　川 Sichuan	350201	316029	18835
贵　州 Guizhou	191695	179367	9435
云　南 Yunnan	235740	221589	7834
西　藏 Tibet	13767	13026	204
陕　西 Shaanxi	206447	190964	10843
甘　肃 Gansu	131752	126740	2729
青　海 Qinghai	29692	28496	419
宁　夏 Ningxia	35833	34531	639
新　疆 Xinjiang	148598	132284	5095

数(总计)

Primary Schools (Regional Aggregates)

单位:人

Unit: in Person

Teachers, Staff & Workers				
教辅人员 Teaching Auxiliarg	工勤人员 Workers	校办工厂、农场职工 Employees in School-run Factories & Farms	代课教师 Substitute Teachers	兼任教师 Part-time Teachers
77662	**145709**	**4594**	**423857**	**20496**
3063	3228	73	167	120
1038	2088	96	462	58
3048	5321	204	18028	748
2994	3942	98	25607	1131
3300	6336	171	4878	652
406	2482	96	3839	1038
5745	4263	111	1519	386
3529	8043	223	1205	214
5192	3851	436	423	322
7027	6636	538	14380	754
2570	5198	316	0	1058
1236	2519	115	15698	1290
1177	2027	56	4287	375
2224	2278	46	6720	800
6587	8348	273	8261	772
5856	6836	161	15988	2774
3620	6308	486	21674	620
2517	5764	140	4278	631
3674	12722	209	46029	786
2490	5403	55	65747	954
495	2541	38	1894	173
1220	4119	97	11277	242
2776	12316	245	28586	1489
839	2043	11	26519	1056
1015	5276	26	26713	331
17	507	13	3287	43
1509	3077	54	30955	450
567	1694	22	22883	666
82	616	79	1319	61
178	484	1	1488	58
1671	9443	105	9746	444

小学教职工

Number of Teachers, Staff & Workers

教职工数

地区 Region	合计 Total	专任教师 Full-time Teachers	行政人员 Adm. Personnel
合　计 Total	**1080931**	**936396**	**77314**
北　京 Beijing	27481	21642	3148
天　津 Tianjin	22882	17905	2940
河　北 Hebei	49638	44017	3057
山　西 Shanxi	38440	33057	2357
内蒙古 Inner Mongolia	28141	24104	2430
辽　宁 Liaoning	57389	47763	8220
吉　林 Jilin	26462	21852	2489
黑龙江 Heilongjiang	38230	31137	3799
上　海 Shanghai	27772	20332	2890
江　苏 Jiangsu	55985	50169	3373
浙　江 Zhejiang	45817	40928	2022
安　徽 Anhui	38108	35327	1420
福　建 Fujian	26608	24449	1172
江　西 Jiangxi	18600	17241	774
山　东 Shandong	83348	73052	5107
河　南 Henan	58099	51334	3400
湖　北 Hubei	66445	58881	3965
湖　南 Hunan	35713	32097	1539
广　东 Guangdong	116612	97912	10059
广　西 Guangxi	26311	23263	1676
海　南 Hainan	7581	6199	354
重　庆 Chongqing	41688	36446	2721
四　川 Sichuan	32758	28450	2109
贵　州 Guizhou	18963	16749	1325
云　南 Yunnan	11565	10366	533
西　藏 Tibet	1741	1608	61
陕　西 Shaanxi	27963	24110	2309
甘　肃 Gansu	15722	14310	724
青　海 Qinghai	4013	3773	167
宁　夏 Ningxia	5643	5324	100
新　疆 Xinjiang	25213	22599	1074

数(城市)
in Primary Schools (Urban)

单位:人

Unit: in Person

Teachers, Staff & Workers				
教辅人员 Teaching Auxiliarg	工勤人员 Workers	校办工厂、农场职工 Employees in School-run Factories & Farms	代课教师 Substitute Teachers	兼任教师 Part-time Teachers
23312	**42123**	**1786**	**32004**	**4130**
1407	1221	63	80	104
542	1448	47	231	33
803	1632	129	877	169
1445	1525	56	1686	158
601	952	54	681	127
190	1182	34	169	260
1260	813	48	261	159
1213	2021	60	235	86
2472	1887	191	237	264
979	1339	125	1151	59
792	1961	114	0	188
374	955	32	1742	24
296	672	19	392	57
173	411	1	87	167
2125	2879	185	787	248
1400	1885	80	1613	517
1484	1982	133	2733	144
628	1391	58	265	203
1871	6649	121	12769	226
447	915	10	1259	176
192	816	20	51	17
616	1834	71	1662	102
597	1531	71	639	149
219	663	7	431	125
127	531	8	33	11
7	65	0	23	0
450	1069	25	610	111
178	501	9	235	89
22	51	0	88	2
38	180	1	74	5
364	1162	14	903	150

小学教职

Number of Teachers, Staff & Workers in

地 区 Region	教职工数 合 计 Total	专任教师 Full-time Teachers	行政人员 Adm. Personnel
合 计 Total	**1260445**	**1120663**	**72317**
北 京 Beijing	20890	16088	2543
天 津 Tianjin	17950	15275	1789
河 北 Hebei	61677	55685	3023
山 西 Shanxi	28721	25489	1169
内蒙古 Inner Mongolia	34518	28648	2682
辽 宁 Liaoning	24819	21409	2789
吉 林 Jilin	42132	33117	5070
黑龙江 Heilongjiang	36617	30441	3153
上 海 Shanghai	24342	17477	2206
江 苏 Jiangsu	47509	42052	2411
浙 江 Zhejiang	109202	99764	4931
安 徽 Anhui	36398	33722	1698
福 建 Fujian	54348	49642	3591
江 西 Jiangxi	66498	63894	1424
山 东 Shandong	76695	68294	3714
河 南 Henan	68350	62220	2386
湖 北 Hubei	29726	27422	695
湖 南 Hunan	58346	54231	1689
广 东 Guangdong	87964	77011	7067
广 西 Guangxi	49233	42617	3492
海 南 Hainan	13363	11917	424
重 庆 Chongqing	34670	30338	2750
四 川 Sichuan	76427	66470	5119
贵 州 Guizhou	36328	33420	2049
云 南 Yunnan	36003	32522	1667
西 藏 Tibet	3430	3174	74
陕 西 Shaanxi	28725	26303	1396
甘 肃 Gansu	22939	21772	531
青 海 Qinghai	7693	7372	107
宁 夏 Ningxia	7241	6901	168
新 疆 Xinjiang	17691	15976	510

工数(县镇)

Primary Schools (County Seats & Towns)

单位:人

Unit: in Person

Teachers, Staff & Workers			代课教师 Substitute Teachers	兼任教师 Part-time Teachers
教辅人员 Teaching Auxiliarg	工勤人员 Workers	校办工厂、农场职工 Employees in School-run Factories & Farms		
24283	**41812**	**1370**	**27208**	**3318**
1081	1173	5	32	11
366	486	34	41	25
1024	1893	52	1764	103
783	1252	28	1718	52
967	2185	36	545	188
62	521	38	119	29
2441	1449	55	145	65
828	2167	28	107	6
2632	1791	236	145	55
1264	1663	119	665	182
1522	2799	186	0	725
286	622	70	955	166
486	619	10	482	90
400	753	27	1767	234
1991	2625	71	970	117
1549	2163	32	843	321
586	986	37	835	33
861	1527	38	357	67
901	2933	52	2884	57
1115	1982	27	3750	112
157	864	1	191	67
404	1165	13	1008	36
1147	3571	120	1401	262
303	555	1	1003	107
401	1400	13	683	44
6	175	1	164	14
314	695	17	1455	29
123	507	6	2739	76
32	182	0	118	9
45	127	0	132	0
206	982	17	190	36

小学教职工

Number of Teachers, Staff &

地 区 Region	合 计 Total	专任教师 Full-time Teachers	行政人员 Adm. Personnel
	教职工数		
合 计 Total	**3914809**	**3645691**	**175839**
北 京 Beijing	14803	12113	1276
天 津 Tianjin	11771	10649	823
河 北 Hebei	241531	229463	9028
山 西 Shanxi	135487	129563	3979
内蒙古 Inner Mongolia	82507	74259	3236
辽 宁 Liaoning	117621	101775	14889
吉 林 Jilin	97998	86394	7551
黑龙江 Heilongjiang	129973	116544	7951
上 海 Shanghai	2043	1599	174
江 苏 Jiangsu	193589	176215	8662
浙 江 Zhejiang	20347	18435	1202
安 徽 Anhui	205142	197409	6202
福 建 Fujian	108071	103157	3756
江 西 Jiangxi	122208	117378	2047
山 东 Shandong	250925	238720	6873
河 南 Henan	390286	374936	9606
湖 北 Hubei	156474	147599	3669
湖 南 Hunan	181752	174376	3458
广 东 Guangdong	242437	214339	24020
广 西 Guangxi	159470	139262	16756
海 南 Hainan	33925	31251	1650
重 庆 Chongqing	52782	48428	3021
四 川 Sichuan	241016	221109	11607
贵 州 Guizhou	136404	129198	6061
云 南 Yunnan	188172	178701	5634
西 藏 Tibet	8596	8244	69
陕 西 Shaanxi	149759	140551	7138
甘 肃 Gansu	93091	90658	1474
青 海 Qinghai	17986	17351	145
宁 夏 Ningxia	22949	22306	371
新 疆 Xinjiang	105694	93709	3511

数(农村)

Workers in Primary Schools (Rural)

单位:人

Unit:in Person

Teachers,Staff & Workers			代课教师 Substitute Teachers	兼任教师 Part-time Teachers
教辅人员 Teaching Auxiliarg	工勤人员 Workers	校办工厂、农场职工 Employees in School-run Factories & Farms		
30067	**61774**	**1438**	**364645**	**13048**
575	834	5	55	5
130	154	15	190	0
1221	1796	23	15387	476
766	1165	14	22203	921
1732	3199	81	3652	337
154	779	24	3551	749
2044	2001	8	1113	162
1488	3855	135	863	122
88	173	9	41	3
4784	3634	294	12564	513
256	438	16	0	145
576	942	13	13001	1100
395	736	27	3413	228
1651	1114	18	4866	399
2471	2844	17	6504	407
2907	2788	49	13532	1936
1550	3340	316	18106	443
1028	2846	44	3656	361
902	3140	36	30376	503
928	2506	18	60738	666
146	861	17	1652	89
200	1120	13	8607	104
1032	7214	54	26546	1078
317	825	3	25085	824
487	3345	5	25997	276
4	267	12	3100	29
745	1313	12	28890	310
266	686	7	19909	501
28	383	79	1113	50
95	177	0	1282	53
1101	7299	74	8653	258

小学教职工总数中社会

Number of Primary Schools Teachers, Staff &

教职工数

地区 Region	合计 Total	专任教师 Full-time Teachers	行政人员 Adm. Personnel
合计 Total	**162825**	**117239**	**10771**
北京 Beijing	797	540	77
天津 Tianjin	564	236	70
河北 Hebei	11650	8150	833
山西 Shanxi	7445	5114	408
内蒙古 Inner Mongolia	2999	2266	277
辽宁 Liaoning	1056	955	73
吉林 Jilin	977	685	105
黑龙江 Heilongjiang	1594	1149	142
上海 Shanghai	2591	2091	183
江苏 Jiangsu	5487	3968	282
浙江 Zhejiang	7875	5567	427
安徽 Anhui	4331	3100	282
福建 Fujian	2635	1913	193
江西 Jiangxi	2781	2126	186
山东 Shandong	9308	6720	629
河南 Henan	12641	9047	778
湖北 Hubei	4079	2962	329
湖南 Hunan	4600	3246	244
广东 Guangdong	41128	28555	2554
广西 Guangxi	6090	4831	543
海南 Hainan	4552	3047	318
重庆 Chongqing	2540	1840	197
四川 Sichuan	7547	6116	362
贵州 Guizhou	5788	4726	432
云南 Yunnan	1521	1012	127
西藏 Tibet	179	137	15
陕西 Shaanxi	6368	4405	440
甘肃 Gansu	714	504	55
青海 Qinghai	334	269	22
宁夏 Ningxia	279	188	13
新疆 Xinjiang	2375	1774	175

力量办教职工数

Workers Maintained by the Communities

单位:人

Unit:in Person

Teachers,Staff & Workers				
教辅人员 Teaching Auxiliarg	工勤人员 Workers	校办工厂、农场职工 Employees in School-run Factories & Farms	代课教师 Substitute Teachers	兼任教师 Part-time Teachers
7555	**26989**	**271**	**13380**	**2524**
122	58	0	20	9
53	205	0	0	22
554	2104	9	922	127
533	1368	22	486	90
128	327	1	304	169
4	24	0	30	32
81	105	1	117	85
77	225	1	0	26
146	171	0	235	232
370	845	22	301	60
410	1466	5	0	318
155	792	2	848	76
90	435	4	202	73
173	296	0	88	6
524	1402	33	536	47
714	2060	42	968	394
180	591	17	506	34
244	866	0	116	36
1609	8324	86	1497	92
172	543	1	1610	133
214	969	4	11	14
118	382	3	827	34
329	738	2	1634	160
74	556	0	752	90
67	315	0	70	0
6	21	0	6	0
257	1259	7	1140	91
38	117	0	73	55
14	21	8	18	0
20	57	1	21	1
79	347	0	42	18

小学女教

Number of Female Teachers,

地　区 Region	合　计 Total	专任教师 Full-time Teachers	教职工数 行政人员 Adm. Personnel
合　计 Total	**3237320**	**3054234**	**80533**
北　京 Beijing	46667	38892	4016
天　津 Tianjin	35374	30866	2755
河　北 Hebei	232394	224730	3667
山　西 Shanxi	134450	128790	2272
内蒙古 Inner Mongolia	78451	72428	2652
辽　宁 Liaoning	126241	114038	10983
吉　林 Jilin	101359	90823	5873
黑龙江 Heilongjiang	121943	110095	6172
上　海 Shanghai	38206	30161	2985
江　苏 Jiangsu	147405	139046	3040
浙　江 Zhejiang	103709	97650	1597
安　徽 Anhui	107958	105229	1094
福　建 Fujian	99882	97218	961
江　西 Jiangxi	84779	82403	766
山　东 Shandong	184168	175848	3228
河　南 Henan	268177	259138	3322
湖　北 Hubei	113999	107864	1852
湖　南 Hunan	137156	132411	1333
广　东 Guangdong	255013	239376	6783
广　西 Guangxi	110726	104264	2643
海　南 Hainan	23782	21560	329
重　庆 Chongqing	60578	57191	1473
四　川 Sichuan	157968	149150	3380
贵　州 Guizhou	77544	74594	1586
云　南 Yunnan	100116	95428	1141
西　藏 Tibet	6126	5882	45
陕　西 Shaanxi	107955	103597	2237
甘　肃 Gansu	49317	47813	443
青　海 Qinghai	13987	13513	129
宁　夏 Ningxia	17157	16779	90
新　疆 Xinjiang	94733	87457	1686

职工数

Staff & Workers in Primary Schools

单位:人

Unit: in Person

Teachers, Staff & Workers					
教辅人员 Teaching Auxiliarg	工勤人员 Workers	校办工厂、农场职工 Employees in School-run Factories & Farms		代课教师 Substitute Teachers	兼任教师 Part-time Teachers
36688	**64176**	**1689**		**249851**	**9710**
1935	1794	30		133	65
658	1064	31		359	42
1607	2266	124		15069	435
1542	1814	32		20895	779
1304	2035	32		3319	384
239	946	35		2865	464
3254	1355	54		957	154
2133	3422	121		838	120
3000	1876	184		335	253
2521	2698	100		9902	382
1368	3011	83		0	799
498	1083	54		9205	408
635	1043	25		3303	159
515	1068	27		3905	200
2347	2653	92		5500	269
2765	2881	71		11111	1287
1656	2441	186		9789	281
1097	2260	55		2639	390
2094	6667	93		32257	447
934	2865	20		37290	511
292	1575	26		728	57
519	1362	33		5514	87
1094	4277	67		14459	400
354	1006	4		8153	400
358	3178	11		11807	106
9	187	3		851	15
696	1404	21		20221	255
209	849	3		10899	310
47	269	29		536	26
65	223	0		815	20
943	4604	43		6197	205

小学专任教师学历、

CBreakdown of Primary Schools Heads and Teachers

地 区 Region	合 计 Total	其中女 Of Which: Female	按学历分 研究生毕业 Graduate	本科毕业 Under-graduate	专科毕业 Associate Bachelor	高中阶段毕业 High School Graduate
合 计 Total	**5702750**	**3054234**	**1018**	**175263**	**2134696**	**3269207**
北 京 Beijing	49843	38892	39	5968	29964	13574
天 津 Tianjin	43829	30866	6	1471	20463	21463
河 北 Hebei	329165	224730	19	7490	160074	160277
山 西 Shanxi	188109	128790	34	4859	70226	110531
内蒙古 Inner Mongolia	127011	72428	15	4712	44316	74876
辽 宁 Liaoning	170947	114038	34	5034	68004	95774
吉 林 Jilin	141363	90823	158	14612	77754	47661
黑龙江 Heilongjiang	178122	110095	42	9400	78427	87555
上 海 Shanghai	39408	30161	9	2085	25418	11502
江 苏 Jiangsu	268436	139046	6	9401	121887	132931
浙 江 Zhejiang	159127	97650	15	5964	67113	83008
安 徽 Anhui	266458	105229	12	5849	70379	187322
福 建 Fujian	177248	97218	0	1233	51447	121065
江 西 Jiangxi	198513	82403	62	5641	50664	134845
山 东 Shandong	380066	175848	137	17207	144114	214703
河 南 henan	488490	259138	78	13622	160852	307036
湖 北 Hubei	233902	107864	35	11463	92397	123471
湖 南 Hunan	260704	132411	42	4913	83652	167802
广 东 Guangdong	389262	239376	81	15460	190585	180029
广 西 Guangxi	205142	104264	32	1443	57545	139058
海 南 Hainan	49367	21560	7	1106	16662	30774
重 庆 Chongqing	115212	57191	27	3180	55346	53679
四 川 Sichuan	316029	149150	38	6628	110874	190153
贵 州 guizhou	179367	74594	4	1537	36491	127352
云 南 Yunnan	221589	95428	2	2421	53217	153475
西 藏 Tibet	13026	5882	0	87	2074	9823
陕 西 Shaanxi	190964	103597	23	3669	71612	109661
甘 肃 Gansu	126740	47813	6	1770	37051	81643
青 海 Qinghai	28496	13513	17	949	12930	13745
宁 夏 Ningxia	34531	16779	2	792	13123	19816
新 疆 Xinjiang	132284	87457	36	5297	60035	64603

职称情况(总计)

by Educational Attainment (Regional Aggregates)

单位:人

Unit: in Person

By Educational Attainment	按职称分 By Rank					
高中阶段毕业以下 Below High School Graduate	中学高级 Senior Secondary	小学高级 Senior Primary	小学一级 1st Grade Primary	小学二级 2st Grade Primary	小学三级 3st Grade Primary	未评职称 Rank Undecided
122566	**15813**	**2037609**	**2534656**	**703780**	**39083**	**371809**
298	141	22569	24065	1610	29	1429
426	199	23640	17641	1657	29	663
1305	480	104406	158995	41423	779	23082
2459	295	55642	92028	22115	1266	16763
3092	698	48178	54632	13929	693	8881
2101	1514	105941	45914	10834	484	6260
1178	267	55094	65961	15203	605	4233
2698	1959	81378	67520	16126	1647	9492
394	72	20444	16846	732	22	1292
4211	482	116490	102863	36297	392	11912
3027	483	59160	71248	18808	471	8957
2896	338	88626	140697	26480	508	9809
3503	436	44940	98742	26426	435	6269
7301	348	63909	101452	23920	1161	7723
3905	2283	160795	172629	29470	767	14122
6902	1534	156900	198037	76263	5782	49974
6536	1338	120752	82607	19038	1501	8666
4295	718	124171	109054	18507	815	7439
3107	443	119031	171910	42229	8902	46747
7064	271	80306	70201	39953	2022	12389
818	64	13266	23022	8783	1503	2729
2980	74	32068	62172	13360	298	7240
8336	474	114429	157158	29196	803	13969
13983	153	30409	92641	35787	3408	16969
12474	115	62915	103202	42716	879	11762
1042	5	897	4546	2851	360	4367
5999	237	42052	81932	36896	1226	28621
6270	121	36001	57418	20293	622	12285
855	25	7353	13234	4527	193	3164
798	66	13060	14121	5371	121	1792
2313	180	32787	62168	22980	1360	12809

小学专任教师学历、

CBreakdown of Primary Schools Heads and Teachers

地 区 Region	合 计 Total	其中女 Of Which: Female	按学历分 研究生毕业 Graduate	本科毕业 Under-graduate	专科毕业 Associate Bachelor	高中阶段毕业 High School Graduate
合 计 Total	**936396**	**720337**	**482**	**87686**	**514889**	**326180**
北 京 Beijing	21642	18600	15	3496	13552	4496
天 津 Tianjin	17905	14999	4	1120	9660	7026
河 北 Hebei	44017	37367	8	2756	27959	13187
山 西 Shanxi	33057	28336	20	2354	18425	12094
内蒙古 Inner Mongolia	24104	19519	12	2274	13013	8600
辽 宁 Liaoning	47763	39576	30	3460	29280	14806
吉 林 Jilin	21852	18587	78	6035	11453	4216
黑龙江 Heilongjiang	31137	25859	18	4788	17151	9029
上 海 Shanghai	20332	17590	4	1158	13107	6003
江 苏 Jiangsu	50169	36651	3	3681	28089	18015
浙 江 Zhejiang	40928	30459	6	3433	21822	15452
安 徽 Anhui	35327	24416	4	2614	16758	15790
福 建 Fujian	24449	18779	0	722	11819	11753
江 西 Jiangxi	17241	13380	8	1549	7926	7524
山 东 Shandong	73052	52961	43	9210	39762	23754
河 南 henan	51334	40875	11	5196	27993	17880
湖 北 Hubei	58881	40191	26	6725	29915	21357
湖 南 Hunan	32097	25627	26	2618	16973	12317
广 东 Guangdong	97912	73775	70	10822	54295	32060
广 西 Guangxi	23263	17915	12	693	11821	10448
海 南 Hainan	6199	4149	6	647	3570	1932
重 庆 Chongqing	36446	21559	16	1975	20287	13560
四 川 Sichuan	28450	21397	15	2985	15090	10082
贵 州 guizhou	16749	12571	2	769	7365	8189
云 南 Yunnan	10366	7980	0	957	5260	3996
西 藏 Tibet	1608	1052	0	36	638	849
陕 西 Shaanxi	24110	19342	9	1935	14848	7147
甘 肃 Gansu	14310	10906	0	708	8429	4928
青 海 Qinghai	3773	2900	8	329	1971	1380
宁 夏 Ningxia	5324	4235	2	387	3002	1853
新 疆 Xinjiang	22599	18784	26	2254	13656	6457

职称情况(城市)

by Educational Attainment (Urban)

单位:人

Unit:in Person

By Educational Attainment	按职称分 By Rank					
高中阶段毕业以下 Below High School Graduate	中学高级 Senior Secondary	小学高级 Senior Primary	小学一级 1st Grade Primary	小学二级 2st Grade Primary	小学三级 3st Grade Primary	未评职称 Rank Undecided
7159	**5521**	**409654**	**372240**	**80304**	**4825**	**63852**
83	107	11292	9111	473	17	642
95	131	11077	5990	379	7	321
107	116	19257	17770	4026	168	2680
164	57	12445	14246	3414	152	2743
205	284	9764	8963	2854	78	2161
187	310	27469	14835	2495	54	2600
70	122	9809	8715	2358	27	821
151	745	16092	10186	2570	96	1448
60	46	10151	9174	369	8	584
381	176	23486	18386	4775	89	3257
215	328	17206	17230	3118	65	2981
161	140	16908	14087	2647	60	1485
155	176	8262	11650	2801	46	1514
234	96	8467	6078	1780	105	715
283	657	29914	33805	5008	200	3468
254	284	19585	21190	6733	317	3225
858	625	29632	21890	3810	171	2753
163	270	18514	10561	1601	96	1055
665	260	33636	37808	10493	1801	13914
289	47	10025	7105	3242	358	2486
44	47	1947	2669	740	102	694
608	51	12552	18507	3549	108	1679
278	147	13329	12224	1102	43	1605
424	59	5423	6895	1776	280	2316
153	17	4938	4080	796	14	521
85	3	326	737	251	25	266
171	69	8355	10514	3236	92	1844
245	34	6131	5894	1144	65	1042
85	4	1809	1202	348	5	405
80	19	2683	1840	499	16	267
206	94	9170	8898	1917	160	2360

小学专任教师学历、

CCBreakdown of Primary Schools Heads and Teachers by

地 区 Region	合 计 Total	其中女 Of Which: Female	按学历分			
			研究生毕业 Graduate	本科毕业 Under-graduate	专科毕业 Associate Bachelor	高中阶段毕业 High School Graduate
合 计 Total	**1120663**	**747075**	**215**	**36558**	**512993**	**557013**
北 京 Beijing	16088	12147	16	1537	9155	5262
天 津 Tianjin	15275	10373	1	219	6536	8347
河 北 Hebei	55685	44245	8	1646	32347	21536
山 西 Shanxi	25489	21631	3	837	12829	11685
内蒙古 Inner Mongolia	28648	20931	2	1057	12472	14736
辽 宁 Liaoning	21409	16878	2	548	10244	10482
吉 林 Jilin	33117	26152	53	3899	19443	9614
黑龙江 Heilongjiang	30441	24813	16	1690	16374	12054
上 海 Shanghai	17477	11561	5	880	11381	4915
江 苏 Jiangsu	42052	28247	1	2241	25412	14138
浙 江 Zhejiang	99764	58465	9	2394	40026	55319
安 徽 Anhui	33722	19813	3	1015	12926	19620
福 建 Fujian	49642	30600	0	271	16914	31868
江 西 Jiangxi	63894	30735	8	2150	19355	40525
山 东 Shandong	68294	41766	49	3702	33322	30742
河 南 henan	62220	46592	7	2552	28794	30467
湖 北 Hubei	27422	17171	3	1541	14733	10764
湖 南 Hunan	54231	35350	0	893	21576	31190
广 东 Guangdong	77011	54754	3	1776	41970	32860
广 西 Guangxi	42617	31224	2	310	16349	25514
海 南 Hainan	11917	6429	0	175	4818	6814
重 庆 Chongqing	30338	17795	5	795	16100	13006
四 川 Sichuan	66470	41813	8	1619	30773	33318
贵 州 guizhou	33420	21602	1	298	10229	21974
云 南 Yunnan	32522	21497	2	533	11849	19328
西 藏 Tibet	3174	1707	0	22	487	2434
陕 西 Shaanxi	26303	19142	0	544	12915	12466
甘 肃 Gansu	21772	11788	0	335	7468	13364
青 海 Qinghai	7372	4528	4	187	3906	3160
宁 夏 Ningxia	6901	4461	0	176	3411	3219
新 疆 Xinjiang	15976	12865	4	716	8879	6292

职称情况(县镇)

Educational Attainment (County Seats & Towns)

单位:人

Unit:in Person

By Educational Attainment	按职称分 By Rank					
高中阶段毕业以下 Below High School Graduate	中学高级 Senior Secondary	小学高级 Senior Primary	小学一级 1st Grade Primary	小学二级 2st Grade Primary	小学三级 3st Grade Primary	未评职称 Rank Undecided
13884	**3367**	**442718**	**495037**	**117177**	**6165**	**56199**
118	27	6652	8264	642	10	493
172	46	7382	6887	714	16	230
148	81	21117	24655	5582	114	4136
135	32	8335	12177	2553	124	2268
381	164	12107	11741	2947	123	1566
133	217	13219	6037	1173	46	717
108	52	14624	14527	2884	214	816
307	535	14786	10805	2502	294	1519
296	25	9506	7010	271	10	655
260	134	19058	16769	3967	63	2061
2016	145	36103	45378	12611	319	5208
158	41	14287	15799	2440	36	1119
589	151	15355	26097	6341	130	1568
1856	133	22221	32405	7055	269	1811
479	500	27241	30478	7300	171	2604
400	237	21012	25005	9139	660	6167
381	275	15357	8294	2541	226	729
572	168	28280	20921	3567	151	1144
402	68	28429	31329	8075	1863	7247
442	78	20545	13272	6623	255	1844
110	7	3927	5288	1915	166	614
432	7	8910	17539	2610	84	1188
752	92	27688	32733	4404	92	1461
918	37	9523	17542	4359	133	1826
810	27	13411	14778	3233	73	1000
231	1	416	1447	615	70	625
378	25	6685	12367	4284	228	2714
605	12	6185	10829	3305	99	1342
115	8	2295	3646	942	36	445
95	17	2710	3050	809	15	300
85	25	5352	7968	1774	75	782

小学专任教师学历、

CCBreakdown of Primary Schools Heads and

地 区 Region	合 计 Total	其中女 Of Which: Female	按学历分 研究生毕业 Graduate	本科毕业 Under-graduate	专科毕业 Associate Bachelor	高中阶段毕业 High School Graduate
合 计 Total	**3645691**	**1586822**	**321**	**51019**	**1106814**	**2386014**
北 京 Beijing	12113	8145	8	935	7257	3816
天 津 Tianjin	10649	5494	1	132	4267	6090
河 北 Hebei	229463	143118	3	3088	99768	125554
山 西 Shanxi	129563	78823	11	1668	38972	86752
内蒙古 Inner Mongolia	74259	31978	1	1381	18831	51540
辽 宁 Liaoning	101775	57584	2	1026	28480	70486
吉 林 Jilin	86394	46084	27	4678	46858	33831
黑龙江 Heilongjiang	116544	59423	8	2922	44902	66472
上 海 Shanghai	1599	1010	0	47	930	584
江 苏 Jiangsu	176215	74148	2	3479	68386	100778
浙 江 Zhejiang	18435	8726	0	137	5265	12237
安 徽 Anhui	197409	61000	5	2220	40695	151912
福 建 Fujian	103157	47839	0	240	22714	77444
江 西 Jiangxi	117378	38288	46	1942	23383	86796
山 东 Shandong	238720	81121	45	4295	71030	160207
河 南 henan	374936	171671	60	5874	104065	258689
湖 北 Hubei	147599	50502	6	3197	47749	91350
湖 南 Hunan	174376	71434	16	1402	45103	124295
广 东 Guangdong	214339	110847	8	2862	94320	115109
广 西 Guangxi	139262	55125	18	440	29375	103096
海 南 Hainan	31251	10982	1	284	8274	22028
重 庆 Chongqing	48428	17837	6	410	18959	27113
四 川 Sichuan	221109	85940	15	2024	65011	146753
贵 州 guizhou	129198	40421	1	470	18897	97189
云 南 Yunnan	178701	65951	0	931	36108	130151
西 藏 Tibet	8244	3123	0	29	949	6540
陕 西 Shaanxi	140551	65113	14	1190	43849	90048
甘 肃 Gansu	90658	25119	6	727	21154	63351
青 海 Qinghai	17351	6085	5	433	7053	9205
宁 夏 Ningxia	22306	8083	0	229	6710	14744
新 疆 Xinjiang	93709	55808	6	2327	37500	51854

职称情况(农村)

CCTeachers by Educational Attainment (Rural)

单位:人

Unit:in Person

By Educational Attainment	按职称分 By Rank					
高中阶段毕业以下 Below High School Graduate	中学高级 Senior Secondary	小学高级 Senior Primary	小学一级 1st Grade Primary	小学二级 2st Grade Primary	小学三级 3st Grade Primary	未评职称 Rank Undecided
101523	**6925**	**1185237**	**1667379**	**506299**	**28093**	**251758**
97	7	4625	6690	495	2	294
159	22	5181	4764	564	6	112
1050	283	64032	116570	31815	497	16266
2160	206	34862	65605	16148	990	11752
2506	250	26307	33928	8128	492	5154
1781	987	65253	25042	7166	384	2943
1000	93	30661	42719	9961	364	2596
2240	679	50500	46529	11054	1257	6525
38	1	787	662	92	4	53
3570	172	73946	67708	27555	240	6594
796	10	5851	8640	3079	87	768
2577	157	57431	110811	21393	412	7205
2759	109	21323	60995	17284	259	3187
5211	119	33221	62969	15085	787	5197
3143	1126	103640	108346	17162	396	8050
6248	1013	116303	151842	60391	4805	40582
5297	438	75763	52423	12687	1104	5184
3560	280	77377	77572	13339	568	5240
2040	115	56966	102773	23661	5238	25586
6333	146	49736	49824	30088	1409	8059
664	10	7392	15065	6128	1235	1421
1940	16	10606	26126	7201	106	4373
7306	235	73412	112201	23690	668	10903
12641	57	15463	68204	29652	2995	12827
11511	71	44566	84344	38687	792	10241
726	1	155	2362	1985	265	3476
5450	143	27012	59051	29376	906	24063
5420	75	23685	40695	15844	458	9901
655	13	3249	8386	3237	152	2314
623	30	7667	9231	4063	90	1225
2022	61	18265	45302	19289	1125	9667

小学办学

Condition of School Buildings in

地　区 Region	学校占地面积 Areas Occupied	校舍建筑面积 Floor Space	教学及辅助用房			
			计 Total	其中		
				普通教室 classroom	实验室 Laboratory	图书室 Library
合　计 Total	**2741459179**	**577161373**	**356746150**	**300882851**	**15589831**	**13593797**
北　京 Beijing	17279176	5049012	2571632	1926224	129092	103754
天　津 Tianjin	14161888	3446301	2098492	1603275	74411	65594
河　北 Hebei	163894672	28052921	19577504	16047413	1306327	1046636
山　西 Shanxi	78981157	16446675	10168386	8769488	422489	450236
内蒙古 Inner Mongolia	112116204	9371884	5754483	4688317	350548	296205
辽　宁 Liaoning	99598352	13852967	9590224	7026791	649638	458624
吉　林 Jilin	96604792	9471727	6534845	5196794	412028	241045
黑龙江 Heilongjiang	128428708	12957312	9097116	7331098	607719	372235
上　海 Shanghai	7918987	3817751	1893361	1177793	192542	107188
江　苏 Jiangsu	138659073	27096364	17463216	14316185	596317	727080
浙　江 Zhejiang	54906193	19816033	11743009	8675851	536015	363133
安　徽 Anhui	130268349	23952069	16228555	14550500	458843	656443
福　建 Fujian	57267906	20360054	12251307	9823217	508597	551183
江　西 Jiangxi	67257907	18827575	11768418	10442316	428534	358715
山　东 Shandong	172904795	29411571	19091790	15378306	1130071	847077
河　南 Henan	196759280	44231787	29446400	25560545	1290072	1301072
湖　北 Hubei	135072112	31327118	17311281	14490794	1108090	829271
湖　南 Hunan	122121004	34450905	19816783	17046701	762116	642832
广　东 Guangdong	187533393	58261545	33029200	26715485	1325998	1266498
广　西 Guangxi	113672365	29095032	18019315	16394052	386744	509135
海　南 Hainan	43956722	4943555	2722398	2378994	92868	128785
重　庆 Chongqing	39213181	13874378	8029798	6938846	260921	190156
四　川 Sichuan	106435979	34633548	20340211	17658575	784623	498957
贵　州 Guizhou	54278372	14104434	9819241	8834408	310124	297039
云　南 Yunnan	94914089	24499754	13851940	12459786	553242	391919
西　藏 Tibet	13780639	1976002	803613	724008	15950	35446
陕　西 Shaanxi	89177074	19318315	11967747	10829233	282603	329183
甘　肃 Gansu	73338521	11355483	7416463	6736250	181546	195986
青　海 Qinghai	16010645	2225578	1297074	1144371	14301	35375
宁　夏 Ningxia	19078838	2533293	1697920	1450950	73566	73018
新　疆 Xinjiang	95868806	8400430	5344428	4566285	343896	223977

条件(一)(总计)

Primary Schools (1)(Regional Aggregates)

单位:平方米

Unit: m^2

Teaching & Assistant Buildings: Of Which: 微机室 Pc-room	Teaching & Assistant Buildings: Of Which: 语音室 Linguistic	行政办公用房 Administritive: 计 Total	行政办公用房 Administritive: 其中教师办公室 Of Which: for Teachers	生活用房 Residential and Welfard	其他用房 Rooms For Other Purposes	校舍面积中 Of the Floor Space: 危房面积 Floor Space of Dilapidated Buildings	校舍面积中 Of the Floor Space: 当年新增 New Floor Space Added in Current Year
5713346	**1838991**	**63228981**	**49322861**	**99565233**	**57621009**	**38568116**	**14999875**
93693	24570	694265	413593	691936	1091179	12587	181525
57883	36618	480560	336528	356966	510283	11883	114032
516759	125098	3491853	2955054	2086906	2896658	906691	619964
158941	44037	3050976	2613184	1712345	1514968	662064	430059
133719	44499	1460622	1204949	1402081	754698	1517525	194692
247952	81860	1805443	1192196	848206	1609094	329761	273290
172685	60158	1380272	996974	481487	1075123	906446	204612
213716	51836	1765192	1354716	746880	1348124	944155	216141
78924	35358	470591	260028	471099	982700	0	118205
400106	117676	2844520	1935114	3725543	3063085	12760	932097
255050	105891	1710818	1142825	4040087	2322119	60564	1058705
140940	40445	2636450	2173611	3603482	1483582	3900674	855009
187098	49082	1447194	1008528	4753734	1907819	624678	448400
131819	48671	1698232	1318237	3914815	1446110	1126090	441990
412413	169695	3958220	3005638	3437058	2924503	1251052	413333
325375	92929	7378766	6329442	4283508	3123113	3413856	936012
218452	62798	2811159	2078555	8170465	3034213	1478604	313410
197290	61061	3565269	2847490	6928326	4140527	1967869	379832
470843	294848	4646958	3184017	11791280	8794107	2266211	1632157
129246	37545	1858863	1522999	6349477	2867377	2752130	427022
30375	11264	324437	238847	1529433	367287	286907	223103
167476	29456	975733	677120	3489096	1379751	1297897	200233
362199	70981	2420382	1831826	9133944	2739011	2305474	770573
119772	19124	1098560	866647	2137561	1049072	577797	475201
74295	28358	1298440	919425	7665567	1683807	4602975	1488994
7195	2460	143989	116505	877476	150924	103631	140447
160231	38431	4041427	3598092	2098824	1210317	2159029	551580
97608	15311	2096194	1930331	1028307	814519	1873274	412492
21909	5907	221987	175617	536918	169599	162557	75867
45615	8247	357515	307318	275318	202540	171140	79514
83767	24777	1094094	787455	997108	964800	881835	391384

小学办学条

Condition of School Buildings in

地 区 Region	学校占地面积 Areas Occupied	校舍建筑面积 Floor Space	教学及辅助用房 计 Total	其中 普通教室 classroom	实验室 Laboratory	图书室 Library
合 计 Total	**243729669**	**92705295**	**54331893**	**40390255**	**2624309**	**2007985**
北 京 Beijing	4335630	2598495	1228958	890793	57670	51617
天 津 Tianjin	2632065	1343528	750067	521185	26046	20583
河 北 Hebei	12295545	3698811	2283239	1789206	120381	85375
山 西 Shanxi	6980127	2547244	1503816	1184784	59146	49290
内蒙古 Inner Mongolia	8077346	1821176	1087971	831281	43047	39362
辽 宁 Liaoning	12090200	4226540	2745668	1737701	109562	98478
吉 林 Jilin	4712995	1744415	1072003	767712	43510	33402
黑龙江 Heilongjiang	8386258	2574810	1577059	1124742	68633	52067
上 海 Shanghai	3050794	2132787	1037707	637368	89377	57384
江 苏 Jiangsu	12838950	5091654	3222582	2267586	149071	126746
浙 江 Zhejiang	11690623	5232196	3133684	2027640	159432	115606
安 徽 Anhui	8952962	2892499	1833788	1501102	83193	79407
福 建 Fujian	4954955	2408717	1487010	1056439	57221	70685
江 西 Jiangxi	3483323	1308094	780803	634397	31622	25797
山 东 Shandong	21711280	6358912	3827729	2733370	189884	139071
河 南 Henan	11130435	4591859	2568469	2043834	105765	85981
湖 北 Hubei	19807940	6287424	3735189	2983036	213905	161349
湖 南 Hunan	8631776	3232847	1945287	1518920	98155	71387
广 东 Guangdong	30959104	14449746	8010420	5756120	460994	314255
广 西 Guangxi	7763475	2461206	1387154	1091809	79563	48696
海 南 Hainan	2122576	713871	322986	256662	17675	17437
重 庆 Chongqing	9907611	4278166	2404275	2020695	85531	62317
四 川 Sichuan	5008027	2826966	1653468	1205894	74327	53786
贵 州 Guizhou	2867001	1233197	764226	623803	29795	23548
云 南 Yunnan	2237996	1091458	642456	515678	43241	22003
西 藏 Tibet	528313	127263	59747	50783	3804	1477
陕 西 Shaanxi	4995552	2111799	1282658	1030443	45808	35894
甘 肃 Gansu	3196660	1098417	675506	539900	22362	21026
青 海 Qinghai	1043117	354855	211676	144743	4015	5277
宁 夏 Ningxia	1526485	390469	263124	210432	8686	8089
新 疆 Xinjiang	5810548	1475874	833168	692197	42888	30593

件(一)(城市)

Primary Schools (1)(Urban)

单位:平方米

Unit:m^2

Teaching & Assistant Buildings		行政办公用房 Administritive		生活用房 Residential and Welfard	其他用房 Rooms For Other Purposes	校舍面积中 Of the Floor Space	
Of Which							
微机室 Pc-room	语音室 Linguistic	计 Total	其中教师办公室 Of Which: for Teachers			危房面积 Floor Space of Dilapidated Buildings	当年新增 New Floor Space Added in Current Year
1690093	**688520**	**10740954**	**6941537**	**14047540**	**13584908**	**1726612**	**2945354**
47731	15136	324529	187651	333467	711541	6972	122297
22701	13463	205101	123976	150905	237455	6580	53895
78684	33994	491485	356201	399069	525018	37536	120134
40242	16158	432864	281356	329334	281230	27582	46239
37341	18776	305034	213989	254871	173300	171927	60263
83817	42319	579869	316998	258584	642419	18418	87401
46441	22869	257986	158999	115948	298478	43233	66786
50509	20667	400896	246082	228437	368418	68958	24382
45667	20523	268181	149618	232370	594529	0	49760
101392	30831	547162	330256	546161	775749	4724	194303
89364	40342	495512	301252	902800	700200	1475	539003
65894	18030	344241	234936	413945	300525	143530	100905
48540	16382	208299	129444	364137	349271	77389	74736
26343	12916	129078	93128	257973	140240	26862	47306
124641	69587	900517	573587	782475	848191	65594	141500
81235	25121	686125	489966	832116	505149	78288	77245
88772	25905	630398	424893	1191352	730485	94128	74720
49852	28678	296692	213651	600701	390167	89025	61173
230116	111691	1313715	810102	2231350	2894261	67201	380447
43047	14175	204975	136506	546978	322099	55751	110953
9426	3390	49370	31823	239468	102047	10673	47513
62667	14894	333403	218572	1064121	476367	359749	62540
57770	20090	284933	187982	582881	305684	36963	85329
24480	5005	127565	85913	222494	118912	13212	55325
18365	9463	112498	65290	212985	123519	53885	94765
1939	728	16294	13802	36403	14819	992	300
42786	13780	326417	236888	312807	189917	48817	53290
21761	6335	161505	119918	109749	151657	44919	37378
6813	2805	38032	27103	62296	42851	20910	9581
11523	4224	62858	48580	21368	43119	4397	3408
30234	10243	205420	133075	209995	227291	46922	62477

小学办学条

Condition of School Buildings in

地　区 Region	学校占地面积 AreasOccupied	校舍建筑面积 FloorSpace	教学及辅助用房			
				其中		
			计 Total	普通教室 classroom	实验室 Laboratory	图书室 Library
合　计 Total	**379368313**	**104007051**	**61075687**	**50376566**	**2632859**	**2105422**
北　京 Beijing	6277481	1334656	740544	575010	33420	25234
天　津 Tianjin	6076117	1259435	773338	605845	27183	23685
河　北 Hebei	22976639	4580526	3040451	2504075	173275	132677
山　西 Shanxi	6695606	1788658	1052448	902240	46747	41219
内蒙古 Inner Mongolia	16873757	1837192	1096349	886732	61312	48015
辽　宁 Liaoning	6566998	1416799	1006553	772467	42920	34574
吉　林 Jilin	12383515	2193179	1421635	1110228	68083	47979
黑龙江 Heilongjiang	9727424	1922567	1304220	1066074	57602	39814
上　海 Shanghai	4249670	1540572	773670	484215	92664	43576
江　苏 Jiangsu	13487111	4140557	2529799	2040229	97205	95811
浙　江 Zhejiang	37237051	12357511	7375217	5625748	325547	219517
安　徽 Anhui	11331479	2947316	1760725	1545650	65743	69405
福　建 Fujian	12868117	5038084	2926647	2375734	119082	125355
江　西 Jiangxi	21651669	6064194	3721840	3298516	131595	116380
山　东 Shandong	26850824	5358640	3139858	2520511	182561	126605
河　南 Henan	16448106	5085499	3191204	2710503	121929	113731
湖　北 Hubei	7893886	2673677	1401282	1185054	73586	49775
湖　南 Hunan	20997758	5953310	3228943	2712525	151766	115434
广　东 Guangdong	25729683	9784576	5500408	4339718	229076	193369
广　西 Guangxi	14915450	4478054	2520240	2249049	60472	72154
海　南 Hainan	6024657	1082738	535297	464072	19417	20370
重　庆 Chongqing	7903614	3132372	1772294	1477769	61231	47539
四　川 Sichuan	15153283	6446756	3342858	2809372	143604	96639
贵　州 Guizhou	7765100	2329185	1445940	1257316	58618	47637
云　南 Yunnan	9290950	3023333	1692433	1483298	68859	54611
西　藏 Tibet	3052590	405277	156284	145290	2212	4383
陕　西 Shaanxi	7379620	2165367	1336747	1190168	39752	35182
甘　肃 Gansu	8840100	1709797	1081579	994627	24581	24210
青　海 Qinghai	3442687	505353	300420	270048	5118	7215
宁　夏 Ningxia	2786635	474591	310231	267728	11552	11580
新　疆 Xinjiang	6490736	977280	596233	506755	36147	21747

件(一)(县镇)

Primary Schools (1) (County Seats & Towns)

单位:平方米

Unit: m²

Teaching & Assistant Buildings		行政办公用房 Administritive		生活用房 Residential and Welfard	其他用房 Rooms For Other Purposes	校舍面积中 Of the Floor Space	
Of Which							
微机室 Pc-room	语音室 Linguistic	计 Total	其中教师办公室 Of Which: for Teachers			危房面积 Floor Space of Dilapidated Buildings	当年新增 New Floor Space Added in Current Year
1455068	**529920**	**11033858**	**7991345**	**20863186**	**11034320**	**4362712**	**3220021**
24618	4830	201521	124511	194595	197996	2010	27609
21294	13221	166778	122603	152300	167019	2128	26403
99709	26566	564033	461131	452770	523272	96344	113671
27191	9465	304611	251660	230386	201213	45570	105376
38361	14007	314496	245674	263824	162523	307869	46373
28329	12908	200902	129522	75957	133387	24596	32500
51777	24563	373358	251735	121364	276822	191623	67292
44673	11886	319680	232468	78847	219820	120875	34586
30506	13441	183594	98501	217363	365945	0	62537
73936	24926	476271	302824	613013	521474	3476	159573
150242	60712	1043801	720672	2512338	1426155	39132	441617
34087	9496	295529	211308	682320	208742	308977	88644
57797	15866	389581	248145	1244330	477526	108227	120618
52561	19011	533052	403266	1349601	459701	305684	165309
90768	45415	707056	508105	954738	556988	203891	85759
75843	21622	776653	625861	728261	389381	263179	137978
40364	16132	262213	181612	792628	217554	79143	38997
61858	17934	578055	425058	1404173	742139	272402	92392
90905	74699	741278	478507	2117921	1424969	221409	368871
51958	12561	310406	233686	1197449	449959	264266	145379
11189	4352	65501	41272	416693	65247	52798	55726
47707	8265	240765	157775	820243	299070	195587	44700
95658	28458	465156	323611	2095459	543283	287512	176211
38740	7225	189416	133311	448324	245505	72164	69847
27892	10596	269003	175211	819493	242404	371226	217289
1445	404	35658	25203	184203	29132	14838	39537
33237	8422	436949	379281	248578	143093	168447	76892
17636	3711	332175	305349	167385	128658	220303	78285
7381	2312	51112	41181	119137	34684	37672	24877
10919	1772	70616	60230	49206	44538	25235	19041
16487	5142	134639	92072	110287	136121	56129	56132

小学办学条

Condition of School Buildings in

地区 Region	学校占地面积 AreasOccupied	校舍建筑面积 FloorSpace	教学及辅助用房 计 Total	其中 普通教室 classroom	实验室 Laboratory	图书室 Library
合　计 Total	**2118361197**	**380449027**	**241338570**	**210116030**	**10332663**	**9480390**
北　京 Beijing	6666065	1115861	602130	460421	38002	26903
天　津 Tianjin	5453706	843338	575087	476245	21182	21326
河　北 Hebei	128622488	19773584	14253814	11754132	1012671	828584
山　西 Shanxi	65305424	12110773	7612122	6682464	316596	359727
内蒙古 Inner Mongolia	87165101	5713516	3570163	2970304	246189	208828
辽　宁 Liaoning	80941154	8209628	5838003	4516623	497156	325572
吉　林 Jilin	79508282	5534133	4041207	3318854	300435	159664
黑龙江 Heilongjiang	110315026	8459935	6215837	5140282	481484	280354
上　海 Shanghai	618523	144392	81984	56210	10501	6228
江　苏 Jiangsu	112333012	17864153	11710835	10008370	350041	504523
浙　江 Zhejiang	5978519	2226326	1234108	1022463	51036	28010
安　徽 Anhui	109983908	18112254	12634042	11503748	309907	507631
福　建 Fujian	39444834	12913253	7837650	6391044	332294	355143
江　西 Jiangxi	42122915	11455287	7265775	6509403	265317	216538
山　东 Shandong	124342691	17694019	12124203	10124425	757626	581401
河　南 Henan	169180739	34554429	23686727	20806208	1062378	1101360
湖　北 Hubei	107370286	22366017	12174810	10322704	820599	618147
湖　南 Hunan	92491470	25264748	14642553	12815256	512195	456011
广　东 Guangdong	130844606	34027223	19518372	16619647	635928	758874
广　西 Guangxi	90993440	22155772	14111921	13053194	246709	388285
海　南 Hainan	35809489	3146946	1864115	1658260	55776	90978
重　庆 Chongqing	21401956	6463840	3853229	3440382	114159	80300
四　川 Sichuan	86274669	25359826	15343885	13643309	566692	348532
贵　州 Guizhou	43646271	10542052	7609075	6953289	221711	225854
云　南 Yunnan	83385143	20384963	11517051	10460810	441142	315305
西　藏 Tibet	10199736	1443462	587582	527935	9934	29586
陕　西 Shaanxi	76801902	15041149	9348342	8608622	197043	258107
甘　肃 Gansu	61301761	8547269	5659378	5201723	134603	150750
青　海 Qinghai	11524841	1365370	784978	729580	5168	22883
宁　夏 Ningxia	14765718	1668233	1124565	972790	53328	53349
新　疆 Xinjiang	83567522	5947276	3915027	3367333	264861	171637

件(一)(农村)

Primary Schools (1)(Rural)

单位:平方米

Unit: m^2

Teaching & Assistant Buildings		行政办公用房 Administritive		生活用房 Residential and Welfard	其他用房 Rooms For Other Purposes	校舍面积中 Of the Floor Space	
Of Which							
微机室 Pc-room	语音室 Linguistic	计 Total	其中教师办公室 Of Which: for Teachers			危房面积 Floor Space of Dilapidated Buildings	当年新增 New Floor Space Added in Current Year
2568185	**620551**	**41454169**	**34389979**	**64654507**	**33001781**	**32478792**	**8834500**
21344	4604	168215	101431	163874	181642	3605	31619
13888	9934	108681	89949	53761	105809	3175	33734
338366	64538	2436335	2137722	1235067	1848368	772811	386159
91508	18414	2313501	2080168	1152625	1032525	588912	278444
58017	11716	841092	745286	883386	418875	1037729	88056
135806	26633	1024672	745676	513665	833288	286747	153389
74467	12726	748928	586240	244175	499823	671590	70534
118534	19283	1044616	876166	439596	759886	754322	157173
2751	1394	18816	11909	21366	22226	0	5908
224778	61919	1821087	1302034	2566369	1765862	4560	578221
15444	4837	171505	120901	624949	195764	19957	78085
40959	12919	1996680	1727367	2507217	974315	3448167	665460
80761	16834	849314	630939	3145267	1081022	439062	253046
52915	16744	1036102	821843	2307241	846169	793544	229375
197004	54693	2350647	1923946	1699845	1519324	981567	186074
168297	46186	5915988	5213615	2723131	2228583	3072389	720789
89316	20761	1918548	1472050	6186485	2086174	1305333	199693
85580	14449	2690522	2208781	4923452	3008221	1606442	226267
149822	108458	2591965	1895408	7442009	4474877	1977601	882839
34241	10809	1343482	1152807	4605050	2095319	2432113	170690
9760	3522	209566	165752	873272	199993	223436	119864
57102	6297	401565	300773	1604732	604314	742561	92993
208771	22433	1670293	1320233	6455604	1890044	1980999	509033
56552	6894	781579	647423	1466743	684655	492421	350029
28038	8299	916939	678924	6633089	1317884	4177864	1176940
3811	1328	92037	77500	656870	106973	87801	100610
84208	16229	3278061	2981923	1537439	877307	1941765	421398
58211	5265	1602514	1505064	751173	534204	1608052	296829
7715	790	132843	107333	355485	92064	103975	41409
23173	2251	224041	198508	204744	114883	141508	57065
37046	9392	754035	562308	676826	601388	778784	272775

小学办学条

Condition of School Buildings in

地　区 Region	体育运动场(馆)面积 (平方米) Sports Areas (m^2)	计算机 (台) PC (set)	图书藏量(册) Books & Magazines in Libraries (Volume)
合　计 Total	**900379183**	**2678411**	**1410676033**
北　京 Beijing	6935367	57009	22966436
天　津 Tianjin	5381202	27857	8830975
河　北 Hebei	68987443	194185	108675352
山　西 Shanxi	26114360	71282	40154450
内蒙古 Inner Mongolia	41497873	49319	21119796
辽　宁 Liaoning	50298133	110650	42873519
吉　林 Jilin	42758702	80808	30873701
黑龙江 Heilongjiang	71758154	99893	29397068
上　海 Shanghai	2638390	49657	15737078
江　苏 Jiangsu	41849757	179766	89539302
浙　江 Zhejiang	22024205	151932	56535022
安　徽 Anhui	38786464	63184	60695835
福　建 Fujian	22497056	112733	49283661
江　西 Jiangxi	22764153	58032	32929551
山　东 Shandong	60151680	183071	72439594
河　南 Henan	53494818	121586	140297366
湖　北 Hubei	42730853	94591	63709353
湖　南 Hunan	31109341	100687	76317271
广　东 Guangdong	55081236	286488	147987575
广　西 Guangxi	26458771	54170	45922498
海　南 Hainan	10349945	16286	9596392
重　庆 Chongqing	12910020	93262	22065728
四　川 Sichuan	33655855	161522	55408703
贵　州 Guizhou	14717633	52843	21947065
云　南 Yunnan	14946771	27502	38845629
西　藏 Tibet	1510518	2872	1836040
陕　西 Shaanxi	28481880	72074	51433013
甘　肃 Gansu	20509325	45104	23798729
青　海 Qinghai	3044838	10607	4119871
宁　夏 Ningxia	5060533	17465	6995889
新　疆 Xinjiang	21873907	31974	18343571

件(二)(总计)

Primary Schools (2)(Regional Aggregates)

电子图书藏量(片) Electronic Books & Magazines in Libraries(disk)	固定资产总值(万元) Total Volue of Fixed Asset (in 10 thousand yuan)			
	计 Total	其中:仪器设备总值(万元) Of Which: Total Volue of Equip & Instru. (in 10 thousand yuan)		
		计 Sub Total	专业实验设备 For Prefession	专业实习设备 For Practice
12346850	**31983379.16**	**3097495.11**	**1849806.00**	**376217.42**
165020	510999.48	71485.43	41622.90	1744.63
14840	188277.13	22780.25	11776.23	2107.18
874136	1689437.76	260177.99	200157.07	23148.75
381360	940294.28	57321.78	35847.41	6515.20
137963	434147.46	46697.23	29164.24	3432.52
54846	746352.00	113832.00	69668.00	7717.00
212718	530440.15	97685.64	69614.67	9112.85
143856	660905.62	72812.82	47809.74	7917.50
114601	430061.93	74297.37	44135.40	3156.79
902469	1941588.63	196889.79	85303.58	12830.11
227491	1319704.58	129480.56	73561.35	0.00
316806	1096854.35	54633.67	32202.27	6570.44
164557	1195563.00	162912.00	148897.00	14015.00
264865	969856.09	177087.41	26393.53	5997.15
282414	1479917.04	138825.90	74554.54	17651.73
1261227	1994355.58	137646.44	83909.16	25571.85
433224	1353560.33	123658.72	80194.68	14376.10
442729	1401463.04	216892.91	123040.94	50369.43
4120444	4541533.17	305985.20	247772.33	58212.87
86091	1037242.71	66580.34	33185.64	8893.90
88787	334867.15	25084.68	11900.74	9976.02
190820	1335442.57	57981.91	35790.15	6206.63
431851	1603292.51	179936.64	79645.31	55158.32
93262	569331.50	34245.71	21296.44	3973.86
38790	930602.46	45075.52	24029.61	2504.44
952	124636.65	4770.74	2215.00	366.12
644554	782371.20	60319.53	31063.91	6783.71
138830	800697.61	63644.39	19970.01	5867.57
25745	237544.25	9147.90	4224.04	924.10
45715	267908.59	14606.05	7071.12	2190.09
45887	534130.34	74998.59	53788.99	2925.56

地 区 Region	体育运动场(馆)面积 (平方米) Sports Areas (m^2)	计算机 (台) PC (set)	图书藏量(册) Books & Magazines in Libraries (Volume)
合 计 Total	**85461015**	**950323**	**281729681**
北 京 Beijing	1422797	32399	11585948
天 津 Tianjin	880954	13092	3338408
河 北 Hebei	4780110	40363	13971514
山 西 Shanxi	2417168	19331	7673867
内蒙古 Inner Mongolia	3196850	18301	6223738
辽 宁 Liaoning	5922955	48307	16831436
吉 林 Jilin	2259453	25476	6807044
黑龙江 Heilongjiang	4006154	32297	6806396
上 海 Shanghai	1082523	30520	9751420
江 苏 Jiangsu	4321737	50953	16827243
浙 江 Zhejiang	4322551	54548	16969714
安 徽 Anhui	2889524	32196	9869824
福 建 Fujian	1797226	31049	8661039
江 西 Jiangxi	1011551	13029	2962998
山 东 Shandong	8004858	78739	17339520
河 南 Henan	3803521	40072	15472773
湖 北 Hubei	6692508	43305	16601777
湖 南 Hunan	2298675	27820	11434098
广 东 Guangdong	9042963	145640	39669325
广 西 Guangxi	2655343	20475	5916261
海 南 Hainan	474108	5273	1275409
重 庆 Chongqing	3099587	38210	6919954
四 川 Sichuan	1655433	27329	5630922
贵 州 Guizhou	1004223	11692	2543156
云 南 Yunnan	644521	8406	3139216
西 藏 Tibet	85147	919	200901
陕 西 Shaanxi	1790832	24297	7520919
甘 肃 Gansu	1256321	12240	3290340
青 海 Qinghai	377303	4429	800960
宁 夏 Ningxia	472040	5941	1267423
新 疆 Xinjiang	1792079	13675	4426138

件(二)(城市)
in Primary Schools (2)(Urban)

电子图书藏量(片) Electronic Books & Magazines in Libraries(disk)	固定资产总值(万元) Total Value of Fixed Asset (in 10 thousand yuan)			
	计 Total	其中:仪器设备总值(万元) Of Which: Total Volue of Equip & Instru. (in 10 thousand yuan)		
		计 Sub Total	专业实验设备 For Prefession	专业实习设备 For Practice
5882816	**8083194.47**	**1199200.68**	**751565.09**	**138417.83**
115179	236076.62	32228.59	15584.47	1024.98
8163	56965.63	11393.28	4431.39	651.13
602383	370602.86	144474.28	116805.52	8443.86
93368	206170.34	18431.94	11377.51	2093.76
70784	113619.67	14341.37	8120.02	1153.10
23175	260671.00	40786.00	22651.00	2389.00
92635	134714.59	21397.50	12641.09	2785.27
57364	163893.89	27329.77	18202.41	1505.29
51727	221207.18	43837.88	23485.29	1574.09
281915	503132.99	80750.83	23103.92	2169.14
77567	476357.28	51970.04	30684.95	0.00
111718	235449.24	22259.58	13209.99	2451.47
72871	295610.00	97016.00	92021.00	4995.00
92092	74557.47	10064.54	5997.36	889.77
115815	543389.24	60741.73	28403.75	5772.78
400073	405088.56	37013.63	23606.25	5712.76
136645	324383.71	44971.45	27478.95	3797.89
203561	340881.68	96685.57	73822.05	2535.49
2698470	1438796.19	125342.85	98520.66	26822.19
20187	132776.49	18821.29	9629.10	2042.40
72582	75546.98	12009.75	4300.36	6899.08
106196	622783.39	25816.77	16033.17	3022.22
97714	290442.14	82338.67	25544.01	43045.27
20888	56078.59	8986.38	4811.99	1201.58
16223	90871.45	10773.97	4100.93	494.36
390	10029.85	1241.51	820.04	63.10
150710	146414.18	18863.83	9791.83	1188.91
39286	100740.14	10780.76	6001.69	1495.10
8868	17962.72	3153.43	1780.89	461.61
20217	28098.40	4368.63	2383.26	881.00
24050	109882.00	21008.86	16220.24	856.23

小学办学

Condition of School Buildings in

地　区 Region	体育运动场(馆)面积 (平方米) Sports Areas (m^2)	计算机 (台) PC (set)	图书藏量(册) Books & Magazines in Libraries (Volume)
合　计 Total	**127249845**	**693268**	**290465291**
北　京 Beijing	2738659	12312	6222530
天　津 Tianjin	2329420	10211	3056742
河　北 Hebei	9034394	40560	19190194
山　西 Shanxi	2144073	12574	5528512
内蒙古 Inner Mongolia	6025673	12778	5574692
辽　宁 Liaoning	3365730	12229	4427810
吉　林 Jilin	5524701	26261	8112119
黑龙江 Heilongjiang	5144703	22246	5154387
上　海 Shanghai	1359898	17582	5353062
江　苏 Jiangsu	4100753	36249	13029096
浙　江 Zhejiang	15214200	87906	35541228
安　徽 Anhui	3641644	15410	8551179
福　建 Fujian	5183251	31105	14897899
江　西 Jiangxi	7129871	23969	11454815
山　东 Shandong	9008452	40113	13931202
河　南 Henan	4600406	30037	17022609
湖　北 Hubei	2522068	16850	6263129
湖　南 Hunan	5237515	28202	17645809
广　东 Guangdong	8102114	51707	28747014
广　西 Guangxi	3406951	20961	10201872
海　南 Hainan	1699836	5802	2434930
重　庆 Chongqing	2646864	24232	6360196
四　川 Sichuan	4798965	44480	13005540
贵　州 Guizhou	2215220	17167	4722069
云　南 Yunnan	1713546	10876	7178217
西　藏 Tibet	273515	609	462021
陕　西 Shaanxi	2491271	16302	7391102
甘　肃 Gansu	2545816	10061	4237416
青　海 Qinghai	682418	2943	909374
宁　夏 Ningxia	811563	4977	1223097
新　疆 Xinjiang	1556355	6557	2635429

条件(二)(县镇)

Primary Schools (2)(County Seats & Towns)

电子图书藏量(片) Electronic Books & Magazines in Libraries(disk)	固定资产总值(万元) Total Value of Fixed Asset (in 10 thousand yuan)			
	计 Total	其中:仪器设备总值(万元) Of Which: Total Volue of Equip & Instru. (in 10 thousand yuan)		
		计 Sub Total	专业实验设备 For Prefession	专业实习设备 For Practice
2287107	**6660174.04**	**581776.85**	**360941.38**	**68922.57**
28593	81628.79	10929.40	3369.16	239.50
4319	69836.65	8111.94	5312.98	847.22
78102	264339.71	27295.97	18543.70	3550.25
62401	192332.67	9375.62	4351.67	1106.25
28051	97538.67	12904.49	9311.01	820.93
5816	96230.00	10571.00	4331.00	1165.00
45632	134010.75	18240.09	11308.92	2312.83
27264	129022.81	15382.86	9551.90	2015.93
60196	197047.56	29567.44	20043.98	1523.92
143755	347308.15	34656.91	20375.36	2159.01
138912	727412.06	70342.91	38942.64	0.00
73087	169733.14	9437.17	6370.79	1610.24
31103	259172.00	18021.00	13874.00	4147.00
85927	378161.77	19527.02	11017.25	2860.21
79654	278133.45	26834.39	15147.29	3976.19
333690	272872.84	22553.02	13118.34	5433.55
64879	220245.28	15365.66	10699.74	2620.35
53699	252969.74	29456.93	16079.51	2720.84
511333	817201.26	67778.93	56524.28	11254.65
45142	204595.14	17104.64	8894.71	3394.70
10342	76602.56	5976.44	3782.73	1623.30
20396	134942.56	16896.99	10354.31	1745.05
138811	376923.97	36128.11	22824.38	4862.14
23806	127134.04	7891.08	4837.99	1480.37
8726	147627.50	9985.44	5694.51	889.06
418	35596.34	582.74	198.87	63.83
149639	129458.14	10083.95	5646.91	1553.03
19320	288748.81	6737.32	3797.60	1372.66
6613	22425.79	2101.04	1152.67	224.59
4600	59849.60	3909.77	1677.16	604.98
2881	71072.29	8026.58	3806.02	744.99

小学办学条
Condition of School Buildings in

地 区 Region	体育运动场(馆)面积 (平方米) Sports Areas (m^2)	计算机 (台) PC (set)	图书藏量(册) Books & Magazines in Libraries (Volume)
合 计 Total	**687668323**	**1034820**	**838481061**
北 京 Beijing	2773911	12298	5157958
天 津 Tianjin	2170828	4554	2435825
河 北 Hebei	55172939	113262	75513644
山 西 Shanxi	21553119	39377	26952071
内蒙古 Inner Mongolia	32275350	18240	9321366
辽 宁 Liaoning	41009448	50114	21614273
吉 林 Jilin	34974548	29071	15954538
黑龙江 Heilongjiang	62607297	45350	17436285
上 海 Shanghai	195969	1555	632596
江 苏 Jiangsu	33427267	92564	59682963
浙 江 Zhejiang	2487454	9478	4024080
安 徽 Anhui	32255296	15578	42274832
福 建 Fujian	15516579	50579	25724723
江 西 Jiangxi	14622731	21034	18511738
山 东 Shandong	43138370	64219	41168872
河 南 Henan	45090891	51477	107801984
湖 北 Hubei	33516277	34436	40844447
湖 南 Hunan	23573151	44665	47237364
广 东 Guangdong	37936159	89141	79571236
广 西 Guangxi	20396477	12734	29804365
海 南 Hainan	8176001	5211	5886053
重 庆 Chongqing	7163569	30820	8785578
四 川 Sichuan	27201457	89713	36772241
贵 州 Guizhou	11498190	23984	14681840
云 南 Yunnan	12588704	8220	28528196
西 藏 Tibet	1151856	1344	1173118
陕 西 Shaanxi	24199777	31475	36520992
甘 肃 Gansu	16707188	22803	16270973
青 海 Qinghai	1985117	3235	2409537
宁 夏 Ningxia	3776930	6547	4505369
新 疆 Xinjiang	18525473	11742	11282004

件(二)(农村)

Primary Schools (2)(Rural)

电子图书藏量(片) Electronic Books & Magazines in Libraries(disk)	固定资产总值(万元) Total Volue of Fixed Asset (in 10 thousand yuan)			
	计 Total	其中:仪器设备总值(万元) Of Which: Total Volue of Equip & Instru. (in 10 thousand yuan)		
		计 Sub Total	专业实验设备 For Prefession	专业实习设备 For Practice
4176927	**17240010.65**	**1316517.58**	**737299.53**	**168877.02**
21248	193294.07	28327.44	22669.27	480.15
2358	61474.85	3275.03	2031.86	608.83
193651	1054495.19	88407.74	64807.85	11154.64
225591	541791.27	29514.22	20118.23	3315.19
39128	222989.12	19451.37	11733.21	1458.49
25855	389451.00	62475.00	42686.00	4163.00
74451	261714.81	58048.05	45664.66	4014.75
59228	367988.92	30100.19	20055.43	4396.28
2678	11807.19	892.05	606.13	58.78
476799	1091147.49	81482.05	41824.30	8501.96
11012	115935.24	7167.61	3933.76	0.00
132001	691671.97	22936.92	12621.49	2508.73
60583	640781.00	47875.00	43002.00	4873.00
86846	517136.85	147495.85	9378.92	2247.17
86945	658394.35	51249.78	31003.50	7902.76
527464	1316394.18	78079.79	47184.57	14425.54
231700	808931.34	63321.61	42015.99	7957.86
185469	807611.62	90750.41	33139.38	45113.10
910641	2285535.72	112863.42	92727.39	20136.03
20762	699871.08	30654.41	14661.83	3456.80
5863	182717.61	7098.49	3817.65	1453.64
64228	577716.62	15268.15	9402.67	1439.36
195326	935926.40	61469.86	31276.92	7250.91
48568	386118.87	17368.25	11646.46	1291.91
13841	692103.51	24316.11	14234.17	1121.02
144	79010.46	2946.49	1196.09	239.19
344205	506498.88	31371.75	15625.17	4041.77
80224	411208.66	46126.31	10170.72	2999.81
10264	197155.74	3893.43	1290.48	237.90
20898	179960.59	6327.65	3010.70	704.11
18956	353176.05	45963.15	33762.73	1324.34

工读学校

Basic Statistics of Correctional

地　区 Region	学校数(所) Schools	班数(个) Classes	离校人数 School Leavers
合　计 Total	**82**	**450**	**3390**
北　京 Beijing	6	38	683
天　津 Tianjin	3	5	107
河　北 Hebei	0	0	0
山　西 Shanxi	2	3	7
内蒙古 Inner Mongolia	1	2	0
辽　宁 Liaoning	10	64	382
吉　林 Jilin	4	14	50
黑龙江 Heilongjiang	1	4	30
上　海 Shanghai	13	136	1163
江　苏 Jiangsu	9	86	202
浙　江 Zhejiang	2	13	59
安　徽 Anhui	3	4	26
福　建 Fujian	0	0	0
江　西 Jiangxi	1	0	0
山　东 Shandong	0	0	0
河　南 Henan	3	11	39
湖　北 Hubei	3	12	298
湖　南 Hunan	1	0	0
广　东 Guangdong	2	16	110
广　西 Guangxi	3	4	0
海　南 Hainan	0	0	0
重　庆 Chongqing	6	15	98
四　川 Sichuan	4	8	45
贵　州 Guizhou	3	5	27
云　南 Yunnan	1	5	40
西　藏 Tibet	0	0	0
陕　西 Shaanxi	1	5	24
甘　肃 Gansu	0	0	0
青　海 Qinghai	0	0	0
宁　夏 Ningxia	0	0	0
新　疆 Xinjiang	0	0	0

基本情况
Work-study Schools

单位:人
Unit:in Person

入校人数 No. of Persons Entered	在校生数 Enrolment	教职工数 Teachers, Staff & Workers 计 Total	其中专任教师 Of Which: Full-time Teachers
3373	**7452**	**2636**	**1580**
493	832	419	220
56	82	113	28
0	0	0	0
2	26	86	60
5	10	68	41
313	1409	329	195
35	288	118	77
51	51	28	26
1143	2904	656	372
247	335	124	72
91	158	51	40
24	32	91	48
0	0	0	0
0	0	5	0
0	0	0	0
26	181	61	45
368	162	61	45
0	0	6	6
176	339	75	54
0	30	37	26
0	0	0	0
67	175	108	72
101	170	70	50
45	57	46	38
105	120	45	36
0	0	0	0
25	91	39	29
0	0	0	0
0	0	0	0
0	0	0	0
0	0	0	0

特殊教育基本

Basic Statistics of Special Education

地　区 Region	学校数(所) Schools	班数(个) Classes	毕业生数 Graduates	招生数 Entrants	在校学生数 合　计 Total	 一年级 Grade 1	 二年级 Grade 2
合　计 Total	**1551**	**12881**	**44533**	**48840**	**364740**	**44774**	**47836**
北　京 Beijing	25	274	1007	647	6177	442	591
天　津 Tianjin	22	174	535	230	3167	257	291
河　北 Hebei	97	671	1987	1794	13481	1560	1739
山　西 Shanxi	36	363	422	782	5852	987	980
内蒙古 Inner Mongolia	31	239	249	402	3037	438	439
辽　宁 Liaoning	75	686	790	803	8429	872	900
吉　林 Jilin	45	408	466	477	4748	495	515
黑龙江 Heilongjiang	71	701	536	830	6404	901	754
上　海 Shanghai	31	486	2143	1361	11563	476	601
江　苏 Jiangsu	108	1127	3988	3857	32222	3464	3848
浙　江 Zhejiang	63	574	2561	1947	15357	1521	1764
安　徽 Anhui	71	479	2032	2582	18849	2699	2999
福　建 Fujian	77	616	6677	5270	40921	4045	4754
江　西 Jiangxi	49	252	1025	2262	14854	2553	2572
山　东 Shandong	138	1261	2012	2308	17154	1852	1810
河　南 Henan	123	937	1977	2634	19146	2770	3031
湖　北 Hubei	76	564	774	1118	7908	1271	1197
湖　南 Hunan	55	384	2192	2154	13634	1562	1655
广　东 Guangdong	67	573	3396	3462	27073	3396	3375
广　西 Guangxi	47	316	1579	2918	15874	2088	2258
海　南 Hainan	4	35	71	213	1665	251	311
重　庆 Chongqing	41	254	1891	1513	14483	1283	1679
四　川 Sichuan	70	469	2090	2550	15839	2209	2339
贵　州 Guizhou	38	244	1237	2051	13812	2377	2415
云　南 Yunnan	25	206	1759	2619	17621	2350	2531
西　藏 Tibet	2	13	11	30	162	40	31
陕　西 Shaanxi	28	236	129	304	2143	353	294
甘　肃 Gansu	14	133	466	975	7673	1450	1354
青　海 Qinghai	8	64	212	240	2383	348	430
宁　夏 Ningxia	6	53	55	138	1246	203	200
新　疆 Xinjiang	8	89	264	369	1863	261	179

情况(总计)

(Regional Aggregates)

单位:人

Unit:in Person

Enrolment

三年级 Grade 3	四年级 Grade 4	五年级 Grade 5	六年级 Grade 6	七年级 Grade 7	八年级 Grade 8	九年级 Grade 9	十年级 Grade 10
50710	**50075**	**49647**	**43318**	**25005**	**25364**	**23814**	**4197**
641	687	798	909	524	592	657	336
365	421	494	626	240	251	209	13
1739	1743	1602	1658	721	1238	1245	236
897	900	778	395	330	296	226	63
443	485	457	227	188	147	184	29
1044	994	951	880	796	788	1197	7
643	638	545	615	410	381	337	169
806	992	881	658	472	425	375	140
931	1164	1285	1012	1394	2126	1918	656
4311	4456	4872	5104	2081	1956	1665	465
1908	2090	2058	1877	1222	1425	1365	127
3224	2842	2890	1324	948	885	907	131
5222	5543	6042	6410	2780	2937	3085	103
2468	2257	1903	666	839	826	699	71
1934	1944	1978	1782	1807	1721	1580	746
3047	2747	2803	1507	1226	1095	694	226
1182	1079	962	902	504	448	320	43
1720	1588	1626	1679	1428	1154	1116	106
3802	3895	3925	4072	1544	1404	1512	148
2256	2196	1877	1617	1417	1286	847	32
315	270	199	184	60	43	32	0
2083	2270	2432	2240	756	877	815	48
2243	2018	2091	1966	1028	913	903	129
2323	2118	1763	1568	498	420	325	5
2637	2546	2388	2266	940	1005	943	15
50	26	15	0	0	0	0	0
328	242	244	204	138	154	105	81
1341	1161	1027	553	289	262	225	11
417	388	376	99	118	75	105	27
231	192	174	105	63	35	43	0
159	183	211	213	244	199	180	34

特殊教育基本

Basic Statistics of Special

地区 Region	学校数(所) Schools	班数(个) Classes	毕业生数 Graduates	招生数 Entrants	在校学生数 合计 Total	一年级 Grade 1	二年级 Grade 2
合计 Total	**705**	**7031**	**14892**	**15173**	**109776**	**12632**	**12265**
北京 Beijing	15	177	629	408	3304	250	261
天津 Tianjin	13	116	327	140	1672	123	136
河北 Hebei	34	330	949	607	5184	483	526
山西 Shanxi	22	241	218	443	3519	526	512
内蒙古 Inner Mongolia	17	156	121	197	1530	228	228
辽宁 Liaoning	40	386	463	420	4719	410	411
吉林 Jilin	22	207	265	230	2127	199	210
黑龙江 Heilongjiang	20	242	216	296	2364	301	281
上海 Shanghai	23	373	1437	926	7945	353	350
江苏 Jiangsu	39	383	1161	1019	8472	865	848
浙江 Zhejiang	46	425	802	935	6546	829	892
安徽 Anhui	29	261	363	523	4124	508	582
福建 Fujian	31	310	1045	847	6297	600	679
江西 Jiangxi	16	126	158	344	1653	324	268
山东 Shandong	78	792	1231	1672	9955	1085	899
河南 Henan	47	417	390	668	5489	696	759
湖北 Hubei	37	311	415	525	3363	503	453
湖南 Hunan	20	218	1261	1000	4427	461	435
广东 Guangdong	29	384	1313	1094	8551	995	874
广西 Guangxi	14	136	176	451	2177	389	371
海南 Hainan	2	30	17	86	413	83	63
重庆 Chongqing	12	104	509	308	3052	206	348
四川 Sichuan	31	209	369	542	3157	609	545
贵州 Guizhou	14	107	329	313	1632	372	242
云南 Yunnan	14	149	316	398	2576	365	339
西藏 Tibet	2	13	11	30	162	40	31
陕西 Shaanxi	13	152	87	215	1607	248	205
甘肃 Gansu	10	107	111	202	1508	191	198
青海 Qinghai	2	31	49	69	564	89	102
宁夏 Ningxia	5	50	26	60	600	76	86
新疆 Xinjiang	8	88	128	205	1087	225	131

情况(城市)

Education(Urban)

单位:人

Unit:in Person

Enrolment

三年级 Grade 3	四年级 Grade 4	五年级 Grade 5	六年级 Grade 6	七年级 Grade 7	八年级 Grade 8	九年级 Grade 9	十年级 Grade 10
12691	**12282**	**12398**	**12106**	**9910**	**10939**	**10668**	**3885**
259	290	323	336	324	404	530	327
174	166	207	321	190	188	157	10
512	518	461	515	321	882	745	221
477	474	441	306	288	246	186	63
217	209	196	147	116	72	90	27
480	558	499	552	452	472	878	7
247	243	219	252	192	221	200	144
268	331	304	248	209	194	160	68
541	626	744	620	959	1582	1515	655
1013	1038	1263	1235	543	635	604	428
791	826	706	679	518	655	530	120
617	467	512	444	328	285	250	131
652	750	754	815	627	618	699	103
247	159	144	108	132	110	92	69
913	921	916	850	1325	1211	1185	650
722	650	618	551	539	494	251	209
445	450	374	345	259	279	212	43
383	324	336	323	821	616	622	106
1004	1046	1101	1224	631	693	835	148
335	281	231	235	122	116	65	32
63	47	40	37	34	26	20	0
449	438	509	556	162	167	173	44
490	316	378	364	131	92	105	127
218	217	150	195	79	83	76	0
388	291	323	308	166	206	179	11
50	26	15	0	0	0	0	0
229	162	171	149	123	134	105	81
211	182	202	182	135	120	87	0
69	75	77	38	32	30	25	27
121	82	60	71	54	24	26	0
106	119	124	100	98	84	66	34

特殊教育基本
Basic Statistics of Special

地区 Region	学校数(所) Schools	班数(个) Classes	毕业生数 Graduates	招生数 Entrants	在校学生数 合计 Total	一年级 Grade 1	二年级 Grade 2
合计 Total	**774**	**5293**	**11868**	**14444**	**97157**	**12572**	**12695**
北京 Beijing	10	91	237	170	1854	127	184
天津 Tianjin	9	58	193	61	1295	115	124
河北 Hebei	56	303	288	576	3163	559	568
山西 Shanxi	11	95	94	167	968	234	203
内蒙古 Inner Mongolia	12	71	88	139	893	123	124
辽宁 Liaoning	31	273	228	303	2878	367	397
吉林 Jilin	23	201	173	218	2213	246	244
黑龙江 Heilongjiang	49	433	223	437	3003	477	364
上海 Shanghai	8	109	661	412	3393	123	249
江苏 Jiangsu	56	604	617	954	7296	1096	930
浙江 Zhejiang	17	149	1589	894	7696	574	722
安徽 Anhui	36	191	325	517	3067	502	493
福建 Fujian	40	276	1961	1800	11978	1217	1321
江西 Jiangxi	33	125	234	585	3611	697	759
山东 Shandong	56	438	583	473	5005	563	615
河南 Henan	73	506	545	877	5755	943	967
湖北 Hubei	37	234	206	386	2338	463	403
湖南 Hunan	30	141	299	452	3227	402	404
广东 Guangdong	35	157	717	835	5522	709	704
广西 Guangxi	32	173	690	1422	4892	527	485
海南 Hainan	2	5	23	34	444	61	115
重庆 Chongqing	27	137	558	598	4425	478	461
四川 Sichuan	39	241	593	843	4374	696	616
贵州 Guizhou	24	125	239	549	2926	586	512
云南 Yunnan	8	55	299	409	2705	304	344
西藏 Tibet	0	0	0	0	0	0	0
陕西 Shaanxi	11	58	33	76	400	90	61
甘肃 Gansu	3	16	66	156	924	174	157
青海 Qinghai	5	24	74	52	641	79	136
宁夏 Ningxia	1	3	14	30	153	30	22
新疆 Xinjiang	0	1	18	19	118	10	11

情况(县镇)

Education(County Seats & Towns)

单位:人

Unit:in Person

Enrolment

三年级 Grade 3	四年级 Grade 4	五年级 Grade 5	六年级 Grade 6	七年级 Grade 7	八年级 Grade 8	九年级 Grade 9	十年级 Grade 10
13071	**12738**	**12344**	**11146**	**8297**	**7655**	**6484**	**155**
243	247	291	356	157	147	93	9
150	235	259	290	37	42	40	3
452	479	424	407	147	63	64	0
165	163	105	44	19	17	18	0
109	152	128	71	59	59	67	1
416	316	338	224	290	275	255	0
334	338	249	282	213	153	129	25
407	357	393	338	235	201	188	43
380	508	501	342	413	495	381	1
1014	888	852	857	625	560	451	23
956	1090	1191	1073	648	697	738	7
474	426	367	290	235	185	95	0
1336	1374	1556	1575	1137	1240	1222	0
634	503	440	182	130	140	126	0
648	638	667	597	429	473	351	24
909	732	813	458	428	304	184	17
409	299	258	234	162	72	38	0
426	430	395	388	310	233	239	0
726	719	756	810	426	339	333	0
419	397	321	296	1026	888	533	0
84	64	44	33	19	13	11	0
581	619	646	596	340	370	334	0
626	596	471	584	321	248	216	0
444	457	281	272	190	116	68	0
372	366	293	376	198	235	215	2
0	0	0	0	0	0	0	0
54	59	59	42	15	20	0	0
152	142	124	62	37	39	37	0
116	114	71	38	33	18	36	0
28	15	31	13	3	3	8	0
7	15	20	16	15	10	14	0

特殊教育基本

Basic Statistics of Special

地区 Region	学校数(所) Schools	班数(个) Classes	毕业生数 Graduates	招生数 Entrants	在校学生数		
					合计 Total	一年级 Grade 1	二年级 Grade 2
合计 Total	**72**	**557**	**17773**	**19223**	**157807**	**19570**	**22876**
北京 Beijing	0	6	141	69	1019	65	146
天津 Tianjin	0	0	15	29	200	19	31
河北 Hebei	7	38	750	611	5134	518	645
山西 Shanxi	3	27	110	172	1365	227	265
内蒙古 Inner Mongolia	2	12	40	66	614	87	87
辽宁 Liaoning	4	27	99	80	832	95	92
吉林 Jilin	0	0	28	29	408	50	61
黑龙江 Heilongjiang	2	26	97	97	1037	123	109
上海 Shanghai	0	4	45	23	225	0	2
江苏 Jiangsu	13	140	2210	1884	16454	1503	2070
浙江 Zhejiang	0	0	170	118	1115	118	150
安徽 Anhui	6	27	1344	1542	11658	1689	1924
福建 Fujian	6	30	3671	2623	22646	2228	2754
江西 Jiangxi	0	1	633	1333	9590	1532	1545
山东 Shandong	4	31	198	163	2194	204	296
河南 Henan	3	14	1042	1089	7902	1131	1305
湖北 Hubei	2	19	153	207	2207	305	341
湖南 Hunan	5	25	632	702	5980	699	816
广东 Guangdong	3	32	1366	1533	13000	1692	1797
广西 Guangxi	1	7	713	1045	8805	1172	1402
海南 Hainan	0	0	31	93	808	107	133
重庆 Chongqing	2	13	824	607	7006	599	870
四川 Sichuan	0	19	1128	1165	8308	904	1178
贵州 Guizhou	0	12	669	1189	9254	1419	1661
云南 Yunnan	3	2	1144	1812	12340	1681	1848
西藏 Tibet	0	0	0	0	0	0	0
陕西 Shaanxi	4	26	9	13	136	15	28
甘肃 Gansu	1	10	289	617	5241	1085	999
青海 Qinghai	1	9	89	119	1178	180	192
宁夏 Ningxia	0	0	15	48	493	97	92
新疆 Xinjiang	0	0	118	145	658	26	37

情况(农村)

Education(Rural)

单位:人

Unit:in Person

Enrolment

三年级 Grade 3	四年级 Grade 4	五年级 Grade 5	六年级 Grade 6	七年级 Grade 7	八年级 Grade 8	九年级 Grade 9	十年级 Grade 10
24948	**25055**	**24905**	**20066**	**6798**	**6770**	**6662**	**157**
139	150	184	217	43	41	34	0
41	20	28	15	13	21	12	0
775	746	717	736	253	293	436	15
255	263	232	45	23	33	22	0
117	124	133	9	13	16	27	1
148	120	114	104	54	41	64	0
62	57	77	81	5	7	8	0
131	304	184	72	28	30	27	29
10	30	40	50	22	49	22	0
2284	2530	2757	3012	913	761	610	14
161	174	161	125	56	73	97	0
2133	1949	2011	590	385	415	562	0
3234	3419	3732	4020	1016	1079	1164	0
1587	1595	1319	376	577	576	481	2
373	385	395	335	53	37	44	72
1416	1365	1372	498	259	297	259	0
328	330	330	323	83	97	70	0
911	834	895	968	297	305	255	0
2072	2130	2068	2038	487	372	344	0
1502	1518	1325	1086	269	282	249	0
168	159	115	114	7	4	1	0
1053	1213	1277	1088	254	340	308	4
1127	1106	1242	1018	576	573	582	2
1661	1444	1332	1101	229	221	181	5
1877	1889	1772	1582	576	564	549	2
0	0	0	0	0	0	0	0
45	21	14	13	0	0	0	0
978	837	701	309	117	103	101	11
232	199	228	23	53	27	44	0
82	95	83	21	6	8	9	0
46	49	67	97	131	105	100	0

地　区 Region	毕业生数 Graduates	招生数 Entrants	在校学生数 合　计 Total	一年级 Grade 1	二年级 Grade 2	三年级 Grade 3
合　计 Total	**16043**	**17677**	**127415**	**15438**	**16385**	**17420**
北　京 Beijing	341	234	2333	152	234	231
天　津 Tianjin	168	75	1115	83	109	132
河　北 Hebei	826	675	4969	564	594	648
山　西 Shanxi	126	309	2260	397	384	353
内蒙古 Inner Mongolia	88	152	1005	159	158	145
辽　宁 Liaoning	282	273	3366	307	352	414
吉　林 Jilin	199	177	1747	165	199	243
黑龙江 Heilongjiang	199	353	2542	359	305	309
上　海 Shanghai	881	516	4574	178	260	365
江　苏 Jiangsu	1335	1383	11160	1193	1371	1476
浙　江 Zhejiang	988	699	5788	543	634	717
安　徽 Anhui	752	938	6651	938	1005	1103
福　建 Fujian	2420	1833	14916	1424	1705	1933
江　西 Jiangxi	264	688	3943	738	688	651
山　东 Shandong	779	882	6335	638	643	710
河　南 Henan	638	897	6378	952	994	973
湖　北 Hubei	284	389	2782	445	428	411
湖　南 Hunan	895	781	4536	485	535	524
广　东 Guangdong	1139	1161	8636	1096	1085	1253
广　西 Guangxi	613	1203	5400	656	698	671
海　南 Hainan	18	56	383	64	59	73
重　庆 Chongqing	631	520	4933	440	585	755
四　川 Sichuan	787	980	5613	849	806	773
贵　州 Guizhou	381	775	4852	911	820	842
云　南 Yunnan	609	970	6196	854	903	920
西　藏 Tibet	0	20	83	21	13	23
陕　西 Shaanxi	56	107	797	126	123	129
甘　肃 Gansu	150	330	2142	402	394	374
青　海 Qinghai	68	75	756	112	136	127
宁　夏 Ningxia	20	66	483	81	85	86
新　疆 Xinjiang	106	160	741	106	80	56

女学生数
in Special Education

单位：人
Unit: in Person

Enrolment

四年级 Grade 4	五年级 Grade 5	六年级 Grade 6	七年级 Grade 7	八年级 Grade 8	九年级 Grade 9	十年级 Grade 10
17040	**16841**	**14663**	**9451**	**9463**	**9048**	**1666**
262	304	337	193	216	265	139
135	164	200	101	97	91	3
611	527	556	255	546	567	101
325	275	162	139	110	92	23
156	150	75	58	41	53	10
361	385	325	363	332	525	2
230	206	226	160	130	121	67
371	352	264	215	166	150	51
441	535	386	559	836	741	273
1525	1693	1700	729	696	578	199
765	760	711	489	578	536	55
1039	1021	459	343	333	363	47
2065	2253	2352	984	1044	1129	27
567	461	171	236	225	183	23
649	677	626	754	674	658	306
6915	925	474	439	384	234	88
6384	358	292	180	165	105	14
493	532	508	525	430	434	70
1202	1202	1251	508	498	491	50
669	507	474	732	567	411	15
73	41	42	11	13	7	0
763	805	732	259	300	272	22
709	715	662	389	317	353	40
715	593	552	161	143	114	1
923	759	751	349	368	361	8
16	10	0	0	0	0	0
97	83	78	51	62	37	11
315	256	152	96	83	67	3
127	132	25	33	26	32	6
68	72	38	26	13	14	0
69	88	82	114	70	64	12

特殊教育学校教职工数(总计)
Number of Teachers, Staff and Workers in Special Education Schools (Regional Aggregates)

单位:人
Unit:in Person

地 区 Region	教职工数 Teachers, Staff & Workers					代课教师 Substitute Teachers	兼任教师 Part-time Teachers
	合 计 Total	专任教师 Full-time Teachers	行政人员 Adm. Personnel	教辅人员 Teaching Auxiliarg	工勤人员 Workers		
合 计 Total	**40853**	**30349**	**3963**	**2140**	**4401**	**831**	**378**
北 京 Beijing	929	667	116	58	88	11	11
天 津 Tianjin	711	458	132	34	87	0	4
河 北 Hebei	2097	1605	176	92	224	26	5
山 西 Shanxi	1116	870	89	35	122	69	25
内蒙古 Inner Mongolia	813	610	91	50	62	21	11
辽 宁 Liaoning	2474	1854	322	91	207	26	26
吉 林 Jilin	1775	1237	295	122	121	8	1
黑龙江 Heilongjiang	2546	1926	251	120	249	0	7
上 海 Shanghai	1629	985	233	154	257	7	7
江 苏 Jiangsu	3346	2456	251	184	455	45	11
浙 江 Zhejiang	1445	1133	105	54	153	0	13
安 徽 Anhui	1295	973	107	84	131	142	38
福 建 Fujian	1505	1251	94	34	126	79	11
江 西 Jiangxi	509	413	48	14	34	30	4
山 东 Shandong	5135	3585	525	381	644	4	19
河 南 Henan	3194	2510	243	202	239	25	74
湖 北 Hubei	1633	1243	162	85	143	32	4
湖 南 Hunan	1219	923	97	63	136	13	3
广 东 Guangdong	1655	1311	137	68	139	113	39
广 西 Guangxi	719	495	65	32	127	25	2
海 南 Hainan	100	65	9	10	16	8	0
重 庆 Chongqing	697	543	66	33	55	24	14
四 川 Sichuan	1278	994	105	41	138	20	12
贵 州 Guizhou	675	517	71	23	64	14	4
云 南 Yunnan	610	442	46	18	104	0	0
西 藏 Tibet	39	23	6	0	10	0	0
陕 西 Shaanxi	662	481	61	17	103	46	24
甘 肃 Gansu	394	294	28	10	62	11	0
青 海 Qinghai	153	128	6	5	14	9	8
宁 夏 Ningxia	149	120	8	4	17	8	1
新 疆 Xinjiang	351	237	18	22	74	15	0

特殊教育学校女教职工数

Number of Female Teachers, Staff and Workers in Special Education Schools

单位:人

Unit:in Person

地　区 Region	教职工数 Teachers, Staff & Workers					代课教师 Substitute Teachers	兼任教师 Part-time Teachers
	合　计 Total	专任教师 Full-time Teachers	行政人员 Adm. Personnel	教辅人员 Teaching Auxiliarg	工勤人员 Workers		
合　计 Total	**27331**	**22005**	**1824**	**1357**	**2145**	**508**	**195**
北　京 Beijing	711	544	78	47	42	3	10
天　津 Tianjin	484	352	64	26	42	0	0
河　北 Hebei	1566	1304	77	59	126	20	3
山　西 Shanxi	803	672	50	24	57	52	12
内蒙古 Inner Mongolia	540	438	29	35	38	19	8
辽　宁 Liaoning	1778	1443	186	63	86	4	16
吉　林 Jilin	1201	934	164	66	37	6	0
黑龙江 Heilongjiang	1636	1368	134	64	70	0	1
上　海 Shanghai	1204	803	154	110	137	7	2
江　苏 Jiangsu	2083	1667	100	94	222	41	9
浙　江 Zhejiang	1048	859	49	44	96	0	12
安　徽 Anhui	809	638	39	54	78	31	15
福　建 Fujian	1113	949	43	27	94	73	9
江　西 Jiangxi	370	319	22	12	17	24	3
山　东 Shandong	2896	2313	153	205	225	3	8
河　南 Henan	2228	1880	101	139	108	21	14
湖　北 Hubei	972	810	50	52	60	24	4
湖　南 Hunan	764	624	30	40	70	10	0
广　东 Guangdong	1173	940	86	53	94	71	36
广　西 Guangxi	562	401	35	26	100	15	1
海　南 Hainan	61	38	6	6	11	5	0
重　庆 Chongqing	470	408	23	16	23	18	10
四　川 Sichuan	842	695	51	29	67	8	5
贵　州 Guizhou	492	394	39	15	44	11	4
云　南 Yunnan	401	301	18	13	69	0	0
西　藏 Tibet	24	13	4	0	7	0	0
陕　西 Shaanxi	422	356	19	6	41	14	8
甘　肃 Gansu	240	187	11	8	34	4	0
青　海 Qinghai	91	80	1	4	6	4	4
宁　夏 Ningxia	101	89	1	4	7	7	1
新　疆 Xinjiang	246	186	7	16	37	13	0

特殊教育学校专任教师

Full-time Teachers in Special Education

地区 Region	合计 Total	其中女 Of Which: Female	按学历分 by Educational Attainment			
			研究生毕业 Graduate	本科毕业 Under-graduate	专科毕业 Associate Bachelor	高中阶段毕业 High School Graduate
合 计 Total	**30349**	**22005**	**48**	**3757**	**15023**	**11140**
北 京 Beijing	667	544	1	116	373	172
天 津 Tianjin	458	352	0	49	227	165
河 北 Hebei	1605	1304	1	157	1041	405
山 西 Shanxi	870	672	0	95	445	321
内蒙古 Inner Mongolia	610	438	0	91	235	271
辽 宁 Liaoning	1854	1443	16	269	1071	476
吉 林 Jilin	1237	934	8	302	567	351
黑龙江 Heilongjiang	1926	1368	2	214	906	779
上 海 Shanghai	985	803	0	162	451	362
江 苏 Jiangsu	2456	1667	0	227	1180	1011
浙 江 Zhejiang	1133	859	0	118	456	537
安 徽 Anhui	973	638	0	104	430	421
福 建 Fujian	1251	949	2	37	479	711
江 西 Jiangxi	413	319	0	38	205	166
山 东 Shandong	3585	2313	3	663	1834	1067
河 南 Henan	2510	1880	1	278	1284	921
湖 北 Hubei	1243	810	5	160	616	446
湖 南 Hunan	923	624	0	89	487	338
广 东 Guangdong	1311	940	1	227	638	440
广 西 Guangxi	495	401	0	13	181	289
海 南 Hainan	65	38	0	10	33	22
重 庆 Chongqing	543	408	1	48	301	192
四 川 Sichuan	994	695	1	71	486	424
贵 州 Guizhou	517	394	0	15	195	281
云 南 Yunnan	442	301	0	60	229	146
西 藏 Tibet	23	13	0	4	3	16
陕 西 Shaanxi	481	356	1	49	268	159
甘 肃 Gansu	294	187	0	14	163	107
青 海 Qinghai	128	80	2	24	60	34
宁 夏 Ningxia	120	89	0	12	68	39
新 疆 Xinjiang	237	186	3	41	111	71

学历、职称情况

Schools Broken Down by Rank and Age

单位:人

Unit:in Person

Attainment	按职称分 by Rank					
高中阶段毕业以下 Below High School Graduate	中学高级 Senior Secondary	小学高级 Senior Primary	小学一级 1st Grade Primary	小学二级 2st Grade Primary	小学三级 3st Grade Primary	未评职称 Rank Undecided
381	**729**	**12321**	**11950**	**3223**	**250**	**1876**
5	12	303	276	33	2	41
17	22	251	173	9	0	3
1	29	599	702	170	0	105
9	6	358	356	99	2	49
13	11	199	220	113	21	46
22	66	1060	539	113	3	73
9	22	608	433	140	2	32
25	92	925	600	193	12	104
10	8	487	396	33	0	61
38	60	1127	823	283	9	154
22	10	500	361	137	6	119
18	23	341	402	127	2	78
22	5	335	645	191	1	74
4	13	139	165	49	2	45
18	136	1286	1709	347	4	103
26	78	861	1005	299	29	238
16	25	552	469	144	10	43
9	30	398	355	80	17	43
5	3	364	532	135	106	171
12	0	187	152	116	2	38
0	2	20	29	13	0	1
1	13	200	258	47	0	25
12	6	440	439	80	2	27
26	9	151	232	74	1	50
7	9	194	153	61	0	25
0	0	2	6	9	1	5
4	14	142	218	51	2	54
10	4	98	123	36	14	19
8	8	48	55	9	0	8
1	2	50	59	5	0	4
11	11	96	65	27	0	38

Condition of School Buildings in

地　区 Region	学校占地面积 Areas Occupied	校舍建筑面积 Floor Space	教学及辅助用房 Teaching & Assistant Buildings					
			计 Total	其中 Of Which				
				普通教室 classroom	实验室 Laboratory	图书室 Library	微机室 PC-room	专用教室
合　计 Total	**10222485**	**3801428**	**1593941**	**1019758**	**67460**	**58770**	**40639**	**231301**
北　京 Beijing	172965	90149	44902	22929	1546	1629	1622	7016
天　津 Tianjin	98564	46662	23707	14020	278	913	917	2191
河　北 Hebei	573699	158867	74412	47022	3223	3295	2195	14578
山　西 Shanxi	210285	95224	26956	17177	486	853	561	5600
内蒙古 Inner Mongolia	228208	60896	26396	18564	960	888	765	4374
辽　宁 Liaoning	503907	170503	80212	40799	4003	3361	2574	13579
吉　林 Jilin	577620	116350	54608	34307	1926	2029	1129	4993
黑龙江 Heilongjiang	459006	142241	70128	38141	3920	3403	1736	12601
上　海 Shanghai	201173	133075	62327	34786	2056	2944	1657	19489
江　苏 Jiangsu	825256	327249	123331	77945	4302	4701	3381	22521
浙　江 Zhejiang	351665	152843	63149	38543	2966	2488	2359	9201
安　徽 Anhui	537423	131935	57109	36660	2023	2258	1673	12233
福　建 Fujian	287014	154024	64270	50135	2546	1782	1265	8542
江　西 Jiangxi	122037	58944	27109	19272	1562	1092	747	2201
山　东 Shandong	1414946	453642	174928	96857	11854	7152	4001	25891
河　南 Henan	656511	200640	81208	58803	2541	2814	1828	10126
湖　北 Hubei	475270	203879	74265	53871	2814	3589	1476	6039
湖　南 Hunan	516927	128061	53811	39616	1071	1528	469	6131
广　东 Guangdong	438592	310295	125674	76799	8847	4091	3186	13935
广　西 Guangxi	147960	74884	42351	31009	1511	1063	953	4676
海　南 Hainan	56860	13014	3626	2280	50	182	160	300
重　庆 Chongqing	159353	97385	41130	26435	1073	861	1027	7188
四　川 Sichuan	267932	157502	71862	45644	1794	1817	1919	8121
贵　州 Guizhou	117828	51714	27205	22222	513	783	432	2126
云　南 Yunnan	221464	94025	29734	22799	1290	963	399	3011
西　藏 Tibet	33204	6215	1886	1408	0	70	134	128
陕　西 Shaanxi	165253	65779	28947	21627	991	757	917	2081
甘　肃 Gansu	70936	31733	12508	9320	728	536	459	551
青　海 Qinghai	81393	17779	7256	6190	162	202	99	602
宁　夏 Ningxia	47316	16796	5805	4746	189	282	225	363
新　疆 Xinjiang	201918	39123	13129	9832	235	444	374	913

校办学条件

Special Education Schools

单位：平方米

Unit: m^2

行政办公用房 Administritive		生活用房 Residential and Welfare	其他用房 Rooms for Other Purposes	校舍面积中 Of the Floor space		图书(册) Books & Magazines in Libraries (Volume)	教学用录像录音带(盘) Tapes for Teaching
计 Total	其中教师办公室 Of Which: for Teachers			危房面积 Floor Space of Dilapidated Buildings	当年新增 New Floor Space Added in Current Year		
450994	**266632**	**1212656**	**543837**	**119247**	**106642**	**2785328**	**87729**
7319	5163	20174	17754	0	4007	130144	4874
9939	4621	6033	6983	0	0	34036	997
20673	14042	35474	28308	3317	11967	81580	1307
13497	8600	37504	17267	6145	2080	35486	834
9958	7746	20845	3697	6433	3676	22108	150
23307	11392	31132	35852	3017	0	153312	1732
14478	8557	28240	19024	13520	-621	64746	441
29569	16087	28762	13782	5085	2685	68152	438
15188	8798	20608	34952	0	1131	183771	4928
37302	19697	111213	55403	300	9568	312068	7840
16327	10931	56805	16562	40	3891	131707	3358
12549	8386	45038	17239	6987	11916	133535	1083
18970	9870	53218	17566	5437	7611	74969	2223
4102	3351	20292	7441	1051	1541	25103	962
64585	32175	153691	60438	9821	6780	305404	7260
33109	22353	56726	29597	11819	9108	127819	4307
19345	10370	71621	38648	9713	240	115697	1088
11561	7761	39158	23531	7371	2519	95275	3190
24623	13269	130096	29902	100	2760	333571	32172
6158	4300	18148	8227	4653	9796	75621	1220
655	415	5788	2945	0	0	3900	150
7361	4737	42413	6481	3348	1220	24836	348
10963	7017	55720	18957	6099	4648	72344	2656
5571	3186	14964	3974	1208	880	23753	430
6105	3122	44482	13704	8170	1096	44824	1511
724	404	3015	590	0	0	0	10
13227	10485	19394	4211	2419	1940	49439	1227
4562	3556	10166	4497	0	0	26968	625
1881	1547	7770	872	321	2533	11838	120
2396	1957	5988	2607	1346	1756	17316	158
4990	2737	18178	2826	1527	1914	6006	90

幼儿园基本

Basic Statistics of Kindergartens

地　区 Region	园数(所) Kindergartens		班数(个) Classes	
	计 Total	其中少数民族幼儿园 Of Which: Minorities	计 Total	其中学前班 Of Which: Pre-School
合　计 Total	**116390**	**568**	**728511**	**325182**
北　京 Beijing	1430	10	7733	1293
天　津 Tianjin	1778	4	6703	554
河　北 Hebei	3765	19	35957	22106
山　西 Shanxi	5137	0	29767	13842
内蒙古 Inner Mongolia	1140	79	12881	8245
辽　宁 Liaoning	7033	111	29668	12546
吉　林 Jilin	2404	75	12637	6737
黑龙江 Heilongjiang	2181	10	15572	9189
上　海 Shanghai	1032	2	8110	33
江　苏 Jiangsu	6875	2	42795	10827
浙　江 Zhejiang	11560	3	44651	1174
安　徽 Anhui	2512	4	25003	14945
福　建 Fujian	7064	54	26721	7131
江　西 Jiangxi	4478	4	22778	10527
山　东 Shandong	17070	15	54998	16107
河　南 Henan	2659	15	47970	33332
湖　北 Hubei	2258	5	21422	11909
湖　南 Hunan	2331	38	25732	17472
广　东 Guangdong	10067	3	71393	26971
广　西 Guangxi	2670	3	31394	21208
海　南 Hainan	662	6	4790	2332
重　庆 Chongqing	3093	0	18840	8686
四　川 Sichuan	8109	33	51272	22631
贵　州 Guizhou	1319	13	17532	11796
云　南 Yunnan	1862	10	24488	15581
西　藏 Tibet	41	0	204	59
陕　西 Shaanxi	2288	4	8371	2400
甘　肃 Gansu	2276	10	14834	7457
青　海 Qinghai	220	11	2908	2071
宁　夏 Ningxia	167	7	3267	2213
新　疆 Xinjiang	909	18	8120	3808

情况(总计)
(Regional Aggregates)

入园(班)人数(人) Enrollment		在园(班)人数(人) Retained		离园(班)人数(人) Leavers	
计 Total	其中学前班 Of Which: Pre-School	计 Total	其中学前班 Of Which: Pre-School	计 Total	其中学前班 Of Which: Pre-School
13167889	**7684152**	**20039061**	**9002399**	**10719922**	**7216334**
86465	27122	199390	35768	76879	24200
65837	18418	199551	20058	79599	17274
653422	436812	926076	537477	458072	362940
403582	175549	680324	267209	416918	256647
220008	158789	290612	176346	208475	174607
376388	204407	675118	282453	350428	255298
198386	122243	259163	140531	150803	112142
248377	170774	345116	202603	354396	322305
88173	11	254821	116	90426	95
589551	159802	1252515	304973	630810	289794
503766	29835	1179558	35652	481852	28562
542361	366247	715064	411782	500390	369082
374629	102792	695822	152752	341930	140102
504672	300657	633073	320120	230973	155585
807095	315941	1432854	447746	655392	343340
1188469	946198	1494284	1037574	861610	749851
425259	274159	597841	315080	282539	214453
566568	409093	657070	429795	338076	284147
1301523	769614	2125196	864849	1145873	730074
693064	551925	843289	585221	527988	473540
79194	48302	113367	56569	55246	44090
407641	228879	572538	285710	313689	235543
1048731	578769	1536444	716372	886670	633665
536093	444463	620089	459251	326541	277542
561942	426027	706551	426027	431444	348245
3005	863	6901	2544	2746	1869
128011	40677	231912	67069	98641	64221
268563	174169	372225	189274	217040	147800
62740	47237	74075	50409	44558	40746
78340	59598	102217	67340	53599	45739
156034	94780	246005	113729	106319	72836

幼儿园基本

Basic Statistics of

地　区 Region	园数(所) Kindergartens 计 Total	其中少数民族幼儿园 Of Which: Minorities	班数(个) Classes 计 Total	其中学前班 Of Which: Pre-School
合　计 Total	**31652**	**104**	**180872**	**33461**
北　京 Beijing	545	4	4254	388
天　津 Tianjin	381	3	2402	337
河　北 Hebei	965	6	6363	1425
山　西 Shanxi	687	0	4563	894
内蒙古 Inner Mongolia	445	16	3125	1134
辽　宁 Liaoning	2991	18	11615	2196
吉　林 Jilin	895	3	3517	1049
黑龙江 Heilongjiang	973	5	4471	1451
上　海 Shanghai	598	2	4591	28
江　苏 Jiangsu	1414	1	9931	1659
浙　江 Zhejiang	2626	0	13275	167
安　徽 Anhui	768	1	4858	1000
福　建 Fujian	1371	1	6547	360
江　西 Jiangxi	640	0	3938	575
山　东 Shandong	3165	10	14737	2603
河　南 Henan	1003	8	8266	1408
湖　北 Hubei	1213	1	8235	2260
湖　南 Hunan	945	0	5178	1275
广　东 Guangdong	4374	1	24370	3156
广　西 Guangxi	599	0	5029	1720
海　南 Hainan	290	0	1577	370
重　庆 Chongqing	1178	0	6494	2659
四　川 Sichuan	1121	0	6789	1513
贵　州 Guizhou	444	0	2955	874
云　南 Yunnan	351	3	2515	370
西　藏 Tibet	29	0	155	48
陕　西 Shaanxi	611	3	3641	724
甘　肃 Gansu	394	8	2755	454
青　海 Qinghai	122	4	686	226
宁　夏 Ningxia	77	2	590	143
新　疆 Xinjiang	437	4	3450	995

情况(城市)

Kindergartens(Urban)

入园(班)人数(人) Enrollment		在园(班)人数(人) Retained		离园(班)人数(人) Leavers	
计 Total	其中学前班 Of Which: Pre-School	计 Total	其中学前班 Of Which: Pre-School	计 Total	其中学前班 Of Which: Pre-School
2594719	**834321**	**5256140**	**1129987**	**2094055**	**886769**
44329	9371	116564	12121	40602	9209
28561	12150	71553	12231	28320	11598
104393	37563	194088	49080	66671	28715
82594	23204	138811	31621	60640	21528
57172	32379	93317	37987	51394	35947
110211	32044	271901	59696	97283	54388
52057	24493	79611	32440	36944	22935
58944	27772	112143	41805	79269	63802
44526	0	138045	0	47650	0
128325	20227	306758	58150	116998	39583
142953	5134	363929	6008	128706	5496
88754	29457	154733	35196	76351	31137
78867	4304	180211	9389	64004	9434
61615	17552	113087	21553	37377	12136
200370	46920	427716	78537	163282	55799
134887	45183	269623	57443	100322	42328
141418	57463	245041	67011	96996	48220
112413	44078	159077	48805	61489	33105
284293	78823	694959	115434	289298	99436
74758	42901	130574	49013	52331	38529
18084	5125	34673	8395	11808	6111
129535	74134	185876	90655	91760	69640
126244	50186	224732	62641	91524	50665
68801	36148	102660	37932	41034	21084
40860	13877	83936	13877	32533	11779
2340	740	5405	2164	2157	1655
51150	11422	118870	26549	41912	22646
46596	15520	85736	18377	29382	11085
16975	8254	23445	9949	6192	4431
10362	3942	22525	5863	6825	3424
52332	23955	106541	30065	43001	20924

幼儿园基本

Basic Statistics of Kindergartens

地 区 Region	园数(所) Kindergartens		班数(个) Classes	
	计 Total	其中少数民族幼儿园 Of Which: Minorities	计 Total	其中学前班 Of Which: Pre-School
合 计 Total	**34177**	**231**	**174666**	**47655**
北 京 Beijing	376	3	1984	535
天 津 Tianjin	1051	1	3267	202
河 北 Hebei	1127	2	6566	3186
山 西 Shanxi	573	0	3761	924
内蒙古 Inner Mongolia	482	51	3312	1460
辽 宁 Liaoning	1196	8	4166	1301
吉 林 Jilin	1154	56	4383	1644
黑龙江 Heilongjiang	824	3	3288	1198
上 海 Shanghai	404	0	3261	0
江 苏 Jiangsu	865	0	7076	1267
浙 江 Zhejiang	7336	3	27911	838
安 徽 Anhui	706	2	3985	1226
福 建 Fujian	2149	2	8180	1378
江 西 Jiangxi	1821	0	8874	3230
山 东 Shandong	2784	3	11057	2986
河 南 Henan	838	3	7865	3536
湖 北 Hubei	532	3	3285	1338
湖 南 Hunan	925	32	5605	2590
广 东 Guangdong	2281	0	14068	3880
广 西 Guangxi	1213	2	7361	2760
海 南 Hainan	225	5	1310	448
重 庆 Chongqing	842	0	5195	1884
四 川 Sichuan	1929	25	10901	3404
贵 州 Guizhou	569	5	4690	1973
云 南 Yunnan	897	1	5832	1540
西 藏 Tibet	12	0	49	11
陕 西 Shaanxi	380	1	1972	497
甘 肃 Gansu	325	2	2455	1009
青 海 Qinghai	73	6	649	358
宁 夏 Ningxia	74	3	808	403
新 疆 Xinjiang	214	9	1550	649

情况(县镇)
(County Seats & Towns)

入园(班)人数(人) Enrollment		在园(班)人数(人) Retained		离园(班)人数(人) Leavers	
计 Total	其中学前班 Of Which: Pre-School	计 Total	其中学前班 Of Which: Pre-School	计 Total	其中学前班 Of Which: Pre-School
3246035	**1395859**	**5378954**	**1705034**	**2566085**	**1388874**
25941	9856	52995	15166	23603	11277
27763	5812	98158	7371	37720	5133
130752	73571	196007	95672	90147	64883
70036	20478	122147	30234	64811	28712
66316	40356	89945	45762	62542	48810
57330	27308	102375	38374	54028	36009
74389	35681	99408	41723	55694	34958
63361	32927	88064	39211	81918	69523
40741	0	110148	0	39990	0
107189	21104	239384	43770	107677	40719
317543	21121	738202	25791	316423	20867
85365	33531	130552	40601	71517	36251
121022	25143	240194	40368	115092	40919
197563	97065	250686	104345	79756	46022
173608	65006	313296	100310	137604	77949
203065	115830	287904	137306	132272	95054
80220	40772	116616	52349	49552	36963
151066	87947	182021	94289	84797	64568
280554	135770	466644	157940	233455	138065
164825	93929	232186	104598	121380	92304
23332	11531	35782	14575	16027	11814
126304	56945	187834	74957	93610	64071
246463	114461	398688	150141	207258	136626
126774	86145	158272	89746	80627	59900
117056	55207	195183	55207	90268	47266
665	123	1496	380	589	214
38124	11437	61230	16865	25574	16425
54273	31248	80067	34239	45745	27899
15581	10109	20108	11363	11979	10307
21538	14545	29201	16489	14344	10473
37276	20901	54161	25892	20086	14893

幼儿园基本

Basic Statistics of

地区 Region	园数(所) Kindergartens		班数(个) Classes	
	计 Total	其中少数民族幼儿园 Of Which: Minorities	计 Total	其中学前班 Of Which: Pre-School
合计 Total	**50561**	**233**	**372973**	**244066**
北京 Beijing	509	3	1495	370
天津 Tianjin	346	0	1034	15
河北 Hebei	1673	11	23028	17495
山西 Shanxi	3877	0	21443	12024
内蒙古 Inner Mongolia	213	12	6444	5651
辽宁 Liaoning	2846	85	13887	9049
吉林 Jilin	355	16	4737	4044
黑龙江 Heilongjiang	384	2	7813	6540
上海 Shanghai	30	0	258	5
江苏 Jiangsu	4596	1	25788	7901
浙江 Zhejiang	1598	0	3465	169
安徽 Anhui	1038	1	16160	12719
福建 Fujian	3544	51	11994	5393
江西 Jiangxi	2017	4	9966	6722
山东 Shandong	11121	2	29204	10518
河南 Henan	818	4	31839	28388
湖北 Hubei	513	1	9902	8311
湖南 Hunan	461	6	14949	13607
广东 Guangdong	3412	2	32955	19935
广西 Guangxi	858	1	19004	16728
海南 Hainan	147	1	1903	1514
重庆 Chongqing	1073	0	7151	4143
四川 Sichuan	5059	8	33582	17714
贵州 Guizhou	306	8	9887	8949
云南 Yunnan	614	6	16141	13671
西藏 Tibet	0	0	0	0
陕西 Shaanxi	1297	0	2758	1179
甘肃 Gansu	1557	0	9624	5994
青海 Qinghai	25	1	1573	1487
宁夏 Ningxia	16	2	1869	1667
新疆 Xinjiang	258	5	3120	2164

情况(农村)

Kindergartens (Rural)

入园(班)人数(人) Enrollment		在园(班)人数(人) Retained		离园(班)人数(人) Leavers	
计 Total	其中学前班 Of Which: Pre-School	计 Total	其中学前班 Of Which: Pre-School	计 Total	其中学前班 Of Which: Pre-School
7327135	**5453972**	**9403967**	**6167378**	**6059782**	**4940691**
16195	7895	29831	8481	12674	3714
9513	456	29840	456	13559	543
418277	325678	535981	392725	301254	269342
250952	131867	419366	205354	291467	206407
96520	86054	107350	92597	94539	89850
208847	145055	300842	184383	199117	164901
71940	62069	80144	66368	58165	54249
126072	110075	144909	121587	193209	188980
2906	11	6628	116	2786	95
354037	118471	706373	203053	406135	209492
43270	3580	77427	3853	36723	2199
368242	303259	429779	335985	352522	301694
174740	73345	275417	102995	162834	89749
245494	186040	269300	194222	113840	97427
433117	204015	691842	268899	354506	209592
850517	785185	936757	842825	629016	612469
203621	175924	236184	195720	135991	129270
303089	277068	315972	286701	191790	186474
736676	555021	963593	591475	623120	492573
453481	415095	480529	431610	354277	342707
37778	31646	42912	33599	27411	26165
151802	97800	198828	120098	128319	101832
676024	414122	913024	503590	587888	446374
340518	322170	359157	331573	204880	196558
404026	356943	427432	356943	308643	289200
0	0	0	0	0	0
38737	17818	51812	23655	31155	25150
167694	127401	206422	136658	141913	108816
30184	28874	30522	29097	26387	26008
46440	41111	50491	44988	32430	31842
66426	49924	85303	57772	43232	37019

幼儿教育中女儿童数

Number of Female Children in Kindergartens

地区 Region	入园(班)人数(人) Enrollment 计 Total	其中学前班 Of Which: Pre-School	在园(班)人数(人) Retained 计 Total	其中学前班 Of Which: Pre-School	离园(班)人数(人) Leavers 计 Total	其中学前班 Of Which: Pre-School
合计 Total	**5912419**	**3459476**	**9067576**	**4055739**	**4847968**	**3274190**
北京 Beijing	39670	12252	93223	16250	34890	10915
天津 Tianjin	30500	8399	94212	9367	37082	8044
河北 Hebei	296646	197974	420890	244161	209730	166346
山西 Shanxi	182828	79053	311527	121262	192358	117927
内蒙古 Inner Mongolia	102751	74364	136146	82491	96768	80986
辽宁 Liaoning	167350	90574	299945	124319	158678	115062
吉林 Jilin	86480	53714	114747	61976	65993	49209
黑龙江 Heilongjiang	115245	79104	162357	93754	168037	152682
上海 Shanghai	41727	7	121678	54	42233	50
江苏 Jiangsu	261043	68814	565148	135227	281906	128867
浙江 Zhejiang	230630	13289	545541	15961	218341	12683
安徽 Anhui	241356	163796	319583	184208	224532	166260
福建 Fujian	164598	44875	307885	66863	149368	60739
江西 Jiangxi	214050	128004	270216	136523	100599	67754
山东 Shandong	366630	141646	658796	201872	298416	154518
河南 Henan	538293	432136	680075	474512	394698	344584
湖北 Hubei	186183	119380	262229	136970	122341	93082
湖南 Hunan	253836	183842	295289	193450	152553	128598
广东 Guangdong	575210	349346	943063	390261	506510	331025
广西 Guangxi	308267	247424	375375	262581	236696	212472
海南 Hainan	32528	20022	47269	23418	22866	18117
重庆 Chongqing	184060	102166	260628	128134	142455	106095
四川 Sichuan	472666	259988	699748	322968	402706	287380
贵州 Guizhou	243030	201417	281996	208174	149335	127296
云南 Yunnan	257722	195201	326441	195201	197857	159414
西藏 Tibet	1365	428	3373	1245	1298	896
陕西 Shaanxi	56856	17951	105630	29652	44318	28478
甘肃 Gansu	122677	80742	168365	87329	99799	69261
青海 Qinghai	29466	21662	34452	23018	20980	19059
宁夏 Ningxia	36546	28089	47710	31752	24964	21454
新疆 Xinjiang	72210	43817	114039	52786	49661	34937

幼儿园教职工数(总计)

Number of Teachers, Staff & Workers in Kindergarten (Regional Aggregates)

单位:人

Unit: in Person

地 区 Region	教职工数 Teachers, Staff & Workers					代课教师 Substitute Teachers	兼任教师 Part-time Teachers
	合 计 Total	园 长 Kindergarten Heads	专任教师 Full-time Teachers	保健员 Health Nurses	其 他 Other		
合 计 Total	**973159**	**96219**	**612856**	**63620**	**200464**	**67750**	**11680**
北 京 Beijing	26324	1569	13056	1261	10438	677	231
天 津 Tianjin	15309	1054	9737	309	4209	0	0
河 北 Hebei	32822	3105	21688	2265	5764	3475	293
山 西 Shanxi	29705	2826	19923	1374	5582	5637	723
内蒙古 Inner Mongolia	15839	1313	9735	950	3841	805	217
辽 宁 Liaoning	42852	6270	24946	2928	8708	1442	435
吉 林 Jilin	16994	2229	10107	1551	3107	1382	99
黑龙江 Heilongjiang	20298	2734	11779	1785	4000	518	238
上 海 Shanghai	25087	1449	15089	1237	7312	941	78
江 苏 Jiangsu	64317	6228	46239	2767	9083	11296	709
浙 江 Zhejiang	83022	8238	54056	5205	15523	0	1750
安 徽 Anhui	19528	2426	14162	1056	1884	1867	369
福 建 Fujian	38671	3399	27238	1654	6380	5637	374
江 西 Jiangxi	26515	3503	17612	1979	3421	514	336
山 东 Shandong	80216	9366	57349	3088	10413	6559	524
河 南 Henan	41756	3073	26242	3198	9243	2666	899
湖 北 Hubei	28905	2740	17815	2157	6193	2306	501
湖 南 Hunan	24208	2592	12662	3893	5061	455	267
广 东 Guangdong	143381	12364	82186	9511	39320	4711	804
广 西 Guangxi	23374	2574	13702	2005	5093	2581	219
海 南 Hainan	7685	828	4308	981	1568	58	64
重 庆 Chongqing	19013	2240	12141	1595	3037	1748	384
四 川 Sichuan	49451	5698	31243	4341	8169	3409	776
贵 州 Guizhou	13994	1374	8751	1136	2733	959	195
云 南 Yunnan	23857	1952	15279	1599	5027	1033	177
西 藏 Tibet	628	66	341	74	147	15	4
陕 西 Shaanxi	21020	1901	12689	1392	5038	3394	296
甘 肃 Gansu	14568	1495	9614	715	2744	2481	488
青 海 Qinghai	3243	259	1825	182	977	138	54
宁 夏 Ningxia	3784	225	2415	208	936	330	27
新 疆 Xinjiang	16793	1129	8927	1224	5513	716	149

幼儿园教职工数(城市)

Number of Teachers,Staff & Workers in Kindergarten(Urban)

单位:人
Unit:in Person

地 区 Region	教职工数 Teachers, Staff & Workers 合 计 Total	园 长 Kindergarten Heads	专任教师 Full-time Teachers	保健员 Health Nurses	其他 Other	代课教师 Substitute Teachers	兼任教师 Part-time Teachers
合 计 Total	**487151**	**40978**	**278633**	**33687**	**133853**	**18556**	**5313**
北 京 Beijing	19109	968	9097	905	8139	344	185
天 津 Tianjin	9195	619	4918	220	3438	0	0
河 北 Hebei	17762	1287	10705	1298	4472	615	120
山 西 Shanxi	13811	929	7978	743	4161	1421	346
内蒙古 Inner Mongolia	8632	584	4895	538	2615	447	138
辽 宁 Liaoning	28256	3830	14894	2168	7364	1011	300
吉 林 Jilin	8279	936	4382	915	2046	415	56
黑龙江 Heilongjiang	11672	1456	6350	1135	2731	383	181
上 海 Shanghai	15595	856	8935	767	5037	314	20
江 苏 Jiangsu	24215	2038	15519	1242	5416	1373	322
浙 江 Zhejiang	31750	2622	19650	2086	7392	0	380
安 徽 Anhui	9871	989	6800	594	1488	640	212
福 建 Fujian	16304	1388	10116	800	4000	1092	209
江 西 Jiangxi	9337	975	5687	753	1922	141	128
山 东 Shandong	35395	3438	22405	1976	7576	1592	306
河 南 Henan	24072	1483	13650	1706	7233	1135	395
湖 北 Hubei	20689	1808	12257	1458	5166	1229	247
湖 南 Hunan	14328	1299	6888	2319	3822	159	177
广 东 Guangdong	78161	6045	43102	5136	23878	1744	400
广 西 Guangxi	9818	798	5448	642	2930	339	62
海 南 Hainan	4025	393	2153	503	976	21	33
重 庆 Chongqing	10437	1221	5742	943	2531	275	172
四 川 Sichuan	17278	1556	9674	1492	4556	577	246
贵 州 Guizhou	6905	592	3771	693	1849	343	103
云 南 Yunnan	7446	511	4562	470	1903	233	75
西 藏 Tibet	481	53	247	55	126	1	4
陕 西 Shaanxi	12462	838	6855	814	3955	1412	156
甘 肃 Gansu	7664	563	4547	407	2147	670	216
青 海 Qinghai	2056	157	1098	134	667	104	35
宁 夏 Ningxia	2038	124	1139	129	646	198	16
新 疆 Xinjiang	10108	622	5169	646	3671	328	73

幼儿园教职工数(县镇)

Number of Teachers, Staff & Workers in Kindergarten (County Seats & Towns)

单位:人

Unit: in Person

地区 Region	教职工数 Teachers, Staff & Workers					代课教师 Substitute Teachers	兼任教师 Part-time Teachers
	合计 Total	园长 Kindergarten Heads	专任教师 Full-time Teachers	保健员 Health Nurses	其他 Other		
合计 Total	**305443**	**30564**	**206556**	**20863**	**47460**	**19494**	**3707**
北京 Beijing	5139	391	2945	268	1535	176	24
天津 Tianjin	5009	347	3882	75	705	0	0
河北 Hebei	9126	861	6523	678	1064	1389	102
山西 Shanxi	7853	609	5704	445	1095	960	123
内蒙古 Inner Mongolia	6389	599	4241	395	1154	307	70
辽宁 Liaoning	6961	1148	4466	441	906	144	88
吉林 Jilin	7346	1060	4760	574	952	785	35
黑龙江 Heilongjiang	6252	915	3808	517	1012	47	44
上海 Shanghai	8664	538	5684	408	2034	609	57
江苏 Jiangsu	13543	1078	10074	578	1813	1676	91
浙江 Zhejiang	47213	5104	31393	2896	7820	0	1240
安徽 Anhui	5785	741	4472	291	281	680	66
福建 Fujian	14950	1365	11245	668	1672	1880	92
江西 Jiangxi	12154	1564	8436	952	1202	267	160
山东 Shandong	16608	1831	12596	621	1560	1720	102
河南 Henan	12652	989	9038	1080	1545	808	232
湖北 Hubei	5971	559	4102	519	791	621	76
湖南 Hunan	8104	973	4773	1300	1058	210	78
广东 Guangdong	33287	2919	20088	2276	8004	1507	235
广西 Guangxi	11465	1283	7044	1164	1974	1290	123
海南 Hainan	2482	285	1515	279	403	33	22
重庆 Chongqing	6421	764	4671	559	427	539	56
四川 Sichuan	16659	1796	11217	1566	2080	1296	228
贵州 Guizhou	5578	575	3854	361	788	364	73
云南 Yunnan	13351	992	8767	889	2703	466	58
西藏 Tibet	147	13	94	19	21	14	0
陕西 Shaanxi	5614	461	3993	382	778	810	72
甘肃 Gansu	4175	356	3144	215	460	567	77
青海 Qinghai	1134	91	691	45	307	28	12
宁夏 Ningxia	1681	96	1217	79	289	128	11
新疆 Xinjiang	3730	261	2119	323	1027	173	60

幼儿园教职工数(农村)

Number of Teachers, Staff & Workers in Kindergarten (Rural)

单位:人
Unit: in Person

地区 Region	教职工数 Teachers, Staff & Workers					代课教师 Substitute Teachers	兼任教师 Part-time Teachers
	合计 Total	园长 Kindergarten Heads	专任教师 Full-time Teachers	保健员 Health Nurses	其他 Other		
合计 Total	**180565**	**24677**	**127667**	**9070**	**19151**	**29700**	**2660**
北京 Beijing	2076	210	1014	88	764	157	22
天津 Tianjin	1105	88	937	14	66	0	0
河北 Hebei	5934	957	4460	289	228	1471	71
山西 Shanxi	8041	1288	6241	186	326	3256	254
内蒙古 Inner Mongolia	818	130	599	17	72	51	9
辽宁 Liaoning	7635	1292	5586	319	438	287	47
吉林 Jilin	1369	233	965	62	109	182	8
黑龙江 Heilongjiang	2374	363	1621	133	257	88	13
上海 Shanghai	828	55	470	62	241	18	1
江苏 Jiangsu	26559	3112	20646	947	1854	8247	296
浙江 Zhejiang	4059	512	3013	223	311	0	130
安徽 Anhui	3872	696	2890	171	115	547	91
福建 Fujian	7417	646	5877	186	708	2665	73
江西 Jiangxi	5024	964	3489	274	297	106	48
山东 Shandong	28213	4097	22348	491	1277	3247	116
河南 Henan	5032	601	3554	412	465	723	272
湖北 Hubei	2245	373	1456	180	236	456	178
湖南 Hunan	1776	320	1001	274	181	86	12
广东 Guangdong	31933	3400	18996	2099	7438	1460	169
广西 Guangxi	2091	493	1210	199	189	952	34
海南 Hainan	1178	150	640	199	189	4	9
重庆 Chongqing	2155	255	1728	93	79	934	156
四川 Sichuan	15514	2346	10352	1283	1533	1536	302
贵州 Guizhou	1511	207	1126	82	96	252	19
云南 Yunnan	3060	449	1950	240	421	334	44
西藏 Tibet	0	0	0	0	0	0	0
陕西 Shaanxi	2944	602	1841	196	305	1172	68
甘肃 Gansu	2729	576	1923	93	137	1244	195
青海 Qinghai	53	11	36	3	3	6	7
宁夏 Ningxia	65	5	59	0	1	4	0
新疆 Xinjiang	2955	246	1639	255	815	215	16

幼儿园女教职工数

Number of Female Teachers, Staff & Workers in Kindergarten

单位:人

Unit: in Person

地区 Region	教职工数 Teachers, Staff & Workers 合计 Total	园长 Kindergarten Heads	专任教师 Full-time Teachers	保健员 Health Nurses	其他 Other	代课教师 Substitute Teachers	兼任教师 Part-time Teachers
合计 Total	**910125**	**89649**	**602235**	**59763**	**158478**	**62403**	**9344**
北京 Beijing	24573	1511	12910	1235	8917	632	179
天津 Tianjin	13871	911	9124	287	3549	0	0
河北 Hebei	29696	2503	20827	2060	4306	2983	216
山西 Shanxi	27988	2600	19590	1304	4494	5216	629
内蒙古 Inner Mongolia	14616	1235	9482	910	2989	659	172
辽宁 Liaoning	39827	5766	24383	2626	7052	1238	336
吉林 Jilin	15911	2066	9881	1491	2473	1231	52
黑龙江 Heilongjiang	19061	2590	11513	1630	3328	488	203
上海 Shanghai	24263	1433	14980	1225	6625	855	66
江苏 Jiangsu	61953	5937	45741	2695	7580	10861	588
浙江 Zhejiang	78386	7897	53712	4817	11960	0	1470
安徽 Anhui	18567	2241	13920	979	1427	1728	299
福建 Fujian	37656	3352	27158	1604	5542	5499	312
江西 Jiangxi	24810	3284	17023	1817	2686	459	256
山东 Shandong	76370	8804	56599	2883	8084	6150	400
河南 Henan	38403	2706	25763	3010	6924	2408	804
湖北 Hubei	26520	2518	17432	2029	4541	1994	410
湖南 Hunan	22319	2406	12471	3721	3721	409	160
广东 Guangdong	132017	11869	81019	9031	30098	4306	606
广西 Guangxi	22037	2456	13447	1876	4258	2438	165
海南 Hainan	7146	788	4266	942	1150	51	47
重庆 Chongqing	17732	2070	11914	1466	2282	1678	322
四川 Sichuan	45671	5326	30622	3963	5760	3005	566
贵州 Guizhou	13191	1282	8601	1078	2230	814	160
云南 Yunnan	22268	1814	14940	1467	4047	876	129
西藏 Tibet	542	53	324	72	93	13	1
陕西 Shaanxi	19331	1643	12451	1307	3930	3064	231
甘肃 Gansu	13366	1092	9331	687	2256	2286	389
青海 Qinghai	2980	231	1793	174	782	126	46
宁夏 Ningxia	3489	209	2296	198	786	274	23
新疆 Xinjiang	15565	1056	8722	1179	4608	662	107

幼儿园园长、专任教师

Breakdown of Kindergarten Heads and Teachers by

地 区 Region	合 计 Total	按学历分 by Educational Attainment				
		研究生毕业 Graduate	本科毕业 Under-graduate	专科毕业 Associate Bachelor	高中阶段毕业 High School Graduate	高中阶段以下毕业 Below High School Graduate
合 计 Total	**709075**	**857**	**25446**	**264567**	**379839**	**38366**
北 京 Beijing	14625	86	988	6799	6396	356
天 津 Tianjin	10791	1	338	3330	6578	544
河 北 Hebei	24793	39	1037	11972	11061	684
山 西 Shanxi	22749	65	1038	9970	10057	1619
内蒙古 Inner Mongolia	11048	7	681	5028	5024	308
辽 宁 Liaoning	31216	114	1402	13914	14001	1785
吉 林 Jilin	12336	63	1456	6475	4056	286
黑龙江 Heilongjiang	14513	23	1021	7067	5912	490
上 海 Shanghai	16538	14	1114	10814	4300	296
江 苏 Jiangsu	52467	22	1663	21593	26584	2605
浙 江 Zhejiang	62294	20	1152	14909	42199	4014
安 徽 Anhui	16588	6	592	6412	8925	653
福 建 Fujian	30637	3	298	8010	20343	1983
江 西 Jiangxi	21115	11	692	6739	11945	1728
山 东 Shandong	66715	76	2300	17685	42396	4258
河 南 Henan	29315	27	1310	12735	14253	990
湖 北 Hubei	20555	13	928	8414	10446	754
湖 南 Hunan	15254	18	738	6380	7610	508
广 东 Guangdong	94550	119	2115	33433	52717	6166
广 西 Guangxi	16276	6	396	6061	9124	689
海 南 Hainan	5136	10	150	1908	2954	114
重 庆 Chongqing	14381	8	549	5126	7558	1140
四 川 Sichuan	36941	24	960	10886	21977	3094
贵 州 Guizhou	10125	13	309	3643	5504	656
云 南 Yunnan	17231	7	498	5710	9933	1083
西 藏 Tibet	407	0	8	74	257	68
陕 西 Shaanxi	14590	26	549	6745	6706	564
甘 肃 Gansu	11109	21	418	4253	5895	522
青 海 Qinghai	2084	2	74	1056	884	68
宁 夏 Ningxia	2640	1	178	1418	953	90
新 疆 Xinjiang	10056	12	494	6008	3291	251

学历、职称情况(总计)

Educational Attainment and Rank(Regional Aggregates)

单位:人

Unit:in Person

按职称分 by Rank					
中学高级 Senior Secondary	小学高级 Senior Primary	小学一级 1st Grade Primary	小学二级 2st Grade Primary	小学三级 3st Grade Primary	未评职称 Rank Undecided
3803	**107427**	**159506**	**69058**	**11672**	**357609**
137	3479	4877	1664	203	4265
92	3921	2637	389	35	3717
167	5620	7416	3301	308	7981
98	3731	7579	2837	431	8073
120	2934	3589	1174	201	3030
561	6311	5218	1901	569	16656
189	2950	3407	1093	224	4473
271	3262	3432	1201	240	6107
110	7505	5974	1216	59	1674
187	7214	12192	5032	602	27240
128	3804	7822	5445	699	44396
29	3733	4954	1397	207	6268
78	2770	8738	3864	279	14908
74	2218	3221	1314	475	13813
314	6505	13593	4982	802	40519
290	5340	7337	4016	624	11708
105	5092	6036	2640	524	6158
153	2275	3043	1365	253	8165
190	6246	14137	9055	2759	62163
69	2843	3516	2431	399	7018
30	516	942	562	114	2972
46	1826	3288	1138	204	7879
135	5353	7264	2238	340	21611
30	1549	3087	1211	200	4048
41	3878	5089	2166	186	5871
9	46	84	33	11	224
72	2053	3476	1931	338	6720
18	1721	3053	1614	155	4548
12	395	510	250	59	858
17	663	874	366	11	709
31	1674	3121	1232	161	3837

幼儿园园长、专任教师
Breakdown of Kindergarten Heads and Teachers

地区 Region	合计 Total	按学历分 by Educational Attainment				
		研究生毕业 Graduate	本科毕业 Undergraduate	专科毕业 Associate Bachelor	高中阶段毕业 High School Graduate	高中阶段以下毕业 Below High School Graduate
合　计 Total	**319611**	**704**	**17388**	**146078**	**144960**	**10481**
北　京 Beijing	10065	78	769	4737	4357	124
天　津 Tianjin	5537	1	273	2396	2792	75
河　北 Hebei	11992	36	653	6180	4864	259
山　西 Shanxi	8907	38	650	4903	2907	409
内蒙古 Inner Mongolia	5479	6	402	2931	1989	151
辽　宁 Liaoning	18724	104	1202	9577	7329	512
吉　林 Jilin	5318	47	845	2965	1391	70
黑龙江 Heilongjiang	7806	16	792	4260	2554	184
上　海 Shanghai	9791	10	714	6694	2282	91
江　苏 Jiangsu	17557	12	832	9070	7215	428
浙　江 Zhejiang	22272	18	848	7692	12922	792
安　徽 Anhui	7789	3	378	3306	3855	247
福　建 Fujian	11504	3	210	3743	7190	358
江　西 Jiangxi	6662	8	368	3013	3012	261
山　东 Shandong	25843	69	1658	10114	13326	676
河　南 Henan	15133	10	902	7351	6532	338
湖　北 Hubei	14065	13	758	6023	6799	472
湖　南 Hunan	8187	18	584	3921	3439	225
广　东 Guangdong	49147	108	1613	19661	25056	2709
广　西 Guangxi	6246	5	256	2822	3032	131
海　南 Hainan	2546	10	99	1029	1386	22
重　庆 Chongqing	6963	5	405	2888	3255	410
四　川 Sichuan	11230	12	485	4765	5525	443
贵　州 Guizhou	4363	12	207	1926	2023	195
云　南 Yunnan	5073	4	265	2042	2441	321
西　藏 Tibet	300	0	6	71	166	57
陕　西 Shaanxi	7693	24	428	4314	2787	140
甘　肃 Gansu	5110	20	316	2462	2112	200
青　海 Qinghai	1255	1	49	645	534	26
宁　夏 Ningxia	1263	1	114	720	385	43
新　疆 Xinjiang	5791	12	307	3857	1503	112

学历、职称情况(城市)

by Educational Attainment and Rank (Urban)

单位:人

Unit:in Person

按职称分 by Rank					
中学高级 Senior Secondary	小学高级 Senior Primary	小学一级 1st Grade Primary	小学二级 2st Grade Primary	小学三级 3st Grade Primary	未评职称 Rank Undecided
2440	**59355**	**79507**	**34780**	**6418**	**137111**
118	2613	3556	1381	166	2231
61	2812	1569	208	24	863
66	2517	3080	1572	200	4557
63	1904	2891	1082	146	2821
77	1403	1688	528	129	1654
341	3979	3675	1396	443	8890
113	1164	1230	591	142	2078
182	2067	1910	679	88	2880
70	4839	3685	468	26	703
73	3416	6107	2255	247	5459
102	2459	4308	2612	315	12476
22	1873	2064	661	145	3024
67	1447	2801	1380	192	5617
44	1002	1377	561	188	3490
208	3902	7014	2496	239	11984
164	3017	3934	2060	289	5669
75	3467	4300	1887	321	4015
138	1429	1897	998	201	3524
134	4024	8471	5146	1750	29622
34	1164	1485	924	143	2496
29	281	367	202	33	1634
37	920	1467	729	125	3685
72	2105	2593	1040	216	5204
20	652	1139	467	133	1952
18	1405	1470	632	89	1459
9	32	38	17	0	204
53	1104	1745	1163	201	3427
7	798	1377	669	85	2174
2	190	249	140	42	632
16	295	386	142	11	413
25	1075	1634	694	89	2274

幼儿园园长、专任教师

Breakdown of Kindergarten Heads and Teachers by

地　区 Region	合　计 Total	按学历分 by Educational Attainment				
		研究生毕业 Graduate	本科毕业 Under-graduate	专科毕业 Associate Bachelor	高中阶段毕业 High School Graduate	高中阶段以下毕业 Below High School Graduate
合　计 Total	**237120**	**105**	**6312**	**83436**	**135109**	**12158**
北　京 Beijing	3336	7	180	1629	1371	149
天　津 Tianjin	4229	0	57	793	3023	356
河　北 Hebei	7384	3	299	3521	3289	272
山　西 Shanxi	6313	9	315	3254	2588	147
内蒙古 Inner Mongolia	4840	0	246	1834	2621	139
辽　宁 Liaoning	5614	9	128	2422	2792	263
吉　林 Jilin	5820	15	538	2865	2213	189
黑龙江 Heilongjiang	4723	7	157	2019	2361	179
上　海 Shanghai	6222	3	384	3841	1832	162
江　苏 Jiangsu	11152	2	509	5260	4991	390
浙　江 Zhejiang	36497	2	296	6843	26814	2542
安　徽 Anhui	5213	2	171	2125	2709	206
福　建 Fujian	12610	0	78	3492	8372	668
江　西 Jiangxi	10000	3	304	3221	5772	700
山　东 Shandong	14427	5	417	3932	9160	913
河　南 Henan	10027	16	366	4274	5074	297
湖　北 Hubei	4661	0	115	1769	2594	183
湖　南 Hunan	5746	0	151	2161	3244	190
广　东 Guangdong	23007	5	352	8090	13259	1301
广　西 Guangxi	8327	1	118	2904	4886	418
海　南 Hainan	1800	0	41	746	974	39
重　庆 Chongqing	5435	3	114	1877	3042	399
四　川 Sichuan	13013	6	347	4474	7528	658
贵　州 Guizhou	4429	1	78	1449	2560	341
云　南 Yunnan	9759	3	198	3210	5817	531
西　藏 Tibet	107	0	2	3	91	11
陕　西 Shaanxi	4454	2	81	1858	2287	226
甘　肃 Gansu	3500	0	78	1300	1984	138
青　海 Qinghai	782	1	25	391	325	40
宁　夏 Ningxia	1313	0	64	681	524	44
新　疆 Xinjiang	2380	0	103	1198	1012	67

学历、职称情况(县镇)

Educational Attainment and Rank (County Seats & Towns)

单位:人

Unit:in Person

按职称分 by Rank					
中学高级 Senior Secondary	小学高级 Senior Primary	小学一级 1st Grade Primary	小学二级 2st Grade Primary	小学三级 3st Grade Primary	未评职称 Rank Undecided
1087	**37372**	**56860**	**22560**	**3247**	**115994**
17	659	1067	210	26	1357
22	799	855	153	9	2391
83	2035	2241	787	72	2166
23	1330	2692	889	137	1242
39	1343	1627	535	69	1227
162	1371	732	164	75	3110
70	1399	1771	391	60	2129
77	798	1041	359	96	2352
39	2542	2098	695	30	818
81	2031	2496	1205	114	5225
24	1262	3365	2706	356	28784
4	1390	1679	356	35	1749
11	1172	4654	1783	69	4921
18	1149	1670	621	240	6302
69	1604	3389	1164	157	8044
98	1878	2714	1349	209	3779
29	1225	1321	565	176	1345
15	792	1051	332	40	3516
44	1900	4085	2292	625	14061
35	1594	1798	1251	177	3472
1	180	372	199	55	993
7	769	1411	317	41	2890
53	2740	3571	725	58	5866
9	763	1519	490	50	1598
21	2220	3093	1178	82	3165
0	14	46	16	11	20
14	774	1496	627	95	1448
6	633	1377	601	46	837
10	197	255	110	15	195
1	356	466	205	0	285
5	453	908	285	22	707

幼儿园园长、专任教师学历、

Breakdown of Kindergarten Heads and Teachers by

地 区 Region	合 计 Total	按学历分 by Educational Attainment				
		研究生毕业 Graduate	本科毕业 Under-graduate	专科毕业 Associate Bachelor	高中阶段毕业 High School Graduate	高中阶段以下毕业 Below High School Graduate
合 计 Total	**152344**	**48**	**1746**	**35053**	**99770**	**15727**
北 京 Beijing	1224	1	39	433	668	83
天 津 Tianjin	1025	0	8	141	763	113
河 北 Hebei	5417	0	85	2271	2908	153
山 西 Shanxi	7529	18	73	1813	4562	1063
内蒙古 Inner Mongolia	729	1	33	263	414	18
辽 宁 Liaoning	6878	1	72	1915	3880	1010
吉 林 Jilin	1198	1	73	645	452	27
黑龙江 Heilongjiang	1984	0	72	788	997	127
上 海 Shanghai	525	1	16	279	186	43
江 苏 Jiangsu	23758	8	322	7263	14378	1787
浙 江 Zhejiang	3525	0	8	374	2463	680
安 徽 Anhui	3586	1	43	981	2361	200
福 建 Fujian	6523	0	10	775	4781	957
江 西 Jiangxi	4453	0	20	505	3161	767
山 东 Shandong	26445	2	225	3639	19910	2669
河 南 Henan	4155	1	42	1110	2647	355
湖 北 Hubei	1829	0	55	622	1053	99
湖 南 Hunan	1321	0	3	298	927	93
广 东 Guangdong	22396	6	150	5682	14402	2156
广 西 Guangxi	1703	0	22	335	1206	140
海 南 Hainan	790	0	10	133	594	53
重 庆 Chongqing	1983	0	30	361	1261	331
四 川 Sichuan	12698	6	128	1647	8924	1993
贵 州 Guizhou	1333	0	24	268	921	120
云 南 Yunnan	2399	0	35	458	1675	231
西 藏 Tibet	0	0	0	0	0	0
陕 西 Shaanxi	2443	0	40	573	1632	198
甘 肃 Gansu	2499	1	24	491	1799	184
青 海 Qinghai	47	0	0	20	25	2
宁 夏 Ningxia	64	0	0	17	44	3
新 疆 Xinjiang	1885	0	84	953	776	72

职称情况(农村)

Educational Attainment and Rank (Rural)

单位:人

Unit: in Person

按职称分 by Rank					
中学高级 Senior Secondary	小学高级 Senior Primary	小学一级 1st Grade Primary	小学二级 2st Grade Primary	小学三级 3st Grade Primary	未评职称 Rank Undecided
276	**10700**	**23139**	**11718**	**2007**	**104504**
2	207	254	73	11	677
9	310	213	28	2	463
18	1068	2095	942	36	1258
12	497	1996	866	148	4010
4	188	274	111	3	149
58	961	811	341	51	4656
6	387	406	111	22	266
12	397	481	163	56	875
1	124	191	53	3	153
33	1767	3589	1572	241	16556
2	83	149	127	28	3136
3	470	1211	380	27	1495
0	151	1283	701	18	4370
12	67	174	132	47	4021
37	999	3190	1322	406	20491
28	445	689	607	126	2260
1	400	415	188	27	798
0	54	95	35	12	1125
12	322	1581	1617	384	18480
0	85	233	256	79	1050
0	55	203	161	26	345
2	137	410	92	38	1304
10	508	1100	473	66	10541
1	134	429	254	17	498
2	253	526	356	15	1247
0	0	0	0	0	0
5	175	235	141	42	1845
5	290	299	344	24	1537
0	8	6	0	2	31
0	12	22	19	0	11
1	146	579	253	50	856

幼儿园校舍及

Statistics of Kindergarten Buildings

地区 Region	学校占地面积 Areas Occupied	校舍建筑面积 Floor Space	教学及辅助用房 Teaching & Assistant Buildings				
			计 Total	其中 Of Which			
				活动室 Recreational	睡眠室 Bed Room	保健室 Health Care	图书室 Picture Books
合　计 Total	**14700128**	**72243577**	**47398161**	**27740756**	**12070832**	**1449363**	**1536522**
北　京 Beijing	3428434	1795443	981548	521171	341197	24780	24746
天　津 Tianjin	1864099	778818	544059	318538	116382	12841	9741
河　北 Hebei	6827531	2137496	1427547	841324	347889	57043	61134
山　西 Shanxi	5346038	2099234	1375554	935257	239286	44959	54310
内蒙古 Inner Mongolia	2598884	897174	555571	305607	160702	15138	19371
辽　宁 Liaoning	6036172	2526706	1732167	917367	533681	75314	65876
吉　林 Jilin	2260404	950397	635132	324863	199832	22494	21117
黑龙江 Heilongjiang	2976231	1248117	801223	423404	250972	32334	27887
上　海 Shanghai	3306390	2066303	1126205	676854	234756	29269	24547
江　苏 Jiangsu	14203171	6045550	4035604	2401279	887095	101843	127236
浙　江 Zhejiang	10997933	6485104	4398455	2572965	1261946	113233	128646
安　徽 Anhui	3409663	1342577	935315	592075	168568	35025	33075
福　建 Fujian	4172607	2659230	1781910	1137870	328225	41630	40255
江　西 Jiangxi	2946164	1774074	1241486	716126	317160	45733	47129
山　东 Shandong	21836871	6238770	4152188	2777340	803172	112298	143870
河　南 Henan	5410435	2734621	1820071	1009695	503644	58518	59368
湖　北 Hubei	4076110	2426604	1584657	861165	482919	56773	46920
湖　南 Hunan	3180336	1856748	1268896	659990	408422	59374	49427
广　东 Guangdong	15865218	12202772	7732031	4504122	2020297	212638	270654
广　西 Guangxi	2889771	1838164	1208885	679435	351598	42158	32911
海　南 Hainan	996270	523845	341815	198463	95547	16537	15990
重　庆 Chongqing	2478869	1465765	997366	582830	209058	36787	33624
四　川 Sichuan	6199672	3629388	2456066	1384192	595836	80903	73174
贵　州 Guizhou	1430363	810231	555059	307485	153063	18250	19051
云　南 Yunnan	2866906	1721096	1095947	590040	338347	29594	28200
西　藏 Tibet	144123	53488	31658	14702	10683	763	492
陕　西 Shaanxi	2690326	1378325	943181	538033	254249	25813	30365
甘　肃 Gansu	2818145	1036688	701202	449896	133534	22380	23148
青　海 Qinghai	453404	184401	110766	61286	33272	3146	2927
宁　夏 Ningxia	453657	218227	141756	73054	50585	4382	3686
新　疆 Xinjiang	2837031	1118221	684841	364328	238915	17413	17645

其他情况(总计)

and Others(Regional Aggregates)

单位:平方米

Unit: m^2

行政办公用房 Administritive 计 Total	其中教师办公室 Of Which: Office	生活用房 Residential and Welfare	其他用房 Forother Purposes	校舍面积中 Of Hoor Space: 危房面积 Floor Space of Dilapidated Buildings	当年新增 New Floor Space Added in Current Year	幼儿园中户外活动场 Areas for Out Door Activities	图书(册) Picture Books	教学用录像录音带(盒) Tapes for Teaching
6126689	**3691762**	**8209309**	**10509418**	**347495**	**1571719**	**62989085**	**51989114**	**6508602**
179277	66702	274731	359887	2767	12317	1440059	1317076	208958
68106	45320	64993	101660	45	2047	965622	548187	77928
231105	158959	185759	293085	10262	47766	3375995	2029469	157338
282352	200692	214539	226789	14669	59080	2440033	2415437	197307
95580	57173	110356	135667	23702	22849	1069141	591538	73382
200233	107436	249586	344720	2316	41124	2973797	2274717	279332
90006	46684	93298	131961	5315	9641	1195308	644745	86985
107310	48512	134700	204884	6069	16013	1214953	657964	95334
168566	74521	303590	467942	0	93602	822304	1212354	86296
530443	316296	609437	870066	6574	140860	5347220	5771825	445109
503760	308651	731522	851367	1102	207293	6099435	5463864	672828
134915	87937	147332	125015	31110	26631	1307421	988214	135344
201367	137246	305770	370183	14267	42452	1840626	1194184	185542
139434	87181	198217	194937	9011	29285	1066888	815445	140684
666502	492372	495899	924181	17958	107899	11338516	4828930	528983
290875	168170	278664	345011	11616	56549	2048238	2072956	264753
191567	103805	352516	297864	14583	24214	1424304	1094399	156917
142505	78629	203978	241369	6042	44746	1044507	1431976	187846
746179	408979	1391565	2332997	12503	123118	6985185	7872036	1347161
113881	64429	288181	227217	24533	109705	1183905	799813	184127
38248	24543	80492	63290	2879	7773	424670	295879	54467
114648	70683	180257	173494	8321	17275	919550	957467	115002
271804	164694	501487	400031	13830	63296	2452723	2321725	290527
62090	37476	93290	99792	14680	26348	432430	584524	61798
126069	65996	284976	214104	29051	116864	1008465	960767	140277
2725	1848	9757	9348	0	80	17375	15887	1432
161608	104648	144830	128706	11106	27479	611245	1103097	131904
121170	86890	90068	124248	24406	32467	479249	937856	95681
16480	8653	24768	32387	4916	11938	130230	121090	13932
22309	13505	23782	30380	3504	9866	210170	143032	17571
105575	53132	140969	186836	20358	41142	1119521	522661	73857

幼儿园校舍及
Statistics of Kindergarten

地　区 Region	学校占地面积 Areas Occupied	校舍建筑面积 Floor Space	教学及辅助用房 Teaching & Assistant Buildings				
			计 Total	其中 Of Which			
				活动室 Recreational	睡眠室 Bed Room	保健室 Health Care	图书室 Pictare Books
合　计 Total	**55249740**	**34211605**	**21731865**	**12155616**	**6491720**	**583493**	**637798**
北　京 Beijing	2052720	1257324	687359	349140	249720	17380	17072
天　津 Tianjin	707896	458993	294595	143972	84757	4969	5500
河　北 Hebei	2351944	1077432	682826	380740	232691	21141	21755
山　西 Shanxi	1522785	877582	547483	297458	167049	14742	18131
内蒙古 Inner Mongolia	1050243	511715	308791	162488	105285	7349	9745
辽　宁 Liaoning	3248360	1684045	1098885	562408	358558	45085	37366
吉　林 Jilin	868536	473873	298041	144417	101753	9029	9868
黑龙江 Heilongjiang	1538253	780857	462649	245031	151620	18501	16586
上　海 Shanghai	1679831	1156815	615126	376502	118350	16052	12325
江　苏 Jiangsu	3387941	2016435	1309778	769463	338227	28016	34013
浙　江 Zhejiang	3381393	2367536	1591235	939038	470538	31591	40960
安　徽 Anhui	1297134	657012	452545	271630	117202	14920	15918
福　建 Fujian	1621018	1250810	821854	482252	201409	17518	18063
江　西 Jiangxi	911854	660114	450036	243824	139632	14401	16512
山　东 Shandong	5997841	2615807	1682085	973605	492509	45829	57082
河　南 Henan	2701269	1596561	1025329	548377	352558	24425	26398
湖　北 Hubei	2311931	1563644	1008369	545417	328055	26066	27358
湖　南 Hunan	1739119	1056518	715854	376822	248084	29591	26384
广　东 Guangdong	7257812	6076521	3768748	2226749	969075	94425	120834
广　西 Guangxi	1050998	724226	449415	254581	139035	9632	9673
海　南 Hainan	384074	264249	175726	100255	55483	6159	7258
重　庆 Chongqing	964629	679637	453494	248201	135423	14406	14057
四　川 Sichuan	1702973	1221409	794894	426414	253577	21795	23161
贵　州 Guizhou	621320	412079	277863	151091	89210	9202	9422
云　南 Yunnan	770646	548420	336493	183826	111693	6320	5931
西　藏 Tibet	92700	35485	19915	10529	5989	684	352
陕　西 Shaanxi	1326424	795892	540140	290781	178139	11181	13248
甘　肃 Gansu	838527	482677	321581	173247	100149	9303	9351
青　海 Qinghai	237239	115129	72105	36679	24165	1654	1685
宁　夏 Ningxia	229076	120328	73257	37319	28173	3110	1874
新　疆 Xinjiang	1403254	672480	395394	203360	143612	9017	9916

其他情况(城市)

Buildings and Others(Urban)

单位:平方米

Unit:m²

行政办公用房 Administrative		生活用房 Residential and Welfare	其他用房 Forother Purposes	校舍面积中 Of Hoor Space:		幼儿园中户外活动场 Areas for Out Door Activities	图书(册) Picture Books	教学用录像录音带(盒) Tapes for Teaching
计 Total	其中教师办公室 Of Which: Office			危房面积 Floor Space of Dilapidated Buildings	当年新增 New Floor Space Added in Current Year			
2719644	**1330608**	**4034552**	**5725544**	**94164**	**731991**	**23179126**	**24372954**	**3456468**
119353	41642	203402	247210	2023	4756	795169	933324	160918
39218	19220	47439	77741	0	1788	314521	261054	48866
105950	60512	110662	177994	2785	26078	1254073	839415	87927
91318	44463	128923	109858	2207	27407	656139	771864	82323
53102	27848	67273	82549	5751	12048	458827	389373	45531
128493	59465	179664	277003	1870	23796	1387166	1311791	195126
46624	16939	53501	75707	587	3645	388641	312464	38812
67527	26769	94861	155820	937	2156	732358	416064	59575
91876	38468	163070	286743	0	48751	419078	553649	49134
153051	70369	219616	333990	380	41494	1279534	1892960	194941
171081	94426	261777	343443	161	99299	1492952	2145115	240987
62993	32784	72355	69119	9252	16838	512639	546395	73501
85171	49327	149098	194687	5767	24220	758044	619089	99800
44293	22481	67169	98616	3427	7117	369909	356334	57318
224455	128469	254600	454667	7292	55372	2977345	2278175	269159
157288	71040	175233	238711	3611	31645	1185546	1241670	161150
128726	60143	220844	205705	7316	19595	895722	712070	113232
76941	37107	102369	161354	3549	24196	587076	790910	101628
385204	191843	652972	1269597	2216	63083	3136465	4022570	795598
44234	20067	121690	108887	9161	67698	559253	415160	113151
18555	12426	37470	32498	220	3870	174146	164353	30885
51129	27458	79013	96001	4273	6586	317897	383746	59413
97176	45726	157874	171465	2155	18916	704465	769762	100309
32116	15954	45305	56795	856	8794	193810	362050	35597
40935	17433	99892	71100	6591	37794	311795	343307	47861
1690	1079	5452	8428	0	80	16838	13398	1222
71346	34498	98606	85800	3619	13418	346450	623234	73981
44163	22196	44937	71996	4757	7631	207386	410219	47256
9255	4874	13430	20339	252	10418	70616	106972	10865
13156	6872	14146	19769	350	1006	109482	80381	11300
63225	28710	91909	121952	2799	22496	565784	306086	49102

幼儿园校舍及

Statistics of Kindergarten Buildings

地 区 Region	学校占地面积 Areas Occupied	校舍建筑面积 Floor Space	教学及辅助用房 Teaching & Assistant Buildings				
			计 Total	其中 Of Which			
				活动室 Recreational	睡眠室 Bed Room	保健室 Health Care	图书室 Pictare Books
合 计 Total	**44336636**	**22217540**	**14880413**	**8715377**	**3694165**	**488403**	**468838**
北 京 Beijing	861489	373240	201794	113291	67999	5289	5261
天 津 Tianjin	798320	244540	195316	135246	27305	6185	2418
河 北 Hebei	1940168	564871	399042	226866	80007	15177	15485
山 西 Shanxi	964489	457625	297962	219736	45068	9385	9196
内蒙古 Inner Mongolia	1185347	320474	204285	116929	50373	6241	7642
辽 宁 Liaoning	875209	390225	287552	151805	86289	15153	15315
吉 林 Jilin	978788	380007	271730	143465	80555	9847	8003
黑龙江 Heilongjiang	742725	309310	216299	116857	65410	9499	7425
上 海 Shanghai	1476325	850310	472520	277769	107751	12270	11688
江 苏 Jiangsu	2461565	1223149	814496	440858	190563	18204	24543
浙 江 Zhejiang	6898298	3780082	2566998	1492734	740251	73496	80174
安 徽 Anhui	1003608	400506	285038	188098	35684	10574	9709
福 建 Fujian	1519242	894004	604889	400836	89520	14780	13994
江 西 Jiangxi	1357312	763994	537870	312997	140845	21419	20404
山 东 Shandong	5061655	1311890	861642	581521	155073	27685	31321
河 南 Henan	1629734	766612	542461	319041	111028	21094	20305
湖 北 Hubei	944274	584479	391799	213476	111990	20885	10355
湖 南 Hunan	1043134	629367	441299	226286	132071	21432	16792
广 东 Guangdong	3408745	2882649	1897377	1111693	522342	54196	62882
广 西 Guangxi	1481542	900652	600056	329478	175576	22784	16774
海 南 Hainan	340162	166733	110650	67914	26327	6288	5502
重 庆 Chongqing	868806	536492	364571	216983	61144	15862	13091
四 川 Sichuan	2134272	1299498	872316	490917	197456	28397	20559
贵 州 Guizhou	581177	304659	211811	118683	52360	6955	7308
云 南 Yunnan	1514367	921109	600059	318463	185912	17206	15495
西 藏 Tibet	51423	18003	11743	4173	4694	79	140
陕 西 Shaanxi	555880	304987	206961	121680	51746	7237	6200
甘 肃 Gansu	637615	259833	171018	123708	21319	4829	4292
青 海 Qinghai	202055	66182	36554	23254	8753	1373	1161
宁 夏 Ningxia	200348	93702	64969	34493	22347	1218	1532
新 疆 Xinjiang	618562	218356	139336	76127	46407	3364	3872

其他情况(县镇)

and Others(County Seats & Towns)

单位:平方米

Unit:m^2

行政办公用房 Administritive		生活用房 Residential and Welfare	其他用房 Forother Purposes	校舍面积中 Of Hoor Space:		幼儿园中户外活动场 Areas for Out Door Activities	图书(册) Picture Books	教学用录像录音带(盒) Tapes for Teaching
计 Total	其中教师办公室 Of Which: Office			危房面积 Floor Space of Dilapidated Buildings	当年新增 New Floor Space Added in Current Year			
1855399	**1178310**	**2636583**	**2845145**	**175224**	**545120**	**19357983**	**15697954**	**1806869**
43553	16134	49392	78501	302	6259	397706	279961	32894
20011	17488	13496	15717	0	259	453243	223141	23752
60552	42899	44271	61006	5133	13603	948095	548519	41539
67024	47839	41527	51112	5202	15412	401217	519522	42725
33776	23110	36968	45445	15268	10085	447677	168115	24076
31895	19466	34109	36669	171	7429	430264	340987	36256
33790	22397	29797	44690	4568	3366	596835	272044	40305
29749	16193	27862	35400	3013	11064	284219	174181	27504
71465	33666	132803	173522	0	44851	368332	630130	33217
102827	53137	123238	182588	1870	25445	769479	1166251	82435
305104	193833	433449	474531	581	104204	4291768	3106495	400538
38170	27683	40902	36396	9462	6901	385025	246026	39620
72660	52597	102737	113718	6835	10185	666202	412955	53822
60318	39286	98452	67354	5156	17830	458789	330987	56972
148402	111488	106299	195547	7142	23492	2660332	1015754	97328
83842	58406	68937	71372	5953	18131	561982	557145	67672
40676	26286	87686	64318	5786	3607	267524	248097	30379
49236	29172	78068	60764	2418	18561	351995	524130	53416
165394	93756	342428	477450	6935	29062	1571629	1907828	261065
55982	34511	145244	99370	11714	19773	506887	318572	56150
10011	7334	30071	16001	1568	3428	151315	96028	17425
42573	26957	73172	56176	3480	8275	343265	372088	38708
86310	56139	213797	127075	8589	25535	831622	876447	91309
21985	15269	38333	32530	11590	15213	156300	179928	20703
65605	35270	142442	113003	19523	59008	513147	481511	72618
1035	769	4305	920	0	0	537	2489	210
43102	31267	27665	27259	7227	10306	124606	250002	25507
31163	24800	23603	34049	9422	13218	83396	277869	18854
6816	3509	11032	11780	4554	1252	54311	12471	2664
8710	6190	9438	10585	3154	8781	85733	58547	6271
23663	11459	25060	30297	8608	10585	194551	99734	10935

幼儿园校舍及

Statistics of Kindergarten

地　区 Region	学校占地面积 Areas Occupied	校舍建筑面积 Floor Space	教学及辅助用房 Teaching & Assistant Buildings				
			计 Total	其中 Of Which			
				活动室 Recreational	睡眠室 Bed Room	保健室 Health Care	图书室 Picture Books
合　计 Total	**47414852**	**15814432**	**10785883**	**6869763**	**1884947**	**377467**	**429886**
北　京 Beijing	514225	164879	92395	58740	23478	2111	2413
天　津 Tianjin	357883	75285	54148	39320	4320	1687	1823
河　北 Hebei	2535419	495193	345679	233718	35191	20725	23894
山　西 Shanxi	2858764	764027	530109	418063	27169	20832	26983
内蒙古 Inner Mongolia	363294	64985	42495	26190	5044	1548	1984
辽　宁 Liaoning	1912603	452436	345730	203154	88834	15076	13195
吉　林 Jilin	413080	96517	65361	36981	17524	3618	3246
黑龙江 Heilongjiang	695253	157950	122275	61516	33942	4334	3876
上　海 Shanghai	150234	59178	38559	22583	8655	947	534
江　苏 Jiangsu	8353665	2805966	1911330	1190958	358305	55623	68680
浙　江 Zhejiang	718242	337486	240222	141193	51157	8146	7512
安　徽 Anhui	1108921	285059	197732	132347	15682	9531	7448
福　建 Fujian	1032347	514416	355167	254782	37296	9332	8198
江　西 Jiangxi	676998	349966	253580	159305	36683	9913	10213
山　东 Shandong	10777375	2311073	1608461	1222214	155590	38784	55467
河　南 Henan	1079432	371448	252281	142277	40058	12999	12665
湖　北 Hubei	819905	278481	184489	102272	42874	9822	9207
湖　南 Hunan	398083	170863	111743	56882	28267	8351	6251
广　东 Guangdong	5198661	3243602	2065906	1165680	528880	64017	86938
广　西 Guangxi	357231	213286	159414	95376	36987	9742	6464
海　南 Hainan	272034	92863	55439	30294	13737	4090	3230
重　庆 Chongqing	645434	249636	179301	117646	12491	6519	6476
四　川 Sichuan	2362427	1108481	788856	466861	144803	30711	29454
贵　州 Guizhou	227866	93493	65385	37711	11493	2093	2321
云　南 Yunnan	581893	251567	159395	87751	40742	6068	6774
西　藏 Tibet	0	0	0	0	0	0	0
陕　西 Shaanxi	808022	277446	196080	125572	24364	7395	10917
甘　肃 Gansu	1342003	294178	208603	152941	12066	8248	9505
青　海 Qinghai	14110	3090	2107	1353	354	119	81
宁　夏 Ningxia	24233	4197	3530	1242	65	54	280
新　疆 Xinjiang	815215	227385	150111	84841	48896	5032	3857

其他情况(农村)
Buildings and Others(Rural)

单位:平方米
Unit:m^2

行政办公用房 Administritive		生活用房 Residential and Welfare	其他用房 Forother Purposes	校舍面积中 Of Hoor Space:		幼儿园中户外活动场 Areas for Out Door Activities	图书(册) Picture Books	教学用录像录音带(盒) Tapes for Teaching
计 Total	其中教师办公室 Of Which: Office			危房面积 Floor Space of Dilapidated Buildings	当年新增 New Floor Space Added in Current Year			
1551646	**1182844**	**1538174**	**1938729**	**78107**	**294608**	**20451976**	**11918206**	**1245265**
16371	8926	21937	34176	442	1302	247184	103791	15146
8877	8612	4058	8202	45	0	197858	63992	5310
64603	55548	30826	54085	2344	8085	1173827	641535	27872
124010	108390	44089	65819	7260	16261	1382677	1124051	72259
8702	6215	6115	7673	2683	716	162637	34050	3775
39845	28505	35813	31048	275	9899	1156367	621939	47950
9592	7348	10000	11564	160	2630	209832	60237	7868
10034	5550	11977	13664	2119	2793	198376	67719	8255
5225	2387	7717	7677	0	0	34894	28575	3945
274565	192790	266583	353488	4324	73921	3298207	2712614	167733
27575	20392	36296	33393	360	3790	314715	212254	31303
33752	27470	34075	19500	12396	2892	409757	195793	22223
43536	35322	53935	61778	1665	8047	416380	162140	31920
34823	25414	32596	28967	428	4338	238190	128124	26394
293645	252415	135000	273967	3524	29035	5700839	1535001	162496
49745	38724	34494	34928	2052	6773	300710	274141	35931
22165	17376	43986	27841	1481	1012	261058	134232	13306
16328	12350	23541	19251	75	1989	105436	116936	32802
195581	123380	396165	585950	3352	30973	2277091	1941638	290498
13665	9851	21247	18960	3658	22234	117765	66081	14826
9682	4783	12951	14791	1091	475	99209	35498	6157
20946	16268	28072	21317	568	2414	258388	201633	16881
88318	62829	129816	101491	3086	18845	916636	675516	98909
7989	6253	9652	10467	2234	2341	82320	42546	5498
19529	13293	42642	30001	2937	20062	183523	135949	19798
0	0	0	0	0	0	0	0	0
47160	38883	18559	15647	260	3755	140189	229861	32416
45844	39894	21528	18203	10227	11618	188467	249768	29571
409	270	306	268	110	268	5303	1647	403
443	443	198	26	0	79	14955	4104	0
18687	12963	24000	34587	8951	8061	359186	116841	13820

第二部分
Part Ⅱ

办 学 条 件
Physical Facilities

一、教育经费
Public Expenditure on Education

全国教育经费来源和支出情况

Sources of Educational Fund and Expenditure for Education

单位：万元

Unit: in 10 thousand Yuan

年份 地区 Year Region	合 计 Total	国家财政性教育经费 Government Appropriation for Education	预算内教育经费 Budgetary	社会团体和公民个人办学经费 Funds of Social Organizations and Citizens for Running Schools	社会捐资和集资办学经费 Donations and Fund-Raising for Running Schools	学费和杂费 Trition and Miscellanecous Fee	其他教育经费 Other Educational Funds
1991	7315028.2	6178286.0	4597308.1		628209.7	323475.6	185056.9
1992	8670490.5	7287505.8	5387381.7		696285.2	439319.3	247380.2
1993	10599374.4	8677618.3	6443914.0	33322.7	701856.1	871476.9	315100.4
1994	14887812.6	11747395.6	8839794.7	107795.2	974487.1	1469228.1	588906.6
1995	18779501.1	14115233.3	10283930.0	203671.5	1628414.0	2012422.5	819759.8
1996	22623393.5	16717045.5	12119133.6	261998.9	1884189.5	2610391.2	1149798.4
1997	25317325.7	18625416.3	13577262.1	301746.4	1706587.6	3260792.0	1422783.4
1998	29490592.0	20324526.0	15655917.0	480314.0	1418537.0	3697474.0	3569741.0
1999	33490416.4	22871756.1	18157597.3	628957.1	1258694.2	4636107.9	4094901.1
2000	38490805.8	25626055.7	20856792.0	858537.2	1139556.9	5948304.3	4918351.7
2001	46376626.2	30570099.5	25823761.9	1280895.2	1128851.8	7456013.5	5940766.2
2002	54800277.6	34914047.5	31142383.3	1725548.7	1272791.0	9227791.7	7660098.7

各地区教育经费来

Sources of Educational Fund and Expenditure

年份 地区 Year Region	合　计 Total	国家财政性教育经费 Government Appropriation for Education	预算内教育经费 Budgetary
北　京 Beijing	3538686.4	2194372.8	2017388.5
天　津 Tianjin	975729.9	596587.8	531016.7
河　北 Hebei	2101071.7	1373880.8	1243140.5
山　西 Shanxi	1176899.9	774618.8	665526.1
内蒙古 Inner Mongolia	854998.4	641468.4	575370.9
辽　宁 Liaoning	1943994.9	1283469.8	1135498.1
吉　林 Jilin	1226407.4	856766.1	757042.8
黑龙江 Heilongjiang	1587805.4	1096737.9	902091.5
上　海 Shanghai	2739674.4	1740616.5	1528275.5
江　苏 Jiangsu	4044278.0	2336580.5	2061504.1
浙　江 Zhejiang	3396099.4	1973232.3	1580231.6
安　徽 Anhui	1640472.5	1061197.5	997076.1
福　建 Fujian	1779257.0	1149599.7	1041590.5
江　西 Jiangxi	1169816.0	684152.4	635353.0
山　东 Shandong	3338764.4	2094603.7	1831983.8
河　南 henan	2288398.7	1555518.4	1437318.2
湖　北 Hubei	2301981.4	1292427.4	1162285.4
湖　南 Hunan	2104947.7	1151360.5	1056543.2
广　东 Guangdong	5203412.4	3247693.4	2910766.1
广　西 Guangxi	1346031.4	924536.3	824650.0
海　南 Hainan	297249.9	195177.6	161222.4
重　庆 Chongqing	1066535.0	645003.9	593211.8
四　川 Sichuan	2437436.8	1519277.4	1380815.2
贵　州 guizhou	867637.9	660740.2	601850.0
云　南 Yunnan	1295046.1	1071094.8	987968.2
西　藏 Tibet	141177.9	134182.8	133970.8
陕　西 Shaanxi	1597678.6	944164.3	882321.2
甘　肃 Gansu	836405.0	606262.4	538792.9
青　海 Qinghai	190401.0	161859.6	155645.5
宁　夏 Ningxia	229622.8	177182.2	164007.4
新　疆 Xinjiang	1082359.3	769681.3	647925.3

源和支出情况(2002)

for Education by Region(2002)

单位：万元

Unit: in 10 thousand Yuan

社会团体和公民个人办学经费 Funds of Social Organizations and Citizens for Running Schools	社会捐资和集资办学经费 Donations and Fund-Raising for Running Schools	学费和杂费 Trition and Miscellanecous Fee	其他教育经费 Other Educational Funds
34576.9	103802.7	386539.3	819394.7
52723.9	4166.4	127788.5	194463.3
62397.8	27553.7	442540.9	194698.5
39826.1	48881.5	203725.9	109847.6
7136.2	4693.8	130614.4	71085.6
40798.2	6659.9	374196.1	238870.9
13881.4	32373.1	176365.5	147021.3
33311.8	4055.6	266404.1	187296.0
102573.6	56915.5	395645.9	443922.9
143341.6	265358.2	633223.9	665773.8
241947.1	142825.4	457234.8	580859.8
28339.9	21756.7	338581.8	190596.6
113997.7	57028.5	249930.5	208700.6
59066.5	10932.3	247321.8	168343.0
142001.1	63321.7	648258.2	390579.7
51568.4	30794.5	413268.6	237248.8
20815.7	58698.4	514210.8	415829.1
60759.7	34565.0	536794.2	321468.3
252941.7	118281.4	1009222.3	575273.6
20981.5	11079.7	233333.3	156100.6
11673.2	6869.8	49000.6	34528.7
19096.7	35628.9	161596.1	205209.4
29612.3	68052.5	379724.4	440770.2
11455.9	6792.2	122255.0	66394.6
15512.0	17414.5	105485.5	85539.3
0.0	436.4	4930.5	1628.2
89388.7	18722.0	331812.5	213591.1
8872.3	9238.7	132539.6	79492.0
957.1	328.2	17769.2	9486.9
648.4	2743.7	27377.7	21670.8
15345.3	2820.1	110099.8	184412.8

各类学校教育经费

Sources of Educational Fund and Expenditure

学校、类别 Type of schools	合计 Total	国家财政性教育经费 Government Appropriation for Education	预算内教育经费 Budgetary
全国总计 National Total	**54800277.6**	**34914047.5**	**31142383.3**
中央 Gentral Government	6581620.7	3531595.2	3042306.7
地方 Local Government	48218656.9	31382452.3	28100076.6
按学校类别分组 Grouped by Type of Schools			
高等学校 Institutions of Higher Education	15832129.1	7875176.1	7548856.1
普通高等学校 Regular IHEs	14878589.8	7521462.8	7243458.6
成人高等学校 IHEs for Adults	953539.3	353713.3	305397.5
中等专业学校 Specialized Sec. Schools	2505373.9	1356574.7	1273760.2
中等技术学校 Technical Schools	1723505.9	931580.0	880751.2
中等师范学校 Teacher Training Schools	375672.7	198849.4	185890.3
成人中专学校 Specialized Secondary Schools for Adults	406195.3	226145.3	207118.7
技工学校 Technical Schools	366761.1	196713.5	137485.3
中学 Secondary Schools	16704638.3	10623978.5	9003381.6
普通中学 Regular Secondary Schools	16682289.8	10613312.8	8995103.4
高级中学 Senior Secondary Schools	3490127.9	1651651.9	1359066.1
完全中学 Complete Secondary Schools	4595595.6	2528159.9	2046846.5
初级中学 Junior Secondary Schools	8596566.3	6433501.0	5589190.8
农村 Rural	4270561.7	3413785.2	3188332.9
成人中学 Secondary Schools for Adults	22348.5	10665.7	8278.2
职业中学 Vocational Schools	1470023.8	888018.6	773302.8
小学 Primary Schools	14485877.7	11641506.9	10473153.2
普通小学 Regular Primary Schools	14480218.2	11636869.2	10469011.1
农村 Rular Areas	8389830.6	7100910.9	6709476.9
成人小学 Primary Schools for Adults	5659.5	4637.7	4142.1
特殊教育学校 Special Edu. Schools	151392.0	133194.5	116767.4
幼儿园 Kindergartens	675844.0	416389.4	397252.8
其他 Others	2608237.7	1782495.3	1418423.9

来源和支出情况(2002)

Education in Various Schools (2002)

单位：万元

Unit: in 10 thousand Yuan

社会团体和公民个人办学经费 Funds of Social Organizations and Citizens for Running Schools	社会捐资和集资办学经费 Donations and Fund-Raising for Running Schools	学费和杂费 Trition and Miscellanecous Fee	其他教育经费 Other Educational Funds
1725548.7	**1272791.0**	**9227791.7**	**7660098.7**
	206891.4	872793.3	1970340.8
1725548.7	1065899.6	8354998.4	5689757.9
417624.1	279514.3	4264516.5	2995298.1
331363.3	278253.4	3906525.7	2840984.6
86260.8	1260.9	357990.8	154313.5
25045.5	8202.9	824107.5	291443.3
10880.8	3094.3	610481.7	167469.1
	2924.1	128563.0	45336.2
14164.7	2184.5	85062.8	78638.0
	1158.8	77188.6	91700.2
898922.3	599213.5	2433370.7	2149153.3
896845.0	599145.5	2428480.0	2144506.5
146228.5	185092.3	853343.9	653811.3
404974.0	217738.3	708894.4	735829.0
345642.5	196314.9	866241.7	754866.2
	87627.5	494221.1	274927.9
2077.3	68.0	4890.7	4646.8
63429.0	14041.5	358983.6	145551.1
320527.8	327885.4	1156260.1	1039697.5
319902.3	327884.7	1156107.3	1039454.7
	175005.8	743639.3	370274.6
625.5	0.7	152.8	242.8
	2868.3	3303.8	12025.4
	14908.1	110060.9	134485.6
	24998.2		800744.2

二、教育基本建设投资

Capital Construction Investment in the Educational Sector

教育基本建设

Data on the Completion of Capital Construction

学校类别 Type of School	投资合计 Total Investment Completed in the Curent yeal (in 10 Thousand Yuan)	本年完成投资按 Investment by source of			
		国家预算内 Budgetary Allocation			
		计 Subtotal	中央 Central	省级 Local	计 Subtotal
合计 Total	**12536600**	**1815779**	**455717**	**1360060**	**8478426**
北京 Beijing	178029	30350	1953	28397	139662
天津 Tianjin	214084	4880	2380	2500	168318
河北 Hebei	565314	47982	15838	32144	477935
山西 Shanxi	204598	16493	9993	6500	157385
内蒙古 Inner Mongolia	145185	30179	15228	14951	101017
辽宁 Liaoning	382851	26349	7711	18638	276465
大连 Dalian	55207	21139	200	20939	30668
吉林 Jilin	246178	19638	13777	5861	170196
黑龙江 Heilongjiang	273177	10741	7330	3411	237675
上海 Shanghai	355600	15484	0	15484	231838
江苏 Jiangsu	1321433	44996	0	44996	956729
浙江 Zhejiang	1272813	105243	10327	94916	931798
宁波 Ningbo	97173	21360	0	21360	72765
安徽 Anhui	432542	66157	12365	53792	304654
福建 Fujian	158161	17360	4700	12660	119157
厦门 Xiamen	48203	27793	75	27718	9391
江西 Jiangxi	421367	26895	17534	9361	229017
山东 Shandong	890276	28406	3178	25228	746271
青岛 Qingdao	38398	100	100	0	38298
河南 henan	661024	69593	22946	46647	463552
湖北 Hubei	518200	23951	12073	11878	412835
湖南 Hunan	397875	38890	15934	22955	292062
广东 Guangdong	1113315	449569	4690	444879	464566
深圳 Shenzhen	214961	176590	250	176340	29934
广西 Guangxi	191725	60137	28841	31296	126000
海南 Hainan	78871	12761	11891	870	49737
重庆 Chongqing	222124	24632	12601	12030	147921
四川 Sichuan	447756	52003	19541	32463	322344
贵州 guizhou	148343	32072	14106	17966	111673
云南 Yunnan	234354	100325	28523	71801	100729
西藏 Tibet	56916	41199	35199	6000	8946
陕西 Shaanxi	456376	35849	13254	22595	263229
甘肃 Gansu	218590	57212	45804	11408	116800
青海 Qinghai	28727	12345	11532	813	12751
宁夏 Ningxia	42835	12810	10780	2030	25176
新疆 Xinjiang	165396	39628	30530	9098	106976
新疆生产建设兵团	38623	14668	14533	135	23956

投资完成情况

Investment in the Educational Sector

资金来源分(万元) Fund (in 10 Thousand Yuan)			本年竣工建筑面积(平方米) Building Floor Area Completed (in m^2)			
自筹资金 Self - raised Fund 其中 Of Which: 学校自筹 Raised by School	个人集资 Individual Donations	其他 Other Sources	合计 Total	教学及辅助用房 Tewaching & Administritive	行政办公用房 Adm. Buildsing Rooms for other purposes	其他用房
6175752	**474745**	**2242395**	**103769342**	**71243142**	**4260392**	**28265808**
98003	246	8017	516395	379251	39723	97421
134322	0	40886	924109	780387	22827	120895
399394	29782	39397	5257107	4076031	203163	977913
110583	22860	30720	2064985	1138558	75851	850576
77879	8203	13989	1328281	932645	49565	346071
228497	14237	80037	2549646	1687979	64399	797268
18013	1360	3400	464852	394094	29280	41478
109766	5860	56344	2369312	1777635	63545	528132
211692	5443	24761	2158731	1395859	65597	697275
138505	483	108278	1340338	1188283	76509	75546
727126	34066	319708	9351568	6743939	284730	2322899
679337	25201	235772	7598837	4752506	615846	2230485
19055	316	3048	608221	451102	41911	115208
252312	10101	61731	4891349	3807130	165159	919060
62222	5225	21644	1513904	1065041	27460	421403
1583	1	11019	229960	96006	10608	123346
168967	10427	165455	4306889	2600204	50404	1656281
605166	77807	115599	6858660	4320732	378310	2159618
20654	0	0	334624	251605	26699	56320
371381	30180	127879	7112587	5122751	377383	1612453
367282	16135	81414	4114419	2515154	172455	1426810
209569	17487	66923	4142662	3044403	125593	972666
229081	11545	199180	7419264	5632338	320576	1466350
23145	0	8437	1059493	782136	61783	215574
83688	11063	5588	2278729	1479102	38034	761593
32118	7251	16373	716267	330011	11018	375238
97645	20454	49571	2655500	1262585	74704	1318211
233453	20715	73409	5492531	3315884	159776	2016871
42525	8584	4598	2467634	1705764	48231	713639
50171	15518	33300	2297138	1717562	29827	549749
376	82	6771	513323	301236	23739	188348
202417	33307	157298	4240540	2710052	231261	1299227
76605	11654	44578	2232505	1722678	96036	413791
4729	4919	3631	285639	210748	4704	70187
9222	1165	4849	373266	261902	49040	62324
64217	10345	18792	1381501	1021251	144146	216104
15052	2723	-1	318576	268598	500	49478

教育基本建设

Data on the Completion of Capital Construction

学校类别 Type of School	投资合计 Total Investment Completed in the Curent yeal (in 10 Thousand Yuan)	本年完成投资按 Investment by source of 国家预算内 Budgetary Allocation 计 Subtotal	中 央 Central	省级 Local	计 Subtotal
总 计 Total	**14195367**	**2165410**	**805348**	**1360060**	**9787561**
普通高等学校 Regular Institutions of Higher Education	7510844	859605	446054	413550	5192508
中等师范学校 Teacher Teaining Schools	73336	940	30	910	64289
普通中学 Regular Secondary Schools	4393986	777611	224824	552785	3037933
职业中学 Vocational Schools	260916	37316	7188	30128	199832
小学 primary Schools	1632505	448406	119523	328884	1048374
特殊教育学校 Special Education Schools	17807	3947	891	3056	13273
幼儿园 Kindergartens	75511	3534	266	3268	59848
其他 Other	230462	34051	6572	27479	171504

投资完成情况

Investment in the Educational Sector

资金来源分(万元) Fund (in 10 Thousand Yuan)			本年竣工建筑面积(平方米) Building Floor Area Completed (in m^2)			
自筹资金 Self - raised Fund		其他 Other Sources				
其中 Of Which:						
学校自筹 Raised by School	个人集资 Individual Donations		合计 Total	教学及辅助用房 Tewaching & Administritive	行政办公用房 Adm. Buildsing Rooms for other purposes	其他用房
7484887	**474745**	**2242396**	**107631770**	**72901362**	**4382952**	**30347456**
4937680	128296	1458731	35476723	18934555	1184829	15357339
43417	1757	8107	519031	319200	30384	169447
1844047	204519	578442	44798307	31734336	1960753	11103218
122028	12421	23768	2797230	1850461	116444	830325
418476	71881	135725	21743825	18603046	971317	2169462
4299	1259	587	161714	127099	4390	30225
27286	4118	12129	599080	527900	15056	56124
87654	50494	24907	1535860	804765	99779	631316

三、仪器设备

Instrument and Equipment

教学、科研仪器设备分省情况

Classification of Instruments and Equipment for Instruction and Scientific Research by Province

单位:万元

Unic: in 10 Thousand Yuan

地 区 Region	教学科研仪器设备数 No. Of Instruments and Equipment for Instruction and Scientific Research		十万元以上仪器设备数 No. Of Instruments and Equipment Valued above 100 Thousand Yuan	
	台、件 Set & Piece	金额(万元) Book Value (in 10 Thousand Yuan)	台、件 Set & Piece	金额(万元) Book Value (in 10 Thousand Yuan)
合 计 Total	**7458006**	**6657829.95**	**68726**	**2185109.23**
北 京 Beijing	618324	818407.17	9909	353300.43
天 津 Tianjin	156504	168559.22	1918	68213.57
河 北 Hebei	309934	243925.13	2318	71995.10
山 西 Shanxi	147374	114260.72	1071	30888.55
内蒙古 Inner Mongolia	75844	50934.64	476	11610.24
辽 宁 Liaoning	351354	291221.28	2855	85900.90
吉 林 Jilin	177147	175269.35	1775	69450.75
黑龙江 Heilongjiang	215639	229416.38	1843	81967.98
上 海 Shanghai	388267	482145.48	5332	207667.34
江 苏 Jiangsu	664198	578987.01	5825	184812.46
浙 江 Zhejiang	395715	338686.29	3528	103802.48
安 徽 Anhui	266681	193584.51	1786	53415.74
福 建 Fujian	180473	146077.17	2734	45211.06
江 西 Jiangxi	228551	161195.41	2521	42533.68
山 东 Shandong	396942	335820.31	3147	107586.18
河 南 henan	274759	205169.99	1753	50465.20
湖 北 Hubei	490941	421818.49	3984	129377.31
湖 南 Hunan	296498	223878.83	2033	56400.41
广 东 Guangdong	432126	371878.65	3438	115299.68
广 西 Guangxi	143333	107585.39	978	30450.83
海 南 Hainan	29487	19790.26	188	4316.60
重 庆 Chongqing	142926	107164.36	886	24932.03
四 川 Sichuan	289900	250211.17	2618	84870.98
贵 州 guizhou	86394	55880.12	516	12265.98
云 南 Yunnan	126658	88419.39	756	19478.01
西 藏 Tibet				
陕 西 Shaanxi	353392	321632.98	3367	104971.59
甘 肃 Gansu	105646	79471.89	657	19263.05
青 海 Qinghai	15700	9240.16	15	280.81
宁 夏 Ningxia	28654	18415.06	115	2686.89
新 疆 Xinjiang	68645	48783.14	384	11693.40

第三部分
Part Ⅲ

科学研究活动及其他
Scientific Research Activites & Other

一、自然科学与技术
Natural Science and Technology

	教学与科研人员 Personnel Engaged in S&T Activities		研究与发展人员 R & D Personnel	
	计 Total	其中:科学家和工程师 Of Which: Scientists & Engineers	计 Total	其中:科学家和工程师 Of Which: Scientists & Engineers
合计: Total	**645177**	**620240**	**263123**	**257949**
按学校规格分 Breakdown by category of HEIs	0	0	0	0
重点院校 Key HEIs	207094	196947	96781	94057
一般院校 Ordinary Degree Level HEIs	403339	389930	157456	155119
高等专科学校 Short-cycle HEIs	34744	33363	8886	8773
按学校隶属分 Breakdown by Control	0	0	0	0
部委院校 HEIs under Other Central Ministries	27703	26143	12755	12298
教育部直属院校 HEIs Under Ministry of Education	183133	174246	82413	80216
地方院校 HEIs Under Local Govermments	434341	419851	167955	165435
按学校类型分 Breakdown by Type of HEIs	0	0	0	0
综合大学 Comprehensive Universities	162991	156116	69144	67612
工科院校 Engineering	214648	206610	92395	90525
农林院校 Agriculture	34763	31963	17130	16502
医药院校 Medicine & Pharmacy	159335	154921	54710	53975
师范院校 Teachers Training	54536	52419	24077	23757
其他院校 Others	18904	18211	5667	5578

科技人力情况
in Regular HEIs

单位:人
Unit: in Person

研究与发展全时人员 R & D FTEs (Full-time Equivalents)		R&D成果应用及科技服务人员 R & D Personnel		R&D成果应用及科技服务全时人员 R & D FTEs(FullJ-time Equivalents)	
计 Total	其中:科学家和工程师 Of Which: Scientists & Engineers	计 Total	其中:科学家和工程师 Of Which: Scientists & Engineers	计 Total	其中:科学家和工程师 Of Which: Scientists & Engineers
148953	**145917**	**52492**	**51193**	**30327**	**29496**
0	0	0	0	0	0
64036	62265	21726	20958	14079	13553
81332	80122	29542	29048	15701	15413
3585	3530	1224	1187	547	530
0	0	0	0	0	0
8000	7722	4342	4253	2543	2489
53946	52503	17300	16607	11539	11053
87007	85692	30850	30333	16245	15954
0	0	0	0	0	0
41140	40190	10408	10100	6217	6011
55610	54432	30450	29825	17926	17526
10934	10544	4025	3775	2321	2160
27077	26739	3996	3944	1994	1963
11763	11619	2707	2671	1445	1424
2429	2393	906	878	424	412

普通高等学校科技人力中科学家

Statistics of Scientists and Engineer Among S & T

	科技活动人员 Personnel Engaged in S&T Activities		
	高级 Senior	中级 Middle	初级 Junior
合计:Total	**209519**	**96301**	**172764**
按学校规格分 Breakdown by category of HEIs	0	0	0
重点院校 Key HEIs	75632	27725	45521
一般院校 Ordinary Degree Level HEIs	123782	59429	117532
高等专科学校 Short-cycle HEIs	10105	9147	9711
按学校隶属分 Breakdown by Control	0	0	0
部委院校 HEIs under Other Central Ministries	11184	4026	5564
教育部直属院校 HEIs Under Ministry of Education	64701	23511	41411
地方院校 HEIs Under Local Govermments	133634	68764	125789
按学校类型分 Breakdown by Type of HEIs	0	0	0
综合大学 Comprehensive Universities	52341	21833	43054
工科院校 Engineering	80833	37781	46594
农林院校 Agriculture	12855	6308	7591
医药院校 Medicine & Pharmacy	38419	13258	56888
师范院校 Teachers Training	19607	11990	13478
其他院校 Others	5464	5131	5159

和工程师技术职务(职称)情况

Manpower in Regular HEIs by Level of Post

单位:人
Unit: in Person

研究与发展人员 R & D Personnel			研究与发展全时人员 R & D FTEs (Full-time Equivalents)		
高级 Senior	中级 Middle	初级 Junior	高级 Senior	中级 Middle	初级 Junior
120658	**93670**	**38998**	**73488**	**50708**	**19297**
0	0	0	0	0	0
47507	32546	12492	33346	20709	7218
69295	57740	25167	38463	28706	11606
3856	3384	1339	1679	1293	473
0	0	0	0	0	0
6646	4058	1304	4374	2378	794
39964	28069	11004	27911	17571	6254
74048	61543	26690	41203	30759	12249
0	0	0	0	0	0
32144	24380	10029	20734	13777	5104
45200	31838	11577	28870	18484	6054
7892	5669	2497	5296	3527	1460
20844	21599	10858	10837	10444	5118
12078	8059	3221	6597	3601	1256
2500	2125	816	1154	875	305

	拨入 Revenues			
	合计 Total	政府资金 Government Funds	企事业单位委托 Contract Research Fund	其他 Others
合计：Total	**25333773**	**11710024**	**10857066**	**2766683**
按学校规格分 Breakdown by category of HEIs				
重点院校 Key HEIs	17398333	8365818	7385361	1647154
一般院校 Ordinary Degree Level HEIs	7779150	3286183	3407320	1085647
高等专科学校 Short-cycle HEIs	156290	58023	64385	33882
按学校隶属分 Breakdown by Control				
部委院校 HEIs under Other Central Ministries	3824207	2567736	1005332	251139
教育部直属院校 HEIs Under Ministry of Education	13404965	5711871	6313630	1379464
地方院校 HEIs Under Local Govermments	8104601	3430417	3538104	1136080
按学校类型分 Breakdown by Type of HEIs				
综合大学 Comprehensive Universities	6364390	2995471	2808236	560683
工科院校 Engineering	15443667	6400411	7475233	1568023
农林院校 Agriculture	1358004	1025840	170156	162008
医药院校 Medicine & Pharmacy	1021512	656795	150292	214425
师范院校 Teachers Training	985252	552926	201055	231271
其他院校 Others	160948	78581	52094	30273

科技经费情况

Regular HEIs

单位：千元

Unit: in Thousand Yuan

支出 Expenditures				
合计 Total	劳务费 Personnel Costs	业务费 Non-Personnel Expenses	转拨外单位经费 Expenses on Extermal Services	其他 Others
23749220	**4323098**	**15736690**	**1471385**	**3873471**
15639972	2399450	10693948	1111324	2245084
7924014	1860005	4943846	357642	1589257
185234	63643	98896	2419	39130
3504730	351061	2679789	172530	356698
11961827	2045250	7877670	921102	1872068
8282663	1926787	5179231	377753	1644705
5863179	1250838	3743500	397953	999039
14169041	2094391	9659167	893788	2131981
1313826	226593	893778	110893	205876
1235110	470259	663981	37609	212030
987687	232836	664835	29584	279502
180377	48181	111429	1558	45043

普通高等学校研究与

Statistics of R & D Projects and

	科技课题 R&D Projects			出版科技专著（部） No. Of Mono-graphs Published
	课题数(项) No. Of projects	投入人数 No. Of Input of S&T Manpower	实际支出 Actual Exp.	
合计：Total	**165200**	**161633**	**16529369**	**6778**
按学校规格分 Breakdown by category of HEIs				
重点院校 Key HEIs	80201	71794	11806647	2792
一般院校 Ordinary Degree Level HEIs	82055	86466	4631641	3894
高等专科学校 Short-cycle HEIs	2944	3373	91081	92
按学校隶属分 Breakdown by Control				
部委院校 HEIs under Other Central Ministries	11041	9413	2491145	350
教育部直属院校 HEIs Under Ministry of Education	67550	60075	9177655	2460
地方院校 HEIs Under Local Govermments	86609	92146	4860569	3968
按学校类型分 Breakdown by Type of HEIs				
综合大学 Comprehensive Universities	44470	43715	4058821	1335
工科院校 Engineering	73900	66018	10751597	2592
农林院校 Agriculture	12880	12176	866581	826
医药院校 Medicine & Pharmacy	19830	25898	392240	1470
师范院校 Teachers Training	11539	11440	376489	446
其他院校 Others	2581	2386	83641	109

发展课题、成果情况

Achievements in Regular HEIs

单位：千元

Unit: in thousand Yuan

发表学术论文（篇）No. Of Papers Published	成果获奖 Achieverments Awards		技术转让 Technological Transfer		知识产权授权数 No. Of Awarded	专利出售 Income from License Arrangements	
	合　计 Total	其中：国家奖 Of Which: National Awards	合同数 No. Of Contracts	收　入 Actual Revenues		项　数 No. Of Items	实现金额 Income
387290	**3859**	**860**	**7809**	**1579611**	**3954**	**611**	**359536**
164090	1843	653	4511	1084153	2729	475	223503
208140	1994	205	3280	494690	1191	134	135633
15060	22	2	18	768	34	2	400
19982	267	196	1145	339728	250	99	91857
143264	1546	492	3743	791297	2469	376	128636
224044	2046	172	2921	448586	1235	136	139043
100803	1097	253	1363	312704	1027	168	79948
157924	1513	484	5193	1132312	2419	402	253575
21045	286	47	406	37791	178	13	11560
61220	754	60	630	72226	132	11	12480
38124	182	15	145	18314	155	15	1753
8174	27	1	72	6264	43	2	220

二、社会科学
Social Science

普通高等学校人文、

Professional Manpower in Regular HEIs in the

		学校数（所）No. Of HEIs	社科活动人员（人）Personnel Engaged in Social Science Research (in Person)				
			合 计 Total	高 级 Senior	中 级 Middle	初级 Junior	辅助人员 Auxiliary
	合计：Total	712	286444	100323	104695	73663	7763
按学校规格分 Breakdown by category of HEIs	重点院校 Key HEIs	85	53717	24488	18901	8910	1418
	一般院校 Ordinary Degree Level HEIs	478	196765	66362	72206	52846	5351
	高等专科学校 Short-cycle HEIs	149	35962	9473	13588	11907	994
按学校隶属关系分 Breakdown by Control	教育部直属院校 HEIs Under Ministry of Education	71	53306	24747	18837	8506	1216
	其他部委院校 HEIs under Other Central Ministries	67	22655	8140	8589	5204	722
	地方院校 HEIs Under Local Govermments	574	210483	67436	77269	59953	5825
按学校类型分 Breakdown by Type of HEIs	综合大学 Comprehensive Universities	72	57602	23786	20855	11579	1382
	全国重点理工农医院校 National Key HEIs Science and Technology, Agriculture and Medicine	298	83073	26354	30932	23064	2723
	师范院校 Teachers Training	192	81053	27219	29101	22742	1991
	语言院校 Languages	15	7819	2575	2964	2097	183
	财经院校 Finance and Economics	57	30675	11070	11441	7561	603
	政法院校 Political Science & Law	23	7869	2719	3031	1932	187
	艺术院校 Art	29	8115	2888	2635	2210	382
	民族院校 Minorities	12	5554	2041	2065	1337	111
	体育院校 Physical Culture	14	4684	1671	1671	1141	201

社会科学人力情况
Fields of the Humanities and Social Acience

研究与发展人员(人) R & D Personnel (in Person)					研究与发展全时人员(人年) R & D FTEs (Man/Year)				
合计 Total	高级 Senior	中级 Middle	初级 Junior	辅助人员 Auxiliary	合计 Total	高级 Senior	中级 Middle	初级 Junior	辅助人员 Auxiliary
92519	49208	30852	11914	545	39284.1	23530.9	11715.1	3865.6	172.5
18403	12201	4911	1183	108	9212.8	6529.3	2136.1	496.9	50.5
65586	33362	22407	9403	414	27128.9	15511.8	8445	3057	115.1
8530	3645	3534	1328	23	2942.4	1489.8	1134	311.7	6.9
19085	12625	5026	1310	124	9456	6729.3	2170.2	505.9	50.6
7759	3987	2769	964	39	3353.8	1959.8	1052.5	331.1	10.4
65675	32596	23057	9640	382	26474.3	14841.8	8492.4	3028.6	111.5
21650	13337	6227	1929	157	10089	6700.3	2616.8	720	51.9
22135	10985	7790	3236	124	9127.3	5071.9	2951.5	1060.6	43.3
27284	13733	9486	3952	113	11604.2	6678.2	3608	1285.4	32.6
2958	1339	1143	464	12	999.1	580.5	327.7	84.3	6.6
10863	5762	3629	1436	36	3992.5	2468.1	1158.1	352.5	13.8
2385	1084	946	328	27	950.3	482.4	355.1	106.9	5.9
1721	970	483	209	59	932.5	560.6	256.2	103.6	12.1
2083	1173	713	190	7	898.3	556.4	262.4	77.8	1.7
1440	825	435	170	10	690.9	432.5	179.3	74.5	4.6

普通高等学校人文、社会科

Humanities and Social Sciences R &

		学校数（所）No. Of HEIs	拨入 Revenues						
			合计 Total	科研事业费 Primary Research Funds	科研基金费 Grants by Research Funds	国家社科规划、基金项目经费 Funds Allocated to Projects Supported by NSSP Funds	中央其他部门社科专项经费 Earmarked SSRF Provided by Other Central Agencies	省市自治区社科专项经费 Earmarked SSRF Provided by Prov. Authorities	企事业单位委托项目经费 Contract Research Funds Provided by Ent. & Inst.
	合计 Total	712	19199909	9395113	80523	571506	905393	1509680	3982040
按学校规格分 Breakdown by category of HEIs	重点院校 Key HEIs	85	8048119.5	2670864	22000	302490	593685	503506	2649772
	一般院校 Ordinary Degree Level HEIs	478	10437675	6212004	58120	263947	302355	951275	1307752
	高等专科学校 Short-cycle HEIs	149	714115	512245.2	403	5070	9353	54900	24516
按学校隶属关系分 Breakdown by Control	教育部直属院校 HEIs Under Ministry of Education	71	8218158.9	2960432	22000	266268	526370	456426	2597318
	其他部委院校 HEIs under Other Central Ministries	67	1296252	640516.2	10500	66617	177158	87862	166440
	地方院校 HEIs Under Local Govermments	574	9685498.2	5794164	48023	238621	201866	965392	1218282
按学校类型分 Breakdown by Type of HEIs	综合大学 Comprehensive Universities	72	6187960.5	2758731	2600	237046	357598	417324	1632038
	全国重点理工农医院校 National Key HEIs Science and Technology, Agriculture and Medicine	298	4818507.1	1699735	52620	118695	278714	617209	1256726
	师范院校 Teachers Training	192	4425181.7	2627716	4803	108896	89012	252901	791384
	语言院校 Languages	15	505749.02	225711.9	0	7943	12804	11037	10274
	财经院校 Finance and Economics	57	1889188.9	1170835	10000	50552	47772	134179	260801
	政法院校 Political Science & Law	23	433374	288925.2	0	10070	29690	18047	20237
	艺术院校 Art	29	387460	313719.2	0	8083	500	24117	5350
	民族院校 Minorities	12	281064	174952.8	10500	17992	12213	9830	3331
	体育院校 Physical Culture	14	271424	134787.4	0	12230	77091	25037	1900

学研究与发展经费情况

D Expenditure in Regular HEIs

单位：百元

Unit: in Hundred Yuan

金融机构贷款 Loans Provided by Financial Inst.	自筹经费 Self-raised Fubds	国外资金 Foreign Funds	其他收入 Others Revenues	支出 Expenditures									
				合计 Total	内部支出 Intramural Expenditures								转拨给外单位经费 Extramural Exp.
					小计 Subtotal	科研人员费 Personnel Costss	业务费 Non-Personnel Expenses	科研基建费 Capital Construction Funds for R&D	仪器设备费 Instruments and Equipment	图书资料费 Books and Information	管理费 Management	其他 Others	
48910	1513944	372744	820057	16801766	16598097	5817983	5530901	131148	1700751	1759973	436675	1220666	203670
20000	392637	253279	639888	6765920	6665396	1658806	2785614	41000	591429	810616	243093	534837	100524
28910	1021608	116207	175497	9354841	9254362	3790341	2627017	86186	1020890	902926	184294	642707	100480
0	99699	3258	4672	681005	678339	368836	118270	3962	88432	46431	9287	43121	2666
20000	471321	261171	636854	6863308	6772218	1649735	2842483	42627	562508	802602	229012	643249	91090
0	109876	11297	25986	1169047	1158602	485304	369608	13988	100016	95461	25372	68854	10445
28910	932748	100275	157217	8769411	8667277	3682943	2318810	74533	1038227	861910	182290	508564	102135
5000	277070	172775	327779	5095827	5050168	1519834	1872502	2500	453927	664918	142061	394426	45659
20000	342880	57705	374223	4153703	4050784	1383637	1553351	72224	306319	312605	154468	268180	102920
23910	378496	94166	53899	4179223	4140109	1521798	1161772	29014	527756	510557	80065	309147	39114
0	212709	5120	20151	453659	453659	223096	84437	60	25711	37303	5609	77442	0
0	181271	5983	27797	1725929	1717464	678489	499778	11200	216256	158454	35911	117376	8465
0	34371	20262	11773	362707	360921	169554	88805	0	57859	20179	4724	19800	1786
0	26418	9033	240	328822	328622	144066	118161	2327	42717	12764	3113	5474	200
0	41525	7600	3120	289344	287044	87702	103193	12823	38848	30114	2945	11418	2300
0	19204	100	1075	212554	209328	89806	48900	1000	31359	13079	7779	17405	3226

普通高等学校人文、社会科学研

Basic Statistics of Humunities and Social Sciences

		课题数(项)No. Of Projects	当年投入人数(人年) Input of Man-year	其中:研究生 Of Which: Graduate Students	当年拨入经费(百元) Revenues (100 Yuan)	当年支出经费(百元) Expenditures (100 Yuan)
	合计:Total	62788	42614	7896	9994188.92	7515927
按学校规格分 Breakdown by category of HEIs	重点院校 Key HEIs	20790	12044	3326	5726605.89	4203999
	一般院校 Ordinary Degree Level HEIs	38555	27739	4433	4064450.37	3169176
	高等专科学校 Short-cycle HEIs	3443	2831	137	203132.66	142752
按学校隶属关系分 Breakdown by Control	教育部直属院校 HEIs Under Ministry of Education	21280	11903	3273	5602014.99	4142402
	其他部委院校 HEIs under Other Central Ministries	3572	3364	557	666885.98	479262
	地方院校 HEIs Under Local Govermments	37936	27348	4067	3725287.95	2894263
按学校类型分 Breakdown by Type of HEIs	综合大学 Comprehensive Universities	19515	12240	2934	3738603.84	2612616
	全国重点理工农医院校 National Key HEIs Science and Technology, Agriculture and Medicine	14335	9628	1657	3045537.29	2168732
	师范院校 Teachers Training	17088	11723	1689	1845980.84	1709502
	语言院校 Languages	1307	854	128	160220.02	106445
	财经院校 Finance and Economics	6703	4841	992	732205.45	583298
	政法院校 Political Science & Law	1342	852	17	158184.18	75709
	艺术院校 Art	784	803	128	77402.5	98084
	民族院校 Minorities	985	928	203	99472.8	89675
	体育院校 Physical Culture	729	745	148	136582	71867

究与发展课题、成果情况

R & D and Achievements in Regular HEIs

出版专著（部） Monographs Published (Titles)	发表论文（篇）No. Of Papers Published				应用成果（项） No. Of Application-oriented Results (Items)	
	合 计 Total	国内学术刊物 In Domestic Journals		国外学术刊物 In Foreign Journals	提交有关部门数 No. Of Results Submitted to Relevant Agencies	鉴定成果数 No. Of Results Appraised
		国内外公开发行 Published an Distributed at Home and Abroad	国内公开发行 Openly Distributed at Home			
8701	211635	126343	82413	2879	15945	4013
3249	53552	29636	22412	1504	6330	739
5084	138408	84938	52182	1288	9197	3143
368	19675	11769	7819	87	418	131
3365	52609	28185	23138	1286	7305	952
576	16912	9304	7287	321	673	77
4760	142114	88854	51988	1272	7967	2984
2956	54270	31520	21778	972	5650	642
1673	53578	29515	23135	928	4645	568
2126	58926	36685	21719	522	2109	300
252	3658	2148	1439	71	214	15
689	27237	19140	7802	295	2278	2383
302	5834	3054	2749	31	592	40
416	2544	950	1587	7	103	15
261	4092	2803	1258	31	224	20
26	1496	528	946	22	130	30

地区 Region	报名总数 Total	性别 Gender		政治面貌 Political Party		年龄分布 Age Distribution		
		男 Male	女 Female	中共党员 Member of C.P.C	共青团员 Member of C.Y.L	18周岁以下 Under 18 Years of age	18(含)-25(含)周岁 18-25 years of age	25周岁以上 Over 25 years of age
总计 Total	**5267760**	**3053170**	**2214590**	**18159**	**5043985**	**605585**	**4639598**	**22577**
比例 Percentage	100%	57.96%	42.04%	0.34%	95.75%	11.50%	88.08%	0.43%
北京 Beijing	87047	41292	45755	103	79601	15542	71404	101
天津 Tianjin	52312	26130	26182	80	50991	325	51952	35
河北 Hebei	300830	159953	140877	1484	285683	38201	262484	145
山西 Shanxi	194170	110801	83369	488	181274	27460	166353	357
内蒙古 Inner Mongolia	137129	72211	64918	486	132755	49839	87225	65
辽宁 Liaoning	185199	94192	91007	227	180618	2350	182692	157
吉林 Jilin	116731	61340	55391	289	114872	2188	114454	89
黑龙江 Heilongjiang	147980	78200	69780	822	145172	2872	144148	960
上海 Shanghai	109246	52663	56583	49	98003	634	107743	869
江苏 Jiangsu	318560	192409	126151	323	309717	27087	291062	411
浙江 Zhejiang	241652	134335	107317	986	234516	25385	216145	122
安徽 Anhui	242533	159069	83464	701	231511	102558	139735	240
福建 Fujian	167268	102814	64454	248	158860	9453	157691	124
江西 Jiangxi	166029	112617	53412	230	155154	33818	132015	196
山东 Shandong	451105	260759	190346	1045	442766	47276	403124	705
河南 Henan	393116	232892	160224	1104	384922	76426	316387	303
湖北 Hubei	287509	170617	116892	421	281093	19733	267638	138
湖南 Hunan	258171	158810	99361	317	250451	11054	246952	165
广东 Guangdong	285608	175770	109838	1283	269655	13909	271615	84
广西 Guangxi	154560	90548	64012	1570	146631	3657	145485	5418
海南 Hainan	26270	17407	8863	72	24080	2153	24076	41
重庆 Chongqing	81846	45763	36083	410	77767	23860	57944	42
四川 Sichuan	227512	133534	93978	2407	217946	24490	202712	310
贵州 Guizhou	80187	51762	28425	488	69494	20007	59283	897
云南 Yunnan	101358	53697	47661	455	99903	3921	94207	3230
西藏 Tibet	6708	3816	2892	64	6415	756	5928	24
陕西 Shaanxi	200980	120367	80613	1065	185606	2845	197995	140
甘肃 Gansu	115151	72537	42614	420	107165	3771	104999	6381
青海 Qinghai	20857	10482	10375	103	18600	3359	17371	127
宁夏 Ningxia	30388	16911	13477	145	28326	1926	28421	41
新疆 Xinjiang	79748	39472	40276	274	74438	8730	70358	660

招生报名情况(2002 年)
Higher Educational Institutions (2002)

单位:人
Unit: in Person

考试类型
Examinations Participated by Applicants

全国统考 National Exam	保送生 For Recommended Students	小语种 non-English Foreign Languages	二学位 Second Beachelor Degree	实践青年 Practising Younth	职教师资 Teachers in the Vocational School	民族体育运动训练 Nation Sport Training	高职班 Class in Tertiary Vocational Education
4870021	**1111**	**3295**	**0**	**1525**	**46298**	**687**	**344823**
92.45%	0.02%	0.06%	0.00%	0.03%	0.88%	0.01%	6.55%
71385	0	0	0	449	0	0	15213
52153	129	30	0	0	0	0	0
277673	76	36	0	0	99	627	22319
171717	0	0	0	0	22453	0	0
126325	0	0	0	0	0	0	10804
165698	0	0	0	0	0	0	19501
109212	0	0	0	0	7519	0	0
138892	0	0	0	0	9088	0	0
92819	132	135	0	0	0	0	16160
289185	250	129	0	0	0	0	28996
205945	0	0	0	0	0	0	35707
242202	34	237	0	0	0	60	0
155385	0	0	0	0	0	0	11883
157601	78	26	0	0	41	0	8283
414706	0	2586	0	1051	0	0	32762
354563	0	0	0	0	0	0	38553
267052	0	0	0	0	0	0	20457
242050	0	0	0	0	0	0	16121
259240	0	0	0	0	0	0	26368
154557	0	3	0	0	0	0	0
25828	0	0	0	25	0	0	417
71353	84	24	0	0	0	0	10385
211549	123	89	0	0	880	0	14871
76096	7	0	0	0	0	0	4084
101358	0	0	0	0	0	0	0
6512	196	0	0	0	0	0	0
189250	0	0	0	0	1997	0	9733
110930	0	0	0	0	4221	0	0
19986	0	0	0	0	0	0	871
29053	0	0	0	0	0	0	1335
79746	2	0	0	0	0	0	0

普通高等学校

Applicants of Student for Regular

地区 Region	应试卷种 Category of Examination Papers to be tested		考生类别 Categories of Applicants					
	汉语卷 Chinese	非汉语卷 Minority Languages	城市应届 Urban Sec. Schools Graduates in Current Year		农村应届 Rural Sec. Schools Graduates in Current Year		城市往届 Urban Sec. Schools Graduates in Previous Year	农村往届 Rural Sec. Schools Graduates in Previous Year
			小计 Total	其中:普通高中应届生 Of which: General Senion Sec. Schools Graduates	小计 Total	其中:普通高中应届生 Of which: General Senior Sec. Schools Graduates		
总　计 Total	**4823784**	**46237**	**2046427**	**1726247**	**1956729**	**1811696**	**523438**	**741166**
比　例 Percentage	99.05%	0.95%	38.85%	32.77%	37.15%	34.39%	9.94%	14.07%
北　京 Bejing	71385	0	62639	47659	11332	9466	11389	1687
天　津 Tianjin	52153	0	33193	31888	11128	11044	5245	2746
河　北 Hebei	277673	0	85371	72069	142024	130934	21719	51716
山　西 Shanxi	171717	0	66655	59937	66773	55079	26537	34205
内蒙古 Inner Mongolia	117821	8504	40251	33625	50565	44647	16807	29506
辽　宁 Liaoning	163111	2587	104786	86502	50516	47227	15103	14794
吉　林 Jilin	104179	5033	64155	56158	23010	22230	18518	11048
黑龙江 Heilongjiang	137400	1492	78049	69409	34577	32100	20291	15063
上　海 Shanghai	92819	0	87599	77430	12133	13428	7447	2067
江　苏 Jiangsu	289185	0	127735	111089	144297	130823	16012	30516
浙　江 Zhejiang	205945	0	76164	73825	109144	107862	22391	33953
安　徽 Anhui	242202	0	86947	85449	69647	68399	46241	39698
福　建 Fujian	155385	0	47343	39934	81896	76485	12587	25442
江　西 Jiangxi	157601	0	68854	61826	56635	53461	22643	17897
山　东 Shandong	414706	0	145346	107046	193506	192334	30647	81606
河　南 Henan	354563	0	103725	73740	170587	126711	37259	81545
湖　北 Hubei	267052	0	122672	107330	102083	94952	25463	37291
湖　南 Hunan	242050	0	77883	76220	113344	110256	25468	41476
广　东 Guangdong	259240	0	135934	133305	103286	102608	23753	22635
广　西 Guangxi	154557	0	56177	52148	59093	57103	15933	23357
海　南 Hainan	25828	0	12866	12302	8401	8206	3090	1913
重　庆 Chongqing	71353	0	41495	35705	29137	24578	5493	5721
四　川 Sichuan	211549	0	82426	75992	93562	83692	20339	31185
贵　州 Guizhou	76096	0	32323	29105	27161	25709	9039	11664
云　南 Yunnan	101358	0	32766	32671	41189	40123	9006	18397
西　藏 Tibet	4961	1551	4152	4078	871	859	833	852
陕　西 Shaanxi	189250	0	73347	66221	69810	66003	27674	30149
甘　肃 Gansu	110407	523	30472	27648	41472	35983	14047	29160
青　海 Qinghai	18636	1350	9630	8762	6557	6466	2408	2262
宁　夏 Ningxia	29053	0	11902	11902	9418	9418	3990	5078
新　疆 Xinjiang	54549	25197	43570	41492	23575	23510	6066	6537

招生报名情况(2002年)(续)

Higher Educational Institutions (2002) (Continue)

单位:人
Unit: in Person

统考科类 Categories of Major Fields								
文理综合 Comprehensive	文史 Literature and History	外语(文) Foreign Languages	艺术(文) Arts	体育(文) Physical Education	理工 Science and Engineering	外语(理) Foreign Languages	艺术(理) Arts	体育(理) Physical Education
1057608	**1086748**	**76789**	**160138**	**14792**	**2259531**	**132600**	**19386**	**62429**
21.72%	22.32%	1.58%	3.29%	0.30%	46.40%	2.72%	0.40%	1.28%
0	22870	0	0	0	48515	0	0	0
0	10560	0	1973	113	38873	0	237	397
0	86939	0	9991	346	174862	0	153	5382
0	43301	0	5998	1064	116936	0	808	3610
0	36190	2740	5038	0	80719	0	0	1638
0	41601	0	11056	631	108070	0	1897	2443
0	31084	0	5138	482	70282	0	411	1815
0	35968	0	7216	182	91864	0	1176	2486
0	44356	0	0	0	48463	0	0	0
289185	0	0	0	0	0	0	0	0
0	61604	0	11061	1058	128642	0	889	2691
0	89166	0	8234	1612	138682	0	502	4006
0	48106	0	1165	0	100420	0	2680	3014
63	36245	2067	9622	2183	102543	604	1229	3045
0	109504	0	28736	0	269217	0	0	7249
354563	0	0	0	0	0	0	0	0
0	77302	0	13690	777	170230	0	1519	3534
0	95978	0	11421	0	127763	0	1073	5815
259240	0	0	0	0	0	0	0	0
154557	0	0	0	0	0	0	0	0
0	8377	0	369	0	16678	0	11	393
0	20936	0	3187	1150	44101	0	1005	974
0	6623	46334	8470	2677	16547	123649	4100	3149
0	26734	0	2208	616	45549	0	207	782
0	33875	4519	3730	796	56835	0	330	1273
0	3948	818	339	294	449	494	51	119
0	44071	6911	5147	0	128884	0	457	3780
0	28205	7956	3631	368	63737	4429	80	2524
0	7937	0	262	97	11557	0	16	117
0	10108	0	544	0	17859	0	0	542
0	25160	5444	1912	346	41254	3424	555	1651

普通高等学校

Applicants of Student for Regular

地　区 Region	毕业类别 Categories of Graduates						应试外 Foregin Languages		
	高中毕业 General Sec. School Graduates	中等师范毕业 Teachers Training School Graduates	其他中专毕业 Specialized Sec. School Graduates	职业高中毕业 Vacational Senior Sec. School Graduates	技工学校毕业 Skilled Worker School Graduates	其他中等学历教育毕业 Others	英语 English	俄语 Russian	日语 Japanese
总　计 Total	**4709523**	**41929**	**144729**	**268792**	**10284**	**92503**	**5164046**	**21248**	**10875**
比　例 Percentage	89.40%	0.80%	2.75%	5.10%	0.20%	1.76%	99.27%	0.41%	0.21%
北　京 Beijing	65835	32	7429	11719	1239	793	86278	4	307
天　津 Tianjin	50500	350	930	359	134	39	52278	3	30
河　北 Hebei	273516	4543	5700	15261	356	1454	299767	827	236
山　西 Shanxi	172958	5740	6092	6481	1828	1071	194136	13	19
内蒙古 Inner Mongolia	123628	642	1618	11014	76	151	118342	2896	999
辽　宁 Liaoning	161212	311	10970	11614	789	303	179405	2548	3246
吉　林 Jilin	106920	1359	5315	2696	177	264	112412	659	3660
黑龙江 Heilongjiang	134470	1860	2346	8489	450	365	135962	10857	1161
上　海 Shanghai	90561	5	1480	630	96	16474	108969	12	149
江　苏 Jiangsu	287748	151	13607	16185	767	102	315092	1	52
浙　江 Zhejiang	200844	350	2202	37970	73	213	241640	37	4
安　徽 Anhui	236787	579	1148	2922	130	967	242293	230	5
福　建 Fujian	152711	947	2803	1839	101	8867	167115	1	152
江　西 JIangxi	155035	835	3264	6531	134	230	165726	1	0
山　东 Shandong	408070	276	35370	6763	110	516	448519	1906	678
河　南 Henan	287652	5962	14119	28845	671	55867	388031	18	24
湖　北 Hubei	263761	1457	8940	12803	89	459	286967	432	61
湖　南 Hunan	239156	1201	6416	11322	34	42	257900	217	47
广　东 Guandgong	255696	695	855	28288	35	39	285373	0	5
广　西 Guangxi	142044	8903	1139	2127	52	295	154550	0	7
海　南 Hainan	25358	283	121	495	6	7	25874	0	0
重　庆 Chongqing	70962	326	1807	7859	47	845	80861	133	8
四　川 Sichuan	210173	1095	2126	13580	86	452	227173	243	17
贵　州 Guizhou	74115	916	1951	2661	169	375	76061	35	2
云　南 Yunnan	92496	2035	1621	1955	1772	1479	101357	0	0
西　藏 Tibet	6163	80	159	57	136	113	6695	13	0
陕　西 Shaanxi	189250	0	0	11730	0	0	189240	9	1
甘　肃 Gansu	109979	199	194	4196	36	547	110288	119	0
青　海 Qinghai	19387	190	976	218	13	73	20856	1	1
宁　夏 Ningxia	28824	0	0	1414	150	0	30375	10	2
新　疆 Xinjiang	73712	607	4031	769	528	101	54511	23	2

招生报名情况(2002 年)(续)

Higher Educational Institutions (2002) (Continue)

单位:人

Unit: in Person

语语种 to be Tested				民族 Nationalities						预计录取总量 Estimated Erollment	预计录取率 Estimated Erollment Rate
德语 German	法语 France	西班牙语 Spanish	其他外语 Other Foregin Languages	汉族 Han	蒙古族 Meng	藏族 Zang	维吾尔族 Wei	朝鲜族 Korean	其他民族 Others		
70	**64**	**33**	**5530**	**4910985**	**45357**	**10005**	**21611**	**11735**	**268067**	**3042440**	**57.76%**
0.00%	0.00%	0.00%	0.11%	93.23%	0.86%	0.19%	0.41%	0.22%	5.09%		
0	0	0	0	80609	401	177	12	94	5754	59945	68.87%
1	0	0	0	50381	65	83	1	19	1763	36620	70.00%
0	0	0	0	283351	1053	4	3	88	16331	158736	52.77%
1	1	0	0	193365	53	1	1	6	744	81754	42.10%
0	0	0	0	99114	29644	5	3	234	8129	69649	50.79%
0	0	0	0	156129	4251	3	3	1663	23150	137556	74.27%
0	0	0	0	101870	1185	0	1	6623	7052	81039	69.42%
0	0	0	0	138184	1114	4	1	2842	5835	93458	63.16%
22	16	16	62	107245	0	0	0	0	2001	79055	72.36%
13	12	0	0	316966	42	2	0	16	1534	216671	68.02%
1	0	0	0	240621	30	284	1	0	716	174129	72.06%
0	2	0	0	239921	1	1	0	1	2609	137720	56.78%
0	0	0	0	165013	36	0	0	3	2216	82175	49.13%
0	0	0	0	165369	34	1	0	5	620	95825	57.72%
4	0	0	0	448352	62	4	1	33	2653	241391	53.51%
2	0	0	0	387086	534	8	20	22	5446	178883	45.50%
19	30	0	0	275343	93	9	760	9	11295	129703	45.11%
4	3	0	0	236405	22	3	39	5	21697	120495	46.67%
0	0	0	0	284080	37	3	1	14	1473	173545	60.76%
0	0	0	0	95178	0	0	0	0	59382	82977	53.69%
0	0	0	0	24135	25	0	0	2	2108	17865	68.01%
0	0	0		76248	12	10	4	2	5570	65329	79.82%
1	0	17	0	222539	106	1306	3	14	3544	145008	63.74%
0	0	0	0	47653	195	9	8	6	32316	60273	75.17%
1	0	0	0	75251	0	0	0	0	26107	59460	58.66%
0	0	0	0	2253	2	4365	4	1	83	4842	72.18%
0	0	0	0	198959	73	4	0	16	1928	100442	49.98%
0	0	0	0	110615	75	1204	1	6	3250	62609	54.37%
0	0	0	0	15237	428	2472	0	3	2717	20913	100.27%
1	0	0	0	25133	4684	0	0	0	571	18701	61.54%
0	0	0	5468	48380	1100	43	20744	8	9473	55672	69.81%

普通高等学校

Applicants of Student for Regular

地区 Region	报名总数 Total	性别 Gender 男 Male	女 Female	政治面貌 Political Party 中共党员 Member of C.P.C	共青团员 Member of C.Y.L	年龄分布 Age Distribution 18周岁以下 Under 18 years of age	18(含)25(含)周岁 Over 25 years of age	25周岁以上 Over 25 years of age
总计 Total	**6124580**	**3481096**	**2643484**	**19416**	**5826643**	**744019**	**5371782**	**8779**
比例 Percentage	100%	56.84%	43.16%	0.32%	95.14%	12.15%	87.71%	0.14%
北京 Beijing	94157	44797	49360	121	84957	3212	90774	171
天津 Tianjin	72989	35884	37105	90	69551	587	72292	110
河北 Hebei	336934	176941	159993	2005	318128	14778	321839	317
山西 Shanxi	212447	119421	93026	470	197665	33633	178539	275
内蒙古 Inner Mongolia	166457	86438	80019	624	160481	60664	105699	94
辽宁 Liaoning	176098	88277	87821	654	171472	29392	146599	107
吉林 Jilin	118866	62651	56215	142	116978	2471	116311	84
黑龙江 Heilongjiang	158923	83148	75775	604	156405	4553	153968	402
上海 Shanghai	118824	57732	61092	40	97508	26384	92399	41
江苏 Jiangsu	366261	215780	150481	226	354700	24811	341347	103
浙江 Zhejiang	268913	144839	124074	1042	256334	33433	235282	198
安徽 Anhui	292083	186256	105827	386	276989	95405	196309	369
福建 Fujian	204570	118998	85572	221	192913	11234	193224	112
江西 Jiangxi	205411	133565	71846	272	190545	41453	163748	210
山东 Shandong	537761	307256	230505	1356	527645	36826	500405	530
河南 Henna	478315	276176	202139	1431	467839	46840	431201	274
湖北 Hubei	331449	193686	137763	422	323364	130934	200401	114
湖南 Hunan	299137	176523	122614	1399	290637	39707	259078	352
广东 Guangdong	335658	200798	134860	1093	314111	14705	320798	155
广西 Guangxi	185465	105073	80392	679	177236	13077	171757	631
海南 Hainan	29160	19105	10055	101	26627	1059	28082	19
重庆 Chongqing	97772	52858	44914	405	93190	6003	91729	40
四川 Sichuan	258810	147477	111333	2109	247674	12130	246436	244
贵州 Guizhou	109121	69205	39916	739	94114	4132	103086	1903
云南 Yunnan	119956	64945	55011	285	113416	10974	108737	245
西藏 Tibet	9436	5148	4288	97	8866	796	7991	649
陕西 Shaanxi	244953	142014	102939	1081	227596	5777	238914	262
甘肃 Gansu	136140	86351	49789	527	125855	5602	130201	337
青海 Qinghai	23716	11715	12001	79	21161	5413	18175	128
宁夏 Ningxia	41342	22409	18933	451	38233	9480	31847	15
新疆 Xinjiang	93456	45630	47826	265	84453	18554	74614	288

招生报名情况(2003 年)

Higher Educational Institutions (2003)

单位:人

Unit: in Person

考试类型 Examinations Participated by Applicants		应试卷种 Category of Examination Papers to be Tested		考生类别 Categories of Applicants					
				城市应届 Urban Sec. Schools Graduates in Current Year		农村应届 Rural Sec. Schools Graduates in Current Year		城市往届 Urban Sec. Schools Graduates in Previous Year	农村往届 Rural Sec. Schools Graduates in Previous Year
全国统考 National Exam.	非全国统考 Non-National Exam.	汉语卷 Chinese	非汉语卷 Minority Languages	小 计 Total	其中:普通高中应届生 Of which: General Senior Sec. Schools Graduates	小 计 Total	其中:普通高中应届生 Of which: General Senior Sec. Schools Graduates		
5665787	**458793**	**6010113**	**74851**	**2313589**	**1932026**	**2449098**	**2246693**	**554676**	**807217**
92.51%	7.49%	98.13%	1.22%	37.78%	31.55%	39.99%	36.68%	9.06%	13.18%
80815	13342	94157	0	64161	51804	13994	12734	13662	2340
57242	15747	72989	0	47344	34989	13694	12352	8673	3278
317247	19687	336897	37	86633	75241	163721	152166	24967	61613
212447	0	212447	0	65734	58296	69839	66980	35425	41449
155354	11103	154865	11592	49432	43551	63407	56948	19801	33817
154337	21761	151694	24404	110010	89674	55426	52063	5540	5122
118866	0	113161	5705	65865	64757	23781	23748	18402	10818
147528	11395	157221	1702	87113	77060	39529	37590	18394	13887
92913	25911	118824	0	96232	68074	11730	11672	8864	1998
341427	24834	366261	0	140903	125554	169746	158983	20031	35581
229052	39861	268913	0	88022	69797	143470	117170	13782	23639
292077	6	292083	0	103997	88902	93360	90001	50949	43777
190819	13751	204570	0	54711	44732	103176	94090	14034	32449
194237	11174	205411	0	93869	84527	65119	62015	27552	18871
483469	54292	529747	0	169379	121666	247301	246022	32640	88664
430258	48057	478315	0	123598	89267	218330	167699	39812	96575
307106	24343	331449	0	134276	119010	133144	122979	24728	39301
284078	15059	299137	0	83264	77323	144417	135452	23836	47620
306381	29277	335402	0	156526	136556	132004	121166	22850	24278
183201	2264	183201	0	64037	58625	81085	78337	18946	21397
28885	275			18983	18632	4204	3998	4388	1585
83785	13987	97772	0	44486	37118	39868	33880	5977	7421
238796	20014	258604	206	88146	80377	121322	108521	17003	32339
102927	6194	109121	0	38031	34620	39811	37857	13026	18253
110046	9910	119956	78	38142	32664	50297	46079	12052	19465
9170	266	9314	122	5237	4993	1708	1700	2048	443
231834	13119	244953	0	84660	75037	101326	94624	26659	32305
131725	4415	135866	274	36135	3924	52666	49550	15273	32066
21252	2464	22265	1451	11819	9415	8078	7978	1828	1991
38785	2557	41342	0	14754	12957	15090	14371	4875	6623
89728	3728	64176	29280	48090	42884	28455	27968	8659	8252

普通高等学校

Applicants of Student for Regular

地区 Region	统考科类 Categories of Major Fields 文理综合 Comprehensive	文史 Literature and History	外语（文） Foreign Languages	艺术（文） Arts	体育（文） Physical Education	理工 Science and Engineering	外语（理） Foreign Languages	艺术（理） Arts	体育（理） Physical Education	高中毕业 General Senior Sec. School Graduates
总计 Total	**1400863**	**1205929**	**73631**	**187974**	**27753**	**2545275**	**138367**	**23050**	**62945**	**5501566**
比例 Percentage	24.72%	21.28%	1.30%	3.32%	0.49%	44.92%	2.44%	0.41%	1.11%	89.83%
北京 Beijing	0	28637	0	0	0	52178	0	0	0	75722
天津 Tianjin	0	12962	0	2217	114	41352	0	218	379	56711
河北 Hebei	0	93717	0	13911	1021	202804	0	588	5206	312857
山西 Shanxi	0	54890	0	10825	3819	133302	0	1937	7674	199385
内蒙古 Inner Mongolia	0	49685	0	7892	0	95991	0	0	1786	153059
辽宁 Liaoning	139596	0	0	11365	3376	0	0	0	0	156747
吉林 Jilin	0	36489	0	0	0	82377	0	0	0	116705
黑龙江 Heilonjiang	0	37128	0	8360	644	97152	0	1411	2833	144569
上海 Shanghai	0	35693	0	0	0	57220	0	0	0	89868
江苏 Jiangsu	341427	0	0	0	0	0	0	0	0	339275
浙江 Zhejiang	0	70836	0	12878	1453	140189	0	1227	2469	221404
安徽 Anhui	0	88533	0	11260	3469	183293	0	1114	4408	286469
福建 Fujian	0	62613	0	1370	0	118849	0	4134	3853	181523
江西 Jiangxi	0	45307	0	12242	3172	128117	0	2273	3126	191176
山东 Shandong	0	122062	0	44045	0	308721	0	0	8641	485364
河南 Henan	430258	0	0	0	0	0	0	0	0	354890
湖北 Hubei	0	82895	0	16202	1948	199299	0	2030	4732	305093
湖南 Hunan	0	113930	0	0	0	170148	0	0	0	282475
广东 Guangdong	306381	0	0	0	0	0	0	0	0	303064
广西 Guangxi	183201	0	0	0	0	0	0	0	0	175915
海南 Hainan	0	9661	287	0	0	18540	0	30	367	28473
重庆 Chongqing	0	27174	0	3723	1481	49320	0	1183	904	83307
四川 Sichuan	0	6666	58936	10435	3698	12659	138367	4651	3384	237075
贵州 Guizhou	0	36770	0	2843	1023	60881	0	395	1015	100743
云南 Yunnan	0	37529	4614	4173	1256	61019	0	488	967	108899
西藏 Tibet	0	5261	0	0	0	3909	0	0	0	8734
陕西 Shaanxi	0	53263	9794	6782	0	155673	0	727	5595	225386
甘肃 Gansu	0	42905	0	4560	502	80953	0	169	2636	130302
青海 Qinghai	0	7464	0	265	119	13172	0	43	189	20716
宁夏 Ningxia	0	11628	0	671	0	25279	0	0	1207	38815
新疆 Xinjiang	0	32231	0	1955	658	52878	0	432	1574	86845

招生报名情况(2003 年)(续)

Higher Educational Institutions (2003)(Continue)

单位:人

Unit: in Person

毕业类别 Categories of Graduates					应试外语语种 Foregin Languages to be Tested						
中等师范毕业 Teachers Training School Graduates	其他中专毕业 Specialized Sec. School Graduates	职业高中毕业 Vacational Senior Sec. School Graduates	技工学校毕业 Skilled Worker School Graduates	其他中等学历教育毕业 Others	英语 English	俄语 Russian	日语 Japanese	德语 German	法语 France	西班牙语 Spanish	其他外语 Other Foregin Languages
36501	**186202**	**274798**	**8440**	**117073**	**6027312**	**19243**	**10897**	**88**	**62**	**8**	**431**
0.60%	3.04%	4.49%	0.14%	1.91%	98.41%	0.31%	0.18%	0.00%	0.00%	0.00%	0.01%
83	7199	9466	995	692	93466	1	213	11	0	0	0
400	8864	4990	938	1086	72923	1	65	0	0	0	0
2997	5176	13606	368	1930	336029	469	436	0	0	0	0
4211	3835	4115	397	504	212410	14	23	0	0	0	0
297	1139	11717	54	191	147233	2889	1235	0	0	0	0
299	8135	9822	749	346	171739	1907	2452	0	0	0	0
294	1009	525	79	254	114645	610	3611	0	0	0	0
265	4594	8098	251	1146	148440	9198	1285	0	0	0	0
4	3415	921	90	24526	118287	27	416	36	20	7	31
163	3168	23602	42	11	366199	1	40	11	10	0	0
264	9834	36213	1049	149	268825	15	72	1	0	0	0
697	1016	2447	95	1359	291751	0	0	0	0	0	332
6622	3535	2551	114	10225	204479	0	91	0	0	0	0
825	5633	7272	117	388	205288	3	4	0	0	1	48
185	44105	7612	138	357	533956	3102	701	2	0	0	0
5191	18942	32664	690	65938	478249	18	45	3	0	0	0
1086	11532	13440	145	153	330890	409	102	17	31	0	0
300	5286	10915	37	124	298864	240	32	1	0	0	0
1572	7654	22086	709	317	335373	2	22	0	0	0	0
4202	1950	2925	47	426	183194	0	3	2	1	0	0
158	118	405	3	3	29145	0	1	0	0	0	0
543	3751	9177	98	896	97664	107	1	0	0	0	0
1093	2961	17086	18	577	258496	133	15	0	0	0	0
1090	3636	2910	256	486	102918	5	4	0	0	0	0
471	3997	6068	380	141	119928	0	7	1	0	0	20
39	520	90	4	49	9433	2	1	0	0	0	0
1558	7713	8878	231	1187	237049	9	11	2	0	0	0
482	434	4224	33	665	131249	43	3	1	0	0	0
183	2579	132	19	87	23715	1	0	0	0	0	0
0	0	0	0	2783	41321	16	5	0	0	0	0
927	4472	841	294	77	64154	21	1	0	0	0	0

普通高等学校招生报名情况(2003 年)(续)

Applicants of Student for Regular Higher Educational Institutions (2003)(Continue)

单位:人

Unit: in Person

地 区 Region	民族 Nationalities 汉族 Han	蒙古族 Meng	藏族 Zang	维吾尔族 Wei	朝鲜族 Korean	其他民族 Others
总 计 Total	**5680070**	**49362**	**13269**	**25148**	**13462**	**343269**
比 例 Percentage	92.74%	0.81%	0.22%	0.41%	0.22%	5.60%
北 京 Beijing	87391	410	217	8	99	6032
天 津 Tianjin	70167	93	87	0	19	2623
河 北 Hebei	315462	1174	2	3	77	20216
山 西 Shanxi	211522	49	0	1	9	866
内蒙古 Inner Mongolia	119268	37250	6	4	250	9679
辽 宁 Liaoning	147619	4132	2	0	1637	22708
吉 林 Jilin	103101	1199	0	1	7366	7199
黑龙江 Heilongjiang	148289	1159	0	1	3160	6314
上 海 Shanghai	117624	0	0	0	0	1200
江 苏 Jiangsu	364512	58	90	4	17	1580
浙 江 Zhejiang	267805	17	1	1	11	1078
安 徽 Auhui	289051	0	0	0	0	3032
福 建 Fujian	201767	41	3	0	2	2757
江 西 Jiangxi	204539	44	2	2	3	821
山 东 Shandong	516944	1062	29	330	689	18963
河 南 Henan	471334	624	11	24	12	6310
湖 北 Hubei	317896	87	46	730	17	12673
湖 南 Hunan	273385	28	82	43	5	25594
广 东 Guangdong	333743	55	2	0	13	1589
广 西 Guangxi	113266	0	0	0	0	72199
海 南 Hainan	26638	0	0	0	0	2522
重 庆 Chongqing	90848	42	79	1	7	6795
四 川 Sichuan	252310	98	1957	1	6	4438
贵 州 Guizhou	62968	242	6	20	14	45871
云 南 Yunnan	87937	142	391	2	3	31481
西 藏 Tibet	3250	3	5940	0	1	242
陕 西 Shaanxi	243417	71	5	3	5	1452
甘 肃 Gansu	131031	85	1127	0	11	3886
青 海 Qinghai	16779	550	3137	0	5	3245
宁 夏 Ningxia	33488	94	10	2	5	7743
新 疆 Xinjiang	56719	553	37	23967	19	12161

附　　表

Appendixes

国内生产总值

Gross Domestic Product

本表按当年价格计算

The data in Value terms in this table are calculated at current prices

单位:亿元

Unit: in 100 Million Yuan

年 份 Year	国民生产总值 Gross National Product	国内生产总值 Gross Domestic Product								人均国内生产总值(元) Per Capita GDP (Yuan)
		合 计 Total	第一产业 Primary Industry	第二产业 Secondary Industry			第三产业 Tertiary Industry			
				小 计 Subtotal	工 业 Industry	建筑业 Construction	小 计 Subtotal	交通运输仓储邮电通信业 Transportation, Post and Telecommunications	批发和零售贸易餐饮业 Wholesale, Retail & Catering Trade	
1952	679.0	679.0	342.9	141.8	119.8	22.0	194.3	29.0	80.3	119
1953	824.0	824.0	378.0	192.5	163.5	29.0	253.5	35.0	115.5	142
1954	859.0	859.0	392.0	211.7	184.7	27.0	255.3	38.0	120.3	144
1955	910.0	910.0	421.0	222.2	191.2	31.0	266.8	39.0	119.8	150
1956	1028.0	1028.0	443.9	280.7	224.7	56.0	303.4	46.0	131.4	165
1957	1068.0	1068.0	430.0	317.0	271.0	46.0	321.0	49.0	133.0	168
1958	1307.0	1307.0	445.9	483.5	414.5	69.0	377.6	71.0	136.6	200
1959	1439.0	1439.0	383.8	615.5	538.5	77.0	439.7	94.0	145.7	216
1960	1457.0	1457.0	340.7	648.2	568.2	80.0	468.1	104.0	133.1	218
1961	1220.0	1220.0	441.1	388.9	362.1	26.8	390.0	69.2	110.8	185
1962	1149.3	1149.3	453.1	359.3	325.4	33.9	336.9	57.4	80.5	173
1963	1233.3	1233.3	497.5	407.6	365.6	42.0	328.2	55.0	76.1	181
1964	1454.0	1454.0	559.0	513.5	161.1	52.4	381.5	58.4	94.0	208
1965	1716.1	1716.1	651.1	602.2	546.5	55.7	462.8	77.4	118.3	240
1966	1868.0	1868.0	702.2	709.5	648.6	60.9	456.3	85.1	148.1	254
1967	1773.9	1773.9	714.2	602.8	544.9	57.9	456.9	72.3	153.5	235
1968	1723.1	1723.1	726.3	537.3	190.3	47.0	459.5	70.5	138.9	222
1969	1937.9	1937.9	736.2	689.1	626.1	63.0	512.6	84.9	163.6	243
1970	2252.7	2252.7	793.3	912.2	828.1	84.1	547.2	100.2	178.1	275
1971	2426.4	2426.4	826.3	1022.8	926.6	96.2	577.3	108.4	178.3	288
1972	2518.1	2518.1	827.4	1084.2	989.9	94.3	606.5	118.0	194.3	292
1973	2720.9	2720.9	907.5	1173.0	1072.5	100.5	640.4	125.5	211.0	309
1974	2789.9	2789.9	945.2	1192.0	1083.6	108.4	652.7	126.1	206.6	310
1975	2997.3	2997.3	971.1	1370.5	1244.9	125.6	655.7	141.6	175.8	327
1976	2943.7	2943.7	967.0	1337.2	1204.6	132.6	639.5	139.6	147.2	316
1977	3201.9	3201.9	942.1	1509.1	1372.4	136.7	750.7	156.9	213.8	339
1978	3624.1	3624.1	1018.4	1745.2	1607.0	138.2	860.5	172.8	265.5	379
1979	4038.2	4038.2	1258.9	1913.5	1769.7	143.8	865.8	184.2	220.2	417
1980	4517.8	4517.8	1359.4	2192.0	1996.5	195.5	966.4	205.0	213.6	460
1981	4860.3	4862.4	1545.6	2255.5	2048.4	207.1	1061.3	211.1	255.7	489
1982	5301.8	5294.7	1761.6	2383.0	2162.3	220.7	1150.1	236.7	198.6	525
1983	5957.4	5934.5	1960.8	2646.2	2375.6	270.6	1327.5	264.9	231.4	580
1984	7206.7	7171.0	2295.5	3105.7	2789.0	316.7	1769.8	327.1	412.4	692
1985	8989.1	8964.4	2541.6	3866.6	3448.7	417.9	2556.2	406.9	878.4	853
1986	10201.4	10202.2	2763.9	4492.7	3967.0	525.7	2945.6	475.6	943.2	956
1987	11954.5	11962.5	3204.3	5251.6	4585.8	665.8	3506.6	544.9	1159.3	1104
1988	14922.3	14928.3	3831.0	6587.2	5777.2	810.0	4510.1	661.0	1618.0	1355
1989	16917.8	16909.2	4228.0	7278.0	6484.0	794.0	5403.2	786.0	1687.0	1512
1990	18598.4	18547.9	5017.0	7717.4	6858.0	859.4	5813.5	1147.5	1419.7	1634
1991	21662.5	21617.8	5288.6	9102.2	8087.1	1015.1	7227.0	1409.7	2087.0	1879
1992	26651.9	26638.1	5800.0	11699.5	10284.5	1415.0	9138.6	1681.8	2735.0	2287
1993	34560.5	34634.4	6882.1	16428.5	14143.8	2284.7	11323.8	2123.2	3090.7	2939
1994	46670.0	46759.4	9457.2	22372.2	19359.6	3012.6	14930.0	2685.9	4050.4	3923
1995	57494.9	58478.1	11993.0	28537.9	24718.3	3819.6	17947.2	3054.7	4932.3	4854
1996	66850.5	67884.6	13844.2	33612.9	29082.6	4530.5	20427.5	3494.0	5560.3	5576
1997	73142.7	74462.6	14211.2	37222.7	32412.1	4810.6	23028.7	3797.2	6159.9	6053
1998	78017.8	79395.7	14599.6	38691.8	33429.8	5262.0	26104.3	5029.3	6609.6	6392
1999	80422.8	81910.9	14457.2	40417.9	34975.2	5442.7	27035.8	4459.5	6842.3	6534
2000	88189.6	89403.6	14212.0	45487.8	39570.3	5917.5	29703.8	4918.6	7306.9	7078
2001	94346.4	95933.3	14609.9	49069.1	42607.1	6462.0	32254.3	5222.1	7823.5	7543
2002	103553.6	104790.6	16117.3	53540.7	46535.7	7005.0	35132.6	6240.9	8215.3	8184

数据来源:摘自国家统计局《2003 中国统计年鉴》。

各地区国内生产总值(2002年)

Gross Domestic Product by Region (2002)

本表绝对数按当年价格计算,指数按可比价格计算

Absolute figures in this table are calculated at current prices while indices are calculated at comparable prices.

单位:亿元

Unit: in 100 Million Yuan

地 区 Region	国内生产总值 Gross Domestic Product							人均国内生产总值(元) Per Capita GDP (Yuan)
	合 计 Total	第一产业 Primary Industry	第二产业 Secondary Industry			第三产业 Tertiary Industry		
			小 计 Subtotal	工 业 Industry	建筑业 Construction	小 计 Subtotal	教育、文化艺术和广播电影电视业 Education, Culture, Arts, Radio, Film and Television	
北 京 Beijing	3212.71	98.05	1116.53	874.15	242.38	1998.13	212.16	28449
天 津 Tianjin	2051.16	84.00	1001.90	909.24	92.66	965.26	85.52	22380
河 北 Hebei	6122.53	957.01	3046.00	2695.69	350.31	2119.52	154.27	9115
山 西 Shanxi	2017.54	197.80	1083.79	921.99	161.80	735.95	57.72	6146
内蒙古 Inner Mongolia	1734.31	374.69	728.34	573.30	155.04	631.28	53.90	7241
辽 宁 Liaoning	5458.22	590.20	2609.85	2331.95	277.90	2258.17	152.08	12986
吉 林 Jilin	2246.12	446.17	978.37	803.53	174.84	821.58	74.80	8334
黑龙江 Heilongjiang	3882.16	447.00	2169.15	1916.04	253.11	1266.01	98.85	10184
上 海 Shanghai	5408.76	88.24	2564.69	2312.77	251.92	2755.83	196.50	40646
江 苏 Jiangsu	10631.75	1119.12	5550.98	4826.58	724.40	3961.65	298.75	14391
浙 江 Zhejiang	7796.00	694.00	3982.00	3580.00	402.00	3120.00	247.48	16838
安 徽 Anhui	3569.10	772.55	1552.21	1290.52	261.69	1244.34	98.83	5817
福 建 Fujian	4682.01	664.78	2159.94	1882.55	277.39	1857.29	131.54	13497
江 西 Jiangxi	2450.48	535.98	951.77	693.18	258.59	962.73	70.84	5829
山 东 Shandong	10552.06	1390.00	5309.54	4629.54	680.00	3852.52	298.76	11645
河 南 Henan	6168.73	1288.36	2951.06	2531.72	419.34	1929.31	153.34	6436
湖 北 Hubei	4975.63	707.00	2446.05	2168.42	277.63	1822.58	153.30	8319
湖 南 Hunan	4340.94	847.25	1737.20	1440.80	296.40	1756.49	196.95	6565
广 东 Guangdong	11769.73	1032.80	5935.63	5288.53	647.10	4801.30	232.79	15030
广 西 Guangxi	2455.36	595.68	863.96	699.16	164.80	995.72	91.53	5099
海 南 Hainan	604.13	228.95	125.33	83.78	41.55	249.85	17.94	7803
重 庆 Chongqing	1971.30	315.78	827.55	651.00	176.55	827.97	83.79	6347
四 川 Sichuan	4875.12	1027.62	1982.44	1551.48	430.96	1865.06	166.60	5766
贵 州 Guizhou	1185.04	280.83	474.68	370.49	104.19	429.53	49.46	3153
云 南 Yunnan	2232.32	470.50	951.48	780.33	171.15	810.34	83.26	5179
西 藏 Tibet	161.42	39.68	32.93	11.61	21.32	88.81	10.97	6093
陕 西 Shaanxi	2035.96	303.79	925.78	691.07	234.71	806.39	96.03	5523
甘 肃 Gansu	1161.43	214.45	530.36	390.61	139.75	416.62	28.10	4493
青 海 Qinghai	341.11	44.90	154.01	100.19	53.82	142.20	15.85	6426
宁 夏 Ningxia	329.28	52.84	151.16	114.80	36.36	125.28	14.74	5804
新 疆 Xinjiang	1598.28	305.00	672.10	473.00	199.10	621.18	65.39	8382

数据来源:摘自国家统计局《2003中国统计年鉴》。

国家财政收支总额及增长速度

Total Government Revenue and Expenditures and Their Increase Rate

年 份 Year	财政收入 (亿元) Total Revenue (100 million Yuan)	财政支出 (亿元) Total Expenditures (100 million Yuan)	收支差额 (亿元) Balance (100 million Yuan)	增长速度 Increase Rate (%) 财政收入 Total Revenue	增长速度 Increase Rate (%) 财政支出 Total Expenditures
1970	662.90	649.41	13.49	25.8	23.5
1971－1975	3919.71	3917.94	1.77	4.2	4.8
1971	744.73	732.17	12.56	12.3	12.7
1972	766.56	765.86	0.70	2.9	4.6
1973	809.67	808.78	0.89	5.6	5.6
1974	783.14	790.25	－7.11	－3.3	－2.3
1975	815.61	820.88	－5.27	4.1	3.8
1976－1980	5089.61	5282.44	－192.83	7.3	8.4
1976	776.58	806.20	－29.62	－4.8	－1.8
1977	874.46	843.53	30.93	12.6	4.6
1978	1132.26	1122.09	10.17	29.5	33.0
1979	1146.38	1281.79	－135.41	1.2	14.2
1980	1159.93	1228.83	－68.90	1.2	－4.1
1981－1985	7402.75	7483.18	－80.43	11.6	10.3
1981	1175.79	1138.41	37.38	1.4	－7.5
1982	1212.33	1229.98	－17.65	3.1	8.0
1983	1366.95	1409.52	－42.57	12.8	14.6
1984	1642.86	1701.02	－58.16	20.2	20.7
1985	2004.82	2004.25	0.57	22.0	17.8
1986－1990	12280.60	12865.67	－585.07	7.9	9.0
1986	2122.01	2204.91	－82.90	5.8	10.0
1987	2199.35	2262.18	－62.83	3.6	2.6
1988	2357.24	2491.21	－133.97	7.2	10.1
1989	2664.90	2823.78	－158.88	13.1	13.3
1990	2937.10	3083.59	－146.49	10.2	9.2
1991－1995	22442.10	24387.46	－1945.36	16.3	17.2
1991	3149.48	3386.62	－237.14	7.2	9.8
1992	3483.37	3742.20	－258.83	10.6	10.5
1993	4348.95	4642.30	－293.35	24.8	24.1
1994	5218.10	5792.62	－574.52	20.0	24.8
1995	6242.20	6823.72	－581.52	19.6	17.8
1996	7407.99	7937.55	－529.56	18.7	16.3
1997	8651.14	9233.56	－582.42	16.8	16.3
1998	9875.95	10798.18	－922.23	14.2	16.9
1999	11444.08	13187.67	－1743.59	15.9	22.1
2000	13395.23	15886.50	－2491.27	17.0	20.5
2001	16386.04	18902.58	－2516.54	22.3	19.0
2002	18903.64	22053.15	－3149.51	15.4	16.7

数据来源：摘自国家统计局《2003 中国统计年鉴》。

中央财政和地方财政收支总额

Total Revenue and Expenditures of Central and Local Governments

单位:亿元

Unit: in 100 million Yuan

年　份 Year	财 政 收 入 Total Revenue			财 政 支 出 Total Expenditures		
	合　计 Total	中　央 Central Government	地　方 Local Government	合　计 Total	中　央 Central Government	地　方 Local Government
1970	662.90	182.95	479.95	649.41	382.37	267.04
1971－1975	3919.71	576.43	3343.28	3919.44	2125.14	1794.30
1975	815.61	96.63	718.98	820.88	409.40	411.48
1976－1980	5089.61	904.32	4185.29	5282.44	2625.34	2657.10
1976	776.58	98.91	677.67	806.20	377.63	428.57
1977	874.46	113.85	760.61	843.53	393.70	449.83
1978	1132.26	175.77	956.49	1122.09	532.12	589.97
1979	1146.38	231.34	915.04	1281.79	655.08	626.71
1980	1159.93	284.45	875.48	1228.83	666.81	562.02
1981－1985	7402.75	2583.02	4819.73	7483.18	3725.64	3757.54
1981	1175.79	311.07	864.72	1138.41	625.65	512.76
1982	1212.33	346.84	865.49	1229.98	651.81	578.17
1983	1366.95	490.01	876.94	1409.52	759.60	649.92
1984	1642.86	665.47	977.39	1701.02	893.33	807.69
1985	2004.82	769.63	1235.19	2004.25	795.25	1209.00
1986－1990	12280.60	4104.41	8176.19	12865.67	4420.27	8445.40
1986	2122.01	778.42	1343.59	2204.91	836.36	1368.55
1987	2199.35	736.29	1463.06	2262.18	845.63	1416.55
1988	2357.24	774.76	1582.48	2491.21	845.04	1646.17
1989	2664.90	822.52	1842.38	2823.78	888.77	1935.01
1990	2937.10	992.42	1944.68	3083.59	1004.47	2079.12
1991－1995	22442.10	9038.39	13403.71	24387.46	7323.13	17064.33
1991	3149.48	938.25	2211.23	3386.62	1090.81	2295.81
1992	3483.37	979.51	2503.86	3742.20	1170.44	2571.76
1993	4348.95	957.51	3391.44	4642.30	1312.06	3330.24
1994	5218.10	2906.50	2311.60	5792.62	1754.43	4038.19
1995	6242.20	3256.62	2985.58	6823.72	1995.39	4828.33
1996	7407.99	3661.07	3746.92	7937.55	2151.27	5786.28
1997	8651.14	4226.92	4424.22	9233.56	2532.50	7672.58
1998	9875.95	4892.00	4983.95	10798.18	3125.60	7672.58
1999	11444.08	5849.21	5594.87	13187.67	4152.33	9035.34
2000	13395.23	6989.17	6406.06	15886.50	5519.85	10366.65
	16386.04	8582.74	7803.30	18902.58	5768.02	13134.56
2001	18903.64	10388.64	8515.00	22053.15	6771.70	15281.45

数据来源:摘自国家统计局《2003 中国统计年鉴》。

人口数及构成

Population and Its Composition

单位:万人

Unit: in 10 thousand persons

年 份 Year	年底总人口 Total Population (year-end)	按性别分 By Gender 男 Male 人口数 Population	比重(%) Proportion	女 Female 人口数 Population	比重(%) Proportion	按城乡分 By Residence 城镇总人口 Urban 人口数 Population	比重(%) Proportion	农村总人口 Rural 人口数 Population	比重(%) Proportion
1978	96259	49567	51.49	46692	48.51	17245	17.92	79014	82.08
1979	97542	50192	51.46	47350	48.54	18495	18.96	79047	81.04
1980	98705	50785	51.45	47920	48.55	19140	19.39	79565	80.61
1981	100072	51519	51.48	48553	48.52	20171	20.16	79901	79.84
1982	101654	52352	51.50	49302	48.50	21480	21.13	80174	78.87
1983	103008	53152	51.60	49856	48.40	22274	21.62	80734	78.38
1984	104357	53848	51.60	50509	48.40	24017	23.01	80340	76.99
1985	105851	54725	51.70	51126	48.30	25094	23.71	80757	76.29
1986	107507	55581	51.70	51926	48.30	26366	24.52	81141	75.48
1987	109300	56290	51.50	53010	48.50	27674	25.32	81626	74.68
1988	111026	57201	51.52	53825	48.48	28661	25.81	82365	74.19
1989	112704	58099	51.55	54605	48.45	29540	26.21	83164	73.79
1990	114333	58904	51.52	55429	48.48	30191	26.41	84142	73.59
1991	115823	59466	51.34	56357	48.66	30543	26.37	85280	73.63
1992	117171	59811	51.05	57360	48.95	32372	27.63	84799	72.37
1993	118517	60472	51.02	58045	48.98	33351	28.14	85166	71.86
1994	119850	61246	51.10	58604	48.90	34301	28.62	85549	71.38
1995	121121	61808	51.03	59313	48.97	35174	29.04	85947	70.96
1996	122389	62200	50.82	60189	49.18	35950	29.37	86439	70.63
1997	123626	63131	51.07	60495	48.93	36989	29.92	86637	70.08
1998	124810	63629	50.98	61181	49.02	37942	30.40	86868	69.60
1999	125909	64189	50.98	61720	49.02	38892	30.89	87017	69.11
2000	126583	65355	51.63	61228	48.37	45844	36.22	80739	63.78
2001	127627	65672	51.46	61955	48.54	48064	37.66	79563	62.34
2002	128453	66115	51.47	62338	48.53	50212	39.09	78241	60.91

注:总人口和城镇人口中包括中国人民解放军现役军人。

Urban Population include the military personnel of Chinese People's Liberation Army.

各地区分性别的15岁及15岁以上文盲半文盲人口

Illterate and Semi-Literate Population Aged 15 and Over by Sex and Region

单位：人，%（person，%）

地 区 Region	15岁及15岁以上人口 Population Aged 15 & Over			文盲、半文盲人口 Illiterate and Semi-literate			文盲半文盲占15岁及以上人口比例 Percentage to total Population Aged 15 & Over（%）		
	合 计 Total	男 Male	女 Female	合 计 Total	男 Male	女 Female	合 计 Total	男 Male	女 Female
合 计 Total	**990974**	**499149**	**491825**	**115284**	**32074**	**83210**	**11.63**	**6.43**	**16.92**
北 京 Beijing	12154	6448	5706	650	144	506	5.35	2.23	8.87
天 津 Tianjin	8511	4200	4311	574	129	445	6.74	3.07	10.32
河 北 Hebei	52391	26246	26145	4091	1095	2996	7.81	4.17	11.46
山 西 Shanxi	24847	12756	12091	1591	499	1092	6.40	3.91	9.03
内蒙古 Inner Mongolia	18989	9727	9262	2555	819	1736	13.46	8.42	18.74
辽 宁 Liaoning	35077	17605	17472	1811	462	1349	5.16	2.62	7.72
吉 林 Jilin	22350	11174	11176	974	319	655	4.36	2.85	5.86
黑龙江 Heilongjiang	31380	15976	15404	2051	656	1395	6.54	4.11	9.06
上 海 Shanghai	14296	7000	7297	1170	249	921	8.18	3.56	12.62
江 苏 Jiangsu	59252	29232	30020	8477	1979	6498	14.31	6.77	21.65
浙 江 Zhejiang	38248	19161	19088	5177	1528	3649	13.54	7.97	19.12
安 徽 Anhui	47593	23887	23706	8510	2478	6032	17.88	10.37	25.45
福 建 Fujian	26930	13875	13055	3680	881	2799	13.67	6.35	21.44
江 西 Jiangxi	31332	15668	15664	3371	813	2558	10.76	5.19	16.33
山 东 Shandong	72804	36380	36423	8180	2004	6176	11.24	5.51	16.96
河 南 Henan	72133	35991	36142	6592	1784	4808	9.14	4.96	13.30
湖 北 Hubei	45591	22902	22690	6896	1910	4985	15.13	8.34	21.97
湖 南 Hunan	52114	26633	25481	4352	1191	3161	8.35	4.47	12.41
广 东 Guangdong	57744	29217	28528	4045	801	3244	7.01	2.74	11.37
广 西 Guangxi	37014	18973	18041	3498	774	2725	9.45	4.08	15.10
海 南 Hainan	5860	3011	2849	520	109	410	8.87	3.62	14.39
重 庆 Chongqing	24695	12440	12255	2547	695	1852	10.31	5.59	15.11
四 川 Sichuan	67689	33464	34225	9172	2748	6424	13.55	8.21	18.77
贵 州 Guizhou	27497	14126	13371	5152	1528	3625	18.74	10.82	27.11
云 南 Yunnan	32138	16414	15724	7425	2244	5181	23.10	13.67	32.95
西 藏 Tibet	1949	920	1029	854	311	543	43.82	33.80	52.77
陕 西 Shaanxi	28186	14305	13881	4385	1504	2881	15.56	10.51	20.75
甘 肃 Gansu	19375	9842	9533	4090	1419	2670	21.11	14.42	28.01
青 海 Qinghai	3851	1970	1881	954	291	663	24.77	14.77	35.25
宁 夏 Ningxia	4093	2087	2006	716	222	495	17.49	10.64	24.68
新 疆 Xinjiang	14891	7519	7373	1223	487	736	8.21	6.48	9.98

注：本表“文盲、半文盲人口”指15岁及15岁以上不识字及识字很少人口。

Illiterate and semi-illiterate population in this table refers to the population aged 15 and over, who are unable or very difficult to read.

数据来源：摘自国家统计局《2003中国统计年鉴》。

各地区按性别和受

Population by Sex, Educational

本表是2002年人口变动情况抽样调查样本数据，抽样比为0.988‰。

地　区 Region	6岁及6岁以上人口 Population Aged 6 and Over			不识字或识字很少 Illterate		
	合计 Total	男 Male	女 Fernale	合计 Total	男 Male	女 Fernale
全　国 National Total	**1178951**	**598979**	**579972**	**120551**	**34743**	**85809**
北　京 Beijing	13239	7009	6230	661	148	513
天　津 Tianjin	9522	4723	4799	606	146	460
河　北 Hebei	62588	31611	30978	4253	1174	3079
山　西 Shanxi	30192	15526	14667	1709	558	1150
内蒙古 Inner Mongolia	22236	11423	10813	2653	868	1785
辽　宁 Liaoning	39676	19986	19691	1969	536	1433
吉　林 Jilin	25500	12825	12675	1103	383	720
黑龙江 Heilongjiang	36007	18418	17589	2202	737	1466
上　海 Shanghai	15469	7592	7877	1182	256	926
江　苏 Jiangsu	69427	34594	34832	8600	2032	6568
浙　江 Zhejiang	43244	21823	21421	5281	1575	3706
安　徽 Anhui	58813	30045	28769	8620	2553	6066
福　建 Fujian	32162	16700	15462	3824	971	2853
江　西 Jiangxi	38249	19449	18801	3479	863	2616
山　东 Shandong	83881	42277	41604	8468	2148	6320
河　南 Henan	88118	44573	43545	6838	1931	4908
湖　北 Hubei	56354	28574	27779	6996	1963	5033
湖　南 Hunan	61435	31673	29762	4441	1240	3201
广　东 Guangdong	71705	36606	35099	4593	1097	3496
广　西 Guangxi	44120	22775	21346	3796	928	2868
海　南 Hainan	7273	3779	3494	573	135	437
重　庆 Chongqing	28823	14640	14183	2682	763	1919
四　川 Sichuan	79863	39892	39972	9775	3054	6721
贵　州 Guizhou	34146	17630	16516	5534	1701	3833
云　南 Yunnan	38413	19747	18667	7799	2418	5380
西　藏 Tibet	2406	1151	1255	914	339	575
陕　西 Shaanxi	34241	17530	16712	4463	1538	2925
甘　肃 Gansu	23833	12203	11630	4317	1532	2785
青　海 Qinghai	4724	2419	2305	1051	333	718
宁　夏 Ningxia	5068	2588	2481	759	242	517
新　疆 Xinjiang	18220	9201	9019	1411	580	831

数据来源：摘自国家统计局《2003中国统计年鉴》。